The Law & Order Presidency

Willard M. Oliver
Radford University

Prentice
Hall

Upper Saddle River, New Jersey 07458

Library of Congress Cataloging-in-Publication Data

Oliver, Willard M.
  The law & order presidency / by Willard M. Oliver.
    p. cm.
  Includes bibliographical references and index.
  ISBN 0-13-026084-3
    1. Criminal justice, Administration of—United States.   2. Presidents—United States.   I.
Title: Law and order presidency.   II. Title.

HV9950 .O45 2003
364.973—dc21

                                                                2001059827

Publisher: Jeff Johnston
Executive Editor: Kim Davies
Assistant Editor: Sarah Holle
Production Editor: Rosie Jones, Clarinda Publication Services
Production Liaison: Barbara Marttine Cappuccio
Director of Production and Manufacturing: Bruce Johnson
Managing Editor: Mary Carnis
Manufacturing Manager: Cathleen Petersen
Creative Director: Cheryl Asherman
Cover Design Coordinator: Miguel Ortiz
Marketing Manager: Jessica Pfaff
Cover Designer: Joe Sengotta
Cover Image: The White House Photo Office
Formatting and Interior Design: The Clarinda Company
Printing and Binding: Phoenix Book Tech Park

Pearson Education LTD, *London*
Pearson Education Australia PTY, Limited, *Sydney*
Pearson Education Singapore, Pte. Ltd.
Pearson Education North Asia Ltd., *Hong Kong*
Pearson Education Canada, Ltd., *Toronto*
Pearson Educación de Mexico, S.A. de C.V.
Pearson Education—Japan, *Tokyo*
Pearson Education Malaysia, Pte. Ltd

10   9   8   7   6   5   4   3   2   1
ISBN 0-13-026084-3

Dedicated to Mark Matthew Oliver

Although I only met you once, I know in my heart you would have been a good son and a loving brother. By the grace of God, I look forward to meeting you again.

Contents

Preface

> "You wanted *law and order* in this town,
> you got it!"
> —*Ronald Reagan*
> *(from the 1953 movie Law & Order)*

The Law & Order Presidency is an acknowledgment that presidents have come to be more involved in the issue of crime policy—a public policy issue that was once relegated to the purview of state and local governments. Throughout the twentieth century, commencing with the Hoover Presidency and with nearly every presidential succession, presidents have become more engaged in such issues as "street crime" and drugs. While this has had a profound impact upon crime policy and the criminal justice system in the United States, it has also had a significant impact upon public opinion of crime. Through the presidents' ability to lead public opinion, supported and promulgated by the media, presidents have come to greatly influence the public's perceptions of crime. The more time and attention the president spends on the topic of crime, the more the American public comes to believe that crime is one of the "most important problems facing the country."

The research at hand utilizes the theory that presidents influence public opinion in order to predict the impact that presidential time and attention on crime has on public opinion of crime (see introduction). Recognizing that there are many assumptions inherent within this hypothesis, the research will attempt to address the three most important assumptions: 1) that presidents have in fact historically allocated time and resources to the issue of crime (see chapter 1); 2) that presidents have some bona fide reasons for engaging in a policy that has traditionally been under the authority of state and local governments (see chapter 2); and 3) that presidents have the means by which they can engage in crime-control policy (chapter 3). Having satisfied the assumptions, the research will then test the hypothesis utilizing a time-series regression analysis of data collected from the Gallup poll's "Most Important Problem" series to represent the dependent variable and from the *Public Papers of the Presidents of the United States* to represent the key independent variable for the years 1945 to 1996, and controlling for other influencing factors such as crime rates, unemployment rates, media influence, and congressional attention to crime (see chapter 4). The conclusion reached by this researcher is that presidential time and attention to crime is found to influence the public's perception that crime is an important issue (see chapter 5).

Recognizing that there exists within the Office of the Presidency a specific role oriented toward addressing issues of domestic crime in the United States—namely the Law & Order presidency—and that this role has had a significant impact upon public opinion, the implications that this has on the public policy of crime is explored. Reaching the conclusions that presidents should not be involved in crime-control policy, while recognizing there is likely no turning back, the author suggests a prescription for the direction the Law & Order presidency should take in order to retain (or obtain) sound crime-control policy in the future.

Acknowledgments

As always, the author must first start with his immediate family without whom this research clearly would not have been possible. A deep heartfelt thanks goes to my wife, Judy, who has endured so much during the preparation, research, and writing of this book. I must also thank my sons, Paul and James, who also had to endure my absence in order that I could conduct my research and write both the original doctoral dissertation and then the conversion into the current book. Their constant talk of "Daddy's Dissertation," however, was always encouraging. I must also recognize my daughter, Sarah Elizabeth, who was born during the writing of this book. She will forever be Daddy's "little girl". Finally, a special dedication goes to Mark Matthew, my third son, who was born and died during this research. This work is dedicated to his memory.

I must also turn to several other family members, especially my Mom, Carol Oliver, and my sister-in-law, Kathy Fellers, who both read, edited, and offered valuable corrections to the first draft. In addition, I must thank all of the rest of my family for their continued support of my efforts. Your kind words and encouragement have not gone unnoticed.

In addition to family, I must thank a number of friends who provided support along the way without always knowing it. They include Jim Hilgenberg and Dan Gutierrez, my fellow graduate students at West Virginia University, and especially Michael and Stephanie Caulfield, along with all of their wonderful children: Maria, Joseph, Catherine, Stephen, Theresa, Timothy, and Peter. My thanks to all of you for your indirect contributions to this book.

A very sincere thank you goes to all of the wonderful people at Prentice Hall for supporting me in this project. To Bryce Dodson who encouraged me to develop this project into a Prentice Hall book, and to Kim Davies and Sarah Holle, two very fine editors and good friends. I must also thank Rosie Jones and the production staff who make the final product a reality. Moreover, I must thank the three reviewers provided by Prentice Hall that provided some valuable insights and suggestions that have greatly enhanced the quality of this publication. I am indebted to Dr. J. D. Jamieson, Southwest Texas State University, San Marcos, TX;

Tere Chipman, Fayetteville Technical Community College, Fayetteville, NC; Junius H. Koonce, Edgecomb Community College, Rocky Mount, NC; and Pamela Hart, Iowa Western Community College, Council Bluffs, IA.

I would also like to thank all of the archivists who work for the National Archives and Records Administration at the various presidential libraries I visited. As these dedicated employees have to endure more than 10,000 researchers a year, handle more than 300,000,000 pages of text, 5,000,000 photographs, 14,000,000 feet of movie film, and 70,000 hours of audio and video recordings, it is a wonder that they were able to not only be helpful and point a confused researcher in the right direction, but to be friendly and professional at the same time. This is truly a remarkable feat. My sincerest thanks goes to all of the employees of the libraries, the foundations, and the National Archives and Records Administration, especially the archivists whom I met at the Gerald R. Ford Library, Ann Arbor, Michigan; Herbert Hoover Library, West Branch, Iowa; Lyndon B. Johnson Library, Austin, Texas; Ronald Reagan Library, Simi Valley California; Franklin D. Roosevelt Library, Hyde Park, New York; as well as the Nixon Project, College Park, Maryland.

In addition to all these wonderful people I have met along the way, I would also like to thank several researchers whom I have never met, but have nonetheless been very influential on my research. The researcher in the presidential field who has perhaps had the most impact upon my research is Barbara Hinckley, a political scientist whose ideas and thoughts are so well communicated in her clear and articulate writing style. In the area of crime-control policy, the first researcher to venture into this area has had a great impact upon my understanding of national crime-control policy from its origins and growth to its current status today. This pioneer is James D. Calder, University of Texas at San Antonio. Finally, the recent work of Nancy Marion, University of Akron, Ohio, has proven to be very insightful and helpful in understanding presidential crime-control policy. I would like to thank all three of these researchers for laying the foundation for my research.

Finally, there is one very important group of individuals who helped pave the way for this research and provided immeasurable assistance throughout the process—my dissertation committee. Words alone cannot express the sincere gratitude that I have for the five distinguished members of this committee, as well as the entire political science department at West Virginia University. They accepted a criminal justice professor into the folds of political science and allowed me the opportunity and provided me the tools to intermix my two areas of interest: crime policy and presidents. The seeds were planted by Dr. Kevin Leyden, my advisor, mentor, and friend, whom it has been a great pleasure to know and work with both under and alongside. The seeds then began to grow under the tutelage of Dr. Jeffrey Worsham whose theoretical and cerebral push were greatly needed, and from Dr. John Kilwein who always had the knack of bringing reality back into my research. The research then took a decidedly quantitative push from two members of the West Virginia University political science faculty who were not on my com-mittee but were nonetheless greatly appreciated, Dr. Robert Duval and Dr. Christopher Mooney (currently at the University of Illinois at Springfield). The re-search then became greatly enhanced in the scholarly field of presidential studies through the help and encouragement of Dr. Robert DiClerico whose passion for the study of the American Presidency I share. In addition, I must also thank Dr. David Williams who provided a different, but very helpful, perspective from the public administration field. Finally, I must return to my advisor, Dr. Kevin Leyden, for all of his advice on making the final draft far better than I could ever have writ-ten myself and for telling me something my wife had told me all along, "cut the fluff."

About the Author

Willard M. Oliver is an assistant professor of Criminal Justice at Radford University in Virginia. He holds a Ph.D. in political science from West Virginia University. He is the author of *Community-Oriented Policing: A Systemic Approach to Policing, Second Edition* (Prentice Hall, 2001) and the editor of *Community Policing: Classical Readings* (Prentice Hall, 2000). He has published numerous scholarly articles and book reviews in such journals as *American Journal of Criminal Justice, Criminal Justice Review, Criminal Justice Policy Review, Journal of Criminal Justice Education, Justice Quarterly, Police Quarterly, Policing: An International Journal of Police Strategies and Management*, and *Police Practice and Research: An International Journal*. He is also a former police officer and military police officer. Finally, and most importantly, he is a husband and father of three boys and a girl.

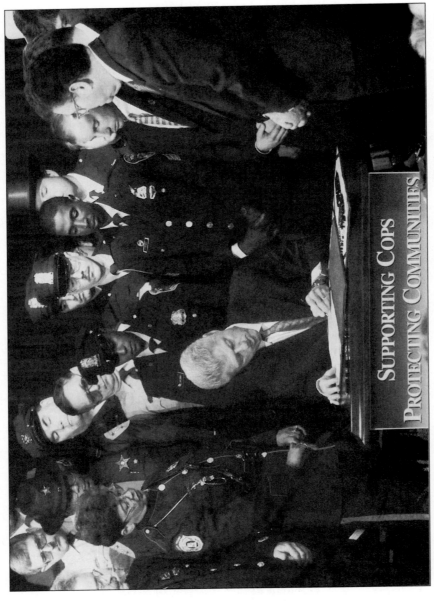

President Bill Clinton, surrounded by law enforcement officers, while signing two crime bills during a ceremony in the Old Executive Office Building in Washington, D.C. on November 13, 1998. Part of the legislation expanded a scholarship program for survivors of federal law enforcement officers killed in the line of duty.

Introduction

> *The first responsibility of government is law and order.*
> *—President Clinton[1]*

The realization of a "law and order" presidency has been widely recognized in much of the literature dealing with presidents and their crime control policies, but has simply not been named as such. Reviewing this literature in 1995, the author was struck by the previous year's political activity over the Violent Crime Control and Law Enforcement Act of 1994, when presidential activity on the topic of crime had reached a new level, but so had the public perception of crime. In fact, crime, for the first time in the Gallup poll's history of asking, "what is the most important problem facing the country," became the number one problem. The correlation between these two events could not be considered two isolated events, but simply had to be seen as being related. The more important question this author began to explore was the relationship of causation between these two events. As the following case study attempts to show, it would appear that this president was largely responsible for crime becoming the "most important problem facing the country" that year.

In 1992, Governor Clinton (D-AR) sought the Democratic party's nomination to run against President Bush, the Republican incumbent. As part of his endeavor to win the Democratic nomination he positioned himself as a "law and order" president from the commencement of his campaign and offered himself as a more moderate Democrat. This was intended to highlight the differences between his stance on crime and the views of his likely Democratic primary contender, New York Governor Mario Cuomo.[2] Governor Cuomo had a strong record of opposing the death penalty which made him vulnerable to attacks and portrayed as being "soft on crime." Clinton had learned from the mistakes made by the Democratic candidate, Governor Michael Dukakis (D-MA), when he ran against

1

then Vice-President Bush in the 1988 Presidential campaign. Bush was able to portray his opponent as soft on crime because of Governor Dukakis' strong views against the death penalty and through his successful use of the "Willie Horton" television ad which depicted a convicted felon who was released on a weekend furlough and raped a young woman.[3] Clinton did not want to repeat these mistakes and created for himself a strong stance on crime, while still retaining many of the traditional liberal policies aimed at rehabilitation, drug treatment, and various programs focused on improving the quality of life in inner cities. The tactic worked and although Clinton did not start off as the Democratic frontrunner, through a shrewd campaign and various political circumstances, he was able to secure the Democratic nomination for president.

Governor Clinton had campaigned heavily on crime while seeking the Democratic nomination and began targeting his rhetoric at President Bush in order to position himself as the candidate who would be toughest on crime. Clinton utilized the 1992 Democratic Party platform as the basis for his crime control strategy which took the stance that "crime is a relentless danger to our communities. Over the last decade, crime has swept through our country at an alarming rate."[4] The platform stated that "Democrats pledge to restore government as the upholder of basic law and order for crime-ravaged communities. The simplest and most direct way to restore order in our cities is to put more police on the streets."[5] In addition to more police, the party platform called for the creation of a Police Corps, modeled after the military's R.O.T.C.,[6] to implement the concepts of community policing, target white collar criminals, favor innovative sentencing and punishment options, as well as expand drug counseling and treatment programs.[7] Clinton promised not only to support the party platform, which, with the exception of the call for drug counseling and treatment, had become more moderate, but also to support a much more conservative approach in his policies on crime control.

The centerpiece of Clinton's campaign on crime was promising to add an additional 100,000 police officers to America's streets under the auspices of community policing and to create a police corps through the use of a "national service trust fund."[8] The initiative was meant to send a clear message to the American electorate that the Democrats could be just as tough on the crime issue as the Republicans, all of which could be delivered through the soundbite: "100,000 Cops." As one author explained, "by encapsulating the crime initiative within the call for 100,000 Cops, the Clinton campaign had accomplished the dual goals of shifting the debate on crime and providing the media and the public a clear message that cut through the complexities of federal crime policy."[9] While this was his most successful initiative regarding crime, it was not his only initiative. It became obvious by the end of the summer and early fall of 1992, that Clinton had an extensive crime control plan that would be underwritten by a host of new and old initiatives.

Clinton supported an expanded use of the federal death penalty and to successfully highlight this fact, during his campaign he returned to Arkansas four times to oversee the execution of death row inmates.[10] He favored the expanded use of juvenile "boot camp" programs for nonviolent, first-time offenders.[11] He advocated an increased use of law enforcement and judicial resources to fight the war on drugs.[12] He also supported background checks on all handgun purchases, as well as a waiting period, and the ban of some automatic weapons.[13] Complementary to the issue of firearms, he heavily favored the passage of the Brady bill, but rather than portraying his reasons in terms of the traditional liberal viewpoint, he articulated that he was a supporter of the second amendment and only wanted to protect Americans and the police.[14] In one campaign speech in Houston, Texas, Clinton, surrounded by police officers stated, "It is crazy to believe that we shouldn't at least try to give our police officers a fair fight in the fight to keep our streets safe. That's why I believe you ought to be for the Brady bill."[15] In addition, he also supported increased cooperation between the federal, state, and local governments, programs oriented on reducing child and spousal abuse, and efforts to make public schools safer environments.[16] Finally, Clinton did support some of the liberal ideas in his campaign anti-crime agenda such as a health and education approach to illegal drugs, but again, Clinton was able to frame the issue and convey a tough stance on a traditionally liberal policy position. In one attack against President Bush on the issue of drug treatment, Clinton argued:

> Bush confuses being tough with being smart, especially on drugs. Bush thinks locking up addicts instead of treating them before they commit crimes . . . is clever politics. That may be, but it certainly isn't sound policy, and the consequences of his cravenness could ruin us.[17]

In sum, as one author concluded:

> . . . Clinton's agenda for crime control in 1992 was varied. It was both conservative and liberal, and included illicit drug abuse, law enforcement issues, victims, domestic violence, firearms, white collar crime, prisons, and safe schools. On the whole, Clinton's agenda was much more conservative than one would ordinarily expect from a liberal candidate for president. It encompassed many areas that were traditionally Republican strongholds but also included liberal approaches as well. This was a surprise to both the Republicans and the public, and helped to get Clinton elected into office that year.[18]

Clinton's crime control policies were most assuredly part of his success with the crime issue. However, it was also in part due to how he handled the crime issue throughout the campaign. For Clinton, crime was an offensive issue, rather than the defensive issue it had been for other Democratic candidates, especially in 1988.[19] He succeeded in making the issue a positive one, one that did not divide the American electorate, but rather united it under a cause that everyone could support. This was illustrated in his campaign speech in Houston, Texas, when he stated:

> We cannot take our country back until we take our neighborhoods back. Four years ago this crime issue was used to divide America. I want to use it to unite America. I

want to be tough on crime and good for civil rights. You can't have civil justice with-out order and safety.[20]

In addition, he worked hard to win the endorsement of the police associa-tions and police unions,[21] he convincingly utilized several television advertise-ments demonstrating his pro-death penalty stance,[22] he incorporated crime, drugs, and gun control into his political agenda publication *Putting People First,* filling up six of 172 pages,[23] and he took advantage of any opportunity to surround him-self with police officers in staged photo opportunities.[24] Clinton's strong stance on crime, coupled with the fact that President Bush downplayed the crime issue in the 1992 campaign, by not mentioning it during the Republican Convention, nor being able to replicate his 1988 crime symbol (namely Willie Horton), gave Clinton the upper hand in regard to the crime issue. As one author so caustically remarked, "there was little about Clinton's crime control record in Arkansas that Bush could taunt him about the way he mocked Dukakis as a patsy for every dark-skinned murderer in Massachusetts."[25] All told, Clinton had succeeded in not only match-ing the Republicans on the crime issue, but by the end of the election, managing to steal it from them.[26] In November of 1992, Clinton won the election over the in-cumbent George Bush, and on January 20, 1993, was sworn in as the forty-second President of the United States, "well-positioned to make crime a key substantive and political success of his administration."[27]

It has been demonstrated that the shift from a campaign for president to actu-ally becoming president is a crucial time period for any candidate in regard to their policy formulation.[28] This would especially be true for President-Elect Clinton who was a Democrat taking over the White House after twelve years of Republi-can rule. During the transition period, he selected two moderates, Al From and Bruce Reed, to handle his domestic policy agenda.[29] They would write a memo in late December 1992, recommending that Clinton capitalize on the momentum he had managed to gain on the crime issue against President Bush by making crime a central issue on his agenda.[30] Their advice was to draft and transmit to Congress, in the first one hundred days in office, a crime bill that would utilize all of his cam-paign promises regarding crime—adding 100,000 new police officers, creating more boot camps for first-time nonviolent offenders, expanding the death penalty, and adhering to his stance on gun control.[31] In addition, they also recommended that he ban the importation of certain assault rifles through the use of an Executive Order.[32] Between his campaign promises and his ability to beat President Bush on the crime issue, coupled with the recommendation of his policy advisors that he focus on crime, the president was left in a strong position to capitalize on the issue of crime. It quickly became apparent, however, that Clinton would lose the initia-tive by ignoring both the advice and his campaign promises.

All presidents come into office with a certain amount of political capital based upon their electoral victory.[33] As DiClerico has pointed out, "Clinton's win provided him with very little capital" due to his low winning percentage.[34] In addition to the political capital upon entering office, presidents also can add to this capital through their reputation for competent leadership and their ability to enhance their public support.[35] In this matter, DiClerico explained that "Clinton has not been particularly successful on either count."[36] As to the crime issue, although he had the political capital coming into office, he did not display competent leadership nor did he do anything to enhance public support for the various initiatives he proposed. Concerning all substantive policy considerations, he completely ignored the issue of crime upon taking office.[37]

This total disregard for the issue of crime is evident in the fact that the White House declined to draft any crime legislation or to pressure Congress to draft and pass a crime bill during the first one hundred days of the Clinton presidency. The majority of his first six months in office were spent dealing with such issues as gays in the military, a deficit-reduction package, motor-voter registration, the family and medical leave act, NAFTA, and his health care initiative.[38] In addition, while the president called for $100 billion in increased spending for sixty-one separate programs, the centerpiece of his campaign on the crime issue, the 100,000 Cops initiative was nowhere to be seen.[39] In fact, in regard to the budget and crime, Clinton actually called for funding cuts, including a $206 million cut from aid to local police agencies, a $40 million cut from the FBI budget, and $331 million in cuts for prison construction.[40] Moreover, although he drafted a number of executive orders in his first one hundred days on abortion counseling, abortions in military hospitals, fetal tissue research, and the RU-486 pill, the order banning the importation of assault rifles was shelved.[41] Finally, in his address before a joint session of Congress on his administration's goals, Clinton did include crime but its emphasis was on signing the Brady bill,[42] and he would make two speeches before law enforcement officials—one in the Rose Garden at the White House[43] and one at the National Law Enforcement Officers Memorial.[44] The former simply mentioned the "100,000 police officers" initiative, while the latter was strictly ceremonial. All told, the president did very little during the first six months in office, leaving one journalist to remark: "President Clinton has not determined to make crime-fighting one of the cornerstones of his administration. And that's a big mistake."[45]

Several authors cite three factors that contributed to Clinton's decision to drop the crime issue: politics, personnel, and priorities.[46] Politically, it was said that President Clinton "concluded that crime had been irrelevant to his victory in the 1992 campaign, and thus was not an essential element of his mandate or important to his political future."[47] As a result, Clinton's capital was spent on other items of his agenda as previously detailed. Personnel-wise, the key to the lack of a focus on crime was a result of the fact that several members of the Clinton transition team, Al From, Will Marshall, and Robert Shapiro, did not become members of his administration.[48] In addition to his White House staff, Clinton also found himself mired with difficulties in getting appointments for crucial members of his cabinet who could have assisted in the area of crime, namely the Attorney General and the Drug Czar. Regarding the appointment of Attorney General, Clinton had to endure public challenges of his first two choices, both of whom ended up withdrawing from the process,[49] and was not able to appoint Janet Reno to the position until March 12, 1993, three months into the administration.[50] Clinton was also slow in announcing the appointment of the Drug Czar, which came on April 28, 1993, and Lee P. Brown was not sworn in to office until July 1, 1993, six months into the administration.[51] Finally, it has been said that Clinton's priorities were simply overshadowed by issues that were not a part of the "New Democrat" ideas, but were relegated to many "old issues" such as the economy, health care reform, and children's welfare.[52] As one Senior White House official stated in an interview:

> If we had done a crime bill at the beginning of the term, it would have passed with bipartisan support, been a great credit to the administration, and set an entirely different tone for the administration. If we had done any of the New Democrat ideas, it would have helped us build a working coalition, so we could do more unpopular stuff later.[53]

In the end, Clinton's first one hundred days in office were marked by a number of political setbacks, an emphasis on several very controversial issues and, although Clinton had a high success rate for legislation being passed that he had supported, most of these bills consisted of narrow margin victories.[54] All of this would contribute to the decline of his public approval rating from a high of 58 percentage points upon taking office to a low of 38 percent by June of 1993—the lowest level for any post-World War II president at that point in his term.[55] Whether due to his inexperience, his poor transition from candidate to president, or his poor handling of the office of the presidency, Clinton's first six months in office were difficult and he was in need of an issue upon which he could win. Crime was potentially that issue.

Clinton's reentry into the crime rhetoric did not come until August 11, 1993, one week after the Republican leadership in Congress had announced it would be proceeding with an omnibus anti-crime bill that it hoped to pass by Thanksgiving. Their plan called for many of the same provisions that had failed to pass Congress two years earlier,[56] as well as many of the bills that had been reformulated the previous year[57] and were believed to have bipartisan support.[58] The proposals consisted of federal aid to local law enforcement, building more prisons, mandatory minimum sentences, a greater use of the death penalty, and the "three strikes" provision which would give life imprisonment to a three-time convicted felon. As a result of this announcement and in dire need of a legislative victory, Clinton seized the anti-crime rhetoric and unveiled his plan on August 11, 1993.

   In order to respond to the Republican proposal and once again seize the crime issue for the Democrats, the White House began drafting a proposal and a speech for Clinton to deliver before the bills could be introduced in either the House or Senate. The proposal was largely based upon the "compromises reached in the conference report on the Bush administration's crime bill, which had been blocked in the Senate in its final stages."[59] It was also composed of a number of the proposals put forth by Clinton during his campaign. What it did not consist of was any input from the Attorney General or the Department of Justice.[60] In the end, the proposal was predominately a one hundred and second Congress bill with some Clinton campaign initiatives tacked on to make it appear that the entire proposal was being put forth by the White House.[61]

   On August 11, 1993, President Clinton would present his plan in a Rose Garden ceremony, surrounded by the Vice President, the Attorney General, Senator Biden (D-DE), Representative Brooks (D-TX), and various members of the law enforcement community. Clinton would argue that "the first duty of any government is to try to keep its citizens safe" and proposed that his plan would add 100,000 police officers to the streets, pass a waiting period on the purchase of handguns, and limit the number of habeas corpus appeals by death row inmates. As if tearing a page from his campaign rhetoric, Clinton would conclude that, "for too long, crime has been used as a way to divide Americans with rhetoric . . . it is time to use crime as a way to unite Americans through action."[62] He would also draft two memorandums to the Secretary of Treasury, directing him to cease the importation of specific assault pistols and to limit the number of gun dealer licences by conducting more intensive background checks and closer oversight.[63] President Clinton would reiterate this initiative to the American people on August 14, 1993, in his weekly radio address.[64]

   Despite Clinton's foray back into the area of crime-control policy, the White House did little to draft the legislation which some cited as evidence that Clinton was merely using the crime event to boost his public rating.[65] In any event, the drafting of the anti-crime legislation was left to Senator Biden and Representative Brooks, who would introduce the legislation in their respective houses on September 23, 1993.[66] Both proposals authorized federal aid to hire 50,000 new police officers, expanded the use of the federal death penalty, revised the rules for death row appeals, and allocated funds for drug treatment.[67] The differences between the two bills were that the House proposal allowed for a waiting period on handgun purchases while the Senate version did not, and the House bill extended the death penalty to sixty-four crimes, while the Senate version limited it to forty-seven.[68] Congress was on the way to passing an omnibus crime control bill.

   President Clinton was slow to respond to the initial introduction of bills in both chambers and it was not until October 9, 1993, in another radio address, that he would raise the issue of crime and call for passage of the crime bill,[69] and repeat the call on October 23, 1993, in yet another radio address.[70] In the meantime, Senator Biden, despite overwhelming odds, managed to get a bipartisan bill passed on November 19, 1993.[71] The House, however, under the leadership of Representative Brooks did not fare as well. Although the House managed to approve eleven single-subject bills, the passage of the main legislation was extremely slow due in part to liberal disillusionment with the way the legislation was developing and obstruction by the Congressional Black Caucus over portions of the bills,[72] as well as a lack of leadership from the White House moving the House toward conference committee.[73] As a result, the Congress was only able to pass a watered-down version of the Brady bill,[74] a parental kidnapping bill,[75] and a child protection bill.[76] The one hundred and third Congress would have to wait until the second session in order to pass the main legislation and President Clinton would have to wait to get his crime bill.

Although Clinton, during the recess, would call for Congress to return in the second session and pass the anti-crime legislation[77] and would invoke a call for the legislation in his State of the Union Address,[78] it became clear that the President was not taking an active role and was leaving the leadership to both Biden and Brooks.[79] Thus the bill would languish in the House subject to additional markups, rather than going directly to conference, until well into the summer of 1994.[80] Despite a continued call for passage of the legislation in a number of radio addresses,[81] Clinton and the Democrats lost the initiative, and by summer, the Republicans were able to walk away from what had been predominately a Democratic bill with bipartisan support without any political damage. They were in a position to take control of the bill and both the Congressional Democrats and the White House were forced into a position of having to compromise.

The Presidential rhetoric increased dramatically during the month of August in the hopes that passage could be achieved and the President utilized every means of communication available to him, including radio addresses, remarks to specific groups such as police organizations,[82] and a number of exchanges with reporters. It was at this point that Clinton began drawing upon the earlier creation of a "war room" to deal with domestic policy issues such as crime, and employing a strategy of direct lobbying, national outreach, and constituency group mobilization, which developed into a form of "reverse lobbying."[83] His appeals managed to win him the support of a number of U.S. city mayors, including New York City Mayor Rudolph Giuliani, a staunch Republican,[84] the support of the public,[85] and the support of a number of interest groups oriented on crime control.[86] While this did take away some of the moderate Republicans from the partisan strategy of the Republican leadership, many of the Democrats walked away from the final bill as well.[87] For the first time, President Clinton became actively involved in the passage of the crime bill beyond the pressure he was trying to keep on public opinion and interest groups. The White House began actively seeking votes from Democrats who had walked away or were undecided and soliciting the help of many of the moderate Republicans.[88]

At the Capitol, the bargaining over the crime bill began on the afternoon of August 19, 1994, and did not end until August 21, 1994. During these negotiations the Republicans were able to achieve a victory by driving down the amounts spent on various social programs, such as drug treatment, and by the afternoon of August 21, a procedural motion was made to bring the bill to the floor.[89] The motion was carried by 239 votes to 189, with 42 Republicans, 196 Democrats, and 1 Independent voting yea. A second vote followed and was defeated on "a motion to recommit the conference report to accompany the bill to the committee of conference."[90] Finally, the bill was voted upon with 235 voting in favor, 195 voting against, and 5 abstaining. In the end, 188 Democrats, 46 Republicans, and 1 Independent voted in favor of the bill. As DiClerico summed up the crime bill, "the circumstances surrounding its passage tarnished much of the luster that might have come the president's way. After a humiliating procedural vote in which 58 House Democrats—including 20 committee and subcommittee chairs and a deputy whip—abandoned the president, a concession forced by Republicans reduced the bill's funding by some $3 billion dollars."[91] In the end, Clinton and the Democrats claimed victory, but so did the Republicans—the Democrats for stealing the crime issue from the Republicans and the Republicans for watering-down the "liberal" components of the crime bill. On September 13, 1994, with much political fanfare on the south lawn of the White House, President Clinton signed the Violent Crime Control and Law Enforcement Act of 1994 into law, with several of his campaign promises intact.[92]

President Clinton's activity on crime during his campaign for President and his tenure in office, and to the point that he signed the crime bill into law, can be summed up from this particular case study as going from very active during the campaign, to almost nonexistent during his first six months in office, to a period of steadily increasing attention to the issue as it revolved around the Congressional anti-crime legislation. Simply put, upon taking office, Clinton did not focus on the topic of crime until the Republican Congress proposed legislation and Clinton began seeking a much needed legislative victory. By looking at the number of speeches President Clinton gave on the topic of crime during this time period (see figure I–1), this fact becomes even more evident. Clinton, slowly but surely, returned to utilizing the issue of crime in his speeches as "it was soon apparent that its political value lay in the possibility of co-opting a traditional Republican issue"[93] as it had successfully done during his presidential campaign. Crime was back on the president's agenda.

The primary emphasis of President Clinton, once he did begin to reintroduce the crime issue, was not to pressure Congress directly, but indirectly, by increasing the pressure on the American people to support the passage of a crime bill.[94] This becomes clear in the fact that he did little to provide leadership in Congress by steering the bill toward conference committee,[95] but he did take the role of spokesman on the crime bill through his public remarks, addresses before such

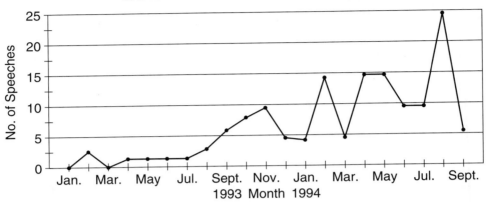

FIGURE I–1   Clinton's Speeches on Crime

Source: Data collected by author from successive volumes of the paper version of *Public Papers of the Presidents* (Washington, D.C.: U.S. Government Printing Office) and the electronic version obtained in *World Book Encyclopedia: American Reference Library* (Orem, Utah: Western Standard Publishing Company). Data includes speeches on the topic of "crime" under the headings of "remarks," "addresses," "interviews," tele-conferences" and "radio addresses."

organizations as the National Association of Police Organizations, the dozen radio addresses he delivered, and the incorporation of the crime bill into his State of the Union Address. All told, Clinton was very active in the public forum in his attempts to influence Congress through the American people in the hopes that enough support could be fostered to pass the crime bill. As the public attention to his rhetoric on crime had worked during the 1992 campaign, Clinton was merely trying to repeat this success and translate it into a legislative victory. By all appearances, Clinton did have an impact on the crime issue through his rhetoric, first and foremost because of the level of media attention to the crime issue during the period of August 1993 through September 1994. A search of the indices of five national newspapers during the time frame of Clinton's entry into office, up to the passage of the crime bill in September of 1994, demonstrates that the crime issue did not become a major national issue until Clinton unveiled his crime agenda in August of 1993 (see figure I-2). The newspaper coverage of Clinton's crime bill then remained fairly consistent until the month of August 1994 when the debate over final passage of the Violent Crime Control and Law Enforcement Act of 1994 became a major political debate. This also appears to hold true for the medium of television evening news coverage in that there were almost no new stories on Clinton and the crime issue until Clinton unveiled his plan in August of 1993 (see figure I-3). Once Clinton revealed his crime plan, the television evening newscasts began carrying a relatively consistent level of coverage. And, once again, there was a dramatic increase of coverage in August of 1994, during the debates over final passage of the crime bill for which President Clinton

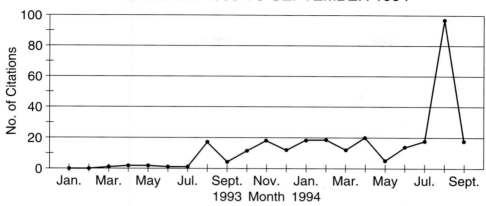

JANUARY 1993 TO SEPTEMBER 1994

FIGURE I–2 Newspaper Coverage of Crime

Source: The original chart, which provided the data from January 1993 to April 1994, appeared in Poveda, Tony G. 1996. "Clinton, Crime, and the Justice Department." *Social Justice.* 21(3): 73–84 on page 81. Data was collected from *The National Newspaper Index* (1992–1994) which is a database that indexes the following newspapers: *New York Times, Wall Street Journal, Washington Post, Christian Science Monitor* and the *Los Angeles Times.* The above chart was created by reevaluating the original data through each of the cited newspapers' individual index from January 1993 to September 1994. In both the original and above charts the keyword search used was "Clinton and Crime."

was dedicating much of his resources. What is perhaps most revealing about the impact Clinton was able to have on the level of media coverage regarding his crime plan is the presence of a high correlation between both mediums of news coverage,[96] as well as the high correlation between Clinton and both newspaper[97] and television[98] coverage on the crime issue. However, what is even more striking is the impact all of this had on the public opinion of crime during this same time period.

In the fall of 1992, as the November elections for President drew near, a Gallup poll asking "What is the most important problem facing the country?" found only 7 percent reporting "crime" to be an important issue and another 6 percent citing "drug abuse."[99] In January of 1993, just prior to Clinton's inauguration, another poll was taken and only 9 percent reported "crime" being the "most important problem" with another 6 percent citing "drug abuse"[100] (see figure I-4). Another public opinion poll taken in June of 1993 also demonstrated that only 9 percent of those polled felt "crime" was the "most important problem."[101] Despite the campaign rhetoric on crime in 1992, crime was not a major issue for the American public at the end of 1992 or the beginning of 1993. However, that would change dramatically in the fall of 1993.

On September 12, 1993, a month after Clinton unveiled his plan, the Gallup poll once again asked the question, "What is the most important problem facing the country?" and the percentage responding "crime" jumped to 16 percent with those responding "drugs" remaining low at 6 percent[102] (see figure I-4). Then just

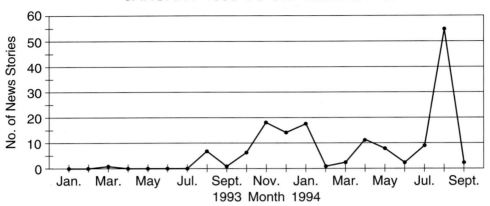

FIGURE I–3 Television Coverage of Crime

Source: Data collected by author from Vanderbilt University. 1998. *Television News Archive.* Nashville: Vanderbilt University. Data obtained from *Television News Archive* Homepage at http://tvnews.vanderbilt.edu/index.html and was downloaded January 2000. The keyword search used "Clinton and Crime."

prior to the State of the Union Address, where Clinton called for the passage of the crime bill, the Gallup poll reported 37 percent reporting "crime" and 9 percent reporting "drugs" as the "most important problem."[103] After the State of the Union Address, the numbers increased to 49 percent citing "crime" and 8 percent citing "drugs."[104] By the fall of 1994, during the debates over the passage of the crime

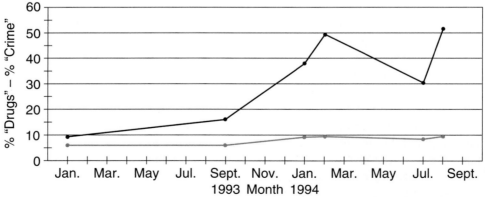

FIGURE I–4 Crime as "Most Important Problem"

Source: Gallup, George. 1945–1996. *The Gallup Poll: Public Opinion.* Wilmington, Delaware: Scholarly Resources, Inc.; *The Gallup Organization Homepage,* "Gallup Social and Economic Indicators—Most Important Problem http://www.gallup.com/poll/indicators/indmip.asp. Data obtained January 2000; and Maguire, Kathleen and Ann. L. Pastore. 1998. *Sourcebook of Criminal Justice Statistics 1997.* Washington, D.C.: Bureau of Justice Statistics.

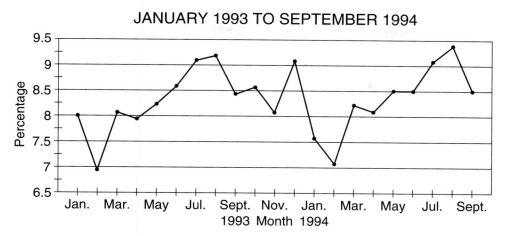

FIGURE I–5   Crime Index Total by Month

Source: Federal Bureau of Investigation. *Uniform Crime Reports—1996.* Washington, D.C.: Federal Bureau of Investigation, U.S. GPO.

bill when President Clinton increased his rhetoric on crime (see figure I-1), the percentage of people reporting crime as the "most important problem facing the nation" was unprecedented. The Gallup poll taken August 16, 1994, reported 52 percent of those polled reporting "crime" as the "most important problem"[105] (see figure I-4) and a number of other public opinion polls taken during this time period clearly demonstrated that crime was in fact the number one problem facing the country.[106] Crime, for some reason, had become a significant issue facing the American people, while drugs were not. The question that many were left asking was why?[107]

The most distinct cause of crime becoming the "most important problem facing the nation" would seem to be crime itself. However, using the total crime index[108] by month during the same time period, January 1993 through September 1994, there is nothing to indicate anything unusual in regard to the occurrence of crime in the United States (see figure I-5). In fact, during the time period of the State of the Union Address by President Clinton in January of 1994, when public opinion of crime rose substantially, the crime rate by month was falling. However, looking at the crime data month by month does tend to mask the overall drop in crime from 1991 to 1994 (see figure I-6).[109] In other words, it should be noted that overall, crime had been falling for the previous two years before crime became the "most important problem facing the nation." This does leave one to wonder what caused crime to rise so dramatically in the minds of the American people, especially in comparison to the open-ended options one has when answering this particular survey question?

In looking at the various graphs, there appears to be a strong relationship between President Clinton's allocation of his resources to speaking out on the

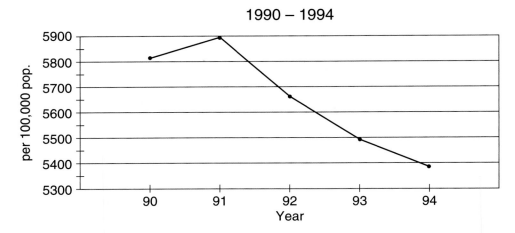

FIGURE I–6   Crime Index by Year

Source: Federal Bureau of Investigation. *Uniform Crime Reports—1996.* Washington, D.C.: Federal Bureau of Investigation, U.S. GPO.

subject of crime (see figure I-1) and the increase in media coverage on the issue (see figures I-2 and I-3). As Clinton speaks, the media reports, and public opinion rises. As a result, the fact that crime became the "most important problem facing the nation" appears to be a direct result of the increase in speeches and reporting. The reason drugs remained relatively stable and low on the list of the "most important problems" is simply because Clinton did not focus on drugs, but rather crime. Finally, as Clinton's speeches precede the media coverage—both the newspaper and television coverage reviewed consisted of media reports on President Clinton and his crime initiative—it would seem that the President, through the media, was able to increase public concern for the issue of crime. As Beckett and Sasson state:

> . . . public concern about crime and drugs has . . . proven quite volatile, susceptible to mobilization by politicians and the mass media. This should hardly come as surprising news; in general, when people are asked about the country's problems, they reflect not on their relatively narrow range of personal experiences but on what they have seen and heard in the mass media from their leaders. This is not to say that politicians can mobilize popular concern about any issue or that public concern about crime is not genuine. But on the relatively rare occasions when the public has put crime or drugs at the top of its list of concerns, it has done so in the context of massive political initiative and media coverage.[110]

In sum, then, it would appear that President Clinton, through the media, was able to greatly influence public opinion of crime through his time and attention to the issue, making it the number one issue facing the nation for the first time in the history of the Gallup poll's famous question. Although this case study is important and provides a great deal of explanation as to why crime surfaced in the fall of 1994 as the "most important problem," it does not tell us whether this President can always influence public opinion of crime, as it may have been solely related to the activity over the crime bill, or whether all presidents have this ability. Do presidents have the ability to influence public opinion of crime? It is the contention of this author that presidents do have this ability and that they have greatly utilized this ability to their advantage over the last half of the twentieth century. Therefore, the research at hand is intended to explore this possibility and determine if, and to what extent, as well as why and how, presidents are able to influence public opinion of crime.

PRESIDENTIAL INFLUENCE OVER PUBLIC OPINION

In 1992, political scientists' Paul Brace and Barbara Hinckley published *Follow the Leader,* which has become a definitive book in the area of presidential leadership and public opinion.[111] In their study of presidential leadership, they focused on major events, the president's handling of these crises, and how the public responded. One of the observations they make, in regard to presidential leadership, is that "implicit in this notion . . . are at least three components: activity, approval, and success."[112] They explain that there must be some type of activity occurring upon which citizens may have formed an opinion. If the president acts in a manner that is responsive to the needs and opinions of the American people, then their public approval will rise. Finally, public approval creates a situation where the president may be able to see legislation that he supports pass Congress, hence success. They further state that, "also implicit is the notion that the president's role is the critical one. The president acts, and Congress and the public respond."[113] This concept is key to understanding presidential leadership, for as a result of the Constitutional boundaries placed upon a president's ability to administer the executive office, the president is placed in a position whereby his power is relegated to the ability to influence. As Richard E. Neustadt has so eloquently stated, his is the "power to persuade."[114] Therefore, presidents find themselves in a position of seeking legislative success by influencing Congress and public opinion through the various activities available to a president. While the former is at least equally important to the president's ability to lead,[115] the research at hand is intended to focus on the latter, for as Brace and Hinckley state, "public mobilization is critical if presidents are to succeed."[116]

There is a rather extensive body of literature that has analyzed the president's ability to take the leadership role in public opinion. The research typically falls into two distinct categories.[117] The first category focuses on the president's ability to manipulate his public approval ratings by engaging in such acts as foreign and domestic trips, giving major speeches, or "going public" through televised speeches.[118] Early research into this ability on the part of the president was suggested to have been possible, but was considered short-lived.[119] More recent research, including the definitive work of Brace and Hinckley, has found some qualifying elements regarding the presidents ability to manipulate their popularity.[120] These qualifications include the fact that major speeches boost popularity ratings, foreign trips have little to no impact, and domestic trips hurt presidential popularity.[121]

The second category focuses on the president's ability to lead public opinion.[122] This category looks at the time and attention a president gives to a specific policy or policies and the effect he is able to have on the policy area by influencing the public. The most common focus of these studies is generally on the president's speeches.[123] There is, however, a qualifying element to this ability as well, in that popular presidents can influence public opinion,[124] but unpopular presidents cannot.[125] Therefore, in a sense, although there are two sets of literature regarding the president's ability to lead public opinion, this is what links them together. In combining the literature from the various perspectives of the president's ability to influence popular support and public opinion, it does become clear that it is a well-accepted theory that presidents can influence the public policy agenda.

Almost as extensive as the above two categories are another two categories of research that attempt to analyze how presidents influence the public.[126] The first looks at the president's ability to influence public opinion through the use of symbolic speeches.[127] These works are based upon the early research of Murray Edelman,[128] who argues that symbolic policies, as delivered through speeches, are those that have no substantive basis and are meant to appeal to beliefs held by the populace, whether those beliefs are true or false.[129] Presidents are then said to deliver speeches that create a psychological, emotional, or social impact, but avoid those statements that contain politics and policy in their statements.[130]

The second set of literature argues that presidents do in fact deliver substantive speeches and provide specific policy attributes when delivering said speeches.[131] In other words, presidents spend a portion of their time issuing substantive policy actions and another portion of their time developing these actions through discussion. Ragsdale, in looking at the presidency from Truman through Carter, found 24 percent of presidential statements are policy actions (both promises and achievements), 62 percent are policy discussions (description of national facts, situations, and backgrounds), while 14 percent consist of nonpolicy remarks.[132] In addition, the work of Paul C. Light, which focuses primarily on the State of Union Addresses, demonstrates that presidents do in fact develop substantive policy and generally deliver it during this yearly speech which serves as their legislative agenda for the upcoming year.[133]

Clearly these last two sets of views on how presidents influence public opinion, symbolic versus substantive speeches, stand in opposition to one another. As

Cohen states, however, "the distinction between symbol and substance is often too starkly drawn in the literature"[134] for, as Cohen continues, "all politics has symbolic as well as substantive implications."[135] Recognizing that in many cases presidents may make calls for what is clearly symbolic policy, for instance calling for federal law to extend the number of crimes for which the death penalty applies, they may also make calls for policy that serves as a cross between symbolism and substance, such as the "100,000 Cops" initiative by President Clinton. This policy was symbolic because the addition of officers played upon public belief that more police officers would reduce crime, but it was substantive policy for the fact it was backed by federal dollars to be delivered to state and local police agencies through hiring grants. Finally, in some cases, speeches are almost entirely substantive, such as when George Bush notified the United States that he would be sending soldiers to Saudi Arabia in support of Kuwait soon after Saddam Hussein had invaded the small Persian Gulf country. In the end, although presidents may attempt to increase their public popularity or attempt to influence public opinion through either symbolic or substantive speeches, the underlying assumption of all of these perspectives is that presidents do have the ability to take the leadership role in public opinion.

This makes intuitive sense as it is the executive branch of government that receives the most media attention, because of the ease of covering one individual rather than 435 representatives, 100 senators, or 9 supreme court justices. It is, therefore, to the president that the public (and the media) looks for understanding of the government's agenda. Although some may argue that Congress has the ability to influence public opinion because of its visibility,[136] and others may argue that it is state governors,[137] it is still the President of the United States who remains the primary focus of public opinion. In a sense, it is the president who leads the country because of his high visibility, the prestige of the office, and his symbolic representation of the United States. Since Richard Neustadt theorized in 1960, in his seminal book *Presidential Power,*[138] that presidents do provide leadership to the United States, it has been the focus of many scholars to determine how presidents influence public opinion and, subsequently, the public agenda. The American people are very reliant on what the president thinks,[139] and the president, through his position in government, in the media, and with the public, stands to influence where the nation focuses its interest. This status has little competition except in international crises that lie largely beyond the president's control.[140] Even in these cases, however, the president can lead the American people in support of intervention, such as in the Persian Gulf War, or away from intervention, such as in the early years of the Balkan wars. In sum, then, presidents do influence public opinion and it is this theory that the study at hand is based upon. And although it will acknowledge the difference between symbolic and substantive policy, this study does not discern any difference between these two viewpoints for the simple fact that both have the capability of influencing public opinion.

Utilizing the theory that presidents influence public opinion, this study will relegate itself to a specific policy area, namely that of crime. It is the contention of this author that presidents have not only the ability to influence public opinion as a whole, but that they also have the capability to influence the public on a specific policy. This is supported by the work of John Kingdon, who has argued that, "no other single actor in the political system has quite the capability of the president to set agendas in given policy areas for all who deal with those policies" and that one of the key reasons for the president's preeminent position in agenda-setting is because of his "command of public attention, which can be converted into pressure on other government officials to adopt the president's agenda."[141] As an extension to Kingdon's point, Cohen and Collier have explained that "the president … is at the center of public attention. No other political figure can compete with the president in this regard."[142] Extending and narrowing the focus even further, Bosso has stated, "the presidency is the single most powerful institutional lever for policy breakthrough [and] is the political system's thermostat, capable of heating up or cooling down the politics of any single issue or of an entire platter of issues."[143] Bosso then summarizes that "the literature on subgovernment politics tends to converge on one point: presidential intervention is a key variable."[144] Research tends to bear this sentiment out in that presidents have been found to have the capability of influencing the public through speeches that are focused on one policy issue, such as welfare, civil rights, or use of force.[145] Presidents are then not only a focal point for public opinion, but they are a focal point for the government's agenda and specific policy issues.

If presidents are able to influence public opinion, and more particularly public opinion in a specific policy area, then it is not beyond reproach that presidents have the capability of influencing public opinion of crime. As the past ten presidents have been found to have increased the amount of attention to the issue of crime with each presidential succession,[146] it would stand to reason that public attention has also increased over the years. It has been theorized that presidents can influence the public's opinion of crime due to the complexity of the crime issue[147] and how it lends itself to the use of symbolic speeches.[148] Limited research has found that presidents do, in fact, use symbolic statements in their speeches on crime,[149] but it has not been determined whether presidents have the capability to influence public opinion of crime.[150] In a broader view, regardless of the differences between symbolic or substantive statements, because it is the president, in his time and attention to crime as well as his speeches through the media, who reaches most Americans in their daily life, if the president focuses on crime, then public opinion of crime should naturally increase. In conclusion, if presidents can influence public opinion through the use of speeches on a single issue, such as crime, regardless of whether they are symbolic or substantive, then presidents should be able to influence public opinion of crime. Therefore, it is the hypothesis of this study that the more time and attention presidents give to crime-control policy the more concerned the public becomes with the issue of crime. Formally stated, the hypothesis of this study is:

Presidents influence public opinion of crime.

SCOPE AND METHOD

As this study is based upon the theory that presidents influence public opinion and the hypothesis states that "presidents influence public opinion of crime," the primary focus will remain on the presidents of the United States across time. While it will most assuredly review all presidents, the emphasis will be on the modern presidents from President Hoover[151] through President Clinton's first term in office. In addition, the focus will also be on the public opinion of crime as it relates to all possible issues of concern, rather than being relegated to direct questions that specifically ask about people's perceptions of crime. Bringing these two together is the limited scope of this study to determine if presidents influence public opinion of crime. Again, it should be plainly stated that presidents are clearly not the only influence on the public's opinion of crime, since Congress, Governors, the U.S. Supreme Court, or crime itself may also be influencing factors. However, this study will be relegated to the influence that presidents have on public opinion as a result of their time and attention to the issue of crime.

The subject matter, it should also be stated, is the specific issue of crime. Because, as LaFree has stated, "crime has … played an increasingly important role in shaping public policy and national politics in the postwar period,"[152] the subject matter is important to understand in conjunction with the presidents' use of the issue in order to influence public opinion. As a result, it is necessary to delineate what is meant by the term "crime." From a formal standpoint, crime can be defined as:

> An act committed or omitted in violation of a law forbidding or commanding it, for which the possible penalties upon conviction for an adult include incarceration, for which a corporation can be penalized by fine or forfeit, or for which a juvenile can be adjudged delinquent or transferred to criminal court for prosecution. Crimes are defined as offenses against the state and … criminal law generally requires proof of both *mens rea*, or a criminal intent or a wrongful purpose, and of the commission of an overt criminal act. Criminal law commonly classifies violations into a) crimes against property, b) crimes against the person, and c) crimes against public safety and morals.[153]

This definition provides an understanding of crime that is broad enough to encompass the subject matter from both the perspective of the presidents and that of the public. It encompasses all categories of crime and it allows for this study to control the changing interpretation of crime across time. Because the types of crime to which presidents, the public, and the criminal justice system dedicate themselves have changed over time, going from prohibition and the mafia in the 1920s–1930s, to juvenile delinquency in the 1950s, to civil and campus unrest in the 1960s–1970s, to drugs in the 1980s and finally to "crime" in the 1990s, the formal definition allows all of these "crime movements" to be captured under a general category of behavior.

Although this study is intent on utilizing a formal definition of crime, adhering to violations of criminal law, the primary focus of crime following World War II has been in the area of what is most often referred to as "street crime."[154] While this term is imprecise, it conjures up what one author has termed "predatory crimes" because they involve offenders who "prey" on other persons or their property.[155] These predatory crimes "evoke the greatest popular fear and concern"[156] and it is to these that the subject matter of crime, especially at the national level, most often turns. It is generally conceded that when the public thinks about crime and when the president talks about crime, the focus is most likely to be in regard to the so-called "street crimes."[157]

Finally, it is necessary to point out the definition of what is meant by the "law and order presidency." As one author, Michael Flamm, has explained, the use of the term "law and order" grew out of the debates in the 1960s and "had special resonance because it combined an understandable concern over the rising number of traditional crimes … with a host of implicit and explicit attitudes and assumptions toward civil rights, urban rioting, antiwar protest, changing moral values, the Supreme Court, and drug use."[158] As a result, Flamm articulates that the politicians "loaded the phrase 'law and order' with layers of meaning virtually impossible to disentangle and turned it into a Rorschach test of public fear and unease. Thus what ultimately gave the issue such potency was precisely its amorphous quality, its ability to represent different concerns to different people at different moments."[159] Because it is so keenly accurate, this definition of "law and order," combined with the specific office of the president, will represent what is meant by the "law and order presidency." In other words, anything that a president chooses to focus on related to the above definition of crime and specifically regarding domestic policy will represent the concept of "law and order," and his time and attention to these issues are thus dubbed the "law and order presidency."

Recognizing the various limitations of this study, it should also be clearly stated that the purpose is to determine whether or not there is evidence to support one hypothesis: do presidents influence public opinion of crime? Although there is the potential for a number of hypotheses regarding presidents, crime, and public opinion, it is the intent of this author to adhere strictly to the one hypothesis. However, it should also be noted that this research will undertake several major objectives aimed at exploring the broad assumptions being made in regard to this hypothesis. The first major objective is to determine whether or not presidents *have* been involved in crime-control policy and that this has been the case across time or whether this has simply been the agenda of one or two presidents in recent years.

If presidents have not been actively involved in crime-control policy, then the assertion that presidential activity on crime influences public opinion of crime would be an erroneous assumption.

The second major objective is, once determining that crime is an issue of the American Presidency, to explore the reasons why presidents would become involved in an issue that for most of American history has been relegated to local governments. Clearly there are limitations to what the chief executive can do regarding crime-control policymaking, so one may ask why presidents find themselves engaged in the issue of crime. Although there are perhaps multiple political, economic, and social reasons, it is important to at least explore the question of "why" because the hypothesis that presidents influence public opinion of crime makes an assumption that there is a reason for doing so.

Finally, a third major objective of the research is to determine how presidents influence public opinion of crime. Although it is important to determine if presidents influence public opinion of crime, it is equally important to have a broader understanding of how they do so. While it would seem that the larger share of the methods for dealing with crime would be found in presidential speech-making, other possibilities for influencing public opinion must be explored. It is not enough that presidents do affect and have reasons for influencing public opinion of crime, part of the underlying assumption to the formally stated hypothesis is that they have the means to influence public opinion. Therefore, it is a major objective of this research to determine how presidents engage in crime-control policy.

In order to test the hypothesis and develop an understanding of these three major objectives, the bulk of the research has come from primary sources with a strong use of secondary sources as supporting evidence.[160] The first primary source utilized was the *Public Papers of the Presidents of the United States,* in both paper and electronic format,[161] which provided qualitative and quantitative data for this study. The papers of all presidents, from Washington through Clinton's first term in office, were reviewed for a qualitative understanding of presidential activity on crime. The papers from President Hoover through Clinton's first term were then utilized to assess both qualitative and quantitative data, primarily descriptive statistics in the latter case, regarding the modern presidents' involvement in the issue of crime. Finally, the papers that cover the post-World War II era, 1945 through 1996, were utilized to derive the primary independent variable, presidential activity on crime, for use in a statistical analysis.

The second primary sources utilized in this study were the various papers of the presidents of the United States and their staffs and administrations available at the libraries of the presidents of the United States where the National Archives and Records Administration oversees these documents.[162] Research was conducted at a number of these libraries in order to develop a deeper understanding of the various assumptions underlying the hypothesis and to be able to satisfy the three major objectives of this study.[163] Although a primary focus of the research at these libraries consisted of reviewing what are known as the White House Central Files, the correspondence and papers of other agencies and departments such as the Department of Justice, Federal Bureau of Investigation, and several crime commissions were also reviewed.

The final use of primary sources for this study consisted of the collection of data for the time-series Ordinary Least Squares regression model. As previously stated, the *Public Papers of the Presidents of the United States* were utilized for purposes of the key independent variable in the study, namely presidential activity on crime. For the dependent variable, public opinion of crime, the percentage of responses regarding crime from the Gallup poll's famous time-series question "What is the Most Important Problem Facing the Nation?" were utilized.[164] Finally, in order to control for other influencing factors, additional data were collected from primary sources to assess other influencing factors such as media, crime, and unemployment.

It should be noted that many other primary sources were utilized, such as the Congressional Record, U.S. government publications regarding crime, and reports from various interest groups regarding crime. In these instances however, there was not a methodical review of these sources across time. In addition, it should also be noted that the secondary sources utilized for this study were not isolated to one academic discipline, but primarily cut across the fields of political science, criminal justice, and sociology. Although it is the intent of this study to analyze the political interaction between presidents and the public, it has often been noted that there is a limited body of research by political scientists in the policy area of crime,[165] thus necessitating the need to cross disciplines.

Finally, recognizing the theory, hypothesis, and methodology of this study are important, as is recognizing the limited scope to which this study addresses itself. However, one looming question asks what importance does answering the question "Do presidents influence public opinion of crime" have? I believe this question is important for several reasons. First, it is often said that the president can utilize the office of the presidency as a "bully pulpit" for addressing and raising awareness on a variety of issues. If this is in fact the case for crime, then the president may be largely responsible for the rising fear of crime among Americans that has been experienced in the United States since the early 1980s.[166] Although it may be true that all politicians contribute to this increased awareness, it is nevertheless true that the president is the most visible of politicians. This may also lead us to an explanation for the paradox that, although the rates of fear have been rising since the early 1980s, the overall rate of crime has been declining over the past twenty years.[167] In truth, all official crime has been falling since 1992.[168] Yet during this same time period we have seen the fear of crime rise to unprecedented levels as was illustrated in the opening case study. In a sense, presidents may be contributing to the artificial construction of a variety of "crime waves," or what Cohen calls a "moral panic,"[169] that has been experienced in the last half of the twentieth century. Crime may be an easier issue for presidents then, if they can successfully rally the public by playing upon their fears, unlike other public policy issues where Americans may not be as concerned and which do not elicit similar fears.

Second, and at a more policy-significant level, it may indicate that the president can control the public agenda on crime, thus securing success with Congress on crime-control policy.[170] If presidents can utilize this power to place certain items on the agenda and keep others off the agenda, the ability to utilize crime for both its symbolic and substantive power may allow presidents to downplay other items.[171] This ability may then allow the president to win in Congress through the passage of a variety of crime bills, thus boosting presidential popularity and providing feedback into legislative success.[172] The president essentially may be able to orchestrate the agenda through the use of symbolic and substantive crime policy, thus assisting in the control of Congress. This is important because, while this may benefit the criminal justice system, it can be detrimental to other areas of social welfare spending.

Finally, despite a number of clearly articulated arguments against the president becoming involved in the policy issue of crime[173] and a number of recent calls for the president and Congress to stop, or at least limit, their focus on the issue of crime,[174] presidents appear to have no reason to stop using the crime issue for political reasons. In other words, it does not appear that the presidents' use of the issue of crime will abate anytime in the near future.[175] Hence, there is a strong potential that presidents, through their time and attention to the issue of crime, will continue to enhance their political base while degrading criminal justice policy and usurping what has historically been a state and local initiative.

PREVIEW OF THE FINDINGS

The "law and order presidency" as a concept that presidents serve in a capacity that requires them to deal with the issue of crime is not a new one. Eighty years ago, Clarence Berdahl wrote about the president's "power of police control."[176] Other influential writers reverberated this sentiment, such as Edward Corwin who spoke of "the president as supervisor of law enforcement,"[177] Clinton Rossiter who described the president as "protector of peace" (both internal and external),[178] and Joseph Kallenback's statement that the president was the "Conservator-in-Chief of Public Order."[179] More recent scholars, notably Calder[180] and Marion,[181] have also explored the role of the chief executive and his involvement in crime-control policy. Recognizing that the president's attention to crime has increased with each presidential succession, this study aims to determine if the "law and order presidency" has gained any advantage in this role, particularly in the ability to influence public opinion of crime. It is the finding of this author that the role of the "law and order president" is successful in influencing public opinion and that this is not merely relegated to one incident or to one president as was described in the introductory case study. Rather, this is a role that has become institutionalized within the office of the presidency and all presidents, choosing to exercise this ability, have the means by which they can influence public opinion of crime.

In order to demonstrate this, the first three chapters will focus on the underlying assumptions made in the hypothesis that "presidents influence public opinion of crime." In chapter one, I ask *if* presidents have been involved in crime control policy. In order to answer this question, I will provide a historical review of presidential involvement in the area of crime commencing with the early Constitutional considerations of law and order as it relates to the office of the president. The chapter will then explore the limited, but evolving, involvement of presidents in crime from Washington through Coolidge. Finally, it will focus on the origins of crime-control policy at the national level and how presidents, starting with Herbert Hoover, incorporate crime into their presidential agendas.

Having articulated that presidents are involved in crime-control policy, chapter two asks *why* presidents have become involved. The chapter will suggest not only why they became involved in crime, but it will suggest what reasons presidents have for remaining involved in the area of crime policy. A number of possibilities are explored, consisting mainly of political, economical, and social reasons, each of which have their own value. As a result, this chapter will not reach a simple answer to the question "Why?" but will suggest that it is the sum of all parts that make crime control an issue valuable to the office of the presidency.

Having articulated why presidents become involved in crime-control policy, chapter three will ask the question *how* presidents involve themselves in crime policy. Although the larger means available to the president clearly lies in his rhetoric, which will be explored most fully, all other options of crime-control activity will also be explored in order to understand how presidents can remain visible and active with this single policy issue.

Having satisfied the three major objectives of this study and effectively dealing with the underlying assumptions of the hypothesis, chapter four will test the hypothesis to determine if there is evidence to support its claims that presidents influence public opinion of crime. Utilizing a time-series, Ordinary Least Squares regression analysis of data collected from the *Public Papers of the Presidents of the United States* and the Gallup poll's "Most Important Problem Facing the Nation" series from 1945 to 1996, and controlling for such variables as official crime rates, unemployment rates, and media influence, it will be demonstrated that presidential attention to crime is found to influence the public's perception that crime is an important issue. In addition, several tests will be made to determine both statistically and theoretically the validity of these findings.

In the final chapter, chapter five, I will reiterate the findings that presidents influence public opinion of crime and conclude that the "law and order presidency" has become a definitive role of the American presidency. I will suggest that, for good or bad, this has several clear and important policy implications. Although the "law and order presidency" is only one role and one institutional factor regarding the office of the presidency, I will attempt to argue that this role is of great importance.

Endnotes

1. Clinton, William J. 1995. *Public Papers of the Presidents of the United States—1994.* Washington D.C.: U.S. G.P.O., p. 1463. Note: italics are the author's.
2. Daly, Christopher B. 1991. "Massachusetts Seen Near Return to Death Penalty." *Washington Post* (August 18): A4.
3. See Jamieson, Kathleen Hall. 1992. *Dirty Politics: Deception, Distraction, and Democracy.* New York: Oxford University Press; West, Darrell M. 1997. *Air Wars: Television Advertising in Election Campaigns 1952–1996.* 2d ed. Washington D.C.: Congressional Quarterly, Inc.
4. Democratic National Convention. "1992 Democratic Party Platform." Reprinted in World Book Encyclopedia. 1998. *American Reference Library.* CD-ROM. Orem: Western Standard Publishing Company.
5. Democratic National Convention. "1992 Democratic Party Platform." Reprinted in World Book Encyclopedia. 1998. *American Reference Library.* CD-ROM. Orem: Western Standard Publishing Company.
6. Reserve Officer Training Corps (R.O.T.C.).
7. Democratic National Convention. "1992 Democratic Party Platform." Reprinted in World Book Encyclopedia. 1998. *American Reference Library.* CD-ROM. Orem: Western Standard Publishing Company.
8. Chernoff, Harry A., Christopher M. Kelly, and John R. Kroger. 1996. "The Politics of Crime." *Harvard Journal on Legislation* 33(2): 527–579; Marion, Nancy E. 1997. "Symbolic Policies in Clinton's Crime Control Agenda." *Buffalo Criminal Law Review* 1(1): 67–108; Zuckman, Jill. 1993. "The President's Call to Serve is Clear but Undefined." *Congressional Quarterly Weekly Report* 218: 51.
9. Shaiko, Ronald G. 1998. "Reverse Lobbying: Interest Group Mobilization from the White House and the Hill." In *Interest Group Politics.* 5th ed. Allan J. Cigler and Burdett A. Loomis, eds. Washington D.C.: Congressional Quarterly Press, pp. 255–282, pp. 259–260.
10. Chernoff, Harry A., Christopher M. Kelly, and John R. Kroger. 1996. "The Politics of Crime." *Harvard Journal on Legislation* 33(2): 527–579; Wattenberg, Ben J. 1996. *Values Matter Most: How Democrats or Republicans or a Third Party Can Win and Renew the American Way of Life.* New York: Regnery Publishing, Inc., pp. 4. Note: One of the death row inmates is reported to have had an I.Q. in the 70's. See Beckett, Katherine and Theodore Sasson. 2000. *The Politics of Injustice.* Thousand Oaks: Pine Forge Press, p. 70.
11. Ifill, Gwen. 1992. "Clinton, in Houston Speech, Assails Bush on Crime Issue." *The New York Times* (July 24): A13.
12. Wallace, Henry Scott. 1992. "Clinton's Real Plan on Crime." *National Law Journal* 12:15.
13. Ifill, Gwen. 1992. "Clinton, in Houston Speech, Assails Bush on Crime Issue." *The New York Times* (July 24): A13; Marion, Nancy E. 1994. A History of Federal Crime Control Initiatives, 1960–1993. Westport: Praeger Publishers.
14. Marion, Nancy E. 1994. *A History of Federal Crime Control Initiatives, 1960–1993.* Westport: Praeger Publishers.
15. Ifill, Gwen. 1992. "Clinton, in Houston Speech, Assails Bush on Crime Issue." *The New York Times* (July 24): A13.

16. Marion, Nancy E. 1997. "Symbolic Policies in Clinton's Crime Control Agenda." *Buffalo Criminal Law Review* 1(1): 67–108.

17. Cited in Bertram, Eva et al. 1996. *Drug War Politics: The Price of Denial.* Berkeley: University of California Press, p. 117.

18. Marion, Nancy E. 1997. "Symbolic Policies in Clinton's Crime Control Agenda." *Buffalo Criminal Law Review* 1(1): 67–108, p. 71.

19. Chernoff, Harry A., Christopher M. Kelly, and John R. Kroger. 1996. "The Politics of Crime." *Harvard Journal on Legislation* 33(2): 527–579, p. 543.

20. Ifill, Gwen. 1992. "Clinton, in Houston Speech, Assails Bush on Crime Issue." *The New York Times* July 24: A13; Walsh, Edward. 1992. "Clinton Charges Bush Uses Crime Issue to Divide." *The Washington Post* (July 24): A16.

21. Devroy, Ann and Ruth Marcus. 1992. "Police Group Gives Bush Its Blessing: President Fought for Endorsement." *The Washington Post* (October 10): A1.

22. Chernoff, Harry A., Christopher M. Kelly, and John R. Kroger. 1996. "The Politics of Crime." *Harvard Journal on Legislation* 33(2): 527–579, p. 543.

23. Clinton, Bill and Al Gore. 1992. *Putting People First.* New York: Times Books.

24. Ifill, Gwen. 1992. "Clinton, in Houston Speech, Assails Bush on Crime Issue." *The New York Times* (July 24): A13; Ifill, Walsh, Edward. 1992. "Clinton Charges Bush Uses Crime Issue to Divide." *The Washington Post* (July 24): A16.

25. Michelowski, Raymond. 1993. "Some Thoughts Regarding the Impact of Clinton's Election on Crime and Justice Policy." *The Criminologist* 18(3): 6.

26. Newsweek poll, March 19–20, 1992, gave Bush a 41% to 35% lead over Clinton on crime. A CBS/New York Times poll, May 6–8, 1992, gave Bush a 36% to 22% lead on "law and order." An ABC News/WP poll, May 8–11, 1992, gave Bush a 39% to 26% lead on crime. An ABC News/WP poll, June 3–7, 1992, gave Bush a 32% to 21% lead on crime. A Gallup/Newsweek poll, July 9–10, 1992, showed Clinton leading Bush on crime 25% to 24%. An U.S. News and World Reports/Princeton Survey Research poll, August 6–9, 1992, demonstrated an equal tie of 38% each. A NBC News/Wall Street Journal poll, August 10–12, 1992, gave Clinton a lead over Bush, 33% to 25%. A Gallup poll, August 10–12, 1992, gave Clinton the lead 51% to 35%. An ABC News/WP poll, October 4, 1992, gave Clinton the lead, 38% to 32%. A Times Mirror poll, October 8–11, 1992, showed Clinton leading 31% to 27%. A Gallup/USA Today/CNN poll, October 9–11, 1992, showed Clinton leading 39% to 34%. Finally, a Princeton Survey Research poll, October 20–22, 1992, showed Clinton leading 35% to 25%. All of these polls are available on LEXIS. See also Chernoff, Harry A., Christopher M. Kelly, and John R. Kroger. 1996. "The Politics of Crime." *Harvard Journal on Legislation* 33(2): 527–579, specifically footnotes 93 and 94.

27. Chernoff, Harry A., Christopher M. Kelly, and John R. Kroger. 1996. "The Politics of Crime." *Harvard Journal on Legislation* 33(2): 544.

28. See Pfiffner, James P. 1996. *The Strategic Presidency: Hitting the Ground Running.* 2d ed., Rev. Lawrence: University Press of Kansas.

29. Chernoff, Harry A., Christopher M. Kelly, and John R. Kroger. 1996. "The Politics of Crime." *Harvard Journal on Legislation* 33(2): 527–579, p. 544.

30. Chernoff, Harry A., Christopher M. Kelly, and John R. Kroger. 1996. "The Politics of Crime." *Harvard Journal on Legislation* 33(2): 527–579, p. 544.

31. Chernoff, Harry A., Christopher M. Kelly, and John R. Kroger. 1996. "The Politics of Crime." *Harvard Journal on Legislation* 33(2): 527–579, p. 545.

32. Chernoff, Harry A., Christopher M. Kelly, and John R. Kroger. 1996. "The Politics of Crime." *Harvard Journal on Legislation* 33(2): 527–579, p. 545.

33. DiClerico, Robert. 1995. The American President. 4th ed. Englewood Cliffs: Prentice Hall, Inc.; DiClerico, Robert. 1996. "Assessing Context and Character." *Society* 33(6): 28–36;

Neustadt, Richard E. 1990. *Presidential Power and the Modern Presidents.* New York: The Free Press; Pfiffner, James P. 1996. *The Strategic Presidency: Hitting the Ground Running.* 2d ed., Rev. Lawrence: University Press of Kansas.

34. DiClerico, Robert. 1996. "Assessing Context and Character." *Society* 33(6): 28–37, p. 28.

35. DiClerico, Robert. 1995. *The American President.* 4th ed. Englewood Cliffs: Prentice Hall, Inc.; DiClerico, Robert. 1996. "Assessing Context and Character." *Society* 33(6): 28–36; Neustadt, Richard E. 1990. *Presidential Power and the Modern Presidents.* New York: The Free Press; Pfiffner, James P. 1996. *The Strategic Presidency: Hitting the Ground Running.* 2d ed., Rev. Lawrence: University Press of Kansas.

36. DiClerico, Robert. 1996. "Assessing Context and Character." *Society* 33(6): 28–37, p. 28.

37. Beckett, Katherine. 1997. *Making Crime Pay: Law and Order in Contemporary American Politics.* New York: Oxford University Press; Beckett, Katherine. 1994. "Setting the Public Agenda: 'Street Crime' and Drug Use in American Politics." *Social Problems* 41(3): 425–447; Beckett, Katherine and Theodore Sasson. 2000. *The Politics of Injustice.* Thousand Oaks: Pine Forge Press; Bertram, Eva et al. 1996. *Drug War Politics: The Price of Denial.* Berkeley: University of California Press; Chernoff, Harry A., Christopher M. Kelly, and John R. Kroger. 1996. "The Politics of Crime." *Harvard Journal on Legislation* 33(2): 527–579; Marion, Nancy E. 1997. "Symbolic Policies in Clinton's Crime Control Agenda." *Buffalo Criminal Law Review* 1(1): 67–108; Massing, Michael. 1998. The Fix. New York: Simon & Schuster; Poveda, Tony G. 1996. *Social Justice* 21(3): 73–84;

38. DiClerico, Robert. 1996. "Assessing Context and Character." *Society* 33(6): 28–36; Clinton, William J. 1994. *Public Papers of the Presidents of the United States—1993.* Washington D.C.: U.S. G.P.O.

39. Chernoff, Harry A., Christopher M. Kelly, and John R. Kroger. 1996. "The Politics of Crime." *Harvard Journal on Legislation* 33(2): 527–579, p. 545.

40. Marion, Nancy E. 1997. "Symbolic Policies in Clinton's Crime Control Agenda." *Buffalo Criminal Law Review* 1(1): 67–108, pp. 73 and 74.

41. Chernoff, Harry A., Christopher M. Kelly, and John R. Kroger. 1996. "The Politics of Crime." *Harvard Journal on Legislation* 33(2): 527–579, p. 545; National Archives and Records Administration. 1999. "Executive Orders Disposition Tables" available on the World Wide Web http://www.nara.gov/fedreg/eo.html. Data downloaded October 19, 1999. See specifically January 1993 through July 1993.

42. Clinton, William J. 1994. "Address Before a Joint Session of Congress on Administration Goals. February 17, 1993." *Public Papers of the Presidents of the United States—1993.* Washington D.C.: U.S. G.P.O., p. 117.

43. Clinton, William J. 1994. "Remarks to Law Enforcement Organizations and an Exchange with Reporters. April 15, 1993." *Public Papers of the Presidents of the United States—1993.* Washington D.C.: U.S. G.P.O., pp. 435–437.

44. Clinton, William J. 1994. "Remarks at the National Law Enforcement Officers Memorial Ceremony. May 13, 1993." *Public Papers of the Presidents of the United States—1993.* Washington D.C.: U.S. G.P.O., pp. 654–656.

45. Kondracke, Morton. 1993. "Hour is Late, But Crime Bill is Finally Coming." *Roll Call* (July 8); as cited in Chernoff, Harry A., Christopher M. Kelly, and John R. Kroger. 1996. "The Politics of Crime." *Harvard Journal on Legislation* 33(2): 527–579, p. 545, footnote 103.

46. Chernoff, Harry A., Christopher M. Kelly, and John R. Kroger. 1996. "The Politics of Crime." *Harvard Journal on Legislation* 33(2): 527–579, p. 545.

47. Chernoff, Harry A., Christopher M. Kelly, and John R. Kroger. 1996. "The Politics of Crime." *Harvard Journal on Legislation* 33(2): 527–579, p. 545.

48. Chernoff, Harry A., Christopher M. Kelly, and John R. Kroger. 1996. "The Politics of Crime." *Harvard Journal on Legislation* 33(2): 527–579, p. 547.

49. The first nomination was for Zoe Baird, Vice President and general counsel to Aetna Life and Casualty Insurance and the second nomination was Kimba Woods, a judge of the U.S. District Court for the Southern District of New York.

50. Chernoff, Harry A., Christopher M. Kelly, and John R. Kroger. 1996. "The Politics of Crime." *Harvard Journal on Legislation* 33(2): 527–579, p. 547; Clinton, William J. 1994. "Remarks on the Swearing-In of Attorney General Janet Reno." *Public Papers of the Presidents of the United States—1993.* Washington D.C.: U.S. G.P.O., p. 279; Windlesham, Lord. 1998. *Politics, Punishment, and Populism.* New York: Oxford University Press, p. 78.

51. Clinton, William J. 1994. *Public Papers of the Presidents of the United States—1993.* Washington D.C.: U.S. G.P.O.; Kohl, Herb. 1996. "Response to "The Politics of Crime." *Harvard Journal on Legislation* 33(2): 527–579, pp. 581–584.

52. Chernoff, Harry A., Christopher M. Kelly, and John R. Kroger. 1996. "The Politics of Crime." *Harvard Journal on Legislation* 33(2): 527–579, pp. 548.

53. Interview with a Senior White House official on January 16, 1996 as cited in Chernoff, Harry A., Christopher M. Kelly, and John R. Kroger. 1996. "The Politics of Crime." *Harvard Journal on Legislation* 33(2): 527–579, pp. 548–549.

54. Chernoff, Harry A., Christopher M. Kelly, and John R. Kroger. 1996. "The Politics of Crime." *Harvard Journal on Legislation* 33(2): 527–579, p. 549; DiClerico, Robert. 1996. "Assessing Context and Character." *Society* 33(6): 28–37.

55. Chernoff, Harry A., Christopher M. Kelly, and John R. Kroger. 1996. "The Politics of Crime." *Harvard Journal on Legislation* 33(2): 527–579, p. 549; Ragsdale, Lyn. 1998. *Vital Statistics on the Presidency: Washington to Clinton.* Rev. ed. Washington D.C.: Congressional Quarterly, Inc., p. 214.

56. Poveda, Tony G. 1996. "Clinton, Crime, and the Justice Department." *Social Justice* 21(3): 73–84, p. 76.

57. Marion, Nancy E. 1997. "Symbolic Policies in Clinton's Crime Control Agenda." *Buffalo Criminal Law Review* 1(1): 67–108.

58. Windlesham, Lord. 1998. *Politics, Punishment, and Populism.* New York: Oxford University Press, p. 35.

59. Windlesham, Lord. 1998. *Politics, Punishment, and Populism.* New York: Oxford University Press, p. 31.

60. Poveda, Tony G. 1996. "Clinton, Crime, and the Justice Department." *Social Justice* 21(3): 73–84.

61. It is not unusual for incoming presidents to support previous legislative bills circulating in Congress because they generally have been worked out in Committees, have reached their final stages, and provide for an instant "win" on the part of the President. See Light, Paul C. 1991. *The President's Agenda: Domestic Policy Choice from Kennedy to Reagan.* Revised Edition. Baltimore: The Johns Hopkins University Press, pp. 122–126.

62. Clinton, William J. 1994. "Remarks Announcing the Anti-crime Initiative and an Exchange with Reporters. August 11, 1993." *Public Papers of the Presidents of the United States—1993.* Washington D.C.: U.S. G.P.O., p. 1360–1363. See Ifill, Gwen. 1992. "Clinton, in Houston Speech, Assails Bush on Crime Issue." *The New York Times* (July 24): A13, for similar remarks.

63. Clinton, William J. 1994. *Public Papers of the Presidents of the United States—1993.* Washington D.C.: U.S. G.P.O., p. 2241; Windlesham, Lord. 1998. *Politics, Punishment, and Populism.* New York: Oxford University Press, pp. 32–33.

64. Clinton, William J. 1994. "The President's Radio Address. August 14, 1993." *Public Papers of the Presidents of the United States—1993.* Washington D.C.: U.S. G.P.O., p. 1379–1380,

65. Chernoff, Harry A., Christopher M. Kelly, and John R. Kroger. 1996. "The Politics of Crime." *Harvard Journal on Legislation* 33(2): 527–579, p. 550.

66. For a comprehensive outline of the history of the Violent Crime Control and Law Enforcement Act of 1994 (H.R. 3355), see Congressional Information Service. 1995. *CIS Annual 1994.* Bethesda: Congressional Information Service, pp. 170–184; 103d Cong., 2d Sess. "Violence Crime Control and Law Enforcement Act of 1994." 1995. *Congressional and Administrative News.* St. Paul: West Publishing, pp. 1801–1880; Houston, James and William W. Parsons. 1998. *Criminal Justice and the Policy Process.* Chicago: Nelson-Hall Publishers, pp. 77–82.

67. "Brooks, Biden Offer Crime Measures." *Congressional Quarterly Weekly Report.* September 25: 51. In the House it was designated House Resolution 3131 and in the Senate, Senate Bill 1488.

68. "Brooks, Biden Offer Crime Measures." *Congressional Quarterly Weekly Report* (September 25): 51; Marion, Nancy E. 1997. "Symbolic Policies in Clinton's Crime Control Agenda." Buffalo Criminal Law Review 1(1): 67–108, p. 77; Windlesham, Lord. 1998. *Politics, Punishment, and Populism.* New York: Oxford University Press, p. 32.

69. Clinton, William J. 1994. "The President's Radio Address. October 9, 1993." *Public Papers of the Presidents of the United States—1993.* Washington D.C.: U.S. G.P.O., p. 1721–1722.

70. Clinton, William J. 1994. "The President's Radio Address. October 23, 1993." *Public Papers of the Presidents of the United States—1993.* Washington D.C.: U.S. G.P.O., pp. 1811–1812.

71. Chernoff, Harry A., Christopher M. Kelly, and John R. Kroger. 1996. "The Politics of Crime." *Harvard Journal on Legislation* 33(2): 527–579, p. 551; Windlesham, Lord. 1998. *Politics, Punishment, and Populism.* New York: Oxford University Press, pp. 35–36.

72. Windlesham, Lord. 1998. *Politics, Punishment, and Populism.* New York: Oxford University Press, p. 36.

73. Chernoff, Harry A., Christopher M. Kelly, and John R. Kroger. 1996. "The Politics of Crime." *Harvard Journal on Legislation* 33(2): 527–579, p. 554.

74. Clinton, William J. 1994. "Remarks on Signing Handgun Control Legislation. November 30, 1993." *Public Papers of the Presidents of the United States—1993.* Washington D.C.: U.S. G.P.O., pp. 2079–2081; DeFrances, Carol J. and Steven K. Smith. 1994. "Federal-State Relations in Gun Control: The 1993 Brady Handgun Violence Prevention Act." *Publius: The Journal of Federalism* 24(Summer): 69–82.

75. Clinton, William J. 1994. "Statement on Signing the International Parental Kidnapping Crime Act of 1993. December 2, 1993." *Public Papers of the Presidents of the United States—1993.* Washington D.C.: U.S. G.P.O., p. 2093.

76. Clinton, William J. 1994. "Statement on Signing the National Child Protection Act of 1993. December 20, 1993." *Public Papers of the Presidents of the United States—1993.* Washington D.C.: U.S. G.P.O., pp. 2192–2193.

77. Clinton, William J. 1994. "The President's Radio Address. December 11, 1993." *Public Papers of the Presidents of the United States—1993.* Washington D.C.: U.S. G.P.O., pp. 2154–2155.

78. Clinton, William J. 1995. "Address Before a Joint Session of the Congress on the State of the Union. January 25, 1994." *Public Papers of the Presidents of the United States—1994.* Washington D.C.: U.S. G.P.O., pp. 126–135, specifically page 133.

79. Chernoff, Harry A., Christopher M. Kelly, and John R. Kroger. 1996. "The Politics of Crime." *Harvard Journal on Legislation* 33(2): 527–579, p. 557; Ifill, Gwen. 1994. "Clinton Embraces Crime Measure, Ever So Vaguely." *The New York Times* (February 21): A13. As cited in the Ifill article, White House press secretary Dee Dee Myers stated, "It is up to Congress to work out all the details" demonstrating a very hands-off approach to the crime legislation by President Clinton.

80. Chernoff, Harry A., Christopher M. Kelly, and John R. Kroger. 1996. "The Politics of Crime." *Harvard Journal on Legislation* 33(2): 527–579, p. 557.

81. Clinton, William J. 1995. *Public Papers of the Presidents of the United States—1994.* Washington D.C.: U.S. G.P.O., see pages 658–660, "The President's Radio Address" April 9, 1994; pages 701–702, "The President's Radio Address" April 16, 1994; pages 766–767, "The President's Radio Address" April 23, 1994; pages 1096–1098, "The President's Radio Address" June 18, 1994; pages 1258–1259, "The President's Radio Address" July 16, 1994; and pages 1340–1341, "The President's Radio Address" July 30, 1994.

82. Many of these were coordinated with the assistance of the White House and their "reverse lobbying" with the various interest groups representing the law enforcement community. See Shaiko, Ronald G. 1998. "Reverse Lobbying: Interest Group Mobilization from the White House and the Hill." In *Interest Group Politics.* 5th ed. Allan J. Cigler and Burdett A. Loomis, eds. Washington D.C.: Congressional Quarterly Press, pp. 255–282.

83. Shaiko, Ronald G. 1998. "Reverse Lobbying: Interest Group Mobilization from the White House and the Hill." In *Interest Group Politics.* 5th ed. Allan J. Cigler and Burdett A. Loomis, eds. Washington D.C.: Congressional Quarterly Press, pp. 255–282.

84. Windlesham, Lord. 1998. *Politics, Punishment, and Populism.* New York: Oxford University Press, p. 96.

85. As Wolpe and Levine explain, "On the evening of August 12, at a rally at the National Association of Police Organizations meeting in Minneapolis, Clinton stood surrounded by uniformed officers and American flags as he blamed special interests for the House vote defeating the rule for floor consideration of HR 3355, as he attacked Republicans for playing politics with America's safety, and as he tapped widespread public support for a ban on assault weapons. The evening news pictures were vintage Reagan. Within a week, a *USA Today* poll showed that confidence in Clinton's handling of crime had bounced up to 42 percent from 29 percent just a month earlier." See Wolpe, Bruce C. and Bertram J. Levine. 1996. *Lobbying Congress: How the System Works.* 2d ed. Washington D.C.: Congressional Quarterly Press, p. 133.

86. Chernoff, Harry A., Christopher M. Kelly, and John R. Kroger. 1996. "The Politics of Crime." *Harvard Journal on Legislation* 33(2): 527–579, p. 570, footnote 251; Shaiko, Ronald G. 1998. "Reverse Lobbying: Interest Group Mobilization from the White House and the Hill." In *Interest Group Politics.* 5th ed. Allan J. Cigler and Burdett A. Loomis, eds. Washington D.C.: Congressional Quarterly Press, pp. 255–282; Windlesham, Lord. 1998. *Politics, Punishment, and Populism.* New York: Oxford University Press, p. 96. According to Shaiko, Clinton was able to obtain support from the following interest groups: Fraternal Order of Police, National Association of Police Organizations, International Union of Police Associations, National Troopers Coalition, International Brotherhood of Police Officers, International Association of Chiefs of Police, Federal Law Enforcement Officers Association, National Organization of Black Law Enforcement Executives, National Sheriffs Association, Major City Police Chiefs Association, Police Executive Research Forum, and the Police Foundation. The only association missing was the Police Benevolent Association which would not support the crime bill because of their unhappiness with the Brady Bill and the Assault Weapons Ban.

87. Chernoff, Harry A., Christopher M. Kelly, and John R. Kroger. 1996. "The Politics of Crime." *Harvard Journal on Legislation* 33(2): 527–579, pp. 570–571.

88. Shaiko, Ronald G. 1998. "Reverse Lobbying: Interest Group Mobilization from the White House and the Hill." In *Interest Group Politics.* 5th ed. Allan J. Cigler and Burdett A. Loomis, eds. Washington D.C.: Congressional Quarterly Press, pp. 255–282, p. 261; Windlesham, Lord. 1998. *Politics, Punishment, and Populism.* New York: Oxford University Press, pp. 100–102. According to Windlesham, "during the final stages of negotiation, a potential swing voter, Representative Susan Molinari (R-NY), pressed for a fundamental change in the judicial process. She wanted evidence of previous charges of sexual offenses to be admissible as evidence in court, even if the defendant had not been convicted of the offense … Molinari had obtained an encouraging response from a surprising quarter. She has said that when she had talked to

Clinton on the telephone, he had expressed his disappointment that two items had been dropped from the bill—the sexual predator notification provision and the provision that would make admissible in court, at the discretion of the judge, a defendant's prior charges of sexual offenses. According to Molinari, Clinton had said that he would try and get them back."

89. Chernoff, Harry A., Christopher M. Kelly, and John R. Kroger. 1996. "The Politics of Crime." *Harvard Journal on Legislation* 33(2): 527–579, pp. 570–573; Windlesham, Lord. 1998. *Politics, Punishment, and Populism.* New York: Oxford University Press, pp. 96–103.

90. Windlesham, Lord. 1998. *Politics, Punishment, and Populism.* New York: Oxford University Press, p. 103.

91. DiClerico, Robert. 1996. "Assessing Context and Character." *Society* 33(6): 28–37.

92. Clinton, William J. 1995. "Remarks on Signing the Violent Crime Control and Law Enforcement Act of 1994. September 13, 1994." *Public Papers of the Presidents of the United States—1994.* Washington D.C.: U.S. G.P.O., pp. 1539–1541.

93. Poveda, Tony G. 1996. "Clinton, Crime, and the Justice Department." *Social Justice* 21(3): 73–84, p. 76.

94. Windlesham, Lord. 1998. *Politics, Punishment, and Populism.* New York: Oxford University Press, p. 97. Note: During the month of August 1994, when the Violent Crime Control and Law Enforcement Act of 1994 was reaching its final stages in Congress, Clinton did resort to more traditional means of directly lobbying individual members of Congress.

95. Windlesham, Lord. 1998. *Politics, Punishment, and Populism.* New York: Oxford University Press, pp. 101–103.

96. Pearson correlation of .94 where p is significant at the .05 level.

97. Pearson correlation of .79 where p is significant at the .05 level.

98. Pearson correlation of .72 where p is significant at the .10 level.

99. Gallup Survey of "Most Important Problem Facing the Nation" September 2, 1992. See Gallup, George. 1945–1996. *The Gallup Poll: Public Opinion.* Wilmington, Delaware: Scholarly Resources, Inc.; *The Gallup Organization Homepage,* "Gallup Social and Economic Indicators—Most Important Problem" http://www.gallup.com/poll/indicators/indmip.asp Data obtained January 2000; Maguire, Kathleen and Ann. L. Pastore. 1998. *Sourcebook of Criminal Justice Statistics 1997.* Washington D.C.: Bureau of Justice Statistics.

100. Gallup Survey of "Most Important Problem Facing the Nation" January 11, 1993. See Gallup, George. 1945–1996. *The Gallup Poll: Public Opinion.* Wilmington, Delaware: Scholarly Resources, Inc.; *The Gallup Organization Homepage,* "Gallup Social and Economic Indicators—Most Important Problem" http://www.gallup.com/poll/indicators/indmip.asp. Data obtained January 2000; and Maguire, Kathleen and Ann. L. Pastore. 1998. *Sourcebook of Criminal Justice Statistics 1997.* Washington D.C.: Bureau of Justice Statistics.

101. Los Angeles Times, Public Opinion Survey as cited in Beckett, Katherine. 1997. *Making Crime Pay: Law and Order in Contemporary American Politics.* New York: Oxford University Press, p. 25; Beckett, Katherine and Theodore Sasson. 2000. *The Politics of Injustice.* Thousand Oaks: Pine Forge Press, p. 71.

102. Gallup Survey of "Most Important Problem Facing the Nation" September 12, 1993. See Gallup, George. 1945–1996. *The Gallup Poll: Public Opinion.* Wilmington, Delaware: Scholarly Resources, Inc.; *The Gallup Organization Homepage,* "Gallup Social and Economic Indicators—Most Important Problem" http://www.gallup.com/poll/indicators/indmip.asp. Data obtained January 2000; and Maguire, Kathleen and Ann. L. Pastore. 1998. *Sourcebook of Criminal Justice Statistics 1997.* Washington D.C.: Bureau of Justice Statistics.

103. Gallup Survey of "Most Important Problem Facing the Nation" January 17, 1994. See Gallup, George. 1945–1996. *The Gallup Poll: Public Opinion.* Wilmington, Delaware: Scholarly Resources, Inc.; *The Gallup Organization Homepage,* "Gallup Social and Economic Indicators—Most Important Problem" http://www.gallup.com/poll/indicators/indmip.asp. Data obtained

January 2000; and Maguire, Kathleen and Ann. L. Pastore. 1998. *Sourcebook of Criminal Justice Statistics 1997.* Washington D.C.: Bureau of Justice Statistics.

104. Gallup Survey of "Most Important Problem Facing the Nation" January 30, 1994. See Gallup, George. 1945–1996. *The Gallup Poll: Public Opinion.* Wilmington, Delaware: Scholarly Resources, Inc.; *The Gallup Organization Homepage,* "Gallup Social and Economic Indicators—Most Important Problem" http://www.gallup.com/poll/indicators/indmip.asp. Data obtained January 2000; and Maguire, Kathleen and Ann. L. Pastore. 1998. *Sourcebook of Criminal Justice Statistics 1997.* Washington D.C.: Bureau of Justice Statistics.

105. Gallup Survey of "Most Important Problem Facing the Nation" August 16, 1994. See Gallup, George. 1945–1996. *The Gallup Poll: Public Opinion.* Wilmington, Delaware: Scholarly Resources, Inc.; *The Gallup Organization Homepage,* "Gallup Social and Economic Indicators—Most Important Problem" http://www.gallup.com/poll/indicators/indmip.asp. Data obtained January 2000; and Maguire, Kathleen and Ann. L. Pastore. 1998. *Sourcebook of Criminal Justice Statistics 1997.* Washington D.C.: Bureau of Justice Statistics.

106. These additional polls include a CBS News, CBS News/New York Times, Wirthlin Group, and Princeton Survey Research Associates public opinion survey. See Warr, Mark. 1995. "The Polls—Poll Trends. Public Opinion on Crime and Punishment." *Public Opinion Quarterly* 59: 296–310. See also Hagan, Michael G. 1995. "The Crime Issue and the 1994 Elections." Paper presented at the annual meeting of the American Political Science Association, Chicago, August 31–September 3; Roberts, Julian V. and Loretta J. Stalans. 1997. *Public Opinion, Crime, and Criminal Justice.* Boulder: Westview Press.

107. See for instance Warr, Mark. 1995. "The Polls—Poll Trends. Public Opinion on Crime and Punishment." *Public Opinion Quarterly* 59: 296–310.

108. The crime index is composed of violent and property crime and is calculated for each 100,000 in the United States Population.

109. Federal Bureau of Investigation. 1996. *Uniform Crime Reports—1995.* Washington D.C.: U.S. Department of Justice.

110. Beckett, Katherine and Theodore Sasson. 2000. *The Politics of Injustice.* Thousand Oaks: Pine Forge Press, p. 127.

111. Brace, Paul and Barbara Hinckley. 1992. *Follow the Leader: Opinion Polls and the Modern Presidents.* New York: Basic Books.

112. Brace, Paul and Barbara Hinckley. 1992. *Follow the Leader: Opinion Polls and the Modern Presidents.* New York: Basic Books, p. 73.

113. Brace, Paul and Barbara Hinckley. 1992. *Follow the Leader: Opinion Polls and the Modern Presidents.* New York: Basic Books, p. 73.

114. Neustadt, Richard E. 1990. *Presidential Power and the Modern Presidents: The Politics of Leadership from Roosevelt to Reagan.* New York: The Free Press. See specifically chapter three, entitled "The Power to Persuade."

115. See for instance Rivers, Douglas and Nancy L. Rose. 1985. "Passing the President's Program: Public Opinion and Presidential Influence in Congress." *American Journal of Political Science* 29: 183–196.

116. Brace, Paul and Barbara Hinckley. 1992. *Follow the Leader: Opinion Polls and the Modern Presidents.* New York: Basic Books, p. 82. This point is reaffirmed by Cohen and Collier when they state, "Presidential ability to affect the congressional agenda can come about through two routes, directly or indirectly through public opinion." See Cohen, Jeffrey E. and Ken Collier. 1999. *Presidential Policymaking: An End-of-Century Assessment.* Edited by Steven A. Shull. Armonk: M. E. Sharpe, p. 43.

117. Cohen, Jeffrey E. 1995. "Presidential Rhetoric and the Public Agenda." *American Journal of Political Science* 39(1): 87–107.

118. Brace, Paul and Barbara Hinckley. 1992. *Follow the Leader: Opinion Polls and the Modern Presidents.* New York: Basic Books; Brace, Paul and Barbara Hinckley. 1993. "Presidential Activities from Truman through Reagan: Timing and Impact." *Journal of Politics* 55: 382–398; Hinckley, Barbara. 1990. *The Symbolic Presidency.* New York: Routledge; Kernell, Samuel. 1997. *Going Public: New Strategies of Presidential Leadership.* 3d ed. Washington D.C.: Congressional Quarterly, Inc.; Ostrom, Charles W., Jr. and Dennis M. Simon. 1985. "Promise and Performance: A Dynamic Model of Presidential Popularity." *American Political Science Review* 79: 334–358; Ostrom, Charles W., Jr. and Dennis M. Simon. 1988. "The President's Public." *American Journal of Political Science* 32: 1096–1119; Ostrom, Charles W., Jr. and Dennis M. Simon. 1989. "The Man in the Teflon Suit: The Environmental Connection, Political Drama and Popular Support in the Reagan Presidency." *Public Opinion Quarterly* 53: 353–387; Ragsdale, Lyn. 1984. "The Politics of Presidential Speechmaking, 1949–1980." *American Political Science Review* 78: 971–984; Ragsdale, Lyn. 1987. "Presidential Speechmaking and the Public Audience: Individual Presidents and Group Attitudes." *Journal of Politics* 49:704–736.

119. MacKuen, Michael B. 1983. "Political Drama, Economic Conditions and the Dynamics of Presidential Popularity." *American Journal of Political Science* 27: 165–192; Ragsdale, Lyn. 1984. "The Politics of Presidential Speechmaking, 1949–1980." *American Political Science Review* 78: 971–984; Ragsdale, Lyn. 1987. "Presidential Speechmaking and the Public Audience: Individual Presidents and Group Attitudes." *Journal of Politics* 49:704–736. See also Cohen, Jeffrey E. 1995. "Presidential Rhetoric and the Public Agenda." *American Journal of Political Science* 39(1): 87–107, for an explanation of this set of literature.

120. Brace, Paul and Barbara Hinckley. 1992. *Follow the Leader: Opinion Polls and the Modern Presidents.* New York: Basic Books; Brace, Paul and Barbara Hinckley. 1993. "Presidential Activities from Truman through Reagan: Timing and Impact." *Journal of Politics* 55: 382–398; Ostrom, Charles W., Jr. and Dennis M. Simon. 1985. "Promise and Performance: A Dynamic Model of Presidential Popularity." *American Political Science Review* 79: 334–358; Ostrom, Charles W., Jr. and Dennis M. Simon. 1988. "The President's Public." *American Journal of Political Science* 32: 1096–1119; Ostrom, Charles W., Jr. and Dennis M. Simon. 1989. "The Man in the Teflon Suit: The Environmental Connection, Political Drama and Popular Support in the Reagan Presidency." *Public Opinion Quarterly* 53: 353–387; Ragsdale, Lyn. 1984. "The Politics of Presidential Speechmaking, 1949–1980." The *American Political Science Review* 78: 971–984; Ragsdale, Lyn. 1987. "Presidential Speechmaking and the Public Audience: Individual Presidents and Group Attitudes." *Journal of Politics* 49: 704–736; Simon, Dennis M. and Charles W. Ostrom, Jr. 1985. "The President and Public Support: A Strategic Perspective." In *The Presidency and Public Policy Making.* George C. Edwards III, Steven A. Shull, and Norman C. Thomas, Eds. Pittsburgh: University of Pittsburgh Press; Simon, Dennis M. and Charles W. Ostrom, Jr. 1988. "The Politics of Prestige: Popular Support and the Modern Presidency." *Presidential Studies Quarterly* 18: 741–759.

121. Brace, Paul and Barbara Hinckley. 1992. *Follow the Leader: Opinion Polls and the Modern Presidents.* New York: Basic Books.

122. Denton, Robert F., Jr. and Dan F. Hahn. 1986. *Presidential Communication.* New York: Praeger Publishers; Edwards, George C. III. 1983. *The Public Presidency: The Pursuit of Popular Support.* New York: St. Martin's Press; Gelderman, C. W. 1995. "All the President's Words." *The Wilson Quarterly* 19: 68–79; Graber, Doris. 1982. *The President and the Public.* Philadelphia: Institute for Study of Human Issues; Kernell, Samuel. 1997. *Going Public: New Strategies of Presidential Leadership.* 3d ed. Washington D.C.: Congressional Quarterly, Inc.; Light, Paul C. 1991. *The President's Agenda: Domestic Policy Choice from Kennedy to Reagan.* rev. ed. Baltimore: Johns Hopkins University Press; Mondak, Jeffrey. 1993. "Source Cues and Policy Approval: The Cognitive Dynamics of Public Support for the Reagan Agenda." *American Journal*

of Political Science 37: 186–212; Page, Benjamin I. and Robert Y. Shapiro. 1984. "Presidents as Opinion Leaders: Some New Evidence." *Policy Studies Journal* 12: 649–661; Page, Benjamin I. and Robert Y. Shapiro. 1992. *The Rational Public: Fifty Years of Trends in Americans' Policy Preferences.* Chicago: University of Chicago Press; Page, Benjamin I., Robert Y. Shapiro, and Glenn R. Dempsey. 1987. "What Moves Public Opinion?" *American Political Science Review* 81: 23–43; Sigelman, Lee. 1980. "Gauging the Public Response to Presidential Leadership." *Presidential Studies Quarterly* 10: 427–433.

123. Cohen, Jeffrey E. 1995. "Presidential Rhetoric and the Public Agenda." *American Journal of Political Science* 39(1): 87–107; Cohen, Jeffrey E. 1997. *Presidential Responsiveness and Public Policy-Making: The Public and the Policies that Presidents Choose.* Ann Arbor: The University of Michigan Press; Gelderman, C. W. 1995. "All the President's Words." *The Wilson Quarterly* 19: 68–79; Ragsdale, Lyn. 1984. "The Politics of Presidential Speechmaking, 1949–1980." *American Political Science Review* 78: 971–984; Ragsdale, Lyn. 1987. "Presidential Speechmaking and the Public Audience: Individual Presidents and Group Attitudes." *Journal of Politics* 49:704–736.

124. Edwards, George C. III. 1983. *The Public Presidency: The Pursuit of Popular Support.* New York: St. Martin's Press; Page, Benjamin I. and Robert Y. Shapiro. 1985. "Presidential Leadership through Public Opinion." In *The Presidency and Public Policy Making.* Edited by George C. Edwards III, Steven A. Shull, and Norman C. Thomas. Pittsburgh: University of Pittsburgh Press, pp. 22–36; Page, Benjamin I. and Robert Y. Shapiro. 1992. *The Rational Public: Fifty Years of Trends in Americans' Policy Preferences.* Chicago: University of Chicago Press.

125. Page, Benjamin I. and Robert Y. Shapiro. 1992. *The Rational Public: Fifty Years of Trends in Americans' Policy Preferences.* Chicago: University of Chicago Press; Sigelman, Lee and Carol K. Sigelman. 1981. "Presidential Leadership of Public Opinion: From 'Benevolent Leader' to 'Kiss of Death'?" In *The Presidency and Public Policy Making.* Edited by George C. Edwards III, Steven A. Shull, and Norman C. Thomas. Pittsburgh: University of Pittsburgh Press.

126. See Cohen, Jeffrey E. 1997. *Presidential Responsiveness and Public Policy-Making: The Public and the Policies that Presidents Choose.* Ann Arbor: The University of Michigan Press, pp. 34–37 for a broader understanding of these two categories.

127. Ceaser, James W. 1985. "The Rhetorical Presidency Revisited." In *Modern Presidents and the Presidency.* Marc Landy, ed. Lexington: Lexington Books, pp. 15–34; Ceaser, James W., Glen E. Thurow, Jeffrey Tulis, and Joseph M. Bessette. 1981. "The Rise of the Rhetorical Presidency." *Presidential Studies Quarterly* 11: 158–171; Cohen, Jeffrey E. 1997. *Presidential Responsiveness and Public Policy-Making: The Public and the Policies that Presidents Choose.* Ann Arbor: The University of Michigan Press; Hart, Roderick P. 1984. "The Language of the Modern Presidency." *Presidential Studies Quarterly* 14: 249–264; Hill, Kim Quaile. 1998. "The Policy Agenda of the President and the Mass Public: A Research Validation and Extension." *American Journal of Political Science* 42: 1328–1334; Hinckley, Barbara. 1990. *The Symbolic Presidency: How Presidents Portray Themselves.* New York: Routledge; Tulis, Jeffrey K. 1987. *The Rhetorical Presidency.* Princeton: Princeton University Press.

128. Edelman, Murray. 1988. *Constructing the Political Spectacle.* Chicago: The University of Chicago Press; Edelman, Murray. 1971. *Politics as Symbolic Action: Mass Arousal and Quiescence.* Chicago: Markham Publishing Company; Edelman, Murray. 1964. *The Symbolic Uses of Politics.* Urbana: University of Illinois Press.

129. Elder, Charles and Roger Cobb. 1983. *The Political Uses of Symbols.* New York: Longman; Gusfield, Joseph. 1963. *Symbolic Crusade.* Urbana: University of Illinois Press; Hinckley, Barbara. 1990. *The Symbolic Presidency: How Presidents Portray Themselves.* New York: Routledge.

130. Hinckley, Barbara. 1990. *The Symbolic Presidency: How Presidents Portray Themselves.* New York: Routledge, p. 73.

131. Kessel, John H. 1974. "Parameters of Presidential Politics." *Social Science Quarterly* 55: 8–24; Kessel, John H. 1977. "Seasons of Presidential Politics." *Social Science Quarterly* 58: 418–435; Light, Paul. 1991. *The President's Agenda: Domestic Policy Choice from Kennedy to Reagan.* Rev. ed. Baltimore: The Johns Hopkins University Press.

132. The data is from Ragsdale, Lyn. 1982. *Presidents and Publics: The Dialogue of Presidential Leadership.* Ph.D. Dissertation, University of Wisconsin—Madison. It is cited in Cohen, Jeffrey E. 1997. *Presidential Responsiveness and Public Policy-Making: The Public and the Policies that Presidents Choose.* Ann Arbor: The University of Michigan Press, p. 35; Hinckley, Barbara. 1990. *The Symbolic Presidency: How Presidents Portray Themselves.* New York: Routledge, pp. 72–73.

133. Light, Paul. 1991. *The President's Agenda: Domestic Policy Choice from Kennedy to Reagan.* Rev. ed. Baltimore: The Johns Hopkins University Press; Light, Paul C. 1993. "Presidential Policy Making." In *Researching the Presidency: Vital Questions, New Approaches.* Edited by George C. Edwards III, John H. Kessel, and Bert A. Rockman. Pittsburgh: University of Pittsburgh Press, pp. 161–199.

134. Cohen, Jeffrey E. 1997. *Presidential Responsiveness and Public Policy-Making: The Public and the Policies that Presidents Choose.* Ann Arbor: The University of Michigan Press, p. 36. Cohen cites Kemp, Kathleen. 1981. "Symbolic and Strict Regulation in the American States." *Social Science Quarterly* 62: 516–526 and Marshall, Thomas R. 1993. "Symbolic versus Policy Representation on the U.S. Supreme Court." *Journal of Politics* 55: 140–150. I would also add Marion, Nancy. 1994. "Symbolism and Federal Crime Control Legislation, 1960–1990." *Journal of Crime and Justice* 17(2): 69–91 and Stolz, Barbara Ann. 1992. "Congress and the War on Drugs: An Exercise in Symbolic Politics." *Journal of Crime and Justice* 15(1): 119–136.

135. Cohen, Jeffrey E. 1997. *Presidential Responsiveness and Public Policy-Making: The Public and the Policies that Presidents Choose.* Ann Arbor: The University of Michigan Press, p. 36.

136. Dodd, Lawrence C. and Bruce I. Oppenheimer. 1997. *Congress Reconsidered.* 6th ed. Washington D.C.: Congressional Quarterly, Inc., see pages 61–80.

137. Davey, Joseph D. 1988. *The Politics of Prison Expansion: Winning Elections by Waging War on Crime.* Westport: Praeger Publishers.

138. Neustadt, Richard E. 1960/1980/1990. *Presidential Power and the Modern Presidents: The Politics of Leadership from Roosevelt to Reagan.* New York: The Free Press.

139. Greenstein, Fred I. 1974. "The Politics of Persuasion." In *Choosing the President.* Edited by James D. Barber. Englewood Cliffs: Prentice Hall, pp. 87–102; Mayer, William G. 1993. *The Changing American Mind: How and Why American Public Opinion Changed Between 1960 and 1988.* Ann Arbor: The University of Michigan Press.

140. Edelman, Murray. 1964. *The Symbolic Uses of Politics.* Urbana: University of Illinois Press.

141. Kingdon, John W. 1995. *Agendas, Alternatives, and Public Policies.* 2d ed. New York: HarperCollins College Publishers, p. 23.

142. Cohen, Jeffrey E. and Ken Collier. 1999. *Presidential Policymaking: An End-of-Century Assessment.* Edited by Steven A. Shull. Armonk: M. E. Sharpe, pp. 42–43.

143. Bosso, Christopher. 1987. *Pesticides and Politics: The Life Cycle of a Public Issue.* Pittsburgh: University of Pittsburgh Press, p. 261.

144. Bosso, Christopher. 1987. *Pesticides and Politics: The Life Cycle of a Public Issue.* Pittsburgh: University of Pittsburgh Press, p. 261.

145. Behr, Roy L. and Shanto Iyengar. 1985. "Television News, Real-World Clues, and Changes in the Public Agenda." *Public Opinion Quarterly* 49: 38–57; Cohen, Jeffrey E. 1995. "Presidential Rhetoric and the Public Agenda." *American Journal of Political Science* 39(1): 87–107; Iyengar, Shanto. 1991. *Is Anyone Responsible? How Television Frames Political Issues.* Chicago: University of Chicago Press; Iyengar, Shanto, and Donald R. Kinder. 1987. *News that Matters: Television and American Public Opinion.* Chicago: University of Chicago Press.

146. Calder, James D. 1981. "Herbert Hoover's Contributions to the Administrative History of Crime Control Policy." Paper presented at the annual meeting of the Southwest Political Science Association, Dallas, Texas; Calder, James D. 1978. *Presidents and Crime Control: Some Limitations on Executive Policy Making.* Ph.D. Dissertation, Claremont University; Caplan, Gerald. 1973. "Reflections on the Nationalization of Crime, 1964–1968." *Law and the Social Order* 1973: 583–635; Finckenauer, James O. 1978. "Crime as a National Political Issue: 1964–1976." *Crime & Delinquency* 24(1): 13–27; Mahoney, Barry. 1976. *The Politics of the Safe Streets Act, 1965–1973: A Case Study in Evolving Federalism and the National Legislative Process.* Ph.D. Dissertation, Columbia University; Marion, Nancy. 1992. "Presidential Agenda Setting in Crime Control." *Criminal Justice Policy Review* 6: 159–184; Marion, Nancy E. 1994. "*A History of Federal Crime Control Initiatives, 1960–1993.* Westport: Praeger Publishers; Marion, Nancy E. 1994. "Symbolism and Federal Crime Control Legislation, 1960–1990." *Journal of Crime and Justice* 17: 69–91; Potter, Claire B. 1998. *War on Crime: Bandits, G-Men, and the Politics of Mass Culture.* New Brunswick: Rutgers University Press. The one exception to this continued increase in attention to crime by each succeeding president is President Carter. Although Carter focused on the issue of crime, his focus was more relative to the notion of dealing with the bureaucracy that addresses the crime issue, rather than dealing with crime itself.

147. Hall, Stuart, Charles Critcher, Tony Jefferson, John Clarke, and Brian Roberts. 1978. *Policing the Crisis: Mugging, the State, and Law and Order.* London: Macmillan; Scheingold, Stuart A. 1984. *The Politics of Law and Order: Street Crime and Public Policy.* New York: Longman; Scheingold, Stuart A. 1991. *The Politics of Street Crime: Criminal Process and Cultural Obsession.* Philadelphia: Temple University Press.

148. Cronin, Thomas E., Tania Z. Cronin, and Michael E. Milakovich. 1981. *U.S. v. Crime in the Streets.* Bloomington: Indiana University Press; Hinckley, Barbara. 1990. *The Symbolic Presidency: How Presidents Portray Themselves.* New York: Routledge; Marion, Nancy. 1992. "Presidential Agenda Setting in Crime Control." *Criminal Justice Policy Review* 6: 159–184; Marion, Nancy E. 1994. "*A History of Federal Crime Control Initiatives, 1960–1993.* Westport: Praeger Publishers; Marion, Nancy E. 1994. "Symbolism and Federal Crime Control Legislation, 1960–1990." *Journal of Crime and Justice* 17: 69–91; Scheingold, Stuart. 1995. "Politics, Public Policy, and Street Crime." *The Annals of the American Academy of Political and Social Science* 539: 141–154.

149. Marion, Nancy E. 1994. "Symbolism and Federal Crime Control Legislation, 1960–1990." *Journal of Crime and Justice* 17:69–91.

150. One study found that "state actors" and "state initiatives" at the federal level do influence public concern about crime, however "state actor" was used to refer to *any* federal actor and was not limited to the president. See Beckett, Katherine. 1994. "Setting the Public Agenda: 'Street Crime' and Drug Use in American Politics." *Social Problems* 41(3): 425–447. A second study, limited to the issue of drugs, covering the period 1984 to 1991, found that public opinion influences the president in regard to the issue of crime. See Gonzenbach, William J. 1996. *The Media, the President, and Public Opinion: A Longitudinal Analysis of the Drug Issue, 1984–1991.* Mahwah: Lawrence Erlbaum Associates, Publishers.

151. While President Hoover is generally not considered a "modern president," he is the last president during the transition to the modern presidency and he was the first to call for the national government to become actively involved in crime-control policy.

152. LaFree, Gary. 1998. *Losing Legitimacy: Street Crime and the Decline of Social Institutions in America.* Boulder: Westview Press, p. 2.

153. Rush, George E. 2000. *The Dictionary of Criminal Justice.* 5th ed. New York: Dushkin/McGraw-Hill, p. 86.

154. LaFree, Gary. 1998. *Losing Legitimacy: Street Crime and the Decline of Social Institutions in America.* Boulder: Westview Press; Scheingold, Stuart A. 1991. *The Politics of Street Crime: Criminal Process and Cultural Obsession.* Philadelphia: Temple University Press; Scheingold, Stuart A. 1995. "Politics, Public Policy, and Street Crime." *The Annals of the American Academy of Political and Social Science* 539: 155–168.

155. Glaser, Daniel. 1978. *Crime in Our Changing Society.* New York: Holt. See also LaFree, Gary. 1998. *Losing Legitimacy: Street Crime and the Decline of Social Institutions in America.* Boulder: Westview Press, p. 3.

156. LaFree, Gary. 1998. *Losing Legitimacy: Street Crime and the Decline of Social Institutions in America.* Boulder: Westview Press, p. 3; Scheingold, Stuart A. 1991. *The Politics of Street Crime: Criminal Process and Cultural Obsession.* Philadelphia: Temple University Press, introduction and chapter one.

157. Scheingold, Stuart A. 1991. *The Politics of Street Crime: Criminal Process and Cultural Obsession.* Philadelphia: Temple University Press.

158. Flamm, Michael William. 1998. *"Law and Order": Street Crime, Civil Disorder, and the Crisis of Liberalism.* Ph.D. Dissertation, Columbia University, abstract.

159. Flamm, Michael William. 1998. *"Law and Order": Street Crime, Civil Disorder, and the Crisis of Liberalism.* Ph.D. Dissertation, Columbia University, abstract.

160. For definitions of primary and secondary sources see Booth, Wayne C., Gregory G. Colomb, and Joseph M. Williams. 1995. *The Craft of Research.* Chicago: The University of Chicago Press, p. 69.

161. See Washington to Clinton. Various years. *Public Papers of the Presidents of the United States.* Washington D.C.: U.S. G.P.O. and World Book Encyclopedia. 1998. *American Reference Library.* Orem: The Western Standard Publishing Company. This electronic version contains most of the president's public papers in a searchable format. In addition, the paper version and electronic version are identical from President Hoover through President Clinton, as the electronic version provides a reference for each paragraph, citing where it can be found in the paper version.

162. See Hyland, Pat. 1995. *Presidential Libraries and Museums: An Illustrated Guide.* Washington D.C.: Congressional Quarterly Books.

163. The specific libraries where research was conducted by this author are as follows: The Franklin and Eleanor Roosevelt Library, Hyde Park, New York; The Gerald R. Ford Library, Ann Arbor, Michigan; The Herbert Hoover Presidential Library, West Branch, Iowa; The Lyndon Baines Johnson Library, Austin, Texas; The Richard M. Nixon Project, College Park, Maryland; The Ronald Reagan Presidential Library, Simi Valley, California.

164. Gallup, George. 1945–1996. *The Gallup Poll: Public Opinion.* Wilmington, Delaware: Scholarly Resources, Inc.; *The Gallup Organization Homepage,* "Gallup Social and Economic Indicators—Most Important Problem" http://www.gallup.com/poll/indicators/indmip.asp. Data obtained January 2000; Maguire, Kathleen and Ann. L. Pastore. 1998. *Sourcebook of Criminal Justice Statistics 1997.* Washington D.C.: Bureau of Justice Statistics.

165. As several authors state, "Political science research on criminal justice is scarce." See Dilulio, John J., Jr., Steven K. Smith, and Aaron J. Saiger. 1995. "The Federal Role in Crime Control." In *Crime.* Edited by James Q. Wilson and Joan Petersilia. San Francisco: Institute for Contemporary Studies, p. 450. Although they limit their citation to Nagel, Stuart, Erika Fairchild, and Anthony Champagne. 1983. *The Political Science of Criminal Justice.* Springfield: Charles C. Thomas. There have been several other earlier works by political scientist's in the area of crime. See Cronin, Thomas E., Tania Z. Cronin, and Michael E. Milakovich. 1981. *U.S. v. Crime in the Streets.* Bloomington: Indiana University Press; Fairchild, Erika S. and Vincent J. Webb. 1985. *The Politics of Crime and Criminal Justice.* Beverly Hills: SAGE Publications; Feeley, Malcolm M. and Austin D. Sarat. 1980. *The Policy Dilemma: Federal Crime Policy and the Law*

Enforcement Assistance Administration. Minneapolis: University of Minnesota Press; Gray, Virginia and Bruce Williams. 1980. *The Organizational Politics of Criminal Justice: Policy In Context.* Lexington: Lexington Books; Scheingold, Stuart A. 1984. *The Politics of Law and Order: Street Crime and Public Policy.* New York: Longman; Scheingold, Stuart A. 1991. *The Politics of Street Crime: Criminal Process and Cultural Obsession.* Philadelphia: Temple University Press; Wilson, James Q. 1975. *Thinking About Crime.* New York: Basic Books, Inc.; Wilson, James Q. 1968. *Varieties of Police Behavior.* Cambridge: Harvard University Press.

166. Gaubatz, Kathlyn Taylor. 1995. *Crime in the Public Mind.* Ann Arbor: The University of Michigan Press.

167. Federal Bureau of Investigation. 1994–1998. *Uniform Crime Reports.* Washington D.C.: U.S. G.P.O.

168. Federal Bureau of Investigation. 1999. *Uniform Crime Reports—1998.* Washington D.C.: U.S. G.P.O.

169. Cohen, Stanley. 1980. *Folk Devils and Moral Panics: The Creation of the Mods and Rockers.* New York: St. Martin's Press. See also Chiricos, Ted. 1998. "The Media, Moral Panics and the Politics of Crime Control." In *The Criminal Justice System: Politics and Policies.* 7th ed. George F. Cole and Marc G. Gertz, eds. Belmont: Wadsworth Publishers, pp. 58–75.

170. Cohen, Jeffrey E. 1995. "Presidential Rhetoric and the Public Agenda." *American Journal of Political Science* 39(1): 87–107.

171. Edelman, Murray. 1988. *Constructing the Political Spectacle.* Chicago: The University of Chicago Press; Edelman, Murray. 1971. *Politics as Symbolic Action: Mass Arousal and Quiescence.* Chicago: Markham Publishing Company; Edelman, Murray. 1964. *The Symbolic Uses of Politics.* Urbana: University of Illinois Press; Marion, Nancy. 1992. "Presidential Agenda Setting in Crime Control." *Criminal Justice Policy Review* 6: 159–184; Marion, Nancy E. 1994. *A History of Federal Crime Control Initiatives, 1960–1993.* Westport: Praeger Publishers; Marion, Nancy E. 1994. "Symbolism and Federal Crime Control Legislation, 1960–1990." *Journal of Crime and Justice* 17: 69–91.

172. Brace, Paul and Barbara Hinckley. 1992. *Follow the Leader: Opinion Polls and the Modern Presidents.* New York: Basic Books; Brace, Paul and Barbara Hinckley. 1993. "Presidential Activities from Truman through Reagan: Timing and Impact." *Journal of Politics* 55: 382–398; Howes, J. S. and J. Twombly. 1996. "Presidents, Political Drama, and Public Approval." Paper presented at the annual meeting of the Northeastern Political Science Association, Boston, Massachusetts; Ostrom, Charles W., Jr. and Dennis M. Simon. 1985. "Promise and Performance: A Dynamic Model of Presidential Popularity." *American Political Science Review* 79: 334–358; Ostrom, Charles W., Jr. and Dennis M. Simon. 1988. "The President's Public." *American Journal of Political Science* 32: 1096–1119; Ostrom, Charles W., Jr. and Dennis M. Simon. 1989. "The Man in the Teflon Suit: The Environmental Connection, Political Drama and Popular Support in the Reagan Presidency." *Public Opinion Quarterly* 53: 353–387; Rivers, Douglas and Nancy L. Rose. 1985. "Passing the President's Program: Public Opinion and Presidential Influence in Congress." *American Journal of Political Science* 29: 183–196; Simon, Dennis M. and Charles W. Ostrom, Jr. 1985. "The President and Public Support: A Strategic Perspective." In *The Presidency and Public Policy Making.* George C. Edwards III, Steven A. Shull, and Norman C. Thomas, eds. Pittsburgh: University of Pittsburgh Press; Simon, Dennis M. and Charles W. Ostrom, Jr. 1988. "The Politics of Prestige: Popular Support and the Modern Presidency." *Presidential Studies Quarterly* 18: 741–759.

173. See Calder, James Doug. 1978. *Presidents and Crime Control: Some Limitations on Executive Policy Making.* Ph.D. Dissertation, Claremont University.

174. See for instance Dilulio, John J., Jr. 1999. "Federal Crime Policy: Time for a Moratorium." *Brookings Review* 17(1): 17–21; Heymann, Philip B. and Mark H. Moore. 1996. "The Federal

Role in Dealing with Violent Street Crime: Principles, Questions, and Cautions." *The Annals of the American Academy of Political and Social Science* 543: 103–115; Marion, Nancy. 1992. "Presidential Agenda Setting in Crime Control." *Criminal Justice Policy Review* 6(2): 159–184, p. 181.

175. See for instance Faucheux, Ron. 1994. "The Politics of Crime." *Campaigns and Elections.* (March): 31–34, which states on page 34, "crime will be a big political issue as long as people fear it." See also Scheingold, Stuart A. 1995. "Politics, Public Policy, and Street Crime." *The Annals of the American Academy of Political and Social Science* 539: 155–168.

176. Berdahl, Clarence A. 1920. *War Powers of the Executive in the United States.* Urbana: University of Illinois Press, p. 182. I was first introduced to these early concepts of the president and crime by the works of James D. Calder. See Calder, James D. 1982. "Presidents and Crime Control: Kennedy, Johnson and Nixon and the Influences of Ideology." *Presidential Studies Quarterly* 12: 574–589; Calder, James D. 1978. *Presidents and Crime Control: Some Limitations on Executive Policy Making.* Ph.D. Dissertation, Claremont University.

177. Corwin, Edward S. 1957. *The President and His Powers 1787 to 1957.* 4th ed. New York: New York University Press, p. 79.

178. Rossiter, Clinton. 1960. *The American Presidency.* 2nd ed. New York: New American Library, p. 26.

179. Kallenbach, Joseph E. 1966. *The American Chief Executive.* New York: Harper and Row, p. 446.

180. Calder, James D. 1981. "Herbert Hoover's Contributions to the Administrative History of Crime Control Policy." Paper presented at the annual meeting of the Southwest Political Science Association, Dallas, Texas; Calder, James D. 1982. "Presidents and Crime Control: Kennedy, Johnson and Nixon and the Influences of Ideology." *Presidential Studies Quarterly* 12: 574–589; Calder, James D. 1978. *Presidents and Crime Control: Some Limitations on Executive Policy Making.* Ph.D. Dissertation, Claremont University.

181. Marion, Nancy. 1992. "Presidential Agenda Setting In Crime Control." *Criminal Justice Policy Review* 6(2): 159–184; Marion, Nancy. 1994. "Symbolism and Federal Crime Control Legislation, 1960–1990." *Journal of Crime and Justice* 17(2): 69–91. Two other works by Nancy Marion do not focus exclusively on the presidents, but include material on presidents and crime: Marion, Nancy E. 1994. *A History of Federal Crime Control Initiatives, 1960–1993.* Westport: Praeger Publishers; Marion, Nancy E. 1995. *A Primer in the Politics of Criminal Justice.* New York: Harrow and Heston Publishers.

President John F. Kennedy making his remarks upon receiving the report of the President's Committee on Juvenile Delinquency and Youth Crime at the White House on May 31, 1962.

PHOTOGRAPH COURTESY OF THE JOHN F. KENNEDY LIBRARY.

chapter 1

A History of Presidents and Crime Policy

. . . that our wish as well as theirs is that the public efforts may be directed honestly to the public good, that peace be cultivated, civil and religious liberty unassailed, [and] law and order preserved.

—Thomas Jefferson[1]

This chapter is about the history of presidents and their involvement in the area of crime, punishment, and the criminal justice system. The intent of this chapter is to demonstrate that presidential involvement in crime policy is really a discussion of evolution. Presidents as early as Washington and Jefferson had to deal with issues that were of a criminal nature. The types of crimes, however, were far different from those with which contemporary presidents have had to deal. In many of these early cases, the types of crime display a more definitive federal jurisdiction—rebellion and treason—whereas presidents today find themselves dealing with issues of street crime and drugs. In addition, presidents in the eighteenth and nineteenth centuries attempted, in most cases, to limit federal intervention in the area of crime and to leave the issue to state governments. This would no longer be the case for most of the twentieth century. The federal government would move heavily into the area of crime by passing significant criminal legislation, federalizing a vast number of state crimes,[2] and providing increased funding to support both state and local criminal justice agencies.[3] Presidents, the Executive branch, and the federal government as a whole, would become heavily involved in the "federalization"[4] and "nationalization"[5] of crime. As Friedman has pointed out, government's "role in the [criminal justice] system has grown to an impressive size, starting from a baseline of close to zero"[6] and that "the big show, the main show, is now Washington D.C.; and the big gun is the president, not the governor or the mayor."[7] As a result, it is necessary to understand how presidential involvement in the issue of crime has evolved from a "baseline of zero" to being the "big show."

This will be done by relating presidential involvement in crime policy into three eras: traditional, transitional, and nationalization. The first era of presidents

41

and crime is the traditional era which spans the years 1776 through 1899[8] and will discuss the limited role presidents played in crime during the eighteenth and nineteenth centuries. The second era is divided into two time periods. The first, covering the years 1900 to 1927, will discuss presidential responses to such social and political events as prohibition and organized crime and is considered the "responsive" period of presidential involvement in crime.[9] The second time period commences with President Hoover's attempt to make crime a national issue thus paving the way for the later nationalization of crime in the last half of the twentieth century.[10] However, primarily because of the Depression, the election of Franklin D. Roosevelt in 1932, and World War II, many of these policy concepts did not become actualized until much later. Hence, the second part of the transitional era is considered to be the developmental period, spanning the years 1928 through 1963.[11] Finally, in 1964 with the presidential election cast between the Democratic incumbent, President Lyndon B. Johnson, and the Republican candidate, Barry Goldwater, crime would become a national issue and the era of presidential involvement in crime would move from the transitional-developmental era to that of the "nationalization" of crime.[12] Therefore, these three eras will provide a categorization of the evolution of presidential involvement in the issue of crime.[13]

CONSTITUTIONAL CONSTRUCTION AND CRIME

Crime has been a part of American life since the founding of the Jamestown settlement. According to one historian, by 1690 crime had already become "a civic problem of the first magnitude."[14] The mid-1700s, the period after the French and Indian wars, was characterized by "an increase in crimes of all sorts: counterfeiting, petty thievery, housebreaking, burglaries of every description, highway robberies, rape, assault, and murder."[15] As a more contemporary report has noted, "violence has been far more intrinsic to our past than we should like to think."[16] In fact, American history prior to the Revolutionary War and the drafting of the Constitution is replete with examples of violence.[17] As one author would later note, "crime is as American as Jesse James."[18] While it becomes clear that crime was an issue for governmental consideration, when the Constitution was constructed in 1787, it was evident that the Constitution intended for the federal government to play a limited role in this policy area.

The most significant event that the American Revolution brought about was the federal system of government as realized through ratification of the United States Constitution. This would have a profound impact on American criminal justice because it would allow the government to separate itself from English law, allowing "the Americans to cast off even more of the archaic English legal heritage and enshrine in the law emerging ideas about crime, punishment, and individual liberty."[19] While the preamble to the United States Constitution speaks of "establishing justice" and "insuring domestic tranquility," the oversight of crime is severely limited in terms of federal jurisdiction over crime and when the federal government can intervene in crimes occurring at the state and local level.

Turning to specifics, the Constitution gave Congress the power "to provide for the punishment of counterfeiting the securities and current coin of the United States," "to constitute tribunals inferior to the supreme court," and "to define and punish piracies and felonies committed on the high seas."[20] It also gave Congress the power to "call forth the militia to execute the laws of the union" and "suppress insurrections."[21] Moreover, it gave the people the right of habeas corpus, considered by many to be a fundamental protection against an arbitrary government,[22] when instructing Congress that "the privilege of the Writ of Habeas Corpus shall not be suspended, unless when in cases of rebellion or invasion the public safety may require it."[23] These were essentially the strict Constitutional limits of the Congress in regard to crime. However, both the so-called elastic clause, that Congress could "make all laws which shall be necessary and proper" and the commerce clause, that Congress could "regulate commerce . . . among the states," would become important at a much later date.[24]

In the case of the judiciary, it created the federal court system,[25] it commanded that "the trial of all crimes, except in cases of impeachment, shall be by jury; and such trial shall be held in the State where the said crimes shall have been committed,"[26] and it defined the crime of treason.[27] Beyond these basic tenets of judicial power, the Constitution was limited in its construction of a court system focused on crime.

Article four of the United States Constitution does provide additional guidance in regard to the issue of crimes in its declaration that "a person charged in any state with treason, felony, or other crime, who shall flee from justice, and be found in another state, shall on demand of the executive authority of the state from which he fled, be delivered up, to be removed to the state having jurisdiction of the crime."[28] Hence, the issue among the states of extraditing criminals was resolved. In addition, Article four also gave Congress the power to "dispose of and make all needful rules and regulations respecting the territory or other property belonging to the United States."[29] This allowed the federal government to establish criminal law and enforce the law in any of its territories that had not become states. As a result of westward expansion generally initiated with territories, this clause, as it relates to crime, would prove significant throughout most of the nineteenth century. Finally, Article four declared that "the United States shall guarantee to every state in this Union a Republican form of government, and shall protect each of them against invasion; and on application of the legislature, or of the executive (when the legislature cannot be convened) against domestic violence."[30] This clause allowed for the federal government, primarily through the actions of the president, to intervene in cases of domestic disturbances upon request of the state government[31] and was most likely a result of Shay's Rebellion in Pennsylvania which occurred just prior to the Constitutional Convention.[32] Although used infrequently, it was a means by which presidents could find themselves "Constitutionally" engaged in the issue of local crime.

The Constitution gave the person holding the office of president the "power to grant reprieves and pardons for offenses against the United States, except in cases of impeachment."[33] This ability to grant pardons is the one definitive power granted to the executive officer that is clearly centered on the issue of crime. The other executive powers, while not as definitive as the power to pardon, allow the president to deal with the issue of crime in an indirect manner. For instance, the president "shall from time to time give to the Congress information of the State of the Union."[34] This allows the president to create and communicate his agenda for possible consideration by the Congress,[35] part of which may be, and has been, focused on the issue of crime. In addition, the president has the power to appoint key personnel to cabinet and staff positions[36] that may be focused on the subject of crime, such as the Attorney General.[37] And finally, the president has the power to veto legislation[38] which may consist of law revolving around the issue of crime. All said and done the president is limited by his office to directly deal with the issue of crime. But over time, presidents have found the means by which they, their administration, and the federal government could be involved in this subject matter.

Although presidential involvement in the issue of crime would evolve, there was a profound realization that local crimes were best left to the state and local governments. Federal intervention in local crimes, the founders agreed, should be a last resort. Madison would highlight this fact, partially to alleviate the fears of the anti-federalist, in the Federalist Papers, Number 43, when he explained:

> Insurrection in a State will rarely induce a federal interposition, unless the number concerned in them bear some proportion to the friends of government. It will be much better that the violence in such cases should be repressed by the superintending power, than that the majority should be left to maintain their cause by a bloody and obstinate contest. The existence of a right to interpose will generally prevent the necessity of exerting it.[39]

However, this is not to say that Madison did not recognize the importance of maintaining civil order and that government, including the national government, had the right to intervene. As Madison explains in Federalist Number 37:

> Energy in government is essential to that security against external and internal danger and to that prompt and salutary execution of the laws which enter into the very definition of good government. Stability in government is essential to national char-

acter and to the advantage annexed to it, as well as to that repose and confidence in the minds of the people, which are among the chief blessings of civil society.[40]

It was, however, Alexander Hamilton, who recognized that granting the state and local governments primary domain over the issue of crime would give them a vested power over the national government. He wrote in Federalist Number 17:

> There is one transcendent advantage belonging to the province of the State governments, which alone suffices to place the matter in a clear and satisfactory light—I mean the ordinary administration of criminal and civil justice. This, of all others, is the most powerful, most universal, and most attractive source of popular obedience and attachment. It is this which, being the immediate and visible guardian of life and property, having its benefits and its terrors in constant activity before the public eye, regulating all those personal interests and familiar concerns to which the sensibility of individuals is more immediately awake, contributes more than any other circumstance to impressing upon the minds of the people affection, esteem, and reverence towards the government. This great cement of society, which will diffuse itself almost wholly through the channels of the particular governments, independent of all other causes of influence, would insure them so decided an empire over their respective citizens as to render them at all times a complete counterpoise, and, not unfrequently, dangerous rivals to the power of the Union.[41]

Although perhaps overstating the case of the power granted to state and local governments through their rights over the criminal justice system, the important aspect of this lengthy quote is the fact that Hamilton recognized that it was the state and local governments who had primary domain over the issue of crime.[42] The national government was a very limited, almost nonexistent, partner. Friedman had stated that the federal government, in regards to crime, had started "from a baseline of close to zero";[43] this was it.

Although the national government was limited by the Constitution as to the role it could play in the issue of crime, there was still the realization that criminal justice in the territories and in the District of Columbia was of a "federal" nature and was in need of its own criminal law. As a result, the first federal crime bill was passed, entitled the Crimes Act of 1790, which defined seventeen crimes against the national government.[44] Some of these crimes consisted of federal violations such as murder or other crimes "within any fort, arsenal, dock-yard, magazine," or other place under federal control or "upon the high seas, or in any river, haven, basin or bay, out of the jurisdiction of any particular state."[45] It also made it a crime to forge any United States certificates or securities, commit perjury in a federal court, or commit treason, piracy, and violence against an ambassador.[46] All told, the majority of these crimes were concerned with criminal issues clearly within the realm of "federal" law.

The following year, the first ten amendments to the Constitution of the United States were ratified and became effective December 15, 1791.[47] Because there was very little language in the Constitution as originally drafted that protected the rights of citizens, several key states, during the ratification process, demanded the inclusion of a "Bill of Rights." As a result, "about half the text of the Bill of Rights, by bulk, is concerned with criminal justice."[48] The fourth amendment protected citizens against "unreasonable searches and seizures." The fifth amendment provided for a grand jury hearing, disallowed trial for the same offense twice, and ensured that a person could not be "deprived of life, liberty, or property, without due process of law." The sixth amendment gave citizens the right to a "speedy and public trial" and the right to confront witnesses. In the seventh amendment, citizens were granted trials by jury and in the eighth amendment they were protected from "excessive bail" and "cruel and unusual punishments." Finally, and of noted significance,[49] the tenth amendment reaffirmed that "the powers not delegated to the United States by the Constitution, nor prohibited by it to the states, are reserved to the states respectively, or to the people." Hence, matters of crime and criminal justice were reaffirmed to be under the control of state and local governments.

It is evident that the founding fathers and the federal system they created, left the primary task of maintaining law and order to the state and local governments. A combination of Article four, Section four, which guaranteed the states a "republican form of government" and the tenth amendment, which reserved the rights not granted by the Constitution to the states, vastly limited the power of the national government to intervene in matters of a criminal nature. Although it could most assuredly deal with crime in its territories and in the District of Columbia as well as on the "high seas," it could not become directly involved in criminal matters unless called upon by the state legislature or state executive when the legislature could not convene. It is clear then, that crime, criminal justice, and the maintenance of law and order was traditionally a state and local government matter and that presidents were greatly limited in their ability to address this issue.

THE TRADITIONAL ERA (1776–1899)

The traditional era of presidents involvement in crime is primarily marked by its limited nature. Presidents were either constrained by the Constitution, did not desire to get involved, or did not have the means by which they could become involved. Most crime, then, was left to the state and local governments unless it had a specific federal nature or the president was called upon to render assistance by the state legislature or executive. As Calder has explained, there are essentially three broad categories under which the federal government could intervene: "1) incidents threatening the unity principle of the federal system of government; 2) incidents threatening the national security and involving foreign nations; and 3) incidents violating a federal law passed by Congress."[50] It was under these three cat-

The President Speaks . . .

The most malign of all these dangers today is disregard and disobedience of law. Crime is increasing. Confidence in rigid and speedy justice is decreasing. I am not prepared to believe that this indicates any decay in the moral fibre of the American people. I am not prepared to believe that it indicates an impotence of the Federal Government to enforce its laws.

It is only in part due to the additional burdens imposed upon our judicial system by the 18th amendment. The problem is much wider than that. Many influences had increasingly complicated and weakened our law enforcement organization long before the adoption of the 18th amendment.

To reestablish the vigor and effectiveness of law enforcement we must critically consider the entire Federal machinery of justice, the redistribution of its functions, the simplification of its procedure, the provision of additional special tribunals, the better selection of juries, and the more effective organization of our agencies of investigation and prosecution that justice may be sure and that it may be swift. While the authority of the Federal Government extends to but part of our vast system of national, State, and local justice, yet the standards which the Federal Government establishes have the most profound influence upon the whole structure.

President Herbert Hoover with the Wickersham Commission on the White House lawn after their first formal meeting on May 28, 1929.
PHOTOGRAPH USED BY PERMISSION FROM AP/WIDE WORLD PHOTOS.

(continued)

The President Speaks . . . — (continued)

We are fortunate in the ability and integrity of our Federal judges and attorneys. But the system which these officers are called upon to administer is in many respects ill adapted to present-day conditions. Its intricate and involved rules of procedure have become the refuge of both big and little criminals. There is a belief abroad that by invoking technicalities, subterfuge, and delay, the ends of justice may be thwarted by those who can pay the cost.

Reform, reorganization, and strengthening of our whole judicial and enforcement system, both in civil and criminal sides, have been advocated for years by statesmen, judges, and bar associations. First steps toward that end should not longer be delayed. Rigid and expeditious justice is the first safeguard of freedom, the basis of all ordered liberty, the vital force of progress. It must not come to be in our Republic that it can be defeated by the indifference of the citizens, by exploitation of the delays and entanglements of the law, or by combinations of criminals. Justice must not fail because the agencies of enforcement are either delinquent or inefficiently organized. To consider these evils, to find their remedy, is the most sore necessity of our times.

—Herbert Hoover
Inaugural Address, March 4, 1929

---

egories that presidents limited the role of the national government in "crime control" during the traditional era.

Upon winning the first presidential election running unopposed, President George Washington would create the office of the presidency—an institution that would establish the standards for all the presidents that would succeed him. His foray into the area of crime and criminal justice were most assuredly limited. However, he would be responsible for establishing several institutions beyond his immediate office that would contribute to the long-term evolution of national intervention in crime. On September 24, 1789, President Washington signed the "Act to Establish the Judicial Courts of the United States."[51] The Judiciary Act, as it was commonly known, provided for the Supreme Court, created the circuit and district courts, and provided a district attorney and marshal for each federal judicial district.[52] In addition, the Judiciary Act also created the office of the Attorney General in the provision that

> . . . there shall also be appointed a meet person, learned in the law, to act as Attorney-General for the United States, who shall be sworn or affirmed to a faithful execution of his office; whose duty it shall be to prosecute and conduct suits in the Supreme Court in which the United States shall be concerned, and to give his advise and opinion upon questions of law when required by the President of the United States, or when requested by the heads of any of the departments, touching any matters that

may concern their departments, and shall receive such compensation for his services as shall by law be provided.[53]

Upon creation of this office, President Washington appointed Edmund Randolph on September 26, 1789. On March 31, 1792, attending his first cabinet meeting, the Attorney General would become a full member of the President's cabinet.[54] Although these two institutions—the court system and the office of the Attorney General—would later contribute to presidential involvement in crime, during the traditional era they assisted in keeping national intervention limited in nature.

President Washington's concerns as they related to crime were chiefly in the area of protecting citizens from violence by the Indians as well as protecting the Indians from violence by the settlers,[55] and dealing with the issue of fugitives.[56] However, the most significant event, and the first intervention by the national government ordered by a president, was the Whiskey Rebellion of 1794. The Whiskey Rebellion came as a result of the first Treasury Secretary Alexander Hamilton's attempt to raise money to fund the debt and pay the expenses of government.[57] One of the methods employed was an excise tax on whiskey distilleries that began in 1791 and was met immediately with violence and refusals to pay.[58] The resistance came to a head when, in July of 1794, sixty tax evaders were summoned to trial at the federal court in Philadelphia. This act sparked a riot and resulted in the burning of the chief tax collector's home and the death of one soldier.[59] Hamilton, with the President's backing, treated the incident as a treason-rebellion threatening federal survival.[60] Fifteen thousand militiamen were called up under the command of General Henry Lee.[61] A total of 12,900 men marched into Pennsylvania, with Hamilton along to force the issue. Upon seeing such a large force, the dissidents fled. Only two individuals were caught and sentenced to hang. They were later pardoned by Washington.[62] In the end, as Johnson explains, "Hamilton thought he had made his point and that the government had gained 'reputation and strength' "[63] and, as a later author would write, this had been "a severe but successful test of the new government in its domestic relations."[64]

The second president of the United States, John Adams, would very nearly repeat the actions of President Washington. He was equally concerned with the violence by and against Indians[65] and he demonstrated a concern for security from "injustice and violence at sea."[66] However, the greatest similarity was in Frie's Rebellion of 1798 when a rebellion against federal authority to directly tax houses, land, and slaves was taken up, again in Pennsylvania. When federal officers entered Bucks County to collect taxes, they were driven off by the local populace with David Frie, a local auctioneer, leading the rabble.[67] As Calder explains:

President John Adams, in ordering Frie's arrest by federal troops declared that the executive branch had been provided by the framers of the Constitution with a

TABLE 1–1   The Presidents

	The Traditional Era
George Washington	1789–1797
John Adams	1797–1801
Thomas Jefferson	1801–1809
James Madison	1809–1817
James Monroe	1817–1825
John Quincy Adams	1825–1829
Andrew Jackson	1829–1837
Martin Van Buren	1837–1841
William Henry Harrison	1841
John Tyler	1841–1845
James K. Polk	1845–1849
Zachary Taylor	1849–1850
Millard Fillmore	1850–1853
Franklin Pierce	1853–1857
James Buchanan	1857–1861
Abraham Lincoln	1861–1865
Andrew Johnson	1865–1869
Ulysses S. Grant	1869–1877
Rutherford B. Hayes	1877–1881
James A. Garfield	1881
Chester A. Arthur	1881–1885
Grover Cleveland	1885–1889
Benjamin Harrison	1889–1893
Grover Cleveland	1893–1897
William McKinley	1897–1901

residuum of power. This residual power derived from his obligation in Article II, Section 1, Paragraph 8: ". . . to the best of my ability preserve, protect and defend the Constitution of the United States." Further, the power to suppress violent opposition to a federal law stemmed from the domestic tranquility clause of the Constitution and the Militia Act of 1792.[68]

As a result, once again, a president had ordered federal intervention primarily under the dictates that it was a violation of federal law and therefore necessitated intervention by the president.

Thomas Jefferson was also concerned with the matter of crime, having spent a great deal of time on the subject in his home state of Virginia.[69] Like Washington and Adams, Jefferson also voiced concern over violence by and against the Indians and found himself concerned with criminal violations by the British government on the seas and in America's ports.[70] He also oversaw the building of a jail in the District of Columbia[71] and was apparently the first president to speak of maintaining and preserving "law and order."[72] Perhaps one of the most intriguing crimes of our nation's history and one that President Jefferson would be closely involved with was the treason charges against Aaron Burr.

Jefferson, having won his first term with Aaron Burr as vice-president, was not fond of the man and considered him an unscrupulous adventurer.[73] Burr was limited by Jefferson in his role as vice-president and when Jefferson was elected for a second term, Burr was dropped from the ticket. Burr, at the same time, was secretly engaged in a variety of anti-Union activity and, as part of his plans, hoped to be elected Governor of New York. Hamilton frustrated this possibility by stating Burr "was a dangerous man and one who ought not to be trusted with the reins of government."[74] These remarks were printed, a duel was proposed, and Burr shot and killed Hamilton. Burr fled and continued seeking to create a new kingdom out of a combination of American territory and states. Jefferson charged him with treason and had him taken into custody. A trial took place in 1807.[75] As a result of partisan politics, Burr was acquitted through Chief Justice Marshall's narrow interpretation of treason, but "the episode demonstrated that even a state's rights president like Jefferson was determined to uphold federal authority as far as it legally stretched."[76] Because they did not "stretch" far, once again presidents were found to be limited in their ability to deal with criminal matters even in cases clearly involving federal law and federal jurisdiction.

Another example of the limits can be found in an incident occurring during President Jefferson's second term in office. By the end of 1807, Jefferson was concerned with the deteriorating foreign situation and sent to Congress a message recommending an embargo of all ships sailing from foreign ports.[77] In his attempt to strangle the British economy, Jefferson was relying on the citizens to bear the hardships associated with the embargo, but was unable to provide definitive leadership and, not surprisingly, the embargo was routinely violated, smuggling became common, and a black market of goods was created.[78] Jefferson's answer was the application of the "principle of *posse comitatus*, a device that enlisted in the embargo enforcement process federal tax collectors, federal marshals, and military contingents."[79] In addition, he ordered federal troops to duty; he required state governors to provide state militiamen; and he also ordered the search and seizure of American vessels for smuggled goods. Although Jefferson had initiated the embargo under concern for national security, the embargo became an issue of law and order—primarily in port cities on the east coast—which required him to deal with the issue of crime. His application of *posse comitatus* would once again stretch the authority of the federal government in dealing with domestic crimes.

President Madison would also have similar concerns for crimes against American citizens by the British, inheriting both the embargo and the road to war from his predecessor. However, after the war years, Madison, in his eighth annual address, would note "that the statutory provisions for the dispensation of criminal justice are deficient" and submitted the question "whether a more enlarged revisal of the criminal code" might be an item for consideration by the legislature.[80] The succeeding presidents, Monroe and Adams, would also take up similar issues in regard to both piracy and Indians. The next president, Andrew Jackson, would contribute significantly to the evolution of federal intervention in crime.

In 1829, Andrew Jackson, a hero of the war against Britain, would become the seventh president. Because of his military background, much of his concern regarding crime was in the area of military law. Jackson, however, would also be faced with a significant event revolving around federal law.[81] Several tariff acts that had been recently passed by Congress were placing undue stress on the state of South Carolina's economy and as a result, South Carolina sought to secede from the Union.[82] While Jackson prepared for a conflict by sending additional troops to the Charleston Harbor, the state of South Carolina assembled its militia. Jackson would render a 9,000 word proclamation in December of 1832 explaining why South Carolina did not have the right of secession.[83] The issue was finally resolved when Congress authorized the use of the army and navy to enforce federal law, while at the same time lowering the federal tariff. South Carolina backed down and the issue was settled. In Calder's terms, this situation had presented a threat to federal unity and Jackson's actions were clearly within federal authority. Jackson was widely praised for his handling of the situation.[84] However, it also demonstrated the power of the national government to enforce its laws and quell domestic disturbances.

When Van Buren became president in 1837, he recognized that the subject of crime and social order was a significant issue and that as America moved westward, the law was often deficient and there was open discussion of secession from the Union. In his inaugural speech he would articulate this by trying to appeal to the sensibilities of the American people by stating, "the capacity of the people for self-government, and their willingness, from a high sense of duty . . . to submit to all needful restraints and exactions of municipal law, have also been favorably exemplified in the history of the American States," but recognizing that "occasionally, it is true, the ardor of public sentiment, outrunning the regular progress of the judicial tribunals or seeking to reach cases not denounced as criminal by the existing law, has displayed itself in a manner calculated to give pain to the friends of free government and to encourage the hopes of those who wish for its overthrow."[85] The very next year, in 1838, as a result of a bitter political contest in Pennsylvania there was discussion of a rebellion and minor acts of rioting which prompted the governor to call upon the president for assistance in accordance with the U.S. Constitution.[86] In this case, what was significant is not so much what the president did, but rather what the president did not do. He refused to send federal soldiers to Pennsylvania on the grounds that federal interference is justified only where domestic violence is such that state authorities have proved inadequate.[87]

Van Buren effectively created a precedent that the states had to first exhaust their resources in dealing with domestic violence before the national government would intervene. This clearly was an example of presidents in the traditional era restricting their activity with regard to state and local crime.

The next president, William Henry Harrison, would meet an untimely death and therefore would have no chance to deal with issues of crime. His successor, John Tyler, would have the opportunity to expand upon the precedent set by Van Buren. The 1842 incident, known as the Dorr Rebellion, came as a result of the Rhode Island Constitution which only allowed property owners the right to vote.[88] Dorr sent letters to the president and met with him in Washington. He later returned to Rhode Island to lead a small band of followers in skirmishes against the state militia.[89] Dorr was then arrested, which only managed to enhance his standing and the rhetoric of a "revolution" ensued. Dorr was released and left the state.[90] The Governor, Samuel King, fearing an invasion, called out the state militia and declared martial law.[91] He then sent a letter to President Tyler requesting intervention against the "impending" attack. Tyler refused and after explaining Article 4, Section 4 of the Constitution, he articulated the reasoning:

> By a careful consideration of the above-recited acts of Congress your excellency will not fail to see that no power is vested in the Executive of the United States to anticipate insurrectionary movements against the government of Rhode Island so as to sanction the interposition of the military authority, but that there must be an actual insurrection, manifested by lawless assemblages of the people or otherwise, to whom a proclamation may be addressed and who may be required to betake themselves to their respective abodes.[92]

President Tyler would then explain that in the event of an actual attack, he would issue a proclamation and allow for federal intervention. As Wiecek, discussing Tyler's actions, concludes:

> He confirmed the widely held assumption that responsibility for execution of the dual promise of guarantee and protection might sometimes fall on the President, as commander in chief of the armed forces, rather than Congress. Yet his caution and moderation served as a warning to future presidents that the great power confided to them was best used with restraint and that the mere threat of action might be more effective than a precipitate dispatch of troops.[93]

In sum, Tyler extended the precedent of President Van Buren's position that state resources must first be exhausted, by adding that an actual threat must have taken place. And, unlike President Adams, Tyler "had not found authority in either the Constitution or the Militia Act of 1792"[94] to intervene. Once again, presidents in the traditional era took a limited role in local issues of crime.

President Tyler's other concerns for crime issues included the possibility of creating a "maritime police," matters of the slave trade, and the expense of supporting a police force in Washington, D.C.[95] His successor, James Polk also spoke of "law and justice" at the federal level and issues revolving around the slave trade. The following two presidents, Zachary Taylor and Millard Fillmore, apparently did not deal with crime in any specific way, however the fourteenth president, Franklin Pierce would find several occasions whereupon he found himself engaged in the subject of domestic crime.

The first issue came about through an increased level of violence in the Kansas Territory that was brought to the attention of President Pierce by the governor of the territory. Pierce drafted a lengthy "special message" to Congress in January of 1856, detailing the level of violence in the Kansas Territory and surmised that the answer to the violence was to initiate the proceedings to make Kansas a member of the Union, rather than attempting to deal with it through increased federal intervention.[96] The second case was from a request by the California Governor that same year in August, requesting federal assistance to stop the "San Francisco Vigilance Committee" from usurping the authority of the state.[97] Pierce, utilizing the precedent set by President Tyler, refused to intervene because there had been no "actual shock of arms" between insurgents and the state, as well as invoking the precedent set by President Van Buren that the state had not exhausted its resources.[98] As a result, the president took no action.

Like President Pierce, when James Buchanan took office, he too would find himself engaged in matters of crime in the Kansas Territory, "violence and lawlessness" on the frontier, and dealing with the issue of the fugitive slave laws. However, it was the presidency of Abraham Lincoln and the Civil War years that would test the president's resolve on a plethora of fronts, including the issue of crime. While it is more difficult to discuss the issue of crime during this time period, primarily because all issues centered on the war itself, Lincoln had a keen ability to separate out the issues while still refusing to allow any state to secede. Before a special session of Congress in July of 1861, Lincoln explained:

> It might seem at first thought to be of little difference whether the present movement of the South be called "secession" or "rebellion." The movers, however, well understand the difference. At the beginning they knew they could never raise their treason to any respectable magnitude by any name which implies violation of law. They knew their people possessed as much of moral sense, as much of devotion to law and order, and as much pride in and reverence for the history and Government of their common country as any other civilized and patriotic people. They knew they could make no advancement directly in the teeth of these strong and noble sentiments.[99]

Lincoln then spoke of the "sophism" used by the secessionists—that states had a right to secede from the Union—which he further stated had no merit. Although Lincoln would effectively deal with the topics of rebellion, treason, the fugitive slave law, slavery itself, military justice, and would suspend the Writ of Habeas Corpus, all of these actions dealing with crime were centered on the war.[100] Equally, when Andrew Johnson assumed the presidency upon the assassination of

Lincoln, he would have to deal with the war's aftermath and Reconstruction. However, he lost control over the Reconstruction efforts, was nearly impeached, and lost the election in 1868.

Ulysses S. Grant, a war hero of the Civil War, entered office in 1869 and found himself responsible for unifying the south with the north rather than defeating it. Although he would deal with such crime issues as ever increasing violence in the territories and the Washington, D.C. police, his primary concern became the enforcement of the Fourteenth Amendment. In order to give the executive office more power in dealing with the Ku Klux Klan, Grant requested that Congress authorize his office with the ability to target this group directly. He was granted this power through the Ku Klux Act of 1871.[101] Grant would declare martial law in nine counties in South Carolina and would follow "Jefferson's lead by forming a *posse comitatus* and sending federal marshals into surrounding states to root out klansmen."[102] In addition, in 1873, upon the request of the Louisiana Governor, he would send troops into New Orleans due to lawlessness resulting from racial problems and again to South Carolina in 1876 during a series of riots. This last act resulted in the Congress's passage of the Posse Comitatus Act in 1878[103] which prohibits the use of the military in civilian law enforcement. Once more, as a result of the war and its aftermath, the powers of the president relating to crime tended to expand. Although the Posse Comitatus Act would contract these powers, the necessity was no longer as great. This was because in the post-reconstruction era, the most significant area of crime that presidents had to deal with was in the area of territorial crimes over which they had jurisdiction.

President Rutherford B. Hayes would also find himself dealing with the issue of territory crimes, while also dealing with a series of riots revolving around the railroad strikes during his first year in office. The railroad strikes and subsequent riots resulted from a price war in a stagnant economy between the factories and the railroads.[104] As the railroads continually increased the work and decreased the pay, the end result was simultaneous strikes occurring in Baltimore, Maryland, and Martinsburg, West Virginia, which then quickly spread across the country.[105] Violence, on such a large scale, had not been seen in the United States since the Civil War. As Polakoff explains:

> State militiamen were too poorly trained and organized to control the situation. In Pittsburgh they fired on people indiscriminately, killing and wounding scores. Immediately, panicky governors appealed to the president for help in restoring order. To his credit, Hayes refused to be stampeded . . . he checked the language of the Constitution and insisted that the governors specify both that their legislatures were not in session and could not be speedily summoned, and that they were confronted with domestic violence that they were powerless to suppress.[106]

As Hayes would later communicate to the Congress, "I am gratified to be able to state that the troops sent in response to these calls for aid in the suppression of domestic violence were able, by the influence of their presence in the disturbed regions, to preserve the peace and restore order without the use of force."[107] Once again, the precedent of limiting intervention in domestic disturbances was restored and presidents found themselves focusing their attention on issues of direct federal concern.

Crime in the United States territories would remain the concern of the following presidents. President Garfield would not have the chance to deal with any issues revolving around crime because of his assassination in July of 1881 by Charles J. Guiteau, a mentally disturbed patronage position seeker. Chester A. Arthur, upon secession to the office of president would primarily deal with this heinous crime against the government as well as the issue of territorial crimes. Grover Cleveland would also find himself engaged in the issue of territorial crime during both of his two separate terms in office. The president between Cleveland's two terms, Benjamin Harrison, would again deal with this issue, as well as with the protection of the United States mail and a variety of issues concerning military justice. In addition, during the administrations of Harrison, Cleveland, and finally William McKinley, they would each render assistance to the Idaho governors regarding a series of disturbances at the Couer D'Alene mines.[108] Finally, on several occasions in President Cleveland's second term, he utilized United States soldiers to intervene in domestic disturbances without a formal proclamation, such as in Montana against "Coxey's Army of Unemployed,"[109] and without the Governor's direct request, such as in Chicago during a series of railroad strikes.[110] Although the governor denied that the president had any right to utilize soldiers, Cleveland responded, "I have neither transcended my authority nor duty . . . In this hour of danger and public distress, discussion may well give way to active efforts on the part of all in authority to restore obedience to the law and to protect life and property."[111] The president's use of troops in this case, however, proved to be a mistake because it failed to preserve order and incited several additional days of rioting in Chicago.[112]

In 1896, with William McKinley elected as the president to lead the country into the twentieth century through a greater expansion of the industrial age and away from the traditional era of president's involvement in crime, he was perhaps somewhat prescient in his inaugural speech when he explained:

> The preservation of public order, the right of discussion, the integrity of courts, and the orderly administration of justice must continue forever [to be] the rock of safety upon which our Government securely rests. One of the lessons taught by the late election, which all can rejoice in, is that the citizens of the United States are both law-respecting and law-abiding people, not easily swerved from the path of patriotism and honor. This is in entire accord with the genius of our institutions, and but emphasizes the advantages of inculcating even a greater love for law and order in the future.[113]

During his tenure in office he would find himself engaged primarily with the impending war (Spanish-American) and foreign matters, giving little attention to the issue of crime despite his inaugural rhetoric. Ironically, he would fall victim to an assassin's bullet, assuredly one of the most heinous crimes possible.

Thus closed a century and an era of presidential activity in crime that was marked by strong restraint resulting from the language of the United States Constitution, but presented a not too consistent policy of intervention. Although Presidents Van Buren and John Tyler created a clear policy relating to federal intervention in domestic disturbances which delineated that there must be an actual disturbance and that states must exhaust their resources first, this policy was not always evident. Several presidents, namely John Adams and Thomas Jefferson, intervened in domestic disturbances through methods aimed at expanding their authority. Others found themselves forced into extreme circumstances that compelled their intervention, namely Lincoln and Johnson. One president intervened forcibly with congressional backing (i.e., Grant) and another without so much as a proclamation (i.e., Cleveland). In the end, however, it is clear that presidents were only involved in issues of major domestic disturbances during the traditional era and not the types of "street crimes" that were proliferating throughout the nineteenth century.[114] In other words, presidents limited themselves, or were limited by law, to only deal with extreme incidents that were well beyond the scope of the state governments. Otherwise, relating to crime, they occupied themselves with issues that clearly had federal jurisdiction and were overseen by federal law, such as military justice, territorial crimes, and crime in the District of Columbia.

THE TRANSITIONAL ERA (1900–1963)

The Responsive Period (1900–1927)

At the beginning of the twentieth century, several factors emerged that would contribute to the increase in federal intervention of crime during the twentieth century. They are: 1) Federal Antitrust suits, 2) Drug Prohibition, and 3) Alcohol Prohibition. Each of these would contribute to some degree to the growing development of federal intervention in street level crime but during the responsive period of 1900 to 1927, the federal government simply took a responsive approach to these various issues. It was not until the election of 1928 when Hoover would become the thirty-first President of the United States that a formal plan would begin to be developed by the national government and the foundation for federal crime intervention throughout the rest of the century would be laid.

The first significant factor, antitrust lawsuits, revolve around a crime that is unique in its status and in its enforcement.[115] The Sherman Antitrust Act was passed by Congress in 1890 as a result of the federal government's attempt to "regulate the movement of commodities and to control economic power."[116] They did this through the use of the commerce clause which grants Congress the authority to "regulate Commerce . . . among the several States."[117] The concept was to break up business monopolies in order that smaller companies would have the chance to compete in the marketplace. The first few years of the Sherman antitrust

The President Speaks . . .

It is important . . . that we recognize clearly the increasing scope and complexity of the problem of criminal law administration. Undoubtedly there are unfortunate aspects of our national life which seriously threaten the American home, increase the danger of juvenile delinquency and multiply offenses against the good order of society. The regulation of the illicit traffic in drugs, the prevention of commerce in stolen goods and, generally, the interstate character of offenses attributable to the roving criminal have presented national problems against which primitive forms of law enforcement are relatively powerless.

It is equally necessary that we realize the importance of common action all along the line, starting with crime prevention itself and carrying this common action all the way through to prosecution and punishment.

Franklin D. Roosevelt's June 28, 1934, "Fireside Chat." In this his fifth "Fireside Chat," Roosevelt comments on the passage of a series of federal crime bills stating they have "strengthened the hand of the Federal Government in its attempt to suppress gangster crime."

PHOTO COURTESY OF THE FRANKLIN DELANO ROOSEVELT LIBRARY, HYDE PARK, NEW YORK.

> We have come to a time when our need is to discover more fully and to direct more purposefully into useful channels that greatest of all natural resources, the genius of the younger generation. Crime is a symptom of social disorder. Widespread increase in capacity to substitute order for disorder is the remedy.
>
> This can come only through expert service in marshalling the assets of home, school, church, community and other social agencies, to work in common purpose with our law enforcement agencies. We deceive ourselves when we fail to realize that it is an interrelated problem of immense difficulty. Scientific research, highly trained personnel, expert service are just as necessary here as in any field of human endeavor.
>
> —*Franklin D. Roosevelt*
> *Address to the Conference on Crime,*
> *December 10, 1934*

laws were tenuous, and by 1895, when a case against the American Sugar Refining Company was thrown out by the Supreme Court, the antitrust laws fell into disuse by the federal government[118] until the presidency of Theodore Roosevelt. Although there is a distinctly economic side to this "crime," what is most significant about the antitrust laws and their impact on crime is best explained by Ashdown, when he writes that "the tiger was now loose. Federal jurisdiction no longer had to be limited to peculiarity federal issues—counterfeiting, piracy, the governance and protection of federal property, and treason. Any activity affecting more than one state or crossing state boundaries was the legitimate subject of federal regulation."[119] Although

TABLE 1–2   The Presidents

	The Transitional Era
Theodore Roosevelt	1901–1909
William H. Taft	1909–1913
Woodrow Wilson	1913–1921
Warren G. Harding	1921–1923
Calvin Coolidge	1923–1929
Herbert Hoover	1929–1933
Franklin D. Roosevelt	1933–1945
Harry S Truman	1945–1953
Dwight D. Eisenhower	1953–1961
John F. Kennedy	1961–1963

little in the area of crime regulation would occur during the responsive period, seeds were planted for later federal intervention.

The second and third factors occurring at the turn of the century came as a direct result of the progressive movement that was largely centered on creating a more moral society through temperance toward drugs and alcohol.[120] As early as 1876, a third party known as the "Prohibition Reform Party" had managed to put forth its platform and party candidate.[121] In each succeeding election, this progressive party would denounce the use of drugs and alcohol and discuss how these vices contributed to the problems of crime. In the case of drugs, because of a rash of adverse reactions to cocaine and a decline in its popularity, the drug became associated with criminals and minorities.[122] In addition, opium had long been considered a drug commonly associated with many Asian groups.[123] Eventually, this would lead to the passage of several anti-drug laws with little to no enforcement behind them. Finally, in the case of alcohol, prohibition laws would be passed in the form of a constitutional amendment, but, in a paradoxical manner, this would ultimately contribute to the need for federal intervention in state and local crime control.

It is perhaps altogether fitting and proper that the president who would lead the country into the twentieth century and commence the transitional period is Theodore Roosevelt, the former president of the New York City Police Department's Police Board, which had effectively made him the city's police commissioner.[124] As a progressive individual, a background on the frontier, his service as the police commissioner, and his assumption of the presidency through McKinley's assassination,[125] Roosevelt was poised to become somewhat of an interventionist in regard to crime at the state and local government level. He was, in fact, greatly concerned about issues such as lynching,[126] child labor laws,[127] and reports of violence against the Japanese in California.[128] He also found himself engaged in such issues as military law, the Washington, D.C. Police Department, and crime in the American territories.[129] But his greatest intervention came not so much from issues at the state and local level, but from his aggressive and successful use of the Sherman Antitrust Act.

Although Roosevelt had mentioned the power of the national government to oversee corporations in his first annual address, it was his second annual address that highlighted his resolve when he stated, "this country cannot afford to sit supine on the plea that under our peculiar system of government we are helpless in the presence of the new conditions. The power of Congress to regulate interstate commerce is an absolute and unqualified grant, and without limitations other than those prescribed by the Constitution."[130] In fact, Roosevelt had already pressed for "the Justice Department to proceed against Northern Securities for violating the Sherman Antitrust Act, on the grounds that it was in restraint of trade."[131] Although no one felt that the suit would be successful and would result in a decision similar to the American Sugar Refining Company case, the Supreme Court in a five-to-four vote, upheld the lowercourt ruling and Roosevelt and the national government had its first win.[132] Although the case was not about crime at the state and local level, by affirming the power of the federal government in the use of the Sherman Antitrust Act, the commerce clause was wide open for the federal government to regulate not only industries, but crimes that occurred interstate.

One final event during the Roosevelt presidency would have some impact upon the power of the national government, especially as it related to government intervention in issues of domestic disturbances. Prior to the Supreme Court decision, but after announcing his intent to pursue the antitrust suit against Northern Securities, Roosevelt was faced with a coal strike in eastern Pennsylvania in May of 1902.[133] In this case, "the operators plainly counted upon a coal shortage and violence and sabotage in the minefields to force President Roosevelt to intervene to put down the strike, as Grover Cleveland had done in the 1894 Pullman strike."[134] However, Roosevelt refused to intervene, citing no threat to the general welfare and by October he would acknowledge that he had "no legal or constitutional duty—and therefore no legal or constitutional right in the matter."[135] Although this seemed to Roosevelt the "right" thing to do, he was cornered by the fact that the public was pressuring him to do something. Often considered to be a "man of action," Roosevelt called a meeting among interested parties which resulted in little movement on either side of the strike and a near-death experience for Roosevelt, but did produce a critical idea that would bring the strike to an end.[136] Roosevelt had gotten the idea to send in troops if so requested by the governor, to seize the mines and run them himself.[137] The threat was enough for the strikers to back down and the owners to enter into arbitration. Roosevelt had found his way out of the corner and his actions were well-received by the public. Although he had managed to continue the policy of non-intervention, albeit through a threat of intervention, and in another case, through a refusal to intervene during a Colorado mining disturbance, he would later reverse course in regard to intervention. In 1907, when the governor of Nevada requested troops, Roosevelt agreed and ordered them in only to discover later through a Presidential investigating committee that the action was not warranted.[138] However, what is most telling about Roosevelt and the power of government to intervene in domestic situations, much as in the vein of Grover Cleveland, is explained by Roosevelt in a letter about his reaction to the railroad strike:

> I did not intend to sit supinely when such a state of things was impending . . . I had to take charge of the matter, as President, on behalf of the Federal Government . . . I knew that this action would form an evil precedent, and that it was one which I should take most reluctantly, but . . . it would have been imperative to act, precedent or no precedent–and I was in readiness.[139]

Finally in 1907, Roosevelt would begin a fight over the creation of a federal detective agency that would continue until the end of his term in office. Although he had proposed the idea, Congress opposed it "in part because two congressmen had recently been prosecuted for fraud and members feared further investigations."[140] Out of frustration with Congress, Roosevelt created the Bureau of Investigation by way of an Executive Order in 1908 and a bitter political fight ensued to the end of his term. Like it or not, the future Federal Bureau of Investigation was born.

President Taft would then succeed Roosevelt who had, at the beginning of his first elected term in office, declared not to run again. Taft would take a largely different tack in regard to Roosevelt's beliefs of federal intervention. Taft believed that "there is no undefined residuum of power which (a president) can exercise because it seems to him to be in the public interest."[141] What is also interesting about Taft, however, is that he had served as a prosecuting attorney and a state court judge and was a large proponent of criminal justice reform.[142] In fact, in his first annual message, he spoke of "the deplorable delays in the administration of civil and criminal law" and stated that he had no "doubt for one moment that much of the lawless violence and cruelty exhibited in lynchings is directly due to the uncertainties and injustice growing out of the delays in trials, judgments, and the executions thereof by our courts."[143] He would go on to recommend an in-depth study of the federal criminal laws and, ultimately, a reorganization of the Department of Justice. Taft would however, for the most part, deal with issues of crime that were relegated to federal authority and federal jurisdiction.

Taft focused some of his attention on the International Maritime Law and continued the Roosevelt administration's stance on antitrust lawsuits. In this regard, the Supreme Court decided in two separate cases against the Standard Oil Company of New Jersey and the American Tobacco Company during Taft's administration.[144] As he would comment, "the violations of the antitrust law present perhaps the most important litigation before the (Justice) Department, and the number of cases filed shows the activity of the Government in enforcing that statute."[145] He also took a strong stance against fraud in the federal government when drafting a resolution which stated, "the primary duty with respect to frauds in the executive service falls upon the Executive to direct proper executive investigation, and upon the discovery of fraud and crime to direct judicial investigation for the purposes of recovering what is due the Government and of bringing to justice the guilty person."[146] Moreover, some of his attention was given to the issue of the Washington, D.C. Police Department and its ability to police the District of Columbia. Finally, Taft would also request from Congress an appropriation of $25,000 for the United States to send a delegation to The Hague in the Netherlands for the purpose of participating in an international conference aimed at controlling the opium trade.[147] The resulting conference was held in 1912, but it was not until 1914, into the next administration, that any action would be taken regarding the passage of law. These activities on the part of Taft were, for the most part, limited to issues of the federal government. However, many of his actions would continue the use of the interstate commerce clause and establish the movement toward federal action in state and local issues of crime.

President Woodrow Wilson became president in 1913 and would find himself predominately engaged in international events ranging from U.S. neutrality before the war to engagement in World War I, and in his push for the creation and membership in the League of Nations.[148] However, two years of his administration, 1914 and 1919, would find him dealing heavily with issues of law and order. In 1914, he became engaged in convincing Congress to pass the Clayton Bill which was intended to clarify and strengthen many of the generalities of the Sherman Antitrust Act of 1890 which, most importantly, when passed, made corporations personally and criminally liable for the acts of their companies.[149] Congress would also pass the Harrison Act which Wilson signed into law effective on March 1, 1915. This law was intended to control the marketing and sale of narcotics but effectively brought the federal government into direct intervention when it came to illegal drugs—a role it would maintain for the rest of the century.[150] Finally, Wilson would find himself sending troops to assist in a Colorado coal mine strike to stop several days of rioting.[151]

Although the emphasis was on United States engagement in World War I during the years 1915–1918, Wilson did act quickly to seek passage of the Adamson Act in 1916 which established the eight-hour workday for interstate railroad workers and averted a nationwide railroad strike.[152] However, it was in 1919 after the end of World War I, that Wilson would again become heavily engaged in issues of crime. In that year, he signed the National Motor Vehicle Theft Act[153] which would bring the crime of grand larceny auto into federal purview when the vehicles were transported across state lines. He would oversee the federal intervention in several domestic disturbances such as the race riots in Washington, D.C. and Omaha without proclamation,[154] and he would create a special Narcotics Division within the Treasury Department in order to enforce the Harrison Act.[155] However, no other event in that year would have as much impact regarding the issue of crime as when Congress, on October 28, 1919, passed the National Prohibition Enforcement Act, despite President Wilson's veto. Congress, through the Eighteenth Amendment, made it illegal to manufacture, sell, or transport alcohol and scheduled the law to take effect January of 1920.[156] The United States was about to enter the era of Prohibition.

President Wilson, as obvious in his veto, was opposed to the law and did little to address violations of the law. President Harding would succeed Wilson in 1921, but he too would do little to address violations of the law. Instead Harding found himself engaged in a corruption scandal revolving around his Attorney General, Harry M. Daugherty. It resulted in a congressional investigation which, despite having found no evidence against Daugherty, continued to plague his administration.[157] Harding also ran into problems when he attempted to avert a railroad strike in 1922 and unsuccessfully encouraged Congress to pass an anti-lynching law.[158] One incident in 1921—a West Virginia coal mine strike—would find the president refusing troops on the basis that state resources had not been exhausted. But after a sudden outburst of violence, he would issue a proclamation and send in the troops.[159] His death would bring President Coolidge into office, setting the stage for the federal government to begin the process of moving into the "developmental period" regarding federal crime-control policy.

President Coolidge, assuming office in August of 1923, was somewhat plagued with the Daugherty scandal during these years, but he was unwilling to remove Harding's beloved attorney general. Upon winning the office in his own right, he would remove Daugherty and nominate Harlan Stone to the position. Stone proceeded to change the damaged image of the Department of Justice.[160] One extension of the corruption extended to the Bureau of Investigation (later the Federal Bureau of Investigation) under the leadership of William Burns who was also removed from office and replaced by the young J. Edgar Hoover.[161] The move, having a profound impact for most of the twentieth century but not realized at the time, was primarily intended as a response to the poor public image of the Bureau. Hoover presented a "clean-cut" image.

As for Prohibition, Coolidge was in a position that kept the issue at bay during his presidency. One author has explained "Coolidge kept Prohibition from becoming a major issue by the expedient of occupying the middle ground between drys and wets. As a consequence, wets were slow to criticize the president for fear that he would become an ardent dry, and most drys were reluctant to criticize him too much for fear that he would do even less to enforce the law."[162] In fact, although Mabel Walker Willebrandt was chosen to supervise Prohibition prosecutions for the Department of Justice during the Harding Administration and although the office grew during Wilson's administration, for the most part, the resources were inadequate to the task.[163] In the end, albeit Prohibition was on the books and had an enforcement team, the reality was a limited enforcement of the law and a sporadic method of prosecution. The primary reason for this fact is that most of the issues in regard to Prohibition and the crimes that were resulting from its illegality were at the state and local level.

Although the enforcement of the Volstead Act was conducted overwhelmingly by state and local criminal justice agencies and many of these agencies simply chose to ignore the law, what could not be ignored was the rising level of "street crimes" that were plaguing every city in the nation.[164] Prohibition was a direct cause of not only the rise in the black market and organized crime, it was also largely associated with the increase in many petty crimes.[165] The decade of the 1920s was clearly marked by a growing concern over crime. In response, a number of states and cities began forming "crime commissions" to look into more effective means of addressing the problems of crime.[166] By the end of the 1920s there were over twenty-five such commissions.[167] A 1920 survey of criminal justice administrations directed by Roscoe Pound and Felix Frankfurter provided the model for the work of most of these crime commissions.[168] Eventually, the issue of crime was so widespread that a national conference was held in Washington, D.C. in 1927 and the "National Crime Commission" was born. The Honorable Newton D. Baker served as the chairman and a number of prominent politicians and criminal justice officials served on various committees analyzing the causes, preventions, and methods to most effectively deal with specific crimes.[169] Although Coolidge supported the work of the state and local crime commission, he did little in the way of offering federal assistance, leaving the work to the state and local governments.[170] As Calder explains, "the Coolidge administration had been unwilling to expand public dialogue on crime beyond preachments about law observance. No connection was envisioned between law observance and social factors or between law observance and the structural integrity of criminal justice administration."[171] Due to growing public awareness of crime, limited activity of the national government in regard to prohibition, and the necessity to address the problems with more than rhetoric on "law observance," the time was ripe for federal intervention in state and local crime and for the development of a federal crime-control policy.

The Developmental Period (1928–1963)

The developmental period of federal crime-control policy commences with President Herbert Hoover's election to office in 1928 since his administration "marks the origins of federal crime-control policy."[172] It became clear during the campaign of 1928 that mere rhetoric like that of President Coolidge would no longer suffice to satisfy America's growing crime problem and that neither candidate, Hoover or Governor Smith, could avoid the issue of Prohibition which was a significant factor in the rise in crime.[173] Hoover called for a national commission on law observance to study what he called "a great social and economic experiment noble in motive and far-reaching in purpose."[174] He would consistently try to tie the issues of Prohibition to the larger issue of law observance by both citizens and government.[175] Ushered into office with a landslide victory, Hoover would set in motion a series of events that would take a long hard look at the criminal justice system, crime, and Prohibition.

Hoover would first demonstrate in rhetoric that he was serious about federal involvement in the issue of crime. In his inaugural speech he opened his address with the view that one of the greatest "dangers today is disregard and disobedience of law." He urged that, in order "to reestablish the vigor and effectiveness of law enforcement, we must critically consider the entire Federal machinery of justice, the redistribution of its functions, the simplification of its procedure, the provision of additional special tribunals, the better selection of juries, and the more effective organization of our agencies of investigation and prosecution that justice may be sure and that it may be swift."[176] He then addressed the issues of the Eighteenth Amendment as they related to crime and reiterated his proposal "to appoint a national commission for a searching investigation of the whole structure of our Federal system of jurisprudence, to include the method of enforcement of the Eighteenth Amendment and the causes of abuses under it."[177] In a follow-up speech titled "Law Enforcement and Respect for the Law," delivered to the Associated

Press on April 22, 1929, Hoover articulated his belief of presidential authority and responsibility relating to crime-control policy:

> It may be said by some that the larger responsibility for the enforcement of laws against crime rests with State and local authorities and it does not concern the Federal Government. But it does concern the President of the United States, both as a citizen and as the one upon whom rests the primary responsibility of leadership for the establishment of standards of law enforcement in this country. Respect for law and obedience to law does not distinguish between Federal and State laws—it is a common conscience.[178]

As Calder explains, "Hoover understood the limitations imposed on a president in expanding federal jurisdiction" for "the vagaries of prohibition made this crystal clear, but Hoover remained philosophically comfortable with widening federal law enforcement power. The federal executive's role, he believed, encompassed investigation of social problems like crime, followed by implementation of model programs for state-level replication."[179] As a result, the development of federal crime-control policy was about to be set into motion.

In May of 1929, President Hoover would, with congressional funding, appoint an eleven-member Commission on Law Observance and Enforcement under the leadership of George W. Wickersham, formerly the Attorney General during Taft's administration. It would come to be known primarily as the "Wickersham Commission." This was the first federal commission created by a president to comprehensively examine the criminal justice system.[180] The commission would begin its work in earnest, with clear directives but little intervention on the part of President Hoover.[181] Although the Commission never reached consensus on Prohibition despite releasing two reports on the subject in the years 1930 and 1931, they would publish an additional twelve reports during these two years. The reports consisted of comprehensive reviews and policy recommendations related to federal law such as the report on processing juvenile offenders in the federal system, but many also dealt with the federal-state issues of crime such as the reports on the costs of crime, causes of crime, criminal statistics, the police, prosecution, correctional practices and, one of the most controversial reports, lawlessness in law enforcement.[182] In the end, however, the Wickersham Commission's recommendations were limited in their implementation because of the additional cost and bureaucratic structures that would have been necessary to carry out these policies. The great depression that ensued in the autumn that they commenced their investigation prevented most of their recommendations from being realized during Hoover's administration. The only recommendation acted upon by Hoover was when the Bureau of Investigation began tracking crime statistics throughout the United States, giving birth to the Uniform Crime Reports published annually by the Federal Bureau of Investigation. Many of the other recommendations would have to wait several decades to see any semblance of implementation.

In addition to forming of the Wickersham Commission and awaiting their recommendations for legislative proposals, Hoover remained busy in regard to crime by focusing on issues that were directly under his control. He immediately began the process of reforming the Department of Justice and Bureau of Investigation, as well as the court system by removing incompetent or corrupt attorneys and improving federal court procedures.[183] He would continue addressing the issue of Prohibition by transferring the Bureau of Prohibition to the Department of Justice.[184] He sought to improve the prison overcrowding situation through his Director of the Bureau of Prisons, Sanford Bates, who created a comprehensive plan to improve federal corrections and build new prison facilities[185] and he insured that those involved in organized crime, specifically Al Capone, would be targeted by federal law enforcement.[186] In addition, Hoover would provide federal assistance to the New Jersey State Police in the Lindbergh baby kidnaping case, and then seek and secure the passage of a federal law against kidnaping.[187] He would continue his rhetoric against the crime of lynching and he would send in federal soldiers to suppress the Bonus Army disturbance in July of 1932.[188]

Despite his earnest efforts to continue his work into a second term, between the public perception that he was doing little in regard to the depression and his adamant campaign stance that the Eighteenth Amendment should not be repealed, Hoover lost a second term to Governor Franklin D. Roosevelt of New York. However, in his one term he managed to take the federal criminal justice system which "lacked organizational codification and direction, . . . focus, and . . . a reform agenda for succeeding years" and managed to "craft the miscellaneous parts of federal justice administration into a comprehensive whole."[189] The developments of the federal criminal justice system and its ability to engage in issues of street crimes were underway, disrupted by World War II, but fully entrenched as an added responsibility of the President of the United States.

During the election of 1932, Governor Roosevelt spent much of his time campaigning against Hoover's adamant stance to continue Prohibition. In an election-year publication, he dedicated a chapter to the issues of "Crime and Criminals."[190] Primarily as a result of the depression, Franklin D. Roosevelt was ushered into office in March of 1933 with his promise of a "New Deal" for the American people. Immediately upon taking office, he began putting his economic recovery plan into effect within the first 100 days of his administration. His first action related to the issue of crime would come in December 1933 when he issued a proclamation regarding the repeal of the Eighteenth Amendment[191] and he urged "all citizens of the United States and upon other residents within the jurisdiction thereof, to cooperate with the Government in its endeavor to restore greater respect for law and order."[192] Roosevelt would reiterate his concern for crime in his first annual message to Congress when he stated that "crimes of organized banditry, cold blooded shooting, lynching and kidnaping have threatened our security . . . and these violations of law call on the strong arm of Government for their immediate suppression."[193] He would also express his belief that "the adoption of the Twenty-first Amendment should give material aid to the elimination of those new forms of crime which came from the illegal traffic in liquor."[194] Despite achieving this key victory, Roosevelt would continue his strong push for additional federal crime-control measures.

In 1934, Roosevelt's administration sent forth to Congress a number of bills aimed at enhancing the federal role in crime control. The bills included additional punishments for killing or assaulting Federal officers,[195] regulating the procedures of criminal cases in the federal courts,[196] limiting appeals in *habeas corpus* proceedings,[197] extending punishments in regards to the federal kidnaping statute,[198] an anti-racketeering bill,[199] a bill allowing pursuit of fleeing felons throughout the U.S.,[200] extending extortion jurisdiction to various forms of communication (e.g., telephone, radio, etc.),[201] punishment of federal prisoners who escape,[202] allowing states to enter into mutual assistance agreements,[203] extending the provisions of the National Motor Vehicle Theft Act,[204] making it a federal crime to rob a national bank,[205] and to regulate the defense of alibis in criminal cases.[206] By May of that same year the majority of these bills and approximately a dozen more were passed and signed into law by Roosevelt. As he explained in a statement upon signing the crime bills, "these laws are a renewed challenge on the part of the Federal Government to inter-state crime. They are also complementary to the broader program designed to curb the evil-doer of whatever class."[207] Finally, at the end of the year, he would follow up on his federal crime-control initiatives by addressing the Attorney General's four-day conference on crime. He spoke of "our constant struggle to safeguard ourselves against the attacks of the lawless and the criminal elements of our population" and he urged the attendees to "plan and construct with scientific care a constantly improving administrative structure" consisting of federal, state, and local law enforcement, as well as "to interpret the problem of crime to the people of this country."[208] Roosevelt, with the assistance of his aid, Louis Howe,[209] by the end of the year, had most assuredly made crime part of his administration's agenda.

The next several years of the Roosevelt administration consisted largely of expanding the federal agencies responsible for crime[210] such as the renamed Federal Bureau of Investigation[211] and the Federal Bureau of Narcotics,[212] as well as targeting specific members of organized crime. He would also oversee a series of judicial reforms in 1937[213] and address a National Parole Conference held at the White House in 1939.[214] Although it is not clear how far Roosevelt would have continued his crime-control policies, by 1936 "he issued the first in a series of directives establishing the domestic intelligence structure and policies of the federal government."[215] This would be the first in a series of moves in response to the growing possibility that the United States would enter World War II and, once it did, the primary objective of Roosevelt's "crime policy" was to target cases of espionage, sabotage, and subversiveness.[216] This would remain the case for the rest of Roosevelt's time in office, until his death in 1945, and to some degree during the administration of Harry S Truman. Crime, because of World War II, would take a back seat to "national security."

Truman's ascension to the presidency would find him dealing with the close of World War II and its aftermath. Truman recognized, however, in a speech to a conference of churches, that "the aftermath of a major war always includes an increase in juvenile delinquency" and that "more often it is the result of everything that is abnormal in war—including the absence of fathers and mothers in the armed forces or in business or in war industries."[217] Although this speech was given in 1946, at the beginning of the greatest population birth cohort the nation would witness, the speech was prescient for the fact that it was not until the 1950s that the issue of juvenile delinquency would become a bona fide problem of epidemic proportions and only as an indirect effect of the war.[218] Although Truman would often acknowledge that crime and juvenile delinquency were issues of concern, in most cases they were framed in terms of either state and local issues[219] or issues of civil rights.[220] He would give a most telling address at the Attorney General's Conference on Law Enforcement Problems in 1950 in which he articulated he was clearly concerned with issues of federalism. Although he wished to assist and have federal agencies work closely with state and local law enforcement, he also wanted to keep the demarcation lines clear as to what was a federal responsibility and what was a state and local responsibility. This became clear in his directions to the attorney general to target violators of the federal tax, narcotics, and organized crime laws.[221] By 1950 and 1951, at the end of Truman's tenure in office, there was a growing awareness of crime becoming a problem in the United States and Senator Estes Kefauver created a Special Crime Investigating Committee. While Truman encouraged departments to cooperate with the investigation,[222] he did not try to take a leadership role at this point and the presidency was passed to Eisenhower.

Eisenhower entered the White House during a time that juvenile delinquency was becoming a prominent issue and there were repeated calls for the government to do something.[223] Yet Eisenhower clearly attempted to downplay the seriousness of the issue as when he responded to a reporter's question that "I don't like to use the words 'juvenile delinquent' because I have a very firm conviction that that term ought to be translated into parental failure; that is what I think."[224] The pressure on the administration, however, began to build when Congress created a special committee on juvenile delinquency and the Secretary of HEW called a national conference on juvenile delinquency in 1954.[225] This forced the hand of Eisenhower and in his 1955 State of the Union Address he announced his plan that in order "to help the States do a better and more timely job, we must strengthen their resources for preventing and dealing with juvenile delinquency" and he proposed "Federal Legislation to assist the States to promote concerted action in dealing with this nation-wide problem."[226] Despite this proposal, subsequent pleas, and twice submitting delinquency control bills, no legislation was enacted by Congress during Eisenhower's administration.[227] Eisenhower would have to settle for issues dealing with crime and the police in Washington, D.C.[228] and giving rhetorical speeches to the law enforcement community.[229]

In 1960, despite both major parties responding to the issue of juvenile delinquency in their platforms,[230] neither juvenile delinquency nor crime became campaign issues. Once Kennedy was elected and his younger brother, Robert Kennedy, was appointed Attorney General, the administration would begin addressing several issues involving crime, namely organized crime and juvenile delinquency.[231] Although Robert Kennedy was assuredly the primary leader on issues of crime,[232] President Kennedy contributed to the initiatives by creating the President's Committee on Juvenile Delinquency and Youth Crime,[233] hosting a White House Conference on Narcotic and Drug Abuse,[234] as well as creating the President's Advisory Committee on Narcotics and Drug Abuse.[235] As a result of the various initiatives, President Kennedy was able to succeed where his predecessor Eisenhower had failed. On September 22, 1961, the Juvenile Delinquency and Youth Offenses Control Act of 1961 was signed into law by President Kennedy.[236] Earlier that month, Kennedy also signed three pieces of legislation aimed at addressing the issues of organized crime.

In the end, Kennedy, with the assistance of his brother, had successfully begun to expand the government's involvement in the issue of crime. Coupled with his assassination in November of 1963—the victim of a heinous crime—and an increasing crime trend in the early 1960s, crime was quickly becoming an issue of national attention. The departure point for crime becoming a definitive issue in national politics would come the following year during the campaign between Presidential incumbent Lyndon B. Johnson and the Republican nominee, Barry Goldwater.

THE NATIONALIZATION ERA (1964–PRESENT)

There is overwhelming evidence to support the fact that the 1964 election between Lyndon B. Johnson, the incumbent, and Barry Goldwater, the Republican challenger, saw crime become a major election issue for the first time, helped define the role of the federal government in crime-control policy, and resulted in increased federal activity on crime.[237] The movement to make crime a national issue was actually begun in the spring of 1964 by Governor George Wallace who used the "law and order" platform to "attract support among northern white ethnic voters" but failed to gain any success as his campaign never fully developed.[238] In the summer of 1964, Goldwater began utilizing the rhetoric of "law and order" with much success and he continued to press the issue all the way up to his acceptance speech at the Republican Convention. As one author has explained, "the accep-

The President Speaks . . .

There has been a substantial postwar increase in crime in this country, particularly in crimes of violence. This is disturbing, but it is one of the inevitable results of war, and the dislocations that spring from war. It is one of the many reasons why we must work with other nations for a permanent peace.

I might remind you that after every war this country has ever been engaged in, we have had exactly the same problems to face. After the Revolutionary War we had almost exactly the same problems with which we are faced now, out of which came the Alien and Sedition laws, which we finally had to repeal because they did not agree with the Bill of Rights. Then, after the War Between the States, or the Civil War, we had all sorts of banditry. My State was famous for some of the great bandits of that time, if you recall. We had the same situation after World War I. We had a terrible time then with the increase in crimes of violence. We managed to handle the situation, and I am just as sure as I stand here that we will do it again.

This postwar increase in crime has been accompanied by a resurgence of underworld forces—forces which thrive on vice and greed. This underworld has used its resources to corrupt the moral fiber of some of our citizens and some of our communities. It carries a large share of the responsibility for the general increase in crime in the last few years.

It is important, therefore, that we work together in combating organized crime in all its forms. We must use our courts and our law enforcement agencies, and the moral forces of our people, to put down organized crime wherever it appears.

The fundamental basis of this Nation's law was given to Moses on the Mount. The fundamental basis of our Bill of Rights comes from the teachings which we get from Exodus and St. Matthew, from Isaiah and St. Paul. I don't think we emphasize that enough these days.

Above all, we must recognize that human misery breeds most of our crime. We must wipe out our slums, improve the health of our citizens, and eliminate the inequalities of opportunity which embitter men and women and turn them toward lawlessness. In the long run, these programs represent the greatest of all anticrime measures.

I am particularly anxious that we should do everything within our power to protect the minds and hearts of our children from the moral corruption that accompanies organized crime. Our children are our greatest resource, and our greatest asset—the hope of our future, and the future of the world. We must not permit the existence of conditions which cause our children to believe that crime is inevitable and normal. We must teach idealism—honor, ethics, decency, the moral law. We must teach that we should do right because it is right, and not in the hope of any material reward. That is

(continued)

tance speech was most notable because it signaled Goldwater's deliberate decision to make "law and order" his major domestic issue."[239] It was there that Goldwater voiced his opinion:

> Tonight there is violence in our streets, corruption in our highest offices, aimlessness among our youth, anxiety among our elderly, and there is a virtual despair among the many who look beyond material success toward the inner meaning of their lives . . . The growing menace in our country tonight, to personal safety, to life, to limb and to property, in homes, in churches, in the playgrounds and places of business, particularly, in our great cities, is the mounting concern of every thoughtful citizen in the United States. Security from domestic violence, no less than from foreign is the most elementary and fundamental purpose of any government, and a government that cannot fulfill this purpose is one that cannot long command the loyalty of its citizens.[240]

This was coupled with a dramatic speech by the former president, Dwight D. Eisenhower, who told the convention to "not be guilty of maudlin sympathy for the criminal who, roaming the streets with switchblade knife and illegal firearms seeking a helpless prey, suddenly becomes upon apprehension a poor, underprivileged person who counts upon the compassion of our society and the laxness or weaknesses of too many courts to forgive his offense." As a result, Goldwater and Eisenhower succeeded, as Theodore White would explain, in "lifting to national discourse a matter of intimate concern to the delegates, creating there before them an issue which touched all fears, North and South. The convention howled."[241]

President Johnson, although having had to deal with several issues regarding crime upon ascension to office, namely the Kennedy assassination and riots, did not utilize the "law and order" rhetoric during the first half of 1964 and little attention was given to crime.[242] Two days after the Republican National Convention, when asked about Goldwater making crime a major campaign issue by a reporter, Johnson's answer was a reminder that "the Constitution provides that responsibility for law and order should be vested in the States and in the local communities, for the protection of the individual."[243] Although Johnson would increase his rhetoric on the issue of crime as the election of 1964 drew near and he would increase his activities on the subject of crime, Johnson was tentative at getting involved in the issue.[244] In addition, some of his activities did not assist him in responding to Goldwater's charges. For instance, during the summer, Johnson asked

TABLE 1–3   The Presidents

	The Nationalization Era
Lyndon B. Johnson	1963–1969
Richard M. Nixon	1969–1974
Gerald R. Ford	1974–1977
Jimmy (James Earl) Carter	1977–1981
Ronald Reagan	1981–1989
George Bush	1989–1993
Bill (William Jefferson) Clinton	1993–2001
George W. Bush	2001–

J. Edgar Hoover to prepare a report regarding the rash of riots occurring across the nation. Johnson's main speech writer, Bill Moyers, upon receiving the report, wrote a memorandum to the president stating that "as written, the report can actually play into Goldwater's hands" and that "if I were writing for the Senator from Arizona, I could use this report."[245] In the end, Johnson was not very forceful on the issue, but it would not matter. Johnson was handed a definitive victory in November of 1964.[246] However, as one author has stated, "although Goldwater lost the 1964 presidential election, he succeeded in setting the scene for debate about crime"[247] Another author wrote that "since that time the crime problem has remained high in public opinion polls concerned with major domestic issues and has been a factor in national politics."[248] Crime had become a national issue.

Although Johnson had not made crime an important part of his campaign, he would come to make crime a central part of his elected term in office. As the authors of Johnson's Crime Commission would later write:

> The previous fall, Barry Goldwater had campaigned on the "lawlessness" theme. Although he had lost the election (for other reasons), the fears upon which this theme played were substantial, and, more importantly, Lyndon Johnson recognized their explosive potential. Johnson is not the sort of politician who overlooks actual or potential political issues, and it was quite clear that Goldwater had touched a sensitive nerve. Undoubtedly he believed that he could preempt the issue by proposing a bundle of anticrime legislation and, simultaneously, a grandiose study of the problem.[249]

If there is anything that best demonstrates Johnson's activity on the crime issue, it is the "bundle of anticrime legislation" his administration proposed and Johnson signed into law consisting of the Criminal Justice Act (1964), the Drug Abuse and Control Act (1965), the Prisoner Rehabilitation Act (1965), the Law Enforcement Assistance Act (1965), the Bail Reform Act (1966), the Narcotic Addict Rehabilitation Act (1966), the Act to Reform Federal Criminal Laws (1966), the Act to Extend the Law Enforcement Assistance Act (1966), the Act to Prohibit Obstruction of Criminal Investigations (1967), the Act to Create the Federal Judicial Center

(1967), the District of Columbia Crime Act (1967), the Act to Provide Indemnity Payments for Police Officers (1968), the Omnibus Crime Control and Safe Streets Act (1968), the Juvenile Delinquency Prevention and Control Act (1968), the Gun Control Act (1968) and the Traffic in or Possession of Drugs Act (1968).[250] In addition, not only would he initiate the "grandiose study" known as the President's Commission on Law Enforcement and Administration of Justice (1965), he would also create four additional crime commissions: the President's Commission on Crime in the District of Columbia (1965), the Commission on Pornography and Obscenity (1966), the National Advisory Commission on Civil Disorders (1968), and the Commission on the Causes and Prevention of Violence (1969). If one adds the Warren Commission, a special commission to investigate the assassination of John F. Kennedy,[251] and the dozens of special speeches on crime, it is clear that a significant portion of Johnson's time and attention was dedicated to the problems of crime and that while he was fighting a war in Vietnam, he was also fighting a "war on crime" at home.[252]

Despite the facts that Johnson had made crime a central part of his domestic policy and he chose not to run for a second term, the two candidates in 1968, Nixon and Wallace, both made crime a central part of their campaign as did their party platforms.[253] The Republican party platform specifically stated that "respect for the law is the cornerstone of a free and well-ordered society"[254] and John Mitchell, Nixon's campaign director promised that the administration would provide an all-out attack on crime.[255] Upon assuming office in 1969, it is said that Nixon told Kissinger that in regard to domestic policy he had only three areas of concern: crime, school integration, and economic matters.[256] Egil Krogh, Jr., Nixon's Domestic Council aide, has also stated that "law and order" was Nixon's principal domestic issue.[257] In the end, Nixon would succeed in expanding federal intervention in crime control beyond anything Johnson was able to accomplish.

Nixon was able to do this first and foremost by way of his "new federalism"[258] policy where he succeeded in moving the funding for the Safe Streets Act of 1968, by way of the newly created office known as the Law Enforcement Assistance Administration (LEAA) within the Department of Justice, to a block-grant format.[259] In this case, the Federal government would issue block grants to state government "planning agencies" which could then provide individual grants to local police departments. By achieving this legislative victory to change the way the funds were allocated, "Nixon held fast to the concept of local determination of and control over crime-control programs."[260] A second means of accomplishing his crime-control agenda was by way of launching the first "war on drugs" along the Mexican border and the successful passage of the Drug Abuse Office and Treatment Act which would combine all drug agencies under one drug superagency, the Drug Enforcement Administration.[261] Finally, he would personally target and oversee the issues of crime, drugs, and juvenile delinquency in the District of Columbia and, like Johnson, he made the nation's capital a test case for his policies.[262] Although even Nixon realized "that in the long run crime itself requires much more far-reaching and subtle approaches"[263] and that "crime will never stop . . . all we can do is slow it down,"[264] it is a result of his initiatives in crime-control policy, as Calder explains, that "law and order had come home to roost."[265] The issue of crime had become an institutionalized part of the office of the president.[266]

The next president, upon assuming office when President Nixon resigned, would automatically be forced to deal with the issue of crime, namely Watergate. President Gerald Ford would take office on August 9, 1974 and on September 8, 1974, he would announce his intentions to grant Nixon an unconditional pardon. As a result of granting the pardon, the fact he had not been elected to the office, and because he attempted to "carry on" most of the Nixon administration's policies, Ford faced strong opposition in most of his legislative proposals.[267] The same would be true for his crime-control policies. Although he would attempt to "carry on" many of the Nixon administration's crime policies, he would also attempt to focus on several issues of his own.[268] He would give three key speeches: one at the Yale Law School,[269] a crime message to Congress,[270] and a speech to the International Association of Chiefs of Police,[271] that would outline his crime-control policies.[272] He clearly demonstrated an interest in continuing the funding for the Law Enforcement Assistance Administration, as well as targeting the problems of drugs.[273] In addition, he supported the movement toward mandatory sentencing and restricting the search capabilities of law enforcement, and he signed into law the Juvenile Justice and Delinquency Act of 1974 and the Public Safety Officers' Benefits Act of 1976.[274] Moreover, it should be noted that Ford was also the target in two assassination attempts on his life. While Ford was apparently concerned about the issue of crime, his administration was too short and chaotic in the aftermath of Watergate to launch or pass any major pieces of legislation.[275]

In the 1976 campaign, the two major party platforms would once more detail their stance on crime[276] and "crime again became a national political issue."[277] One key issue that Carter would raise during the campaign would ultimately be very telling about how Carter, the eventual winner, attempted to address the issue of crime. He repeatedly condemned the Law Enforcement Assistance Administration (LEAA) for its waste of millions of dollars "while making almost no contribution to reducing crime."[278] Carter promised to either reorganize the LEAA or to abolish it altogether.[279] Carter's concern for controlling the bureaucracy and his label as an outsider handicapped his abilities to achieve many domestic policy victories.[280] Crime policy was no exception. Although he had appointed a task force from the Department of Justice to study the LEAA program in 1977, and they too recommended eliminating the agency, Carter could not convince Congress to take action in 1978. The following year, several changes were made by adding some new offices, abolishing some old ones, and changing some of the funding mechanisms of the LEAA,[281] but Carter's vision of major reforms or abolishment never occurred. Although Carter's main emphasis for crime-control policy was dealing with the LEAA, this is not to say that he did not address other issues. Carter would deal with issues of organized crime, drugs, juvenile crime, judicial reforms, crime in the District of Columbia, and prison reform.[282] However, Carter's time and attention to each of these issues was limited and he saw no major legislative success in the area of crime. Although crime had not completely drifted from the institution of the presidency, there was, to be sure, a temporary "lull."[283]

This lull would not last long. It ended with the victory of Ronald Reagan over President Carter in the 1980 election. The party platforms would again call for tougher crime-control policies[284] and the challenger, Ronald Reagan, would use the issue of crime against the president. In one campaign speech, Reagan voiced the sentiment that "in recent years, a murderous epidemic of drug abuse has swept our country. Mr. Carter, through his policies and his personnel, has demonstrated little interest in stopping its ravages."[285] This speech, and many like it, are telling about Reagan's crime-control policy. Although he would return to the "law and order" approach to crime first espoused by Barry Goldwater and similar to that of Nixon and Ford,[286] Reagan was able to reframe the issue of crime and associated it heavily with the issue of drugs. Crime and drugs were synonymous to Reagan, but the topic of drugs offered a new appeal.[287]

Needless to say, Reagan's primary emphasis on crime was by way of addressing the problems of illicit drugs. He would look to revise the concept of "organized crime" by concentrating on the modern day organized crime associations centered on the commerce of drugs, by appointing a President's Commission on Organized Crime,[288] by calling for a reorganization of the federal mechanism for targeting drugs, by amending the Posse Comitatus Act to allow the military to assist civilian law enforcement, by creating a model multi-jurisdictional task force known as the South Florida Task Force, for which he placed Vice-President Bush in the leadership role, and through the efforts of his wife, Nancy, in the "Just say no" campaign.[289] Although he would focus on several other items, Marion sums up Reagan's crime-control agenda by saying it "was limited . . . to drugs (which included a war against organized crime), the formation of a comprehensive, anti-crime reform of the federal criminal code (which included the death penalty, the exclusionary rule, *habeas corpus*, and the insanity defense), gun control, child pornography, victims of crime, prison reform, and juvenile crime."[290] As a result, Reagan would achieve several legislative victories in the passage of the Comprehensive Crime Control Act of 1984, the Anti-Drug Abuse Act of 1986, and the Anti-Drug Abuse Act of 1988.

Upon completion of two terms in office, the 1988 campaign would see Reagan's Vice-President, George Bush, challenge the Democratic nominee, Michael Dukakis, then Governor of Massachusetts, for the office of the presidency. Playing on the theme of crime, the Bush campaign utilized a series of campaign ads depicting a black convicted murderer who raped a Maryland woman and stabbed her fiancé while on a prison furlough, which most assuredly assisted the Bush campaign in its stance to appear "tough on crime."[291] This, and many other factors, would allow Bush to succeed his predecessor, and the crime policies of Ronald Reagan would be continued for another four years with a dramatic increase in "fighting the war on drugs." President Bush's four years in office were marked primarily by his strong stance on drugs, but were coupled with the issue of crime.[292]

Like Reagan, Bush considered the issue of drugs to be synonymous with the issue of crime. He would achieve several legislative victories regarding crime, including the passage of the Crime Control Act of 1990, but would fail to win reelection in 1992. In 1993, President William J. Clinton entered office under a campaign theme of "getting tough on crime," and despite a temporary neglect of the issue upon taking office, he would move on to achieve a legislative success in 1994 with the passage of the Violent Crime Control and Law Enforcement Act,[293] the largest federal crime control package to date (see Introduction). Clinton would go on to utilize this victory and his "tough on crime" rhetoric to win the 1996 campaign against the Republican nominee, Bob Dole.

Conclusions

In reviewing presidential activity regarding the issue of crime in the United States across time, it becomes evident that presidents have always had to deal with issues centered on crime, but there has been an evolution in regard to their level of involvement. Dividing American history into three eras, for purposes of looking at presidents and crime, helps to sort out how this evolution has occurred through the use of a simple heuristic device. The first era—the traditional era which runs from 1776 to 1899—shows a time period in which presidents, for the most part, limited their activity to intervention as dictated by the Constitution for assistance in domestic disturbances. The second era—the transitional era—is best divided into two time periods. The first period is the responsive, ranging from 1900 to 1927, where the government became more involved in the issue of local crime control but only as a response to problems of crime resulting from prohibition and organized crime. Also during this time there was a growth in the federal bureaucracy that dealt with issues of crime. The second time period of the transitional era is labeled the developmental period and spans the years 1928–1963, from the election of President Hoover through the assassination of President Kennedy. This time period is marked largely by a development in the federal role in state and local crime control, primarily rising out of the Prohibition and post-World War II eras, both witnessing the growing problems of crime for which local criminal justice agencies were ill-equipped to handle. Finally, with the campaign debate between Johnson and Goldwater in 1964, crime became a national political issue—one that would become an integral part of every president's domestic agenda with the exception of a limited activity on the part of President Carter.

In sum, presidents over time have become far more involved in the issues of crime in the United States, and whether framed in terms of "street crime," "drugs," or "law and order," attention to the issue of crime has become a part of the American presidency. Recognizing this to be the case, there then looms the question "Why?" Why have presidents become more engaged in an issue that has always been under state and local purview? Why do presidents exert their valuable resources to address a problem over which they cannot expect to have a great amount of control? Why has crime become an issue for the office of the presidency, an issue not limited to one or two presidents or simply one party or the other? Why have presidents become so heavily involved in the issue of crime-control policy? It is to these questions that the next chapter turns.

Endnotes

1. Thomas Jefferson. *Messages and Papers of the Presidents*. 1: 369–370. Derived from World Book Encyclopedia. *American Reference Library*. Orem: The Western Standard Publishing Company. The text comes from Jefferson's Second Inaugural Address. Italics are the author's.
2. Task Force on the Federalization of Criminal Law. 1998. *The Federalization of Criminal Law: Defending Liberty, Pursuing Justice*. Washington D.C.: American Bar Association.
3. See for instance Friedman, Lawrence M. 1993. *Crime and Punishment in American History*. New York: Basic Books; Walker, Samuel. 1998. *Popular Justice: A History of American Criminal Justice*. 2d ed. New York: Oxford University Press.
4. The term "federalization" is often used synonymously with the term "nationalization." However, when used as a distinct term in regards to the "federalization of crime" it is defined as the movement of a criminal law or criminal jurisdiction from the exclusive purview of the state and local governments and making it a federal crime under federal jurisdiction.
5. The term "nationalization" is often used synonymously with the term "federalization." However, when used as a distinct term in regards to the "nationalization of crime" it is defined as the movement of the political issue of crime from a policy issue for the state and local governments to deal with, to one that moves to the attention of the entire nation.
6. Friedman, Lawrence M. 1993. *Crime and Punishment in American History*. New York: Basic Books, p. 262.
7. Friedman, Lawrence M. 1993. *Crime and Punishment in American History*. New York: Basic Books, p. 263.
8. Lawrence M. Friedman in his seminal work on criminal justice history divides his analysis into the "Colonial Period" and "From the Revolution to the Close of the Nineteenth Century." Samuel Walker in his seminal work on criminal justice history considers this both the Colonial Era (1776–1820) and the time period of "Building the Criminal Justice System" from 1820–1900. See Friedman, Lawrence M. 1993. *Crime and Punishment in American History*. New York: Basic Books; Walker, Samuel. 1998. *Popular Justice: A History of American Criminal Justice*. 2d ed. New York: Oxford University Press.
9. Samuel Walker looks at the time period of 1900–1920 as "Completing the System: Reform in the Progressive Era." See Walker, Samuel. 1998. *Popular Justice: A History of American Criminal Justice*. 2d ed. New York: Oxford University Press.
10. Calder, James D. 1993. *The Origins and Development of Federal Crime-control policy: Herbert Hoover's Initiatives*. Westport: Praeger Publishers.
11. Samuel Walker looks at the time period of 1920 to 1960 as being a time of "Consolidation and Change" during the "Modern Era." See Walker, Samuel. 1998. *Popular Justice: A History of American Criminal Justice*. 2d ed. New York: Oxford University Press.
12. Friedman writes of the "National System" and Walker dubs the time period of 1960–1975 as the "National Crisis over Crime and Justice" and 1975–1995 as "Criminal Justice in a Conservative Era." See Friedmann, Lawrence M. 1993. *Crime and Punishment in American History*. New York: Basic Books; Walker, Samuel. 1998. *Popular Justice: A History of American Criminal Justice*. 2d ed. New York: Oxford University Press.
13. Author's note: While the information contained in these eras is an historical review of presidents and their involvement in crime, it is not meant to be a detailed history but

rather a sweeping review of each president's involvement based upon an analysis of their *Public Papers*.

14. Bridenbaugh, Carl. 1938. *Cities in the Wilderness: The First Century of Urban Life in America*. New York: The Ronald Press Company, p. 68. See also Mahoney, Barry. 1976. *The Politics of the Safe Streets Act, 1965–1973: A Case Study in Evolving Federalism and the National Legislative Process*. Ph.D. Dissertation, Columbia University.

15. Bridenbaugh, Carl. 1955. *Cities in Revolt: Urban Life in America, 1743–1776*. New York: Alfred A. Knopf, p. 299. See also Mahoney, Barry. 1976. *The Politics of the Safe Streets Act, 1965–1973: A Case Study in Evolving Federalism and the National Legislative Process*. Ph.D. Dissertation, Columbia University.

16. National Commission on the Causes and Prevention of Violence. 1969. *To Insure Domestic Tranquility*. Washington D.C.: U.S. G.P.O.

17. See Graham, Hugh D. and Ted R. Gurr, eds. 1969. *Violence in America: Historical and Comparative Perspectives*. A Report to the National Commission on the Causes and Prevention of Violence. Vols. 1 and 2. New York: New American Library Inc.; Hofstadter, Richard and Michael Wallace, eds. 1971. *American Violence: A Documentary History*. New York: Vintage Books; Lane, Roger. 1976. "Criminal Violence in America: The First Hundred Years." *The Annals of the American Academy of Political and Social Science* 423: 1–13; National Commission on the Causes and Prevention of Violence. 1969. *To Insure Domestic Tranquility*. Washington D.C.: U.S. G.P.O.; Pepinsky, Harold E. 1976. "The Growth of Crime in the United States." *The Annals of the American Academy of Political and Social Science* 423: 23–30; Wilson, James Q. 1976. "Crime and Punishment, 1776 to 1976. Bicentennial Essay." *Time* (April) 26: 82–85.

18. See chapter two of Silberman, Charles E. 1978. *Criminal Violence, Criminal Justice*. New York: Vintage Books.

19. Walker, Samuel. 1998. *Popular Justice: A History of American Criminal Justice*. 2d ed. New York: Oxford University Press, p. 37. See also Greenburg, Douglas. 1974. *Crime and Law Enforcement in the Colony of New York, 1691–1776*. Ithaca: Cornell University Press, p. 56.

20. United States Constitution. Article 1, Section 8.

21. United States Constitution. Article 1, Section 8.

22. Bordenhamer, David J. 1992. *Fair Trial: Rights of the Accused in American History*. New York: Oxford University Press, p. 14; Walker, Samuel. 1998. *Popular Justice: A History of American Criminal Justice*. 2d ed. New York: Oxford University Press, p. 38.

23. United States Constitution. Article 1, Section 9.

24. United States Constitution. Article 1, Section 8.

25. United States Constitution. Article 3, Section 1.

26. United States Constitution. Article 3, Section 2.

27. United States Constitution. Article 3, Section 3. Treason was defined as follows: "Treason against the United States, shall consist only in levying war against them, or in adhering to their enemies, giving them aid and comfort. No person shall be convicted of treason unless on the testimony of two witnesses to the same overt act, or on confession in open court." In addition, "the Congress shall have power to declare the punishment of treason, but no attainder of treason shall work corruption of blood, or forfeiture, except during the life of the person attainted." Madison would explain in Federalist No. 43, "As treason may be committed against the United States, the authority of the United States ought to be enabled to punish it; but as newfangled and artificial treasons have been the great engines by which violent factions, the natural offspring of free governments, have usually wreaked their alternative malignity on each other, the convention have, with great judgement, opposed a barrier to this peculiar danger, by inserting a constitutional definition of the crime, fixing the proof necessary for conviction of it, and restraining the congress, even in punishing it, from extending the consequence of guilt beyond the person of its author."

28. United States Constitution. Article 4, Section 2.

29. United States Constitution. Article 4, Section 3.

30. United States Constitution. Article 4, Section 3. According to James Madison's notes, there was actually much debate over this specific clause during the Constitutional Convention. Luther Martin, a delegate to the convention from Maryland, "opposed it as giving a dangerous and unnecessary power. The consent of the State ought to precede the introduction of any extraneous force whatever." In addition, "Mr. Gerry was against letting loose the myrmidons of the United States on a State without its own consent. The States will be the best Judges in such cases. More blood would have been spilt in Massachusetts in the late insurrection, if the General authority had intermeddled." Governor Morris of Pennsylvania is also reported to have remarked, "We are acting a very strange part. We first form a strong man to protect us, and at the same time wish to tie his hands behind him." Finally, George Mason remarked, "If the General Government should have no right to suppress rebellions against particular States, it will be a bad situation indeed."

31. The State legislature was preferred to make the decision of calling for federal assistance because it was feared that a future insurrection might occur by way of a despotic governor attempting to assume dictatorial powers over the people of that state.

32. Cronin, Thomas E., Tania Z. Cronin, and Michael E. Milakovich. 1981. *U.S. v. Crime in the Streets*. Bloomington: Indiana University Press, p. 2; Mahoney, Barry. 1976. *The Politics of the Safe Streets Act, 1965–1973: A Case Study in Evolving Federalism and the National Legislative Process*. Ph.D. Dissertation, Columbia University, p. 12. See also the discussion by Hamilton in Federalist Papers Number 74, in Rossiter, Clinton. 1961. *The Federalist Papers*. New York: New American Library, pp. 447–449.

33. United States Constitution. Article 2, Section 2.

34. United States Constitution. Article 2, Section 3.

35. Light, Paul C. 1991. *The President's Agenda: Domestic Policy Choice from Kennedy to Reagan*. Rev. ed. Baltimore: The Johns Hopkins University Press.

36. United States Constitution. Article 2, Section 2.

37. Meador, Daniel J. 1980. *The President, the Attorney General, and the Department of Justice*. Charlottesville: White Burkett Miller Center of Public Affairs, University of Virginia.

38. United States Constitution. Article 1, Section 7.

39. Rossiter, Clinton. 1961. *The Federalist Papers*. New York: New American Library, p. 276.

40. Rossiter, Clinton. 1961. *The Federalist Papers*. New York: New American Library, p. 226.

41. Rossiter, Clinton. 1961. *The Federalist Papers*. New York: New American Library, p. 120.

42. Hamilton would also state in speaking before the New York Ratifying Convention on June 28, 1788, ". . . but the laws of Congress are restricted to a certain sphere, and when they depart from this sphere, they are no longer supreme or binding. In the same manner the states have certain independent powers, in which their laws are supreme: for example, in making and executing laws concerning the punishment of certain crimes, such as murder, theft, etc., the states cannot be controlled." In addition he would also explain, "the state officers will ever be important, because they are necessary and useful. Their powers are such as are extremely interesting among the people; such as affect their property, their liberty, and life. What is more important than the administration of justice and the executive of the civil and criminal laws?"

43. Friedman, Lawrence M. 1993. *Crime and Punishment in American History*. New York: Basic Books, p. 262.

44. Ashdown, Gerald G. 1996. "Federalism, Federalization, and the Politics of Crime." *West Virginia Law Review* 98: 789–813; Friedman, Lawrence M. 1993. *Crime and Punishment in American History*. New York: Basic Books.

45. Friedman, Lawrence M. 1993. *Crime and Punishment in American History*. New York: Basic Books, p. 71.

46. Ashdown, Gerald G. 1996. "Federalism, Federalization, and the Politics of Crime." *West Virginia Law Review* 98: 789–813, p. 790, footnote 5.

47. It should be noted that the Bill of Rights pertained only to the national government, not to the states. The Supreme Court would affirm this in Barron v. Baltimore, 32 U.S. (7 Pet.) 243 (1833). See Friedman, Lawrence M. 1993. *Crime and Punishment in American History*. New York: Basic Books, p. 72.

48. Friedman, Lawrence M. 1993. *Crime and Punishment in American History*. New York: Basic Books, p. 72.

49. Ashdown, Gerald G. 1996. "Federalism, Federalization, and the Politics of Crime." *West Virginia Law Review* 98: 789–813, p. 790; Lumbard, Eliot H. 1971. "State and Local Government Crime Control." In *The Challenge of Crime in a Free Society*. Henry S. Ruth, Jr., et al., eds. New York: Da Capo Press, pp. 79–97.

50. Calder, James D. 1978. *Presidents and Crime Control: Some Limitations on Executive Police Making*. Ph.D. Dissertation, Claremont University. Calder explains that these categories are purposely broad and that they were derived from reading several historical accounts by noted historians and political scientists of presidential intervention and justifications for such intervention.

51. Act of September 24, 1789, Ch. 20, 1 Stat. 73. See Meador, Daniel J. 1980. *The President, the Attorney General, and The Department of State*. Charlottesville: White Burkett Miller Center of Public Affairs, University of Virginia, p. 5, footnote 7.

52. Meador, Daniel J. 1980. *The President, the Attorney General, and The Department of State*. Charlottesville: White Burkett Miller Center of Public Affairs, University of Virginia, p. 5.

53. Act of September 24, 1789, Ch. 20, 1 Stat. 73. See Meador, Daniel J. 1980. *The President, the Attorney General, and The Department of State*. Charlottesville: White Burkett Miller Center of Public Affairs, University of Virginia, pp. 5–6, footnotes 7 and 8.

54. Meador, Daniel J. 1980. *The President, the Attorney General, and The Department of State*. Charlottesville: White Burkett Miller Center of Public Affairs, University of Virginia, p. 6. Although the Attorney General began attending cabinet meetings at this time, he was considered the lowest ranking member until his rank as fourth in the cabinet was fixed by Congress in 1886.

55. Washington, George. *Messages and Papers of the Presidents of the United States*. Vol. 1, p. 51 regarding "protection of citizens from violence (Indians)", Vol. 1, p. 129, regarding proclamation to bring those who destroyed an Indian town to justice; Vol. 1, pp. 139–140 regarding crimes by and against Indians in the territories. Citation obtained from World Book Encyclopedia. 1998. *American Reference Library*. CD-ROM. Orem: The Western Standard Publishing Company.

56. Washington, George. *Messages and Papers of the Presidents of the United States*. Vol. 1, p. 103 regarding message to the Senate and House of Representatives concerning fugitives fleeing from Pennsylvania into Virginia; Vol. 1, pp. 139–140 regarding "mutual exchange of fugitives from justice." Citation obtained from World Book Encyclopedia. 1998. *American Reference Library*. CD-ROM. Orem: The Western Standard Publishing Company.

57. Johnson, Paul. 1997. *A History of the American People*. New York: HarperCollins Publishers, p. 213.

58. Johnson, Paul. 1997. *A History of the American People*. New York: HarperCollins Publishers, p. 214.

59. Johnson, Paul. 1997. *A History of the American People*. New York: HarperCollins Publishers, p. 214.

60. Calder, James D. 1978. *Presidents and Crime Control: Some Limitations on Executive Police Making*. Ph.D. Dissertation, Claremont University, p. 55.

61. Johnson, Paul. 1997. *A History of the American People*. New York: HarperCollins Publishers, p. 214.

62. Johnson, Paul. 1997. *A History of the American People*. New York: HarperCollins Publishers, p. 214.
63. Johnson, Paul. 1997. *A History of the American People*. New York: HarperCollins Publishers, p. 214.
64. Morrison, Samuel E. 1965. *The Oxford History of the American People*. New York: Oxford University Press.
65. Adams, John. *Messages and Papers of the Presidents of the United States*. Vol. 1, p. 245. Citation obtained from World Book Encyclopedia. 1998. *American Reference Library*. CD-ROM. Orem: The Western Standard Publishing Company.
66. Adams, John. *Messages and Papers of the Presidents of the United States*. Vol. 1, p. 240. Citation obtained from World Book Encyclopedia. 1998. *American Reference Library*. CD-ROM. Orem: The Western Standard Publishing Company.
67. Morrison, Samuel E. 1965. *The Oxford History of the American People*. New York: Oxford University Press, p. 355.
68. Calder, James D. 1978. *Presidents and Crime Control: Some Limitations on Executive Police Making*. Ph.D. Dissertation, Claremont University, p. 56.
69. Walker, Samuel. 1998. *Popular Justice: A History of American Criminal Justice*. New York: Oxford University Press, p. 39.
70. Jefferson, Thomas. *Messages and Papers of the Presidents of the United States*. Vol. 1, pp. 349–350; pp. 369–370; and p. 411. Citation obtained from World Book Encyclopedia. 1998. *American Reference Library*. CD-ROM. Orem: The Western Standard Publishing Company.
71. Jefferson, Thomas. *Messages and Papers of the Presidents of the United States*. Vol. 1, p. 343. Citation obtained from World Book Encyclopedia. 1998. *American Reference Library*. CD-ROM. Orem: The Western Standard Publishing Company.
72. Jefferson, Thomas. *Messages and Papers of the Presidents of the United States*. Vol. 1, p. 349. Here he states that the federal government has the right "to establish in our harbors such a police as may maintain law and order." He would also call for the preservation of law and order. See footnote 1. Citation obtained from World Book Encyclopedia. 1998. *American Reference Library*. CD-ROM. Orem: The Western Standard Publishing Company.
73. Johnson, Paul. 1997. *A History of the American People*. New York: HarperCollins Publishers, p. 250; Malone, Dumas. 1970. *Jefferson the President: First Term 1801–1805*. Boston: Little, Brown, and Company.
74. Ellis, Joseph J. 1997. *American Sphinx: The Character of Thomas Jefferson*. New York: Alfred A. Knopf; Johnson, Paul. 1997. *A History of the American People*. New York: HarperCollins Publishers, p. 250.
75. Ellis, Joseph J. 1997. *American Sphinx: The Character of Thomas Jefferson*. New York: Alfred A. Knopf; Johnson, Paul. 1997. *A History of the American People*. New York: HarperCollins Publishers; Malone, Dumas. 1970. *Jefferson the President: First Term 1801–1805*. Boston: Little, Brown, and Company; Peterson, Merrill D. 1997. "Thomas Jefferson." In *The Presidents: A Reference History*. 2d ed. Henry F. Graff, ed. New York: Simon & Schuster Macmillan.
76. Johnson, Paul. 1997. *A History of the American People*. New York: HarperCollins Publishers, p. 251.
77. Malone, Dumas. 1970. *Jefferson the President: First Term 1801–1805*. Boston: Little, Brown, and Company; Peterson, Merrill D. 1997. "Thomas Jefferson." In *The Presidents: A Reference History*. 2d ed. Edited by Henry F. Graff. New York: Simon & Schuster Macmillan.
78. Peterson, Merrill D. 1997. "Thomas Jefferson." In *The Presidents: A Reference History*. 2d ed. Henry F. Graff, ed. New York: Simon & Schuster Macmillan.
79. Calder, James D. 1978. *Presidents and Crime Control: Some Limitations on Executive Police Making*. Ph.D. Dissertation, Claremont University, p. 61.

80. Madison, James. *Messages and Papers of the Presidents of the United States.* Vol. 1, pp. 561–562. Dated December 3, 1816. Citation obtained from World Book Encyclopedia. 1998. *American Reference Library.* CD-ROM. Orem: The Western Standard Publishing Company.

81. The concern here is not so much for the violation of crimes, but rather the violation of federal law and the intended use of the national government to deal with this domestic problem.

82. Latner, Richard B. 1997. "Andrew Jackson." In *The Presidents*: *A Reference History.* 2d ed. Henry F. Graff, ed. New York: Simon & Schuster Macmillan.

83. Jackson, Andrew. *Messages and Papers of the United States.* Vol. 1. "The Nullification Proclamation." December 10, 1832. See World Book Encyclopedia. 1998. *American Reference Library.* CD-ROM. Orem: The Western Standard Publishing Company.

84. Calder, James D. 1978. *Presidents and Crime Control: Some Limitations on Executive Police Making.* Ph.D. Dissertation, Claremont University.

85. Van Buren, Martin. *Messages and Papers of the Presidents.* Vol. 2, p. 1533. Citation obtained from World Book Encyclopedia. 1998. *American Reference Library.* CD-ROM. Orem: The Western Standard Publishing Company.

86. Article 4, Section 4.

87. The National Advisory Commission on Civil Disorders. 1968. *Report of the National Advisory Commission on Civil Disorders.* New York: Bantam Books.

88. Calder, James D. 1978. *Presidents and Crime Control: Some Limitations on Executive Police Making.* Ph.D. Dissertation, Claremont University, p. 58.

89. Tyler, John. *Messages and Papers of the Presidents.* Vol. 3. See World Book Encyclopedia. 1998. *American Reference Library.* CD-ROM. Orem: The Western Standard Publishing Company.

90. Calder, James D. 1978. *Presidents and Crime Control: Some Limitations on Executive Police Making.* Ph.D. Dissertation, Claremont University, pp. 58–59.

91. The National Advisory Commission on Civil Disorders. 1968. *Report of the National Advisory Commission on Civil Disorders.* New York: Bantam Books.

92. Tyler, John. *Messages and Papers of the Presidents.* Vol. 3, pp. 2144–2145. Citation obtained from World Book Encyclopedia. 1998. *American Reference Library.* CD-ROM. Orem: The Western Standard Publishing Company.

93. Wiecek, William M. 1972. *The Guarantee Clause of the U.S. Constitution.* Ithaca: Cornell University Press, p. 107; as cited in Calder, James D. 1978. *Presidents and Crime Control: Some Limitations on Executive Police Making.* Ph.D. Dissertation, Claremont University, p. 59.

94. Calder, James D. 1978. *Presidents and Crime Control: Some Limitations on Executive Police Making.* Ph.D. Dissertation, Claremont University, p. 59.

95. Tyler, John. *Messages and Papers of the Presidents.* Vol. 3. See World Book Encyclopedia. 1998. *American Reference Library.* CD-ROM. Orem: The Western Standard Publishing Company.

96. Pierce, Franklin. *Messages and Papers of the Presidents.* Vol. 4, pp. 2885–2893. Citation obtained from World Book Encyclopedia. 1998. *American Reference Library.* CD-ROM. Orem: The Western Standard Publishing Company.

97. Pierce, Franklin. *Messages and Papers of the Presidents.* Vol. 4, p. 2916. Citation obtained from World Book Encyclopedia. 1998. *American Reference Library.* CD-ROM. Orem: The Western Standard Publishing Company.

98. The National Advisory Commission on Civil Disorders. 1968. *Report of the National Advisory Commission on Civil Disorders.* New York: Bantam Books.

99. Lincoln, Abraham. *Messages and Papers of the Presidents.* Vol. 5, pp. 3227–3228. Citation obtained from World Book Encyclopedia. 1998. *American Reference Library.* CD-ROM. Orem: The Western Standard Publishing Company.

100. Donald, Herbert D. 1995. *Lincoln.* New York: Simon & Schuster. See especially pp. 441–443.

101. Simon, John Y. 1997. "Ulysses S. Grant." In *The Presidents*: *A Reference History.* 2d ed. Henry F. Graff, ed. New York: Simon & Schuster Macmillan, p. 252.

102. Calder, James D. 1978. *Presidents and Crime Control: Some Limitations on Executive Police Making*. Ph.D. Dissertation, Claremont University, p. 66.

103. Army Appropriations Act, ch. 263, § 15, 20 Stat. 145, 152 (1878) (codified as amended at 18 U.S.C. § 1385 (1994)). See Hammond, Matthew Carlton. 1997. "The Posse Comitatus Act: A Principle in Need of Renewal." *Washington University Law Quarterly* 72(2). Available at http://www.wulaw.wustl.edu/WULQ/75-2/752-10.html

104. The National Advisory Commission on Civil Disorders. 1968. *Report of the National Advisory Commission on Civil Disorders*. New York: Bantam Books.

105. Polakoff, Keith Ian. 1997. "Rutherford B. Hayes." In *The Presidents: A Reference History*. 2d ed. Henry F. Graff, ed. New York: Simon & Schuster Macmillan, p. 266.

106. Polakoff, Keith Ian. 1997. "Rutherford B. Hayes." In *The Presidents: A Reference History*. 2d ed. Henry F. Graff, ed. New York: Simon & Schuster Macmillan, p. 266.

107. Hayes, Rutherford B. *Messages and Papers of the Presidents*. Vol. 6, p. 4424. Citation obtained from World Book Encyclopedia. 1998. *American Reference Library*. CD-ROM. Orem: The Western Standard Publishing Company.

108. The National Advisory Commission on Civil Disorders. 1968. *Report of the National Advisory Commission on Civil Disorders*. New York: Bantam Books.

109. The National Advisory Commission on Civil Disorders. 1968. *Report of the National Advisory Commission on Civil Disorders*. New York: Bantam Books.

110. Garraty, John A. 1997. "Grover Cleveland." In *The Presidents: A Reference History*. 2d ed. Edited by Henry F. Graff. New York: Simon & Schuster Macmillan, p. 290.

111. Garraty, John A. 1997. "Grover Cleveland." In *The Presidents: A Reference History*. 2d ed. Edited by Henry F. Graff. New York: Simon & Schuster Macmillan, p. 290.

112. Garraty, John A. 1997. "Grover Cleveland." In *The Presidents: A Reference History*. 2d ed. Edited by Henry F. Graff. New York: Simon & Schuster Macmillan, p. 290.

113. McKinley, William. *Messages and Papers of the Presidents*. Vol. 8, p. 6240. Citation obtained from World Book Encyclopedia. 1998. *American Reference Library*. CD-ROM. Orem: The Western Standard Publishing Company.

114. Friedman, Lawrence M. 1993. *Crime and Punishment in American History*. New York: Basic Books; Mahoney, Barry. 1976. *The Politics of the Safe Streets Act, 1965–1973: A Case Study in Evolving Federalism and the National Legislative Process*. Ph.D. Dissertation, Columbia University, p. 16; Walker, Samuel. 1998. *Popular Justice: A History of American Criminal Justice*. 2d ed. New York: Oxford University Press.

115. The Antitrust lawsuits are criminal in form, but are selectively enforced. See Ashdown, Gerald G. 1996. "Federalism, Federalization, and the Politics of Crime." *West Virginia Law Review* 98: 789–813.

116. Ashdown, Gerald G. 1996. "Federalism, Federalization, and the Politics of Crime." *West Virginia Law Review* 98: 789–813, p. 790.

117. U.S. Constitution, Article 1, Section 8.

118. Abrams, Richard M. 1997. "Theodore Roosevelt." In *The Presidents: A Reference History*. 2d ed. Edited by Henry F. Graff. New York: Simon & Schuster Macmillan, p. 332; Miller, Nathan. 1992. *Theodore Roosevelt: A Life*. New York: William Morrow, p. 368.

119. Ashdown, Gerald G. 1996. "Federalism, Federalization, and the Politics of Crime." *West Virginia Law Review* 98: 789–813, p. 791.

120. McWilliams, John C. 1991. "Through the Past Darkly: The Politics and Policies of America's Drug War." *Journal of Policy History* 3(4): 356–392.

121. See the Prohibition Platforms of 1872, 1880, 1884, 1888, 1892, and 1900. In World Book Encyclopedia. 1998. *American Reference Library*. CD-ROM. Orem: The Western Standard Publishing Company.

122. McWilliams, John C. 1991. "Through the Past Darkly: The Politics and Policies of America's Drug War." *Journal of Policy History* 3(4): 356–392; Goldberg, Raymond. 1997. *Drugs Across the Spectrum*. Englewood: Morton Publishing Company.

123. Inciardi, James A. 1986. *The War on Drugs: Heroin, Cocaine, Crime and Public Policy*. Palo Alto: Mayfield Publishers; McWilliams, John C. 1991. "Through the Past Darkly: The Politics and Policies of America's Drug War." *Journal of Policy History* 3(4): 356–392; Goldberg, Raymond. 1997. *Drugs Across the Spectrum*. Englewood: Morton Publishing Company.

124. Roosevelt would become the president of the police board on May 8, 1895 and retained the position until 1896, when he became the Assistant Secretary of the Navy. See Abrams, Richard M. 1997. "Theodore Roosevelt." In *The Presidents: A Reference History*. 2d ed. Henry F. Graff, ed. New York: Simon & Schuster Macmillan, p. 329; Miller, Nathan. 1992. *Theodore Roosevelt: A Life*. New York: William Morrow, p. 228.

125. Leon Czolgosz was the assassin of President McKinley, an apparent anarchist. After McKinley's death he was quickly tried, convicted, and executed. It is reported that Roosevelt had stated that "Awful though this crime was against the President it was a thousand-fold worse crime against this Republic and against free government all over the world." See Miller, Nathan. 1992. *Theodore Roosevelt: A Life*. New York: William Morrow, p. 348–349.

126. Curriden, Mark and Leroy Phillips, Jr. 1999. *Contempt of Court: The Turn-of-the-Century Lynching that Launched a Hundred Years of Federalism*. New York: Oxford; Roosevelt, Theodore. *Messages and Papers of the Presidents*. Vol. 10, pp. 7409–7411. Citation obtained from World Book Encyclopedia. 1998. *American Reference Library*. CD-ROM. Orem: The Western Standard Publishing Company.

127. Roosevelt, Theodore. *Messages and Papers of the Presidents*. Vol. 10, pp. 7736–7737 and 7740. Citation obtained from World Book Encyclopedia. 1998. *American Reference Library*. CD-ROM. Orem: The Western Standard Publishing Company.

128. Roosevelt, Theodore. *Messages and Papers of the Presidents*. Vol. 10, pp. 7744–7745. Citation obtained from World Book Encyclopedia. 1998. *American Reference Library*. CD-ROM. Orem: The Western Standard Publishing Company.

129. Roosevelt, Theodore. *Messages and Papers of the Presidents*. Vol. 10. Citation obtained from World Book Encyclopedia. 1998. *American Reference Library*. CD-ROM. Orem: The Western Standard Publishing Company.

130. Roosevelt, Theodore. *Messages and Papers of the Presidents*. Vol. 9, pp. 6749–6769. December 8, 1902. Citation obtained from World Book Encyclopedia. 1998. *American Reference Library*. CD-ROM. Orem: The Western Standard Publishing Company.

131. Miller, Nathan. 1992. *Theodore Roosevelt: A Life*. New York: William Morrow, p. 364.

132. Abrams, Richard M. 1997. "Theodore Roosevelt." In *The Presidents: A Reference History*. 2d ed. Henry F. Graff, ed. New York: Simon & Schuster Macmillan; Miller, Nathan. 1992. *Theodore Roosevelt: A Life*. New York: William Morrow.

133. Abrams, Richard M. 1997. "Theodore Roosevelt." In *The Presidents: A Reference History*. 2d ed. Henry F. Graff, ed. New York: Simon & Schuster Macmillan, p. 332; Miller, Nathan. 1992. *Theodore Roosevelt: A Life*. New York: William Morrow, p. 370.

134. Miller, Nathan. 1992. *Theodore Roosevelt: A Life*. New York: William Morrow, p. 371.

135. Miller, Nathan. 1992. *Theodore Roosevelt: A Life*. New York: William Morrow, p. 371. The quote by Theodore Roosevelt is from p. 373.

136. Miller, Nathan. 1992. *Theodore Roosevelt: A Life*. New York: William Morrow, p. 371. The quote by Theodore Roosevelt is from pp. 372–378.

137. Miller, Nathan. 1992. *Theodore Roosevelt: A Life*. New York: William Morrow, p. 371. The quote by Theodore Roosevelt is from pp. 372–378.

138. The National Advisory Commission on Civil Disorders. 1968. *Report of the National Advisory Commission on Civil Disorders*. New York: Bantam Books.

139. Roosevelt, Theodore as cited in Abrams, Richard M. 1997. "Theodore Roosevelt." In *The Presidents*: *A Reference History*. 2d ed. Henry F. Graff, ed. New York: Simon & Schuster Macmillan, p. 337.

140. Walker, Samuel. 1998. *Popular Justice*: *A History of American Criminal Justice*. 2d ed. New York: Oxford University Press, p. 138.

141. Taft, William Howard. As Cited in Coletta, Paolo E. 1997. "William Howard Taft." In *The Presidents*: *A Reference History*. 2d ed. Henry F. Graff, ed. New York: Simon & Schuster Macmillan, p. 348.

142. Alpheus, Thomas Mason. 1955. *William Howard Taft*: *Chief Justice*. New York: Simon & Schuster.

143. Taft, William H. *Messages and Papers of the Presidents*. Vol. 10, pp. 7810–7811. December 7, 1909. Citation obtained from World Book Encyclopedia. 1998. *American Reference Library*. CD-ROM. Orem: The Western Standard Publishing Company.

144. The cases would be decided on May 15, 1911, and May 29, 1911, respectively. As cited in Coletta, Paolo E. 1997. "William Howard Taft." In *The Presidents*: *A Reference History*. 2d ed. Henry F. Graff, ed. New York: Simon & Schuster Macmillan, p. 355.

145. Taft, William H. *Messages and Papers of the Presidents*. Vol. 10, p. 7902. Second Annual Message. Citation obtained from World Book Encyclopedia. 1998. *American Reference Library*. CD-ROM. Orem: The Western Standard Publishing Company.

146. Taft, William H. *Messages and Papers of the Presidents*. Vol. 10, p. 7863. April 14, 1909. Citation obtained from World Book Encyclopedia. 1998. *American Reference Library*. CD-ROM. Orem: The Western Standard Publishing Company.

147. Goldberg, Raymond. 1997. *Drugs Across the Spectrum*. Englewood: Morton Publishing Company, pp. 67–68; Taft, William H. *Messages and Papers of the Presidents*. Vol. 10, pp. 7849–7850. February 25, 1910. Citation obtained from World Book Encyclopedia. 1998. *American Reference Library*. CD-ROM. Orem: The Western Standard Publishing Company.

148. Barber, James D. 1992. *The Presidential Character*: *Predicting Performance in the White House*. 4th ed. Englewood Cliffs: Prentice Hall, pp. 13–18.

149. Link, Arthur S. 1997. "Woodrow Wilson." In *The Presidents*: *A Reference History*. 2d ed. Henry F. Graff, ed. New York: Simon & Schuster Macmillan, pp. 370–371.

150. Jensen, Eric L. and Jurg Gerber. 1998. "The Social Construction of Drug Problems: An Historical Overview." In *The New War on Drugs*: *Symbolic Politics and Criminal Justice Policy*. Eric L. Jensen and Jurg Gerber, eds. Cincinnati: Academy of Criminal Justice Sciences and Anderson Publishing, p. 8; McWilliams, John C. 1991. "Through the Past Darkly: The Politics and Policies of America's Drug War." *Journal of Policy History* 3(4): 356–392.

151. The National Advisory Commission on Civil Disorders. 1968. *Report of the National Advisory Commission on Civil Disorders*. New York: Bantam Books.

152. Link, Arthur S. 1997. "Woodrow Wilson." In *The Presidents*: *A Reference History*. 2d ed. Henry F. Graff, ed. New York: Simon & Schuster Macmillan, p. 372.

153. National Motor Vehicle Theft (Dyer) Act., Chapter 89, 41 Stat. 324 (1919). See Ashdown, Gerald G. 1996. "Federalism, Federalization, and the Politics of Crime." *West Virginia Law Review* 98: 789–813, p. 791.

154. The National Advisory Commission on Civil Disorders. 1968. *Report of the National Advisory Commission on Civil Disorders*. New York: Bantam Books.

155. Enforcement was placed under the Treasury Department because the Harrison Act was framed as a revenue act. Jensen, Eric L. and Jurg Gerber. 1998. "The Social Construction of Drug Problems: An Historical Overview." In *The New War on Drugs*: *Symbolic Politics and Criminal Justice Policy*. Edited by Eric L. Jensen and Jurg Gerber. Cincinnati: Academy of Criminal Justice Sciences and Anderson Publishing, pp. 6–9; McWilliams, John C. 1991. "Through the Past Darkly: The Politics and Policies of America's Drug War." *Journal of Policy History* 3(4):

356–392, pp. 363–364; Meier, Kenneth J. 1994. *The Politics of Sin: Drugs, Alcohol, and Public Policy.* Armonk: M.E. Sharpe, pp. 24–32.

156. Volstead Act, Chapter 85, 41 Stat. 305 (1919).

157. Murray, Robert K. 1997. "Warren G. Harding." In *The Presidents: A Reference History.* 2d ed. Henry F. Graff, ed. New York: Simon & Schuster Macmillan, pp. 395–398.

158. Murray, Robert K. 1997. "Warren G. Harding." In *The Presidents: A Reference History.* 2d ed. Henry F. Graff, ed. New York: Simon & Schuster Macmillan, pp. 395–396.

159. The National Advisory Commission on Civil Disorders. 1968. *Report of the National Advisory Commission on Civil Disorders.* New York: Bantam Books.

160. McCoy, Donald R. 1997. "Calvin Coolidge." In *The Presidents: A Reference History.* 2d ed. Henry F. Graff, ed. New York: Simon & Schuster Macmillan, pp. 404–405.

161. Potter, Claire Bond. 1998. *War on Crime: Bandits, G-Men, and the Politics of Mass Culture.* New Brunswick: Rutgers University Press, chapter 2.

162. McCoy, Donald R. 1997. "Calvin Coolidge." In *The Presidents: A Reference History.* 2d ed. Henry F. Graff, ed. New York: Simon & Schuster Macmillan, p. 409.

163. Potter, Claire Bond. 1998. *War on Crime: Bandits, G-Men, and the Politics of Mass Culture.* New Brunswick: Rutgers University Press, p. 16. See also Calder, James D. 1993. *The Origins and Development of Federal Crime-control policy: Herbert Hoover's Initiatives.* Westport: Praeger Publishers, p. 57.

164. Calder, James D. 1993. *The Origins and Development of Federal Crime-control policy: Herbert Hoover's Initiatives.* Westport: Praeger Publishers; Friedman, Lawrence M. 1993. *Crime and Punishment in American History.* New York: Basic Books; Potter, Claire Bond. 1998. *War on Crime: Bandits, G-Men, and the Politics of Mass Culture.* New Brunswick: Rutgers University Press; Walker, Samuel. 1998. *Popular Justice: A History of American Criminal Justice.* 2d ed. New York: Oxford University Press.

165. Nelli, Humbert S. 1985. "American Syndicate Crime: A Legacy of Prohibition." In *Law, Alcohol, and Order: Perspectives on National Prohibition.* Edited by David E. Kyvig. Westport: Greenwood Press, pp. 123–137.

166. Pfiffner, John M. 1929. "The Activities and Results of Crime Surveys." *American Political Science Review* 23: 930–955.

167. "Summary of State and Local Crime Commissions." 1929. "Crime." Box 113, Presidential Papers Subject File, Herbert Hoover Library. A list of crime commissions that existed by the year 1929, included official State Crime Commissions in New York (under Franklin D. Roosevelt), California, Pennsylvania, Montana, Minnesota, Georgia, and Kansas; unofficial State Commissions were located in Missouri, Rhode Island, Illinois, North Carolina, Nebraska, and Minnesota; Bureaus of Criminal Research were created from or in lieu of State Commissions were found in Indiana, Louisiana, Ohio, and Oklahoma; and Crime Commissions in cities included Baltimore, Cleveland, Chicago, Detroit, Dallas, Evanston, Minneapolis, Cincinnati, Philadelphia, Des Moines, and Houston.

168. Pound, Roscoe and Felix Frankfurter, eds. 1968 (1922). *Criminal Justice in Cleveland: Reports of Cleveland Foundation Survey of the Administration of Criminal Justice in Cleveland, Ohio.* Montclair: Patterson-Smith.

169. An organizational chart of how the "National Crime Commission" appeared in 1929 can be found at "National Crime Commission—Organization Chart 1929." 1929. "Crime." Box 113, Presidential Papers Subject File, Herbert Hoover Library.

170. It has been reported on a number of occasions that President Calvin Coolidge created a "National Crime Commission" similar to the one created by President Herbert Hoover. This was not the case. The confusion appears to lie with the use of the state and local crime commissions' joint organization title, which was, in fact, the "National Crime Commission." However, no supporting evidence can be found to support the claims that he actually created the commission.

For citations to the contrary see Beckett, Katherine. 1997. *Making Crime Pay: Law and Order in Contemporary American Politics*. New York: Oxford University Press, p. 29; Kadish, Sanford H. 1983. "Crime Commissions." *Encyclopedia of Crime and Justice*. Vol. 1. New York: The Free Press; Levy, Leonard W. and Louis Fisher, eds. 1994. "Crime, Policy On." *Encyclopedia of the American Presidency*. Vol. 1. New York: Simon & Schuster.

171. Calder, James D. 1993. *The Origins and Development of Federal Crime-control policy: Herbert Hoover's Initiatives*. Westport: Praeger Publisher, p. 28.

172. Calder, James D. 1993. *The Origins and Development of Federal Crime-control policy: Herbert Hoover's Initiatives*. Westport: Praeger Publisher, p. 1. See also Calder, James D. 1981. "Herbert Hoover's Contributions to the Administrative History of Crime-control policy." Unpublished paper presented at the annual meeting of the Southwest Political Science Association, Dallas, Texas. This author relies heavily on the work of James D. Calder in regard to President Hoover's crime-control initiatives. It should also be noted that research conducted at the Herbert Hoover Library by this author also reached very similar conclusions regarding Calder's work.

173. Calder, James D. 1981. "Herbert Hoover's Contributions to the Administrative History of Crime-control policy." Unpublished paper presented at the annual meeting of the Southwest Political Science Association, Dallas, Texas, p. 2.

174. Burner, David. 1997. "Herbert Hoover." In *The Presidents: A Reference History*. 2d ed. Henry F. Graff, ed. New York: Simon & Schuster Macmillan, p. 417.

175. Calder, James D. 1993. *The Origins and Development of Federal Crime-control policy: Herbert Hoover's Initiatives*. Westport: Praeger Publisher, pp. 28–33, section titled "Crime and Justice in the Campaign of 1928."

176. Hoover, Herbert. 1974. "Inaugural Address. March 4, 1929." *Public Papers of the Presidents of the United States—Herbert Hoover*. Washington D.C.: U.S. G.P.O., p. 2.

177. Hoover, Herbert. 1974. "Inaugural Address. March 4, 1929." *Public Papers of the Presidents of the United States—Herbert Hoover*. Washington D.C.: U.S. G.P.O., pp. 3–4.

178. Hoover, Herbert. 1974. "Address to the Associated Press: Law Enforcement and Respect for the Law. April 22, 1929." *Public Papers of the Presidents of the United States—Herbert Hoover*. Washington D.C.: U.S. G.P.O., p. 103.

179. Calder, James D. 1993. *The Origins and Development of Federal Crime-control policy: Herbert Hoover's Initiatives*. Westport: Praeger Publisher, p. 33.

180. Calder, James D. 1993. *The Origins and Development of Federal Crime-control policy: Herbert Hoover's Initiatives*. Westport: Praeger Publishers, p. 77. See also Friedmann, Lawrence M. 1993. *Crime and Punishment in American History*. New York: Basic Books; Mahoney, Barry. 1976. *The Politics of the Safe Streets Act, 1965–1973: A Case Study in Evolving Federalism and the National Legislative Process*. Ph.D. Dissertation, Columbia University; Potter, Claire Bond. 1998. *War on Crime: Bandits, G-Men, and the Politics of Mass Culture*. New Brunswick: Rutgers University Press; Walker, Samuel. 1998. *Popular Justice: A History of American Criminal Justice*. 2d ed. New York: Oxford University Press. See also endnote number 167 for discussion of "first national crime commission."

181. Hoover, Herbert. 1974. "Remarks at the First Meeting of the National Commission on Law Observance and Enforcement. May 28, 1929." *Public Papers of the Presidents of the United States—Herbert Hoover*. Washington D.C.: U.S. G.P.O., pp. 159–161. President Hoover stated at the meeting that "It is my hope that the Commission shall secure an accurate determination of fact and cause, following them with constructive, courageous conclusions which will bring public understanding and command public support of its solutions."

182. Boehm, Randolph. 1997. *Records of the Wickersham Commission on Law Observance and Enforcement (Research Collections in American Legal History)*. New York: University Publications of America. See also Calder, James D. 1993. *The Origins and Development of Federal Crime-control policy: Herbert Hoover's Initiatives*. Westport: Praeger Publisher, chapter 4,

"Scientific Investigation: The Wickersham Commission"; "National Commission on Law Observance and Enforcement." Various boxes, but especially 203, 204, and 208. National Commission on Law Observance and Enforcement. Presidential Papers—Subject File. Herbert Hoover Library; "Final report of the National Commission on Law Observance and Enforcement." Memorandum to the President from George Wickersham, dated August 31, 1931. Box 208. National Commission on Law Observance and Enforcement. Presidential Papers—Subject Files. Herbert Hoover Library.

183. Calder, James D. 1993. *The Origins and Development of Federal Crime-control policy: Herbert Hoover's Initiatives*. Westport: Praeger Publisher, chapter 5, "Reforming Federal Cops and Courts."

184. "Memorandum for the Attorney General, Re: Accomplishments in Prohibition Matters." See specifically "Administering Transfer to the Department of Justice." Memorandum dated February 17, 1933. Box 26, Bureau of Prohibition. Presidential Papers—Cabinet Offices. Herbert Hoover Library.

185. Calder, James D. 1993. *The Origins and Development of Federal Crime-control policy: Herbert Hoover's Initiatives*. Westport: Praeger Publisher, chapter 7, "Federal Prison Reforms." See also "Accomplishments of the Bureau of Prisons since March 4, 1929." Memorandum dated February 15, 1933. Box 226, Bureau of Prisons. Presidential Papers—Subject Files. Herbert Hoover Library; Burner, David. 1979. *Herbert Hoover: A Public Life*. New York: Alfred A. Knopf, 217–219.

186. Calder, James D. 1993. *The Origins and Development of Federal Crime-control policy: Herbert Hoover's Initiatives*. Westport: Praeger Publisher, chapter 6, "Al Capone and the Campaign against Organized Crime"; Potter, Claire Bond. 1998. *War on Crime: Bandits, G-Men, and the Politics of Mass Culture*. New Brunswick: Rutgers University Press; Schoenberg, Robert J. 1992. Mr. Capone. New York: William Morrow and Company, Inc., chapter 22, "Get Capone."

187. Lindbergh Kidnaping Act, Chapter 271, 47 L. (1932).

188. Burner, David. 1997. "Herbert Hoover." In *The ... idents: A Reference History*. 2d ed. Henry F. Graff, ed. New York: Simon & Schuster Mac ... n, p. 418; Calder, James D. 1993. *The Origins and Development of Federal Crime-control p ... cy: Herbert Hoover's Initiatives*. Westport: Praeger Publisher, chapter 8, "Marginal Concerns ... ynching, Massie, Pardons, Lindbergh, and Bonus Army."

189. Calder, James D. 1993. *The Origins and Developm ... t of Federal Crime-control policy: Herbert Hoover's Initiatives*. Westport: Praeger Publisher ... . 214. See also Herbert Hoover's own reflections on the issues of crime in Hoover, Herbe ... 1952. *The Memories of Herbert Hoover: The Cabinet and the Presidency* 1920–1933. New ... ork: The Macmillan Company, chapter 38, "Reform in Law Enforcement."

190. Roosevelt, Franklin D. 1933. *Looking Forward*. R ... way: The John Day Company, Inc., chapter 12, "Crime and Criminals." Roosevelt also wrote ... short piece for the magazine *Liberty* titled "Winning the War Against Crime: How Modern M ... hods of Handling Prisoners are Reforming the Criminal" when he was governor. See the Febr ... ry 13, 1932 issue, p. 59.

191. The Eighteenth Amendment was repealed by vi ... e of the Twenty-first Amendment to the United States Constitution which was ratified on ... December 5, 1933 and was announced in Proclamation Number 2065. Roosevelt, Franklin D ... "The President Proclaims the Repeal of the Eighteenth Amendment. Proclamation No. 2065. ... ecember 5, 1933." *The Public Papers and Addresses of Franklin D. Roosevelt*. Vol. II. New Y ... k: Russell and Russell, pp. 510–514.

192. Roosevelt, Franklin D. "The President Proclaims ... e Repeal of the Eighteenth Amendment. Proclamation No. 2065. December 5, 1933." *The ... blic Papers and Addresses of Franklin D. Roosevelt*. Vol. II. New York: Russell and Russell, ... 511.

193. Roosevelt, Franklin D. "Annual Message to the Co ... ress. January 3, 1934." *The Public Papers and Addresses of Franklin D. Roosevelt*. Vol. III. N ... York: Russell and Russell, pp. 12–13.

194. Roosevelt, Franklin D. "Annual Message to the Co ... ress. January 3, 1934." *The Public Papers and Addresses of Franklin D. Roosevelt*. Vol. III. N ... York: Russell and Russell, p. 13.

195. Senate Bill 2080, January 8, 1934. See Papers of Louis McHenry Howe. Box 72 and 73. Memorandums and Various Bill proposals with comments. Franklin D. Roosevelt Library.

196. Senate Bill 2077, House Resolution 7748 and 6607, January 8, 1934. See Papers of Louis McHenry Howe. Box 72 and 73. Memorandums and Various Bill proposals with comments. Franklin D. Roosevelt Library.

197. Senate Bill 2254, January 8, 1934. See Papers of Louis McHenry Howe. Box 72 and 73. Memorandums and Various Bill proposals with comments. Franklin D. Roosevelt Library.

198. Senate Bill 2252, January 11, 1934. See Papers of Louis McHenry Howe. Box 72 and 73. Memorandums and Various Bill proposals with comments. Franklin D. Roosevelt Library.

199. Senate Bill 2248, January 11, 1934. Eventually the Hobbs Anti-Racketeering Act would be codified at Chapter 569, 48 Stat. 929 (1934). See Papers of Louis McHenry Howe. Box 72 and 73. Memorandums and Various Bill proposals with comments. Franklin D. Roosevelt Library.

200. Senate Bill 2253, January 11, 1934. Eventually the Fugitive Felon Law would be codified at Chapter 301, 48 Stat. 301 (1934). See Papers of Louis McHenry Howe. Box 72 and 73. Memorandums and Various Bill proposals with comments. Franklin D. Roosevelt Library.

201. Senate Bill 2249, January 11, 1934. See Papers of Louis McHenry Howe. Box 72 and 73. Memorandums and Various Bill proposals with comments. Franklin D. Roosevelt Library.

202. Senate Bill 2575, January 23, 1934. See Papers of Louis McHenry Howe. Box 72 and 73. Memorandums and Various Bill proposals with comments. Franklin D. Roosevelt Library.

203. House Resolution 7353, February 20, 1934. See Papers of Louis McHenry Howe. Box 72 and 73. Memorandums and Various Bill proposals with comments. Franklin D. Roosevelt Library.

204. Senate Bill 2845, February 20, 1934. See Papers of Louis McHenry Howe. Box 72 and 73. Memorandums and Various Bill proposals with comments. Franklin D. Roosevelt Library.

205. Senate Bill 2841, February 20, 1934. See Papers of Louis McHenry Howe. Box 72 and 73. Memorandums and Various Bill proposals with comments. Franklin D. Roosevelt Library.

206. Senate Bill 2843, February 20, 1934. See Papers of Louis McHenry Howe. Box 72 and 73. Memorandums and Various Bill proposals with comments. Franklin D. Roosevelt Library.

207. Roosevelt, Franklin D. "Statement on Signing Bill to Help the Federal Government Wage War on Crime and Gangsters. May 19, 1934." *The Public Papers and Addresses of Franklin D. Roosevelt*. Vol. III. New York: Russell and Russell, pp. 242–245. In a note written later by Roosevelt he lists eleven of the statutes passed which he deems to be the most important.

208. Roosevelt, Franklin D. "Address to the Conference on Crime Called by the Attorney General of the United States. December 10, 1934." *The Public Papers and Addresses of Franklin D. Roosevelt*. Vol. III. New York: Russell and Russell, pp. 492–495.

209. Rollins explains that Howe assisted in a number of administrative initiatives but had three specific interests, one of which was "the anti-crime crusade." Stiles supports this conclusion. Rollins, Alfred B. Jr. 1962. *Roosevelt and Howe*. New York: Alfred A. Knopf, chapter 26, "The Call of the Crusades"; Stiles, Lela. 1954. *The Man Behind Roosevelt: The Story of Louis McHenry Howe*. Cleveland: The World Publishing Company.

210. Friedman, Lawrence M. 1993. *Crime and Punishment in American History*. New York: Basic Books, p. 271; Walker, Samuel. 1998. Popular Justice: *A History of American Criminal Justice*. 2d ed. New York: Oxford University Press, p. 160.

211. Potter, Claire Bond. 1998. *War on Crime: Bandits, G-Men, and the Politics of Mass Culture*. New Brunswick: Rutgers University Press.

212. The Federal Bureau of Narcotics would have a long and significant history of federal activity involving drugs under its director Harry Anslinger. See McWilliams, John C. 1989. "Unsung Partner Against Crime: Harry J. Anslinger and the Federal Bureau of Narcotics, 1930–1962." *The Pennsylvania Magazine of History & Biography* 113(2): 207–236; Meier, Kenneth J. 1994. *The Politics of Sin: Drugs, Alcohol, and Public Policy*. Armonk: M. E. Sharpe, chapter two.

213. Roosevelt, Franklin D. "Memorandum of Approval of Bill for Judicial Reform. August 26, 1937." *The Public Papers and Addresses of Franklin D. Roosevelt.* Vol. VI. New York: Russell and Russell, pp. 338–342.

214. Roosevelt, Franklin D. "Public Protection Against Law Breakers Demands Efficient Police Work, Able and Fearless Prosecutions, Prompt, Fair Trials, and the Intelligent and Constructive Treatment of the Guilty . . . Address at the National Parole Conference, White House, Washington D.C. April 17, 1939." *The Public Papers and Addresses of Franklin D. Roosevelt.* Vol. VIII. New York: Russell and Russell, pp. 217–227.

215. Berens, John F. 1980. "The FBI and Civil Liberties from Franklin Roosevelt to Jimmy Carter—An Historical Overview." *Michigan Academician* 13(Fall): 131–144, p. 133.

216. Berens, John F. 1980. "The FBI and Civil Liberties from Franklin Roosevelt to Jimmy Carter–An Historical Overview." *Michigan Academician* 13(Fall): 131–144; O'Reilly, Kenneth. 1982. "A New Deal for the FBI: The Roosevelt Administration, Crime Control, and National Security." *The Journal of American History* (3): 638–658.

217. Truman, Harry S. 1962. "Address in Columbus a Conference of the Federal Council of Churches. March 6, 1946." *Public Papers of the Presidents of the United States.* Washington D.C.: U.S. G.P.O., p. 142.

218. See LaFree who convincingly argues that the early postwar period, 1940–1950, witnessed low, stable crime rates. LaFree, Gary. 1998. *Losing Legitimacy: Street Crime and the Decline of Social Institutions in America.* Boulder: Westview Press.

219. See, for instance, Truman, Harry S. 1964. "Address Before the United States Conference of Mayors. March 21, 1949." *Public Papers of the Presidents of the United States.* Washington D.C.: U.S. G.P.O., p. 175.

220. See, for instance, Truman, Harry S. 1963. "Annual Message to the Congress on the State of the Union. January 6, 1947." *Public Papers of the Presidents of the United States.* Washington D.C.: U.S. G.P.O., p. 9.

221. See, in general, Truman, Harry S. 1965. "The President's News Conference of March 29, 1951." *Public Papers of the Presidents of the United States.* Washington D.C.: U.S. G.P.O., p. 201. In regard to narcotics, see Truman, Harry S. 1965. "Statement by the President Upon Signing Bill Relating to Narcotics Laws Violations. November 2, 1951." *Public Papers of the Presidents of the United States.* Washington D.C.: U.S. G.P.O., pp. 617–618.

222. Truman, Harry S. 1965. "Memorandum to Department and Agency Heads Requesting Their Cooperation With the Senate Special Crime Investigation Committee. June 17, 1950." *Public Papers of the Presidents of the United States.* Washington D.C.: U.S. G.P.O., p. 484.

223. See, for instance, Adlow, Elijah. 1955. "Teen-Age Criminals." *The Atlantic Monthly* 196(1): 46–50, which discusses the "growing problem of juvenile crime" after World War II and its prevalence in the 1950s.

224. Eisenhower, Dwight D. 1953. "The President's News Conference of December 16, 1953." *Public Papers of the Presidents of the United States.* Washington D.C.: U.S. G.P.O., p. 266.

225. Moore, John E. 1969. "Controlling Delinquency: Executive, Congressional and Juvenile, 1961–1964." In *Congress and Urban Problems.* Edited by Frederick N. Cleaveland. Washington D.C.: Brookings Institution; U.S. Senate. 1955. *Juvenile Delinquency: Hearings Before the Special Subcommittee on Juvenile Delinquency of the Senate Committee on Labor and Public Welfare.* Eighty-fourth Congress, First Session.

226. Eisenhower, Dwight D. 1955. "Annual Message to the Congress on the State of the Union. January 6, 1955." *Public Papers of the Presidents of the United States.* Washington D.C.: U.S. G.P.O., p. 25.

227. Mahoney, Barry. 1976. *The Politics of the Safe Streets Act, 1965–1973: A Case Study in Evolving Federalism and the National Legislative Process.* Ph.D. Dissertation, Columbia University; Moore, John E. 1969. "Controlling Delinquency: Executive, Congressional and Juvenile, 1961–1964." In *Congress and Urban Problems.* Edited by Frederick N. Cleaveland. Washington

D.C.: Brookings Institution; Sundquist, James N. 1969. *Politics and Policy: The Eisenhower, Kennedy, and Johnson Years*. Washington D.C.: Brookings Institution, p. 118.

228. Eisenhower, Dwight D. 1953. "Statement by the President Upon Signing Bill Providing for the Treatment of Narcotics Users in the District of Columbia. June 24, 1953." *Public Papers of the Presidents of the United States*. Washington D.C.: U.S. G.P.O., pp. 448–449; Eisenhower, Dwight D. 1954. "Statement by the President Upon Signing Bill Governing the Keeping and Public Inspection of Arrest Books in the District of Columbia. August 20, 1954." *Public Papers of the Presidents of the United States*. Washington D.C.: U.S. G.P.O., pp. 742–743.

229. Eisenhower, Dwight D. 1957. "Remarks at the Graduation Exercises of the FBI National Academy. November 8, 1957." *Public Papers of the Presidents of the United States*. Washington D.C.: U.S. G.P.O., pp. 802–805; Eisenhower, Dwight D. 1960. "Remarks at the 67th Annual Conference of the International Association of Chiefs of Police. October 4, 1960." *Public Papers of the Presidents of the United States*. Washington D.C.: U.S. G.P.O., pp. 745–746.

230. National Party Platforms, Democratic Platform of 1960, p. 598 and National Party Platforms, Republican Platform of 1960, p. 618. As cited in World Book Encyclopedia. *American Reference Library*. CR-ROM. Orem: The Western Standard Publishing Company.

231. Calder, James D. 1978. *Presidents and Crime Control: Some Limitations on Executive Policy Making*. Ph.D. Dissertation, Claremont University, chapter four, "John F. Kennedy and Functionalist Initiative"; Mahoney, Barry. 1976. *The Politics of the Safe Streets Act, 1965–1973: A Case Study in Evolving Federalism and the National Legislative Process*. Ph.D. Dissertation, Columbia University, chapter three, "Kennedy Initiatives, 1961–1964"; Marion, Nancy E. 1994. *A History of Federal Crime Control Initiatives, 1960–1993*. Westport: Praeger Publishers, pp. 25–27.

232. Kennedy, Robert F. 1960. *The Enemy Within*. New York: Harper & Brothers; Mahoney, Barry. 1976. *The Politics of the Safe Streets Act, 1965–1973: A Case Study in Evolving Federalism and the National Legislative Process*. Ph.D. Dissertation, Columbia University, chapter three, "Kennedy Initiatives, 1961–1964"; Navasky, Victor S. 1971. *Kennedy Justice*. New York: Atheneum.

233. Executive Order 10940, May 11, 1961. See also Kennedy, John F. 1963. "Remarks Upon Receiving Report of the President's Committee on Juvenile Delinquency and Youth Crime. May 31, 1962." *Public Papers of the Presidents of the United States*. Washington D.C.: U.S. G.P.O., pp. 447–448.

234. Kennedy, John F. 1963. "Remarks to the White House Conference on Narcotic and Drug Abuse. September 27, 1962." *Public Papers of the Presidents of the United States*. Washington D.C.: U.S. G.P.O., pp. 716–718.

235. Executive Order 11076, January 16, 1963. See also Kennedy, John F. 1964. "Letter to the Chairman in Response to the Interim Report of the President's Advisory Commission on Narcotic and Drug Abuse. April 4, 1963." *Public Papers of the Presidents of the United States*. Washington D.C.: U.S. G.P.O., p. 312.

236. Kennedy, John F. 1962. "Remarks on Signing the Juvenile Delinquency and Youth Offenses Control Act. September 22, 1961." *Public Papers of the Presidents of the United States*. Washington D.C.: U.S. G.P.O., p. 382.

237. Anderson, David C. 1988. *Crimes of Justice: Improving the Police, the Courts, the Prisons*. New York: Times Books, pp. 46–47; Beckett, Katherine and Theodore Sasson. 2000. *The Politics of Injustice*. Thousand Oaks: Pine Forge Press, p. 50; Calder, James D. 1982. "Presidents and Crime Control: Kennedy, Johnson and Nixon and the Influences of Ideology." *Presidential Studies Quarterly* 12: 574–589; Calder, James D. 1978. *Presidents and Crime Control: Some Limitations on Executive Policy Making*. Ph.D. Dissertation, Claremont University, chapter five; Caplan, Gerald. 1973. "Reflections on the Nationalization of Crime, 1964–1968." *Law and the Social Order: Arizona State University Law Journal* 1973: 583–635; Donziger, Steven R. 1996. *The Real War on Crime: The Report of the National Criminal Justice Commission*. New York: Harper Perennial, p. 65; Feeley, Malcolm M. and Austin D. Sarat. 1980. *The Policy Dilemma: Federal Crime Policy and the Law Enforcement*

Assistance Administration. Minneapolis: University of Minnesota Press, pp. 34–35; Finckenauer, James O. 1978. "Crime as a National Political Issue: 1964–76: From Law and Order to Domestic Tranquility." *Crime & Delinquency* (January): 13–27; Flamm, Michael William. 1998. "*Law and Order*": *Street Crime, Civil Disorder, and the Crisis of Liberalism*. Ph.D. Dissertation, Columbia University, chapter two; Friedman, Lawrence M. 1993. *Crime and Punishment in American History*. New York: Basic Books, p. 274; Mahoney, Barry. 1976. *The Politics of the Safe Streets Act, 1965–1973: A Case Study in Evolving Federalism and the National Legislative Process*. Ph.D. Dissertation, Columbia University, pp. 72–73; Marion, Nancy E. 1994. *A History of Federal Crime Control Initiatives, 1960–1993*. Westport: Praeger, p. 39; Rosch, Joel. 1985. "Crime as an Issue in American Politics." In *The Politics of Crime and Criminal Justice*. Erika S. Fairchild and Vincent J. Webb, eds. Beverly Hills: Sage Publications, pp. 19–35; Scheingold, Stuart A. 1984. *The Politics of Law and Order*. New York: Longman, pp. 77–78; Scheingold, Stuart A. 1995. "Politics, Public Policy, and Street Crime." *The Annals of the American Academy of Political and Social Science* 539: 155–168, p. 164; Walker, Samuel. 1998. *Popular Justice: A History of American Criminal Justice*. 2d ed. New York: Oxford University Press, p. 202; Walker, Samuel. 1978. "Reexamining the President's Crime Commission: The Challenge of Crime in a Free Society after Ten Years." *Crime & Delinquency* (January): 1–12.

238. Carter, Dan T. 1995. *The Politics of Rage: George Wallace, the Origins of the New Conservatism, and the Transformation of American Politics*. New York: Simon & Schuster; Feeley, Malcolm M. and Austin D. Sarat. 1980. *The Policy Dilemma: Federal Crime Policy and the Law Enforcement Assistance Administration*. Minneapolis: University of Minnesota Press, pp. 34–35; Flamm, Michael William. 1998. "*Law and Order*": *Street Crime, Civil Disorder, and the Crisis of Liberalism*. Ph.D. Dissertation, Columbia University, chapter two.

239. Flamm, Michael William. 1998. "*Law and Order*": *Street Crime, Civil Disorder, and the Crisis of Liberalism*. Ph.D. Dissertation, Columbia University, p. 82.

240. Goldwater, Barry. 1964. "Republican Nomination Acceptance Speech." *New York Times*. January 10, 1964: A10; reprinted in Feeley, Malcolm M. and Austin D. Sarat. 1980. *The Policy Dilemma: Federal Crime Policy and the Law Enforcement Assistance Administration*. Minneapolis: University of Minnesota Press, p. 35.

241. White, Theodore H. 1965. *The Making of the President 1964*. New York: Atheneum Publishers, p. 200.

242. See Johnson, Lyndon B. 1965. *The Public Papers of the Presidents of the United States*. Washington D.C.: U.S. G.P.O. In volume one of 1963–64, running November 22, 1963 to June 30, 1964, the only references regarding crime revolve around the assassination of former President, John F. Kennedy.

243. Johnson, Lyndon B. 1965. "The President's News Conference at the LBJ Ranch. July 18, 1964." *The Public Papers of the Presidents of the United States*. Volume II, 1963–64. Washington D.C.: U.S. G.P.O., p. 868.

244. President Johnson would answer additional reporter's questions in July (See "The President's News Conference of July 24, 1964"), but it was not until August, in a speech to the American Bar Association, that he would finally begin addressing the crime issue in a speech. (See "Remarks in New York City Before the American Bar Association. August 12, 1964."). In addition, he would write a letter to the Attorney General regarding a program to deal with juvenile delinquency in Washington D.C. (See "Letter to the Attorney General on a Program to Combat Juvenile Delinquency in the District of Columbia. August 22, 1964.") and write another regarding a report on crime and law enforcement that he received from the Attorney General (See "Letter to the Attorney General in Response to a Report on Crime and Law Enforcement. November 1, 1964."). Both of these were clearly designed to show that Johnson was attentive to the issue of crime. Johnson, Lyndon B. 1965. *The Public Papers of the Presidents of the United States*. Volume II, 1963–64. Washington D.C.: U.S. G.P.O.

245. Memorandum for the President from Bill Moyers. September 23, 1964. "Release of the FBI Report on Riots." Office Files of Bill Moyers. Box 39. "Crime." Lyndon Baines Johnson Library.

246. Johnson would win 43,126,506 of the popular votes and 486 electoral votes to Goldwater's 27,176,799 popular votes and 52 electoral votes.

247. Rosch, Joel. 1985. "Crime as an Issue in American Politics." In *The Politics of Crime and Criminal Justice*. Erika S. Fairchild and Vincent J. Webb, eds. Beverly Hills: Sage Publications, p. 25.

248. Finckenauer, James O. 1978. "Crime as a National Political Issue: 1964–76: From Law and Order to Domestic Tranquility." *Crime & Delinquency* (January): 13–27, p. 16.

249. President's Commission on Law Enforcement and Administration of Justice. 1968. *The Challenge of Crime in a Free Society*. New York: An Avon Book, p. 18.

250. See successive volumes of Johnson, Lyndon B. 1963–1969. *Public Papers of the Presidents of the United States*. Washington D.C.: U.S. G.P.O.; see also Calder, James D. 1978. *Presidents and Crime Control: Some Limitation on Executive Policy Making*. Ph.D. Dissertation, Claremont University, chapter five, entitled "Lyndon B. Johnson and Functionalist Implementation"; Caplan, Gerald. 1973. "Reflections on the Nationalization of Crime, 1964–1968." *Law and the Social Order: Arizona State University Law Journal* 1973: 583–635; Feeley, Malcolm M. and Austin D. Sarat. 1980. *The Policy Dilemma: Federal Crime Policy and the Law Enforcement Assistance Administration*. Minneapolis: University of Minnesota Press; Flamm, Michael William. 1998. *"Law and Order": Street Crime, Civil Disorder, and the Crisis of Liberalism*. Ph.D. Dissertation, Columbia University; Mahoney, Barry. 1976. *The Politics of the Safe Streets Act, 1965–1973: A Case Study in Evolving Federalism and the National Legislative Process*. Ph.D. Dissertation, Columbia University; Marion, Nancy E. 1994. *A History of Federal Crime Control Initiatives, 1960–1993*. Westport: Praeger Publishers, chapter three, entitled "The Johnson Administration: A Continuation and Expansion of Activities from the Kennedy Years."

251. Johnson, Lyndon. 1965. "White House Statement on the Appointment of a Special Commission to Investigate the Assassination of President Kennedy. November 29, 1963." *Public Papers of the Presidents of the United States*. 1963–64, Volume I. Washington D.C.: U.S. G.P.O., p. 13.

252. Flamm, Michael William. 1998. *"Law and Order": Street Crime, Civil Disorder, and the Crisis of Liberalism*. Ph.D. Dissertation, Columbia University.

253. Cronin, Thomas E., Tania Z. Cronin, and Michael Milakovich. 1981. *U.S. v. Crime in the Streets*. Bloomington: Indiana University Press, chapter five, entitled "Law and Order in the 1968 Elections"; Finckenauer, James O. 1978. "Crime as a National Political Issue: 1964–76." *Crime & Delinquency* 24(1): 13–27; Harris, Richard. 1969. *Justice: The Crisis of Law, Order, and Freedom in America*. New York: E. P. Dutton and Company, Inc.; Rosch, Joel. 1985. "Crime as an Issue in American Politics." In *The Politics of Crime and Criminal Justice*. Erika S. Fairchild and Vincent J. Webb, eds. Beverly Hills: Sage Publications, pp. 19–35. For the party platforms, see National Party Platforms, Democratic Platform of 1968, pp. 721–722, 734, 741–742; and National Party Platforms, Republican Platform of 1968, pp. 750–752. Citation obtained from World Book Encyclopedia. 1998. *American Reference Library*. CD-ROM. Orem: The Western Standard Publishing Company.

254. See National Party Platforms, Republican Platform of 1968, p. 750. Citation obtained from World Book Encyclopedia. 1998. *American Reference Library*. CD-ROM. Orem: The Western Standard Publishing Company.

255. Marion, Nancy E. 1994. *A History of Federal Crime Control Initiatives*, 1960–1993. Westport: Praeger, p. 72. See also "Crime: Nixon Approach, Its Cost and Results." *Congressional Quarterly Weekly Report*. 29(April 30, 1971): 985–988.

256. Burke, John P. 1992. *The Institutional Presidency*. Baltimore: The Johns Hopkins University Press, p. 71.

257. Cronin, Thomas E., Tania Z. Cronin, and Mich[ae]l Milakovich. 1981. *U.S. v. Crime in the Streets*. Bloomington: Indiana University Press, [pp.] 82–83. See also the Papers and other His[torica]l Files, Staff Member and Office Files, Egil Krogh, White House Spe[cial] Files, Staff Member and Office Files, Egil Krogh, 1969–1973. Especially Boxes 1–5, 10, [1]2, 18, and 32–39. National Archives and Records Administration's Nixon Project, College [Pa]rk, Maryland.

258. Conlan, Timothy. 1988. *New Federalism: Interg[ov]ernmental Reform from Nixon to Reagan*. Washington D.C.: The Brookings Institution.

259. Calder, James D. 1978. *Presidents and Crime C[ontrol: Some Limitations on Executive Policy Making*. Ph.D. Dissertation, Claremont Universit[y, c]hapter six, entitled "Richard M. Nixon and Mechanist Control"; Marion, Nancy E. 1994. A [Hi]story of Federal Crime Control Initiatives, 1960–1993. Westport: Praeger, chapter four, entitl[ed] "The Nixon Administration: A Shift in Federal Crime-control policy." For a good review of th[e i]ssues of the Safe Streets Act of 1968 and the Law Enforcement Assistance Administration, see [Fe]ley, Malcolm M. and Austin D. Sarat. 1980. *The Policy Dilemma: Federal Crime Policy and the [L]aw Enforcement Assistance Administration*. Minneapolis: University of Minnesota Press; Gray[, V]irginia and Bruce Williams. 1980. *The Or[ganizational Politics of Criminal Justice: Policy in [C]ontext*. Lexington: Lexington Books.

260. Calder, James D. 1978. *Presidents and Crime C[ontrol: Some Limitations on Executive Policy Making*. Ph.D. Dissertation, Claremont Universit[y, p]. 252.

261. For an excellent review of Nixon's activities on dr[ug]s see Betram, Eva, Morris Blachman, Kenneth Sharpe, and Peter Andreas. 1996. *Drug W[ars: Politics: The Price of Denial*. Berkeley: University of California Press, chapter six, entit[led] "Presidential Drug Wars and the Narco-Enforcement Complex." See also Baum, Dan. 199[6. *Smoke and Mirrors: The War on Drugs and the Politics of Failure*. Boston: Little, Brown and [Co]mpany; Massing, Michael. 1998. The Fix. New York: Simon & Schuster.

262. Calder, James D. 1978. *Presidents and Crime C[ontrol: Some Limitations on Executive Policy Making*. Ph.D. Dissertation, Claremont University[, p]. 236; Marion, Nancy E. 1994. *A History of Federal Crime Control Initiatives*, 1960–1993. W[est]port: Praeger, p. 77.

263. As cited in Cronin, Thomas E., Tania Z. Cronin, [and] Michael Milakovich. 1981. *U.S. v. Crime in the Streets*. Bloomington: Indiana University P[res]s, p. 83.

264. As cited in Calder, James D. 1978. *Presidents and [C]rime Control: Some Limitations on Executive Policy Making*. Ph.D. Dissertation, Claremon[t U]niversity, p. 253.

265. Calder, James D. 1978. *Presidents and Crime C[ontrol: Some Limitations on Executive Policy Making*. Ph.D. Dissertation, Claremont Universit[y, p]. 238.

266. For issues of institutionalization, see Burke, Joh[n. 1992. *The Institutional Presidency*. Baltimore: the Johns Hopkins University Press, p. 27; [H]argrove, Erwin C. 1974. *The Power of the Modern Presidency*. New York: Alfred A. Kn[op]f, Inc., p. 81; Henderson, Phillip. 1988. *Managing the Presidency: The Eisenhower Lega[cy from Kennedy to Reagan*. Boulder: Westview Publishers, p. 14; Warshaw, Shirley Anne. 1[99]7. *The Domestic Presidency: Policy Making in the White House*. Boston: Allyn and Bacon, c[ha]pter one, titled "The Institutionalization of White House Control of Domestic Policy."

267. Parmet, Herbert S. 1997. "Gerald R. Ford." *The [Pre]sidents: A Reference History*. 2d ed. Henry F. Graff, ed. New York: Simon & Schuster Macm[ill]an.

268. One publication states that neither "President Ford [n]or President Carter mentioned crime-related issues in their State of the Union Addresses or too[k m]uch legislative action on those issues." See Beckett, Katherine and Theodore Sasson. 2000. *T[he Politics of Injustice: Crime and Punishment in America*. Thousand Oaks: Pine Forge Press, p. 6[. T]hese authors also cite, as evidence, Baum, Dan. 1996. *Smoke and Mirrors: The War on Dru[gs and the Politics of Failure*. Boston: Little, Brown and Company. Although Ford did not menti[on] crime in his State of the Union Addresses, he did deliver several speeches on the subject, as well [as] a Special Message to Congress. He clearly desired to make crime part of his domestic polic[y,]s, but all of this was overshadowed by the

aftermath effects of Watergate. Regarding Ford's activity on crime, see Felkenes, George T. 1993. "Domestic Tranquility: President Ford's Policy Positions on Criminal Justice Issues." *Presidential Studies Quarterly* 23(3): 519–532; Felkenes, George T. 1992. "Liberty, Restraint, and Criminal Justice: Gerald Ford's Presidential Concerns." *Journal of Criminal Justice* 20:147–160; Marion, Nancy E. 1994. *A History of Federal Crime Control Initiatives*, 1960–1993. Westport: Praeger, chapter five, entitled "The Ford Administration: A Continuation of Nixon, with Some Variation."

269. Ford, Gerald R. 1977. "Address at the Yale University Law School Sesquicentennial Convocation Dinner. April 25, 1975." *Public Papers of the Presidents of the United States*. 1975, Volume I. Washington D.C.: U.S. G.P.O.

270. Ford, Gerald R. 1977. "Special Message to the Congress on Crime. June 19, 1975." *Public Papers of the Presidents of the United States*. 1975, Volume I. Washington D.C.: U.S. G.P.O.

271. Ford, Gerald R. 1975. "Remarks to the Annual Convention of the International Association of Chiefs of Police. September 24, 1974." *Public Papers of the Presidents of the United States*. 1974. Washington D.C.: U.S. G.P.O. See also Ford, Gerald. 1979. *A Time to Heal: The Autobiography of Gerald R. Ford*. New York: Harper & Row, Publishers and the Reader's Digest Association, Inc. pp. 269–293.

272. Felkenes, George T. 1993. "Domestic Tranquility: President Ford's Policy Positions on Criminal Justice Issues." *Presidential Studies Quarterly* 23(3): 519–532; Felkenes, George T. 1992. "Liberty, Restraint, and Criminal Justice: Gerald Ford's Presidential Concerns." *Journal of Criminal Justice* 20: 147–160.

273. Felkenes, George T. 1993. "Domestic Tranquility: President Ford's Policy Positions on Criminal Justice Issues." *Presidential Studies Quarterly* 23(3): 519–532; Felkenes, George T. 1992. "Liberty, Restraint, and Criminal Justice: Gerald Ford's Presidential Concerns." *Journal of Criminal Justice* 20: 147–160.

274. Felkenes, George T. 1993. "Domestic Tranquility: President Ford's Policy Positions on Criminal Justice Issues." *Presidential Studies Quarterly* 23(3): 519–532; Felkenes, George T. 1992. "Liberty, Restraint, and Criminal Justice: Gerald Ford's Presidential Concerns." *Journal of Criminal Justice* 20: 147–160.

275. Marion, Nancy E. 1994. *A History of Federal Crime Control Initiatives*, 1960–1993. Westport: Praeger, pp. 103, 112–113.

276. National Party Platforms, Democratic Platform, 1976, pp. 916, 923, 928–931 and National Party Platforms, Republican Platform, 1976, p. 7, 14. Citations obtained from World Book Encyclopedia. 1998. *American Reference Library*. CD-ROM. Orem: The Western Standard Publishing Company.

277. Finckenauer, James O. 1978. "Crime as a National Political Issue: 1964–76." *Crime & Delinquency* 24(1): 13–27, p. 22. Two separate authors cite the fact that crime was not a significant issue in the 1976 campaign. However their rationale is based on the fact that, by and large, the candidates agreed with one another that the federal government needed to "get tough on crime" and as a result, the issue did not become a central campaign issue as it was in 1964 and 1968. See Cronin, Thomas E., Tania Z. Cronin, and Michael Milakovich. 1981. *U.S. v. Crime in the Streets*. Bloomington: Indiana University Press, pp. 118–119; Marion, Nancy E. 1994. *A History of Federal Crime Control Initiatives, 1960–1993*. Westport: Praeger, p. 118.

278. "Carter Plan Would Reshuffle LEAA Program." *Congressional Quarterly Weekly Report*. 36 (July 15, 1978): 1821–1822.

279. Cronin, Thomas E., Tania Z. Cronin, and Michael Milakovich. 1981. *U.S. v. Crime in the Streets*. Bloomington: Indiana University Press, pp. 119–123; Diegelman, Robert F. 1982. "Federal Financial Assistance for Crime Control: Lessons of the LEAA Experience." *Journal of Criminal Law and Criminology* 73(3): 994–1011; Gray, Virginia and Bruce Williams. 1980.

The Organizational Politics of Criminal Justice: *Policy in Context*. Lexington: Lexington Books, p. 51; Marion, Nancy E. 1994. *A History of Federal Crime Control Initiatives, 1960–1993*. Westport: Praeger, pp. 117–118.

280. Kikendall, Richard S. 1997. "Jimmy Carter." In *The Presidents*: *A Reference History*. 2d ed. Henry F. Graff, ed. New York: Simon & Schuster Macmillan, pp. 551–567.

281. Cronin, Thomas E., Tania Z. Cronin, and Michael Milakovich. 1981. *U.S. v. Crime in the Streets*. Bloomington: Indiana University Press, chapter seven, "The Decline of the LEAA."

282. Marion, Nancy E. 1994. *A History of Federal Crime Control Initiatives, 1960–1993*. Westport: Praeger, chapter six, "The Carter Administration: A Temporary Lull in Federal Criminal Justice Policy."

283. Marion, Nancy E. 1994. *A History of Federal Crime Control Initiatives, 1960–1993*. Westport: Praeger, chapter six, "The Carter Administration: A Temporary Lull in Federal Criminal Justice Policy."

284. See National Party Platform, Democratic Platform, 1980, pp. 9–13, 30 and National Party Platforms, Republican Platform of 1980, pp. 13–15. Citation obtained from World Book Encyclopedia. 1998. *American Reference Library*. CD-ROM. Orem: The Western Standard Publishing Company.

285. Cited in Marion, Nancy E. 1994. *A History of Federal Crime Control Initiatives, 1960–1993*. Westport: Praeger, p. 143.

286. Marion, Nancy E. 1994. *A History of Federal Crime Control Initiatives, 1960–1993*. Westport: Praeger, chapter seven, entitled "The Reagan Administration: A Return to 'Law and Order.'"

287. Bertram, Eva, Morris Blachman, Kenneth Sharpe, and Peter Andreas. 1996. *Drug War Politics*: *The Price of Denial*. Berkeley: University of California Press, pp. 110–112; see also Jensen, Eric L. and Jurg Gerber. 1998. *The New Drug War*: *Symbolic Politics and Criminal Justice Policy*. Cincinnati: Academy of Criminal Justice Sciences/Anderson Publishing; Sharp, Elaine B. 1994. *The Dilemma of Drug Policy in the United States*. New York: HarperCollins College Publishers.

288. For an excellent review of the politics revolving around the creation of the Attorney General's Task Force on Violent Crime, see Davis, David S. 1983. "The Production of Crime Policies." *Crime and Social Justice* (20): 121–137.

289. Bertram, Eva, Morris Blachman, Kenneth Sharpe, and Peter Andreas. 1996. *Drug War Politics*: *The Price of Denial*. Berkeley: University of California Press, pp. 110–113; Caringella-MacDonald, Susan. 1990. "State Crises and the Crackdown on Crime under Reagan." Contemporary Crises 14: 91–118; Marion, Nancy E. 1994. *A History of Federal Crime Control Initiatives, 1960–1993*. Westport: Praeger, chapter seven, entitled "The Reagan Administration: A Return to 'Law and Order' "; Platt, Tony. 1987. "U.S. Criminal Justice in the Reagan Era: An Assessment." *Crime and Social Justice* 29: 58–69. For an insider account of many of these policies, see Smith, William French. 1991. *Law and Justice in the Reagan Administration*: *Memoirs of an Attorney General*. Stanford: Hoover Institution Press.

290. Marion, Nancy E. 1994. *A History of Federal Crime Control Initiatives, 1960–1993*. Westport: Praeger, p. 150.

291. For an excellent review of the Willie Horton ads, see chapter one, "The Role of Drama and Data in Political Decisions" in Jamieson, Kathleen Hall. 1992. *Dirty Politics*: *Deception, Distraction, and Democracy*. New York: Oxford University Press.

292. Marion, Nancy E. 1994. *A History of Federal Crime Control Initiatives, 1960–1993*. Westport: Praeger, chapter eight, entitled "The Bush Administration: A Continuation of Reagan's Administration."

293. Chernoff, Harry A., Christopher M. Kelly, and John R. Kroger. 1996. "The Politics of Crime." *Harvard Journal on Legislation* 33(2): 527–579.

President Harry S Truman aiming a rifle at a cameraman with other people looking on during a campaign stop in Sun Valley, Idaho during his "western trip."

chapter 2

Why Crime?

> It may be said by some that the larger responsibility for the enforcement of laws against crime rests with State and local authorities and it does not concern the Federal Government. But it does concern the President of the United States, both as a citizen and as the one upon whom rests the primary responsibility of leadership for the establishment of standards of law enforcement in this country.
>
> —Herbert Hoover[1]

With the groundwork laid in the last chapter for understanding that presidents have increasingly been engaged in crime-control policy, this chapter turns to exploring the explanations of why presidents have placed crime on their agenda. As the last chapter demonstrates, there is ample evidence to support the belief that crime has increasingly become an issue which presidents place on their agenda and, since the 1964 election, crime has in fact become a national issue that all presidents have addressed in some form or fashion. The more difficult task, however, is to delve into the question of "why?" Because all presidents make certain choices among numerous options and often the situations in which they make their choices contribute to the outcome, answering why presidents do anything is tenuous at best. However, because more than one president has made the choice to address the issue of crime, there is enough of a pattern that explanations, mixed with some speculation, can be derived in order that a fuller understanding can be reached explaining why presidents have come to be engaged in an issue that was once the primary responsibility of state and local governments.

In order to fully fathom the reasons why the "law and order presidency" has developed over time, an understanding of how issues find their way onto the government's agenda is crucial. Comprehending how problems are perceived, defined, and discussed assists in understanding why the national government is willing to address these problems by placing them on their agenda. From there, one

The President Speaks . . .

For a few minutes this evening I want to speak to you about the serious situation that has arisen in Little Rock. To make this talk I have come to the President's office in the White House. I could have spoken from Rhode Island, where I have been staying recently, but I felt that, in speaking from the house of Lincoln, of Jackson and of Wilson, my words would better convey both the sadness I feel in the action I was compelled today to take and the firmness with which I intend to pursue this course until the orders of the Federal Court at Little Rock can be executed without unlawful interference.

In that city, under the leadership of demagogic extremists, disorderly mobs have deliberately prevented the carrying out of proper orders from a Federal Court. Local authorities have not eliminated that violent opposition and, under the law, I yesterday issued a Proclamation calling upon the mob to disperse.

This morning the mob again gathered in front of the Central High School of Little Rock, obviously for the purpose of again, preventing the carrying out of the Court's order relating to the admission of Negro children to that school.

Whenever normal agencies prove inadequate to the task and it becomes necessary for the Executive Branch of the Federal Government to use its powers and authority to uphold Federal Courts, the President's responsibility is inescapable.

President Dwight D. Eisenhower delivering a speech at the White House Conference on Children and Youth where he discussed the problem of juvenile delinquency in America on March 27, 1960.

PHOTOGRAPH WAS TAKEN BY THE NATIONAL PARKS SERVICE, COURTESY OF THE DWIGHT D. EISENHOWER LIBRARY.

In accordance with that responsibility, I have today issued an Executive Order directing the use of troops under Federal authority to aid in the execution of Federal law at Little Rock, Arkansas. This became necessary when my Proclamation of yesterday was not observed, and the obstruction of justice still continues.

It is important that the reasons for my action be understood by all our citizens.

As you know, the Supreme Court of the United States has decided that separate public educational facilities for the races are inherently unequal and therefore compulsory school segregation laws are unconstitutional.

Our personal opinions about the decision have no bearing on the matter of enforcement; the responsibility and authority of the Supreme Court to interpret the Constitution are very clear. Local Federal Courts were instructed by the Supreme Court to issue such orders and decrees as might be necessary to achieve admission to public schools without regard to race—and with all deliberate speed.

During the past several years, many communities in our Southern States have instituted public school plans for gradual progress in the enrollment and attendance of school children of all races in order to bring themselves into compliance with the law of the land. They thus demonstrated to the world that we are a nation in which laws, not men, are supreme. I regret to say that this truth—the cornerstone of our liberties—was not observed in this instance.

It was my hope that this localized situation would be brought under control by city and State authorities. If the use of local police powers had been sufficient, our traditional method of leaving the problems in those hands would have been pursued. But when large gatherings of obstructionists made it impossible for the decrees of the Court to be carried out, both the law and the national interest demanded that the President take action.

—*Dwight D. Eisenhower*
Radio and Television Address to the American People on the Situation in Little Rock, September 24, 1957

---

can then more readily understand why issues find their way onto the president's agenda and, more specifically, why crime has become a major facet of the president's domestic agenda.

Turning to the major explanations for why presidents have become engaged in crime-control policy, this chapter will posit that there are three key reasons: 1) because crime is a national crisis issue and the public looks to the president for assistance; 2) because crime is an issue that provides presidents with substantive policy; and 3) because it provides presidents with an issue that easily plays on symbolic, valence, and racial politics. Additional reasons include a plethora of political explanations—crime is an excellent campaign issue; national political parties have adopted crime platforms; and as this research will attempt to demonstrate, crime control has a significant influence on public opinion. Finally, this chapter will look at possible ideological explanations, specifically world-view and character, to explain why presidents engage in crime control policy. In sum, this chapter will look at the subject of agenda setting, turn to the specifics of the president's agenda, and then explore the key reasons, as well as political and ideological reasons, why presidents have placed crime on their agenda.

AGENDA SETTING

The term *agenda* has been defined as "the list of subjects or problems to which governmental officials and people outside of government closely associated with those officials are paying some serious attention at any given time."[2] These government officials generally include a variety of political actors at the national, as well as the state and local levels. At the national level this may include the president and his staff, Congress, the Supreme Court, and the bureaucracy. At the state and local levels this may include the governors, the legislatures, the state courts, and their various bureaucracies. In addition, non-government officials, such as special interest groups or the media, are found at all levels and can greatly influence the issues being considered. The agenda, then, is the issues to which these various actors are giving serious attention and consideration.

Crime has always been an item on the agenda of state and local governments simply because it has always been their responsibility to address the issues of law and order. Crime has also found a place on the national government's agenda, but it was sporadic and limited throughout most of the nineteenth century. It was only in the early twentieth century that the issue of crime became a significant agenda item and not until 1964 with the nationalization of crime, that it became a fixed part of the agenda in some form or fashion.

Moving to the concept of "agenda-setting," Ripley defines it as the process "by which problems get selected for governmental action."[3] Others, such as Nelson, have defined it as the process where "public officials learn about new problems, decide to give them their personal attention, and mobilize their organizations to respond to them."[4] Simply put, agenda-setting is how these issues come to the attention of the political actors and then find their way onto the agenda.

Because crime was a serious issue for state and local governments, the agenda-setting process for crime at this level was clearly established when the state governments were formed. As state governments were guaranteed a "republican form of government" and the national government could only assist in issues of "domestic violence" when called upon, state governments were given near total control of addressing the issues of crime. Local governments, upon creation, had to request from their state governments the authority to establish local law and order. These requests were generally granted and hence the issue of crime was clearly set on local government's agendas as well. As for the national government, the agenda-setting process of crime did not come about until the late nineteenth and early twentieth century. For the most part, the regulation of "inter-state commerce" would give the national government the legitimacy needed to address the issue of crime on their agenda and the rising crime rates caused by the prohibition era (a federal law itself) would see the government actively seeking to place crime high on their agenda. With the election of 1964 decided, the issue of crime appearing in a variety of forms, had become a fixed part of the agenda and a problem that the government had actively addressed.[5]

Delving deeper, Cobb and Elder have helped to distinguish that there are several types of agendas which include the systemic agenda and the institutional agenda.[6] The systemic agenda "consists of all issues that are commonly perceived by members of the political community as meriting public attention and as involving matters within the legitimate jurisdiction of existing governmental authority."[7] In order for an issue to find its way onto the systemic agenda it must have broad appeal to a wide audience; there must be agreement that some action is required; and it must fall under the authority of the government addressing the problem. In other words, the systemic agenda is the entire universe of potential issues that government has the capability of addressing.

The institutional agenda, on the other hand, consists of all of the issues that government and the public are openly addressing or, as Cobb and Elder explain, it is "that set of items explicitly up for the active and serious consideration of authoritative decision-makers."[8] These are items that are currently on the agenda and that are being reviewed for possible "relief or redress." In a sense, then, there are those issues that are formally on the agenda (institutional) and there are those that are being discussed behind closed doors and waiting to appear on the formal agenda (systemic). As Marion has stated, "crime is always on the systemic agendas of the presidents, but the placement of crime on the institutional agenda changes."[9] She illustrates one such change through the example of gun control which was an item that was on the systemic agenda at the beginning of the 1980s.[10] In March of 1981, with the attempted assassination of President Reagan, gun control found itself moving from the systemic agenda to the institutional agenda. The fact that the attempted assassination received the attention of a wide audience, that there was a general consensus that something must be done about gun violence, and that it was believed that the national government had the authority to regulate these crimes, gun control moved from the systemic to the institutional agenda and would, nearly ten years later, see the passage of the Brady Bill.[11]

Although Cobb and Elders' original work on agenda-setting is useful for understanding the agenda-setting process, another early work attempted to explain why items find themselves receiving so much attention and hence, find themselves moving from the systemic to the institutional agenda. The work of Downs and his conceptual discussion of the "issue-attention cycle" helped to illustrate this process.[12] Downs articulated that, like the world of economics, there is a cyclical effect to domestic issues, and that the issues currently under active consideration arrive there in such a manner. Downs explained the five stages in the "issue atten-tion cycle": 1) the "pre-problem stage" where "some highly undesirable social condition exists but has not yet captured much public attention"; 2) the "alarmed discovery and euphoric enthusiasm" stage where "some dramatic series of events, or, for other reasons, the public suddenly becomes both aware of and alarmed about the evils of a particular problem"; 3) the realization stage, where there is a "realization that the cost of 'solving' the problem is very high"; 4) the "gradual de-cline of intense public interest"; and 5) the "post-problem stage" where the issue is no longer at the center of the public's concern until there is once again the "alarmed discovery and euphoric enthusiasm" for the issue once again.[13]

Downs' "issue-attention cycle" can be witnessed in a number of issues re-lated to crime. One example is the well-researched work of Nelson in her applica-tion of the "issue-attention cycle" to the crime of child abuse.[14] In the early 1980s, this crime, which has long existed, was euphorically discovered and the issue moved from the systemic agenda to the institutional agenda. There was a realiza-tion of the significant costs to address the problem of child abuse, hence the issue gradually declined from public interest. Other examples of the "issue-attention cycle" as applied to the subject of crime can be found in the cyclical nature of the problem of drugs in the United States which had witnessed "alarmed discovery" in the early 1900s, resulting in the Harrison Act; in the 1930s, which resulted in the Marijuana Tax Act; in the early 1960s under President Johnson, resulting in sev-eral pieces of legislation dealing with illegal drugs; in the early 1970s under Pres-ident Nixon, giving us the "first war on drugs," and again in the mid-1980s under Reagan and Bush, resulting in an ever-increasing dedication of national resources to address the problems of drugs.[15] Between these time periods there is evidence that the realized cost to make significant progress caused public interest to decline and the problem would move into the "post-problem" stage until it was "dis-covered" again.

While the "issue-attention cycle" clearly has application to a number of crimes, it does not necessarily apply to crime in a generic sense. In other words, overall, crime is always a problem and may not be cyclical in nature despite the fact that specific crimes may exhibit these tendencies. This may especially be the case when certain crimes become redefined or when problems were previously perceived as conditions and situations, such as domestic violence or drugs. One other aspect that raises questions of the applicability of the "issue-attention cycle" to crime, especially at the national level, is the fact that once crime became a na-tionalized issue in 1964, it has apparently remained an issue of the government's attention. Despite a vast amount of money and resources being poured into the crime issue, there has been little evidence of a realization that the cost of "solving" the problem exists. In fact, as one author has explained in regard to crime control in America, "nothing succeeds like failure."[16] While it is true that Downs did not specify a time frame for the various stages, it can be believed, circumspectly, that he did not envision a policy lasting in the euphoric stage for over forty years.

Another early and significant contribution to the agenda-setting research came from Cobb, Ross, and Ross when they delineated three different models of agenda-setting.[17] The first model, the outside initiative model, relates to issues raised by non-governmental groups, reaching a large enough audience to find a place on the public agenda, and finally moved to the formal agenda. The second model, the mobilization model, "considers issues which are initiated inside government and consequently achieve formal agenda status almost automatically."[18] These issues find themselves on the formal or government agenda and then through a process of "mobilizing" the public, they find a place on the public agenda. Finally, the third model, the inside initiative model "describes issues which arise within the governmental sphere and whose supporters do not try to expand them to the mass public."[19] These issues are purposely placed on the agenda by governmental actors but are kept from public view in order to avoid any interference from the possibility of becoming policy.

The issue of crime lends itself more readily to the first and second models, with perhaps some instances of the third model being evident. Examples of outside initiatives as related to crime are evident in such issues as domestic violence, driving while intoxicated (DWI), and gun control. There are also a number of examples where crime has found its way on the agenda through the second model. Examples include the creation of a drug problem by the Nixon administration in 1972 which launched the first "war on drugs,"[20] the creation of a "crack epidemic" in the mid-1980s during the Reagan administration,[21] and the example utilized in the introduction when the Clinton administration focused its attention on crime, creating a "crime wave" despite the fact that official crime rates had been falling for several years. These issues were placed on the agenda by the government and only afterward was the public solicited to place the issue on its agenda. The last model, inside initiative, is limited in its application to the issue of crime. Although there are perhaps some instances of its use, such as issues of military law and foreign drug eradication programs, for the most part, issues of crime clearly fall under the outside initiatives and mobilization models of agenda-setting.

One of the most significant contributions to the topic of agenda setting came from Kingdon in 1984, with the publication of his book on the agenda-setting process.[22] His conceptual model of the agenda-setting process consists of the three separate "streams" of information: 1) the problem stream, 2) the policy stream, and 3) the political stream.[23] The problem stream consists of events or crises that may come to the attention of government. Kingdon highlights that problems may be derived from two sources: official indicators such as rising unemployment rates or official crime rates that may signal a potential problem as well as certain "focusing events" such as natural disasters, riots, or bombings. The policy stream

consists of a variety of ideas, interests, and policy proposals that might solve or redress the problem. The policy stream is generally made up of experts, both inside
and outside government, who spend time addressing the problem and looking for
solutions. Finally, the political stream consists of the political environmental factors that can affect the solution to a problem such as partisan conflicts, public
opinion, the national mood, electoral politics, and interest-group activity. Kingdon
then goes on to explain that, on occasion, these three separate streams will intersect creating a "window of opportunity" for governmental action. Kingdon, however, also points out that these policy windows are short-lived and must be taken
advantage of when they occur. Otherwise, the initiative is lost and government
cannot seize the initiative until the streams intersect once more.

The Kingdon model, while at face value appears simple, incorporates all of the
critical concepts of policy studies, namely the realization that problems exist as do
the ideas, interests, and institutions behind governmental activity to address these
problems.[24] As a result, the conceptual model is highly complementary to the study
of agenda-setting in any policy area. Although there has not been a full treatment of
crime policy utilizing Kingdon's model, several authors cite the Kingdon material,[25]
some have used it when analyzing the effects of the media on federal crime policy,[26]
and still others have looked at it in relation to the issue of drug policy-making.[27] This
latter treatment found ample evidence that throughout the twentieth century: drugs
continued to provide a steady stream of problems that could be addressed; the federal government continued to expand its bureaucracy to address the problems of
crime; and political rhetoric and activity, especially on the part of the presidents, has
helped this specific type of crime to stay on the government's agenda.

One final scholarly work on agenda-setting that expands our understanding
of how issues appear on the government's agenda is by Baumgartner and Jones
and their distinction of how policies are understood.[28] They distinguish between
policy images, how policies are understood and discussed, and policy venues
which are the institutional locations where authoritative decisions are made concerning a given issue.[29] In addition, they note that many policies evolve over time
through a highly incremental approach. But they also note that many issues appear
on the agenda almost literally overnight. By focusing on this latter occurrence
which they call "punctuated equilibrium," they are "able to account for both long
periods of stability and short, violent periods of change."[30] Moreover, they discuss
the issue of "policy tone" which details the fact that a policy image may consist of
one understanding at one point in time, but this may change over time (or
overnight) and be couched by an entirely new policy image. Finally, often resulting from the change in tone, there may come a change in policy venue regarding
which agency has the responsibility for addressing the issue.

This discussion of how policy issues find a place on the government's agenda
has a distinct application to the issue of crime. Baumgartner and Jones, in their
book, analyze three issues related to crime in regard to their theory of agenda

setting: drug abuse, alcohol abuse,[31] and child abuse.[32] Jones, in a follow-up book, also expands the discussion of drugs and details how the issue has been understood and reframed over time.[33] Their findings demonstrate that "national policies toward drug abuse underwent a sea change during the 1960s" when the "issue emerged high onto the systemic agenda" and resulted in a change in tone, becoming far more severe and punitive in nature.[34] Throughout the 1940s and 1950s, the issue of drug abuse was a policy that was incrementally evolving. During the 1960s, with an expanded population of young adults, usage of drugs began to rise and the equilibrium that had been established in regard to drug policy was "punctuated." The tone of the policy image changed from one of treatment to one focused on law enforcement and punishment. As a result, the policy venue changed from one that was dealt with by health care professionals to one that was dealt with by the law enforcement community. Baumgartner and Jones point out that "sometime issues change over time, becoming rooted in a new issue area" and that "a number of issues that were once in the exclusive domain of states and localities in the United States have shifted toward the federal level."[35] This statement could be no truer in regard to the issues of crime and, as they demonstrate, in the issue of drugs. As a result, images and venues play an important role in the agenda-setting process.

In looking at our understanding of the agenda-setting process, it becomes clear that a number of factors are involved in the process of moving an item onto the institutional, or governmental agenda. Situations or conditions must be recognized as problems. These problems must come to the attention of government officials and there must be a policy over which they have legitimate jurisdiction. There must be some form of solution to the problem that government could potentially implement. The political environment has to be ready for government to intervene. And finally, the "window of opportunity" must be seized. As a result, it becomes clear that one person, in this case the president, does not control the agenda, but it is an amorphous process affected by a variety of ideas, interests, and institutional factors. Therefore, explaining why presidents may focus their time and attention on the issue of crime may come as a result of the agenda-setting process, a process over which they do not have total control. In other words, rather than the president placing crime on his agenda, crime may be placed on the agenda for him by factors beyond his control. This is not to say, however, that presidents do not have some control over the government's agenda, for their agenda is a significant benchmark to the total government agenda. But it is rather to say that sometimes issues may simply be beyond their control. One only has to think back to 1964 when a nation began experiencing riots in the streets and the public looked to the national government for assistance and how the campaign that year placed crime at the forefront of the American agenda. Johnson had little choice in the matter of whether crime would be part of the government's agenda, but what he did have control over was how much it would be a part of the president's agenda. It is to this specific agenda we now turn.

THE PRESIDENT'S AGENDA

The president's agenda is only one aspect of the total government agenda, but it carries significant weight in the realm of moving policies from the systemic to the institutional agenda. The old saying that "the president proposes and Congress disposes" highlights this importance in the agenda-setting process.[36] As Kingdon explains, "no other single actor in the political system has quite the capability of the president to set agendas in given policy areas for all who deal with those policies."[37] Shull also highlights the fact that presidents have "a far greater role in initiating national policies in the twentieth century than they did previously"[38] and Miroff believes that the president has come to "monopolize the public space."[39] Finally, as Bosso colorfully articulates, "the presidency is the single most powerful institutional lever for policy breakthrough" and the president "is the political system's thermostat, capable of heating up or cooling down the politics of any single issue or of an entire platter of issues."[40] Bosso then further states that in relation to the process of moving issues onto the government's agenda, that "presidential intervention is a key variable."[41] Once we recognize the importance of the president's agenda in relation to the total government agenda, it is important to understand what is meant by the president's agenda, why the president has so much influence, and how this relates to crime policy.

Paul Light's seminal book, *The President's Agenda,* has become the definitive book on understanding the president's agenda, especially as it relates to domestic policy choices.[42] Light explains that:

> . . . the President's agenda is a remarkable list. It is rarely written down. It constantly shifts and evolves. It is often in flux even for the President and the top staff. Items move onto the agenda one day and off the next. Because of its status in the policy process, the President's agenda is the subject of intense conflict. The infighting is resolved sometimes through mutual consent and "collegial" bargaining, sometimes through marked struggle and domination.[43]

Light goes on to say that:

> . . . the President's agenda is perhaps best understood as a *signal.* It indicates what the President believes to be the most important issues facing his administration. It identifies what the President finds to be the most appropriate alternatives for solving the problems. It identifies what the President deems to be the highest priorities.[44]

In sum, the president's agenda stands as a fluid list of what the president and his top staff consider to be the most important problems coupled with what are considered to be the best alternatives for solving these problems in order to create a prioritized "list" of policy related items. However, like understanding the process of how items find their way from the systemic agenda to the institutional agenda which explains why the government chooses certain policies for their agenda, it is equally important to understand how certain policies like crime find their way onto the president's agenda.

The key, according to Light, comes from understanding presidential power and the resources at his disposal.[45] Light articulates that presidents have internal resources such as time, information, expertise, and energy.[46] Kingdon adds to the list institutional resources, "including the veto and the prerogative to hire and fire," organizational resources such as the fact that the executive branch has a more enhanced ability for making unitary decisions than Congress, a command of public attention, "which can be converted into pressure on other government officials to adopt the president's agenda," and finally, like Light, the president's involvement (time and energy) in specific policy issues.[47] Light also delineates several external resources available to the president, such as party support in Congress, public approval, electoral margin, and patronage.[48] These resources must then be understood as being either increasing or diminishing resources. For instance, in regard to the internal sources, presidents face the increasing resources of expertise and information. These two resources are not always readily available to a president when he enters office and must be built over his tenure. However, the other two internal resources are diminishing resources—time and energy—as the president moves further into his term. There is a clear conflict in these internal resources. As the president does move further into his term, he is finally in a position of having enhanced his expertise in the political arena and of having the information to affect policy, but he is assuredly running out of time and, most likely, energy to affect said policies. In regard to external resources, party support in Congress often diminishes in the mid-term elections and public approval typically diminishes throughout the president's four years, leaving him with little capital at the end of his term. Thus, all of these resources, internal and external, come to bear on the president's ability to place items on his agenda and to push them through Congress to achieve a legislative victory.

Light goes on to explain the process of how items find their way onto the president's agenda by first looking at the opportunities the president has for making choices.[49] He notes that the policy cycle, often dictated by the political election cycle, influences the items a president places on his agenda.[50] Light also explains that presidents select issues not just because they are pressing systemic issues, but also because the president considers his chances for reelection, wishes to establish himself historically, and wants to see "good policy" pass the legislature.[51] In a sense, the president is seeking benefits from the policies he chooses. Light further explains that the source of policy ideas plays a role in the policies the president places on his agenda.[52] The president may be influenced by external sources such as Congress, national events and crises, the bureaucrats, and public opinion polls, as well as political parties, interest groups, and the media. In addition, he may be influenced by internal sources such as the party platform under which he ran his campaign, the campaign promises he made along the way, and members of his staff. All of these factors come to bear on the president who must then make the decision as to what issues to address and what issues not to address.

Once the president makes the decision to have his administration move forward on a particular issue such as crime, he must then prioritize his agenda and determine how best to address each issue.[53] This is generally done by establishing the direction he wants the policy issue to take, but is then forced to make several choices along the way. He must determine whether or not the program will be a new one or an old one and whether he will push the policy through legislative or administrative means. He must determine the size of the program and what type of budget the program will receive.[54] He must then weigh the political cost, the economic cost, and the technical ("workability") costs of the policy proposal before moving on the policy.[55] Finally, the president must determine how committed he is to the policy as it moves through the political process.[56] This last part ultimately returns to the issue of the president's resources and how he chooses to employ them. He must determine how much support already exists for the policy (external resources) and how much time and energy he is willing to devote to the policy himself (internal resources).

In recognizing the importance of the president's agenda in defining the issues that the national government places on the institutional agenda, it is important to understand the president's agenda as it relates to crime. Although various aspects of presidents and crime control have been explored by researchers,[57] the most extensive analysis comes from only two researchers, Calder[58] and Marion.[59] The first work, a Ph.D. dissertation, came from James D. Calder and his work in the late 1970s and early 1980s which for the first time, dealt specifically with presidents and their crime-control policies.[60] Calder focused on two aspects of presidents and crime-control policy. The first was centered on the "formal limitation on presidential powers and capabilities" which drew upon aspects of the history of presidential intervention in foreign and domestic affairs, federal assistance to suppress domestic violence, and various issues related to the problems of "street crime." The second part of his dissertation concentrated on the "ideological limitations" of presidents focusing on crime-control policy and utilized case studies of the Kennedy, Johnson, and Nixon administrations to present evidence of these limitations. This section would eventually be published as a journal article in 1982, in the *Presidential Studies Quarterly.*[61] The key emphasis of this section and article was based on the theory that "presidents come from identifiable ideological positions about crime" and that this would influence their policy decisions regarding crime.[62] Calder would demonstrate through his research that Kennedy and Johnson would share a functionalist ideology[63] which would cause them to focus on underlying causes of crime, while Nixon had a more mechanist ideology[64] which resulted in his policies regarding crime to be based on responsibility for one's own actions, thus focusing on disciplining law violators.[65] In the end, Calder's dissertation would conclude that the issue of "law and order" was not a policy area in which presidents would have great control, primarily due to the number of political, informational, and ideological limitations exhibited by this particular policy.

While Calder's research looked primarily at ideological reasons for president's involvement in crime, it was not until 1992 that another author, Nancy E. Marion, would look more specifically at "presidential agenda-setting in crime control."[66] Marion conducted research on the presidential agendas in crime control from 1963 to 1990 by looking at presidential speeches on crime from the *Public Papers of the Presidents of the United States.* Her research was primarily focused on identifying policy trends regarding this one specific policy area. She elaborated five specific hypotheses in her study: 1) the number of crime initiatives will increase over time, 2) Republican and Democratic presidents will suggest different approaches to crime control, 3) Democratic presidents will have described more crime-related initiatives than will Republican presidents, 4) there should be more speeches given in the first year in office than in other years, and 5) it is expected that there will be more crime-related speeches in election years than in off-election years.[67]

Marion analyzed the total number of speeches by presidents that mentioned crime, divided that number into both election and non-election speeches, then determined the average for each administration.[68] She then furthered her analysis by looking at speeches that were solely dedicated to the issue of crime, determining the number of election and non-election speeches as well as their sum and how they averaged over each administration.[69] Finally, she assessed the top five issues related to crime for each year and collapsed these into the top five issues for each president.[70] Her findings indicated that, other than the first hypothesis which stated "that the number of crime proposals would increase each year,"[71] there was no support for any of the hypotheses. And in regard to the first hypothesis, it was "supported only slightly."[72]

The lack of findings in regard to Marion's hypotheses are important, but what was more important was that her research was the first foray into the area of presidential agenda-setting and crime control policies. As she would conclude based on her findings, "it is expected that crime will be on the systemic agenda of all presidents in the future, and that the government will become more involved in crime control to the extent that it can."[73] She would also note that "presidents are using crime as a symbolic function or gesture to gather support and appease public sentiment."[74] This finding would lead her to follow up her original research with the theory that presidential crime control policies are "symbolic policies" and she would demonstrate through additional research that patterns of symbolism exist but that their specific nature and pattern remained unclear.[75] In other words, presidents do invoke symbols in their crime policy which are "used to evoke a particular response from the public without providing any tangible reward, deriving its meaning from the reaction or response of the public." However, it is still unknown whether or not there is a specific intent on the part of the presidents when they employ these symbols because a specific pattern to their usage is lacking.

The President Speaks . . .

I am happy to approve S. 279, Juvenile Delinquency and Youth Offenses Control Act of 1961.

The future of our country depends upon our younger people who will occupy positions of responsibility and leadership in the coming days. Yet for 11 years juvenile delinquency has been increasing. No city or State in our country has been immune. This is a matter of national concern and requires national action.

With this legislation the Federal Government becomes an active partner with States and local communities to prevent and control the spread of delinquency. Though initiative and primary responsibility for coping with delinquency reside with families and local communities, the Federal Government can provide leadership, guidance and assistance.

The Secretary of HEW (Health, Education, and Welfare) will administer the act. He will, however, work closely with the Committee on Juvenile Delinquency and Youth Crime, which I have appointed to bring about a more effective coordination of Federal resources in this field. This Committee

President John F. Kennedy consulting in the Oval Office on February 23, 1961, with J. Edgar Hoover, the Director of the Federal Bureau of Investigation, and the President's brother, Robert F. Kennedy, the Attorney General and head of the U.S. Department of Justice.
PHOTOGRAPH COURTESY OF THE JOHN F. KENNEDY LIBRARY.

includes the Attorney General as Chairman, and the Secretary of Labor, along with the Secretary of HEW.

The resources provided under this program will help local communities in their efforts to stem the tide of juvenile delinquency and youthful offenses, and thus contribute to the preservation of human resources in this vital area of the life of our Nation.

—*John F. Kennedy*
Remarks Upon Signing the Juvenile Delinquency and Youth Offenses Control Act, September 22, 1961

Finally, Marion would publish what is assuredly the definitive book on federal crime policy, *A History of Federal Crime Control Initiatives, 1960–1993*, which analyzes the institutional agenda related to crime-control policy from the Kennedy administration through the Bush administration.[76] In an additional publication, she would follow up the book with an article specifically focused on Clinton's crime agenda from the 1992 presidential campaign through the 1996 presidential campaign.[77] In both of these publications, Marion continued her discussion and research based on the theory that presidents and their crime control policies are simply a result of presidents engaging in symbolic rhetoric.

Much can be gleaned from these two authors' research regarding the presidential agenda-setting process and the presidential focus on crime which contributes to the understanding of why presidents focus on crime-control policy. The work of Calder lends evidence that there are ideological reasons for their engagement in the area of crime policy. The work of Marion lends evidence that they become engaged for reasons of political benefits from the "symbolic" nature of the issue. While both of these perspectives are valuable and cannot be dismissed, the agenda-setting works of Light and Kingdon also raise other possibilities for why presidents have become active in a policy area that, for most of American history, has been relegated to state and local governments. Drawing upon all of the agenda-setting literature which looks at how issues move onto the government's agenda, for which the president's agenda is the "political system's thermostat,"[78] and the previous research on presidential agenda-setting and crime, this chapter will move to explore, with more depth, various possibilities that may explain why presidents have placed crime on their agenda.

EXPLANATIONS TO THE QUESTION: "WHY CRIME?"

In order to explore the question, "why presidents focus on crime control" with greater depth, an understanding of the agenda-setting literature must be combined with both theories and speculation regarding why presidents make certain decisions. The process by which presidents make decisions involving certain policies, as we have already seen in the discussion of agenda-setting, is complex. This process is not at all easy to describe, let alone explain. However, delving into the possible explanations can provide a better understanding of the "law and order presidency." While this complex process could be explored through a variety of means, the rest of this chapter will attempt to draw upon many of the explanations of why presidents engage in certain policies and, more importantly, why they engage in crime control policy.

It is the contention of this author that there are three key reasons why presidents engage in crime-control policy. The first is simply that crime is inevitable and that during each presidential administration there are a number of crimes which naturally rise to the nation's attention. Since the president represents the leader of the nation, when these events occur, people turn to him for guidance. The second is that crime presents the president an opportunity to engage in a substantive policy issue where policy can be turned into tangible rewards such as funding more police officers, additional judges, and new prisons. Crime, then, is attractive to presidents and other politicians, because it provides them with a policy that has a substantive nature. And third, although somewhat in opposition to the second explanation, as Marion has explained, crime lends itself most readily to the use of symbols. Also, as an extension, crime is a valence issue that provides little to no opposition—as no one is "for crime"—and finally, more disturbingly, it provides a veiled symbol for racism that presidents can, and have, played on.

Although the three reasons cited above appear to be the primary reasons why presidents engage in crime control, there are also a number of issues that do not specifically fall into any of these three categories. Rather, they tend to emphasize two other categories that should not be dismissed as influencing factors for presidential involvement in crime, specifically political and ideological explanations. The former provide a simple political benefits explanation for why presidents would engage in issues of crime-control policy, while the latter focuses more on explaining it as being related to the president's world view and personal character which may influence him to engage in the issue of crime.

Crisis

The first key explanation may simply lie in two realities. The first is that crime is inevitable and that many crimes will rise to the level of national awareness. Second, throughout the twentieth century, presidents have become more and more a focal point for American policy, politics, and leadership.[79] When an international crisis occurs, people look to the president for guidance, direction, and leadership. Likewise, when there is a major national crisis, such as a riot, a mass murder, or a bombing, people look to the president. As a result, the president is naturally inclined to respond, or rather, is forced to respond, to the event.

This leadership role carries some political influence and these dramatic events can have either a positive or negative effect, in that they can either unify the nation around the president or they can dramatize and highlight the nation's conflicts and problems.[80] Examples of presidents and national crises revolving around criminal related events include: President Hoover and the Lindbergh baby kidnaping,[81] President Johnson and the series of urban riots occurring in a number of major cities across the United States,[82] President Clinton and both the World Trade Center and Oklahoma City bombings, and, more recently, President Bush and the terrorist attacks in both New York City and Arlington, Virginia. In each of these cases, the public looked to the president for guidance and the presidents responded. Hoover would send in Federal Bureau of Investigation agents without federal jurisdiction to "assist" in the case. Johnson would ultimately create a crime commission to address the issue of civil disorders, known as the Kerner Commission. Clinton would use the full powers of both his rhetoric and administration to respond and investigate these bombings. And Bush created the Office of Homeland Security—a cabinet level position. Perhaps President Johnson explained it best in his memoirs which were published in 1971. Although there is still a hint of incredulity in his writing, the fact that the public looks to the president in times of crises is highlighted when he stated:

> The average American was concerned about the rising crime rate and failed to understand that under our Constitution the preservation of law and order is basically the responsibility of local government. Somehow, in the minds of most Americans the breakdown of local authority became the fault of the federal government.[83]

In the end, whether or not crime is a state or local issue does not seem to matter much. What matters in the case of a crime that rises to the level of national attention is that presidents assume their leadership role. Most presidents, even Johnson, have not ignored this responsibility.

Substantive Policy

The second explanation for why presidents focus on crime-control policy may be derived from the possibility that crime is the type of issue that gives the president the ability to engage in substantive policy. The concept of substantive policy, as utilized here, is meant to denote the fact that the policy passed has a real and demonstrative nature. This then allows presidents the capability of passing "good policy." As Light explains, "there can be little question that Presidents do engage in the search for programmatic benefits" and that "Presidents do have notions of what constitutes good policy."[84] This can also be further explained in relation to the discussion by Theodore Lowi who argues that "good policy" today is seen as "one which is open-ended, ambiguous, and flexible."[85] He argues effective policies require clarity, choice, and closure.[86] In other words, according to Lowi, policies should be more definitive. Crime lends itself to all of these factors in that crime policy can often be real, demonstrative, and definitive in nature.

There are numerous examples of the substantive aspects of crime policy. One such example can be derived from President Johnson's Crime Commission in the 1960s which published the report known as *The Challenge of Crime in a Free Society*.[87] This would result in legislation known as the Omnibus Crime Control and Safe Streets Act of 1968 which established the Law Enforcement Assistance Administration (LEAA) within the Department of Justice. This agency would create a program known as the Law Enforcement Education Program (LEEP), designed to assist and encourage police officers to attend college and work toward furthering their education. This program would ultimately contribute to the creation and evolution of a number of criminal justice programs in institutes of higher education today.[88] Other examples include the rapid increase of federal prison facilities being built across the United States during the last two decades of the twentieth century which have been termed by some the "prison-industrial complex."[89] Regardless of whether one considers prison expansion a "good" or "bad" policy, it can clearly be categorized as being a substantive policy and has a demonstrative effect. Finally, another example that illustrates this point, broached in my Introduction, is President Clinton's "100,000 Cops" initiative. Although this was most certainly used for its symbolic effect, one can hardly argue that the passage of the Violent Crime Control and Law Enforcement Act of 1994 by Congress, which allocated $8.8 billion dollars for local law enforcement and has been dispersed to police agencies across the country to hire additional officers, train them, and purchase new equipment, was merely "symbolic" in nature.

Drawing upon these examples, the substantive aspects of president's involvement in crime-control policy can be categorized as resulting in either the increase in policy funding, the passage of tougher laws, or ultimately, the expansion of governmental powers. A growing body of research has centered on this first category. Budget expenditures by the federal government have grown significantly over the past forty years in the area of crime policy[90] and some "persuasive evidence indicates that both Congress and the President increase public expenditures for the full spectrum of law enforcement as the incidence of crime increases."[91] More particularly, Baumgartner and Jones point out that "the president's position can lead to vast budgetary commitments toward the solution set he is proposing"[92] which, if passed by Congress, can most assuredly strengthen his position. In fact, there is some evidence to suggest that presidents, or at a minimum their policy advisors, recognize this fact.

In the summer of 1966, a series of meetings would take place between several of Johnson's key advisors in the area of crime, specifically Joseph Califano, Nicholas Katzenbach, and James Vorenberg, to formulate ideas for the 1967 legislative program on crime. In a December 10 meeting, one key issue discussed and recorded by James C. Gaither, a staff assistant to Califano, was "how to get $ to local law enforcement."[93] Another example is found early in the Reagan administration by his key policy advisor for drug abuse, Ian MacDonald, when in the upper margins of a document dated July 1981 and titled, "Departments and Agencies with Drug Abuse Program Responsibilities" he would note "Money in this area!!"[94] Clearly there is an advantage to the issue of crime in that the expansion of the budget in this area appears relatively easy to achieve and has steadily grown over time.

In 1992, the federal government spent over $17 billion to fight crime.[95] The corresponding expenditure for 1965 was $535 million—an increase of over 2,000 percent.[96] If the timeframe is narrowed, the trend is still evident. Between 1971–1990, there was a 668 percent increase in expenditures on crime.[97] Although the majority of the federal expenditures on crime are direct expenditures, such as funding for the Federal Bureau of Investigation or the Drug Enforcement Administration, a substantial portion of the funds are intergovernmental expenditures, such as funding for local drug task forces and equipment purchases (see Table 2–1). No matter how one figures the change over time, even controlling for inflation,[98] there has been a significant increase in the dollars the federal government is willing to spend on crime. Moreover, when looking at a specific type of expenditure within the crime issue, varying degrees of growth can be found, such as the steady increase in funding for federal agencies dealing with crime[99] or in the overall figures of federal drug control spending in the last two decades of the twentieth century (see Figure 2–1).[100] Finally, the increases become even more dramatic when one considers the growth rate (or lack of it) in other types of discretionary federal spending. In recent years, spending on many other social programs has been drastically cut, leaving federal expenditures on crime far exceeding the amount spent on many other programs including education.[101] For instance, "nationwide expenditures on criminal justice increased 150 percent between 1972 and 1988, while expenditures on education increased by 46 percent."[102]

The resulting effect of the increase in the federal government's expenditures on crime has come by many to be equated with the concepts first articulated in Eisenhower's farewell speech when he spoke of the dangers of a "military-industrial complex." A number of authors, in the wake of a rapid growth in federal drug control expenditures, have come to forecast warnings of a "narco-industrial complex,"[103] while others, due to a rapid increase in expenditures by the federal government to build more federal prisons, have articulated the problem of a "prison-industrial complex."[104] In reality, taking the sum of these so-called industrial complexes as well as all of the various expenditures on crime, a more accurate description would perhaps be that we have achieved a "criminal justice-industrial complex." The modern day government–private build-up has come, not as a result of the cold war, but rather as a result of the federal government's various wars on crime and drugs. And the reason presidents can effectively request, and generally get, more expenditures on the crime issue is centered on the fact that this issue

TABLE 2–1 **Federal Criminal Justice Expenditures, 1971–1993***
(dollar amounts in thousands)

Year	Total Federal	Direct Expenditures	Intergovernmental Expenditures
1971	1,448,335	1,214,857	233,478
1972	1,876,345	1,502,463	373,882
1973	2,260,959	1,650,881	609,218
1974	2,601,959	1,859,113	742,846
1975	3,018,566	2,187,875	830,691
1976	3,322,073	2,450,229	871,844
1977	3,601,647	2,788,710	822,937
1978	3,834,607	3,122,290	712,317
1979	3,950,686	3,269,381	681,305
1980	—	—	—
1981	—	—	—
1982	4,458,000	—	—
1983	4,844,000	—	—
1984	5,868,000	5,787,000	81,000
1985	6,416,000	6,279,000	137,000
1986	6,595,000	6,430,000	165,000
1987	7,496,000	6,878,000	220,000
1988	8,851,000	7,483,724	330,412
1989	9,674,000	8,110,000	545,000
1990	12,798,000	9,330,923	727,812
1991	15,231,000	11,450,000	1,110,000
1992	17,423,000	13,529,000	3,894,000
1993	18,591,000	14,429,000	4,162,000

**Note:* Data is missing for the years 1980 and 1981 due to a change in agency responsible for reporting the data. Direct and intergovernmental expenditure data is not available for 1982 and 1983 due to the fact the agency did not include this data in the first two years of their reporting scheme. The data is reported in real dollars.

Source: Data collected by author from successive volumes of Bureau of Justice Statistics. 1972–1998. *Sourcebook of Criminal Justice Statistics.* Washington D.C.: Bureau of Justice Statistics.

receives such wide support from the public, the media, and Congress. In fact, related to the perceptions of the public when asked if the government was spending "too little" on "halting the rising crime rate" or "dealing with drug addiction," there has been an overwhelming response that too little has been spent despite rapid increases in expenditures by all level of government during this time period (see Table 2–2). The result, then, is that presidents wield political power in regard to crime expenditures because people think too little is being spent, because crime is always a problem, and because, more than likely, they can achieve legislative victory on issues of crime.

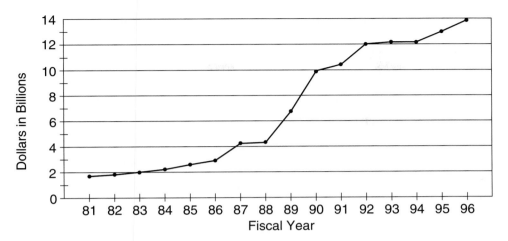

FIGURE 2–1   Federal Drug Control Spending
Source: Office of National Drug Control Policy. *National Drug Control Strategy, 1996.* Washington D.C.: U.S. G.P.O.

This, then, leads to the second category for substantive explanation. Presidents, in proposing new laws, tougher sanctions, and increased expenditures on the issue of crime, stand in a powerful position to achieve legislative success. Although there is an abundant amount of anecdotal evidence to suggest that presidents, when proposing crime-control policy, are successful more often than not, there has been no systematic research to indicate whether this is an accurate perception. The evidence that does exist however, tends to suggest that presidents when proposing new federal crimes and tougher sanctions for previously existing crimes, have been very successful.[105] In addition, although there are sometimes very divisive arguments over crime bills, such as in the cases of President Johnson and the Omnibus Crime Control and Safe Streets Act of 1968, or President Clinton and the Violent Crime Control and Law Enforcement Act of 1994, these policies are also generally passed in the end.[106] In referencing the presidency of Ronald Reagan, one author has gone so far as to explain that "the politics of 'law and order'—with its emphasis on tough punishments, an unimpeded police and legal system, the death penalty, and a rejection of social programs—came to dominate the political discourse about crime and to reflect a bipartisan consensus in Congress during the 1980s."[107] As a result, Reagan, despite having a Democratic Congress for most of his two terms in office, was successful in nearly all of his crime policy proposals. Finally, as Senator Joseph Biden has explained after voting with ninety of his colleagues to impose mandatory life sentences for those convicted of a third violent felony, "if someone came to the Senate floor and said we should barbwire the ankles of anyone who jaywalks, I think it would

TABLE 2–2   Respondents Responding Too Little is Spent on Crime and Drug Addiction in This Country

Question: "We are faced with many problems in this country, none of which can be solved easily or inexpensively. I'm going to name some of the problems, and for each one I'd like you to tell me whether you think we're spending too much money on it, too little money, or about the right amount. First (problem) are we spending too much, too little, or about the right amount on (problem)?"

Year	% Responding too little to "Halting the Rising Crime Rate"	% Responding too little to "Dealing with Drug Addiction"
1973	64%	65%
1974	66	60
1975	65	55
1976	65	58
1977	65	55
1978	64	55
1981	69	59
1982	71	57
1983	67	60
1984	68	63
1985	63	62
1986	64	58
1987	68	65
1988	72	71
1989	73	71
1990	70	64
1991	65	58
1993	71	60
1994	75	60
1996	67	58

Source: Adapted from Kathleen Maguire and Ann Pastore, eds., *Sourcebook of Criminal Justice Statistics 1997.* Washington D.C.: U.S. GPO. Original Source: National Opinion Research Center. 1996. *General Social Surveys, 1972–96.* Storrs: The Roper Center for Public Opinion Research.

pass."[108] This would at least suggest that presidents can achieve a legislative victory in their crime-control policy proposals.

The combination of legislative victories and increased budgets by the federal government in the area of crime provides an understanding for the last substantive explanation for why presidents become engaged in crime-control policies. The explanation, simply put, is that it allows the president to expand the federal government's control over the issue of crime control, hence expanding the powers of the presidency. Stated in a different context, it allows the president to legitimate the government's authority over state and local crimes, to establish a national presence, and to expand government bureaucracy related to crime-control policy.

   The legitimation of its authority actually began at the beginning of the twentieth century with the movement by President Theodore Roosevelt to regulate interstate commerce.[109] It would expand greatly during the prohibition era, as well as in its wake, and would be reestablished in the 1960s.[110] As Lowi has explained, "shoring up all crime-fighting units of local governments became a major program of the Johnson Administration" and "the fact seems to be that we had nationalized local disorders, just as we had nationalized commerce. All of the peripheries of this country now felt the glow of national presence."[111] There is strong evidence of this fact in several of the early meetings between Johnson's policy advisors when formulating the Safe Streets Act of 1968. When discussing the legitimatization of federal government intervention, they articulated that "we won't tell 40,000 local agencies how to do their job—but we'll help."[112] In addition, one proposal they entertained, which had the support of President Johnson, was the expansion of the Internal Revenue Service's (I.R.S.) investigation unit, despite the fact the I.R.S. did not want this expanded power.[113] One other example that is very telling is when John Ehrlichman, a key domestic policy advisor to President Nixon would explain to a Senate Subcommittee investigation that:

> Narcotics suppression is a very sexy political issue. It usually has high media visibility. Parents who are voters are worried about narcotics. They listen to a politician when he talks about drug suppression just as they seem to tune him out when he makes speeches about the energy problem. Therefore, the White House often wants to be involved in narcotics problems even when it doesn't need to be . . . for example, the Feds went into street enforcement partly in response to the obvious political mileage to be gained.[114]

As a result, once federal intervention in crime control was legitimated and a national presence established, the expansion of the federal bureaucracy through various legislation passed by Congress, which most assuredly increases their budgets, has been relatively easy for presidents to achieve. Most of this, it should also be pointed out, has occurred under Republican presidents, specifically Nixon, Ford, Reagan, and Bush. This is truly interesting, for as Mahoney has articulated, "the diminution of the states' role and the expansion of the federal role have taken place despite the fact that Republican presidents, publicly committed to the concept of reducing federal involvement in the administration of grant-in-aid programs, have occupied the White House."[115] All of this can perhaps be best explained in the terms of Foucault who notes that the "scarcely sustainable visibility of the monarch is turned into the unavoidable visibility of the subjects. And it is this inversion of visibility in the functioning of the disciplines that was to assure the exercise of power even in its lowest manifestations."[116] The resulting effect, as Lyons explains, is "the legitimation of state power becomes more anonymous, but the exercise of this power by the state becomes more visible."[117] The legitimation of the national government's crime control policy is not clearly defined, but the president's visibility on the crime issue has certainly increased over time.

This concept of crime as substantive policy does stand somewhat in opposition to Marion's belief that presidents engage in crime-control policy merely for symbolic reasons. In reference to the "100,000 Cops" initiative, she argues that "it appears as if President Clinton has created tangible policies to combat crime and drug use in the country" but that "an analysis of those policies actually show otherwise."[118] Her argument is based on the fact that "the majority of anti-crime legislation must come from the states" and that "any anti-crime legislation is therefore symbolic since it is not a product of the primary crime control body in the country."[119] The key disagreement hinges on the fact that the federal legislation on crime, like the Crime Bill of 1994, "offers no real solutions to the crime problem."[120] While this latter point can be agreed upon, this does not necessarily mean that a policy is devoid of any substantive policy because it does not offer "real solutions" or because the policy is not derived from "the primary crime control body in the country." Tangible results are still achieved. Money is allocated. New programs are created. Prisons are built. New police officers are hired. New equipment is purchased. Crime policy has both real and demonstrative effects. Some crime policy has substance.

Symbolic, Valence, and Racism Explanations

Having stated that the second key reason for presidential involvement in crime-control policy is for substantive policy reasons, it must also be stated that there is still much validity in Marion's assertions that crime is used extensively by presidents for purposes of symbolic politics.[121] The pioneering work by Joseph Gusfield[122] and Murray Edelman[123] provided much of our understanding about the use of symbols. Edelman explains that "every symbol stands for something other than itself, and it also evokes an attitude, a set of impressions, or a pattern of events associated through time, through space, through logic, or through imagination with the symbol."[124] He goes further in saying that "symbols become that facet of experiencing the material world that gives it a specific meaning."[125] In other words, symbols derive their meaning not from content but from the value of how people perceive them. This has clear application for politics in that politicians can utilize political symbols to convey a value, an attitude, or a sentiment, without having to provide details or issue substantive policies. Political symbols can then be defined as "the communication by political actors to others for a purpose, in which the specific object referred to conveys a larger range of meaning, typically with emotional, moral, or psychological impact. This larger meaning need not be independently or factually true, but will tap ideas people want to believe in as true."[126]

The landmark work of Barbara Hinckley was the first to fully apply the symbolic literature[127] to the presidents of the United States[128] and she demonstrated clear evidence that presidents do engage heavily in symbolic politics. The title of her book, *The Symbolic Presidency,* says it all.[129] Marion takes this material further to explain in categorical fashion why presidents engage in symbolic politics.[130] The first reason is that by conveying to the electorate that they are doing something about the problem, it enhances the popularity and electability of the president.[131] The second reason is because it allows the president to "reassure the public that something can be done to solve the problem quickly and easily."[132] Third, it allows the president to use simple symbolics to convey complex problems and solutions.[133] Fourth, it can "provide policy direction to states."[134] Fifth, it can provide a method for presidents to divert the attention of the public toward "more general concerns about unwelcome changes in the social order."[135] Sixth, it allows the president to issue moral imperatives,[136] and finally, it allows presidents to educate the public about the problem and the possible solutions.[137]

Presidents have most assuredly found the use of political symbols in the area of crime policy to be of significant value.[138] Scheingold has explained that "the symbolic forms that define the politicization of street crime are more salient in national than in local politics."[139] Several other authors have explained that crime was used in the early 1960s by "presidents and would-be presidents" who "used the crime issue for a short-term political advantage."[140] They further explain that "crime in the streets as a national issue was *manufactured* and milked by presidential candidates who began a sorry stream of symbolic politics rather than attending to practicalities and management in the war on crime."[141] As a result, presidents became engaged in the issue of street crime, but for the most part, they have dealt more with symbolic politics, rather than substantive politics. The reason for this focus being the role of the national government in crime-control policy is still somewhat limited and presidents have succeeded more in politicizing crime policy, rather than federalizing crime policy. As Scheingold has concluded, "the policy limitations of the politics of law and order are, in part, a product of the symbolic character of politicization."[142] Despite these limitations, presidents for nearly three decades have continued to draw upon the issue of crime and a large portion of their attention has been purely symbolic.

An example of the use of symbolic politics can be demonstrated through the Nixon presidency. During the presidential campaign of 1968, Nixon's campaign speeches were full of pledges to reduce the problem of crime in the nation.[143] It is reported that he told his aides, "scrape away all the crap and just pick three issues that will give us a sharp image" and that they "shouldn't be concerned if it is something we will actually accomplish . . . rather, we should look in terms of how we create issues. We need an enemy."[144] Upon entering office, Nixon listed only three areas upon which he wanted to concentrate domestically: crime, school integration, and economic matters.[145] Shortly thereafter, Nixon would realistically comment "that in the long run crime itself also requires much more far-reaching and subtle approaches." Yet he still believed that "the rapidly mounting urgency of the crime crisis . . . marks immediate, direct anti-crime measures as the first priority task."[146] Despite the efforts of the administration, as his Attorney General, John Mitchell, would lament, "even if the federal government found an indirect way of intervening in the problem, the local government would get the credit for diminishing those classes of crimes."[147] As a result, "the administration concluded that the only thing they could do was 'exercise vigorous symbolic-leadership.'" and they "therefore waged war on crime by adopting 'tough-sounding rhetoric' and pressing for largely ineffectual but highly symbolic legislation."[148] Four years later, President Nixon would speak often about the issues of crime with such statements as "we have fought the frightening trend of crime and anarchy to a standstill" and referencing the "war on drugs" he would emphatically state "we are winning this war."[149] He would continue to offer more empty symbolic rhetoric as typified by one radio address when he stated, "let us make the next four years a period of new respect for law, order, and justice in America, a time of new hope in a land free of fear and a world at peace."[150]

It is evident from these types of statements that crime easily lends itself to the use of symbolic politics. It is also evident that symbolic statements do not have to employ much in the way of truth or as Edelman has put it, "words that succeed and policies that fail."[151] Hinckley further explains that "some of the problems may not actually exist—they may be artifacts of false perceptions."[152] Marion has elaborated still further that "crime is an area where perceptions are, at times, more influential than reality" and "presidents can use symbolic language to address those perceptions."[153] As Donald Sanatarelli, the Associate Deputy Attorney General under President Nixon, explained:

> . . . the reach of the federal government's power in law enforcement does not penetrate to the state and local level . . . where most of the "street crime" people were afraid of existed . . . the federal government simply did not have the machinery or authority to deal with crime in America outside of the District of Columbia . . . in the rest of America, the only thing we could do was to exercise vigorous symbolic leadership.[154]

In sum, presidents, like Nixon, have come to capitalize on the issue of crime not so much because they can offer new substantive policies, but because it provides an issue full of rhetorical symbols.

A related explanation to the argument that crime is a symbolic issue comes from the fact that crime is also a valence issue. A valence issue can be defined as one in "which the overwhelming number of voters have a single position" and that "prevailing opinion is so strong that no opposing position seems possible."[155] The concept was actually first articulated by Butler and Stokes in their book *Political Change in Britain.*[156] The point these authors were trying to make was that most issues are position issues, where there are clearly two opposing viewpoints.[157] Examples in the area of crime and justice include the death penalty and gun control. We speak of pro-death penalty and anti-death penalty, as well as being either for or against gun control. As these authors would then explain, "such a distinction between *position* issues, on which the parties may appeal to rival bodies of opinion, and *valence* issues, on which there is essentially one body of opinion on values or goals, is too often neglected in political commentary."[158] As a result, a slow, but increased attention has been given to this concept.

In 1992, Stokes would expand upon the valence thesis.[159] He explained that a valence issue is one that does "not present even two alternative positions that divide the parties and leaders on the one hand and divide the electorate on the other."[160] In addition, "a valence issue can be displaced by a position issue if political debate centres on a disagreement as to the *means* to reach an agreed-upon end or if the public sees a trade-off between *two* high-consensus goals or ends."[161] Moreover, Stokes explains that we may "speak of a *valence politics,* in which the parties mount their appeals by choosing from a larger set of potential valence issues those on which their identification with positive symbols and their opponent's with negative symbols will be most to their advantage."[162] And finally he states, "valence issues typically involve pairs of positive and negative symbols."[163] In sum, valence issues are those issues upon which people demonstrate a consensus, but may disagree as to the means by which to address the issue and that politicians use these valence issues, coupled with symbolics, to make themselves appear positive, while their opponents are painted in a negative manner.

Crime is most assuredly a valence issue. As some authors have stated, "no one is for it; therefore being against it is a safe political issue."[164] As Jones has explained, "for a politician in an election to decry crime does not lead an opponent to defend it. Valence issues are important because politicians often link the raising of an issue to a policy solution; a crime wave demands harsher penalties."[165] This then feeds into the process whereby politicians utilize the positive and negative symbols by trying to paint their opponent as "soft on crime" and themselves as "tough on crime." What generally results is a consensus that crime is an important issue, but the debate then shifts to one centered on the means by which crime should be addressed. In generic terms, it falls into the punishment versus rehabilitation debate. Although the policy issue of crime is replete with many position issues, such as the death penalty and gun control, it is also teeming with many examples of valence issues, such as child abuse, alcohol abuse, and drug abuse, as well as the issue of "street crime" itself.[166]

Presidents have also played heavily on the fact that street crime is a valence issue. As Scheingold explains, "national politicians also have a strong incentive to politicize street crime . . . for them it provides a unifying theme and thus a valence issue."[167] As a result, "in national politics, especially presidential politics, street crime has been a valence issue—and more."[168] Scheingold further highlights the fact that "not only is there overwhelming agreement that street crime should be reduced, but it has the added attraction of arousing strong emotions—something capable of gaining a firm grip on the public imagination."[169] One such example illustrated by Jones, is the increased attention Vice-President Bush paid to the issue of drug abuse during his 1988 campaign and upon entering the office of the presidency, despite any evidence that there was in fact a drug epidemic.[170] He was successfully able to portray his opponent, Governor Michael Dukakis (D-MA), as "weak on crime" while strengthening his position as being "tough on crime." President Bush, in his first major television address on September 5, 1989, would then announce his "war on drugs." What occurred afterwards was an eight-fold increase in television coverage of the problem[171] and a thirty-six percent increase in drugs being listed as the "most important problem facing the country."[172] In the end, "a peak in awareness of the drug problem was caused primarily by presidential attention to it."[173] Bush had effectively used the valence issues of crime and drugs to not only win the office of the presidency, but to continue garnering support for addressing an issue which had little to no opposition.

Finally, a more deeply related explanation for why presidents have focused their attention on the issue of crime draws upon the symbolic and valence discussion to emphasize one of the most sinister, but effective uses of the crime issue, and that is to link the issue of crime with racism. There is a growing body of evidence that as the civil rights movement began to take hold, public sentiment toward minorities, predominately blacks, began to change. It was no longer politically feasible to openly decry blacks.[174] Research indicates that to some degree this phenomenon had been driven underground and replaced with an emphasis on decrying those social events that are perceived to be highly associated with blacks.[175] For instance, the issues of welfare and affirmative action are often associated with blacks and are decried by a large portion of Americans. What some research has begun to suggest is that negative opinions toward these policies are partly a result of masked racist sentiments.[176] In regard to crime, there is also a growing body of research that has begun to uncover this phenomenon, demonstrating that in many instances hatred for "criminals" and "drug abusers" is really a code-word for hatred towards blacks and other minorities.[177] As a result, presidents, whether intentionally or not, by focusing their attention on crime policy, may in reality be connecting racist sentiments with anti-crime sentiments. Hence, crime becomes a symbol for racism.

Although it is clearly difficult to disentangle the intent of the president in this regard, there is some evidence that this has been used by presidents as "a shorthand signal to a crucial group of white voters, for broader issues of social disorder, evoking powerful ideas about authority, status, morality, self-control, and race."[178] One clear example comes from the Nixon administration, in comments made by Nixon's two key advisors, Haldeman and Ehrlichman. Haldeman is quoted from an entry in his personal diary as saying: "He [President Nixon] emphasized that you have to face the fact that the whole problem is really the blacks. The key is to devise a system that recognizes this while not appearing to."[179] Ehrlichman, in describing the 1968 presidential campaign, explained, "We'll go after the racists. That subliminal appeal to the anti-black voter was always present in Nixon's statements and speeches."[180] In addition, various works by Michael Tonry have demonstrated that both Reagan and Bush were targeting issues of crime and drugs knowing there would be an "adverse differential effect on blacks" and that "the justification . . . [was] entirely political."[181] Finally, there is perhaps no better example of crime posited as a surrogate for race then the infamous 1988 presidential campaign commercial detailing the convicted rapist Willie Horton.[182]

In the television commercial, created by a pro-Bush political action committee, Willie Horton, a black male rapist was granted a weekend furlough by Bush's Democratic challenger, then Governor Michael Dukakis. During the weekend furlough, Willie Horton raped and murdered a white female victim. The commercial was designed to raise the issue of crime and make the statement that Dukakis was "soft on crime." While it succeeded in the endeavor, it also linked the issue of crime with the offender most often feared by white America, namely, a black male. As Jamieson explains, "the Horton story magnifies fear of crime, identifies that fear with Dukakis, and offers a surefire way of alleviating the anxiety—vote for Bush."[183] As a result, crime, in this case, became a surrogate for race-hatred and the two issues became linked. While it was not considered acceptable to voice negative attitudes towards blacks, it was perfectly acceptable to target negative attitudes toward criminals.

The Political Explanations

The political reasons for why presidents engage in crime-control policy present an interesting laundry list of explanations. In each of these explanations, presidents at one point or another are attempting to gain politically from their engagement in crime-control policy. While presidents may find themselves focused on only one of the political explanations detailed below, most likely these explanations are working in concert. Therefore, while all of these are important considerations for understanding why presidents engage in crime-control policy, one is not necessarily more important than the others. They all can be equally important explanations.

The first political explanation lies in the time period before a president assumes the office of the presidency—along the campaign trail. It is during this time period that many future presidents first begin utilizing the issue of crime for political purposes, namely to win votes. The use of substantive, symbolic, and valence politics is often very evident during presidential campaigns. As presidents are making promises about how they will govern, they are seeking to get their policy views communicated to the public, and they are always looking for new and innovative policies, primarily because the media is always looking for new and interesting stories.[184] As a result, crime policy has become a very attractive issue upon which to campaign. As Scheingold explains, "politicians ordinarily gain electoral success by telling the public what it wants to hear . . . when fear of street crime runs high, politicians have every reason to believe that the public is looking for promises to crack down on criminals fairly and expeditiously."[185] In fact, Milakovich and Weis go so far as to say, "well-publicized concern about the problem of crime is often a prerequisite for a successful political campaign in which crime, either an all-out war or a brush-fire response to an increase or a promised decrease, is made a key issue."[186] As crime is always an issue in the media, providing examples upon which to draw, crime has played a role in every presidential campaign since the 1964 election between Johnson and Goldwater.[187] It has also been demonstrated time and time again that crime provides a key issue upon which to propose new laws[188] and policy,[189] such as Clinton's "100,000 Cops" (substantive policy), to generate photo and campaign commercial opportunities,[190] such as the candidate being surrounded by uniformed police officers (symbolic politics), and to portray themselves as being "tough on crime" (valence politics).

There is, however, a nagging belief that once in office, presidents do not keep their promises and only utilize the issues and promises to get elected. As Scheingold has stated, "whether they realize it or not during the campaign, political candidates end up making promises that they cannot possibly keep."[191] If presidential candidates promised to end all crime or drugs, these are assuredly false promises, but in most cases presidents do try to live up to their campaign promises.[192] As a result, campaign promises to "get tough on crime" often result in policy proposals by the White House to do just that. As Egil Krogh, a policy advisor to President Nixon on the issue of crime, explains:

> The president had campaigned on his desire to reduce crime, to reduce crime nationwide. Crime had to be stopped. I don't think as a matter of intelligent politics he could have been in office for one year and then said, "I've discovered that the federal government has little jurisdiction over street crime . . . and therefore it is a matter for the states to handle. Good luck![193]

The effect that campaign promises have on the president's policy once elected is profound and anti-crime rhetoric is often translated into presidential policy proposals. Carried a little further, the resulting effect is "good campaign politics" translated into "good politics."[194] John Ehrlichman was clearly aware of this when, in January of 1972, an election year, the Nixon administration established the Office of Drug Abuse Law Enforcement (ODALE) to address the problem of street-level drug dealing. On February 8, 1972, Ehrlichman would write President Nixon that "the street pusher program is good politics and has widespread acceptance wherever it's talked about."[195] In sum, there are political benefits to be gained from presidential candidates campaigning on issues of "law and order," and these bene-fits continue when they are translated into policy proposals and carried into the Of-fice of the Presidency.

The second political explanation is closely related to the first, that both the national parties, Republican and Democrat, have included crime as part of their party platform since the 1960 election year.[196] In fact, while the first modern elec-tion party platforms to mention crime only consisted of a few phrases referencing "soaring crime rates," by the 1996 campaign, both parties reserved several pages to address the issue of crime and drugs.[197] Although many have concluded that party platforms should not be taken seriously because candidates use them to "run on" not to "stand on,"[198] there is some evidence that suggests presidents sometimes adhere to the party platform and that in many cases, presidents up for reelection essentially write the platforms.[199] While adhering to the party platform on crime can assuredly benefit the candidate in regard to the party members themselves, a unified party-president relationship on crime cannot hurt the president and may, in fact, by way of communicating the candidate's views on crime, provide a political benefit with the electorate.

The third political explanation deals with the type of policy in which crime can be categorized. Understanding how crime is dealt with at the federal level al-lows for a deeper comprehension of the reasons why presidents have focused on crime-control policy. According to Lowi, there is a simple understanding that government can either influence individuals or the environment and that its influ-ence can either be immediate or limited.[200] Lowi further explains that when gov-ernment coercion is likely to immediately affect individuals, the possibility for controversy is high and when the likelihood of coercion is limited, controversy is likely to be low.[201] What can be derived from this understanding are four policy categories which consist of regulatory, redistributive, distributive, and constituent policies.[202] When government is immediately coercive and intends to control in-dividual conduct, this type of policy is known as regulatory policy.[203] Govern-ment generally acts through the passage of laws and policies, as well as the cre-ation of regulatory agencies within the administration to implement these policies. When the government is being immediately coercive, but is attempting to influence the environment, this is known as redistributive policy, which most often comes in the form of a taxation of all citizens and the redistribution of said funds to a specific group of people.[204] When government coercion is low and it attempts to give benefits to a specific group for the sake of the award and not to shape conduct, this is known as distributive policy.[205] These types of "distributive programs allocate direct or indirect subsidies to a recipient in a manner that does not make one recipient's allocation dependent on what another recipient re-ceives."[206] Mayhew has referred to this as "particularized governmental bene-fits,"[207] while most people refer to it affectionately as "pork barrel politics." Fi-nally, when government is not being immediately coercive, but is trying to shape the environment, this is known as constituent policy, which many have come to call morality policy.[208] Crime has, in one form or fashion, been categorized as all four policy types.

Crime, for the most part, has long been considered an area of regulatory policy. Meier has suggested that crime-control efforts are obviously regulatory in nature when he stated, "at the state and local level, one major form of regulation is the legal restriction of criminal activity."[209] Spitzer has also explained that "crime control legislation, which usually includes specific prohibitions backed by firm sanctions, is classic regulatory policy."[210] Crime's relationship to regulatory policy is perhaps best explained in an historical framework. As Eisner has pointed out, "the history of regulation is the history of state economy relations and institutional change."[211] Crime's regulatory policy aspects are historically derived from its relationship, at the federal level, with the movement in the late nineteenth century to regulate interstate commerce. This would eventually lead to the creation, by President Theodore Roosevelt during the progressive era, of what would become the Federal Bureau of Investigation. As the Task Force on the Federalization of Criminal Law, sponsored by the American Bar Association, would explain, "the last third of the nineteenth century saw a significant increase in the assertion of federal jurisdiction, marked initially by a series of Congressional statutes dealing with the misuse of the mails and asserting federal jurisdiction in connection with interstate commerce."[212] The New Deal initiatives then created a new burst of federal regulation of crime, largely coming on the heels of the prohibition movement, with a specific flurry of dozens of crime bills in 1934 (see chapter one). Then, "almost four decades after the election of Franklin Roosevelt, the nation experienced another burst of regulatory policy-making"[213] and crime was no exception. Again, the Task Force explained that "in the 1960s and 1970s . . . concern with organized crime, drugs, street violence, and other social ills precipitated a particularly significant rise in federal legislation tending to criminalize activity involving more local conduct, conduct previously left to state regulation."[214] Dilulio has added that the federal government's role in crime also "grew as the power to regulate interstate commerce was more broadly interpreted by the U.S. Supreme Court."[215] Finally, we have seen "in the 1980s and 1990s, the trend to federalize crime has continued dramatically, covering more conduct formerly left exclusively to state prosecution."[216] What had started initially at the end of the nineteenth century as economic regulation, ultimately turned into an emphasis on social regulation in the 1960s and its expansion ever since.[217]

One explanation for presidential involvement can be explained as the simple fact that presidents have been swept up in this movement and that the expansion of regulation and the growth of the institutions that enforce the regulation have simply grown as a matter of course. The counterargument would be that presidents, like the two Roosevelts and Johnson, have been the orchestrators of this growth and they have done so for purposes of expanding the powers of government.[218] Another way of looking at it is from the perspective of Theodore Lowi, who explains:

> . . .a more consistent line of argument would be that both political parties had become committed to the positive, discretionary, liberal state and that each administration, regardless of party, was drawn into doing whatever seemed necessary to cope with the problems of this kind of state. Federal troops and federal regulators were drawn into local matters as the federal government became more and more involved in local transactions. This is inherent in the notion of establishing a national *presence.* Intervention at all levels is built into the logic of this situation, as President Bill Clinton confirmed with his war-on-crime proposals of 1994.[219]

Whichever explanation one finds more valid assists, albeit from different perspectives, in our understanding of why presidents have become engaged in crime control. The first would argue that it was just an outgrowth of the move to regulate all interstate commerce, while the latter would argue that it was to gain political power and increase the national "presence."

Another way of looking at crime policy has been to define it as having the qualities of being both morality and redistributive policy. Morality policy has been defined as one segment of society attempting by government fiat to impose their values on the rest of society.[220] In the case of crime, these may include such specific issues as drugs, alcohol, prostitution, and gambling—crimes that are often referred to as "victimless crimes."[221] In a sense, these issues can also be defined as redistributive policies in the sense that they are redistributing values rather than income.[222] However, these issues tend to be highly salient and often leave little room for expertise because information by one side is challenged by the other side or is often simply ignored. As a result, these are not issues that presidents obviously want to be drawn into because of their divisiveness and because they tend to split the electorate. But in many cases the salience of the issue forces them into a position to either "choose a side" or attempt to find some type of "common ground" where there often isn't any.

Finally, crime policy has also demonstrated many tendencies in the past forty years of resembling distributive policy. While crime has been defined as being "pork" by a variety of people,[223] it has evidently not been explored much in public policy studies. There is some evidence to suggest that one of the earliest crime policies, resulting from the Omnibus Crime Control and Safe Streets Act of 1968 which created the Law Enforcement Assistance Administration (LEAA) under the Department of Justice, was essentially a distributive policy. As Cronin, Cronin, and Milakovich explain, "not only were LEAA funds a generous pork barrel, but everyone seemed to have a piece of the action when it came to how LEAA was to be managed and even what it was supposed to do."[224] The more recent crime bill of 1994, The Violent Crime Control and Law Enforcement Act, created a similar agency known as the Office of Community Oriented Policing Services (COPS) within the Department of Justice and, for over six years, handed out grants for hiring, training, and equipment to any agency that applied. Since the beginning of the year 2000, over eight billion dollars in grants have been awarded to state and local agencies throughout the United States, suggesting that crime policy, at least in this case, fits the category of distributive policy.[225]

The benefits that a president can derive from this type of policy are clear. Because the distribution of this policy is not a zero-sum gain, primarily because "one recipient's allocation" is not "dependent on what another receives,"[226] this creates a win-win situation for the president in that not only can he credit claim for these "particularized benefits," but so can members of Congress. As a result there is a tendency to "distribute" these benefits universally, across all states, local governments, and, of course, throughout congressional districts. In the end then, it becomes clear that the only means by which presidents, and the federal government as a whole, can address the problem of crime is through either regulatory policy making coupled with administrative enforcement, or through policy funding.

The fourth political explanation for why presidents focus on crime results from their relationship with public opinion. It has been recognized by Brace and Hinckley that "public mobilization is critical if presidents are to succeed"[227] and this is equally true in the area of crime policy. There is, however, a transcendent advantage to mobilizing public opinion of crime—public opinion, or rather public fear of crime, has remained relatively steady and high over time.[228] In addition, crime is always a staple of the daily media. As a result, presidents have the capability of capitalizing on these facts by attempting to influence public opinion, thereby making the president's "visibility" on crime become the public's "visibility" on crime.[229] In other words, it is believed that presidents have the ability to influence public opinion of crime.

There is no doubt that presidents recognize this opportunity as a means to capitalize on the crime issue. Presidents since Johnson have routinely surrounded themselves with uniformed police officers for photo opportunities, and speeches to law enforcement groups have become a mainstay of the presidency. Egil Krogh, a key policy advisor on crime in the Nixon Administration, in a set of notes during a meeting with President Nixon in June of 1971, made the notation, "RN [Richard Nixon] shakes hands of <u>every</u> policeman he sees" and "must get more <u>PUBLIC</u> <u>recognition</u> of what is being done of <u>our</u> support for the police."[230] And, in the Ford Administration, a position paper was created on mandatory sentencing and it was commented that "by taking the lead on this issue, the President can: identify himself (with) concerns and fear held by very large parts of the population, demonstrate an ability to take decisive action, [and] place the Democrats in an extremely difficult situation. If they try to outbid him on the issue, they risk losing their civil libertarians left. If they oppose him, they risk being on the wrong side of public opinion. If they pass his program, he will have scored a major public triumph."[231] There is little doubt that presidents recognize this political power over public opinion, but the central question to this research still remains: do presidents influence public opinion of crime? Although it has been found that "federal state actors," of which the president is one, do influence public opinion of crime,[232] no research to date has explored the specific ability of the presidents to influence public opinion of crime.[233] This specific issue will be returned to in a later chapter.

The fifth political explanation is highly related to the last, as well as to many of the other explanations offered, and that is the president's relationship with the media. The president, by virtue of his office, has the full time and attention of the various forms of media. Whatever issue is on the president's agenda most often becomes the media's issue of the moment.[234] This actuality, coupled with the fact that most people receive their information through the media[235] and the media reports heavily on the issue of crime,[236] combines to form a relationship that, while difficult to untangle, most certainly has an effect upon the American people's perception of crime in the United States. As the president mainly communicates to the American people through the primary forms of media (e.g., television, radio, newspapers, and news magazines), the media, and the president's access to it, becomes a political explanation for why presidents focus on crime.

The sixth and final political explanation lies in the fact that over the past thirty years there have developed a number of interest groups related to the issue of crime and they have become more effective in influencing criminal justice policy.[237] While there are certainly the traditional interest groups that often find themselves embroiled in issues of crime-control policy such as the National Rifle Association, Handgun Control, Inc., and the American Civil Liberties Union, there are a number of well established and well organized interest groups that have specifically organized to deal with issues of crime.[238] Finally, a more recent development in this specific area is not the traditional interest group lobbying in which interest groups seek the support of the president, but rather a form of "reverse lobbying" where presidents seek the support of the interest groups.[239] This occurrence, while a relatively new method of public mobilization, was used by President Clinton in his attempts to garner support for his crime bill.

The Ideological Explanations

One final explanation for the law and order presidency comes simply from the possibility that presidents, whether it is something about their character or ideological world view, feel it is right to address the issue of crime. As Barber has explained, "character is the way the President orients himself toward life" and a "President's world view consists of his primary, politically relevant beliefs, particularly his conceptions of social causality, human nature, and the central moral conflicts of the time."[240] Therefore, it is possible that something within the president's life regarding the issue of crime may have had a profound impact in shaping his character, "not for the moment,"[241] but for life. Equally, the president's life shapes his assumptions and conceptions about how the world works, thus providing a specific world view in regard to crime and hence, as president, generates an ideological response to the issue.

An example of the issue of character can be seen in the life of President Ronald Reagan. There is the possibility that his character was shaped by both his parents and many of his early experiences. In regard to his parents, although he reports both as being loving and caring, it is reported his father was an alcoholic. This fact may have contributed to Reagan's profound hatred for drugs and addicts, contributing to his tough stance on drug abuse. One of his early experiences, described by Reagan in his autobiography, may also explain his future stance on crime and centers on his time as a lifeguard. As he explains:

> About my second year in high school, I got one of the best jobs I ever had: I began the first of seven summers working as a lifeguard at Lowell Park . . . I'd taken a course on lifesaving at the YMCA and when an opening for a lifeguard came up, I went to my old employer in the construction business and told him I was going to have to quit. I worked seven days a week, ten to twelve hours a day, for $15—later $20—a week and one of the proudest statistics in my life is seventy-seven—the number of people I saved during those seven summers.[242]

This concept of being the rescuer, the "lifesaver," can have a profound effect upon an individual and perhaps Reagan saw himself in this role. Hence, when the opportunity came to address problems of crime and drugs, he continued to see himself in this role. Finally, one has to wonder if Reagan's days as a film star, almost always playing the hero, did not have an impact upon his character, hence influencing his views on law and order.

Another example of how a dramatic incident can impact a president's life comes from the example of Franklin D. Roosevelt. As Governor of New York, he had received a kidnaping threat. As he explained in a letter to Joseph P. Kennedy, head of the Securities and Exchange Commission, "a kidnaping threat is not academic to me because we went through it two years ago and it is extremely unpleasant, to put it mildly."[243] This event may have contributed to Roosevelt's orientation toward the issue of crime and hence contributed to his administration's activity in this area.

Finally, a president's world view may influence his activity in the area of crime, but, more importantly, may also influence how he goes about addressing the issue. Calder, who has given this a much fuller treatment,[244] explains "that ideological predispositions restrict the President's ability to effect measurable reductions in ordinary crime."[245] As he further explains, "presidents are not unlike other people in that they arrive at their positions in life as a consequence of the actions and opportunities that they have capitalized on along the way. Their experiences and training have molded their beliefs that are subsequently incorporated in their policy positions."[246] By way of three case studies on the Kennedy, Johnson, and Nixon presidencies, Calder demonstrates that the first two, Kennedy and

The President Speaks . . .

Crime has become a malignant enemy in America's midst. Since 1940 the crime rate in this country has doubled. It has increased five times as fast as our population since 1958. In dollars the cost of crime runs to tens of billions annually. The human costs are simply not measurable.

The problems run deep and will not yield to quick and easy answers. We must identify and eliminate the causes of criminal activity whether they lie in the environment around us or deep in the nature of individual men. This is a major purpose of all we are doing in combating poverty and improving education, health, welfare, housing, and recreation.

President Lyndon Baines Johnson surrounded by the White House Uniformed Secret Service on November 22, 1968.

PHOTOGRAPH TAKEN BY WHITE HOUSE PHOTOGRAPHER FRANK WOLFE, COURTESY OF THE LYNDON BAINES JOHNSON LIBRARY, AUSTIN, TEXAS.

(continued)

The President Speaks . . . —cont.

All these are vital, but they are not enough. Crime will not wait while we pull it up by the roots. We must arrest and reverse the trend toward lawlessness.

This active combat against crime calls for a fair and efficient system of law enforcement to deal with those who break our laws. It means giving new priority to the methods and institutions of law enforcement:

—to our police, who are our front line, both offensive and defensive, in the fight against crime. There is a great need not only for improved training of policemen but for all people to learn about, to understand, and to assist the policeman in his work.

—to our courts, traditionally the symbol and guardian of our cherished freedoms. Local criminal courts are so overloaded that their functioning is impeded and their effectiveness weakened. More courts and judges is one answer, but every possibility of improvement must be explored.

—to our correctional agencies. We cannot tolerate an endless, self-defeating cycle of imprisonment, release, and reimprisonment which fails to alter undesirable attitudes and behavior. We must find ways to help the first offender avoid a continuing career of crime.

No right is more elemental to our society than the right to personal security and no right needs more urgent protection. Our streets must be safe. Our homes and places of business must be secure. Experience and wisdom dictate that one of the most legitimate functions of government is the preservation of law and order.

Our system rejects the concept of a national police force. The protection responsibilities lie primarily with state and local governments.

That is right and proper.

Yet, crime is no longer merely a local problem. Every city, every state is troubled by the same hard statistical—and human—facts. The extent and seriousness of the problem have made it of great national concern.

Crime is as old as history. It is hardly new to America. But in our increasingly mobile, urban society, crime problems are not only greater, they are immensely more complex.

We have not stood idly by in the face of these problems. Many cities and states, as well as the federal government, have developed new programs reflecting their growing concern.

Yet the crime rate continues to increase. The time has come now, to check that growth—to contain its spread—and to reduce its toll of lives and property.

I believe the way to do so is to give new recognition to the fact that crime is a national problem . . . That recognition does not carry with it any threat to the basic prerogatives of state and local governments. It means, rather, that the Federal Government will henceforth take a more meaningful role in meeting the whole spectrum of problems posed by crime.

It means that the Federal Government will seek to exercise leadership and to assist local authorities in meeting their responsibilities.

> It means that we will make a national effort to resolve the problems of law enforcement and the administration of justice—and to direct the attention of the Nation to the problems of crime and the steps that must be taken to meet them.
>
> This effort will involve great difficulties.
>
> It will not produce dramatic, visible results overnight. But it is an effort we must begin now.
>
> —*Lyndon B. Johnson*
> *Special Message to the Congress on Law Enforcement and the*
> *Administration of Justice, March 8, 1965.*

Johnson, had a functionalist ideology which caused them to view crime as resulting "from the inadequate socialization of the individual into the socially acceptable norms of the community."[247] Hence, their commitments to resolving the issue of crime centered on addressing the social environment, not specifically targeting criminals. Nixon, on the other hand, was demonstrated to have a mechanist ideology which viewed crime as being a result of "poor upbringing and insufficient moral guidance by the family and lack of respect for the law."[248] As a result, his commitment to resolving the crime problem was more of an enforcement of the laws and a demand for the respect of the law.

Conclusions

In conclusion, while it is difficult to explain why presidents engage in the various policies they do, and more particularly, why they would engage in the issue of crime, this chapter has attempted to outline some of the possibilities. Whether it is a part of the agenda-setting process or, more specifically, the president's agenda-setting process, crime has come to be a common issue with which the American president must contend. The key explanations consist of the facts that crime, in the form of a national crisis, demands the response of the president and that crime policy lends itself not only to substantive policy creation, but to the employment of symbolic and valence politics, as well as the more sinister creation of race-hatred disguised as crime-hatred.

In addition, the political explanations demonstrate that presidents engage in crime policy for purposes of obtaining political benefits, thus providing a still deeper understanding of why presidents engage in issues of crime. And finally, one last explanation that has been offered up which should not be summarily dismissed, is the possibility that a president's ideology may lead him to engage in issues of crime-control policy because it fits his world view and complements his personal character.

All of these explanations do not necessarily provide conclusive reasons why presidents engage in crime-control policy, nor, when taken as a whole, do they present a complete portrait of why presidents have focused on what was once primarily a state and local issue. However, what it does provide is some evidence to support the assumptions underlying the fact that presidents do focus on crime policy for specific reasons rather than being a random occurrence or happenstance. Recognizing this to be the case—that presidents do in fact have reasons for focusing on this issue of crime—it is important to understand how presidents have involved themselves in the area of crime-control policy and what they can do to affect this policy.

Endnotes

1. Hoover, Herbert. 1974. "Address to the Associated Press: Law Enforcement and Respect for the Law. April 22, 1929." *Public Papers of the Presidents of the United States*. Washington D.C.: U.S. G.P.O., p. 103.

2. Kingdon, John W. 1995. *Agendas, Alternatives, and Public Policies*. 2d ed. New York: Harper-Collins College Publishers, p. 3.

3. Ripley, Randall B. 1985. *Policy Analysis in Political Science*. New York: Nelson-Hall, Inc., p. 23.

4. Nelson, Barbara J. 1984. *Making an Issue of Child Abuse*. Chicago: University of Chicago Press, p. 20. Still others, such as Cobb and Elder have explained it "as a set of political controversies that will be viewed as falling within the range of legitimate concerns meriting the attention of the policy" and "a set of items scheduled for active and serious attention by a decision-making body." See Cobb, Roger W. and Charles D. Elder. 1972. *Participation in American Politics: The Dynamics of Agenda-Building*. Baltimore: The Johns Hopkins University Press; Cobb, Roger W. and Charles D. Elder. 1971. "The Politics of Agenda-Building." *Journal of Politics* 33(4): 892–915.

5. One critical point to understanding the topic of "problems" is the fact that we can generally conceive a variety of problems that need to be addressed, and once addressed, the problem becomes defined as an issue. Yet, it has been pointed out that in many cases issues do not begin so much as problems, but rather as conditions or situations. Conditions are those common events or occurrences that we "put up with" every day. They include such things as snowstorms, traffic delays, and reports of poverty in overseas countries. These "conditions become defined as problems when we come to believe that we should do something about them" (see Kingdon, John W. 1995. *Agendas, Alternatives, and Public Policies*. 2d ed. New York: HarperCollins College Publishers, pp. 109–110). This results in a better understanding of what is meant by a "problem" which can be defined as a "condition or situation that produces needs or dissatisfaction on the part of people for which relief or redress is sought" (see Anderson, James E. 1990. *Public Policymaking: An Introduction*. Boston: Houghton Mifflin, p. 78). Once identified as a problem there is a call for the item to be placed on the agenda in order that the "relief or redress" can be achieved. Thus it becomes a matter of placing the problem on the agenda.

6. Cobb, Roger W. and Charles D. Elder. 1972. *Participation in American Politics: The Dynamics of Agenda-Building*. Baltimore: The Johns Hopkins University Press, p. 3.

7. Cobb, Roger W. and Charles D. Elder. 1972. *Participation in American Politics: The Dynamics of Agenda-Building*. Baltimore: The Johns Hopkins University Press, p. 5.

8. Cobb, Roger W. and Charles D. Elder. 1972. *Participation in American Politics: The Dynamics of Agenda-Building*. Baltimore: The Johns Hopkins University Press, p. 6.

9. Marion, Nancy. 1992. "Presidential Agenda-setting in Crime Control." *Criminal Justice Policy Review* 6(2): 159–184, p. 179.

10. Marion, Nancy E. 1994. *A History of Federal Crime Control Initiatives, 1960–1993.* Westport: Praeger Publishers, pp. 3–6.

11. Patterson, Samuel C. and Keith R. Eakins. 1998. "Congress and Gun Control." In *The Changing Politics of Gun Control.* John M. Bruce and Clyde Wilcox, eds. Lanham: Rowman and Littlefield Publishers, Inc., pp. 45–73; Spitzer, Robert J. 1995. *The Politics of Gun Control.* Chatham: Chatham House Publishers, Inc., pp. 157–163. In addition to the issue of gun control, the attempted assassination of President Reagan also illustrates the movement of another issue from the systemic to the institutional agenda and that is the problem of the "insanity defense." Prior to the Reagan assassination attempt, the issue of the insanity defense was largely an academic issue. But once Reagan's would-be assassin, John Hinckley, utilized the defense to avoid a trial, the "problem" became widely debated, a consensus that something must be done was formed, and the national government had legitimate control over the use of the insanity defense for federal crimes. Eventually Congress would change the laws governing the use of the insanity defense and President Reagan would sign it into law. See Friedman, Lawrence M. 1993. *Crime and Punishment in American History.* New York: Basic Books, p. 405.

12. Downs, Anthony. 1972. "Up and Down with Ecology—The 'Issue Attention Cycle.'" *The Public Interest* 28(Summer): 38–50.

13. Downs, Anthony. 1972. "Up and Down with Ecology—The 'Issue Attention Cycle.'" *The Public Interest* 28(Summer): 38–50, pp. 40–41.

14. Nelson, Barbara J. 1984. *Making an Issue of Child Abuse.* Chicago: University of Chicago Press. Nelson herself offers up another understanding of the agenda-setting process which divides this process into four distinct stages: 1) issue recognition, 2) issue adoption, 3) issue prioritization, and 4) issue maintenance. In the first stage, a problem is recognized and, in the vein of Cobb and Elder, must be considered a legitimate issue for governmental intervention. The second stage however, presents a new consideration and that is whether or not the issue should be adopted. In this stage, government must determine if the issue has an appropriate response available. If so, the problem can move into the third stage where a re-ordering of the current agenda must be made so that government can accommodate the new problem. In the last stage, the issue advances into the process of decision making and as long as proposals are being considered, the issue is maintained on the agenda.

    Nelson's work, especially since it dealt with a criminal issue, namely child abuse, helps to build an understanding of the agenda-setting process. Because Nelson recognizes that issues must not only be recognized and adopted, but that the agenda must be reprioritized each time, it demonstrates that the issue must be seen as an important and significant issue, otherwise it will not find a place on the agenda. Because there is little doubt that crime, especially street crimes such as murder, rape, and robbery, is an important issue, demonstrating that some issues have a strong staying power. This may explain why crime is not necessarily a cyclical issue as in Downs' model, but one that has a distinctive staying power which has caused crime, at the national level, to become an issue that has been maintained for nearly four decades.

15. Bertram, Eva, Morris Blachman, Kenneth Sharpe, and Peter Andreas. 1996. *Drug War Politics: The Price of Denial.* Berkeley: University of California Press; Walker, Samuel. 1994. *Sense and Nonsense about Crime and Drugs: A Policy Guide.* 3d ed. Belmont: Wadsworth Publishing Company, p. 12.

16. Reiman, Jeffrey. 1995. *The Rich Get Richer and the Poor Get Prison: Ideology, Class, and Criminal Justice.* Boston: Allyn and Bacon, chapter one.

17. Cobb, Roger, Jennie-Keith Ross, and Marc Howard Ross. 1976. "Agenda Building as a Comparative Political Process." *American Political Science Review* 70: 126–138.

18. Cobb, Roger, Jennie-Keith Ross, and Marc Howard Ross. 1976. "Agenda Building as a Comparative Political Process." *The American Political Science Review* 70: 126–138, p. 127.

19. Cobb, Roger, Jennie-Keith Ross, and Marc Howard Ross. 1976. "Agenda Building as a Comparative Political Process." *The American Political Science Review* 70: 126–138, p. 128.

20. Walker, Samuel. 1994. *Sense and Nonsense about Crime and Drugs*: *A Policy Guide*. 3d ed. Belmont: Wadsworth Publishing Company, p. 12.

21. Baum, Dan. 1996. *Smoke and Mirrors*: *The War on Drugs and the Politics of Failure*. Boston: Little, Brown and Company; Caringella-MacDonald, Susan. 1990. "State Crises and the Crackdown on Crime under Reagan." *Contemporary Crises* 14: 91–118; Platt, Tony. 1987. "U.S. Criminal Justice in the Reagan Era: An Assessment." *Social Justice* 29: 58–69.

22. Kingdon, John W. 1984. *Agendas, Alternatives, and Public Policies*. Boston: Little, Brown and Company. See also Kingdon, John W. 1994. *Agendas, Alternatives, and Public Policies*. 2d ed. New York: HarperCollins College Publishers.

23. Kingdon, John W. 1994. *Agendas, Alternatives, and Public Policies*. 2d ed. New York: HarperCollins College Publishers, pp. 16–18.

24. For an excellent article on the importance of these three building blocks of political science: ideas, interests, and institutions, see Heclo, Hugh. 1994. "Ideas, Interests, and Institutions." In *The Dynamics of American Politics*: *Approaches and Interpretations*. Lawrence C. Dodd and Calvin Jillson, eds. Boulder: Westview Press, pp. 366–392.

25. Marion, Nancy E. 1994. *A History of Federal Crime Control Initiatives, 1960–1993*. Westport: Praeger Publishers; Marion, Nancy. 1992. "Presidential Agenda-setting in Crime Control." *Criminal Justice Policy Review* 6(2): 159–184; Scheingold, Stuart A. 1991. *The Politics of Street Crime*: *Criminal Process and Cultural Obsession*. Philadelphia: Temple University Press.

26. Chermak, Steven M. and Alexander Weiss. 1997. "The Effects of the Media on Federal Criminal Justice Policy." *Criminal Justice Policy Review* 8(4): 323–342.

27. Sharp, Elaine B. 1994. *The Dilemma of Drug Policy in the United States*. New York: HarperCollins College Publishers.

28. Baumgartner, Frank R. and Bryan D. Jones. 1993. *Agendas and Instability in American Politics*. Chicago: The University of Chicago Press.

29. Baumgartner, Frank R. and Bryan D. Jones. 1993. *Agendas and Instability in American Politics*. Chicago: The University of Chicago Press, pp. 31–32.

30. Baumgartner, Frank R. and Bryan D. Jones. 1993. *Agendas and Instability in American Politics*. Chicago: The University of Chicago Press, p. 4.

31. See also Meier, Kenneth J. 1994. *The Politics of Sin*: *Drugs, Alcohol and Public Policy*. Armonk: M. E. Sharpe.

32. Baumgartner, Frank R. and Bryan D. Jones. 1993. *Agendas and Instability in American Politics*. Chicago: The University of Chicago Press, chapter eight. For the issue of child abuse, see also Nelson, Barbara J. 1984. *Making an Issue of Child Abuse*. Chicago: University of Chicago Press.

33. Jones, Bryan D. 1994. *Reconceiving Decision-Making in Democratic Politics*: *Attention, Choice and Public Policy*. Chicago: The University of Chicago Press, chapter five.

34. Baumgartner, Frank R. and Bryan D. Jones. 1993. *Agendas and Instability in American Politics*. Chicago: The University of Chicago Press, p. 155.

35. Baumgartner, Frank R. and Bryan D. Jones. 1993. *Agendas and Instability in American Politics*. Chicago: The University of Chicago Press, p. 35.

36. Kingdon, John W. 1994. *Agendas, Alternatives, and Public Policies.* 2d ed. New York: Harper-Collins College Publishers, p. 23.

37. Kingdon, John W. 1994. *Agendas, Alternatives, and Public Policies.* 2d ed. New York: Harper-Collins College Publishers, p. 23.

38. Shull, Steven A. 1983. *Domestic Policy Formation*: *Presidential-Congressional Partnership?* Westport: Greenwood Press, p. 17.

39. Miroff, Bruce. 1982. "Monopolizing the Public Space: The President as a Problem for Democratic Politics." In *Rethinking the Presidency.* Edited by Thomas Cronin. Boston: Little, Brown, and Company, pp. 218–232.

40. Bosso, Christopher. 1987. *Pesticides and Politics*: *The Life Cycle of a Public Issue.* Pittsburgh: University of Pittsburgh Press, p. 261.

41. Bosso, Christopher. 1987. *Pesticides and Politics*: *The Life Cycle of a Public Issue.* Pittsburgh: University of Pittsburgh Press, p. 261.

42. Light, Paul C. 1991. *The President's Agenda*: *Domestic Policy Choice from Kennedy to Reagan.* Revised Edition. Baltimore: The Johns Hopkins University Press.

43. Light, Paul C. 1991. *The President's Agenda*: *Domestic Policy Choice from Kennedy to Reagan.* Revised Edition. Baltimore: The Johns Hopkins University Press, p. 1.

44. Light, Paul C. 1991. *The President's Agenda*: *Domestic Policy Choice from Kennedy to Reagan.* Revised Edition. Baltimore: The Johns Hopkins University Press, pp. 2–3.

45. Light, Paul C. 1991. *The President's Agenda*: *Domestic Policy Choice from Kennedy to Reagan.* Revised Edition. Baltimore: The Johns Hopkins University Press, chapter one.

46. Light, Paul C. 1991. *The President's Agenda*: *Domestic Policy Choice from Kennedy to Reagan.* Revised Edition. Baltimore: The Johns Hopkins University Press, p. 15.

47. Kingdon, John W. 1994. *Agendas, Alternatives, and Public Policies.* 2d ed. New York: Harper-Collins College Publishers, pp. 24–27.

48. Light, Paul C. 1991. *The President's Agenda*: *Domestic Policy Choice from Kennedy to Reagan.* Revised Edition. Baltimore: The Johns Hopkins University Press, p. 15.

49. Light, Paul C. 1991. *The President's Agenda*: *Domestic Policy Choice from Kennedy to Reagan.* Revised Edition. Baltimore: The Johns Hopkins University Press, chapter two.

50. Light, Paul C. 1991. *The President's Agenda*: *Domestic Policy Choice from Kennedy to Reagan.* Revised Edition. Baltimore: The Johns Hopkins University Press, chapter two.

51. Light, Paul C. 1991. *The President's Agenda*: *Domestic Policy Choice from Kennedy to Reagan.* Revised Edition. Baltimore: The Johns Hopkins University Press, chapter three.

52. Light, Paul C. 1991. *The President's Agenda*: *Domestic Policy Choice from Kennedy to Reagan.* Rev. ed. Baltimore: The Johns Hopkins University Press, chapter four.

53. Light, Paul C. 1991. *The President's Agenda*: *Domestic Policy Choice from Kennedy to Reagan.* Rev. ed. Baltimore: The Johns Hopkins University Press, chapter five.

54. Light, Paul C. 1991. *The President's Agenda*: *Domestic Policy Choice from Kennedy to Reagan.* Rev. ed. Baltimore: The Johns Hopkins University Press, chapter five.

55. Light, Paul C. 1991. *The President's Agenda*: *Domestic Policy Choice from Kennedy to Reagan.* Rev. ed. Baltimore: The Johns Hopkins University Press, chapter six.

56. Light, Paul C. 1991. *The President's Agenda*: *Domestic Policy Choice from Kennedy to Reagan.* Rev. ed. Baltimore: The Johns Hopkins University Press, chapter seven.

57. Generally the research has focused on individual presidents and their specific agenda on crime. For Hoover, see Calder, James D. 1981. "Herbert Hoover's Contributions to the Administrative History of Crime Control Policy." Unpublished paper presented at the annual meeting of the Southwest Political Science Association, Dallas, Texas; Calder, James D. 1993. *The Origins and Development of Federal Crime Control Policy*: *Herbert Hoover's Initiatives.* Westport: Praeger Publishers. For Johnson, see Cronin, Thomas E., Tania Z. Cronin, and Michael E.

Milakovich. 1981. *U.S. v. Crime in the Streets*. Bloomington: Indiana University Press. For Ford, see Felkenes, George T. 1993. "Domestic Tranquility: President Ford's Policy Positions on Criminal Justice Issues." *Presidential Studies Quarterly* 23(3): 519–532; Felkenes, George T. 1992. "Liberty, Restraint, and Criminal Justice: Gerald Ford's Presidential Concerns." *Journal of Criminal Justice* 20: 147–160. For Reagan, see Caringella-MacDonald, Susan. 1990. "State Crises and the Crackdown on Crime under Reagan." *Contemporary Crises* 14: 91–118; Platt, Tony. 1987. "U.S. Criminal Justice in the Reagan Era: An Assessment." *Social Justice* 29: 58–69. For Clinton, see Poveda, Tony G. "Clinton, Crime and the Justice Department." *Social Justice* 21(3): 73–84. For specifics on the Presidents and Drug policy, see Bertram, Eva, Morris Blachman, Kenneth Sharpe, and Peter Andreas. 1996. *Drug War Politics: The Price of Denial*. Berkeley: University of California Press, chapter six, entitled "Presidential Drug Wars and the Narco-Enforcement Complex." In most other instances, the issue of Presidents and Crime is presented in terms of the political process rather than focusing on a specific president and his crime-control policies.

58. Calder, James D. 1982. "Presidents and Crime Control: Kennedy, Johnson, and Nixon and the Influences of Ideology." *Presidential Studies Quarterly* 12: 574–589; Calder, James D. 1978. *Presidents and Crime Control: Some Limitations on Executive Policy Making*. Ph.D. Dissertation, Claremont University.

59. Marion, Nancy E. 1994. *A History of Federal Crime Control Initiatives*, 1960–1993. Westport: Praeger Publishers; Marion, Nancy E. 1992. "Presidential Agenda-setting in Crime Control." *Criminal Justice Policy Review* 6: 159–184; Marion, Nancy E. 1997. "Symbolic Policies in Clinton's Crime Control Agenda." *Buffalo Criminal Law Review* 1(1): 67–108; Marion, Nancy E. 1994. "Symbolism and Federal Crime Control Legislation, 1960–1994." *Journal of Crime and Justice* 17: 69–91.

60. Calder, James D. 1978. *Presidents and Crime Control: Some Limitations on Executive Policy Making*. Ph.D. Dissertation, Claremont University.

61. Calder, James D. 1982. "Presidents and Crime Control: Kennedy, Johnson, and Nixon and the Influences of Ideology." *Presidential Studies Quarterly* 12: 574–589.

62. Calder, James D. 1978. *Presidents and Crime Control: Some Limitations on Executive Policy Making*. Ph.D. Dissertation, Claremont University, p. 163.

63. Calder cites Professor Gerald I. Jordan in regard to the "functionalist-cooperative model" being defined as a model "which claims that social change derives from the cooperation of all of the elements of the government and the citizenry." Calder, James D. 1978. *Presidents and Crime Control: Some Limitations on Executive Policy Making*. Ph.D. Dissertation, Claremont University, p. 162.

64. Calder cites Professor Gerald I. Jordan in regard to the "mechanist-conflict model" being defined as a model "which generally asserts a bipolar relationship between the individual and government and which envisions the wishes of the nation being met as long as the branches of government remain in a competitive state." Calder, James D. 1978. *Presidents and Crime Control: Some Limitations on Executive Policy Making*. Ph.D. Dissertation, Claremont University, p. 162.

65. Calder, James D. 1982. "Presidents and Crime Control: Kennedy, Johnson, and Nixon and the Influences of Ideology." *Presidential Studies Quarterly* 12: 574–589; Calder, James D. 1978. *Presidents and Crime Control: Some Limitations on Executive Policy Making*. Ph.D. Dissertation, Claremont University.

66. Marion, Nancy E. 1992. "Presidential Agenda Setting in Crime Control." *Criminal Justice Policy Review* 6: 159–184.

67. Marion, Nancy E. 1992. "Presidential Agenda Setting in Crime Control." *Criminal Justice Policy Review* 6: 159–184, p. 165.

68. Marion, Nancy E. 1992. "Presidential Agenda Setting in Crime Control." *Criminal Justice Policy Review* 6: 159–184. Marion reported the averages in the following table:

President	Average # of Speeches	Average # of Non-Election Speeches
Kennedy (D)	11.0	11.0
Johnson (D)	28.6	27.2
Nixon (R)	27.8	21.2
Ford (R)	20.7	18.3
Carter (D)	8.8	8.8
Reagan (R)	41.5	37.4
Bush (R)	119.5	99.5

69. Marion, Nancy E. 1992. "Presidential Agenda Setting in Crime Control." *Criminal Justice Policy Review* 6: 159–184. Marion reported the averages in the following table:

President	Average # of Detailed Speeches	Average # of Non-Election Detailed Speeches
Kennedy (D)	5.0	5.0
Johnson (D)	17.0	17.0
Nixon (R)	12.2	12.2
Ford (R)	12.0	12.0
Carter (D)	6.0	6.0
Reagan (R)	19.3	19.3
Bush (R)	38.5	38.5

70. Marion, Nancy E. 1992. "Presidential Agenda Setting in Crime Control." *Criminal Justice Policy Review* 6: 159–184. Marion reported the following as the top three issues by president:

President	#1 Issue	#2 Issue	#3 Issue
Kennedy	Juveniles	Civil Rights	Legislation/General
Johnson	Law Enforcement	General	Grants
Nixon	Drugs	Law Enforcement	Organized Crime/General
Ford	Drugs	Mand. Sentencing	Grants
Carter	Personnel	Grants	General
Reagan	Drugs	International	Law Enforcement
Bush	Drugs	International	Law Enforcement

71. Marion, Nancy E. 1992. "Presidential Agenda Setting in Crime Control." *Criminal Justice Policy Review* 6: 159–184, p. 179.
72. Marion, Nancy E. 1992. "Presidential Agenda Setting in Crime Control." *Criminal Justice Policy Review* 6: 159–184, p. 179.
73. Marion, Nancy E. 1992. "Presidential Agenda Setting in Crime Control." *Criminal Justice Policy Review* 6: 159–184, p. 181.
74. Marion, Nancy E. 1992. "Presidential Agenda Setting in Crime Control." *Criminal Justice Policy Review* 6: 159–184, p. 182.

75. Marion, Nancy E. 1994. "Symbolism and Federal Crime Control Legislation, 1960–1994." *Journal of Crime and Justice* 17: 69–91.

76. Marion, Nancy E. 1994. *A History of Federal Crime Control Initiatives, 1960–1993*. Westport: Praeger Publishers.

77. Marion, Nancy E. 1997. "Symbolic Policies in Clinton's Crime Control Agenda." *Buffalo Criminal Law Review* 1(1): 67–108. In this article she provides a detailed list of Clinton's agenda by year, indicating the number of mentions for each topic. Using her information, the top issues for Clinton by year are as follows:

Year	#1 Issue	#2 Issue	#3 Issue
1993	100,000 Cops	Brady Bill	Crime Bill Passage
1994	Crime Bill Passage	100,000 Cops	Assault Weapons Ban
1995	100,000 Cops	Crime Bill	OK Bombing/Drugs/Assault Weapons Ban
1996	100,000 Cops	Youth Crime/Gangs	Brady Bill

78. Bosso, Christopher. 1987. *Pesticides and Politics: The Life Cycle of a Public Issue*. Pittsburgh: University of Pittsburgh Press, p. 261.

79. Kernell, Samuel. 1997. *Going Public: New Strategies of Presidential Leadership*. 3d ed. Washington D.C.: Congressional Quarterly Press.

80. Brace, Paul and Barbara Hinckley. 1992. *Follow the Leader: Opinion Polls and the Modern Presidents*. New York: Basic Books, pp. 27–30.

81. Calder, James D. 1993. *The Origins and Development of Federal Crime-control policy: Herbert Hoover's Initiatives*. Westport: Praeger Publishers, pp. 198–203.

82. Flamm, Michael William. 1998. *"Law and Order": Street Crime, Civil Disorder, and the Crisis of Liberalism*. Ph.D. Dissertation, Columbia University; Scruggs, Donald Lee. 1980. *Lyndon Baines Johnson and the National Advisory Commission on Civil Disorders (The Kerner Commission): A Study of the Johnson Domestic Policy Making System*. Ph.D. Dissertation, University of Oklahoma.

83. Johnson, Lyndon Baines. 1971. *The Vantage Point: Perspectives of the Presidency, 1963–1969*. New York: Holt, Rinehart and Winston, p. 549.

84. Light, Paul C. 1991. *The President's Agenda: Domestic Policy Choice from Kennedy to Reagan*. Rev. ed. Baltimore: The Johns Hopkins University Press, p. 69.

85. Feeley, Malcolm and Austin D. Sarat. 1980. *The Policy Dilemma: Federal Crime Policy and the Law Enforcement Assistance Administration*. Minneapolis: University of Minnesota Press, p. 19.

86. Lowi, Theodore J. 1979. *The End of Liberalism: The Second Republic of the United States*. 2d ed. New York: W.W. Norton and Company, pp. 292–294.

87. President's Commission on Law Enforcement and Administration of Justice. 1968. *The Challenge of Crime in a Free Society*. New York: Avon Books.

88. As Freda Adler, past president of the Academy of Criminal Justice Sciences, explains "the LEEP fund program which, for the first time, brought education and training into the various organs of government that are concerned with crime control" and that the "LEAA spent $7 billion." She then goes on to say, "let us never forget that without that massive expenditure of government funds, our profession would not exist, our schools and programs would have remained pipe dreams." See Adler, Freda. 1995. "Who are We? A Self-Analysis of Criminal Justice Specialists." *ACJS Today*. 14(1): 1–21, p. 1. Also, another past-president of the Academy of Criminal Justice Sciences has stated, "Undoubtedly the Law Enforcement Assistance Administration, or

LEAA, was the catalyst for the expansion of undergraduate programs. It was also instrumental in the creation of doctoral programs at John Jay College of Criminal Justice, the University of Albany, and Michigan State University." See Hale, Donna C. 1998. "Presidential Address: Delivered at the 34th Annual Meeting of the Academy of Criminal Justice Sciences, Louisville, Kentucky, March 1997. Criminal Justice Education: Traditions in Transition." *Justice Quarterly* 15(3): 385–394, p. 387.

89. Donziger, Steven R. 1996. *The Real War on Crime*: *The Report of the National Criminal Justice Commission*. New York: Harper Perennial, chapters two and three; Schlosser, Eric. 1998. "The Prison-Industrial Complex." *The Atlantic Monthly* (December): 51–77.

90. Barlow, David E., Melissa Hickman-Barlow, and W. Wesley Johnson. 1996. "The Political Economy of Criminal Justice Policy: A Time-Series Analysis of Economic Conditions, Crime, and Federal Criminal Justice Legislation, 1948–1987. *Justice Quarterly* 13 (2): 223–241; Dilulio, John J., Steven K. Smith, and Aaron J. Saiger. 1995. "The Federal Role in Crime Control." In *Crime*. James Q. Wilson and Joan Petersilia, eds. San Francisco: ICS Press; Gray, Virginia and Bruce Williams. 1980. *The Organizational Politics of Criminal Justice*: Policy in Context. Lexington: Lexington Books.

91. Caldeira, Gregory A. 1983. "Elections and the Politics of Crime: Budgetary Choices and Priorities in America." *In The Political Science of Criminal Justice*. Stuart Nagel, Erika Fairchild, and Anthony Champagne, eds. Springfield: Charles C. Thomas Publishers, pp. 238–252, p. 239. See also Caldeira, Gregory A. and Andrew T. Cowart. 1980. "Budgets, Institutions, and Change: Criminal Justice Policy in America." *American Journal of Political Science* 24: 413–438.

92. Baumgartner, Frank R. and Bryan D. Jones. 1993. *Agendas and Instability in American Politics*. Chicago: The University of Chicago Press, p. 169.

93. Notes of James C. Gaither with cover letter entitled "Summary Description of the Safe Streets and Crime Control Act of 1968" which was addressed "For the Files" by "James C. Gaither." December 10, 1966. Box 1. White House Central Files, Legislative Background of Safe Streets Act. Lyndon Baines Johnson Presidential Library.

94. Notes of Ian MacDonald. Letter entitled "Departments and Agencies with Drug Abuse Program Responsibilities." July 1981. Box 19057. White House Staff and Office Files, Ian MacDonald. Ronald Reagan Presidential Library.

95. Congressional Digest. 1994. "The Federal Role in Crime Control." *Congressional Digest* 73(No. 6/7): 161–192.

96. Congressional Digest. 1994. "The Federal Role in Crime Control." *Congressional Digest* 73(No. 6/7): 161–192. Note: this figure did not take into account inflation of the dollar.

97. Maguire, Kathleen and Ann L. Pastore. 1998. *Bureau of Justice Statistics Sourcebook of Criminal Justice Statistics—1997*. Washington D.C.: U.S. Department of Justice.

98. The use of 1979 and 1991 constant dollars were utilized to assess the inflation of the dollar.

99. Caldeira, Gregory A. and Andrew T. Cowart. 1980. "Budgets, Institutions, and Change: Criminal Justice Policy in America." *American Journal of Political Science* 24: 413–438; Caldeira, Gregory A. 1983. "Elections and the Politics of Crime: Budgetary Choices and Priorities in America." In *The Political Science of Criminal Justice*. Stuart Nagel, Erika Fairchild, and Anthony Champagne, eds. Springfield: Charles C. Thomas Publishers, pp. 238–252, p. 239.

100. Office of National Drug Control Policy. *National Drug Control Strategy*, 1996. Washington D.C.: U.S. G.P.O.

101. Chambliss, William J. 1994. "Policing the Ghetto Underclass: The Politics of Law and Law Enforcement." *Social Problems* 41(2): 177–194.

102. Chambliss, William J. 1994. "Policing the Ghetto Underclass: The Politics of Law and Law Enforcement." *Social Problems* 41(2): 177–194, pp. 183–184.

103. Bertram, Eva, Morris Blachman, Kenneth Sharpe, and Peter Andreas. 1996. *Drug War Politics*: *The Price of Denial*. Berkeley: University of California Press, chapter six, titled "Presidential Drug Wars and the Narco-Enforcement Complex."

104. Donziger, Steven R. 1996. *The Real War on Crime*: *The Report of the National Criminal Justice Commission*. New York: Harper Perennial, chapter three, titled "Fear, Politics, and the Prison-Industrial Complex"; Schlosser, Eric. 1998. "The Prison-Industrial Complex." *The Atlantic Monthly* 282(6): 51–77.

105. Ashdown, Gerald G. 1996. "Federalism, Federalization, and the Politics of Crime." *West Virginia Law Review* 98: 789–813; Task Force on the Federalization of Criminal Law. 1998. *The Federalization of Criminal Law*. Washington D.C.: American Bar Association.

106. Ashdown, Gerald G. 1996. "Federalism, Federalization, and the Politics of Crime." *West Virginia Law Review* 98: 789–813. As examples, Ashdown cites the Omnibus Crime Control and Safe Streets Act of 1968, the Organized Crime Control Act of 1970, the Comprehensive Drug Abuse Prevention and Control Act of 1970, the Comprehensive Crime Control Act of 1984, the Anti-Drug Abuse Act of 1986, the Anti-Drug Abuse Act of 1988, the Crime Control Act of 1990, and the Violent Crime Control and Law Enforcement Act of 1994.

107. Platt, Tony. 1987. "U.S. Criminal Justice in the Reagan Era: An Assessment." *Social Justice* 29: 58–69.

108. Cited in Kaminer, Wendy. 1994. "Federal Offense." *The Atlantic Monthly* (June): 102–114, p. 105.

109. Potter, Claire Bond. 1998. *War on Crime*: *Bandits, G-Men, and the Politics of Mass Culture*. New Brunswick: Rutgers University Press.

110. Potter, Claire Bond. 1998. *War on Crime*: *Bandits, G-Men, and the Politics of Mass Culture*. New Brunswick: Rutgers University Press.

111. Lowi, Theodore J. 1979. *The End of Liberalism*: *The Second Republic of the United States*. 2d ed. New York: W.W. Norton and Company, pp. 276–277.

112. Notes of James C. Gaither with cover letter entitled "Summary Description of the Safe Streets and Crime Control Act of 1968" which was addressed "For the Files" by "James C. Gaither." December 10, 1966. Box 1. White House Central Files, Legislative Background of Safe Streets Act. Lyndon Baines Johnson Presidential Library.

113. Notes of James C. Gaither with cover letter entitled "Summary Description of the Safe Streets and Crime Control Act of 1968" which was addressed "For the Files" by "James C. Gaither." December 3, 1966. Box 1. White House Central Files, Legislative Background of Safe Streets Act. Lyndon Baines Johnson Presidential Library.

114. Senate Subcommittee on Investigations. Testimony of John Ehrlichman on July 28, 1976. As cited in Baum, Dan. 1996. *Smoke and Mirrors*: *The War on Drugs and the Politics of Failure*. Boston: Little, Brown and Company, p. 67.

115. Mahoney, Barry. 1976. *The Politics of the Safe Streets Act, 1965–1973: A Case Study in Evolving Federalism and the National Legislative Process*. Ph.D. Dissertation, Columbia University, p. 298.

116. Foucault, Michel. 1977. *Discipline and Punish*: *The Birth of the Prison*. New York: Vintage Press, p. 189. This citation was first discovered in Lyons, William. 1999. *The Politics of Community Policing*: *Rearranging the Power to Punish*. Ann Arbor: The University of Michigan Press, p. 11.

117. Lyons, William. 1999. *The Politics of Community Policing*: *Rearranging the Power to Punish*. Ann Arbor: The University of Michigan Press, p. 11.

118. Marion, Nancy E. 1997. "Symbolic Policies in Clinton's Crime Control Agenda." *Buffalo Criminal Law Review* 1(1): 67–108, p. 103.

119. Marion, Nancy E. 1997. "Symbolic Policies in Clinton's Crime Control Agenda." *Buffalo Criminal Law Review* 1(1): 67–108, p. 104.

120. Marion, Nancy E. 1997. "Symbolic Policies in Clinton's Crime Control Agenda." *Buffalo Criminal Law Review* 1(1): 67–108, p. 104.

121. Marion, Nancy E. 1994. *A History of Federal Crime Control Initiatives*, 1960–1993. Westport: Praeger Publishers; Marion, Nancy E. 1992. "Presidential Agenda Setting in Crime Control." *Criminal Justice Policy Review* 6: 159–184; Marion, Nancy E. 1997. "Symbolic Policies in Clinton's Crime Control Agenda." *Buffalo Criminal Law Review* 1(1): 67–108; Marion, Nancy. 1994. "Symbolism and Federal Crime Control Legislation, 1960–1990." *Journal of Crime and Justice* 17(2): 69–91.

122. Gusfield, Joseph. 1963. *Symbolic Crusade: Status Politics and the American Temperance Movement*. Urbana: University of Illinois Press.

123. Edelman, Murray. 1988. *Constructing the Political Spectacle*. Chicago: The University of Chicago Press; Edelman, Murray. 1964. *The Symbolic Uses of Politics*. Urbana: University of Illinois Press; Edelman, Murray. 1971. *Politics as Symbolic Action*: Mass Arousal and Quiescence. Chicago: Markham Publishing Company.

124. Edelman, Murray. 1964. *The Symbolic Uses of Politics*. Urbana: University of Illinois Press, p. 6.

125. Edelman, Murray. 1988. *Constructing the Political Spectacle*. Chicago: The University of Chicago Press, p. 8.

126. Hinckley, Barbara. 1990. *The Symbolic Presidency: How Presidents Portray Themselves*. New York: Routledge, Chapman, and Hall, Inc., p. 7.

127. Hinckley draws primarily upon the following works: Edelman, Murray. 1988. *Constructing the Political Spectacle*. Chicago: The University of Chicago Press; Edelman, Murray. 1964. *The Symbolic Uses of Politics*. Urbana: University of Illinois Press; Edelman, Murray. 1971. *Politics as Symbolic Action: Mass Arousal and Quiescence*. Chicago: Markham Publishing Company; Elder, Charles and Roger Cobb. 1983. *The Political Uses of Symbols*. New York: Longman; Novak, Michael. 1974. *Choosing Our King: Powerful Symbols in Presidential Politics*. New York: Macmillan. For additional works, see Hinckley's Bibliography, section 1, titled "Symbolic Politics: General." Hinckley, Barbara. 1990. *The Symbolic Presidency: How Presidents Portray Themselves*. New York: Routledge, Chapman, and Hall, Inc., pp. 183–184.

128. Hinckley draws upon a number of works that had previously dealt with presidents and symbolics, many of which focused on presidential rhetoric. Several key works included: Ceaser, James et al. 1981. "The Rise of the Rhetorical Presidency." *Presidential Studies Quarterly* (Spring): 158–171; Dallek, Robert. 1984. *Ronald Reagan and the Politics of Symbolism*. Cambridge: Harvard University Press; Hart, Roderick. 1984. "The Language of the Modern Presidency." *Presidential Studies Quarterly* 14(2): 249–264; Ragsdale, Lyn. 1984. "The Politics of Presidential Speechmaking." *American Political Science Review* 78: 971–984; Ragsdale, Lyn. 1987. "Presidential Speechmaking and the Public Audience." *Journal of Politics* 49(3): 704–736; Tulis, Jeffrey. 1987. *The Rhetorical Presidency*. Princeton: Princeton University Press; Windt, Theodore. 1983. *Presidential Rhetoric: 1961 to the Present*. 3d ed. Dubuque: Kendall-Hunt. For additional works, see Hinckley's Bibliography, section 2, titled "Presidents and Symbolic Politics." Hinckley, Barbara. 1990. *The Symbolic Presidency: How Presidents Portray Themselves*. New York: Routledge, Chapman, and Hall, Inc., pp. 184–186.

129. Hinckley, Barbara. 1990. *The Symbolic Presidency: How Presidents Portray Themselves*. New York: Routledge, Chapman, and Hall, Inc.

130. Marion, Nancy E. 1997. "Symbolic Policies in Clinton's Crime Control Agenda." *Buffalo Criminal Law Review* 1(1): 67–108; Marion, Nancy. 1994. "Symbolism and Federal Crime Control Legislation, 1960–1990." *Journal of Crime and Justice* 17(2): 69–91.

131. Marion, Nancy E. 1997. "Symbolic Policies in Clinton's Crime Control Agenda." *Buffalo Criminal Law Review* 1(1): 67–108, p. 67; Marion, Nancy. 1994. "Symbolism and Federal Crime Control Legislation, 1960–1990." *Journal of Crime and Justice* 17(2): 69–91, p. 70.

132. Marion, Nancy E. 1997. "Symbolic Policies in Clinton's Crime Control Agenda." *Buffalo Criminal Law Review* 1(1): 67–108, p. 68. See also Elder, Charles D. and Roger G. Cobb. 1983. *Political Uses of Symbols*. New York: Longman Press, pp. 13–15; Marion, Nancy. 1994. "Symbolism and Federal Crime Control Legislation, 1960–1990." *Journal of Crime and Justice* 17(2): 69–91, p. 70; Stolz, Barbara A. 1983. "Congress and Capital Punishment." *Law and Policy Quarterly* 5: 157–180, p. 176.

133. Cronin, Thomas E., Tania Z. Cronin, and Michael Milakovich. 1981. *U.S. v. Crime in the Streets*. Bloomington: Indiana University Press, p. 170; Marion, Nancy E. 1997. "Symbolic Policies in Clinton's Crime Control Agenda." *Buffalo Criminal Law Review* 1(1): 67–108, p. 68.

134. Marion, Nancy E. 1997. "Symbolic Policies in Clinton's Crime Control Agenda." *Buffalo Criminal Law Review* 1(1): 67–108, p. 68; Marion, Nancy. 1994. "Symbolism and Federal Crime Control Legislation, 1960–1990." *Journal of Crime and Justice* 17(2): 69–91, p. 71; Stolz, Barbara A. 1992. "Congress and the War on Drugs: An Exercise in Symbolic Politics." *Journal of Crime and Justice* 15(1): 119–136.

135. Scheingold, Stuart A. 1984. *The Politics of Law and Order*. New York: Longman Press, p. 226; Marion, Nancy. 1994. "Symbolism and Federal Crime Control Legislation, 1960–1990." *Journal of Crime and Justice* 17(2): 69–91, p. 71.

136. Marion, Nancy E. 1997. "Symbolic Policies in Clinton's Crime Control Agenda." *Buffalo Criminal Law Review* 1(1): 67–108, p. 67; Stolz, Barbara A. 1992. "Congress and the War on Drugs: An Exercise in Symbolic Politics." *Journal of Crime and Justice* 15(1): 119–136.

137. Marion, Nancy E. 1997. "Symbolic Policies in Clinton's Crime Control Agenda." *Buffalo Criminal Law Review* 1(1): 67–108, p. 68; Marion, Nancy. 1994. "Symbolism and Federal Crime Control Legislation, 1960–1990." *Journal of Crime and Justice* 17(2): 69–91, p. 71.

138. Cronin, Thomas E., Tania Z. Cronin, and Michael Milakovich. 1981. *U.S. v. Crime in the Streets*. Bloomington: Indiana University Press; Hagan, John. 1983. "The Symbolic Politics of Criminal Sanctions." In *The Political Science of Criminal Justice*. Stuart Nagel, Erika Fairchild, and Anthony Champagne, eds. Springfield: Charles C. Thomas Publishers; Marion, Nancy E. 1994. *A History of Federal Crime Control Initiatives, 1960–1993*. Westport: Praeger Publishers; Marion, Nancy E. 1997. "Symbolic Policies in Clinton's Crime Control Agenda." *Buffalo Criminal Law Review* 1(1): 67–108; Marion, Nancy. 1994. "Symbolism and Federal Crime Control Legislation, 1960–1990." *Journal of Crime and Justice* 17(2): 69–91; Rosch, Joel. 1985. " Crime as an Issue in American Politics." In *The Politics of Crime and Criminal Justice*. Erika S. Fairchild and Vincent J. Webb, eds. Beverly Hills: Sage Publications; Scheingold, Stuart A. 1984. *The Politics of Law and Order*. New York: Longman Press; Scheingold, Stuart A. 1991. *The Politics of Street Crime: Criminal Process and Cultural Obsession*. Philadelphia: Temple University Press; Stolz, Barbara A. 1992. "Congress and the War on Drugs: An Exercise in Symbolic Politics." *Journal of Crime and Justice* 15(1): 119–136.

139. Scheingold, Stuart A. 1991. *The Politics of Street Crime: Criminal Process and Cultural Obsession*. Philadelphia: Temple University Press, p. 177.

140. Cronin, Thomas E., Tania Z. Cronin, and Michael Milakovich. 1981. *U.S. v. Crime in the Streets*. Bloomington: Indiana University Press, p. 170.

141. Cronin, Thomas E., Tania Z. Cronin, and Michael Milakovich. 1981. *U.S. v. Crime in the Streets*. Bloomington: Indiana University Press, p. 170.

142. Scheingold, Stuart A. 1984. *The Politics of Law and Order. New York*: Longman Press, p. 87.

143. Cronin, Thomas E., Tania Z. Cronin, and Michael Milakovich. 1981. *U.S. v. Crime in the Streets*. Bloomington: Indiana University Press.

144. Cited in Carter, Dan. 1995. *The Politics of Rage*. New York: Simon and Schuster, p. 398.

145. Burke, John P. 1992. *The Institutional Presidency*. Baltimore: The Johns Hopkins University Press, p. 71.

146. From Nixon's speech on crime in the District of Columbia, November 1970. Cited in Cronin, Thomas E., Tania Z. Cronin, and Michael Milakovich. 1981. *U.S. v. Crime in the Streets*. Bloomington: Indiana University Press, p. 83.

147. Cited in Epstein, Edward. 1977. *Agency of Fear: Opiates and Political Power in America*. New York: Random House, p. 65.

148. Beckett, Katherine and Theodore Sasson. 2000. *The Politics of Injustice: Crime and Punishment in America*. Thousand Oaks: Pine Forge Press, p. 58.

149. Nixon, Richard M. 1974. "Radio Address on Crime and Drug Abuse. October 15, 1972." *Public Papers of the Presidents of the United States*. Washington D.C.: U.S. G.P.O., pp. 982–986.

150. Nixon, Richard M. 1974. "Radio Address on Crime and Drug Abuse. October 15, 1972." *Public Papers of the Presidents of the United States*. Washington D.C.: U.S. G.P.O., pp. 982–986.

151. Edelman, Murray. 1977. *Political Language: Words that Succeed and Policies that Fail*. New York: Academic Press.

152. Hinckley, Barbara. 1990. *The Symbolic Presidency: How Presidents Portray Themselves*. New York: Routledge, Chapman, and Hall, Inc., p. 144.

153. Marion, Nancy. 1994. "Symbolism and Federal Crime Control Legislation, 1960–1990." *Journal of Crime and Justice* 17(2): 69–91, p. 88.

154. Schell, Jonathan. 1976. *The Time of Illusion*. New York: Alfred A. Knopf, p. 45.

155. Jones, Bryan D. 1994. *Reconceiving Decision-Making in Democratic Politics: Attention, Choice, and Public Policy*. Chicago: The University of Chicago Press, p. 106.

156. Butler, David and Donald Stokes. 1974. *Political Change in Britain: The Evolution of Electoral Choice*. 2d ed. New York: Macmillan.

157. Butler, David and Donald Stokes. 1974. *Political Change in Britain: The Evolution of Electoral Choice*. 2d ed. New York: Macmillan.

158. Butler, David and Donald Stokes. 1974. *Political Change in Britain: The Evolution of Electoral Choice*. 2d ed. New York: Macmillan, p. 292.

159. Stokes, Donald. 1992. "Valence Politics." In *Electoral Politics*. Edited by Dennis Kavanagh. Oxford: Clarendon Press.

160. Stokes, Donald. 1992. "Valence Politics." In *Electoral Politics*. Edited by Dennis Kavanagh. Oxford: Clarendon Press, p. 144.

161. Stokes, Donald. 1992. "Valence Politics." In *Electoral Politics*. Edited by Dennis Kavanagh. Oxford: Clarendon Press, p. 145.

162. Stokes, Donald. 1992. "Valence Politics." In *Electoral Politics*. Edited by Dennis Kavanagh. Oxford: Clarendon Press, p. 146.

163. Stokes, Donald. 1992. "Valence Politics." In *Electoral Politics*. Edited by Dennis Kavanagh. Oxford: Clarendon Press, p. 146.

164. Kappeler, Victor E., Mark Blumberg, and Gary W. Potter. 1996. *The Mythology of Crime and Criminal Justice*. 2d ed. Prospect Heights: Waveland Press, Inc., p. 49.

165. Jones, Bryan D. 1994. *Reconceiving Decision-Making in Democratic Politics: Attention, Choice, and Public Policy*. Chicago: The University of Chicago Press, p. 106.

166. Jones, Bryan D. 1994. *Reconceiving Decision-Making in Democratic Politics: Attention, Choice, and Public Policy*. Chicago: The University of Chicago Press; Baumgartner, Frank R. and Bryan D. Jones. 1993. *Agendas and Instability in American Politics*. Chicago: The University of Chicago Press; Meier, Kenneth J. 1994. *The Politics of Sin: Drugs, Alcohol, and Public Policy*. Armonk: M. E. Sharpe; Nelson, Barbara J. 1984. *Making an Issue of Child Abuse: Political Agenda-setting for Social Problems*. Chicago: University of Chicago Press.

167. Scheingold, Stuart A. 1991. *The Politics of Street Crime: Criminal Process and Cultural Obsession*. Philadelphia: Temple University Press, p. 178.

168. Scheingold, Stuart A. 1995. "Politics, Public Policy, and Street Crime." *The Annals of the American Academy of Political and Social Sciences* 539: 155–168, p. 166.

169. Scheingold, Stuart A. 1995. "Politics, Public Policy, and Street Crime." *The Annals of the American Academy of Political and Social Sciences* 539: 155–168, p. 166.

170. Jones, Bryan D. 1994. *Reconceiving Decision-Making in Democratic Politics: Attention, Choice, and Public Policy.* Chicago: The University of Chicago Press, chapter five.

171. Barrett, Paul. 1990. "Moving On: Though the Drug War Isn't Over, Spotlight Turns to Other Issues." *Wall Street Journal* 11(November); Jones, Bryan D. 1994. *Reconceiving Decision-Making in Democratic Politics: Attention, Choice, and Public Policy.* Chicago: The University of Chicago Press, p. 107.

172. The three previous Gallup poll surveys asking respondents "What is the most important problem facing the country" received a 27 percent response of "Drug Abuse." These polls were conducted on May 7, 1989; July 21, 1989; and August 4, 1989. The President's speech was on September 5, 1989, and on September 10, 1989, when asked the same question, the response citing "Drug Abuse" rose to 63 percentage points. Drugs were, for the first time in the history of the Gallup poll, the "most important problem." See Gallup, George. 1945–1996. *The Gallup Poll: Public Opinion.* Wilmington: Scholarly Resources, Inc.; *The Gallup Organization Homepage*, "Gallup Social and Economic Indicators—Most Important Problem." http://www.gallup.com/poll/indicators/indmip.asp. Data obtained January 2000; Maguire, Kathleen and Ann L. Pastore. 1998. *Sourcebook of Criminal Justice Statistics 1997.* Washington D.C.: Bureau of Justice Statistics.

173. Jones, Bryan D. 1994. *Reconceiving Decision-Making in Democratic Politics: Attention, Choice, and Public Policy.* Chicago: The University of Chicago Press, p. 107.

174. Alvarez, R. Michael and John Brehm. 1997. "Are Americans Ambivalent Towards Racial Policies?" *American Journal of Political Science* 41(2): 345–374; Bobo, Lawrence and James R. Kluegal. 1993. "Opposition to Race Targeting: Self-Interest, Stratification Ideology, or Racial Attitudes?" *American Sociological Review* 58: 443–464; Sniderman, Paul M. and Thomas Piazza. 1993. *The Scar of Race.* Cambridge: Harvard University Press; Sniderman, Paul M., Thomas Piazza, Philip E. Tetlock, and Ann Kendrick. 1991. "The New Racism." *American Journal of Political Science* 35: 423–447.

175. Edsall, Thomas Bryne and Mary D. Edsall. 1991. *Chain Reaction: The Impact of Race, Rights, and Taxes on American Politics.* New York: W.W. Norton.

176. Gilens, Martin. 1995. "Radial Attitudes and Opposition to Welfare." *The Journal of Politics* 57(4): 994–1014; Kuklinksi, James H., Paul M. Sniderman, Kathleen Knight, Thomas Piazza, Philip E. Tetlock, Gordon R. Lawrence and Barbara Mellers. 1997. "Racial Prejudice and Attitudes Toward Affirmative Action." *American Journal of Political Science* 41(2): 402–419; Peffley, Mark, Jon Hurwitz, and Paul M. Sniderman. 1997. "Racial Stereotypes and Whites' Political Views of Blacks in the Context of Welfare and Crime." *American Journal of Political Science* 41(1): 30–60.

177. Barkan, Steven E. and Steven F. Cohn. 1998. "Racial Prejudice and Support by Whites for Police Use of Force: A Research Note." *Justice Quarterly* 15(4): 743–753; Gaubatz, Kathlyn Taylor. 1995. *Crime in the Public Mind.* Ann Arbor: The University of Michigan Press; Hurwitz, Jon and Mark Peffley. 1997. "Public Perceptions of Race and Crime: The Role of Racial Stereotypes." *American Journal of Political Science* 41(2): 375–401; Leyden, Kevin M., John C. Kilwein, and Willard M. Oliver. 1996. "Public Opinion and Crime: Who Fears Crime and Why?" Unpublished paper presented at the Northeastern Political Science Association's annual meeting, Boston, Massachusetts; Meier, Kenneth J. 1990. "The Politics of Drug Abuse: Laws, Implementation and Consequences." *The Western Political Quarterly* 45: 41–69; Meier, Kenneth J. 1994. *The Politics of Sin: Drugs, Alcohol, and Public Policy.* Armonk: M. E. Sharpe; Oliver, Willard M., Kevin M. Leyden, and John C. Kilwein. 1997. "Drowning: The

Subterfuge of Race by the Issue of Crime." Unpublished paper presented at the Southern Criminal Justice Association's annual meeting, Richmond, Virginia; Omni, Michael and Howard Winant. 1986. *Racial Formation in the United States.* New York: Routledge; Peffley, Mark, Jon Hurwitz, and Paul M. Sniderman. 1997. "Racial Stereotypes and Whites' Political Views of Blacks in the Context of Welfare and Crime." *American Journal of Political Science* 41(1): 30–60; Peffley, Mark, Todd Shields, and Bruce Williams. 1996. "The Intersection of Race and Crime in Television News Stories: An Experimental Study." *Political Communication* 13: 309–327.

178. Edsall, Thomas Bryne and Mary D. Edsall. 1991. "Race." *The Atlantic Monthly* 267(5): 77.

179. Cited in Baum, Dan. 1996. *Smoke and Mirrors: The War on Drugs and the Politics of Failure.* Boston: Little, Brown, and Company, p. 13.

180. Ehrlichman, John. 1982. *Witness to Power: The Nixon Years.* New York: Simon & Schuster, p. 233.

181. Tonry, Michael. 1995. *Malign Neglect: Race, Crime, and Punishment in America.* New York: Oxford University Press; Tonry, Michael. 1994. "Racial Politics, Racial Disparities, and the War on Crime." *Crime & Delinquency* 40(4) 475–494. See also Donziger, Steven R. 1996. *The Real War on Crime: The Report of the National Criminal Justice Commission.* New York: Harper Perennial, chapter four, titled "Race and Criminal Justice" and Walker, Samuel, Cassia Spohn, and Miriam DeLone. 1996. *The Color of Justice: Race, Ethnicity, and Crime in America.* Belmont: Wadsworth Publishing Company.

182. For an excellent discussion of the Willie Horton commercial and its political ramifications, see Jamieson, Kathleen Hall. 1992. *Dirty Politics: Deception, Distraction, and Democracy.* New York: Oxford University Press.

183. Jamieson, Kathleen Hall. 1992. *Dirty Politics: Deception, Distraction, and Democracy.* New York: Oxford University Press, p. 41.

184. Patterson, Thomas E. 1994. *Out of Order.* New York: Vintage Books.

185. Scheingold, Stuart A. 1984. *The Politics of Law and Order: Street Crime and Public Policy.* New York: Longman, p. 87.

186. Milakovich, Michael E., and Kurt Weis. 1975. "Politics and Measures of Success in the War on Crime." *Crime and Delinquency* 21(1): 1–10, p. 3.

187. Marion, Nancy E. 1995. *A Primer in The Politics of Criminal Justice.* New York: Harrow and Heston, chapter seven, titled "Campaigns, Elections, and the Issue of Crime."

188. Task Force on the Federalization of Criminal Law, American Bar Association, Criminal Justice Section. 1998. *The Federalization of Criminal Law.* Washington D.C.: American Bar Association.

189. Marion, Nancy E. 1994. *A History of Federal Crime Control Initiatives, 1960–1993.* Westport: Praeger Publishers.

190. Jamieson, Kathleen Hall. 1992. *Dirty Politics: Deception, Distraction, and Democracy.* New York: Oxford University Press; West, Darrell M. 1997. *Air Wars: Television Advertising in Election Campaigns 1952–1996.* 2d ed. Washington D.C.: Congressional Quarterly Press.

191. Scheingold, Stuart A. 1984. *The Politics of Law and Order: Street Crime and Public Policy.* New York: Longman, p. 87.

192. Fishel, Jeff. 1985. *Presidents and Promises: From Campaign Pledge to Presidential Performance.* Washington D.C.: Congressional Quarterly Press, p. 38; Patterson, Thomas E. 1994. *Out of Order.* New York: Vintage Books, p. 12.

193. Quoted in Epstein, Edward J. 1977. *Agency of Fear.* New York: G. P. Putnam's Sons, pp. 225–226.

194. See Faucheux, Ron. 1994. "The Politics of Crime." *Campaigns & Elections* (March): 30–34.

195. See papers of John Ehrlichman. Memorandum from John Ehrlichman to President Nixon, titled "The Street Pusher Program." Dated February 8, 1972. Nixon Project, College Park, Maryland.

196. See National Party Platform, Democratic Platform, and National Party Platform, Republican Platform. 1960–1996. Platforms obtained from World Book Encyclopedia. 1998. *American Reference Library*. CD-ROM. Orem: The Western Standard Publishing Company.

197. See National Party Platform, Democratic Platform, and National Party Platform, Republican Platform. 1960–1996. Platforms obtained from World Book Encyclopedia. 1998. *American Reference Library*. CD-ROM. Orem: The Western Standard Publishing Company. This is clearly an area where more research is needed to comprehend not only how the issue of crime has expanded on the party platforms, but to see how the policy stances have converged over time and how closely presidents have adhered to this specific portion of the party platform.

198. Thomas, Norman C., and Joseph A. Pika. 1996. *The Politics of the Presidency*. 4th ed. Washington D.C.: Congressional Quarterly Press, p. 135.

199. Fishel, Jeff. 1985. *Presidents and Promises: From Campaign Pledge to Presidential Performance*. Washington D.C.: Congressional Quarterly Press; Pomper, Gerald and Susan Lederman. 1980. *Elections in America: Control and Influence in Democratic Politics*. 2d ed. New York: Longman.

200. Lowi, Theodore J. 1964. "American Business, Public Policy, Case Studies, and Political Theory." *World Politics* 16(July): 677–715; Lowi, Theodore J. 1972. "Four Systems of Policy, Politics, and Choice." *Public Administration Review* 32(July/August): 298–310; Meier, Kenneth J. 1993. *Politics and the Bureaucracy: Policymaking in the Fourth Branch of Government*. 3d ed. Belmont: Wadsworth Publishing Company, chapter four.

201. Lowi, Theodore J. 1964. "American Business, Public Policy, Case Studies, and Political Theory." *World Politics* 16(July): 677–715; Lowi, Theodore J. 1972. "Four Systems of Policy, Politics, and Choice." *Public Administration Review* 32(July/August): 298–310; Meier, Kenneth J. 1993. *Politics and the Bureaucracy: Policymaking in the Fourth Branch of Government*. 3d ed. Belmont: Wadsworth Publishing Company, chapter four.

202. Lowi, Theodore J. 1964. "American Business, Public Policy, Case Studies, and Political Theory." *World Politics* 16(July): 677–715; Lowi, Theodore J. 1972. "Four Systems of Policy, Politics, and Choice." *Public Administration Review* 32(July/August): 298–310; Meier, Kenneth J. 1993. *Politics and the Bureaucracy: Policymaking in the Fourth Branch of Government*. 3d ed. Belmont: Wadsworth Publishing Company, chapter four.

203. Lowi, Theodore J. 1964. "American Business, Public Policy, Case Studies, and Political Theory." *World Politics* 16(July): 677–715; Lowi, Theodore J. 1972. "Four Systems of Policy, Politics, and Choice." *Public Administration Review* 32(July/August): 298–310; Meier, Kenneth J. 1993. *Politics and the Bureaucracy: Policymaking in the Fourth Branch of Government*. 3d ed. Belmont: Wadsworth Publishing Company, chapter four; Ripley, Randall and Grace A. Franklin. 1991. *Congress, the Bureaucracy and Public Policy*. California: Brooks/Cole Publishers, p. 21; Stein, Robert M. and Kenneth M. Bickers. 1995. *Perpetuating the Pork Barrel*. Cambridge: Cambridge University Press, p. 17.

204. Lowi, Theodore J. 1964. "American Business, Public Policy, Case Studies, and Political Theory." *World Politics* 16(July): 677–715; Lowi, Theodore J. 1972. "Four Systems of Policy, Politics, and Choice." *Public Administration Review* 32(July/August): 298–310; Meier, Kenneth J. 1993. *Politics and the Bureaucracy: Policymaking in the Fourth Branch of Government*. 3d ed. Belmont: Wadsworth Publishing Company, chapter four.

205. Lowi, Theodore J. 1964. "American Business, Public Policy, Case Studies, and Political Theory." *World Politics* 16(July): 677–715; Lowi, Theodore J. 1972. "Four Systems of Policy, Politics, and Choice." *Public Administration Review* 32(July/August): 298–310; Meier, Kenneth J. 1993. *Politics and the Bureaucracy: Policymaking in the Fourth Branch of Government*. 3d ed. Belmont: Wadsworth Publishing Company, chapter four.

206. Stein, Robert M. and Kenneth M. Bickers. 1995. *Perpetuating the Pork Barrel*. Cambridge: Cambridge University Press, p. 17.

207. Mayhew, David R. 1974. *Congress: The Electoral Connection*. New Haven: Yale University Press, pp. 53–54.

208. See Bryner, Gary. 1998. *Politics and Public Morality*. New York: W.W. Norton and Company, Inc.; Mooney, Christopher Z. 2000. *The Public Clash of Private Values: The Politics of Morality Policy*. New York: Seven Bridges Press.

209. Meier, Kenneth J. 1993. *Politics and the Bureaucracy: Policymaking in the Fourth Branch of Government*. 3d ed. Belmont: Wadsworth Publishing Company, p. 83.

210. Spitzer, Robert J. 1987. "Promoting Policy Theory: Revising the Arenas of Power." *Policy Studies Journal* 15: 675–689, p. 677.

211. Eisner, Marc Allen. 1993. *Regulatory Politics in Transition*. Baltimore: The Johns Hopkins University Press, p. 202.

212. Task Force on the Federalization of Criminal Law. 1998. *The Federalization of Criminal Law*. Washington D.C.: American Bar Association, p. 6.

213. Eisner, Marc Allen. 1993. *Regulatory Politics in Transition*. Baltimore: The Johns Hopkins University Press, p. 204.

214. Task Force on the Federalization of Criminal Law. 1998. *The Federalization of Criminal Law*. Washington D.C.: American Bar Association, p. 7.

215. Dilulio, John J., Jr. 1999. "Federal Crime Policy: Time for a Moratorium." *Brookings Review* 17(1): 17–21, p. 17.

216. Task Force on the Federalization of Criminal Law. 1998. *The Federalization of Criminal Law*. Washington D.C.: American Bar Association, p. 7.

217. Tatalovich, Raymond and Bryon Daynes. 1998. *Moral Controversies in American Politics*. Armonk: M. E. Sharpe Inc.; Tatalovich, Raymond and Bryon Daynes. 1988. *Social Regulatory Policy*. Boulder: Westview Press.

218. For a similar argument, couched in terms of Democratic and Republican views, see Lowi, Theodore J. 1995. *The End of the Republican Era*. Norman: University of Oklahoma Press, p. 57.

219. Lowi, Theodore J. 1995. *The End of the Republican Era*. Norman: University of Oklahoma Press, p. 57. See also Lowi, Theodore J. 1979. *The End of Liberalism: The Second Republic of the United States*. 2d ed. New York: W.W. Norton and Company, p. 116.

220. Gusfield, Joseph R. 1963. *Symbolic Crusade: Status Politics and the American Temperance Movement*. Urbana: University of Illinois Press.

221. Meier, Robert F. and Gilbert Geis. 1997. *Victimless Crimes?* Los Angeles: Roxbury Publishing Company; Schurr, Edwin M. 1965. *Crimes Without Victims*. Englewood Cliffs: Prentice Hall.

222. Tatalovich, Raymond and Bryon Daynes. 1988. *Social Regulatory Policy*. Boulder: Westview Press.

223. E.g., Klein, Joe. 1994. "Crime Bill Garbage Barge." *Newsweek* 123 (February 28): 35.

224. Cronin, Thomas E., Tania Z. Cronin, and Michael E. Milakovich. 1981. *U.S. v. Crime in the Streets*. Bloomington: Indiana University Press, p. 172.

225. Leyden, Kevin M., Willard M. Oliver, and John C. Kilwein. 1999. "Is Crime-control policy Another Form of Pork Barrel Politics?" Unpublished paper presented at the annual meeting of the Western Political Science Association, Seattle, Washington.

226. Stein, Robert M. and Kenneth M. Bickers. 1995. *Perpetuating the Pork Barrel*. Cambridge: Cambridge University Press, p. 17.

227. Brace, Paul and Barbara Hinckley. 1992. *Follow the Leader: Opinion Polls and the Modern Presidency*. New York: Basic Books, p. 82.

228. Flanagan, Timothy J. and Dennis R. Longmire. 1996. *Americans View Crime and Justice: A National Public Opinion Survey*. Thousand Oaks: SAGE Publications; Mayer, William G. 1995. *The Changing American Mind: How and Why American Public Opinion Changed Between*

1960 and 1988. Ann Arbor: The University of Michigan Press; Page, Benjamin I. and Robert Y. Shapiro. 1992. *The Rational Public: Fifty Years of Trends in Americans' Policy Preferences.* Chicago: The University of Chicago Press; Warr, Mark. 1995. "The Polls—Poll Trends: Public Opinion on Crime and Punishment." *Public Opinion Quarterly* 59: 296–310.

229. Foucault, Michel. 1977. *Discipline and Punish: The Birth of the Prison.* New York: Vintage Press, p. 189. This citation was first discovered in Lyons, William. 1999. *The Politics of Community Policing: Rearranging the Power to Punish.* Ann Arbor: The University of Michigan Press, p. 11.

230. Handwritten Notes of Egil Krogh. "Meeting with President and other." June 3, 1971. White House Special Files. Staff Member and Office Files. Box 32. Egil Krogh, 1969–1973. Nixon Project. College Park, Maryland.

231. "Crime Theme." Files of James E. Connor, Staff Secretary. "Crime Message." Box 9. White House Staff Member and Office Files. Ford Library. Ann Arbor, Michigan.

232. Beckett, Katherine. 1994. "Setting the Public Agenda: 'Street Crime' and Drug Use in American Politics." *Social Problems* 41(3): 425–447.

233. The one exception, not withstanding, is an earlier publication of this research. See Oliver, Willard M. 1998. "Presidential Rhetoric on Crime and Public Opinion." *Criminal Justice Review* 23(2): 139–160.

234. Brace, Paul and Barbara Hinckley. 1992. *Follow the Leader: Opinion Polls and the Modern Presidency.* New York: Basic Books; Cornwell, Elmer E. 1965. *Presidential Leadership of Public Opinion.* Bloomington: Indiana University Press; Grossman, Michael B. and Martha Joynt. 1981. *The White House and the News Media.* Baltimore: The Johns Hopkins University Press; Hess, Stephen. 2000. "I Am On TV Therefore I Am." In *Media Power in Politics.* Doris A. Graber, ed. Washington D.C.: Congressional Quarterly Press, pp. 246–254. Rubin, Richard. 1981. *Press, Party, and Presidency.* New York: W.W. Norton and Company.

235. Graber, Doris. 1980. *Crime News and the Public.* New York: Praeger Publishers; Graber, Doris. 1989. *Mass Media and American Politics.* Washington D.C.: Congressional Quarterly Press.

236. Graber, Doris. 1980. *Crime News and the Public.* New York: Praeger Publishers; Kaiser Family Foundation/Center for Media and Public Affairs Report. 1998. *Assessing Local Television News Coverage of Health Issues.* Menlo Park: The Henry J. Kaiser Family Foundation; Surette, Ray. *Media, Crime, and Criminal Justice: Images and Realities.* 2d ed. Belmont: West/Wadsworth Publishers.

237. Melone, Albert P. and Robert Slagter. 1983. "Interest Group Politics and the Reform of the Criminal Code." In *The Political Science of Criminal Justice.* Erika Fairchild and Anthony Champagne, eds. Springfield: Charles C. Thomas Publishers, pp. 41–55; Shaiko, Ronald G. 1998. "Reverse Lobbying: Interest Group Mobilization from the White House and the Hill." In *Interest Group Politics.* 5th ed. Washington, D.C.: Congressional Quarterly Press, pp. 255–282.

238. See appendix in Houston, James and William W. Parsons. 1998. *Criminal Justice and the Policy Process.* Chicago: Nelson-Hall Publishers.

239. Shaiko, Ronald G. 1998. "Reverse Lobbying: Interest Group Mobilization from the White House and the Hill." In *Interest Group Politics.* 5th ed. Washington, D.C.: Congressional Quarterly Press, pp. 255–282.

240. Barber, James David. 1992. *The Presidential Character: Predicting Performance in the White House.* 4th ed. Englewood Cliffs: Prentice Hall, p. 5.

241. Barber, James David. 1992. *The Presidential Character: Predicting Performance in the White House.* 4th ed. Englewood Cliffs: Prentice Hall, p. 5.

242. Reagan, Ronald. 1990. *An American Life.* New York: Simon & Schuster, p. 40.

243. Memorandum to the Honorable Joseph P. Kennedy from Franklin D. Roosevelt. February 6, 1935. White House Official Files. Box 117. "Crime." Franklin D. Roosevelt Library. Hyde Park, New York.

244. Calder, James D. 1982. "Presidents and Crime Control: Kennedy, Johnson and Nixon and the Influences of Ideology." *Presidential Studies Quarterly* 12: 574–589; Calder, James D. 1978. *Presidents and Crime Control: Some Limitations on Executive Policy Making*. Ph.D. Dissertation, Claremont University.
245. Calder, James D. 1978. *Presidents and Crime Control: Some Limitations on Executive Policy Making*. Ph.D. Dissertation, Claremont University, p. 161.
246. Calder, James D. 1978. *Presidents and Crime Control: Some Limitations on Executive Policy Making*. Ph.D. Dissertation, Claremont University, p. 161.
247. Calder, James D. 1982. "Presidents and Crime Control: Kennedy, Johnson and Nixon and the Influences of Ideology." *Presidential Studies Quarterly* 12: 574–589; Calder, James D. 1978. *Presidents and Crime Control: Some Limitations on Executive Policy Making*. Ph.D. Dissertation, Claremont University.
248. Calder, James D. 1982. "Presidents and Crime Control: Kennedy, Johnson and Nixon and the Influences of Ideology." *Presidential Studies Quarterly* 12: 574–589; Calder, James D. 1978. *Presidents and Crime Control: Some Limitations on Executive Policy Making*. Ph.D. Dissertation, Claremont University.

President Lyndon Baines Johnson receiving a t-shirt from a member of the Police Athletic League (PAL) on March 29, 1968.

PHOTO TAKEN BY WHITE HOUSE PHOTOGRAPHER FRANK WOLFE, COURTESY OF THE LYNDON BAINES JOHNSON LIBRARY, AUSTIN, TEXAS.

chapter 3

How Presidents Promote Crime Policy

I am establishing the President's Commission on Law Enforcement and Administration of Justice.

—Lyndon B. Johnson[1]

The purpose of this chapter is to understand that Presidents do have various means by which they can engage in crime-control policy and to specifically explore how presidents have done so to date. As the president must influence both the public and Congress to support new policy and increased funding, the president is placed in a position whereby he must persuade people that the national government has a legitimate role in crime-control and that it can effectively have an impact upon crime under the right circumstances. The president must then bring all of his resources to bear on the problem of crime in order to win the passage of new policies and laws, increase responsibility for his administration, and increase funding to support these endeavors. The matter, then, that this chapter will attempt to address is understanding the resources presidents have at their disposal to deal with the issue of crime. In other words, how do presidents promote their crime policies?

The chapter will be divided into two parts, the Constitutional and the Institutional, which will analyze how presidents engage in crime-control policy issues. Another way of explaining the division is simply that some of the powers of the president are "enumerated powers" or those provided for by the United States Constitution, and the others are "implied powers" or powers necessary for the president to perform his various roles.[2] Therefore, the first part will discuss the enumerated and formal powers of the president and the second part will focus on the implied and informal powers of the president as they both relate to crime-control policy.

The President Speaks . . .

In referring to budget cuts, there is one area where I have ordered an increase rather than a cut—and that is the requests of those agencies with the responsibilities for law enforcement.

We have heard a great deal of overblown rhetoric during the sixties in which the word "war" has perhaps too often been used—the war on poverty, the war on misery, the war on disease, the war on hunger. But if there is one area where the word "war" is appropriate it is in the fight against crime. We must declare and win the war against the criminal elements which increasingly threaten our cities, our homes, and our lives.

We have a tragic example of this problem in the Nation's Capital, for whose safety the Congress and the Executive have the primary responsibility. I doubt if many Members of this Congress who live more than a few blocks from here would dare leave their cars in the Capitol garage and walk home alone tonight.

Last year this administration sent to the Congress 13 separate pieces of legislation dealing with organized crime, pornography, street crime, narcotics, crime in the District of Columbia.

None of these bills has reached my desk for signature.

President Richard M. Nixon greeting members of the White House Uniformed Secret Service on the White House Lawn.

PHOTO COURTESY OF THE NATIONAL ARCHIVES AND RECORDS ADMINISTRATION "NIXON PROJECT," COLLEGE PARK, MARYLAND.

I am confident that the Congress will act now to adopt the legislation I placed before you last year. We in the Executive have done everything we can under existing law, but new and stronger weapons are needed in that fight.

While it is true that State and local law enforcement agencies are the cutting edge in the effort to eliminate street crime, burglaries, murder, my proposals to you have embodied my belief that the Federal Government should play a greater role in working in partnership with these agencies.

That is why 1971 Federal spending for local law enforcement will double that budgeted for 1970.

The primary responsibility for crimes that affect individuals is with local and State rather than with Federal Government. But in the field of organized crime, narcotics, pornography, the Federal Government has a special responsibility it should fulfill. And we should make Washington, D.C., where we have the primary responsibility, an example to the Nation and the world of respect for law rather than lawlessness.

—*Richard M. Nixon*
State of the Union Address, January 22, 1970

CONSTITUTIONAL POWERS

The first category is deemed the Constitutional powers as they are, in fact, the enumerated powers derived directly from the United States Constitution. They consist of the presidential power to appoint members to his cabinet and designate key administrators; to grant pardons; to deliver a message to Congress "from time to time" on the "State of the Union"; to propose legislation to Congress; to share with Congress the power to create and administer the federal bureaucracy; to veto legislation; and to respond to formal requests for assistance in cases of domestic disturbances. All of these enumerated powers have been utilized by presidents to address the issue of crime at one time or another and, as presidents' attention to crime has increased over time, so has their frequency.

The Constitution of the United States of America, in Article II, sets forth that the "executive power shall be vested in a President of the United States of America." There are only four sections to Article II: Section 1 details how the president is to be elected, Section 2 details his powers, Section 3 speaks to his duties, and Section 4 articulates the requirements for removal from office. While the president is granted a number of powers such as his designation as Commander-in-Chief of the Army and Navy, and is given a number of duties such as receiving ambassadors and other public ministers, there are only a few select powers and duties that are germane to the discussion at hand. In regard to the president's ability to deal with issues of crime, Section 2 gives the president the power to appoint and the power to grant reprieves and pardons. Section 3 states that the president has the duty to "from time to time give to Congress information of the State of the Union," that he shall recommend to Congress "such measures as he shall judge necessary and expedient," and "he shall take care that the laws be faithfully executed." In addition, Article I, Section 7 gives the president the power to veto Congressional legislation and Article IV, Section 4 gives the president the power to, upon application by the states, intervene in cases of domestic violence.

One of the powers of the president which has long been considered one of his greatest resources, found in Article II, Section 2 is the power to appoint key officials in the national government. These officials range from cabinet secretaries and under-secretaries to bureau and agency heads, as well as the Justices of the Supreme Court. As the Constitution stipulates:

> . . . he shall nominate, and by and with the Advice and Consent of the Senate, shall appoint Ambassadors, other public Ministers and Consuls, Judges of the supreme Court, and all other Officers of the United States, whose Appointments are not herein otherwise provided for, and which shall be established by Law: but the Congress may by Law vest the Appointment of such inferior Officers, as they think proper, in the President alone, in the Courts of Law, or in the Heads of Departments.[3]

As a result, the president has the power to appoint many of the key leaders in the national government who stand in a position to exercise the will of the president or potentially either their own will or that of the agency they oversee.

In traditional legal theory, this power of appointment has been considered a source of authority and control for the president, resulting from the "chain-of-command."[4] However, more contemporary thought has focused on the realization that many of the presidential appointees, including his cabinet, become co-opted by their respective agencies. This has led Richard Neustadt to comment that "the probabilities of power do not derive from the literary theory of the Constitution"[5] and Pfiffner argues that what has been witnessed over the twentieth century is essentially the demise of "cabinet government."[6] In addition, Pfiffner finds that while presidents do consult and meet with their cabinet early in the administration, by the end of their four years, they generally emphasize the white house staff.[7] John Ehrlichman, a key advisor to President Nixon, reflects this belief. He "has observed that presidents begin their terms with strong cabinets and end them with dominant White House staffs."[8] This is not to say that the power to appoint has no influence on the direction of the national government, but rather to say it is simply not an "absolute" power as previously believed.[9]

Although the cabinet has expanded over time and currently stands at fourteen cabinet heads,[10] research by Thomas E. Cronin has found that certain cabinet members tend to be more influential than others.[11] These members, which include the Secretary of State, Secretary of the Treasury, the Secretary of Defense, and the Attorney General, are often referred to as the "inner cabinet."[12] Cronin points out that because these departments deal more with foreign affairs and macro-level domestic policy while the "outer cabinet" deals more with Congress's proprietary interest in the clientele agencies, presidents tend to work closer with these four cabinet secretaries.[13] This is also not too surprising since these four positions are also the oldest of the cabinet positions.[14] This is also highly relevant to the discussion of Presidents and crime-control policy because the Attorney General, who oversees the Department of Justice, and the Secretary of the Treasury are the key members of the cabinet that deal with crime-related issues. In the case of the former, the Attorney General can be seen as the president's primary appointment in dealing with issues of crime, while the latter has within his or her control a number of agencies oriented toward the enforcement of federal law.

The concept of an Attorney General originated from England and was developed on the English model in colonial America.[15] When the United States established its own government, the issue of an Attorney General was not discussed and the First Congress only created three executive departments—the Departments of Foreign Affairs (later State), Treasury, and War (later Defense)—each headed by a Secretary.[16] The concept of creating a legal counsel to the president was only considered in the terms of the creation of the judiciary and when President Washington, on September 24, 1789, signed into law the "Act to Establish the Judicial Courts of the United States" a provision was made for the office of the Attorney General.[17] Edmund Randolph was appointed on September 26, 1789, as the first Attorney General and when he attended his first cabinet meeting on March 31, 1792, the office would become a permanent fixture of the president's cabinet. However, the office was very weak without any staff or department and, despite a number of attempts to expand its powers, it was often the case that most of the legal powers regarding lawsuits by the national government were vested in the Department of the Treasury.[18] It was not until 1850 that the concept of a "Department of Justice" was suggested by Alexander H. H. Stuart, secretary of the newly established Department of the Interior, and finally proposed and passed by both houses on February 25, 1870.[19] President Grant would then sign the bill into law on June 22, 1870, and the Department of Justice, with the Attorney General as its head, came into formal existence on July 1, 1870.[20]

The Attorney General's responsibilities have grown dramatically since the year 1870, and the Department of Justice has grown significantly as well. According to the Department of Justice itself, the Attorney General is considered the "head of the Department of Justice" and serves as the "chief law enforcement officer of the Federal Government, represents the United States in legal matters generally and gives advice and opinions to the president and to the heads of the executive departments of the Government when so requested." In addition, "the Attorney General appears in person to represent the Government before the U.S. Supreme Court in cases of exceptional gravity or importance." It is evident then, that the Attorney General is the most important appointment by a president regarding the issue of crime and this has essentially been the case since President

Herbert Hoover began the process of nationalizing crime-control policy (see Table 3-1).

In order for the Attorney General to carry out all of the duties of the office, the Department of Justice has had to expand greatly since 1870. In that year there was only a handful of employees and no divisions. But by the turn of the century, it is estimated that there were more than 1,500 employees and a number of divisions.[21] However, the greatest expansion of the Department of Justice would come as a result of the prohibition era and continue through the end of the twentieth century. As of the turn of the last century, it is estimated that there were well over 110,000 employees and dozens of divisions and bureaus within the Department of Justice.[22] In order to clarify the functions of these various divisions and bureaus, one author has classified them into two categories: "1) the lawyering functions, embracing the original and long-standing responsibilities of the Attorney General

TABLE 3–1 Attorney Generals by Presidential Administration (Hoover to Bush)

Hoover	William DeWitt Mitchell	(1929–33)
Roosevelt	Homer S. Cummings	(1933–39)
	Frank Murphy	(1939–40)
	Robert H. Jackson	(1940–41)
	Francis B. Biddle	(1941–45)
Truman	Francis B. Biddle	(1945)
	Thomas C. Clark	(1945–49)
	J. Howard McGrath	(1949–52)
Eisenhower	Herbert Brownell, Jr.	(1953–57)
	William P. Rogers	(1957–61)
Kennedy	Robert F. Kennedy	(1961–63)
Johnson	Robert F. Kennedy	(1963–65)
	Nicholas Katzenbach	(1965–67)
	Ramsey Clark	(1967–69)
Nixon	John N. Mitchell	(1969–72)
	Richard G. Kleindienst	(1972–73)
	Elliot L. Richardson	(1973)
	William B. Saxbe	(1974)
Ford	William B. Saxbe	(1974–75)
	Edward H. Levi	(1975–77)
Carter	Griffin B. Bell	(1977–79)
	Benjamin R. Civiletti	(1979–81)
Reagan	William French Smith	(1981–85)
	Edwin Meese	(1985–88)
	Dick Thornburgh	(1988–89)
Bush	Dick Thornburgh	(1989–91)
	William P. Barr	(1991–93)
Clinton	Janet Reno	(1993–2001)
Bush	John Ashcroft	(2001–)

Source: U.S. Department of Justice, Attorney General Homepage available at http://www.usdoj.gov

for handling government litigation, civil, and criminal, and for giving legal advice to the President and the cabinet; or 2) the non-lawyering functions, embracing all of the Justice Department activities, agencies, and services which are not part of the offices and divisions through which the lawyering role is performed."[23]

The lawyering function has been primarily dealt with through the Attorney General's office, but has assistance from such divisions as the Solicitor General, the Antitrust Division, the Civil Division, the Criminal Division, and the Office of Legal Counsel.[24] The non-lawyering functions can be divided into various bureaus such as the Federal Bureau of Investigation, Drug Enforcement Administration, Immigration and Naturalization Service, Bureau of Prisons, and the U.S. Marshal Services.[25] While all of these bureaus and divisions are important in regard to the appointment process, the two which are perhaps most important, besides the Attorney General and both the Deputy and Associate Attorney Generals, are the Solicitor General and the Director of the Federal Bureau of Investigation.

The primary importance of the presidential appointment of the Solicitor General (see Table 3-2) is that he is an employee of the executive branch and

TABLE 3–2   Solicitors General by Presidential Administration (Hoover to Bush)

Hoover	Charles Evans Hughes, Jr.	(1929–1930)
	Thomas D. Thacher	(1930–1933)
Roosevelt	James Crawford Biggs	(1933–1935)
	Stanley Reed	(1935–1938)
	Robert H. Jackson	(1938–1940)
	Francis Biddle	(1940–1941)
	Charles Fahy	(1941–1945)
Truman	J. Howard McGrath	(1945–1946)
	Philip B. Perlman	(1947–1952)
	Walter J. Cummings, Jr.	(1952–1953)
	Simon E. Sobeloff	(1954–1956)
	J. Lee Rankin	(1956–1961)
Kennedy	Archibald Cox	(1961–1965)
Johnson	Thurgood Marshall	(1965–1967)
	Erwin N. Griswold	(1967–1973)
Nixon	Robert H. Bork	(1973–1977)
Ford		
Carter	Wade H. McCree	(1977–1981)
Reagan	Rex Lee	(1981–1985)
	Charles Fried	(1985–1989)
Bush	Kenneth W. Starr	(1989–1993)
Clinton	Drew S. Days, III	(1993–1996)
	Walter Dellinger (Acting)	(1996–1997)
	Seth P. Waxman	(1997–2001)
Bush	Theodore B. Olson	(2001–)

Source: U.S. Department of Justice, Solicitor General Homepage, available at
http://www.usdoj.gov/osg/aboutosg/sglist.html

officially represents the interest of the national government which can also be interpreted as representing the interests of the president before the United States Supreme Court.[26] In these cases, the Solicitor General has been found to be highly influential with regard to the Supreme Court.[27] In addition, he is largely responsible for setting the agenda of the federal appellate courts.[28] His importance in the judicial process has been highlighted and studied to such a degree that many refer to him as the "tenth justice," referencing the nine justices that serve on the Supreme Court.[29] Although prior to 1870, the Attorney General had direct responsibility to appear before the United States Supreme Court in matters of interest to the national government, the office of the Solicitor General was created as part of the Department of Justice and, in fact, held the number two position within this department until 1952 when all administrative duties were removed from the office.[30] Although Francis Biddle once wrote, "the Solicitor General has no master to serve except his country," there is little doubt that the Solicitor General is, in fact, not only answerable to the Attorney General, but is ultimately answerable to the President of the United States.

The second important presidential appointment following that of the Attorney General is most assuredly the Director of the Federal Bureau of Investigation (F.B.I.) (see Table 3-3). Commencing with the creation of the office by President Theodore Roosevelt in 1908 and becoming a critical governmental agency after the appointment of J. Edgar Hoover as its Director in 1924,[31] the Federal Bureau of Investigation has become a very powerful institution centered on addressing issues of crime in the United States.[32] The appointment of J. Edgar Hoover by President Coolidge and the expansion of his office under President Herbert Hoover gave way to the office becoming a key means by which presidents have dealt with the issue of crime. While most bureau and division heads generally have access to the president through their respective cabinet-level director, the Director of the Federal Bureau of Investigation has maintained a direct line of communication with the president.[33] This has assuredly been the case with Hoover, Roosevelt, Johnson, and Nixon, in regard to J. Edgar Hoover, but it has also been the case with Presidents Ford and Reagan with their respective F.B.I. Directors. There is nothing to indicate that this has not been the case with the other Presidents as well.

While the Attorney General and the Department of Justice are assuredly the leading appointment and agency, respectively, in regard to crime, the Secretary of the Treasury has under his or her responsibility a number of agencies that are oriented toward crime control.[34] These agencies include the U.S. Customs Service,[35] Alcohol, Tobacco, and Firearms,[36] the United States Secret Service,[37] and they oversee the Federal Law Enforcement Training Center (F.L.E.T.C.)[38] in Glynco, Georgia. Therefore, in regard to the law and order presidency, these appointments can be critical to the success of the president in addressing the issues of crime.

One final aspect of the power to appoint comes in the form of judicial appointments by the president.[39] The president has the ability to appoint, with ap-

TABLE 3–3   Directors of the Federal Bureau of Investigation*

Director	Assumed Office
Stanley W. Finch	July 26, 1908
A. Bruce Bielaski	April 30, 1912
William E. Allen, act.	February 10, 1919
William J. Flynn	July 1, 1919
William J. Burns	August 22, 1921
J. Edgar Hoover, act.	May 10, 1924
J. Edgar Hoover	December 10, 1924
L. Patrick Gray, act.	May 3, 1972
William D. Ruckelshaus, act.	April 27, 1973
Clarence M. Kelley	July 9, 1973
William H. Webster	February 23, 1978
John E. Otto, act.	May 26, 1987
William S. Sessions	November 2, 1987
Floyd I. Clarke, act.	July 19, 1993
Louis J. Freeh	September 1, 1993
Thomas J. Pickard, act.	June 25, 2001
Robert S. Mueller, III	September 4, 2001

* The Federal Bureau of Investigation was created July 26, 1908, and was referred to as the Office of Chief Examiner. It became the Bureau of Investigation (March 16, 1909), United States Bureau of Investigation (July 1, 1932), Division of Investigation (August 10, 1933), and Federal Bureau of Investigation (July 1, 1935).

Source: Farmighetti, Robert. 1999. *The World Almanac and Book of Facts, 1998.* New York: World Almanac Books.

proval of the Senate, the nine Supreme Court Justices, as well as all federal judges. One only has to look to the era of the Warren court in order to understand the impact that these appointments can have on issues of crime. Under the Warren court, cases such as Mapp v. Ohio (1961),[40] Miranda v. Arizona (1966),[41] and Gideon v. Wainwright (1963),[42] greatly impacted the criminal justice system and continue to have such an impact today. Therefore, presidential appointment of federal judges, although not a direct influence on crime policy, can have a significant impact in this policy area.

The second constitutional power granted to the president under Article II, Section 2 is the power to grant pardons. The president is assisted in this area by the Attorney General and through the Office of the Pardon Attorney within the Department of Justice which handles "all requests for executive clemency" and "prepares the Department's recommendation to the President for final disposition of each application."[43] The pardons may be granted in several forms including both conditional and unconditional pardons, commutation, remission of fine, and reprieves."[44] What is perhaps the most famous presidential pardon was the one granted by President Gerald Ford to former President Nixon for his role in the

Watergate scandal.[45] Ford would issue the pardon on September 8, 1974, a mere
month after taking office and prior to any conviction or indictment of Nixon for his
role in the scandal. In the pardon, he stated "I, Gerald Ford, President of the United
States, pursuant to the pardon power conferred upon me by Article II, Section 2, of
the Constitution, have granted and by these presents do grant a full, free, and absolute pardon unto Richard Nixon for all offenses against the United States which
he, Richard Nixon, has committed or may have committed or taken part in during
the period from January 20, 1969 through August 9, 1974."[46] As a result, upon
Nixon's acceptance of the presidential pardon, the President Ford had exercised
his constitutional powers, and although he was accused of subverting the legal
process, his power of the pardon was never disputed.[47]

It can be safely stated that the majority of presidential pardons never arise to
such levels as the pardon of former President Nixon, but all presidents have
granted pardons during their tenure in office. President Ford granted a number of
executive warrants for clemency to citizens who evaded the draft during the Vietnam war[48] and President Carter would pardon all "draft resisters and asked the Defense Department to consider the cases of military deserters during that war on an
individual basis."[49] President Eisenhower granted the commutation of an inmate's
death sentence with the provision that he never be paroled and President Nixon
granted executive clemency to former labor leader James Hoffa with the strict
condition that he no longer engage in union activities.[50] It is evident then that presidents are granted the constitutional power of the pardon, that they use it, and that
it is generally undisputed.

In Article II, Section 3, the Constitution states that the president "shall
from time to time give to the Congress Information of the State of the Union."
Although throughout most of the nineteenth century the delivery of a "State of
the Union Speech" was given from "time to time," the speech would ultimately
become a permanent yearly institution by the twentieth century. According to
Light, the State of the Union has become a means by which presidents transmit their agenda for the following year.[51] In a sense, it has become the "must
list" and a means for setting priorities.[52] As Light explains, "at least since
Theodore Roosevelt, Presidents have used the message as a statement of both
foreign and domestic priorities."[53] Ragsdale further comments, "since Truman,
presidents have used State of the Union messages to capture congressional and
national attention for their legislative programs."[54] As a result, Kessel explains
that:

> Cabinet members, White House aides, and others are quite aware of the significance
> of getting material included in the State of the Union message. Favorable mentions of
> a policy gives visibility to it and confers presidential backing to the enterprise at one
> and the same time. Since there are obvious limits to the number of policies that can
> be thus favored, very real contests take place over control of this scarce resource.[55]

In sum, the State of the Union message has become an important constitutional power granted to the President of the United States and when specific policy proposals or mentions are found within its pages, one can be assured that presidents and their cabinet and staff desire to make that policy issue part of the president's agenda.

Crime first made an appearance in the December 3, 1929, State of the Union message by President Herbert Hoover, who was the first president to begin addressing the responsibilities of the national government in regard to crime control.[56] In this message he would articulate the need to focus on the inadequate state of federal prisons, to restrict and enforce the number of immigrants coming into the country, to enforce the laws related to the eighteenth amendment, and to focus on "law enforcement and observance."[57] Hoover explained that "under the authority of Congress I have appointed a National Commission on Law Observance and Enforcement, for an exhaustive study of the entire problem of the enforcement of our laws and the improvement of our judicial system" and that "pending further legislation, the Department of Justice . . . is seeking systematically to strengthen the law enforcement agencies week by week and month by month, not by dramatic displays but by steady pressure."[58] Although no president until Johnson would reserve as much space in the State of the Union regarding the issue of crime, all of the presidents in the intervening years—Roosevelt, Truman, Eisenhower, and Kennedy—did employ the issue of crime at one time or another in their yearly message. One example was when Franklin D. Roosevelt used his 1934 message to rail against the fact that "crimes of organized banditry, cold-blooded shootings, lynching and kidnapping have threatened our security" and he expressed his belief that "these violations of ethics and these violations of law call on the strong arm of Government for their immediate suppression; they call also on the country for an aroused public opinion."[59]

President Johnson would expand upon the issues of crime during his presidency and once again elevated crime as a key component of the State of the Union message. At the beginning of his tenure, Johnson would articulate in the January 4, 1965, State of the Union message that in order "to help control crime, we will recommend programs: to train local law enforcement officers; to put the best techniques of modern science at their disposal; to discover the causes of crime and better ways to prevent it." He further stated, "I will soon assemble a panel of outstanding experts of this Nation to search out answers to the national problem of crime and delinquency, and I welcome the recommendations and the constructive efforts of the Congress."[60] Then, in 1968, Johnson would not only repeat many of his earlier calls, but he explained, "there is no more urgent business before this Congress than to pass the Safe Streets Act this year that I proposed last year."[61] As Ragsdale has articulated,[62] the president was utilizing his speech to influence the public and Congress in order to garner support for his legislative proposal. In the end, Congress would pass the Omnibus Crime Control and Safe

Streets Act of 1968 at the behest of the president, but not without several drastic changes.

Since President Johnson's significant incorporation of crime into the State of the Union message during his presidency, every president has included crime and crime related issues in their State of the Union messages. Although many such as Ford and Carter have limited their attention, and others such as Reagan, Bush, and Clinton have expanded upon their use, crime has become a common policy issue within this yearly message to Congress. Presidents such as Reagan have expressed the belief that "of all the changes in the past twenty years, none has more threatened our sense of national well-being than the explosion of violent crime"[63] and Clinton, in 1994, stated that "while Americans are more secure from threats abroad, I think we all know that in many ways we are less secure from threats here at home."[64] As a result, from the time that President Hoover incorporated crime into his first State of the Union Message through President Clinton's 1996 message, crime has appeared in thirty-seven of the sixty-seven messages. And if the years are limited to President Kennedy's first message through Clinton's 1996 message, then presidents have included crime in thirty out of thirty-five messages.[65] In sum, the use of crime policy in the State of the Union Message has clearly become a constitutional power that presidents have come to widely use.

The second power granted to the president under Article II, Section 3, is that the president may recommend to Congress "such measures as he shall judge necessary and expedient." This power affords the presidents another means by which Presidents can affect crime control which is through legislation on crime (see Table 3-4). Although presidents do not have direct legislative authority, they do have several means to influence the passage or non-passage of a bill.[66] In some cases presidents may utilize their constitutional powers to sign a bill into law or to veto the legislation. In other cases they utilize many of their institutional powers to influence legislation through such means as the administration, the Office of Congressional Relations, or their power of speech. Although the relationship with Congress and the president's ability to influence Congress is far more complex than this, suffice it to say, presidents play a significant role in the legislative process.

This role has been very clear in the area of crime policy as presidents since Franklin D. Roosevelt have been actively engaged in legislation related to crime. A number of the major pieces of crime legislation were in fact proposed to Congress by a president, such as the Omnibus Crime Control and Safe Streets Act of 1968. In other cases the legislation was Congress-initiated and president-supported, such as in the case of President Ford's signing of the Juvenile Justice and Delinquency Prevention Act. Still, in other cases, whether president- or Congress-initiated, presidents have found themselves in a position where they opposed a crime bill but would sign it into law anyway. An example of this actually includes the Omnibus Crime Control and Safe Streets Act of 1968 which, after congressional alterations, was a watered-down version of the original proposal and

TABLE 3–4 Major Legislation Relating to Crime

Year	Administration	Legislative Title
1914	Wilson	Harrison Act
1919	Wilson	National Motor Vehicle Theft Act
1922	Harding	Narcotic Drug Import and Export Act
1932	Roosevelt	Lindbergh Kidnapping Act of 1932
1934	Roosevelt	National Firearms Act of 1934
1934	Roosevelt	Fugitive Felon Act of 1934
1937	Roosevelt	Marihuana (*sic*) Tax Act
1938	Roosevelt	Federal Firearms Act of 1938
1956	Eisenhower	Narcotics Control Act of 1956
1961	Kennedy	Juvenile Delinquency and Youth Offenses Control Act
1964	Johnson	Criminal Justice Act of 1964
1965	Johnson	Drug Abuse and Control Act of 1965
1965	Johnson	Prisoner Rehabilitation Act of 1965
1965	Johnson	Law Enforcement Assistance Act of 1965
1966	Johnson	Bail Reform Act of 1966
1966	Johnson	Narcotic Addict Rehabilitation Act of 1966
1966	Johnson	Federal Criminal Law Reform Act of 1966
1966	Johnson	Act to Extend the Law Enforcement Assistance Act of 1965
1967	Johnson	Act to Prohibit Obstruction of Criminal Investigations
1967	Johnson	Act to Create the Federal Judicial Center
1967	Johnson	District of Columbia Crime Act of 1967
1968	Johnson	Act to Provide Indemnity Payments for Police Officers
1968	Johnson	Omnibus Crime Control and Safe Streets Act of 1968
1968	Johnson	Juvenile Delinquency Prevention and Control Act of 1968
1968	Johnson	Gun Control Act of 1968
1968	Johnson	Traffic in or Possession of Drugs Act of 1968
1970	Nixon	District of Columbian Reorganization and Criminal Procedure Act
1970	Nixon	Organized Crime Control Act of 1970
1970	Nixon	Comprehensive Drug Abuse Prevention and Control Act of 1970
1974	Ford	Juvenile Justice and Delinquency Prevention Act
1984	Reagan	Comprehensive Crime Control Act of 1984
1986	Reagan	Anti-Drug Abuse Act of 1986
1986	Reagan	The Firearms Owners' Protection Act of 1986
1988	Reagan	Anti-Drug Abuse Act of 1988
1990	Bush	Crime Control Act of 1990
1990	Bush	Gun-Free School Zones Act of 1990
1993	Clinton	Brady Handgun Violence Prevention Act of 1993
1994	Clinton	Violent Crime Control and Law Enforcement Act of 1994

had a number of controversial items, especially Title II, which was intended to overturn the U.S. Supreme Court decision of Miranda v. Arizona. As Cronin, Cronin and Milakovich explained:

> When the Omnibus Crime Control and Safe Streets legislation finally reached Johnson's desk in early June 1968, it was difficult to claim it as presidential legislation. The law included what Johnson advisors termed "repressive" and "obnoxious" provisions, but the president was in no position to choose. As Johnson's counsel [resignedly] told the president, "I recognize that you must sign this bill. But it is the worst bill you have signed since you took office."[67]

Despite the drawbacks, after consulting with his advisors, President Johnson signed it into law on the last day possible.[68] Finally, it must be noted that there have been numerous proposals for crime-control policy that have failed to become law, but the mere fact that they are proposed and circulated gives power to the president, and Congress for that matter, to continue addressing the issue of crime.[69]

The third power granted to the President of the United States that is related to the issue of crime and is derived from Article II, Section 3, is found in the clause that the president "shall take Care that the Law be faithfully executed." This clause essentially provides an imperative that it should be the president who controls the bureaucracy in order to assist him in "executing" the law. Yet, it is well established that both the president and Congress share this role and that because the president is often seen as an outsider to the bureaucracy, he wields even less control despite being hierarchically superior to the bureaucracy.[70] As a result, "to a large extent, the president's influence over the bureaucracy is tied to the ability to persuade—to convince others of the rightness or political expediency of actions the president desires."[71] Presidents do, in fact, have multiple means such as those previously discussed by which they can influence the bureaucracy: the power to appoint as well as the power to remove key officials within the bureaucracy. Presidents have also developed a number of institutional means, such as expansion and reorganization of the bureaucracy, executive orders, and the White House staff, all of which will be detailed in the next section. At this point, suffice it to say that presidents can exercise their constitutional powers of faithfully executing the laws by a "general support for law enforcement" and through the creation of—with the approval of Congress—new bureaucracies intent on dealing with crime related issues.[72] As was seen in chapter one, presidents have increasingly demonstrated a strong support for law enforcement over time and, as detailed earlier in this chapter, they do have multiple bureaucratic mechanisms to address the issues of crime, primarily in the Departments of Justice and Treasury.

The president is also granted two additional constitutional powers, both of which lay outside of Article II, namely the power to veto Congressional bills and the power to intervene in domestic disturbances when called upon by the state legislatures or executives. The first power, the power to veto, is granted in Article I,

The President Speaks . . .

In many other areas, it is the responsibility of the Federal Government to augment the enforcement efforts of the States when it becomes necessary.

What else can we do? The Federal Code can be modified to make more sentences mandatory and, therefore, punishment more certain for those convicted of violent crimes.

What can the White House do about this? The Federal role is limited, because most violent crimes are matters for State and local authorities. Further, the creation of criminal sanctions and their interpretation are the concerns of the legislative and judicial branches as well as the executive branch.

The principal role of the Federal Government in the area of crime control has centered in providing financial and technical assistance to the several States. However, while we are all aware that the actual control of crime in this country is a matter primarily of State responsibility under the Constitution, there are several areas in which it is the chief responsibility of the Federal Government.

President Gerald R. Ford shakes hands with a line of uniformed motorcycle police from the California Highway Patrol, lined up on front of Air Force One while on a campaign trip to California on May 24, 1976.

PHOTO COURTESY OF THE GERALD R. FORD LIBRARY.

(continued)

The President Speaks . . . — *(continued)*

We can provide leadership in making funds available to add judges, prosecutors, and public defenders to the Federal system. This Federal model should encourage States to adopt similar priorities for the use of their own funds and those provided by the Law Enforcement Assistance Administration.

We can encourage better use of existing prison facilities to minimize detention of persons convicted of minor crimes, thus making more room for the convicted felons to be imprisoned. There are a number of estimates of how much the crime rate would be reduced if all convicted criminals with major records were sent to prison instead of being set free after conviction, as too many are today.

Although we might expect the certainty of a prison sentence to serve as a deterrent, let us remember that one obvious effect of prison is to separate lawbreakers from the law-abiding society. In totalitarian states it's easier to assure law and order. Dictators eliminate freedom of movement, of speech, and of choice. They control the news media and the educational system. They conscript the entire society and deprive people of basic civil liberties. By such methods, crime can be strictly controlled. But in effect, the entire society becomes one huge prison. This is not a choice we are willing to consider.

Edmund Burke commented appropriately in his "Reflections on the French Revolution." Burke said, and I quote: "To make a government requires no great prudence. Settle the seat of power, teach obedience, and the work is done. To give freedom is still more easy. It is not necessary to guide; it only requires to let go the rein. But to form a free government, that is, to temper together these opposite elements of liberty and restraint in one consistent work, requires much thought, deep reflection, a sagacious, powerful, and combining mind."

Since these words were written, the world has changed profoundly. But the old question still remains: Can a free people restrain crime without sacrificing fundamental liberties and a heritage of compassion?

I am confident of the American answer. Let it become a vital element on America's new agenda. Let us show that we can temper together those opposite elements of liberty and restraint into one consistent whole.

Let us set an example for the world of a law-abiding America glorying in its freedom as well as its respect for law. Let us, at last, fulfill the constitutional promise of domestic tranquility for all of our law-abiding citizens.

Thank you very much.

—*Gerald R. Ford*
Address at the Yale University Law School Sesquicentennial Convocation Dinner, April 25, 1975.

Section 7, which states that "every Order, Resolution, or Vote to which the Concurrence of the Senate and House of Representatives may be necessary shall be presented to the President of the United States; and before the Same shall take Effect, shall be approved by him, or being disapproved by him, shall be repassed by two thirds of the Senate and House of Representatives, according to the Rules and Limitations prescribed in the Case of a Bill." Woodrow Wilson, in his classic book, *Congressional Government,* wrote of the importance of the presidential veto when he explained that "in the exercise of his power to veto, which is, of course, beyond all comparison, his most formidable prerogative, the president acts not as the executive but as a third branch of the legislature."[73] The power of the veto is a formidable one and its use has been studied by many scholars.[74] It has been utilized for various crime legislation passed by Congress and examples include President Ford's veto of legislation to reclassify and upgrade Deputy United States Marshals because he felt it was discriminatory against other federal law enforcement agencies,[75] President Reagan's veto of a bill concerning contract services for drug dependent federal offenders primarily because it would have created a cabinet-level drug czar,[76] and President Clinton's veto of a Department of Justice appropriation bill because of the lack of funds to implement the president's crime related initiatives.[77]

Finally, the last presidential power related to crime that is drawn from the president's constitutional powers comes from Article IV, Section 4, which as previously explained, details that "the United States shall guarantee to every State in this Union a Republican Form of Government, and shall protect each of them against Invasion; and on Application of the Legislature, or of the Executive (when the Legislature cannot be convened) against domestic Violence." Presidents since Washington have employed the use of this Constitutional power and examples such as those reviewed in chapter one abound. In most instances these domestic disturbances are in fact state and local crimes, but rise to such a level that the state is no longer effectively able to deal with the crime. As a result, governors typically have applied to the president for assistance in domestic disturbances. More modern examples include President Franklin D. Roosevelt's use of federal troops to quell the Detroit race riots on June 21, 1943,[78] and what appeared to be a complete repeat on July 24, 1967, when President Johnson would send federal troops into Detroit during the race riots that summer.[79] In the latter case, Johnson wanted to avoid sending in troops but realized he had to commit the troops due to the rapidly deteriorating situation and because his advisors were telling him to sign the Executive Order.[80] Johnson recognized the weight of the constitutional power he had been granted when he would record in his memoirs:

> I knew what I had to do, but I could not erase from my mind the awful prospect of American soldiers possibly having to shoot American citizens. The thought of blood

being spilled in the streets of Detroit was like a nightmare. I could imagine the in-flammatory photographs appearing within hours on television and on the front pages of newspapers around the world.[81]

Johnson would commit the troops which quelled the disturbance, but the scenario would repeat itself several times throughout the United States and eventually, in April of 1968, it would reach the White House steps. Johnson again sent in U.S. soldiers. Afterwards when his aide Califano urged Johnson to send his promised message to Congress on crime, Johnson responded, "NO!" and wrote in the margins of the memorandum, "I promised nothing. I stated my intentions only! Since changed by riots."[82] Johnson was clearly transformed by the use of his formal powers, overtly illustrating the importance and impact of the constitutional powers granted to the President of the United States.

INSTITUTIONAL POWERS

The second category of powers that presidents have in order to exert some influence over crime-control policy are those powers that fall into the institutional powers of the presidency. The institutional powers can be defined as the implied or informal powers that presidents obtain through broad interpretations of the Constitution, through the many roles they play in national governance, and through the requirement to ensure that the laws are "faithfully executed." According to Warshaw, "the existence of an institutional process for domestic policy is one that has been evolving for over seventy years, even before Franklin Delano Roosevelt aggressively sought to control the national agenda through the creation of the Executive Office of the President."[83] This same statement could be made regarding Presidents and their domestic crime policy, for it, too, has greatly evolved over the past seventy years and, for the most part, throughout all of the twentieth century.

The institutional powers related to crime that presidents managed to build during the twentieth century are plentiful. While in many cases they resemble the same institutional powers and means by which presidents address issues other than crime, these powers have been used definitively to address the specific issue of crime. In addition, these methods of engaging in crime-control policy are not relegated to only one president, but demonstrably have been utilized by the office of the presidency across time. Although certain presidents may favor one means over another and some presidents may not have utilized the powers available, none of the institutional powers are relegated to only one president. Finally, it is important to note that while presidents and their staff often think in terms of how they can address a specific issue, in most instances, the choices are not relegated to one specific response, but rather they incorporate multiple means of addressing the crime issue in crafting their administration's response.

A good example of how presidents or minimally their staff utilize multiple institutional powers to address a specific crime policy can be found in the second term of the Reagan administration. Although crime and drugs had been a domestic policy issue of the Reagan administration during his first term in office, it was not until his second term that the issue of drugs moved to the forefront of Reagan's agenda. On September 14, 1986, both President Reagan and his wife Nancy, would address the nation on the campaign against drug abuse.[84] A renewed drug war was underway and additional policies were being formulated to address the issue of crime. President Reagan would articulate six policy goals which consisted of 1) drug-free workforce, 2) drug-free schools, 3) expanded treatment and research, 4) expanded international cooperation, 5) strengthened law enforcement, and 6) increased public awareness and prevention. These goals became the primary focus of his administration as well as the focus of his policy advisors. The National Drug Policy Board (NDPB), an advisory council to Ronald Reagan on drug policy, would submit recommendations to the administration for "1988 anti-drug measures." The NDPB would highlight a number of specific recommendations under each of the president's stated goals and would deliver their proposals to the White House. Dr. Donald Ian MacDonald, the Director of the Drug Abuse Policy Office, who was the key policy advisor to President Reagan on issues of drugs would take the copy and work through the proposals by thinking in terms of the institutional powers of the presidency. In the upper margins he would highlight a coding scheme which consisted of "EO = Executive Order, L = Legislation, B = Budget (may be Legislature to authorize or appropriate $'s), and A = Administrative (internal policy)."[85] MacDonald would then go through each of the recommendations and, utilizing his code, place a letter in the margin corresponding with the institutional means to address each of the NDPB's recommendations. In the margin next to the recommendation that the administration "require private sector companies that receive federal funds to have drug-free workforce plans consistent with the goals and objectives of Executive Order 12564 (The Drug-Free Federal Workplace Order[86]), MacDonald would note, "A and EO, and possibly L to strengthen."[87] His use of the institutional powers to address the issues in this case centered on enforcing the policy through the administration by way of internal policy, as well as using an Executive order to enhance the policy. Beyond that, probably realizing that the administrative policy and Executive order may not have the strength needed to support the policy, MacDonald entertained the notion that a legislative proposal may be necessary. In the case of the recommendation that the administration "require institutions of higher learning to have drug prevention policies and programs through the provision of federal student aid programs under the Higher Education Act of 1965, as amended," MacDonald clearly saw this as a legislative proposal for he marked "L" in the margins.[88] Finally, one last example is found in the NDPB's recommendation to "expand the domestic eradication campaign with additional support by the National Guard in conjunction with the

Drug Enforcement Administration's strategy," MacDonald would mark a "B" in the margins, noting that he saw this as primarily a budgetary issue and that it could be addressed in this manner.[89] In sum, as the example demonstrates, presidents and their staff have multiple means by which to address specific policy issues and often think in terms of how a specific policy proposal or recommendation can best be handled by the administration.

Although the use of Executive orders, legislation, budgets, and administrative (internal policies) are most certainly key powers at the president's disposal to address the issue of crime, they are not the only means available. In fact, it would appear that presidents have at least six key methods at their disposal.[90] They can utilize the Office of the Presidency in a number of ways to promote crime policy, from key advisors to the White House staff and from special councils to the bureaucracy. Presidents can utilize various types of crime commissions and task forces to address crimes, use executive orders, and host White House conferences. Moreover, as MacDonald pointed out, presidents have used the budget to address crime policy. Finally, presidents have used one of their primary tools to address the issue of crime—the institutional power that is granted to the Office of the Presidency for making speeches. The focus, then, of the rest of this chapter will be on these six institutional powers.

The first institutional power that presidents have to implement crime-control policy comes from the Office of the Presidency. Although this power contains various components of the executive office, it has either been or has come to be central to the institutional powers that presidents posess to affect policy. Relating to crime-control policy, this consists of specific aides that deal with crime or crime related issues, those components of the executive office that oversee aspects of crime policy (e.g., the Domestic Policy Council, the Office of National Drug Control Policy), and through the president's ability to not only create a cabinet and the bureaucracy, as was noted under the Constitutional powers, but to expand and reorganize it. It is through these entities within the executive office that presidents have come to affect crime-control policy in the United States.

Presidents throughout the twentieth century have witnessed, if not had a hand in, the continued growth of the federal bureaucracy and they have, most assuredly, increased the number of advisors within the Executive Office. Despite having a cabinet of advisors, numerous administrative agencies, and the large executive office—all of which have the ability to advise the president on crime related issues—one noticeable characteristic of all presidents since Hoover is the fact that each has typically had one individual who has served as the primary source of information in the area of crime control. In several cases this individual also served as the Attorney General, such as was the case of President Hoover and his Attorney General William D. Mitchell and President Kennedy and his brother, Attorney General Robert F. Kennedy. In other cases it has simply been a key aide to the president such as Louis McHenry Howe, who has often been called the "man behind President Roosevelt."[91] In this case it was a mutual agreement. Louis Howe actively sought to become involved in issues of crime and President Roosevelt gave him the majority of work in this area.[92] For both Presidents Reagan and Bush, since their primary concern in the area of crime was related to drugs, a key policy advisor on drugs presented himself as the primary source for information to the president. In the case of Reagan, it was Dr. Carlton E. Turner who had the title of Special Assistant to the President for Drug Abuse Policy and in the case of Bush, it was William Bennet who would become the first "drug czar," taking over the newly created Office of National Drug Control Policy. Finally, in other examples, President Johnson relied heavily upon Joseph Califano; President Nixon relied on Egil "Bud" Krogh (through John Ehrlichman); and President Ford relied on Richard "Dick" Parsons. In each of these cases, despite having several other sources to which they could and often did, go for advice, these individuals remained the "point men" on issues related to crime.

Although presidents may rely on a specific individual for advice on crime-control policy, presidents throughout the twentieth century have still created various mechanisms to expand the White House staff in order to have additional people working on the issue. Presidents prior to Franklin D. Roosevelt typically maintained only a handful of aides which generally served as secretaries and clerks to the president.[93] In 1936, President Roosevelt would create the President's Committee on Administrative Management, generally referred to as the Brownlow Committee, which in 1937 made the recommendation that the president needed additional assistance in order to run the executive office.[94] This resulted in the creation of the Executive Office of the President in 1939, "giving future Presidents a permanent organization to assist them."[95] This has allowed Presidents to create various offices within the Executive Branch in order to deal with specific policy areas.

The most important of these offices to the president is the White House Office which consists of the key policy advisors to the president. This office has increased from a handful of staffers to approximately sixty persons during Roosevelt's tenure in office, then increased to over 300 under Truman and 400 under Eisenhower, finally reaching a peak of over 500 under Nixon. Since then the number of staffers has been scaled back but continues to remain at somewhere around 400 to 500 staffers.[96] In addition, when combining the other various offices, such as the National Security Council, the Office of the Vice President, or the Office of Management and Budget, the total number of employees within the Executive Office of the President is well over 2,000 employees.[97] However, for the discussion here, it is those offices within the Executive Office that deal with issues related to crimes that are of utmost importance.

Those offices within the Executive Office of the President that have been central to the issue of crime policy have been the Domestic Policy Council, the Office of National Drug Control Policy, and the Office of Congressional Relations. Although each of these have seen a number of name changes from administration to administration, the intent of the office and its strategic importance to crime policy have remained. The first has concentrated on many aspects of crime policy, including street crime, drugs, and white collar crime. The second, which has also seen a number of name changes, has consistently focused on the creation of an overarching drug policy for the United States. And finally, the third has maintained a liaison with the Congress in order to articulate and press for passage of the president's crime-control policies.

The presidents from Roosevelt through Johnson typically utilized a small group of senior staff as advisors to consult with them on issues of domestic policy and in the area of crime. As previously stated, they generally had a single person with whom to consult.[98] When Nixon entered office in 1969, it was his intent to create the Urban Affairs Council (UAC) which would be "the domestic policy equivalent of the National Security Council in foreign affairs."[99] The original plan did not work to anyone's liking, including the president's, and resulted in John Ehrlichman proposing a "Domestic Council," which the President supported and Congress ultimately approved.[100] Every president since Nixon has had some form of Domestic Policy Council under the Executive Office, despite a number of name changes primarily resulting from the secession of each new president. President Ford would continue the title of Domestic Council;[101] Carter would merge both the policy staffs of domestic and economics into the Domestic Policy Staff; and Reagan would change it to the Office of Policy Development.[102] As Edwin Meese, a chief policy advisor to President Reagan would comment after having made this last change at the beginning of the Reagan Administration, "if nothing else, new administrations do a lot for sign painters in the federal service."[103] The Clinton Administration would make the next significant change, keeping the title of Office of Policy Development. The president would place under it the newly named Domestic Policy Council and the newly created National Economic Council.[104] Despite these frequent changes, however, the primary intent of the newly dubbed Office of Policy Development would remain to advise the president on issues of domestic affairs.

A part of the Domestic Policy Council, under whichever rubric was popular at the time, consisted of dealing with issues of crime. In the Nixon Administration, a specially designated area of "law enforcement and drug abuse" was created and two committees were formed: the committee on drug abuse and the committee on criminal justice.[105] The criminal justice committee was responsible for issues of gun control, "crime in the streets," juveniles, the Law Enforcement Assistance Administration (LEAA), organized crime, prisons/corrections, and crime statistics.[106] As specific issues were raised, it was their responsibility to create policy option papers on crime that could be forwarded to John Ehrlichman and, upon his approval, to the President for final decisions. A similar structure would be created under other presidential administrations following Nixon with varying degrees of success. However, the key point to be made is the fact that in all administrations since Nixon's, crime policy has often been derived from the Domestic Policy Council.

A closely related area that would eventually develop in a slightly different manner involved the various crimes related to illegal drugs. As stated previously, the Domestic Council under President Nixon had a focal area of "law enforcement and drug abuse" which was divided into two parts. The second committee was on drug abuse and it was divided still further into three sections: domestic drugs, foreign drugs, and military drugs.[107] Again, the administration was concerned with the issue of drugs and it was the responsibility of these committees to forward policy options to Ehrlichman who would then, upon his approval, forward them to the President. Nixon, finding the need to elevate the issue of drugs in his administration would eventually, by way of Executive Order and then congressional approval, create the Special Action Office for Drug Abuse Prevention (SAODAP) as part of the Executive Office.[108] This would eventually be transformed into the Office of Drug Abuse Policy during the Ford administration and would remain as such until the Bush administration. It was under the Bush administration that the Office of Drug Abuse Policy would be reformulated by congressional authority, creating the Office of National Drug Control Policy (ONDCP), which would become an executive agency within the executive office, exercising control over all agencies that had responsibility for the issue of illegal drugs, either domestic or foreign. Despite having the elevated office for drug control policy, the Domestic Policy Council can still address issues related to drugs, as well as issues centered on other types of crimes. Hence, these two entities provide Presidents with two means for the generation of crime/drug control policy.

One final office of the Executive branch that assists in issues of crime-control policy is the Office of Congressional Relations (OCR).[109] Prior to the Eisenhower administration the relationship with Congress to support the president's policy proposals were more informal. Under Eisenhower, they would begin the process toward institutionalizing, within the White House, a mechanism for presidential support of administrative policy in Congress. The responsibility of the OCR is essentially to lobby Congress for the passage of the administration's policies which also include lobbying for support of the administration's crime-control policies. This has been the case for a number of presidential policies related to crime including passage of the Omnibus Crime Control and Safe Streets Act of 1968, the 1986 Anti-Drug Abuse Act, and the Crime Control Act of 1990. More recently, the OCR was an important liaison between the White House and Congress during the passage of the Violent Crime Control and Law Enforcement Act of 1994 as detailed in the introduction.[110] It should also be added that more recently one other office that works closely with the OCR in support of presidential policy is the Office of Public Liaison which "mobilizes interest groups to support the president's agenda."[111] In sum, the president has at his disposal several institutional mechanisms for not only creating crime policy (e.g., the Domestic Policy Council, the

Office of National Drug Control Policy), but for attempting to push the policy through Congress (e.g., the Office of Congressional Relations, the Office of Public Liaison).

One final aspect in regard to the ability of presidents to influence crime-control policy through the executive office is by way of their control over the bureaucracy. Although, as DiClerico has pointed out, "the Constitution accords to Congress the responsibility for establishing, altering, or abolishing departments and agencies in the executive branch, for some time now the primary initiative in this area has rested with the president."[112] The modern presidents have had a strong influence on creating, expanding, and reorganizing agencies with the executive branch to assist them in their implementation of policy. This is perhaps no truer than in the area of crime where presidents have created a number of new agencies, expanded existing agencies, and reorganized a number of agencies to more effectively deal with the issues of crime.

The twentieth century is replete with examples regarding the creation of new agencies to deal with the issues of crime. The Federal Bureau of Investigation, the Federal Bureau of Prohibition, and the Federal Bureau of Narcotics were all created in the early twentieth century for the purpose of addressing varying problems of crime.[113] A more recent example of the creation of new agencies came from the Nixon Administration's efforts to address the problems of drugs. When Nixon assumed office, there was essentially only one agency responsible for addressing the national issue of drug abuse. Prior to Nixon's first term in office, the Federal Bureau of Narcotics (FBN) which was created during the Franklin D. Roosevelt Administration and the Bureau of Drug Abuse Control which was housed under the Department of Health, Education, and Welfare and was created in 1965, had been combined in the last year of Johnson's Administration in order to create the Bureau of Narcotics and Dangerous Drugs (BNDD).[114] When the Nixon Administration attempted to have the BNDD move its enforcement focus from the high-level drug dealers to a street-level focus, the BNDD resisted and Nixon established the Office of Drug Abuse Law Enforcement (ODALE) under White House control.[115] ODALE would come under heavy criticism for its excessive use of no-knock warrants,[116] creating a political problem, which would result in a drastic change in 1973, when "the Nixon administration consolidated the BNDD, ODALE, the Office of National Narcotics Intelligence, and the Customs Service Drug Investigation Unit into a new drug superagency: the Drug Enforcement Administration (DEA)."[117] Finally, other new agencies have been created for the purpose of delivering grants to state and local governments such as the Office of Law Enforcement Assistance (OLEA),[118] the Law Enforcement Assistance Administration (LEAA),[119] the Bureau of Justice Assistance (BJA),[120] and the Office of Community Oriented Policing Services (COPS).[121]

In the case of expanding the various federal agencies to address the issue of crime, the presidencies of Hoover[122] and Roosevelt[123] provided the first significant expansion of federal law enforcement agencies in American history. This trend would continue throughout the twentieth century with nearly all of the federal agencies responsible for dealing with issues of crime expanding in numbers and in their budget authorizations. One example is recalling the increase of the Department of Justice which from the turn of the twentieth century had approximately 1,500 employees[124] and by the turn of the twenty-first century, well over 110,000.[125] Another example is found in the rapid increase of federal prosecutors in United States Attorney's Offices which has "increased from approximately 3000 in the mid-1970s to more than 8000 in the 1990s."[126] Finally, one only has to note the rapid expansion of federal prisons over the past twenty to thirty years to recognize that one means by which presidents can impact issues of crime is through the expansion of previously existing agencies that are responsible for issues of law and order.[127]

The last power of the president in regard to the bureaucracy is found in the power of reorganization. As Watson and Thomas have pointed out, "it has been almost an article of faith among political leaders and public administration theorists that executive reorganization can increase presidential power over the bureaucracy."[128] Much of this power lies in the effect that reorganizing a bureaucracy can have when presidents place the agency in either a supportive or unsupportive organization.[129] In addition, as Meier explains, "reorganizations are able to control both agency policy and some of the consequences of that policy."[130] One example of federal crime-control agencies being reorganized is actually found in the abolishment of an agency. The Law Enforcement Assistance Administration (LEAA) created under the Omnibus Crime Control and Safe Streets Act of 1968 and set into motion by President Nixon, would eventually receive a high level of criticism from President Carter and its annual budget decreased. When President Reagan entered office in 1981, he quietly phased out the LEAA, but would create several new agencies that would assume most of LEAA's duties which included the Bureau of Justice Assistance, the Bureau of Justice Statistics, and the Office of Justice Programs.[131] However, perhaps the best example of the power of reorganization as it relates to crime, comes from the example cited previously regarding the drug law enforcement agencies. The numerous reorganizations under President Nixon of the various drug agencies and the creation of a super agency, the Drug Enforcement Administration (DEA), resulted in increased control of drug policy issues by the White House and achieved major increases in the level of drug law enforcement.[132]

The second institutional power of the president to affect crime-control policy comes from his ability to create commissions to advise him on specific issues such as crime. Smith, Leyden, and Borrelli have pointed out that "presidential commissions, known variously as 'advisory commissions,' 'blue-ribbon panels,' 'task forces,' or 'expert commissions,' have been frequent, although always temporary, additions to the office of the modern presidency."[133] They go on to explain that "officially, nearly all of these commissions carry the same presidential mandate: to study and propose alternatives in response to particularly new and/or particularly difficult problems."[134] However, they and other researchers have pointed out that commissions' reports are often ignored and they become a political issue *because* presidents often do not follow the advice.[135] And, although these commissions are "often appointed to defuse highly sensitive issues," they "often blur critical issues" or the "commissions may make findings and suggestions that embarrass the president."[136] Despite these drawbacks, presidents still create commissions to study various issues and crime has been no different.

There have been a number of crime commissions throughout the twentieth century (see Table 3-5). The first, officially known as the President's Commission on Law Observance and Enforcement, commenced in 1929 under President

TABLE 3–5   Presidential Commissions on Crime (or Related)

Administration	Years	Commission Title
Hoover	1929–1931	The President's Commission on Law Observance and Enforcement
Truman	1951–1952	President's Commission on Civil Rights (Lynchings)
Kennedy	1962–1963	President's Commission on Narcotics and Drug Abuse
Kennedy	1961–1963	Committe on Juvenile Delinquency and Youth Crime
Johnson	1963–1967	Commission to Report upon Kennedy Assassination
Johnson	1965–1966	President's Commission on Crime in the District of Columbia
Johnson	1967–1970	Commission on Obscenity and Pornography
Johnson	1965–1967	President's Commission on Law Enforcement and Administration of Justice
Johnson	1966–1967	President's Task Force on Crime
Johnson	1967–1968	National Advisory Commission on Civil Disorders
Johnson	1968–1969	National Commission on the Causes and Prevention of Violence
Nixon	1970–1971	National Council on Organized Crime
Nixon	1970–1972	President's Commission on Campus Unrest
Nixon	1971–1972	National Commission on Marihuana (sic) and Drug Abuse
Nixon	1971–1973	National Advisory Commission on Criminal Justice Standards and Goals
Reagan	1982–1983	Presidential Commission on Drunk Driving
Reagan	1982–1983	President's Task Force on Victims of Crime
Reagan	1983–1987	President's Commission on Organized Crime
Bush	1989–1991	President's Drug Advisory Council
Clinton	1996–1997	President's Council on Counter-Narcotics
Clinton	1999–2000	Working Group on Unlawful Conduct on Internet
Clinton	2000–2001	Task Force on Drug Use in Sports

Source: Public Papers of the Presidents. Washington, D.C.: U.S. G.P.O.

Herbert Hoover.[137] Hoover would appoint George Wickersham, the former Attorney General in the Taft Administration, as the chairman along with eight other members of notable reputation in various areas of criminal justice. By 1931, the so-called "Wickersham Commission" would publish fourteen volumes dealing with a variety of administrative and social issues calling for a number of reforms within the criminal justice system.[138] In the end, little in the way of reform was enacted primarily due to the economic conditions at the time that the reports were released. The decrease was caused by the Great Depression, as well as the fact that President Hoover was losing much of his political clout not only over the Depression but for his hardliner stance on Prohibition.[139] Although a few recommendations would ultimately be acted upon, it was not until a similar commission was formed during the Johnson administration that the issue of criminal justice reform would be addressed.

Although both Truman and Kennedy would have commissions dealing with issues related to crime and Johnson would create the President's Commission on Crime in the District of Columbia primarily for political purposes, it was the creation of the President's Commission on Law Enforcement and Administration of Justice by President Johnson in 1965 that would have a profound impact upon the criminal justice system.[140] The Attorney General, Nicholas deB. Katzenbach was appointed as the chairman and the commission set out in similar fashion to the Wickersham Commission.[141] By 1967, the Commission would publish their report entitled *The Challenge of Crime in a Free Society*,[142] which included over 200 recommendations for changes in the criminal justice system as well as a number of additional suggestions. The recommendations themselves were not prioritized, but rather laid out in terms of topics, such as the police, organized crime, and research. In the end, many of the recommendations would find their way into the Omnibus Crime Control and Safe Streets Act of 1968—often in a watered-down version— and would see aspects of implementation through the Law Enforcement Assistance Administration. Although there are a variety of perspectives on the success and failure of the Katzenbach Commission, the one fact that seems to be well agreed upon is that the report did have a significant impact upon the criminal justice system.[143] It should also be noted that the report, like many others, encouraged a more active role for the federal government in dealing with the issue of crime.[144]

Other crime commissions have not fared as well as Johnson's Commission on Law Enforcement and Administration of Justice for a variety of reasons. In order to assist in the implementation of the commission's recommendations, Johnson created a Task Force on Crime under the leadership of James Q. Wilson, to speed up the process of translating recommendations into policy.[145] Its impact was negligible, but it also encouraged a greater role for the national government in crime. The National Advisory Commission on Civil Disorders, known as the Kerner Commission, was created as a reaction to the riots of 1967 and 1968, but the conclusions did not set well with Johnson and he chose to "snub" the report.[146]

Another commission created under Johnson, the Commission on Pornography and Obscenity, would move to release their report during the early years of the Nixon Administration. However Nixon, not liking the conclusions, rejected the report.[147] Finally, two other examples are the National Commission on the Causes and Prevention of Violence and the National Advisory Commission on Criminal Justice Standards and Goals, both of which published reports that would ultimately be ignored.[148] In sum, crime commissions, like other presidential commissions, have fared little better because presidents often ignore the advice or find themselves in a political situation when they disagree with the commissions' recommendations.

The third institutional power of the president comes from the use of executive orders. Although presidents were not given any direct legislative authority by the Constitution, many have exercised this power under Article II to "take care that the laws be faithfully executed," and it has been said that "most modern presidents have followed Theodore Roosevelt's 'stewardship' theory of executive power, which holds that Article II confers on them inherent power to take whatever actions they deem necessary in the national interest unless prohibited from doing so by the Constitution or by law."[149] The power of executive orders has been one means by which presidents have managed to exercise some authority.

It is unknown how many executive orders have been issued by presidents because a precise definition of such orders and their publication did not take place until 1935.[150] Since that time, over 13,000 executive orders have been numbered sequentially and published in the *Federal Register*.[151] There is little doubt that "executive orders have played a major role in presidential policy making" for presidents have used these orders "in such areas as civil rights, economic stabilization, and national security." These orders have also played an important role in the presidents' implementation of their crime-control policies.

Presidents prior to Kennedy utilized executive orders to address crime only sporadically and to address issues indirectly related to crime. When President Kennedy entered office, the use of executive orders to deal with issues of crime would become a common, albeit limited, fixture of White House means to implement crime-control policy (see Table 3-6). On average, presidents have only issued one or two executive orders a year related to crime and these only account for a small percentage of the total number of executive orders (see Table 3-6). However, it must be noted that many of these orders have had a significant impact upon the federal mechanisms for addressing crime as well as the entire criminal justice system. During the Kennedy and Johnson administrations, many of the executive orders issued were directed toward domestic disturbances resulting from the civil rights movement[152] and one of Reagan's executive orders brought about drug testing of federal employees.[153] Other executive orders have been used to assist the president in establishing crime-control policy by either 1) the creation of crime commissions such as the executive orders creating the President's Commission on Law Enforcement and Administration[154] and the National Advisory Commission on Civil Disorders,[155] the creation of executive offices such as the establishment of the Special Action Office for Drug Abuse Prevention[156] and the Office of National Narcotics Intelligence[157] both by President Nixon; or 2) to establish mechanisms for generating crime-control policy such as the creation of the National Drug Policy Board by President Reagan.[158] In some cases, the executive orders were merely ceremonial such as the one recognizing the death of J. Edgar Hoover[159] or the one establishing the official seal of the Office of National Drug Control Policy.[160]

TABLE 3–6   Presidential Executive Orders Related to Crime, 1961–1996

President	Year	Total # of E.O.s	Total # of E.O.s Related to Crime	Total % of E.O.s Related to Crime
Kennedy	1961	70	1	.014
	1962	89	1	.011
	1963	55	3	.055
	Total	214	5	.023
Johnson	1963	7	1	.143
	1964	56	1	.018
	1965	74	3	.041
	1966	57	0	0
	1967	65	2	.031
	1968	56	5	.089
	1969	9	0	0
	Total	324	12	.037
Nixon	1969	52	1	.019
	1970	72	4	.055
	1971	63	1	.016
	1972	55	4	.073
	1973	64	3	.047
	1974	40	0	0
	Total	346	13	.038
Ford	1974	29	2	.068
	1975	67	4	.059
	1976	56	1	.018
	1977	17	0	0
	Total	169	6	.041
Carter	1977	66	2	.030
	1978	78	2	.026
	1979	77	1	.013
	1980	73	1	.014
	1981	26	0	0
	Total	320	6	.018

(continued)

TABLE 3–6   Continued

President	Year	Total # of E.O.s	Total # of E.O.s Related to Crime	Total % of E.O.s Related to Crime
Reagan	1981	50	1	.020
	1982	63	4	.063
	1983	57	3	.053
	1984	41	0	0
	1985	45	1	.022
	1986	37	1	.027
	1987	43	4	.093
	1988	40	0	0
	1989	5	0	0
	Total	381	14	.037
Bush	1989	31	2	.065
	1990	43	0	0
	1991	46	1	.022
	1992	40	2	.050
	1993	6	0	0
	Total	166	5	.030
Clinton	1993	57	1	.017
	1994	54	1	.018
	1995	40	1	.025
	1996	49	2	.041
	Total	200	5	.025

Source: National Archives and Records Administration, Executive Orders Disposition Tables, January 21, 1961–October 6, 1999. http://www.nara.gov/fedreg/eo.html#top. Data downloaded on October 19, 1999 and October 1, 2001.

The fourth institutional means by which presidents can focus on crime policy are largely ceremonial and symbolic in nature and operate on a more limited scale than presidential commissions—White House conferences. These "conferences bring together groups of experts and distinguished citizens for public forums held under presidential auspices" and "their principal function is to build support among experts, political leaders, and relevant interests for presidential leadership to deal with the problems at issue."[161] Since the Hoover Administration, one of these problems has consistently been the issue of crime (see Table 3-7). All of the modern presidents have hosted a White House conference related to the topic of crime. The majority of these conferences have generally come late in the president's term in office and none have had any significant impact on crime policy.[162] In addition, many of these conferences are simply used to highlight a policy that the administration has previously addressed in order to make them appear more active in the area. However, most have made various recommendations for im-

TABLE 3–7   White House Conferences Related to Crime

Year	Administration	Date	Conference Title
1930	Hoover	11/19/30	WH Conference on Children (Delinquents)
1934	FDR	12/10/34	AG's WH Crime Conference on Crime
1939	FDR	4/17/39	WH Parole Conference (Crime)
1939	FDR	4/23/39	WH Conference on Children (Crime prevention)
1950	Truman	2/15/50	AG's WH Conference on Crime
1958	Eisenhower	12/16/58	WH Conference on Children (Delinquents)
1960	Eisenhower	3/27/60	WH Conference on Children (Delinquents)
1962	Kennedy	9/27/62	WH Conference on Narcotics (Drug Abuse)
1965	Johnson	11/16/65	WH Conference on Rights (Violence and Crime)
1967	Johnson	3/18/67	WH Conference of Governors (Crime)
1967	Johnson	3/28/67	National Conference on Crime Control
1972	Nixon	2/3/72	WH Conference on Drug Abuse
1975	Ford	9/12/75	WH Conference on Domestic Policy
1988	Reagan	2/29/88	WH Conference on a Drug Free America
1990	Bush	12/11/90	WH Conference on DWI
1991	Bush	4/22/91	WH Conference on Crime Victims Week
1995	Clinton	5/20/95	WH Conference on Character Building (Crime)

Source: Data collected by author from successive volumes of the *Public Papers of the Presidents of the United States.* Washington D.C.: U.S. G.P.O.

proving the criminal justice system and nearly all of them have recommended an expansion of the national government's role in crime control.

The fifth institutional power of the presidents to affect crime-control policy can be found in the budgetary process where the president proposes the annual budget and then delivers the budget to Congress for their approval.[163] Congress does wield the "power of the purse" and can increase, decrease, or eliminate any of the president's proposals. As Aaron Wildavsky has explained, "the president has the first and last moves in the budget process. He can both check and use Congress, and it can both check and use him."[164] However, in the case of budget allocations for federal crime control, there appears to rarely be anything but increases in expenditures when looking at the data over time. One indication can be found in looking at the budget category "administration of justice" in the federal budget which "since 1965 . . . has risen from $535 million to an estimated $11.7 billion in Fiscal Year 1992, an increase of over 2,000 percent."[165] Some research has indicated that presidents have been highly responsive to rising crime rates by increasing the budget of federal law enforcement agencies[166] and more recent research has found significant growth rates in all of the agencies.[167] For instance, Martinek, Meier, and Keiser, have found that between 1970 and 1995 there was a 692% increase in the Alcohol, Tobacco and Firearms annual budget, 860% for the Federal

Bureau of Investigation, 900% for Immigrations, 1,389% for Customs, 1,400% for the Secret Service, and 3,233% for the Drug Enforcement Administration.[168] Finally, when looking at the total federal expenditures on crime over time (see Table 3-8) or the breakdown between direct expenditures (those to federal law enforcement agencies), and intergovernmental expenditures (those to state and local governments), it is evident that the national government has become more active in crime control at both the national and state and local levels over the last three decades of the twentieth century.

One additional means of assessing the power of the budget is through more specific programs related to crime control policy, proposed or encouraged by presidents. One of the first significant expenditures by the national government on

TABLE 3–8   Federal Criminal Justice Expenditures, 1971-1993*
(dollar amounts in thousands)

Year	Total Federal	Direct Expenditures	Intergovernmental Expenditures
1971	1,448,335	1,214,857	233,478
1972	1,876,345	1,502,463	373,882
1973	2,260,959	1,650,881	609,218
1974	2,601,959	1,859,113	742,846
1975	3,018,566	2,187,875	830,691
1976	3,322,073	2,450,229	871,844
1977	3,601,647	2,788,710	822,937
1978	3,834,607	3,122,290	712,317
1979	3,950,686	3,269,381	681,305
1980	—	—	—
1981	—	—	—
1982	4,458,000	—	—
1983	4,844,000	—	—
1984	5,868,000	5,787,000	81,000
1985	6,416,000	6,279,000	137,000
1986	6,595,000	6,430,000	165,000
1987	7,496,000	6,878,000	220,000
1988	8,851,000	7,483,724	330,412
1989	9,674,000	8,110,000	545,000
1990	12,798,000	9,330,923	727,812
1991	15,231,000	11,450,000	1,110,000
1992	17,423,000	13,529,000	3,894,000
1993	18,591,000	14,429,000	4,162,000

*Note: Data are missing for the years 1980 and 1981 due to a change in agency responsible for reporting the data. The direct and intergovernmental expenditure data are not available for 1982 and 1983 due to the fact the agency did not include these data in the first two years of their reporting scheme.

Source: Data collected by author from successive volumes of Bureau of Justice Statistics. 1972–1998. *Sourcebook of Criminal Justice Statistics.* Washington D.C.: Bureau of Justice Statistics.

crime-control policy came as a result of the Omnibus Crime Control and Safe Streets Act of 1968 through its grant funding mechanism, the Law Enforcement Assistance Administration. By analyzing their budget history it is evident that a vast amount of funds were given to state and local agencies in order to address the various problems of crime throughout the 1970s (see Figure 3-1). In addition, the 1986 and 1988 Anti-Drug Abuse Acts would provide additional funds under the Bryne Memorial State and Local Law Enforcement grants which would increase from over $118 million a year in 1989 to $505 million a year by 1998 (see Figure 3-2), causing the national drug control budget to increase from $1.5 billion in 1981 to over $14 billion by 1996 (see Figure 2-1). Finally, more recently, the Violent Crime Control and Law Enforcement Act of 1994, in order to fund the "100,000 Cops" initiative under the auspices of community policing, allocated over $8.8 billion dollars to be delivered to state and local agencies between 1994 and the year 2000. It would appear then, that in regard to budgetary allocations in the area of crime, presidents can be very successful through their requests to increase the expenditures by the national government, either for direct or intergovernmental expenditures, in advancing their crime-control policies.

The sixth and last institutional power of the American president to be reviewed, which is perhaps his strongest asset, is the power of speech. Because presidents sit in a position of power and public attention, coupled with media attention which is focused on the president, he has the ability to deliver speeches that will be disseminated to the American people. Presidents, therefore, have the means by which they can deliver speeches to a largely captive audience. At a very simple level, as Marion explains, "presidents use their speeches to communicate their

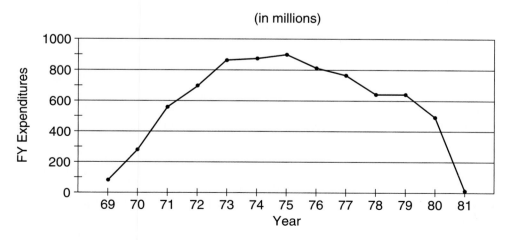

FIGURE 3–1 LEAA Budget History

Source: Law Enforcement Assistance Administration. 1981. *LEAA Twelfth Annual Report: Fiscal Year 1980.* Washington D.C.: U.S. Department of Justice, p. 97.

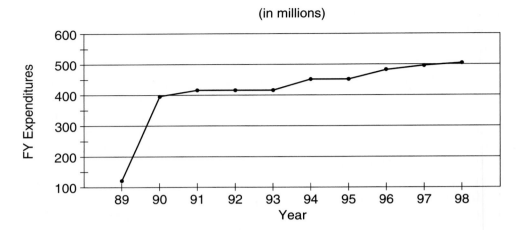

FIGURE 3–2   Bryne Grant Budget History

Source: Bureau of Justice Statistics. 1992–1998. *Edward Bryne Memorial State and Local Law Enforcement Assistance: Fact Sheet.* Washington D.C.: U.S. Department of Justice.

agenda."[169] Shull further elaborates that it is through their use of rhetoric that "presidents set an agenda to promote and communicate their policy preferences to those inside and outside government."[170] As a result, "much of what appears on the public agenda can be traced to the rhetoric in presidential statements."[171] Finally, as one author who has extensively studied the rhetoric of American presidents, Lyn Ragsdale, explains, "presidential speeches to the nation, even relatively mundane ones, have captured considerable attention in contemporary American politics."[172] He further states,

> . . . through the speeches, presidents gain immediate access to the public. In preempting regular broadcasting, they receive the all-but-automatic and undivided attention of millions of radio listeners and television viewers. The forum presents presidents as sole speakers, uninterrupted by queries of news reporters and challenged only afterwards by the rebuttals of partisan foes or the interpretations of political commentators. . . . In this solitary setting, presidents can appear as leaders of the nation; stirring public emotions and proposing solutions to national problems.[173]

Therefore, presidents have a significant power that has developed over time and has become itself an American institution. It has also become clear that this power has translated into a more focused attention on the president in American politics,[174] as well as providing the president with a more refined strategy for influencing public policy.[175]

It must also be noted that presidential speeches today are still the well-planned oratory events that they were in the nineteenth century. Although presidents give more speeches than ever before, "today, a president has an assembly-line of speechwriters that enable him to say something on every conceivable occasion."[176] In addition, it has been noted that in many cases, "speeches are written to become the events to which people react no less than 'real' events themselves."[177] Moreover, because multiple parties are involved in the writing of a speech, a formal format has developed within the twentieth century for the creation of presidential speeches.[178] It has generally been the case that when an item is on the president's agenda, which both the president and his staff believe should be addressed publicly, it will be scheduled well in advance to coincide with a complementary event. The various staff members, cabinet heads, and agencies are then consulted for their input as to what should go into the speech which is then forwarded to the key advisor to the president on that subject. The advisor will generate a draft including the key points of the speech and from there it is sent to the presidential speech writers. Once they formulate a more polished draft, it is circulated for review and ultimately lands on the desk of the president for his personal review and comments. Most presidents make minor changes to the speech and send the speech back to the advisors and speech writers for final editing. Then, on the day of the event, the president delivers the speech possibly adding last minute details to highlight current events or complement the audience being addressed.

Finally, it should be noted that the delivery of presidential speeches is also intended to coincide with other events centered on the same topic such as the issuance of an executive order or the release of a report. An example of the former would be the remarks President Johnson made on crime control on July 16, 1965[179] which were followed by the signing of Executive Order 11236, establishing the President's Commission on Law Enforcement and Administration of Justice on July 23, 1965, thus allowing for the release of a statement regarding the president's actions.[180] An example of the latter case can be found in the impact of this executive order, when President Johnson would deliver a "Special Message to Congress on Crime in America"[181] which was followed by the release of the report *The Challenge of Crime in a Free Society* by the President's Commission on Law Enforcement and the Administration of Justice.[182] Presidents then, attempt to extract as many political benefits as possible from their speeches by delivering them, not in a vacuum, but in relation to as many constitutional and institutional means available.

In sum, presidents utilize the institutional power of speech derived from their office in order to communicate their preferred policies and agenda for the purposes of influencing the people. In regard to speeches related to the issue of crime, presidents have demonstrated a strong penchant for utilizing this power to communicate to the American people their crime-control policies. As Marion explains, "presidents express their solutions for crime in speeches, the public reacts to the symbols in the speeches and are reassured that the government is doing something about crime."[183] Whether the public reacts to the symbols or the substance is a matter for discussion, but the most important aspect of presidential speeches related to crime is that the people are reassured and that they support the president's policies. In order to influence the people through their speeches, it should be noted that presidents have multiple forums for delivering speeches and each of these has been used to one degree or another to address the issues of crime. These include what are considered the two most important speeches by the president, the Inaugural and State of the Union Speeches, as well as other major speeches delivered to a national audience. In addition, they include minor speeches to more specific and limited audiences, as well as news conferences and question-and-answer sessions, either between reporters and the president or in such forums as "town hall" meetings. And finally, they include the use of statements, proclamations/messages, and letters/memoranda which occasionally are read by the president, but more often are read by one of the president's advisors. Each of these will be discussed in turn.

The earliest speeches of the president that received the widest dissemination are the Inaugural speeches and the Annual Address, now known as the State of the Union Address.[184] These speeches have been called the obligatory speeches of the president because they are obliged, "regardless of their desire to and regardless of what may be happening politically," to deliver these speeches.[185] The Inaugural Address, generally an address on the president's philosophy and how he will operate over his term in office, has not often incorporated the subject of crime. In fact, only two Inaugural Addresses have included references to the issue of crime, the first by President Hoover on March 4, 1929 when he spoke of "the failures of our system of criminal justice,"[186] and the second by President Bush on January 20, 1989 when he spoke of "high moral principle(s)" and that "there is crime to be conquered, the rough crime of the streets."[187] The State of the Union Addresses, however, as previously reviewed, have consistently incorporated the matter of crime since the first State of the Union Address that dealt with the issue of crime by President Hoover on December 3, 1929. Since then, from 1929 to 1996, thirty-seven out of sixty-seven State of the Union Addresses have incorporated the issue of crime. This is a significant finding, because if Cohen is right—that presidential attention to specific issue areas in his State of the Union Address affects public concern with those issue areas—when presidents talk about crime in this annual address they have the potential to influence public opinion of crime.[188]

Although the Inaugural and State of the Union Addresses are considered to be "major addresses," other speeches by the president are also considered to be major addresses. These are defined as those addresses "delivered to a national audience during evening listening hours."[189] It has also been articulated that "of the major addresses, the most dramatic and potentially the most effective are special reports the president delivers to the nation on prime-time television."[190] Because of their significance, these speeches are considered to be the "most fully developed form of institutional public behavior and arguably the most important"[191] for the president, in that "presidents define their public audience as a unified people with a genuinely consensual public opinion and a commonly agreed upon public interest."[192] Regarding major presidential speeches on crime (including Inaugural and State of the Union Addresses), presidents from Hoover through Kennedy were more likely to mention crime in these addresses rather than dedicating an entire major address to the subject. Once Johnson made the issue of crime a central part of his domestic policy and delivered the first major address dedicated to crime, nearly every president since then, with the exception of Carter, has delivered a major speech dedicated to the issue of crime (see Table 3-9). In addition to major speeches that have a national audience, presidents deliver a number of minor speeches each year which are speeches that "involve substantive policy remarks made to a specific group or in a certain forum."[193] Examples may include speeches to the National Press Club, the Conference of Governors, or the International Association of Chiefs of Police. The overall use of minor speeches by presidents has continually increased since the Hoover presidency[194] and there is evidence that this has also been the case in regard to minor speeches dedicated to crime, as well as those mentioning the issue of crime (see Table 3-9). Once again, there is evidence that these minor speeches, either dedicated to or mentioning crime, became more of a mainstay of presidential activity with the Johnson Administration and that, on average, President Bush delivered the most minor speeches dedicated to the issue of crime (24 speeches per year), while President Clinton made it an art form to incorporate the subject of crime into his minor speeches during his first term in office (62 speeches per year) (see Table 3-9).

Presidents also have other means of communicating that go beyond major and minor speeches and include the formal news conferences and the more informal question-and-answer sessions that presidents often have with the public through such forums as "town-hall meetings."[195] In these cases, presidents may deliver a short speech, but reporters, citizens, or both, are given an opportunity to question the president, hence creating a forum by which participants "may respond to, probe, or even dispute what presidents have said."[196] It is often the case that these questions revolve around issues of crime. In looking at the total number of exchanges between the president and either reporters or citizens over time, it is clear that, like the major and minor speeches, this has been a growth area throughout the twentieth century. Although there were more exchanges on a yearly average[197] with President Hoover than the following three presidents, this was primarily because Hoover made crime one of his key policy issues. It is not until Kennedy that the issue of crime became a more common topic of discussion in both the news conference and question-and-answer forums with the yearly average increasing significantly during the Reagan, Bush, and Clinton Presidencies (see Table 3-10).

Presidents also have other means of communicating their policy positions. These include the use of statements, messages, and letters or memorandums. In some cases, the president may read the statement or message, but in most

TABLE 3–9   Presidential Speeches on Crime—Hoover to Clinton, I

President/Year	Major	Major (Mention)	Minor	Minor (Mention)
Hoover				
1929	0	3	2	1
1930	0	1	1	3
1931	0	2	1	5
1932	0	0	1	5
Total	0	6	5	14
Yearly Av.	0	1.5	1.25	3.5
FDR I				
1933	0	0	0	2
1934	0	2	2	1
1935	0	1	0	1
1936	0	0	0	4
Total	0	3	2	8
Yearly Av.	0	.75	.5	2
FDR II				
1937	0	1	0	3
1938	0	1	0	1
1939	1	0	0	1
1940	0	1	0	0
Total	1	3	0	5
Yearly Av.	.25	.75	0	1.25
FDR III/IV				
1941	0	0	0	0
1942	0	0	0	0
1943	0	1	0	0
1944	0	0	0	0
1945	0	0	0	0
Total	0	1	0	0
Yearly Av.	0	.2	0	0
Truman I				
1945	0	0	0	0
1946	0	0	0	1
1947	0	1	0	1
1948	0	1	0	1
Total	0	2	0	3
Yearly Av.	0	.5	0	.75
Truman II				
1949	0	0	0	2
1950	0	0	2	2
1951	0	0	0	3
1952	0	0	0	7
Total	0	0	2	14
Yearly Av.	0	0	.5	3.5

TABLE 3–9   Continued

President/Year	Major	Major (Mention)	Minor	Minor (Mention)
Eisenhower I				
1953	0	2	0	2
1954	0	2	0	8
1955	0	1	0	1
1956	0	0	0	1
Total	0	5	0	12
Yearly Av.	0	1.25	0	3
Eisenhower II				
1957	0	0	1	1
1958	0	0	0	2
1959	0	0	0	0
1960	0	0	1	1
Total	0	0	2	4
Yearly Av.	0	0	.5	2
Kennedy				
1961	0	1	2	3
1962	0	1	4	4
1963	0	2	1	2
Total	0	4	7	9
Yearly Av.	0	1.33	2.33	3
Johnson				
1963-4	0	1	3	19
1965	1	1	4	15
1966	0	1	4	8
1967	2	2	7	10
1968	1	4	9	26
Total	4	9	27	78
Yearly Av.	.8	1.8	5.4	15.6
Nixon I				
1969	0	1	3	21
1970	0	1	7	31
1971	0	3	6	6
1972	1	4	9	5
Total	1	9	25	63
Yearly Av.	.25	2.25	6.25	15.75
Nixon II				
1973	2	0	4	1
1974	0	3	1	0
Total	2	3	5	1
Yearly Av.	1	1.5	2.5	.5

(continued)

TABLE 3–9   Continued

President/Year	Major	Major (Mention)	Minor	Minor (Mention)
Ford				
1974	0	1	3	1
1975	2	2	5	3
1976	1	4	8	2
Total	3	7	16	6
Yearly Av.	1	2.33	5.33	2
Carter				
1977	0	3	2	5
1978	0	3	2	7
1979	0	0	2	0
1980	0	3	1	6
Total	0	9	7	18
Yearly Av.	0	2.25	1.75	4.5
Reagan I				
1981	0	0	1	4
1982	2	1	9	8
1983	1	3	9	20
1984	5	5	10	29
Total	8	9	29	61
Yearly Av.	2	2.25	7.25	15.25
Reagan II				
1985	0	6	7	10
1986	2	10	10	16
1987	1	6	8	13
1988	4	11	12	61
Total	7	33	37	100
Yearly Av.	1.75	8.25	9.25	25
Bush				
1989	1	2	23	50
1990	0	0	26	54
1991	0	1	18	8
1992	2	3	30	16
Total	3	6	97	128
Yearly Av.	.75	1.5	24.25	32
Clinton I				
1993	5	5	12	33
1994	10	7	25	60
1995	18	6	15	54
1996	8	8	19	102
Total	41	26	71	249
Yearly Av.	10.25	6.5	17.75	62.25

Source: Coded and calculated by the author from successive volumes of the paper version of *Public Papers of the Presidents* (Washington D.C.: U.S. Government Printing Office) and the electronic version obtained in *World Book Encyclopedia: American Reference Library* (Orem, Utah: Western Standard Publishing Company). Format of table is derived from Ragsdale, Lyn. 1998. *Vital Statistics on the Presidency: Washington to Clinton.* Rev. ed. Washington D.C.: Congressional Quarterly, Inc.

TABLE 3–10 Presidential Activity on Crime (Other than Speeches) Hoover to Clinton, I

President/Year	News Conference/ Question & Answer	Statement	Message	Letter/ Memorandums
Hoover				
1929	19	6	5	6
1930	11	7	6	4
1931	0	1	3	3
1932	2	8	6	3
Total	32	22	20	16
Yearly Av.	8	5.5	5	4
FDR I				
1933	1	0	3	5
1934	0	1	1	2
1935	2	1	0	2
1936	0	0	0	0
Total	3	2	4	9
Yearly Av.	.75	.5	1	2.25
FDR II				
1937	0	2	0	1
1938	0	1	0	1
1939	1	1	1	0
1940	1	1	3	3
Total	2	5	4	5
Yearly Av.	.5	1.25	1	1.25
FDR III/IV				
1941	0	0	0	0
1942	0	0	0	2
1943	0	3	0	0
1944	1	0	0	0
1945	1	0	1	0
Total	2	3	1	2
Yearly Av.	.4	.6	.2	.4
Truman I				
1945	0	0	0	0
1946	0	0	1	1
1947	2	0	4	3
1948	2	0	4	3
Total	4	0	9	7
Yearly Av.	1	0	2.25	1.75
Truman II				
1949	4	0	1	2
1950	7	2	2	2
1951	3	1	1	1
1952	12	2	1	0
Total	26	5	5	5
Yearly Av.	6.5	1.25	1.25	1.25

(continued)

TABLE 3–10   Continued

President/Year	News Conference/ Question & Answer	Statement	Message	Letter/ Memorandums
Eisenhower I				
1953	3	4	0	0
1954	8	3	2	2
1955	4	0	2	0
1956	12	1	2	2
Total	27	8	6	4
Yearly Av.	6.75	2	1.5	1
Eisenhower II				
1957	4	2	1	3
1958	6	1	0	0
1959	3	0	1	1
1960	2	2	1	1
Total	15	5	3	5
Yearly Av.	3.75	1.25	.75	1.25
Kennedy				
1961	9	6	6	5
1962	5	2	1	4
1963	21	6	6	8
Total	35	14	13	17
Yearly Av.	11.66	4.66	4.33	5.66
Johnson				
1963-4	17	8	3	7
1965	9	9	7	8
1966	17	11	8	9
1967	20	16	11	12
1968	9	20	13	10
Total	72	64	42	46
Yearly Av.	14.4	12.8	8.4	9.2
Nixon I				
1969	8	9	8	3
1970	4	9	6	4
1971	4	5	12	4
1972	3	8	6	3
Total	19	31	26	14
Yearly Av.	4.75	7.75	6.5	3.5
Nixon II				
1973	3	3	4	1
1974	0	0	1	0
Total	3	3	5	1
Yearly Av.	1.5	1.5	2.5	.5

TABLE 3–10   Continued

President/Year	News Conference/ Question & Answer	Statement	Message	Letter/ Memorandums
Ford				
1974	2	4	6	4
1975	11	4	2	2
1976	14	4	4	5
Total	27	12	12	11
Yearly Av.	9	4	4	3.66
Carter				
1977	13	3	15	10
1978	11	4	12	3
1979	4	1	10	4
1980	6	10	13	1
Total	34	18	50	18
Yearly Av.	8.5	4.5	12.5	4.5
Reagan I				
1981	11	15	24	1
1982	13	8	29	1
1983	35	8	31	2
1984	46	11	33	3
Total	105	42	117	7
Yearly Av.	26.25	10.5	29.25	1.75
Reagan II				
1985	15	4	21	0
1986	59	11	20	4
1987	54	5	25	3
1988	134	14	40	4
Total	262	34	106	11
Yearly Av.	65.5	8.5	26.5	2.75
Bush				
1989	99	8	25	4
1990	9	3	3	0
1991	107	2	10	3
1992	121	11	14	5
Total	336	24	52	12
Yearly Av.	84	6	13	3
Clinton I				
1993	215	8	7	6
1994	164	11	3	7
1995	156	14	9	7
1996	131	13	4	12
Total	666	46	23	32
Yearly Av.	166.5	11.5	5.75	8

Source: Coded and calculated by the author from successive volumes of the paper version of *Public Papers of the Presidents* (Washington D.C.: U.S. Government Printing Office) and the electronic version obtained in *World Book Encyclopedia: American Reference Library* (Orem, Utah: Western Standard Publishing Company). Format of table is derived from Ragsdale, Lyn. 1998. *Vital Statistics on the Presidency: Washington to Clinton.* Rev. ed. Washington D.C.: Congressional Quarterly, Inc.

The President Speaks . . .

Drug abuse continues to be a serious social problem in America. The lives of hundreds of thousands of people are blighted by their dependence on drugs. Many communities remain unsafe because of drug-related street crime, and the immense profits made in the illicit drug traffic help support the power and influence of organized crime. Among young American men aged 18–24 years, drugs are the fourth most common cause of death: only automobile accidents, homicides, and suicides rank higher. The estimated cost of drug abuse in America exceeds 15 billion dollars each year. Among some minority groups, the incidence of addiction and the harm it inflicts are disproportionate.

Drug addiction, which in recent years was viewed as a problem peculiar to America, now affects people throughout the world. We can no longer concern ourselves merely with keeping illicit drugs out of the United States, but we must join with other nations to deal with this global problem by com-

President Jimmy Carter shaking hands with an Iowa State Police patrolman during the 1980 Presidential campaign.
PHOTO COURTESY OF THE JIMMY CARTER LIBRARY.

(continued)

bating drug traffickers and sharing our knowledge and resources to help treat addiction wherever it occurs. We must set realistic objectives, giving our foremost attention domestically to those drugs that pose the greatest threat to health, and to our ability to reduce crime. Since heroin, barbiturates and other sedative/hypnotic drugs account for 90 percent of the deaths from drug abuse, they should receive our principal emphasis.

My goals are to discourage all drug abuse in America—and also discourage the excessive use of alcohol and tobacco—and to reduce to a minimum the harm drug abuse causes when it does occur. To achieve these goals with the resources available, effective management and direction are essential. Because the federal effort is currently divided among more than twenty different, and often competing, agencies, I have directed my staff to coordinate Federal action and to formulate a comprehensive national policy. This will end the long-standing fragmentation among our international programs, drug law enforcement, treatment and rehabilitation, prevention, and regulatory activities. I will also seek the counsel and active involvement of members of the Cabinet and heads of major independent agencies on all drug abuse policy questions, through a revitalized Strategy Council on Drug Abuse. My staff will examine the functions of the various agencies involved in this field and will recommend to me whatever organizational changes are appropriate.

—*Jimmy Carter*
Drug Abuse Message to the Congress, August 2, 1977.

instances all three are either presented by an aide for the president or published for the record. A statement is generally a brief communication that states the president's position on a specific policy, bill, or event. A message is generally a longer and more detailed explanation of the president's position on a specific policy area and includes his recommendations for how Congress and/or the administration should proceed to address this issue. And finally, a letter or memorandum is generally a more formal written communication that is sent to a specific person, such as a cabinet member or a member of Congress, detailing the president's position on a specific issue. In regard to the issue of crime, the number of statements, messages, and letters/memorandums were limited until President Kennedy's tenure in office. They then began to increase with the Johnson presidency and subsequently fluctuated depending upon the president in office.

In order to more fully understand the president's institutional ability to address the issue of crime through the power of speech coupled with the written word by combining the above eight categories (tables 3-09 and 3-10), an overview of the total number of activities related to crime and their yearly average by presidential administration assists in understanding how active presidents

TABLE 3–11   Level of Crime Activity of Presidents Hoover to Clinton, I

President	Total Activities	Yearly Average
Hoover	119	29.75
Roosevelt, I	31	17.75
Roosevelt, II	26	6.5
Roosevelt, III/IV	9	1.8
Truman, I	25	6.25
Truman, II	59	14.75
Eisenhower, I	62	15.5
Eisenhower, II	38	9.5
Kennedy	99	33
Johnson	347	69.4
Nixon, I	193	48.25
Nixon, II	24	12
Ford	95	31.66
Carter	157	39.25
Reagan, I	378	94.5
Reagan, II	598	149.5
Bush	659	164.75
Clinton, I	1154	288.5

Note: Crime activity is defined as including all major and minor speeches (including mentions), news conferences, statements, messages, and letters related to crime.

Source: Coded and calculated by the author from successive volumes of the paper version of *Public Papers of the Presidents* (Washington D.C.: U.S. Government Printing Office) and the electronic version obtained in *World Book Encyclopedia: American Reference Library* (Orem, Utah: Western Standard Publishing Company). Format of table is derived from Ragsdale, Lyn. 1998. *Vital Statistics on the Presidency: Washington to Clinton.* Rev. ed. Washington D.C.: Congressional Quarterly, Inc.

have been in regard to crime-control policy (see Table 3-11). It becomes clear that President Roosevelt and all of the succeeding presidents until Johnson did not dedicate as much time to the issue. [198] Hoover did in fact spend a large portion of his time addressing the issues of crime and President Johnson, as has been alluded to throughout this research, did allocate a vast amount of his resources toward addressing the issue of crime. And, despite the consistent belief that Nixon focused so heavily on issues of crime, no president would match Johnson's attention to the issue until President Reagan's first term in office and it has been all uphill ever since.

Conclusions

In reviewing both the constitutional and institutional means available to presidents in order to address the issue of crime, it is evident that not only do presidents have the means to address crime, but in fact they have addressed the issue on a fairly regular basis since President Johnson's tenure in office. Understanding how presidents have addressed the issue of crime-control policy assists in clarifying the third and final assumption in regard to the belief that presidents influence public opinion of crime. Having demonstrated that presidents have focused on issues of crime and that this has increased significantly in the twentieth century (chapter one); that there is a host of reasons for presidents to focus on the issue of crime, including the symbolic, substantive, and political reasons why (chapter two); and that presidents do have means, both constitutional and institutional, by which they can become involved in issues of crime and crime-control policy (this chapter); then the three assumptions appear to be validated. The question to address, then, is whether or not this has any affect on public opinion. In other words, does it matter? As presidents have given more time and attention to the issue of crime control throughout the twentieth century, does this increased time and attention to crime influence public opinion of crime, thus providing presidents with a valuable benefit for allocating resources on an issue that for most of American history has been a state and local issue? The following chapter will assess this impact by testing the hypothesis that presidents influence public opinion of crime.

Endnotes

1. Johnson, Lyndon B. 1966. "Special Message to the Congress on Law Enforcement and the Administration of Justice. March 8, 1965." *Public Papers of the Presidents of the United States, 1965*. Washington D.C.: U.S. G.P.O., p. 269.
2. LeLoup, Lance T. and Steven A. Shull. 1999. *The President and Congress: Collaboration and Combat in National Policymaking*. Boston: Allyn and Bacon, p. 40. And yet, still another means of understanding the division of these two presidential powers comes from Thomas and Pika in their delineation of "the formal powers vested in him by the Constitution and by statute and the informal resources inherent in the office." See Thomas, Norman C. and Joseph A. Pika. 1996. *The Politics of the Presidency*. 4th ed. Washington D.C.: Congressional Quarterly Press, p. 211.
3. United States Constitution. Article II, Section 2.
4. Corwin, Edwards S. 1957. *The President: Office and Powers*. 4th ed. New York: New York University Press.
5. Neustadt, Richard E. 1990. *Presidential Power and the Modern Presidents: the Politics of Leadership from Roosevelt to Reagan*. New York: The Free Press, p. 37.
6. Pfiffner, James P. 1996. *The Strategic Presidency: Hitting the Ground Running*. 2d ed., rev. Lawrence: The University Press of Kansas, chapter two, titled "The Holy Grail of 'True' Cabinet Government."
7. Pfiffner, James P. 1996. *The Strategic Presidency: Hitting the Ground Running*. 2d ed., rev. Lawrence: The University Press of Kansas.
8. As cited in Pfiffner, James P. 1996. *The Strategic Presidency: Hitting the Ground Running*. 2d ed., rev. Lawrence: The University Press of Kansas, p. 35.
9. See Thomas, Norman C. and Joseph A. Pika. 1996. *The Politics of the Presidency*. 4th ed. Washington D.C.: Congressional Quarterly Press, p. 257.
10. The fourteen Cabinet Department Heads follow: Secretary of State, Secretary of the Treasury, Secretary of Defense, Attorney General, Secretary of the Interior, Secretary of Agriculture, Secretary of Commerce, Secretary of Labor, Secretary of Health and Human Services, Secretary of

Housing and Urban Development, Secretary of Transportation, Secretary of Energy, Secretary of Education, and Secretary of Veterans Affairs.

11. Cronin, Thomas E. 1980. *The State of the Presidency*. Boston: Little, Brown, and Company, p. 276.

12. Cronin, Thomas E. 1980. *The State of the Presidency*. Boston: Little, Brown, and Company, p. 276.

13. Cronin, Thomas E. 1980. *The State of the Presidency*. Boston: Little, Brown, and Company, p. 276.

14. When President Washington formed the "cabinet," the members included the Secretary of State, the Secretary of the Treasury, the Secretary of War, and the Attorney General (which did not oversee the Department of Justice as this department was not created until 1870). For a history of the U.S. Cabinet, See Hoxie, R. Gordon. 1984. "The Cabinet in the American Presidency, 1789–1984." *Presidential Studies Quarterly* (Spring): 209–230.

15. Meador, Daniel J. 1980. *The President, the Attorney General, and the Department of Justice*. Charlottesville: White Burkett Miller Center of Public Affairs, University of Virginia, p. 4.

16. Act of July 27, 1789, ch. 4, 1 Stat. 28 (Foreign Affairs); Act of Aug. 7, 1789, ch. 6, 1 Stat. 49 (War); and Act of Sept. 2, 1789, ch. 12, 1 Stat. 65 (Treasury). See Meador, Daniel J. 1980. *The President, the Attorney General, and the Department of Justice*. Charlottesville: White Burkett Miller Center of Public Affairs, University of Virginia, p. 5.

17. Act of Sept. 24, 1789, ch. 20, 1 Stat. 73. See Meador, Daniel J. 1980. *The President, the Attorney General, and the Department of Justice*. Charlottesville: White Burkett Miller Center of Public Affairs, University of Virginia, p. 5.

18. Meador, Daniel J. 1980. *The President, the Attorney General, and the Department of Justice*. Charlottesville: White Burkett Miller Center of Public Affairs, University of Virginia, pp. 6–7.

19. Meador, Daniel J. 1980. *The President, the Attorney General, and the Department of Justice*. Charlottesville: White Burkett Miller Center of Public Affairs, University of Virginia, pp. 7–9.

20. Meador, Daniel J. 1980. *The President, the Attorney General, and the Department of Justice*. Charlottesville: White Burkett Miller Center of Public Affairs, University of Virginia, p. 10.

21. Meador, Daniel J. 1980. *The President, the Attorney General, and the Department of Justice*. Charlottesville: White Burkett Miller Center of Public Affairs, University of Virginia, p. 11.

22. See "U.S. Department of Justice Website" online at http://www.usdoj.gov

23. Meador, Daniel J. 1980. *The President, the Attorney General, and the Department of Justice*. Charlottesville: White Burkett Miller Center of Public Affairs, University of Virginia, p. 13.

24. See "Department of Justice Organizational Chart" with links to each respective division. http://www.usdoj.gov/dojorg.htm

25. See "Department of Justice Organizational Chart" with links to each respective division. http://www.usdoj.gov/dojorg.htm

26. Edwards, George C. III and Stephen J. Wayne. 1990. *Presidential Leadership: Politics and Policy Making*. 2d ed. New York: St. Martin's Press, pp. 334–335; Segal, Jeffrey A. 1990. "Supreme Court Support for the Solicitor General: The Effect of Presidential Appointments." *Western Political Quarterly* 43: 137–152; Thomas, Norman C. and Joseph A. Pika. 1996. *The Politics of the Presidency*. 4th ed. Washington D.C.: Congressional Quarterly Press, pp. 305–308.

27. Baum, Lawrence. 1998. *The Supreme Court*. 6th ed. Washington D.C.: Congressional Quarterly Press, pp. 118–119; Handberg, Roger and Harold F. Hill, Jr. 1980. "Court Curbing, Court Reversals, and Judicial Review: The Supreme Court versus Congress." *Law and Society Review* 14: 309–322; Scigliana, Robert. 1971. *The Supreme Court and the Presidency*. New York: The Free Press; Segal, Jeffrey A. 1984. "Predicting Supreme Court Decisions Probabilistically: The Search and Seizure Cases (1962–1981)." *American Political Science Review* 78: 891–900; Segal, Jeffrey A. 1988. "Amicus Curiae Briefs by the Solicitor General During the Warren and Burger Courts." *Western Political Quarterly* 41: 135–144; Segal, Jeffrey A. 1990. "Supreme Court Support for the Solicitor General: The Effect of Presidential Appointments." *Western Political Quarterly* 43: 137–152; Segal, Jeffrey A. and Cheryl D. Reedy. 1988. "The Supreme Court and Sec Discrimination: The Role of the Solicitor General." *Western Political Quarterly* 41: 553–568.

28. Thomas, Norman C. and Joseph A. Pika. 1996. *The Politics of the Presidency*. 4th ed. Washington D.C.: Congressional Quarterly Press, p. 305.

29. Caplan, Lincoln. 1987. *The Tenth Justice: The Solicitor General and the Rule of Law*. New York: Random House; Segal, Jeffrey A. 1991. *The American Courts: A Critical Assessment*. John B. Gates and Charles A. Johnson, eds. Washington D.C.: Congressional Quarterly Press, pp. 373–393, p. 376.

30. Waxman, Seth P. 1998. "'Presenting the Case of the United States As It Should Be': The Solicitor General in Historical Context." Address to the Supreme Court Historical Society. Available online at http://www.usdoj.gov/osg/aboutosg/sgarticle.html

31. Federal Bureau of Investigation. 1998. "History of the Federal Bureau of Investigation." Available online at http://www.fbi.gov/yourfbi/history/hist.htm

32. Potter, Claire Bond. 1998. *War on Crime: Bandits, G-Men, and the Politics of Mass Culture*. New Brunswick: Rutgers University Press.

33. This assertion is based upon the author's research at several of the presidential libraries. Research has included reviewing the papers of the Presidents of the United States, the White House Staff, the Department of Justice, the Federal Bureau of Investigation, and recorded phone conversations between presidents and the Federal Bureau of Investigation Directors conducted at the Herbert Hoover Presidential Library, West Branch, Iowa; Franklin D. Roosevelt Presidential Library, Hyde Park, New York; Lyndon B. Johnson Presidential Library, Austin, Texas; the Nixon Project, College Park, Maryland; and the Ronald Reagan Presidential Library, Simi Valley, California.

34. See U.S. Treasury Website online at http://www.treas.gov

35. See U.S. Customs Service Website online at http://www.customs.treas.gov

36. See Alcohol, Tobacco, and Firearms Website online at http://www.atf.treas.gov

37. See U.S. Secret Service Website online at http://www.treas.gov/usss

38. See F.L.E.T.C. Website online at http://www.treas.gov/fletc

39. Segal, Jeffrey A. and Robert M. Howard. 1999. "Justices and Presidents." In *Presidential Policymaking: An End-of-Century Assessment*. Edited by Steven A. Shull. Armonk: M. E. Sharpe, pp. 168–182.

40. Mapp v. Ohio 367 U.S. 643, 6 L.Ed. 2d 1081, 81 S. Ct. 1684 (1961).

41. Miranda v. Arizona 384 U.S. 436, 16 L.Ed. 2d 694, 86 S. Ct. 1602 (1966).

42. Gideon v. Wainwright 372 U.S. 335, 9 L.Ed. 2d 799, 83 S. Ct. 814 (1963).

43. Office of the Pardon Attorney, U.S. Department of Justice Website online at http://www.usdoj.gov/opa/opa.html

44. Edwards, George C. III and Stephen J. Wayne. 1990. *Presidential Leadership: Politics and Policy Making*. 2d ed. New York: St. Martin's Press, p. 342; Office of the Pardon Attorney, U.S. Department of Justice Website online at http://www.usdoj.gov/opa/opa.html

45. Edwards, George C. III and Stephen J. Wayne. 1990. *Presidential Leadership: Politics and Policy Making*. 2d ed. New York: St. Martin's Press, p. 342; Marion, Nancy E. 1994. *A History of Federal Crime-controlInitiatives, 1960–1993*. Westport: Praeger Publishers, pp. 103–104; Simon, David R. and Stanley D. Eitzen. 1993. *Elite Deviance*. 4th ed. Boston: Allyn and Bacon.

46. Ford, Gerald R. 1975. "Proclamation 4311, Granting Pardon to Richard Nixon. September 8, 1974." *Public Papers of the Presidents of the United States*. Washington D.C.: U.S. G.P.O., p. 104.

47. Edwards, George C. III and Stephen J. Wayne. 1990. *Presidential Leadership: Politics and Policy Making*. 2d ed. New York: St. Martin's Press, p. 342.

48. Ford, Gerald R. 1975. "Remarks on Signing 18 Executive Warrants for Clemency. November 29, 1974." *Public Papers of the Presidents of the United States*. Washington D.C.: U.S. G.P.O., pp. 672–266.

49. Carter, Jimmy. 1978. "Presidential Proclamation of Pardon. January 21, 1977." *Public Papers of the Presidents of the United States*. Washington D.C.: U.S. G.P.O., p. 5–6; Edwards, George

C. III and Stephen J. Wayne. 1990. *Presidential Leadership: Politics and Policy Making.* 2d ed. New York: St. Martin's Press, p. 342.

50. Edwards, George C. III and Stephen J. Wayne. 1990. *Presidential Leadership: Politics and Policy Making.* 2d ed. New York: St. Martin's Press, p. 342.

51. Light, Paul C. 1991. *The President's Agenda: Domestic Policy Choice from Kennedy to Reagan.* Rev. ed. Baltimore: The Johns Hopkins University Press, pp. 158–160.

52. Light, Paul C. 1991. *The President's Agenda: Domestic Policy Choice from Kennedy to Reagan.* Rev. ed. Baltimore: The Johns Hopkins University Press, p. 160.

53. Light, Paul C. 1991. *The President's Agenda: Domestic Policy Choice from Kennedy to Reagan.* Rev. ed. Baltimore: The Johns Hopkins University Press, p. 160.

54. Ragsdale, Lyn. 1998. *Vital Statistics on the Presidency.* Rev. ed. Washington D.C.: Congressional Quarterly Press, p. 366.

55. Kessel, John H. 1972. "The Parameters of Presidential Politics." Paper delivered at the American Political Science Association, New York, p. 3, as cited in Light, Paul C. 1991. *The President's Agenda: Domestic Policy Choice from Kennedy to Reagan.* Rev. ed. Baltimore: The Johns Hopkins University Press, p. 160.

56. Calder, James D. 1993. *The Origins and Development of Federal Crime-control policy: Herbert Hoover's Initiatives.* Westport: Praeger Publishers.

57. Hoover, Herbert 1974. "Annual Message to the Congress on the State of the Union. December 3, 1929." *Public Papers of the Presidents of the United States.* Washington D.C.: U.S. G.P.O., pp. 404–436.

58. Hoover, Herbert 1974. "Annual Message to the Congress on the State of the Union. December 3, 1929." *Public Papers of the Presidents of the United States.* Washington D.C.: U.S. G.P.O., pp. 434–435.

59. Roosevelt, Franklin D. 1938. "Annual Message to the Congress. January 3, 1934." *The Public Papers and Addresses of Franklin D. Roosevelt.* New York: Russell and Russell, pp. 12–13.

60. Johnson, Lyndon B. 1966. "Annual Message of the Congress on the State of the Union. January 4, 1965." *Public Papers of the Presidents of the United States.* Washington D.C.: U.S. G.P.O., p. 7.

61. Johnson, Lyndon B. 1970. "Annual Message to the Congress on the State of the Union. January 17, 1968." *Public Papers of the Presidents of the United States.* Washington D.C.: U.S. G.P.O., pp. 14–15.

62. Ragsdale, Lyn. 1998. *Vital Statistics on the Presidency.* Rev. ed. Washington D.C.: Congressional Quarterly Press, p. 366.

63. Reagan, Ronald. 1988. "Address Before a Joint Session of the Congress on the State of the Union. February 6, 1985." *Public Papers of the Presidents of the United States.* Washington D.C.: U.S. G.P.O., p. 134.

64. Clinton, William J. 1995. "Address Before a Joint Session of the Congress on the State of the Union. January 25, 1994." *Public Papers of the Presidents of the United States.* Washington D.C.: U.S. G.P.O., p. 133.

65. These data were tabulated by the author utilizing successive volumes of the *Public Papers of the Presidents of the United States.* Washington D.C.: U.S. G.P.O and the electronic versions of the "Public Papers" available on CD-ROM from World Book Encyclopedia. 1998. *American Reference Library.* Orem: Western Standard Publishing Company.

66. DiClerico, Robert E. 1995. *The American President.* 4th Ed. Englewood Cliffs: Prentice Hall, chapter three, titled "The President and Congress"; Thomas, Norman C. and Joseph A. Pika. 1996. *The Politics of the Presidency.* 4th Ed. Washington D.C.: Congressional Quarterly Press, p. 211.

67. Cronin, Thomas E., Tania Z. Cronin, and Michael E. Milakovich. 1981. *U.S. v. Crime in the Streets.* Bloomington: Indiana University Press, p. 58.

68. "Legislative Background - Safe Streets Act." Box 4. White House Central Files. Lyndon B. Johnson Library, Austin, Texas.

69. Marion, Nancy E. 1994. *A History of Federal Crime-controlInitiatives, 1960–1993*. Westport: Praeger Publishers.

70. Meier, Kenneth J. 1993. *Politics and the Bureaucracy: Policymaking in the Fourth Branch of Government*. 3d ed. Belmont: Wadsworth Publishing, pp. 167–168; West, William F. 1995. *Controlling the Bureaucracy: Institutional Constraints in Theory and Practice*. Armonk: M. E. Sharpe, chapter four, titled "The Administrative Presidency."

71. West, William F. 1995. *Controlling the Bureaucracy: Institutional Constraints in Theory and Practice*. Armonk: M. E. Sharpe, p. 94.

72. Meier, Kenneth J. 1994. *The Politics of Sin: Drugs, Alcohol, and Public Policy*. Armonk: M. E. Sharpe, p. 68.

73. Wilson, Woodrow. 1973. *Congressional Government*. Cleveland: World Publishing, p. 53.

74. Davidson, Roger H. and Walter J. Oleszek. 1998. *Congress and Its Members*. 6th ed. Washington D.C.: Congressional Quarterly Press, pp. 283–288; Edwards, George C. III and Stephen J. Wayne. 1990. *Presidential Leadership: Politics and Policy Making*. 2d ed. New York: St. Martin's Press, pp. 312–316; Ragsdale, Lyn. 1998. *Vital Statistics on the Presidency: Washington to Clinton*. Rev. ed. Washington D.C.: Congressional Quarterly Press, pp. 366–375; Thomas, Norman C. and Joseph A. Pika. 1996. *The Politics of the Presidency*. 4th ed. Washington D.C.: Congressional Quarterly Press, pp. 213–216.

75. Ford, Gerald R. 1975. "Veto of Legislation to Reclassify and Upgrade Deputy United States Marshals. August 13, 1974." *Public Papers of the Presidents of the United State*. Washington D.C.: U.S. G. P.O., pp. 13–14.

76. Reagan, Ronald. 1984. " Memorandum Returning Without Approval a Bill Concerning Contract Services for Drug Dependent Federal Offenses. January 14, 1983." *Public Papers of the Presidents of the United States*. Washington D.C.: U.S. G.P.O., pp. 49–50.

77. Clinton, William J. 1996. "Message to the House of Representatives Returning Without Approval the Departments of Commerce, Justice, and State, the Judiciary, and Related Agencies Appropriations Act, 1996. December 19, 1995." *Public Papers of the Presidents of the United States*. Washington D.C.: U.S. G.P.O., pp. 1910–1911.

78. Roosevelt, Franklin D. 1943. "The President Directs the Detroit Race Rioters to Disperse. Proclamation No. 2588. June 21, 1943." *The Public Papers and Addresses of Franklin D. Roosevelt*. New York: Russell and Russell, pp. 258–259.

79. Johnson, Lyndon B. 1968. "Telegram in Reply to Governor Romney's Request for Federal Troop Assistance in Detroit. July 24, 1967." *Public Papers of the Presidents of the United States*. Washington D.C.: U.S. G.P.O., pp. 714–715.

80. Flamm, Michael William. 1998. *"Law and Order": Street Crime, Civil Disorder, and the Crisis of Liberalism*. Ph.D. Dissertation, Columbia University, p. 98. See also Scruggs, Donald Lee. 1980. *Lyndon Baines Johnson and the National Advisory Commission on Civil Disorders (The Kerner Commission): A Study of the Johnson Domestic Policy Making System*. Ph.D. Dissertation, The University of Oklahoma; Stark, Rodney. 1972. *Police Riots*. Belmont: Wadsworth Publishing Company.

81. Johnson, Lyndon B. 1971. *The Vantage Point: Perspectives of the Presidency, 1963–1969*. New York: Hold, Rinehart, and Winston, p. 170.

82. Memorandum from Califano to President Johnson. April 10, 1968. White House Office Files of Joseph Califano, White House Central Files, Box 20, Lyndon Baines Johnson Library, Austin, Texas.

83. Warshaw, Shirley Anne. 1997. *The Domestic Presidency: Policy Making in the White House*. Boston: Allyn and Bacon, pp. 5–6.

84. Reagan, Ronald. 1989. "Address to the Nation on the Campaign Against Drug Abuse. September 14, 1986." *Public Papers of the Presidents of the United States*. Washington D.C.: U.S. G.P.O., pp. 1178–1182.

85. MacDonald, Donald Ian. "NDPB Recommendations for 1988 Anti-Drug Measures." From the Office files of Ian MacDonald. Box 19057. White House Staff and Office Files. Ronald Reagan Presidential Library, Simi Valley, California.

86. Reagan, Ronald. 1989. "Executive Order 12564—Drug-Free Federal Workplace. September 15, 1986." *Public Papers of the Presidents of the United States.* Washington D.C.: U.S. G.P.O., pp. 1183–1187.

87. MacDonald, Donald Ian. "NDPB Recommendations for 1988 Anti-Drug Measures." From the Office files of Ian MacDonald. Box 19057. White House Staff and Office Files. Ronald Reagan Presidential Library, Simi Valley, California.

88. MacDonald, Donald Ian. "NDPB Recommendations for 1988 Anti-Drug Measures." From the Office files of Ian MacDonald. Box 19057. White House Staff and Office Files. Ronald Reagan Presidential Library, Simi Valley, California.

89. MacDonald, Donald Ian. "NDPB Recommendations for 1988 Anti-Drug Measures." From the Office files of Ian MacDonald. Box 19057. White House Staff and Office Files. Ronald Reagan Presidential Library, Simi Valley, California.

90. It should be noted that many of the methods by which presidents can implement their crime-control policies are also explanations for "why" they engage in crime-control policy. For instance, a president's response to a crisis, the inclusion of the crime issue in presidential campaigns, and the fact the national political party's platforms include a position on crime, are all explanations for why presidents engage in crime-control policy (see chapter two), but they also stand as an explanation for how they engage in crime-control policies as well.

91. Stiles, Lela. 1954. *The Man Behind Roosevelt: The Story of Louis McHenry Howe.* Cleveland: The World Publishing Company.

92. Rollins, Alfred B., Jr. 1962. *Roosevelt and Howe.* New York: Alfred A. Knopf, pp. 402–404; Stiles, Lela. 1954. *The Man Behind Roosevelt: The Story of Louis McHenry Howe.* Cleveland: The World Publishing Company, pp. 95–96.

93. Warshaw, Shirley Anne. 1999. "Staffing Patterns in the Modern White House." In *Presidential Policymaking: An End-of-Century Assessment.* Steven A. Shull, ed. Armonk: M. E. Sharpe, pp. 131–149.

94. Pfiffner, James P. 1994. *The Modern Presidency.* New York: St. Martin's Press, pp. 93–95; Watson, Richard A. and Norman C. Thomas. 1983. *The Politics of the Presidency.* New York: John Wiley & Sons, p. 313.

95. LeLoup, Lance T. and Steven A. Shull. 1999. *The President and Congress: Collaboration and Combat in National Policymaking.* Boston: Allyn and Bacon, p. 50.

96. LeLoup, Lance T. and Steven A. Shull. 1999. *The President and Congress: Collaboration and Combat in National Policymaking.* Boston: Allyn and Bacon, p. 71; Pfiffner, James P. 1994. *The Modern Presidency.* New York: St. Martin's Press, pp. 92–93; Warshaw, Shirley Anne. 1999. "Staffing Patterns in the Modern White House." In *Presidential Policymaking: An End-of-Century Assessment.* Steven A. Shull, ed. Armonk: M. E. Sharpe, pp. 131–149; Watson, Richard A. and Norman C. Thomas. 1983. *The Politics of the Presidency.* New York: John Wiley & Sons, p. 314; West, William F. 1995. *Controlling the Bureaucracy: Institutional Constraints in Theory and Practice.* Armonk: M. E. Sharpe, pp. 86–87.

97. Pfiffner, James P. 1994. *The Modern Presidency.* New York: St. Martin's Press, p. 96; Warshaw, Shirley Anne. 1999. "Staffing Patterns in the Modern White House." In *Presidential Policymaking: An End-of-Century Assessment.* Steven A. Shull.ed. Armonk: M. E. Sharpe, pp. 131–149.

98. See Warshaw, Shirley Anne. 1999. "Staffing Patterns in the Modern White House." In *Presidential Policymaking: An End-of-Century Assessment.* Steven A. Shull, ed. Armonk: M. E. Sharpe, pp. 131–149.

99. Nixon, Richard. 1978. *RN: Memoirs of Richard Nixon.* New York: Grosset and Dunlap, p. 342.

100. DiClerico, Robert E. 2000. *The American President.* 5th ed. Upper Saddle River: Prentice Hall, pp. 221–223; Warshaw, Shirley Anne. 1999. "Staffing Patterns in the Modern White House." In

Presidential Policymaking: An End-of-Century Assessment. Steven A. Shull, ed. Armonk: M. E. Sharpe, pp. 131–149.

101. Warshaw, Shirley Anne and John Robert Greene. 1994. "'Brushfires': The Departments, the Domestic Council, and Policy Agendas in the Ford White House." *Congress & The Presidency* 21 (2): 83–97.

102. DiClerico, Robert E. 2000. *The American President*. 5th ed. Upper Saddle River: Prentice Hall, pp. 221–223; Edwards, George C. III and Stephen J. Wayne. 1990. *Presidential Leadership: Politics and Policy Making*. 2d ed. New York: St. Martin's Press, pp. 357–362; Thomas, Norman C. and Joseph A. Pika. 1996. *The Politics of the Presidency*. 4th ed. Washington D.C.: Congressional Quarterly Press, pp. 345–349; Warshaw, Shirley Anne. 1999. "Staffing Patterns in the Modern White House." In *Presidential Policymaking: An End-of-Century Assessment*. Steven A. Shull, ed. Armonk: M. E. Sharpe, pp. 131–149.

103. Meese, Edwin III. 1981. "Presidential Decision Making." A speech before the graduating class of West Point Cadets on March 27, 1981. Video Recording reviewed at Ronald Reagan Library, Simi Valley, California.

104. DiClerico, Robert E. 2000. *The American President*. 5th ed. Upper Saddle River: Prentice Hall, p. 223.

105. Domestic Council. Box 4. FG 6–15. "Domestic Council Members." White House Central Files, Subject Files. Nixon Project. College Park, Maryland.

106. Domestic Council. Box 4. FG 6–15. "Domestic Council Members." White House Central Files, Subject Files. Nixon Project. College Park, Maryland.

107. Domestic Council. Box 4. FG 6–15. "Domestic Council Members." White House Central Files, Subject Files. Nixon Project. College Park, Maryland.

108. Executive Order 11599, Establishing a Special Action Office for Drug Abuse Prevention. Signed June 17, 1971. This was nullified by Public Law 92–255 (86 Stat. 65, 21 U.S.C. 1101). See also Sharp, Elaine B. 1994. *The Dilemmas of Drug Policy in the United States*. New York: Harper Collins College Publishers, p. 27.

109. LeLoup, Lance T. and Steven A. Shull. 1999. *The President and Congress: Collaboration and Combat in National Policymaking*. Boston: Allyn and Bacon, p. 72; Pfiffner, James P. 1994. *The Modern Presidency*. New York: St. Martin's Press, p. 97; Thomas, Norman C. and Joseph A. Pika. 1996. *The Politics of the Presidency*. 4th ed. Washington D.C.: Congressional Quarterly Press, pp. 224–225.

110. Windlesham, Lord. 1998. *Politics, Punishment, and Populism*. New York: Oxford University Press, p. 94.

111. Edwards, George C. III and Stephen J. Wayne. 1990. *Presidential Leadership: Politics and Policy Making*. New York: St. Martin's Press, p. 303; Pfiffner, James P. 1999. "Presidential Constraints and Transitions." In *Presidential Policymaking: An End-of-Century Assessment*. Edited by Steven A. Shull. Armonk: M. E. Sharpe, pp. 19–37, p. 24.

112. DiClerico, Robert E. 1995. *The American President*. 4th ed. Englewood Cliffs: Prentice Hall, pp. 173–174.

113. Potter, Claire Bond. 1998. *War on Crime: Bandits, G-Men, and the Politics of Mass Culture*. New Brunswick: Rutgers University Press.

114. Bertram, Eva, Morris Blachman, Kenneth Sharpe, and Peter Andreas. 1996. *Drug War Politics: The Price of Denial*. Berkeley: University of California Press, p. 107.

115. Bertram, Eva, Morris Blachman, Kenneth Sharpe, and Peter Andreas. 1996. *Drug War Politics: The Price of Denial*. Berkeley: University of California Press, p. 107.

116. Epstein, Edward Jay. 1990. *Agency of Fear: Opiates and Political Power in America*. Rev. Ed. New York: Verso Books.

117. Bertram, Eva, Morris Blachman, Kenneth Sharpe, and Peter Andreas. 1996. *Drug War Politics: The Price of Denial*. Berkeley: University of California Press, pp. 107–108; Massing, Michael. 1998. The Fix. New York: Simon & Schuster; McWilliams, John C. 1991. "Through the Past

Darkly: The Politics and Policies of America's Drug War." *Journal of Policy History* 3 (4): 356–392.

118. Caplan, Gerald. 1973. "Reflections on the Nationalization of Crime, 1964–1968." *Law and the Social Order* 1973: 583–635; Flamm, Michael William. 1998. *"Law and Order": Street Crime, Civil Disorder, and the Crisis of Liberalism.* Ph.D. Dissertation, Columbia University, pp. 155–156; Massing, Michael. 1998. *The Fix.* New York: Simon & Schuster; McWilliams, John C. 1991. "Through the Past Darkly: The Politics and Policies of America's Drug War." *Journal of Policy History* 3 (4): 356–392.

119. Cronin, Thomas E., Tania Z. Cronin, and Michael E. Milakovich. 1981. *U.S. v. Crime in the Streets.* Bloomington: Indiana University Press; Diegelman, Robert F. 1982. "Federal Financial Assistance for Crime Control: Lessons of the LEAA Experience." *The Journal of Criminal Law and Criminology* 73 (3): 994–1011; Feeley, Malcolm M. and Austin D. Sarat. 1980. *The Policy Dilemma: Federal Crime Policy and the Law Enforcement Assistance Administration.* Minneapolis: University of Minnesota Press; Gray, Virginia and Bruce Williams. 1980. *The Organizational Politics of Criminal Justice.* Lexington: Lexington Books.

120. Bureau of Justice Assistance. 1992–1998. *Edward Bryne Memorial State and Local Law Enforcement Assistance: Fact Sheet.* Washington D.C.: U.S. Department of Justice. See also Bureau of Justice Assistance Webpage available online at http://www.ojp.usdoj.gov/BJA

121. See Office of Community Oriented Policing Services Webpage available online at http://www.usdoj.gov/cops

122. Calder, James D. 1993. *The Origins and Development of Federal Crime-control policy: Herbert Hoover's Initiatives.* Westport: Praeger Publishers.

123. Potter, Claire Bond. 1998. *War on Crime: Bandits , G-Men, and the Politics of Mass Culture.* New Brunswick: Rutgers University Press.

124. Meador, Daniel J. 1980. *The President, the Attorney General, and the Department of Justice.* Charlottesville: White Burkett Miller Center for Public Affairs, University of Virginia, p. 11.

125. See U.S. Department of Justice Webpage available online at http://www.usdoj.gov

126. Beale, Sara Sun. 1996. "Federalizing Crime: Assessing the Impact on the Federal Courts." *The Annals of the American Academy of Political and Social Science* 543: 39–51, p. 45.

127. Davey, Joseph Dillon. 1998. *The Politics of Prison Expansion.* Westport: Praeger Publishers; Schlosser, Eric. 1998. "The Prison-Industrial Complex." *The Atlantic Monthly* 282 (6): 51–77.

128. Thomas, Norman C. and Joseph A. Pika. 1996. *The Politics of the Presidency.* 4th ed. Washington D.C.: Congressional Quarterly Press, p. 274; Watson, Richard A. and Norman C. Thomas. 1983. *The Politics of the Presidency.* New York: John Wiley & Sons, p. 319.

129. Meier, Kenneth J. 1994. *The Politics of Sin: Drugs, Alcohol, and Public Policy.* Armonk: M. E. Sharpe, p. 97.

130. Meier, Kenneth J. 1994. *The Politics of Sin: Drugs, Alcohol, and Public Policy.* Armonk: M. E. Sharpe, p. 97.

131. Dilulio, John J., Jr., Steven K. Smith, and Aaron J. Saiger. 1994. "The Federal Role in Crime Control." In *Crime.* Edited by James Q. Wilson and Joan Petersilia. San Francisco: ICS Press, pp. 445–462.

132. Meier, Kenneth J. 1993. *Politics and the Bureaucracy: Policymaking in the Fourth Branch of Government.* Belmont: Wadsworth Publishing Company; Meier, Kenneth J. 1994. *The Politics of Sin: Drugs, Alcohol, and Public Policy.* Armonk: M. E. Sharpe.

133. Smith, Daniel A., Kevin M. Leyden, and Stephen A. Borrelli. 1998. "Predicting the Outcomes of Presidential Commissions: Evidence from the Johnson and Nixon Years." *Presidential Studies Quarterly* 28 (2): 269–285, p. 270.

134. Smith, Daniel A., Kevin M. Leyden, and Stephen A. Borrelli. 1998. "Predicting the Outcomes of Presidential Commissions: Evidence from the Johnson and Nixon Years." *Presidential Studies Quarterly* 28 (2): 269–285, p. 270.

135. Calder, James Doug. 1978. *Presidents and Crime Control: Some Limitations on Executive Policy Making*. Ph.D. Dissertation, Claremont University, pp. 138–145; Popper, Frank. 1970. *President's Commissions*. New York: Twentieth Century Fund; Smith, Daniel A., Kevin M. Leyden, and Stephen A. Borrelli. 1998. "Predicting the Outcomes of Presidential Commissions: Evidence from the Johnson and Nixon Years." *Presidential Studies Quarterly* 28 (2): 269–285; Wolanin, Thomas. 1975. *Presidential Advisory Commissions*. Madison: University of Wisconsin Press.

136. Thomas, Norman C. and Joseph A. Pika. 1996. *The Politics of the Presidency*. 4th ed. Washington D.C.: Congressional Quarterly Press, p. 344.

137. Calder, James D. 1981. "Herbert Hoover's Contributions to the Administrative History of Crime-control Policy." Unpublished paper presented at the annual meeting of the Southwest Political Science Association, Dallas, Texas, March 25–28; Calder, James Doug. 1978. *Presidents and Crime Control: Some Limitations on Executive Policy Making*. Ph.D. Dissertation, Claremont University, 139–142; Calder, James D. 1993. *The Origins and Development of Federal Crime-control policy: Herbert Hoover's Initiatives*. Westport: Praeger Publishers, chapter four, titled "Scientific Investigation: The Wickersham Commission."

138. See Boehm, Randolph (Editor). 1997. *Records of the Wickersham Commission on Law Observance and Enforcement (Research Collections in American Legal History)*. New York: University Publications.

139. Ruth, Henry S., Jr. 1968. "To Dust Shall Ye Return?" *Notre Dame Lawyer* 43: 811–833.

140. Calder, James Doug. 1978. *Presidents and Crime Control: Some Limitations on Executive Policy Making*. Ph.D. Dissertation, Claremont University, pp. 138–145.

141. Caplan, Gerald. 1973. "Reflections on the Nationalization of Crime, 1964–1968." *Law and the Social Order* 1973: 583–635.

142. President's Commission on Law Enforcement and Administration of Justice. 1968. *The Challenge of Crime in a Free Society*. New York: Avon Books.

143. Conley, John A. 1994. *The 1967 President's Crime Commission Report: Its Impact 25 Years Later*. Cincinnati: Anderson Publishing Company/Academy of Criminal Justice Sciences; U.S. Department of Justice, Office of Justice Programs. 1997. *The Challenge of Crime in a Free Society: Looking Back, Looking Forward*. Washington D.C.: U.S. Department of Justice; Walker, Samuel. 1978. "Reexamining the President's Crime Commission: The Challenge of Crime in a Free Society after Ten Years." *Crime & Delinquency* 24 (1): 1–12.

144. National Advisory Commission on Civil Disorders. *National Advisory Commission on Civil Disorders Report*. Washington D.C.: U.S. G.P.O., pp. 229–230; National Commission on the Cause and Prevention of Violence. *National Commission on the Causes and Prevention of Violence Final Report*. Washington D.C.: U.S. G.P.O., p. 272; President's Commission on Law Enforcement and Administration of Justice. 1968. *The Challenge of Crime in a Free Society*. New York: Avon Books, p. 284.

145. The President's Task Force on Crime. 1968. *The Report of the President's Task Force on Crime*. As obtained in the "1966–1967 Task Force on Crime" folder. Box 1. White House Central Files, Legislative Background Safe Streets. Nixon Project, College Park, Maryland.

146. Flamm, Michael William. 1998. *"Law and Order": Street Crime, Civil Disorder, and the Crisis of Liberalism*. Ph.D. Dissertation, Columbia University; Scruggs, Donald Lee. 1980. *Lyndon Baines Johnson and the National Advisory Commission on Civil Disorders (The Kerner Commission): A Study of the Johnson Domestic Policy Making System*. Ph.D. Dissertation, The University of Oklahoma.

147. See "Commission on Obscenity and Pornography, 1969–1970." Box 1. White House Central Files-Subject Files. Nixon Project, College Park, Maryland.

148. Clear, Todd. 1997. "Societal Responses to the President's Crime Commission: A Thirty-Year Retrospective." In *The Challenge of Crime in a Free Society: Looking Back, Looking Forward*. Washington D.C.: U.S. Department of Justice, pp. 131–158.

149. Thomas, Norman C. and Joseph A. Pika. 1996. *The Politics of the Presidency*. 4th Ed. Washington D.C.: Congressional Quarterly Press, p. 264; Watson, Richard A. and Norman C. Thomas. 1983. *The Politics of the Presidency*. New York: John Wiley & Sons, p. 305.

150. Watson, Richard A. and Norman C. Thomas. 1983. *The Politics of the Presidency*. New York: John Wiley & Sons, p. 305.

151. National Archives and Records Administration, Executive Orders Disposition Tables, January 21, 1961–October 6, 1999. http://www.nara.gov/fedreg/eo.html#top. Data downloaded on October 19, 1999.

152. Executive Order 11111, Providing assistance for the removal of obstructions of justice and suppression of unlawful combinations within the State of Alabama, Signed: June 11, 1963, Federal Register page and date: 28 FR 5709; June 12, 1963; Executive Order 11118, Providing assistance for removal of unlawful obstructions of justice in the State of Alabama, Signed: September 10, 1963, Federal Register page and date: 28 FR 9863; September 11, 1963; Executive Order 11364, Providing for the restoration of law and order in the State of Michigan, Signed: July 24, 1967, Federal Register page and date: 32 FR 10907; July 26, 1967; Executive Order 11403; Providing for the restoration of law and order in the Washington Metropolitan Area, Signed: April 5, 1968, Federal Register page and date: 33 FR 5501; April 9, 1968; Executive Order 11404, Providing for the restoration of law and order in the State of Illinois, Signed: April 7, 1968, Federal Register page and date: 33 FR 5503; April 9, 1968; Executive Order 11405, Providing for the restoration of law and order in the State of Maryland, Signed: April 7, 1968, Federal Register page and date: 33 FR 5505; April 9, 1968.

153. Executive Order 12564, Drug_Free Federal Workplace, Signed: September 15, 1986, Federal Register page and date: 51 FR 32889; September 17, 1986. See also Crowley, Donald W. 1998. "Drug Testing in the Rehnquist Era." In *The New War on Drugs: Symbolic Politics and Criminal Justice Policy*. Eric L. Jensen and Jurg Gerber, eds. Cincinnati: Anderson Publishing/Academy of Criminal Justice Sciences, pp. 123–139.

154. Executive Order 11236, Establishing the President's Commission on Law Enforcement and Administration of Justice, Signed: July 23, 1965, Federal Register page and date: 30 FR 9349; July 28, 1965.

155. Executive Order 11365, Establishing a National Advisory Commission on Civil Disorders, Signed: July 29, 1967, Federal Register page and date: 32 FR 11111; August 1, 1967.

156. Executive Order 11599, Establishing a special action office for drug abuse prevention,

157. Executive Order 11676, Providing for the establishment of an Office of National Narcotics Intelligence within the Department of Justice, Signed: July 27, 1972, Federal Register page and date: 37 FR 15125; July 28, 1972.

158. Executive Order 12590, National Drug Policy Board, Signed: March 26, 1987, Federal Register page and date: 52 FR 10021; March 30, 1987.

159. Executive Order 11669, J. Edgar Hoover, Signed: May 2, 1972, Federal Register page and date: 37 FR 9013; May 4, 1972.

160. Executive Order 12911, Seal for the Office of National Drug Control Policy, Signed: April 25, 1994, Federal Register page and date: 59 FR 21121; April 28, 1994.

161. Thomas, Norman C. and Joseph A. Pika. 1996. *The Politics of the Presidency*. 4th ed. Washington D.C.: Congressional Quarterly Press, p. 345.

162. Thomas, Norman C. and Joseph A. Pika. 1996. *The Politics of the Presidency*. 4th ed. Washington D.C.: Congressional Quarterly Press, p. 345.

163. LeLoup, Lance T. 1999. "Budget Policy Transformations." In *Presidential Policymaking: An End-of-Century Assessment*. Steven A. Shull, ed. Armonk: M.E. Sharpe, pp. 204–223; Thomas, Norman C. and Joseph A. Pika. 1996. *The Politics of the Presidency*. 4th ed. Washington D.C.:

Congressional Quarterly Press, pp. 268–271; Wildavsky, Aaron. 1992. *The New Politics of the Budgetary Process.* 2d ed. New York: Harper Collins Publishers.

164. Wildavsky, Aaron. 1992. *The New Politics of the Budgetary Process.* 2d ed. New York: Harper Collins Publishers, p. 21

165. Congressional Digest. 1994. "Federal Crime-control Efforts." *Congressional Digest* 73 (6–7): 161–192.

166. Caldeira, Gregory A. 1983. "Elections and the Politics of Crime: Budgetary Choices and Priorities in America." In *The Political Science of Criminal Justice.* Stuart Nagel, Erika Fairchild, and Anthony Champagne, eds. Springfield: Charles C. Thomas Publishers, pp. 238–252; Caldeira, Greg A. and Andrew T. Cowart. 1980. "Budgets, Institutions, and Change: Criminal Justice Policy in America." *American Journal of Political Science* 24 (3): 413–438.

167. Martinek, Wendy L., Kenneth J. Meier, and Lael R. Keiser. 1998. "Jackboots or Lace Panties? The Bureau of Alcohol, Tobacco and Firearms." In *The Changing Politics of Gun Control.* John M. Bruce and Clyde Wilcox, eds. Lanham: Rowman & Littlefield Publishers, Inc., pp. 17–44.

168. Martinek, Wendy L., Kenneth J. Meier, and Lael R. Keiser. 1998. "Jackboots or Lace Panties? The Bureau of Alcohol, Tobacco and Firearms." In *The Changing Politics of Gun Control.* John M. Bruce and Clyde Wilcox, eds. Lanham: Rowman & Littlefield Publishers, Inc., pp. 17–44, p. 24.

169. Marion, Nancy. 1992. "Presidential Agenda Setting in Crime Control." *Criminal Justice Policy Review* 6 (2): 159–184, p. 162.

170. Shull, Steven A. 1983. *Domestic Policy Formation: Presidential–Congressional Partnership?* Westport: Praeger Publishers, p. 31.

171. Shull, Steven A. 1983. *Domestic Policy Formation: Presidential–Congressional Partnership?* Westport: Praeger Publishers, p. 31.

172. Ragsdale, Lyn. 1984. "The Politics of Presidential Speechmaking, 1949–1980." *The American Political Science Review* 78: 971–984, p. 971.

173. Ragsdale, Lyn. 1984. "The Politics of Presidential Speechmaking, 1949–1980." *The American Political Science Review* 78: 971–984, p. 971.

174. Lowi, Theodore J. 1985. *The Personal President: Power Invested, Promises Unfulfilled.* Ithaca: Cornell University Press; Wattenberg, Martin P. 1991. *The Rise of Candidate–Centered Politics.* Cambridge: Harvard University Press.

175. Kernell, Samuel. 1997. *Going Public: New Strategies of Presidential Leadership.* 3d ed. Washington D.C.: Congressional Quarterly Press.

176. Ceaser, James W., Glen Thurow, Jeffrey Tulis, and Joseph M. Bessette. 1981. "The Rise of the Rhetorical Presidency." *Presidential Studies Quarterly* (Spring): 158–171, p. 159.

177. Ceaser, James W., Glen Thurow, Jeffrey Tulis, and Joseph M. Bessette. 1981. "The Rise of the Rhetorical Presidency." *Presidential Studies Quarterly* (Spring): 158–171, p. 159.

178. Ceaser, James W., Glen Thurow, Jeffrey Tulis, and Joseph M. Bessette. 1981. "The Rise of the Rhetorical Presidency." *Presidential Studies Quarterly* (Spring): 158–171. This is also based upon the author's review of presidential speeches on crime at the following presidential libraries: Herbert Hoover Library, West Branch, Iowa; Franklin D. Roosevelt Library, Hyde Park, New York; Lyndon B. Johnson Library, Austin, Texas; Nixon Project, College Park, Maryland; Gerald Ford Library, Ann Arbor, Michigan; Ronald Reagan Library, Simi Valley, California.

179. Johnson, Lyndon B. 1966. "Remarks on Crime Control at the Signing of the District of Columbia Appropriations Bill. July 16, 1965." *Public Papers of the Presidents of the United States.* Washington D.C.: U.S. G.P.O., p. 759.

180. Johnson, Lyndon B. 1966. "Statement by the President on Establishing the President's Commission on Law Enforcement and Administration of Justice. July 26, 1965." *Public Papers of the Presidents of the United States.* Washington D.C.: U.S. G.P.O., p. 785.

181. Johnson, Lyndon B. 1968. "Special Message to the Congress on Crime in America. February 6, 1967." *Public Papers of the Presidents of the United States*. Washington D.C.: U.S. G.P.O., pp. 134–145.

182. Flamm, Michael William. 1998. *"Law and Order": Street Crime, Civil Disorder, and the Crisis of Liberalism*. Ph.D. Dissertation, Columbia University, p. 172; Memorandum to Joseph A. Califano, Jr. from Nicholas deB. Katzenbach, Reference: Timing of the President's Crime Message and Release of the Commission's Report." Dated January 24, 1967. Box 3. White House Central Files, Legislative Background, Safe Streets and Crime Control. Lyndon B. Johnson Library, Austin, Texas; President's Commission on Law Enforcement and Administration of Justice. 1968. *The Challenge of Crime in a Free Society*. New York: Avon Books.

183. Marion, Nancy. 1994. "Symbolism and Federal Crime-control Legislation, 1960–1990." *Journal of Crime and Justice* 17 (2): 69–91.

184. Ceaser, James W., Glen E. Thurow, Jeffrey Tulis, and Joseph M. Bessette. 1981. "The Rise of the Rhetorical Presidency." *Presidential Studies Quarterly* (Spring): 158–171, p. 162.

185. Ragsdale, Lyn. 1984. "The Politics of Presidential Speechmaking, 1949–1980." *The American Political Science Review* 78: 971–984, p. 973.

186. Hoover, Herbert. 1974. "Inaugural Address. March 4, 1929." *Public Papers of the Presidents of the United States*. Washington D.C.: U.S. G.P.O., p. 1.

187. Bush, George. 1990. "Inaugural Address. January 20, 1989." *Public Papers of the Presidents of the United States*. Washington D.C.: U.S. G.P.O., p. 2.

188. Cohen, Jeffrey. 1997. *Presidential Responsiveness and Public Policy-Making: The Public and the Policies that Presidents Choose*. Ann Arbor: The University of Michigan Press; Cohen, Jeffrey. 1995. "Presidential Rhetoric and the Public Agenda." *American Journal of Political Science* 39: 87–107.

189. Ragsdale, Lyn. 1998. *Vital Statistics on the Presidency: Washington to Clinton*. Rev. ed. Washington D.C.: Congressional Quarterly Inc., p. 150.

190. Kernell, Samuel. 1997. *Going Public: New Strategies of Presidential Leadership*. 3d ed. Washington D.C.: Congressional Quarterly Press, p. 107.

191. Ragsdale, Lyn. 1998. *Vital Statistics on the Presidency: Washington to Clinton*. Rev. ed. Washington D.C.: Congressional Quarterly Inc., p. 150.

192. Ragsdale, Lyn. 1987. "Presidential Speechmaking and the Public Audience: Individual Presidents and Group Attitudes." *Journal of Politics* 49 (3): 704–736, pp. 704–705.

193. Ragsdale, Lyn. 1998. *Vital Statistics on the Presidency: Washington to Clinton*. Rev. ed. Washington D.C.: Congressional Quarterly Inc., p. 153.

194. Kernell, Samuel. 1997. *Going Public: New Strategies of Presidential Leadership*. 3d ed. Washington D.C.: Congressional Quarterly Press, p. 115; Ragsdale, Lyn. 1998. *Vital Statistics on the Presidency: Washington to Clinton*. Rev. ed. Washington D.C.: Congressional Quarterly Inc., pp. 153–154.

195. Kernell, Samuel. 1997. *Going Public: New Strategies of Presidential Leadership*. 3d ed. Washington D.C.: Congressional Quarterly Press, pp. 117–123; Ragsdale, Lyn. 1998. *Vital Statistics on the Presidency: Washington to Clinton*. Rev. ed. Washington D.C.: Congressional Quarterly Inc., pp. 152–156.

196. Ragsdale, Lyn. 1984. "The Politics of Presidential Speechmaking, 1949–1980." *The American Political Science Review* 78: 971–984, p. 971.

197. The yearly average of news conferences and questions-and-answers for coding purposes were based on the total number of exchanges between the president and either reporters or citizens. For instance, if a news conference was held and the exchange between the president and the reporter was on "crime in the street," that would be counted as one exchange. If later in the news conference, whether the same reporter or a different one asked about the topic of

"drugs," this was counted as a different exchange. In the case of follow-up questions on a specific topic, these were not counted as a new exchange, but rather as part the previous exchange.
198. Calder, James D. 1993. *The Origins and Development of Federal Crime Control Policy: Herbert Hoover's Initiatives.* Westport: Praeger Publishers; Calder, James D. 1978. *Presidents and Crime Control: Some Limitations on Executive Policy Making.* Ph.D. Dissertation, Claremont University.

President Lyndon Baines Johnson receiving the President's Commission on Law Enforcement and Administration of Justice's report titled The Challenge of Crime in a Free Society, *on February 16, 1967.*

PHOTOGRAPH TAKEN BY WHITE HOUSE PHOTOGRAPHER VOICHI R. OKAMOTO, COURTESY OF THE LYNDON BAINES JOHNSON LIBRARY, AUSTIN, TEXAS.

chapter 4

Do Presidents Influence Public Opinion of Crime?

◆◆◆

> I believe that the overwhelming majority of Americans will join in preserving law and order and reject resolutely those who espouse violence no matter what the cause.
>
> —Lyndon B. Johnson[1]

The previous chapters have laid the groundwork for this chapter by dealing with the three key assumptions being made under the hypothesis that presidents influence public opinion of crime. They include: 1) that presidents do in fact address issues of crime, 2) that presidents have reasons for addressing issues of crime, and 3) that presidents have the means available to address the issues of crime. Having demonstrated that each of these assumptions are both valid and reliable in the previous three chapters, it can be clearly articulated with some assurance of accuracy that presidents do attempt to influence public opinion of crime and that they have done so in the past for various reasons through a number of means available to them. The question that should naturally follow is: has this had any impact? Or, another way of stating this is through the question: "Do presidents influence public opinion of crime?"

This chapter will attempt to address this question by utilizing the theory that presidents influence public opinion and testing the hypothesis that presidents influence public opinion of crime. It will do so by concentrating on what is meant by "public opinion," the dependent variable, and presidents influencing capabilities—the key independent variable. In addition, because there may be other influencing factors on public opinion of crime such as the media, economics, or official crime rates, these possibilities will also be explored. Each of these variables will then be operationalized into quantifiable data lending itself more readily to a statistical analysis. Through the use of an Ordinary Least Squares time-series regression model, the impact that presidents have on the public opinion of crime will be assessed. Additional models will be entertained and other variables will be added to test alternative possibilities in order to

The President Speaks . . .

Good evening. Usually, I talk with you from my office in the West Wing of the White House. But tonight there's something special to talk about, and I've asked someone very special to join me. Nancy and I are here in the West Hall of the White House, and around us are the rooms in which we live. It's the home you've provided for us, of which we merely have temporary custody.

Nancy's joining me because the message this evening is not my message but ours. And we speak to you not simply as fellow citizens but as fellow parents and grandparents and as concerned neighbors. It's back-to-school time for America's children. And while drug and alcohol abuse cuts across all generations, it's especially damaging to the young people on whom our future depends. So tonight, from our family to yours, from our home to yours, thank you for joining us.

America has accomplished so much in these last few years, whether it's been rebuilding our economy or serving the cause of freedom in the world. What we've been able to achieve has been done with your help—with us working together as a nation united. Now, we need your support again. Drugs are menacing our society. They're threatening our values and undercutting our institutions. They're killing our children.

President Ronald Reagan with members of the United States Park Police in the White House Oval Office on December 19, 1985.
PHOTO COURTESY OF THE RONALD REAGAN LIBRARY, SIMI VALLEY, CALIFORNIA.

From the beginning of our administration, we've taken strong steps to do something about this horror. Tonight I can report to you that we've made much progress. Thirty-seven Federal agencies are working together in a vigorous national effort, and by next year our spending for drug law enforcement will have more than tripled from its 1981 levels. We have increased seizures of illegal drugs. Shortages of marijuana are now being reported. Last year alone over 10,000 drug criminals were convicted and nearly $250 million of their assets were seized by the DEA, the Drug Enforcement Administration.

And in the most important area, individual use, we see progress. In 4 years the number of high school seniors using marijuana on a daily basis has dropped from 1 in 14 to 1 in 20. The U.S. military has cut the use of illegal drugs among its personnel by 67 percent since 1980. These are a measure of our commitment and emerging signs that we can defeat this enemy. But we still have much to do.

Despite our best efforts, illegal cocaine is coming into our country at alarming levels, and 4 to 5 million people regularly use it. Five hundred thousand Americans are hooked on heroin. One in twelve persons smokes marijuana regularly. Regular drug use is even higher among the age group 18 to 25—most likely just entering the workforce. Today there's a new epidemic: smokable cocaine, otherwise known as crack. It is an explosively destructive and often lethal substance which is crushing its users. It is an uncontrolled fire.

And drug abuse is not a so-called victimless crime. Everyone's safety is at stake when drugs and excessive alcohol are used by people on the highways or by those transporting our citizens or operating industrial equipment. Drug abuse costs you and your fellow Americans at least $60 billion a year.

From the early days of our administration, Nancy has been intensely involved in the effort to fight. . . . Nancy's personal crusade, like that of so many other wonderful individuals, should become our national crusade. It must include a combination of government and private efforts which complement one another. Last month I announced six initiatives which we believe will do just that.

First, we seek a drug-free workplace at all levels of government and in the private sector. Second, we'll work toward drug-free schools. Third, we want to ensure that the public is protected and that treatment is available to substance abusers and the chemically dependent. Our fourth goal is to expand international cooperation while treating drug trafficking as a threat to our national security. In October I will be meeting with key U.S. Ambassadors to discuss what can be done to support our friends abroad. Fifth, we must move to strengthen law enforcement activities such as those initiated by Vice President Bush and Attorney General Meese. And finally, we seek to expand public awareness and prevention.

(continued)

The President Speaks . . . — (continued)

Your government will continue to act aggressively, but nothing would be more effective than for Americans simply to quit using illegal drugs. We seek to create a massive change in national attitudes which ultimately will separate the drugs from the customer, to take the user away from the supply. I believe, quite simply, that we can help them quit, and that's where you come in.

My generation will remember how America swung into action when we were attacked in World War II. The war was not just fought by the fellows flying the planes or driving the tanks. It was fought at home by a mobilized nation—men and women alike—building planes and ships, clothing sailors and soldiers, feeding marines and airmen; and it was fought by children planting victory gardens and collecting cans. Well, now we're in another war for our freedom, and it's time for all of us to pull together again. So, for example, if your friend or neighbor or a family member has a drug or alcohol problem, don't turn the other way. Go to his help or to hers. Get others involved with you—clubs, service groups, and community organizations—and provide support and strength. And, of course, many of you've been cured through treatment and self-help. Well, you're the combat veterans, and you have a critical role to play. You can help others by telling your story and providing a willing hand to those in need. Being friends to others is the best way of being friends to ourselves. It's time, as Nancy said, for America to "just say no" to drugs.

—Ronald Reagan
Address to the Nation on the Campaign Against Drug Abuse,
September 14, 1986.

---

clearly understand the relation and interaction among the variables addressed. Moreover, measures will be taken to test the possibility that the counterhypothesis that public opinion influences the president is not the more credible theory. Finally, this chapter will conclude with a discussion of the findings related to the hypothesis and theoretical construct that presidents influence public opinion, demonstrating that presidents do, in fact, influence public opinion of crime.

PUBLIC OPINION/PUBLIC AGENDA

The study of public opinion throughout the twentieth century has yielded a very broad and vast multi-disciplinary body of evidence.[2] Early work in the area of public opinion by such people as the social commentator Walter Lippmann[3] and the political scientist V. O. Key[4] argued that the American people lacked the knowledge to understand the issues placed before them and therefore had no ability to formulate policy through public opinion.[5] Rather than seeing public opinion shape policy preferences, supporting the ideas of a true democracy, these individuals argued that policy was in reality formulated by elites.[6] A response to this argument would begin appearing in the 1970s and 1980s, when this counterassumption to American democracy was challenged by a number of researchers. What would subsequently develop was a debate over how rational public opinion has been in Americans' policy preferences. Page and Shapiro would argue that these policy preferences have been consistent over time,[7] while Mayer would counterargue and explain that American public opinion has changed significantly from the early 1960s to the late 1980s.[8] As a result of the conflicting perspectives it becomes more difficult to assess the congruence between American public opinion and governmental policies. It can perhaps only be categorically stated "that the collective decision of government institutions have been strongly related to public opinion."[9] While it is true that there is a significant body of evidence to support the assertion that public opinion influences public policy in the United States,[10] specifically how and what impact it has had is still largely debated.[11] Finally, it should be noted that some research has demonstrated that politicians influence, or provide leadership in, specific policy areas[12] and, more recently, Jacobs and Shapiro have demonstrated, despite conventional wisdom to the contrary, that neither Congress nor the president pander to public opinion. [13]

Similar debates exist in the area of public opinion of crime and its relationship with crime policy. The questions of public opinion of crime affecting crime policy and the debate over whether or not public opinion of crime is rational in the United States are greatly debated. Gaubatz adequately expressed the problem when she explained that "while the body of available information about public opinion on crime and criminal justice is large, it is not sufficient."[14] Despite this insufficiency, two other authors, Hurwitz and Peffley, perhaps stated the issue more succinctly when they explained that "we know two things about public opinion on crime—it is salient and it matters."[15] Research on public opinion of crime, like other areas of public opinion research, has demonstrated time and time again that there is a strong relationship between public opinion of crime and crime policy in the United States, but understanding how and what impact it has is still not very clear.[16] Not only has crime been consistently found to be a highly salient issue,[17] but it has also been demonstrated to be a highly volatile issue in regard to both the public and political agendas. As Scheingold has argued, "the movement of crime on and off the political agenda is not readily explicable in terms of the salience of the issue to the public."[18] The problem over salience, however, is more often than not a derivative of the difficulty in understanding what is meant by the concept of "public opinion of crime."

It is generally the case that when the issue of the "public opinion of crime" is considered, the discussion centers around the concept of the public's "fear of crime." However, this concept, explored across multiple disciplines, has generally demonstrated little agreement over what is meant by these terms.[19] While most people believe they understand what is meant by "fear" and "crime," these terms have the potential for multiple interpretations which becomes important for understanding the phenomenon of "public opinion of crime." The term "crime" is perhaps the easier of the two to define because, as described in the introduction, most people tend to associate the term with what is often referred to as "street crimes."[20] Although the definition of crime can also include such things as white-collar crimes, political crime, and computer related crime, these are generally not the images that the American people conjure up when someone mentions the word "crime." What are generally envisioned are homicides, rapes, and robberies, as well as the more "contemporary crimes" such as carjackings, domestic violence, and mass murders by disgruntled employees.

The more troublesome aspect is defining what is meant by the word "fear." Warr summarizes the problem when he explains that "the phrase 'fear of crime' has acquired so many divergent meanings in the literature that it is in danger of losing any specificity whatsoever."[21] In a scholarly sense it has lost much of its meaning, but the term still invokes a certain understanding from the layperson. While scholars have attempted to adjust their understanding of the public's perception of the term, they have managed to generate additional explanations of the terms that provide a deeper and fuller understanding of this generic phrase.

Some scholars have suggested that "fear of crime" is in reality a "concern for crime" in that people understand crime to be a serious problem in their community and the level of "fear" is actually the level of "concern" they feel due to their understanding of the number, types, and seriousness of the crimes in their neighborhoods.[22] Citizens may become more concerned as they hear from the local media of more friends, relatives, neighbors, and associates being victimized, or from seeing the "symbols" that they attach to crime occurring in their neighborhoods, such as graffiti, broken windows, and abandoned vehicles in the streets. Fear of crime is then a level of concern for crime rather than an emotional fear of crime or of fearing personal bodily harm or loss.

In some cases, the term "fear of crime" is often not about crime per se, but about the perceived risk of victimization.[23] This is not inherently about the emotional reaction that people have in fearing crime, but rather a perception of the "risk" they face in becoming a victim of a crime. It is reasoned that those who perceive a high risk of crime or are concerned that they or a friend may become a victim of a crime will be more afraid. Hence, they do not have a "fear of crime," but they experience what is seen as a "fear of victimization."

Another approach to the "fear of crime" is to look at the threat of crime one believes they face.[24] In this definition the focus is on the threat that people believe they face if they were to place themselves in a specific situation. This "threat" perspective is usually generated from the survey questions that ask, "Is there any area where you live—that is, within a mile—where you would be afraid to walk alone at night? How about at home at night—do you feel safe and secure or not?" These types of questions do not necessarily focus on the behaviors one exhibits, such as walking around one's neighborhood at night, but focus on the level of threat an individual perceives they would face if they did take that midnight stroll.

Finally, the last perspective on "fear of crime" is oriented on the behavior that people exhibit.[25] It is one thing to say one is concerned about crime, fears the victimization of crime, or perceives a threat by crime, but it is an entirely different matter to say that one does in fact change or alter their behavior out of fear for their safety. If people lock their doors at night and refuse to go outside after dark, they are engaging in avoidance behavior and hence the fear for their safety, or the "fear of crime," has altered their lifestyle. While a large majority of people may adjust their behavior in response to crime, either consciously or unconsciously, it is really a matter of degree as to the level of fear one has of crime in this instance. While people may lock their doors at night before going to bed in response to concern for their safety, this behavior may not translate into actual "fear of crime."

While the literature and studies on citizens' fear of crime is mixed and the definitions often muddled, one thing that can be drawn from the discussion is that Americans fear of crime is a complex issue. The literature does not definitively state that all American's fear crime and are paralyzed by this fear. However, it also does not provide us with a definitive answer that crime is not a concern of the American people and the fear of crime is a complete social fabrication. That in turn leaves us somewhere in the middle, struggling to determine to what degree Americans fear crime and to what degree this is driving America's public policy on crime. As a result, it is important to utilize the indicators available to understand the level of fear that Americans have of crime.

In order to gauge the level of fear in the United States the use of survey questions is the primary means available and there are essentially two methods that can be employed, either the direct or indirect. The direct method of assessing public opinion of crime, or "fear of crime," is to raise the issue of crime immediately, providing the respondent time to think only about the issue of crime and then assess to what degree they fear crime. As the issue of crime is raised for them, it is expected that the response that crime is a problem would consistently be high. The indirect method is to assess public opinion by couching the question, not in terms of a specific issue such as crime, but in terms of all the issues they are currently facing or believe are important. In this manner, the salience of crime may be high or low, depending upon how pressing the issue of crime is to the respondent in terms of all the possible issues they feel are important. By looking at the responses to both direct and indirect questions over time, a better assessment of American's fear of crime, concern for crime, and the salience of crime, can be made.

When people are asked directly as to how much they fear crime, the results are often mixed and tend to fluctuate. A study conducted in 1980 asked Americans if they were "highly fearful" of becoming the victim of a violent crime and 40 percent of those surveyed answered in the affirmative.[26] However, a similar study conducted in 1989, asking a similar question found that only 12 percent of those surveyed reported being "very fearful," while 44 percent reported they were "somewhat fearful."[27] There is often a great deal of fluctuation in these types of questions which are asked sporadically and in various formats thus providing little understanding of American's fear of crime. Questions that are asked fairly consistently across time (trend data) are not abundant but do appear to provide a better estimate for the level of fear in the United States.

The two well known public opinion polls, Gallup and Harris, have asked the American people for over three decades the key questions that have been utilized to gauge public opinion of crime.[28] The Gallup poll has asked the question, "Is there any area near where you live—that is, within a mile—where you would be afraid to walk alone at night?"[29] The response to this is very informative. In 1965 the percentage of respondents that answered "yes" was 34 percent and in 1975, a decade later, it had risen to 45 percent. However, in 1981 it was 45 percent, in 1989 it was 43 percent, and in 1993 it was 43 percent. Despite a modest gain from the mid-1960s to the mid-1970s, the answer to the question has remained very constant over time (see Table 4-1). In addition, this survey question has been in-

TABLE 4–1   Respondents Reporting Fear of Walking Alone and Feeling Unsafe at Home at Night, 1965–1997

Question: "Is there any area near where you live—that is, within a mile—where you would be afraid to walk alone at night? How about when you're at home at night—do you feel safe and secure, or not?"

Year	Afraid to Walk Alone at Night	Feel Unsafe at Home at Night
1965	34%	NA
1967	31	NA
1972	42	17
1975	45	20
1977	45	15
1981	45	16
1983	45	16
1989	43	10
1990	40	10
1992	44	11
1993	43	NA
1996	39	9
1997	38	9

Source: Adapted from Kathleen Maguire and Ann Pastore, eds., *Sourcebook of Criminal Justice Statistics 1997.* Washington D.C.: U.S. GPO. Original Source: George Gallup, Jr. 1997. *The Gallup Poll Monthly.* No. 386. Princeton: The Gallup Poll.

TABLE 4–2   Respondents Reporting Whether They Feel Afraid to Walk Alone at Night in Their Own Neighborhood

Question: "Is there any area right around here—that is, within a mile—where you would be afraid to walk alone at night?"

Year	Yes	No
1973	41%	59%
1974	45	55
1976	44	56
1977	45	54
1980	43	56
1982	47	53
1984	42	57
1985	40	59
1987	38	51
1988	40	59
1989	40	60
1990	41	58
1991	43	56
1993	43	57
1994	47	52
1996	42	57

Source: Adapted from Kathleen Maguire and Ann Pastore, eds., *Sourcebook of Criminal Justice Statistics 1997.* Washington D.C.: U.S. GPO. Original Source: National Opinion Research Center. 1996. *General Social Surveys, 1972–96.* Storrs: The Roper Center for Public Opinion Research.

cluded in the General Social Survey (GSS) from 1973 to the present, and it reports similar findings with the percentage levels of respondents stating "yes" at low to mid-40 percentage points, with only the year 1987 deviating from this with a response rate of 38 percentage points (see Table 4-2).

In turning to the Harris poll which has asked the question "In the past year, do you feel the crime rate in your area has been increasing, decreasing, or has it remained the same as it was before?" we find that the responses are very similar in that they are moderately high and remain relatively stable over time (see Table 4-3).[30] This would lead to the conclusion that the fear of crime has altered little over time despite the rising and declining crime rates during this same period.[31] In addition, despite the fact that many argue these two questions are poorly worded—that the Gallup and GSS questions fail to mention the word "crime," and the Harris poll utilizes the term "crime rates" rather than simply "crime"[32]—these two questions are the longest running questions attempting to assess Americans' fear of crime that are available for understanding this phenomenon. As a result, they have become well-used in a variety of disciplines for understanding Americans' fear of crime.

Because the two questions have often been criticized, two more recent questions have entered into the Gallup poll's repertoire of public opinion questions

TABLE 4–3   Attitudes Toward Crime Rate in Own Area

Question: "In the past year, do you feel the crime rate in your area has been increasing, decreasing, or has it remained the same as it was before?"

Year	Increasing	Decreasing	Remained Same	Not Sure
1967	46%	4%	43%	7%
1970	62	3	30	5
1973	48	7	40	5
1975	70	3	24	3
1978	46	7	42	5
1981	68	4	27	1
1982	59	6	34	1
1983	41	15	43	1
1984	33	21	44	2
1985	40	17	42	1
1991	55	5	39	1
1993	54	5	39	2

Source: Adapted from Kathleen Maguire and Ann Pastore, eds., *Sourcebook of Criminal Justice Statistics 1997.* Washington D.C.: U.S. GPO. Original Source: Louis Harris. 1993. *The Harris Poll.* Los Angeles: Creators Syndicate, Inc.

related to the issue of crime. The first asks, "Is there more crime in your area than there was a year ago, or less?" This question presents the word "crime" in the question and remains focused on the respondents' "area" providing for a more specific answer to the issue of crime. Once again, the respondents' answers have remained fairly high and consistent over time by the reply that there has been more crime in their area (See Table 4-4). In addition, a second question which has been utilized by the Gallup poll has shifted the focus from the respondents' "area" to asking about the level of crime throughout the United States. Surprisingly, the answers overwhelming state that there is more crime in the United States than the previous year. However, there has been some decline in the high response rates in the years 1996 and 1997 which would be consistent with the fact that overall crime rates had been consistently falling throughout the 1990s (see Table 4-5). In sum then it is clear that when asked specifically about the issue of crime, citizens tend to respond in the affirmative that crime is a problem and that these responses have, for the most part, remained fairly consistent over time. Although this is assuredly not indicative of the actual rise and fall of the crime rates over time, it is an indicator that when Americans are asked specifically about the problem of crime, there is a tendency for them to respond that it is a problem, that they fear crime, and that there is more, rather than less, crime in their area and in the United States.

According to several researchers, because direct, or closed questions can "sharply restrict frames of reference by focusing attention on the alternatives of-

TABLE 4–4   Attitudes Toward Level of Crime in Own Area

Question: "Is there more crime in your area than there was a year ago, or less?"

Year	More	Less	Same	No Opinion
1972	51%	10%	27%	12%
1975	50	12	29	9
1977	43	17	32	8
1981	54	8	29	9
1983	37	17	36	10
1989	53	18	22	7
1990	51	18	24	8
1992	54	19	23	4
1996	46	24	25	5
1997	46	32	20	2

Source: Adapted from Kathleen Maguire and Ann Pastore, eds., *Sourcebook of Criminal Justice Statistics 1997.* Washington D.C.: U.S. GPO. Original Source: George Gallup, Jr. 1997. *The Gallup Poll Monthly.* No. 386. Princeton: The Gallup Poll.

TABLE 4–5   Attitudes Toward Level of Crime in the United States

Question: "Is there more crime in the U.S. than there was a year ago, or less?"

Year	More	Less	Same	No Opinion
1989	84%	5%	5%	6%
1990	84	3	7	6
1992	89	3	4	4
1996	71	15	8	6
1997	64	25	6	5

Source: Adapted from Kathleen Maguire and Ann Pastore, eds., *Sourcebook of Criminal Justice Statistics 1997.* Washington D.C.: U.S. GPO. Original Source: George Gallup, Jr. 1997. *The Gallup Poll Monthly,* No. 386. Princeton: The Gallup Poll.

fered, no matter how impoverished those alternatives may be and no matter how much effort is made to offer respondents freedom to depart from them,"[33] the use of open and essentially indirect questions on crime are preferred. The most prominent of the indirect questions related to public opinion of crime comes from the Gallup poll's question that has been asked consistently over time for the past fifty years and that is, "What do you think is the most important problem facing the country today?"[34] This question has been dubbed the "most important problem" time-series question and is considered to be the best available gauge of the public's opinion, as well as the public's agenda.[35] It can be considered a gauge of the public's agenda for the fact it provides an understanding of what the American people focus their attention on at any given time.[36] It is the citizen's policy preferences and what they would like to see addressed by the government. In most cases the public's agenda is operationalized through public opinion.[37] The public's opinion at any given moment on what they consider to be the most serious issue that the United States currently faces creates the "list" of policy issues that are deemed the public's "highest priorities."[38] This list, then, provides a legitimization process for government to begin addressing various issues through allocation of resources, implementation, and evaluation of various programs and policies.

The specific question asks the respondents to voice their opinion as to what they feel is the most important problem facing the nation and the aggregated data is then utilized to detail where the public's concerns lie. This allows for the top problems facing the country to be examined and assessed against the entire world of problems facing the country. In regard to crime, it demonstrates that crime has been a highly salient issue which has had an on and off relationship over time. In the 1940s and 1950s, the aggregate response to the question was typically less than one percent. In the early 1960s, the responses jumped to levels averaging around two percent. It was not until 1968 that the response rate to crime being the "most important problem" would rise to such a level that it was considered the third most important problem (see Table 4-6). Crime would not become the number one problem facing the country until 1994, coinciding with President Clinton's support for the passage of the Violent Crime Control and Law Enforcement Act of 1994 and his "100,000 Cops" initiative. That year 52 percent of those responding to the question felt that crime was serious enough to be the "most important problem" and several other national surveys supported these high response rates.[39] The following year, in 1995, once again crime would be considered the "most important problem facing the country" and in 1996 it would move to the position of second "most important problem."

In the years since this unprecedented level crime has begun to drop off, demonstrating that the salience of crime, especially in relation to all of the potential problems that Americans could cite, is a sporadic phenomenon. Finally, it must be noted that in light of the fact that overall crime rates in the United States have been falling consistently since 1992, it does not appear that the salience of crime is related to the actual rate of crime. In other words, as all official crime rates, including murder, rapes and robberies, have been falling throughout the 1990s,[40] crime became the number one problem for two years in a row and the second most important problem in 1996. Therefore, this method of asking an indirect question regarding public opinion of crime appears, as a number of authors have expressed, to demonstrate that in terms of all possible issues, crime is highly salient.[41] The question then is what makes crime such a highly salient issue if it is not crime as expressed through official crime rates? There is a growing body of evidence that it is related to a combination of the media and politicians[42] and, as this research will argue, a growing level of attention to the issue of crime by the presidents of the United States.

TABLE 4–6   "Most Important Problem" Over Time, 1964–1996

Question: "What do you think is the most important problem facing the country
today?"

Year	Most Important	Second Most Important	Third Most Important
1964	Race Problems	Foreign Problems	Unemployment
1965	Vietnam	Civil Rights	Threat of War
1966	Vietnam	Cost of Living	Civil Rights
1967	Vietnam	Civil Rights	Cost of Living
1968	Vietnam	Race Relations	**Crime**
1969	Vietnam	**Crime**	Race Relations
1970	Campus Unrest	Vietnam	Foreign Problems
1971	Vietnam	Economy	Foreign Problems
1972	Vietnam	Inflation	**Drugs**
1973	Cost of Living	**Drugs**	**Crime**
1974	Energy Crisis	Cost of Living	Government Corruption
1975	Cost of Living	Unemployment	Government Corruption
1976	Cost of Living	Unemployment	**Crime**
1977	Cost of Living	Unemployment	Energy Problems
1978	Cost of Living	Energy Problems	Unemployment
1979	Cost of Living	Foreign Problems	Energy Problems
1980	Foreign Problems	Cost of Living	Energy Problems
1981	Cost of Living	Unemployment	**Crime**
1982	Cost of Living	Unemployment	Budget Cuts
1983	Unemployment	Inflation	Fear of Wars
1984	Threat of War	Unemployment	Government Spending
1985	Threat of War	Unemployment	Government Spending
1986	Foreign Tensions	Unemployment	Federal Deficit
1987	Unemployment	Federal Deficit	Economy
1988	Federal Deficit	Economy	**Drugs**
1989	Economy	**Drugs**	Poverty
1990	**Drugs**	Federal Deficit	Poverty
1991	Economy	**Drugs**	Poverty
1992	Economy	Unemployment	Poverty
1993	Economy	Unemployment	Poverty
1994	**Crime**	Economy	Unemployment
1995	**Crime**	Economy	Federal Deficit
1996	Economy	**Crime**	Federal Deficit

Source: Adapted by author from Gallup, George. *The Gallup Poll: Public Opinion.* Wilmington: Scholarly Resources,
Inc., 1964–1996 and *The Gallup Organization Homepage,* "Gallup Social and Economic Indicators—Most Important
Problem" http://www.gallup.com/poll/indicators/indmip.asp. Data obtained January 2000.

THE PRESIDENTIAL AGENDA

The study of the president's agenda, as previously detailed in chapter two, is also a field of research that has provided a very large and rich body of knowledge allowing for a deeper understanding of the presidents and their agenda. The president's agenda is, again, a personal list of policy issues that the president finds to be most important to the nation. It is a list of policy issues that the president considers the "most important problem facing the country." As Light has explained, "the president's agenda is perhaps best understood as a signal" and it "identifies what the president deems to be the highest priorities."[43] Every agenda item addresses an issue, involves specific alternatives, and has some priority in the domestic agenda.[44] It is on this list that the president focuses his attention, discusses possible policy solutions, and bases his requests to Congress for legislative policy that subsequently shapes the domestic agenda.[45] It then becomes not only a focus of the president's time and attention, but also the method by which resources are allocated.[46] Therefore, every legislative proposal, every speech, and every business trip—both foreign and domestic—are largely about the president's agenda.

The presidential agenda has been identified through several methods by various researchers. The first is through the use of the president's speeches and written correspondence as cataloged each year in the publication *Public Papers of the Presidents of the United States.*[47] The second is through the use of the president's State of the Union address[48] and the third is through some variation of presidential rhetoric generally consisting of a more narrow analysis on a specific president or a type of speech, such as major or minor addresses.[49] All of these center upon the speeches and written correspondence of the presidents as a reflection of the presidential agenda in that these speeches and letters are generally prepared well in advance of their delivery, are designed to include the policy and agenda of the administration, and are often delivered to articulate a specific policy. The primary power of the presidency is in fact the "bully pulpit," and it is with these tactics that the president must attempt to influence both Congress and the American people. These speeches and letters are then collected each year and catalogued in the *Public Papers of the President of the United States,* thus becoming a written record of the president's agenda. These speeches and letters include national, state, and local speeches, press speeches, inaugural addresses, farewell addresses, veto messages, and letters to various organizations, cabinet members, and Congressmen. Each is written and delivered to support a policy position.[50]

The *Public Papers of the President of the United States* also includes the State of the Union Addresses which generally provide a detailed list of the many issues that the president believes must be addressed.[51] The State of the Union Address is a requirement of the president specified by the United States Constitution which states in Article II, Section 3, "He shall from time to time give to the Congress Information of the State of the Union, and recommend to their Consideration such Measures as he shall judge necessary and expedient." The State of the Union

Address has become an American institution and is considered "the statement of legislative priorities."[52] Since President Theodore Roosevelt, most presidents have utilized the address to articulate not only to Congress but to the entire nation their priorities on both foreign and domestic issues.[53] Therefore, the State of the Union Address and all of the other speeches and letters delivered by the president throughout a given year, clearly determine the president's agenda. [54]

In regard to the president's agenda on crime, only the recent work of Nancy Marion has focused on this specific policy area. In her first study she analyzed the president's agenda setting on crime control and found specific trends within each presidential administration for the type of crime policies on which they focused.[55] In another piece of research she found that most of the presidents' speeches on crime were laden with symbolic rhetoric, suggesting that presidents use crime speeches for symbolic purposes rather than for proposing substantive policy.[56] In addition, she traced the agenda-setting process of both the president and Congress from Kennedy through Bush as it related to crime-control policy and included some discussion of the public's agenda as well.[57] Finally, she recently updated this analysis by specifically focusing on President Clinton's first term in office.[58] Taken as a whole, Marion's research has been extremely valuable to this area of interest for scholarship on this subject has been most assuredly lacking. However, as George Edwards has explained, most "authors of these fine works concentrate on analyzing *what* the president said. In the process, they make numerous inferences regarding the impact of the president's rhetoric on public opinion. However, scholars of presidential rhetoric virtually never provide evidence for their inferences about the president's impact."[59] Therefore, assessing the impact that the president's rhetoric, and specifically his time and attention to a particular policy issue such as crime, is needed. It is to that end that this research is focused by testing the hypothesis that presidents influence public opinion of crime.

OTHER INFLUENCING FACTORS

Although this study is attempting to test the influence presidents have on public opinion of crime, it is recognized that presidents are not the only influencing factor on mass opinion. There are clearly other causal influences involved and they are identified as: 1) the media, 2) crime, 3) party affiliation, 4) election year, 5) the president's first year in office, and 6) the economy. These all have the potential for influencing the public's opinion of crime and are therefore utilized as control variables.

The first control variable, and perhaps the most significant, is found in the media's influence on the issue of crime. As Jacobs and Shapiro articulate "there is substantial evidence now that public opinion is influenced by the messages and interpretations communicated through the mass media."[60] There is also now an equally substantial body of evidence indicating that public opinion of crime is influenced by the messages and interpretations communicated through such mass media venues as television, newspapers, and magazines.[61] As one author would find in the early 1980s, 95 percent of the respondents in her study stated their primary source for information on crime was the media.[62] It is no wonder that by the mid-1990s another researcher would conclude that the mass media both reflect and form public opinion of crime.[63] Although there is still some debate over specifically how the media impacts the public perception of crime,[64] suffice it to say there is a very strong relationship. What is most important for this study, however, is to ensure that it is the president's influence on the public's opinion of crime that is being measured and not the media's. Therefore, it is hypothesized the media will have some influence upon public opinion of crime.

The second influencing factor on public opinion of crime may in reality be crime itself. Although Americans' perception of how much crime there is in the United States is limited and there appears to be a limited relationship between crime rates and public concern for crime,[65] it is nevertheless hypothesized to have some effect on opinion. If in fact this is the case, when crime rates are high it would follow that the salience of crime would rise as well. When crime rates are low, the salience of crime should be low. Therefore, the rate of crime must be utilized to control for its influence on the public's perception of crime. The best gauge for crime rates in the United States is the yearly compilation of violent and property crime by the Federal Bureau of Investigation in the Uniform Crime Reports.[66] This is primarily because it is the longest time-series data collection of crimes reported to the police in the United States and because, over time, experts on crime, the media, and the government itself, tend to highlight the "rising" or "falling" crime rates when discussing the issue of crime.[67] Although the reports are faced with many internal and external validity problems,[68] they are still considered by most to be the best assessment of crime in the United States and will be operationalized to assess its influence on public opinion. Therefore, it is hypothesized that the official crime rates as reported through the Uniform Crime Reports will influence public opinion of crime.

The third influencing variable may derive from party affiliation. It has been a long-held belief that crime is a Republican issue.[69] It has been further held that Republican presidents are more focused on law and order issues and, as most of the emphasis over the past several decades has been concentrated on adding more police and building more prisons, it has been hypothesized that Republicans would be more successful in this area.[70] Finally, it has been theorized that Republican presidents rely more heavily on symbolism in their speeches[71] and, because the issue of crime is very complimentary to symbolic politics, it can be extended that Republican presidents would take advantage of this opportunity more readily. Therefore, it is hypothesized that Republican presidents will influence public opinion of crime more than Democratic presidents.

The President Speaks . . .

Good evening. This is the first time since taking the oath of office that I felt an issue was so important, so threatening, that it warranted talking directly with you, the American people. All of us agree that the gravest domestic threat facing our nation today is drugs. Drugs have strained our faith in our system of justice. Our courts, our prisons, our legal system, are stretched to the breaking point. The social costs of drugs are mounting. In short, drugs are sapping our strength as a nation. Turn on the evening news or pick up the morning paper and you'll see what some Americans know just by stepping out their front door: Our most serious problem today is cocaine, and in particular, crack.

Who's responsible? Let me tell you straight out—everyone who uses drugs, everyone who sells drugs, and everyone who looks the other way.

. . . No one among us is out of harm's way. When 4-year-olds play in playgrounds strewn with discarded hypodermic needles and crack vials, it breaks my heart. When cocaine, one of the most deadly and addictive illegal drugs, is available to school kids—it's an outrage. And when hundreds of thousands of babies are born each year to mothers who use drugs—premature babies born desperately sick—then even the most defenseless among us are at risk.

President George Bush showing crack cocaine allegedly seized by police across the street from the White House during his first national televised speech on the National Drug Control Strategy on September 5, 1989.

PHOTOGRAPH COURTESY OF THE GEORGE BUSH PRESIDENTIAL LIBRARY.

(continued)

The President Speaks . . . —(continued)

These are the tragedies behind the statistics, but the numbers also have quite a story to tell. Let me share with you the results of the recently completed household survey of the National Institute on Drug Abuse. It compares recent drug use to 3 years ago. It tells us some good news and some very bad news. First, the good. As you can see in the chart, in 1985 the Government estimated that 23 million Americans were using drugs on a "current" basis; that is, at least once in the preceding month. Last year that number fell by more than a third. That means almost 9 million fewer Americans are casual drug users. Good news.

Because we changed our national attitude toward drugs, casual drug use has declined. We have many to thank: our brave law enforcement officers, religious leaders, teachers, community activists, and leaders of business and labor. We should also thank the media for their exhaustive news and editorial coverage and for their air time and space for anti-drug messages. And finally, I want to thank President and Mrs. Reagan for their leadership. All of these good people told the truth: that drug use is wrong and dangerous.

. . . Tonight, I'm announcing a strategy that reflects the coordinated, cooperative commitment of all our Federal agencies. In short, this plan is as comprehensive as the problem. With this strategy, we now finally have a plan that coordinates our resources, our programs, and the people who run them. Our weapons in this strategy are the law and criminal justice system, our foreign policy, our treatment systems, and our schools and drug prevention programs. So, the basic weapons we need are the ones we already have. What's been lacking is a strategy to effectively use them.

Let me address four of the major elements of our strategy. First, we are determined to enforce the law, to make our streets and neighborhoods safe. So, to start, I'm proposing that we more than double Federal assistance to State and local law enforcement. Americans have a right to safety in and around their homes. And we won't have safe neighborhoods unless we're tough on drug criminals—much tougher than we are now. Sometimes that means tougher penalties, but more often it just means punishment that is swift and certain. We've all heard stories about drug dealers who are caught and arrested again and again but never punished. Well, here the rules have changed: If you sell drugs, you will be caught. And when you're caught, you will be prosecuted. And once you're convicted, you will do time. Caught—prosecuted—punished.

I'm also proposing that we enlarge our criminal justice system across the board—at the local, State, and Federal levels alike. We need more prisons, more jails, more courts, more prosecutors. So, tonight I'm requesting—all together—an almost $1.5 billion increase in drug-related Federal spending on law enforcement.

. . . The second element of our strategy looks beyond our borders, where the cocaine and crack bought on America's streets is grown and processed.

. . . The third part of our strategy concerns drug treatment. Experts believe that there are 2 million American drug users who may be able to get off drugs with proper treatment, but right now only 40 percent of them are actually getting help. This is simply not good enough. Many people who need treatment won't seek it on their own, and some who do seek it are put on a waiting list. Most programs were set up to deal with heroin addicts, but today the major problem is cocaine users. It's time we expand our treatment systems and do a better job of providing services to those who need them.

And so, tonight I'm proposing an increase of $321 million in Federal spending on drug treatment. With this strategy, we will do more. We will work with the States. We will encourage employers to establish employee assistance programs to cope with drug use; and because addiction is such a cruel inheritance, we will intensify our search for ways to help expectant mothers who use drugs.

Fourth, we must stop illegal drug use before it starts. Unfortunately, it begins early—for many kids, before their teens. But it doesn't start the way you might think, from a dealer or an addict hanging around a school playground. More often, our kids first get their drugs free, from friends or even from older brothers or sisters. Peer pressure spreads drug use; peer pressure can help stop it. I am proposing a quarter-of-a-billion-dollar increase in Federal funds for school and community prevention programs that help young people and adults reject enticements to try drugs. And I'm proposing something else. Every school, college, and university, and every workplace must adopt tough but fair policies about drug use by students and employees. And those that will not adopt such policies will not get Federal funds—period!

As President, one of my first missions is to keep the national focus on our offensive against drugs. And so, next week I will take the anti-drug message to the classrooms of America in a special television address, one that I hope will reach every school, every young American. But drug education doesn't begin in class or on TV. It must begin at home and in the neighborhood. Parents and families must set the first example of a drug-free life. And when families are broken, caring friends and neighbors must step in.

. . . If we fight this war as a divided nation, then the war is lost. But if we face this evil as a nation united, this will be nothing but a handful of useless chemicals. Victory—victory over drugs—is our cause, a just cause. And with your help, we are going to win.

—*George Bush*
Address to the Nation on the National Drug Control Strategy,
September 5, 1989.

The fourth variable is focused on the theory that presidents are more influential and more popular in an election year, whereas the fifth variable focuses on research indicating that presidents have strong public approval ratings and are more successful in their first year in office after which public opinion begins to erode.[72] Because of such high activity during these two time periods of the presidency, it is possible they may inflate the awareness of specific issues such as crime, and hence may have a greater influence upon public opinion. Therefore, it is hypothesized that a president's activity on crime control will be higher in election years and in his first year in office.

Finally, perhaps one of the most important variables in influencing public opinion on a number of issues including crime, is the economy. It has generally been found, as epitomized in Clinton's 1992 campaign theme, "It's the economy, stupid," that the economic status of the United States plays a direct role in the public's level of support for a president.[73] If the economy is doing well, the president's popularity is generally high; if the economy is doing poorly, the president's popularity is generally low. In the case of crime, it is possible that fear of crime may rise when the economy is doing badly and that people may turn their attention to things other than crime when the economy is doing well. One question is whether these two statements may be linked in such a way that, when the economy is doing poorly, people may be concerned about crime but a politician may not be in a position to influence public opinion. To complicate matters further, the link between crime as a highly salient issue and the strength of the economy is not found in the actual growth or decline of the economy but rather in the issue of poverty. It has long been argued that there is an inextricable link between crime and poverty, as well as between official crime rates and official unemployment rates.[74] Although the relationship is tenuous at best, it is generally agreed that there is some correlation. If people perceive causation, high unemployment rates may cause some to perceive high crime rates, thus raising the salience of crime. For this reason, the official unemployment rates are utilized to control for the fluctuation in the economy and the effect that the perception of this may have on the salience of crime. In sum, then, it is hypothesized that unemployment rates will have a positive influence on public opinion of crime.

METHODOLOGY

As previously indicated, the Gallup poll's "Most Important Problem" time-series has been widely considered to be one of the best indicators of both public opinion in general and the public's agenda more specifically,[75] and will therefore be used for the dependent variable in this study. The responses related to crime in the Gallup poll's survey question, "what is the most important problem facing the country," will become the determinant of whether or not presidential activity on the issue of crime has any impact on public opinion of crime. Because the Gallup poll has repeatedly asked this question since the beginning of its surveying, the entire span of years could potentially be used for the purposes of this model. There is, however, a general consensus that the very early years of the Gallup poll's surveys are questionable due to errors in sampling.[76] In most instances, the year 1948 is considered to be the first most accurate year of the Gallup public opinion polls because "since 1948, the Gallup poll and all the other major polls have used probability methods to choose their samples."[77] However, the first year that reveals some response to the issue of crime is found in the 1945 responses to the Gallup poll's question. The subsequent years of 1946 and 1947, elicited no response referencing crime on the Gallup poll's question. In spite of the fact the first three years (1945–1947) do not fall within the "golden age of surveying,"[78] the responses will be utilized because they are minimal and because it increases the number of cases in the statistical model. In addition, the year 1996 will be utilized as the last year of data collection due to the fact information for later years was not readily available during this study and because the year captures both an election year and the end of Clinton's first term in office.

The Gallup poll's "most important problem" question was collected from several sources. The data was first obtained from various publications of the Gallup poll organization, including monthly publications and compilations of their data.[79] The years 1960 through 1993 were then cross-referenced with the data previously collected by Nancy Marion in her publication titled, *A History of Federal Crime Control Initiatives, 1960–1993.*[80] Additionally, the years 1970 through 1994 were also cross-referenced with the Bureau of Justice Statistics annual compilation of criminal justice data in the *Sourcebook of Criminal Justice Statistics.*[81] Finally, the data was reassessed through a review of the Gallup poll's website which maintains a series of Gallup poll's social and economic indicators, including the "most important problem." [82] The date, or dates, for sometimes the polling would take place over several days, were recorded for all of the polls taken from 1945 through 1996 in order to create a database for the dependent variable. This revealed that the question has been asked at erratic intervals, having been asked at least twice a year and sometimes as often as 13 times in a given year.

As the Gallup poll's question specifically asks for what people feel is the "most important problem facing the country," the percentage of those responding to the question by answering with something related to the issue of crime was the basis of data collection. Each Gallup poll asking for the "most important problem" was reviewed for words related to the issue of crime and the following terms were utilized to represent crime: "juvenile delinquency," "narcotics, drugs," "crime," "law enforcement," "drug addiction," "law & order," "alcohol," "lawlessness," "drugs," and "drug abuse." The total percentage responding to each of the above categories was then recorded into a database and the total responses related to crime were summed. For instance, in a given survey, if two percent responded "crime" was a problem and another four percent responded "drugs," the total responding would be summed as six percent. These totals were then averaged by dividing this total percentage of responses related to crime by the number of times the question was asked each year. This reported a yearly assessment of the public's opinion of crime thus representing the dependent variable (see Table 4-7).

In addition to the Gallup poll's "most important problem" time-series being well used in the literature, the *Public Papers of the Presidents of the United States,* have also been well used to assess the president's agenda on specific issues.[83] As Hinckley explains, "the *Public Papers,* in annual volumes, lists all presidential addresses, radio and television broadcasts, speeches to Congress, short messages, news conferences, and speeches on the road."[84] She further stipulates that it in-

TABLE 4–7 Crime Related Attitudes as a Percentage of the "Most Important Problem Facing the Country." (averaged for the years 1945–1996)

Year	Yearly Average	Year	Yearly Average
1945	1.5	1971	15
1946	0	1972	16.33
1947	0	1973	15
1948	0	1974	4.4
1949	0	1975	6.66
1950	0	1976	9
1951	1	1977	11.75
1952	0	1978	4
1953	0	1979	3.75
1954	0.66	1980	2.5
1955	0	1981	4.25
1956	0.66	1982	3.57
1957	1.33	1983	2.75
1958	0	1984	4.5
1959	0	1985	7
1960	3	1986	5.66
1961	1	1987	11.66
1962	2	1988	11
1963	0.5	1989	40
1964	1.375	1990	21
1965	2.44	1991	13
1966	2	1992	14.66
1967	3	1993	18.5
1968	10.25	1994	50.25
1969	6	1995	34
1970	14	1996	31.66

Source: Calculated by author from successive volumes of the paper version of Gallup, George. *The Gallup Poll: Public Opinion.* Wilmington: Scholarly Resources, Inc. and the electronic version obtained at *The Gallup Organization Homepage,* "Gallup Social and Economic Indicators—Most Important Problem" http://www.gallup.com/poll/indicators/indmip.asp. Data obtained January 2000.

cludes all veto messages and executive orders and summarizes the value of the *Public Papers,* when she states, "in short, the compilation provides a comprehensive and authoritative record of the president's public and verbal activity, from George Washington to the present."[85] Hinckley, however, rightly notes that "this record is limited to actions that are presidentially defined and excludes the following categories: nonpublic actions, . . . actions by other officials, . . . and purely nonverbal appearances."[86] However, despite these missing actions from the *Public Papers*, this public record provides a very in-depth tool for analyzing the president's activities on a broad array of topics.

This study, therefore, utilized the *Public Papers of the Presidents of the United States* to represent the key independent variable, presidential activity related to the issue of crime. The same time frame was employed from 1945 through 1996, by reviewing the activity of presidents on the issue of crime through a content analysis of the *Public Papers*.[87] The index was first reviewed for all topics related to crime for each of the years in question. The key words that were utilized to represent crime consisted of: "crime," "drugs," "narcotics," "Federal Bureau of Investigation," "U.S. Department of Justice," "justice," "juvenile delinquency," "law and order," "law enforcement," "police," "criminal justice," "corrections," "violence," "guns," "law," and "courts." In the early years of the *Public Papers,* most of these topics were found in the index by the term employed. In the later years, most were collapsed into only a few categories consisting of the "U.S. Department of Justice" and "Law Enforcement and Crime." Although the indexing of the *Public Papers* changed across time, the search for related topics by the coders did not. In addition, as the speeches and letters in the *Public Papers* were often cross-indexed, each speech was collected by speech "number" and was recorded in the data collection. Then a process of eliminating duplicate "numbers" allowed for all speeches and letters related to the topic of crime to be recorded and counted. There were four trained data collectors and this author involved in the data collection for purposes of inter-coder reliability, and a comparison of the number counts and coding for the years 1945 through 1994 revealed an inter-coder reliability of 96 percent.

The author then went through this data which provided a number count of activity but also served as an index for the years 1945 through 1994, and utilizing the paper version of the *Public Papers,* looked up each document in order to code it into a larger database. At this point the author would verify that the speech did belong in the database or that it was not relevant to the issue of crime and therefore needed to be excluded. Reasons for exclusion consisted of such criteria as whether the document dealt solely with international issues or the document used the word but had no application to crime such as the use of "drugs" in relation to drugs for those on medicaid and medicare. The information was then recorded by the appropriate year, president, and the specific date of the document. The topic and subtopics of the document were then recorded and identified as being one of the following: major address on crime, major address mentioning crime, minor address, minor address mentioning crime, news conference/question and answer session, statement, message, or letter/memorandum (see chapter three). This database allowed for the researcher to analyze the key independent variable in both a qualitative and quantitative manner, as well as by president and year in question. The resulting number of documents related to crime for each of the years 1945 through 1994 was then used to represent the key independent variable. In order to test the reliability of this coding, several methods were utilized, with little discrepancy found. [88]

Finally, the original coding occurred prior to the known availability of an electronic version of the *Public Papers,* therefore, when this version was obtained by the author, a process of verification was made utilizing the same terms but on a slightly expanded method due to the exactness of the electronic search engine. For instance, the term "guns" was changed to consist of the terms: "gun," "guns," "gun control," "firearms," and "weapons," in order to ensure that no document would be overlooked. In addition, because the electronic format was available through the year 1996, the data collection was updated and a verification of the paper version for the years 1995 and 1996 was conducted by the author. In order to determine the intercoder reliability of both the paper and electronic version, a reliability test was conducted revealing a 98 percent reliability with only five years demonstrating any discrepancy. In each of these cases only one or two documents were either missing or were originally improperly coded. The resulting data was then used to assess the total activities and yearly average by presidential administration (see chapter three) and it was used to assess the total number of activities for each year from 1945 through 1996 (see Table 4-8). This last number thus serves as the key independent variable for this study.

In addition to the dependent and key independent variables, the other independent or control variables also had to be operationalized. The first control variable to be operationalized was the media. Because this time series spans from 1945 through 1996, the use of a television variable was not conducive to the study. Therefore, in order to operationalize the variable for media, the print medium was utilized for this purpose. Past research on assessing the role of the mass media and its relationship with the national agenda have utilized either the *New York Times Index* or the *Readers' Guide to Periodical Literature.*[89] The former is considered to be indicative of national media coverage. It sets the agenda for other major newspapers and network newscasts across the United States, and it has been found to be thorough and reliable.[90] The latter is also considered to be indicative of the national media coverage of issues encompassing a wider reading audience and is also considered to be thorough and reliable.[91] In sum, each of these measurements of the mass media, despite minor fluctuations in the number of articles for a specific time period, have demonstrated that "the trends of emergence or recession from the public agenda can be clearly ascertained from any of them."[92] Therefore, because the national public opinion of crime was desired, for

TABLE 4–8   Presidential Activity on Crime by Year 1945–1996

Year	Total	Year	Total
1945	2	1971	40
1946	3	1972	36
1947	11	1973	18
1948	10	1974	27
1949	9	1975	29
1950	18	1976	42
1951	8	1977	52
1952	23	1978	40
1953	12	1979	21
1954	25	1980	39
1955	8	1981	59
1956	18	1982	71
1957	12	1983	109
1958	9	1984	142
1959	5	1985	63
1960	8	1986	132
1961	36	1987	115
1962	21	1988	280
1963	52	1989	220
1964	52	1990	95
1965	54	1991	149
1966	58	1992	202
1967	80	1993	292
1968	92	1994	287
1969	57	1995	279
1970	60	1996	297

Note: Crime activity is defined as including all major and minor speeches (including mentions), news conferences, statements, messages, and letters related to crime.

Source: Coded and calculated by the author from successive volumes of the paper version of *Public Papers of the Presidents* (Washington D.C.: U.S. Government Printing Office) and the electronic version obtained in *World Book Encyclopedia: American Reference Library* (Orem, Utah: Western Standard Publishing Company). Format of table is derived from Ragsdale, Lyn. 1998. *Vital Statistics on the Presidency: Washington to Clinton.* Rev. ed. Washington D.C.: Congressional Quarterly, Inc.

the purposes of this study, the author utilized the *Readers' Guide to Periodical Literature.*

The *Readers' Guide* indexes the most popular magazines by year and includes such titles as *Time, Newsweek,* and *U.S. News and World Report.* The magazines and periodicals that are indexed in the *Readers' Guide* have changed over time as when certain popular magazines such as the *Saturday Evening Post* and *Life* are discontinued, or when new magazines are inaugurated, for example when *U.S. News and World Report* began publishing to compete with *Time* and *Newsweek.* However, the rise and fall of the public's agenda can still be easily assessed by reviewing the index for the quantity of articles on a particular topic such as crime at a particular point in time. As Baumgartner and Jones explain, "when we want to know whether an issue is news, therefore, it is not difficult: we simply count the number of articles published in an index of media attention for a given year."[93] Therefore, a number count of articles in the *Readers' Guide* becomes the method by which the media variable was quantified.

The number of articles on the subject of crime was collected for the years 1945 through 1994 by the same four data collectors involved in collecting data from the *Public Papers of the Presidents of the United States* and this author. In those volumes where more than one year is included in the *Readers' Guide,* the number of articles was counted and recorded by their respective years as recorded in that particular volume.[94] The topic of crime has been consistently indexed by the *Readers' Guide* over time under the subject heading "Crime and Criminals," and has remained constant over the 50 years in question. In addition, there is a sub-heading under the subject heading "Crime and Criminals" titled "See Also" which refers to other major headings concerning crime. The number of "See Also" sub-headings ranged from 19 in the 1945 edition to 129 in the 1994 edition. The articles under the heading "Crime and Criminals" as well as those under the "See Also" subheadings were counted by each of the data collectors and the final numbers per year were correlated. The rate of inter-coder reliability was 90 percent, and each year's average of article number counts on the topic of crime was utilized for the study. Finally, in order to expand the database by two additional years, the author collected the number count for the years 1995 and 1996, utilizing the same methodology. The number count was conducted on three separate occasions in order to ensure reliability and the correlation between all three counts was slightly

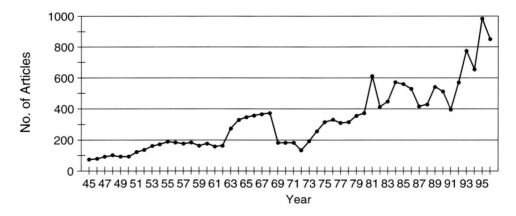

FIGURE 4–1   Media Reporting on Crime

Source: Data collected by author from The H. W. Wilson Company. 1946–1997. *The Readers' Guide to Periodical Literature* Dublin: The H. W. Wilson Company.

over 99 percent. The resulting data presents a variable for the media's attention to the issue of crime for the years 1945 through 1996 (see Figure 4-1).

The second independent variable to be operationalized is that of the official crime rates in the United States. These data can be obtained from the Federal Bureau of Investigation's Uniform Crime Reports (UCR)—an annual collection of crime statistics from police agencies across the country accounting for approximately 98 percent of the population in urban areas and 90 percent of the population in rural areas.[95] In addition, because the UCR data collection system has remained consistent over time, "crime definitions, classifications, and modes of data collection are virtually the same today as they were in 1930."[96] The crimes that have been consistently collected over time by the UCR and are considered to be the most reliable include: murder, rape, robbery, aggravated assault, burglary, larceny, and motor vehicle theft, as well as the more recently added crime of arson.[97] Taken together, these create the Part I offenses of the Uniform Crime Reports, and reported as a rate of crime per 100,000 population in the United States controlling for changing population throughout the time-series, it will become the means of assessing the influence of crime on public opinion of crime. In addition, it should be noted that to accurately assess not only the influence of crime on public opinion but the influence that the release of the UCR data has upon public opinion of crime,[98] the variable will be lagged by one year in the same manner as Haynie did in her study on fear of crime.[99] Thus, for example, the 1993 UCR index crimes per 100,000 population will be associated with the 1994 level of public opinion of crime. The resulting data of official crime rates per 100,000 population for the years 1945 through 1996 represents the variable of crime in the United States for purposes of this study (see Figure 4-2).

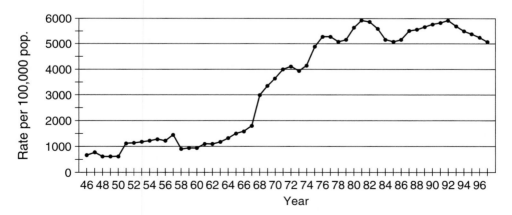

FIGURE 4–2   Crime in the United States

Source: Federal Bureau of Investigation. 1946–1997. *Uniform Crime Reports.* Washington D.C.: U.S. Department of Justice.

The third control variable is found in the party affiliation of the President of the United States. Because it is hypothesized that Republican presidents will be more active on the crime issue than Democratic presidents, a dummy variable will be used to assess party affiliation.[100] The coding scheme employed by year was represented as 1 = Republican and 0 = Democrat. In addition, a dummy variable is employed for the election year variable by coding 1 = yes—it was an election year, and 0 = no—it was not an election year. Finally, one final dummy variable is employed for assessing the president's first year in office by coding 1 = yes—it was the president's first year in office, and 0 = no—it was not the president's first year in office.

The last independent variable to be operationalized was the unemployment rate in the United States. Utilizing data from the U.S. Census Bureau for the years 1945 through 1996, the national unemployment rate was utilized for this variable. The resulting data thus provides a quantifiable analysis of the level of unemployment in the United States (see Figure 4-3).

The data collected thus forms the basic model for this research which will test the hypothesis that presidents influence public opinion of crime. It will do so by using the Gallup poll's "Most Important Problem" time-series as the dependent variable and the number count of presidential activity on crime as the key independent variable. In addition, the other variables reviewed will be entered into the model as additional independent variables, controlling for other possible influencing factors on the public opinion of crime. The data will first be analyzed visually to assess the relationship between the presidents' activity and the public's opinion on crime and then an Ordinary Least Squares time-series regression

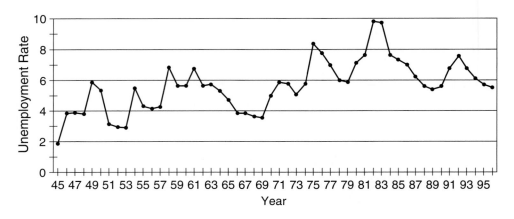

FIGURE 4–3   Unemployment in the United States

Source: Data collected by author from Bureau of Labor Statistics. *Unemployment in the United States.* Washington, D.C.: U.S. Department of Labor.

model will be utilized to test the hypothesis. In addition, alterations to the original model and several tests will be used to ensure the validity of this statistical analysis.

FINDINGS

It is generally agreed that in time-series analysis "the order of the observations is of extreme importance" because this allows us to see trends in the data.[101] It is therefore generally recommended that the data be "eyeballed" in order to recognize how the variable reacts over time.[102] In simply looking at the data plots of the public's response to the "Most Important Problem" question (see Figure 4-4), several rises in public opinion of crime can be captured in the late 1960s and early 1970s, the late 1980s, and the early 1990s. The first is indicative of a culmination of crime-related events including the riots in the late 1960s, campus unrest, the first "war on drugs," and the Nixon Administration's strong "law and order" stance.[103] The second rise is associated with the "crack epidemic" of the mid-1980s and the Reagan Administration's hard line stance against drug dealers and drug users.[104] Finally, the last "spike" of public opinion of crime came during 1993 and 1994—a time period when official crime rates were falling but the president was attempting to pass comprehensive legislation on crime. It was in 1994 that crime became, for the first time in the history of the Gallup poll's survey question, the "most important problem facing the country."

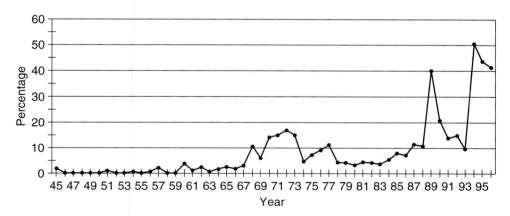

FIGURE 4–4 Public Opinion of Crime

Source: Data collected by author from George Gallup, Jr. 1946–1997. *The Gallup Poll: Public Opinion.* Wilmington: Scholarly Resources, Inc. and the electronic version obtained at *The Gallup Organization Homepage.* "Gallup Social and Economic Indicators—Most Important Problem" http://www.gallup.com/poll/indicators/indmip.asp. Data obtained January 2000.

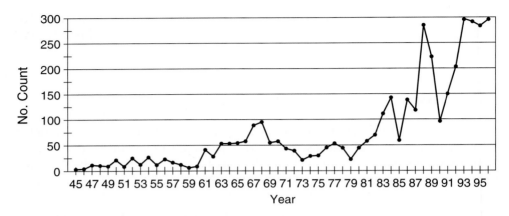

FIGURE 4–5   Presidential Attention to Crime

Source: Data collected by author from successive volumes of *The Public Papers of the Presidents of the United States.* (1946–1997). Washington D.C.: U.S. GPO.

In looking at the trend data on the president's activity on crime (see Figure 4-5), similar circumstances are revealed. Clearly, the first president to pay a vast amount of attention to the issue of crime was President Johnson as seen in the years 1963 through 1968. Although President Nixon was often credited with being the "law and order president," his time and attention to the issue of crime was equal to Johnson's at the beginning of his first term but began to fall off throughout his tenure in office. Ford would renew presidential activity on the issue of crime only to see it once again fade with President Carter's tenure in office. What is remarkable are the dramatic increases during the Reagan, Bush, and Clinton presidencies demonstrating that nearly the last two decades of the twentieth century have been a time period when the concept of the "law and order presidency" has clearly taken hold.

Finally, if one compares the data together, there is an apparent relationship which can be seen in the corresponding increases in the late 1960s and early 1970s, the late 1980s, and the early 1990s (see Figures 4-3 and 4-4). In addition, it appears that public opinion of crime is preceded by an increase in the presidential activity on crime. This is perhaps most apparent in the several "spikes" in presidential activity that occurred from 1967 to 1968, in 1988, and from 1993 to 1994, respectively. These dramatic increases in activity by the presidents are easily explained. In both 1967 and 1968, President Johnson was pushing for Congress to pass the omnibus crime control package and the year 1968 was an election year. The bill was introduced into the House Judiciary Committee on February 8, 1967 and was eventually passed by the full House on August 8, 1967. The Senate did not pass its version until May 23, 1968, whereupon the House voted to approve the Senate's version. On June 19, 1968, President Johnson would sign the Omnibus Crime Control and Safe Streets Act of 1968 into law.[105] In regard to the increase in presidential activity in 1988—another election year—President Reagan increased his activity on crime largely in support of Vice President Bush's presidential campaign which heavily emphasised the "crime" theme.[106] Finally in 1993 and 1994, President Clinton, like President Johnson, became heavily engaged in trying to pressure Congress to pass what would become the most comprehensive crime control package to date, the Violent Crime Control and Law Enforcement Act of 1994 (see Introduction).

What can be inferred from this comparison of the dependent and key independent variable data is that increases in presidential activity on crime appear to precede increases in the public opinion of crime, thus lending some support to the primary hypothesis of this study. At first blush, the evidence tends to support a study by Jones that demonstrated President Bush's attention to the issue of crime. Drugs increased the salience of the issue in the late 1980s.[107] A study by Beckett which convincingly demonstrated that political initiatives precede public concern about crime, for which she also used the Gallup poll's "most important problem" time series as the dependent variable,[108] is in line with the assertions of Chambliss.[109]

In turning to the utilization of a time series, Ordinary Least Squares (OLS) regression, the results support the hypothesis that president's activity on crime does have a significant impact upon the public's opinion of crime ($t < .001$, one-tailed test) (see Table 4-9). The model demonstrates that within a given year, the more the president addresses the issue of crime through his speeches, news conferences, and correspondence, the more the American people will become aware of crime as an important issue in their lives and will shape their opinion that crime is truly an important problem. The results also indicate a fairly strong model ($R^2 = .6324$), that show there is a positive relationship between the president and public opinion and reveal that despite the many other possible influences such as the

TABLE 4–9   Explaining Public Opinion of Crime
            OLS Regression

Independent Variables	Coefficient	Standard Error	t-value
Constant	7.221	3.963	1.822
Presidential Activity	8.306	2.367	3.508***
Media	−5.448	1.092	−0.498
Crime Rate $(t-1)$	2.190	8.868	2.470**
Party	0.457	2.252	0.203
Election Year	−2.949	2.453	−1.202
First Year in Office	−1.184	2.335	−0.507
Unemployment	−1.848	0.847	−2.179*
$n = 52$, $R^2 = .6324$, Adj.$R^2 = .5739$, DW = 1.8397			

$* p < .05$, $** p < .01$, $*** p < .001$. All tests are one-tailed.

media, official unemployment rates, and crime itself, the president still has the most significant impact upon the public. The other variable that is significant in the model is the official crime rates ($t < .01$, one-tailed test), in that as crime rises so too does the public's opinion of crime, demonstrating that the president does not have total control over public opinion, but that crime rates as reported by the Federal Bureau of Investigation also play a role in the public belief that crime is truly an important problem facing the country. The model does not find either the media, party affiliation, election year, or first year in office to be significant variables, which at least suggests the conclusion that presidential activity on crime has a strong influence over public opinion of crime.

In assessing the model (Table 4-9), each of the assumptions of the OLS model was reviewed to ensure that there were no violations.[110] The two assumptions that this model was most likely to violate, and hence that were of greatest concern, were autocorrelation and multicollinearity.[111] Because all of the data collected by the author through primary data collection or from secondary sources were time series, there was a strong possibility for autocorrelation. OLS assumes that the data at one point in time is not influenced by data at a previous point in time or, in other words, there must be no correlation between data points. If the data is influenced by previous time points then the time series has autocorrelated error terms and while the coefficients remain unbiased, the standard deviation and variance are underestimated, hence the tests of significance will be inaccurate.[112] An appropriate test for the presence of autocorrelation is the Durbin-Watson Test which tests for first-order autocorrelation.[113] In the case of this OLS time-series model, the use of the Durbin-Watson Test indicated first-order autocorrelation was *not* present. [114]

In regard to the issue of multicollinearity, the issue centers around the fact that all of the variables may have some level of relationship among themselves.[115] A correlation matrix was generated to analyze this possibility and many of the variables were in fact found to be correlated, such as media with president, media with crime, and crime with unemployment. The most significant relationship was between the president and the media,[116] indicating a high level of multicollinearity.[117] However, this was not unexpected, as the media influences both the president and the public, and when the president speaks, it is often reported by the media.[118] Since the issue of multicollinearity is really one of degree and since it violates no regression assumptions, the presence of multicollinearity is one that must be taken into consideration in regard to estimation of the model. [119]

Although the model presents findings that support the key hypothesis, the observation that specific spikes in presidential activity are followed by dramatic increases in public concern, raises the issue of timing. The model assumes presidential activity and public opinion of crime occur simultaneously or at least within the one-year time frame. Therefore, a second model was created with the same variables as the first but with the president variable lagged one year so that presi-

**TABLE 4–10   Explaining Public Opinion of Crime
(with One-Year Lag)
OLS Regression**

Independent Variables	Coefficient	Standard Error	t-value
Constant	1.375	2.956	0.465
Presidential Activity $(t-1)$	0.157	1.803	8.709***
Media	−2.771	7.771	−3.594***
Crime Rate $(t-1)$	1.366	6.251	2.186*
Party	−0.908	1.561	−0.582
Election Year	0.718	1.706	0.421
First Year in Office	−0.355	1.634	−0.217
Unemployment	5.416	0.661	0.081
$n = 51$, $R^2 = .8290$, Adj.$R^2 = .8012$, DW = 1.7005			

* $p < .05$, **$p < .01$, ***$p < .001$. All tests are one-tailed.

dential activity one year will influence public opinion of crime the following year (see Table 4-10). The findings greatly strengthen the original model, as both the R^2 and the adjusted R^2 rose dramatically, demonstrating a very strong model explaining the public opinion of crime.[120] The variables for presidential activity and the media were found to be highly significant ($t < .001$, one-tailed test). In addition, the crime variable was found also to be significant in this lagged model ($t < .05$, one-tailed test). Again the assumptions of the OLS model remain unviolated: to include specifically the fact that the Durbin-Watson Test again indicated no presence of first-order autocorrelation.[121] In sum, although the first model supported the hypothesis that the president influences public opinion of crime, it would appear that the greater impact, as found in the second model (Table 4-10), is presidential activity during one year influencing public opinion the next year, controlling for all other variables.

Carrying this logic one step further as previously seen in the data plots, many times several years of increases in presidential activity on crime appears to influence public opinion. Therefore, lagging the presidential variable by two years may provide additional insight. In lagging the presidential variable two time periods so that presidential activity one year influences public opinion of crime two years later, the results once again suggest that presidents influence public opinion of crime (see Table 4-11). In fact, in the case of two lags, the presidential variable remained highly significant ($t < .001$, one-tailed test) and the only other variable found to be significant was the crime rate ($t < .05$, one-tailed test). However, of particular interest is the fact that with the introduction of two-lags, the media variable became positively related. Moreover, the model remained a fairly strong model ($R^2 = .61$) and no violations of the OLS assumptions were detected in this

TABLE 4–11   Explaining Public Opinion of Crime
(with Two-Year Lag)
OLS Regression

Independent Variables	Coefficient	Standard Error	t-value
Constant	3.520	4.705	0.748
Presidential Activity $(t-2)$	8.138	0.026	3.072***
Media	5.680	1.056	0.053
Crime Rate $(t-1)$	1.884	9.603	1.962*
Party	−0.712	2.404	−0.296
Election Year	−9.486	2.646	−0.035
First Year in Office	0.920	2.625	0.350
Unemployment	−1.282	1.005	−1.276
$n = 50$, $R^2 = .6100$, Adj.$R^2 = .5450$, DW = 2.1080			

$* p < .05$, $**p < .01$, $***p < .001$. All tests are one-tailed.

model, with particular attention again paid to the possibility of autocorrelation.[122] Finally, it should be noted that, an additional model was constructed to test if presidential activity one year influenced public opinion three years later, and the results were inconclusive due to the presence of first-order correlation by the Durbin-Watson Test. No measures to correct for autocorrelation were taken due to the fact the presidential variable with three lags had no theoretical basis.

In order to test these suggestive findings, the researcher constructed additional models to further understand the relationship between presidential activity on crime and public opinion of crime. The first issue addressed was the fact that in both models there was a negative relationship between the media and public opinion. Articulating this relationship further, it would appear at face value that as the salience of crime with the media falls, public opinion of crime rises. Intuitively this does not make much sense, but as previously stated, it is not surprising to find such a strong relationship between the media, president, and public opinion of crime issue. Therefore, in order to determine the influence of both the media and president on public opinion, a comparison of two models which isolated each variable by excluding the other from the model was generated in order to see if the negative correlation found in the media variable changes to a positive relationship and to see if the presidential model remains significant (see Table 4-12). In the case of the media-only model the media variable becomes positively related, meaning that the more the media reports on the issue of crime, the more concerned the public becomes with the issue ($t < .01$, one-tailed test). In addition, both the crime and unemployment variables remain a significant influence on public opinion ($t < .01$, one-tailed test).[123] In the case of the president-only model, the president remains highly significant ($t < .001$), as do the crime and unemployment variables ($t < .01$, one-tailed test). In comparing the two models together, both the

**TABLE 4–12 Explaining Public Opinion of Crime
OLS Regression**

Independent Variables	President Only			Media Only		
	Coefficient	Standard Error	t-value	Coefficients	Standard Error	t-value
Constant	7.033	3.912	1.797	7.617	4.431	1.718
President	7.439	1.594	−4.664***	—	—	—
Media	—	—	—	2.268	8.304	2.731**
Crime ($t-1$)	2.038	8.254	2.469**	2.694	9.789	2.752**
Party	0.722	2.170	0.332	0.356	2.519	0.141
Election Year	−2.890	2.429	−1.189	−2.012	2.727	−0.737
First Year in Office	−1.255	2.311	−0.543	−1.721	2.606	−0.660
Unemployment	−1.944	0.818	−2.376*	−2.723	0.906	−3004**
	$n = 52$			$n = 52$		
	$R^2 = .6302$			$R^2 = .5295$		
	Adj.$R^2 = .5810$			Adj.$R^2 = .4668$		
	DW = 1.8302			DW = 1.7355		

* $p < .05$, ** $p < .01$, *** $p < .001$. All tests are one-tailed.

R^2 (.6302) and adjusted R^2 (.5810) demonstrate that the president-only model is the better fitted model. [124]

While the hypothesis that presidents influence public opinion of crime is still supported in the models specified so far, there is the possibility that another political variable may greatly influence public opinion of crime and that is the amount of attention, or activity, Congress spends on the issue of crime. Congress has the power to introduce not only presidential proposals on crime, but they may introduce their own as well, as Congress has done so very often over the past thirty years.[125] In addition, like the president, the Congress has a variety of means by which to deal with the issue of crime. Although congressional committees have evolved over the time frame of analysis (1945–1996), have changed names, and have changed responsibilities, generally speaking, the House and Senate Judiciary Committees have had responsibility for issues related to crime, and very often have created subcommittees to handle specific issues such as street crime, organized crime, and juvenile crime.[126] Finally, if Congressional members—especially those of the House—believe that crime is an important issue to their constituents, they will spend time articulating their position on crime when they return to their congressional district.[127] Therefore, assessing congressional activity on crime may be as important as assessing presidential activity, but in light of the relationship between Congress and the president,[128] it is at least advisable to control the influence between these two political entities.

In order to operationalize congressional activity on crime, the author turned to the work of Frank R. Baumgartner and Bryan D. Jones in their widely received publication *Agendas and Instability in American Politics.* [129] Resulting from their research was the establishment of the *Center for American Politics and Public Policy's* "Policy Agendas Project" which made available their collected data on all publicly available congressional hearings conducted from 1947 through 1994. [130]Information was downloaded and evaluated September through October 1999. According to the "Congressional Hearings Data Description" "the hearings included are those of committees, subcommittees, task forces, panels and commissions, and the joint committees of Congress."[131] It should be noted that not included were "committee reports, publications, supplementary materials, and declassified materials," as well as any hearings not released for public record.[132] All of the hearings were coded by their policy content which consisted of 19 major topics and 220 minor topics.

In order to construct a congressional activity on crime variable, the author downloaded all of the data for House, Senate, and Joint Committees related to the issue of crime.[133] The data was then reviewed for all topics, both major and minor, related to crime. The list included House committee hearings on "crime investigation" by the District of Columbia Committee and "crime and criminal justice" hearings by the Judiciary Committee. Senate Committee hearings included "juvenile justice" and "criminal law" hearings by the Judiciary Committee and "investigate crime and law enforcement" hearings by the Committee on the District of Columbia. Finally, any Joint Committee hearings on crime were also included. A number count assessing the total number of hearings for all House, Senate, and Joint Committees related to crime was conducted and the sum total was utilized to represent congressional attention to crime (see Figure 4-6).

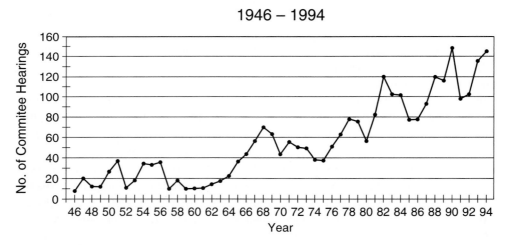

FIGURE 4–6   Congressional Attention to Crime

Source: Data collected by author from Frank Baumgartner and Bryan Jones. *"Policy Agendas Project." Center for American Politics and Public Policy.* The Policy Agendas Project is available at http://depts.washington.edu/ampol/agendasproject.html. The data was downloaded September–October 1999.

As discussed earlier, the concept of "eyeballing" trend data can provide some interesting insight into the variable in question. In the case of congressional attention to the issue of crime, there appeared to be some rise in attention in the late 1940s and throughout the 1950s, most of which was associated with the issue of juvenile crime. The rising trend in the 1960s was most likely in large response to President Johnson's high level of activity on crime and the number of proposals he put forth during his tenure in office (see Table 3-4 for a complete list of Johnson-supported legislation). Finally, it appears that as the presidential activity on crime increased dramatically in the last two decades of the twentieth century, so too did the activity on the part of Congress. Recognizing that these two variables may be related—if one political entity is actively involved in a specific policy area, it only follows that the other will follow suit—the first question to answer was how closely related were these variables.

In assessing the correlation between the presidential variable and the activity on the part of the House (.77) and between the presidential variable and the Senate, there were fairly strong correlations (.69). There was not, however, a strong correlation between the president and Joint Committee hearings on crime (.06), primarily due to the fact that there were so few during this time period. Finally, when taken together as a whole, representing congressional activity on the issue of crime, the correlation between the president and Congress was a strikingly strong correlation (.81).[134] This means there is, in fact, a strong correlation between presidential attention to crime and congressional attention to crime, generating the plausible hypothesis Congress may very well compete with presidents in influencing public opinion of crime. Although the peaks of congressional attention to the issue appear to have less in relation to the public opinion variable, the hypothesis that Congress influences public opinion of crime seems plausible.

To test this hypothesis, the variable of congressional activity was added to the original model and the results assessed for the years 1947 through 1994, due to the more limited availability of data related to congressional hearings on crime (see Table 4-13). The model did not indicate that the congressional variable had any impact upon public opinion of crime. However, once again the presidential variable proved to be highly significant ($t < .01$, one-tailed test) and in this case, the only significant variable explaining public opinion of crime. The model remained fairly strong ($R^2 = .5712$) and there were no indications of any violations of the OLS assumptions to include the presence of autocorrelation.[135] Thus, the hypothesis that Congress influences public opinion of crime was not substantiated.

One other possibility related to the congressional variable may be found in the relationship with the president as discovered in the second model (see Table 4-10), where presidential activity one year influences public opinion the next year. Taking this same line of reasoning to the Congress, the congressional variable was lagged one year, alongside the one year lagged presidential variable, to determine

TABLE 4–13   **Explaining Public Opinion of Crime
(with Congressional Variable)
OLS Regression**

Independent Variables	Coefficient	Standard Error	t-value
Constant	6.479	4.365	1.484
Presidential Activity	7.695	2.787	2.760**
Congressional Activity	5.209	8.147	0.639
Media	−2.162	1.359	−1.590
Crime Rate ($t-1$)	2.102	1.254	1.676
Party	0.511	2.261	0.226
Election Year	−2.290	2.706	−0.846
First Year in Office	0.462	2.619	0.176
Unemployment	−1.401	0.929	−1.508
$n = 49$, $R^2 = .5712$, Adj.$R^2 = .4855$, DW = 1.9321			

* $p < .05$, **$p < .01$, ***$p < .001$. All tests are one-tailed.

TABLE 4–14   **Explaining Public Opinion of Crime
(Presidential and Congressional Variables with One-Year Lag)
OLS Regression**

Independent Variables	Coefficient	Standard Error	t-value
Constant	2.282	3.109	0.734
Presidential Activity ($t-1$)	0.170	2.148	7.943***
Congressional Activity ($t-1$)	−0.065	4.925	−1.334
Media	−2.719	7.959	−3.416***
Crime Rate ($t-1$)	2.116	8.289	2.553**
Party	−0.680	1.604	−0.424
Election Year	0.222	1.798	0.123
First Year in Office	−1.014	1.727	−0.587
Unemployment	−6.936	0.675	−0.102
$n = 48$, $R^2 = .8176$, Adj.$R^2 = .7812$, DW = 1.8681			

* $p < .05$, **$p < .01$, ***$p < .001$. All tests are one-tailed.

if the congressional variable became significant (see Table 4-14). The results proved interesting, but it did not demonstrate the congressional variable to be significant. What it did demonstrate however, was that, once again, the presidential variable was highly significant ($t < .001$, one-tailed test). In addition, the media and official crime rate variables were also found to be highly significant ($t < .001$, one-tailed test). Again, no violations of the OLS assumptions were detected to include the presence of first-order autocorrelation,[136] but the degree of multicollinearity once again raises the issue of the estimation of the model.

In order to address the issue of multicollinearity with the inclusion of a new variable into the original model, namely the congressional variable, two additional models were created in order to isolate each of the highly correlated variables. Therefore, a model indicating president-only and Congress-only were created for comparison purposes (see Table 4-15). In the case of the president-only model, the president remains highly significant ($t < .001$, one-tailed test) and the model remains fairly strong ($R^2 = .6323$).[137] In the case of the Congress-only model, the only significant variable is Congress itself ($t < .05$, one-tailed test).[138] In comparing the two models, utilizing the R^2 as a measure to determine which is the better model, the president-only model appears to be somewhat stronger ($R^2 = .6324$), than the Congress-only model ($R^2 = .4896$). This at least suggests that the president is more influential on public opinion of crime, but that the influence of Congress cannot be dismissed. Rather, it would appear that the relationship between the president and Congress, compounded by the addition of the media, creates a highly complex web of influence on the public's perception that crime is a very important problem facing the country. Recognizing this complex relationship between the president, Congress, and the media, one final issue centered on this last variable must be addressed.

A final critique of all of the models constructed thus far would clearly be found in the media variable. Although the use of the *Readers' Guide to Periodical Literature* has been found to be a robust indicator of media attention to specific issues,[139] one could easily argue the one key influencing factor on the public opinion of crime has been the medium of television news. There is ample evidence the

**TABLE 4–15   Explaining Public Opinion of Crime
OLS Regression**

Independent Variables	President Only			Congress Only		
	Coefficient	Standard Error	t-value	Coefficients	Standard Error	t-value
Constant	7.221	3.963	1.822	4.829	4.660	1.036
President	8.306	2.367	3.508***	—	—	—
Congress	—	—	—	0.169	7.484	2.266*
Media	−5.448	1.092	−0.498	−8.353	1.370	−0.609
Crime $(t-1)$	2.190	8.868	2.476**	1.159	1.300	0.891
Party	0.457	2.252	0.203	0.244	2.434	0.100
Election Year	−2.949	2.453	−1.202	−0.382	2.820	−0.135
First Year in Office	−1.184	2.335	−0.507	1.469	2.795	0.525
Unemployment	−1.848	0.847	−2.179*	−1.613	0.998	−1.616
	$n = 49$			$n = 49$		
	$R^2 = .6324$			$R^2 = .4896$		
	Adj.$R^2 = .5739$			Adj.$R^2 = .4024$		
	DW = 1.8397			DW = 1.7		

* $p < .05$, ** $p < .01$, *** $p < .001$. All tests are one-tailed.

news media has had an impact upon public opinion and public understanding of the crime issue.[140] One recent study on the coverage of crime of the three major networks' evening news (ABC, CBS, and NBC) found that during the early 1990s when crime rates were falling, the number of stories tripled from 571 stories in 1991 to 1,632 stories in 1994.[141] In another study conducted in the last three months of 1996, the local newscasts from 13 cities were recorded and the total number of stories analyzed was 17,074.[142] The most common local television news story was related to crime at 20 percent of total news coverage, with the weather coming in second with only 11 percent of the total news stories.[143] In addition, given that another study has demonstrated that 95 percent of the respondents stated their primary source for information was through the television,[144] it is clear this medium would have a profound influence on public opinion of crime. Therefore, it is important to attempt to assess television news coverage of crime.

In order to operationalize the television variable, the author turned to the "Television News Archive" maintained by Vanderbilt University.[145] The News Archive is an online collection of more "than 30,000 individual network evening news broadcasts and more than 9,000 hours of special news-related programming."[146] The News Archive "has consistently recorded, indexed, and preserved network television news for research, review, and study."[147] The main emphasis of the News Archive is found in their "evening news abstracts" which is derived from the archive's efforts to record the three major networks, ABC, CBS, and NBC broadcasts since 1968 and make available a search-engine index of available abstracts from each edition of the evening news. Each abstract provides the date it was aired, the main topic for each segment including subtopics, and how long the segment aired. In addition, a short one-to-three sentence abstract is then made available describing the main emphasis of the news report.

In order to construct a television news on crime variable, the author conducted a search for each year pertinent to the study, namely the years 1968 though 1996. At first the author attempted to use a variety of terms, such as "crime," "drugs," "drug abuse," "violence," "campus unrest," and "guns." However, after reviewing each of the news abstracts for all of these categories, those that remained applicable to the variable of television news on crime were all found under the one search using the term "crime." As a result, using the total number of abstracts derived from the keyword search for "crime" in the evening news abstracts for the years 1968 through 1996, was the method employed for operationalizing the television news on crime variable.

It must be noted however, that there are several drawbacks to the use of this variable as representing television news on crime. The first is the fact that during the time period of this study, other news shows have developed that often report on issues of crime but are not indexed in the News Archive. These include as 60 Minutes, 20/20, or Dateline NBC. In addition, other shows purporting to be news, but best described as tabloid television, have made their appearances on television during this time period and have also "reported" on the issue of crime. Second, it must be pointed out that many of the more recent shows often considered to be "info-tainment" or "shockumentaries" such as "Cops," "America's Most Wanted," and specials such as Fox's "World's Scariest Police Shootouts" and "World's Scariest Police Chases," often give people the perception that they are news-oriented because they blur the lines between reality and entertainment. They are not included in the variable. A third drawback actually lying in the search method by the News Archive is that the search will only retrieve up to 200 "hits" for each search. Therefore, only 200 hits for each given year searched using the keyword "crime" would be available to the researcher. For the years 1968 through 1992, this was not an issue since the number of evening news stories fell below the 200 retrievable abstracts. However, for the years 1993 through 1996, the data was limited to only 200 abstracts—below the actual number for each year. As there was no means of obtaining the missing data, the data for each of these time points were entered as "200." This recognizes that the estimation of the model will be limited. But due to the fact other variables related to crime reporting rose during this time period, it is believed that the numbers would actually be higher than 200, thus the model will be somewhat underestimated. Finally, it should be noted that the time series data available from the News Archive is limited due to the fact that the data collection did not start until 1968. Thus the time series is limited to the time period 1968 through 1996, for a total of 29 time points.

Again, the concept of "eyeballing" the data first reveals some interesting findings (see Figure 4-7). The first year of data appeared to be strikingly low in comparison to the years 1969 through 1974, and some additional research discov-

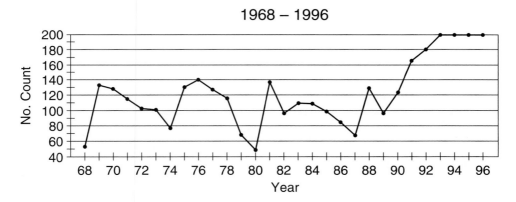

FIGURE 4–7   Crime Reports on Television

Note: The Vanderbilt University Television News Archive only allows for those conducting a search by year to retrieve the first 200 hits. In the case of crime, there were over 200 "hits" for the years 1993–1996. Also, it is important to note that those "hits" under the term "drugs" were all included in a search of the term "crime." Therefore, this chart represents a search using solely the term "crime."

Source: Data collected by author from Vanderbilt University. *Television News Archive.* Nashville: Vanderbilt University. The Television News Archive is available at http://tvnews.vanderbilt.edu/index.html. The data was downloaded January 2000.

ered the data collection for the News Archive did not start until August 5, 1968, hence the data for 1968 are for only a partial year. The data from 1969 through 1974 appear to follow the waning attention to crime during the Nixon administration with a rebound during the Ford Administration and then, once again, a steady decline during the Carter Administration. The variable rebounds dramatically with the entry of Ronald Reagan to the presidency, then begins to taper off until Reagan's emphasis on drugs and Bush's renewed efforts to fight the "war on drugs." Finally, with the entry of President Clinton into office, the level of reporting on crime continues to rise during the 1990s. Recognizing the relationship between presidential activity on crime and the level of news reporting on crime, a correlation of these two variables was conducted demonstrating a fairly strong correlation (.67).[148] Therefore, since the additional hypothesis that television news reporting on crime influences public opinion of crime appears plausible and because there is a fairly strong relationship between the two variables, the question is which has more influence over public opinion of crime.

To test this new hypothesis, the variable of television crime news was added to the strongest model of presidential activity with one lag and the results assessed for the years 1968 through 1996 (see Table 4-16). The model did not indicate that television media had any impact upon public opinion of crime. However, once again, the presidential variable proved to be significant ($t < .001$, one-tailed test) and in this case, was the only significant variable explaining public opinion of crime. The model was a very strong model ($R^2 = .7258$) and there were no indications of any violations of the OLS assumptions to include the presence of autocorrelation.[149] Despite the possibility that the estimators were low due to the data reported for the years 1993 through 1996, the president still was the strong

**TABLE 4–16 Explaining Public Opinion of Crime
(with Television News Variable)
OLS Regression**

Independent Variables	Coefficient	Standard Error	t-value
Constant	13.570	9.547	1.421
Presidential Activity ($t-1$)	0.102	2.426	4.245***
Television	2.860	3.946	0.724
Crime Rate ($t-1$)	−1.422	2.836	−0.501
Party	0.336	3.076	0.109
Election Year	−1.524	3.265	−0.466
First Year in Office	−2.588	3.314	−0.781
Unemployment	−1.075	1.578	−0.680
$n = 29$, $R^2 = .7258$, Adj.$R^2 = .6344$, DW = 1.9883			

* $p < .05$, **$p < .01$, ***$p < .001$. All tests are one-tailed.

The President Speaks . . .

. . . But while Americans are more secure from threats abroad, I think we all know that in many ways we are less secure from threats here at home. Every day the national peace is shattered by crime. In Petaluma, California, an innocent slumber party gives way to agonizing tragedy for the family of Polly Klaas. An ordinary train ride on Long Island ends in a hail of 9-millimeter rounds. A tourist in Florida is nearly burned alive by bigots simply because he is black. Right here in our Nation's Capital, a brave young man named Jason White, a policeman, the son and grandson of policemen, is ruthlessly gunned down. Violent crime and the fear it provokes are crippling our society, limiting personal freedom, and fraying the ties that bind us.

The crime bill before Congress gives you a chance to do something about it, a chance to be tough and smart. What does that mean? Let me begin by saying I care a lot about this issue. Many years ago, when I started out in public life, I was the attorney general of my State. I served as a Governor for a dozen years. I know what it's like to sign laws increasing penalties, to build

President Clinton hands James Brady a pen after signing the Brady bill in the East room of the White House Nov. 30, 1993. Applauding behind them, from left are: Vice President Gore, Attorney General Janet Reno, Sarah Brady and Scott Brady. The law requires a five-day waiting period and background check on handgun buyers and will take effect in 90 days.

PHOTOGRAPH COURTESY OF AP WIDE WORLD PHOTOS.

(continued)

The President Speaks . . . — *(continued)*

more prison cells, to carry out the death penalty. I understand this issue. And it is not a simple thing.

First, we must recognize that most violent crimes are committed by a small percentage of criminals who too often break the laws even when they are on parole. Now those who commit crimes should be punished. And those who commit repeated, violent crimes should be told, "When you commit a third violent crime, you will be put away, and put away for good. Three strikes, and you are out."

Second, we must take serious steps to reduce violence and prevent crime, beginning with more police officers and more community policing. We know right now that police who work the streets, know the folks, have the respect of the neighborhood kids, focus on high crime areas, we know that they are more likely to prevent crime as well as catch criminals. Look at the experience of Houston, where the crime rate dropped 17 percent in one year when that approach was taken.

Here tonight is one of those community policemen, a brave, young detective, Kevin Jett, whose beat is eight square blocks in one of the toughest neighborhoods in New York. Every day he restores some sanity and safety and a sense of values and connections to the people whose lives he protects. I'd like to ask him to stand up and be recognized tonight. Thank you, sir.

You will be given a chance to give the children of this country, the law-abiding working people of this country—and don't forget, in the toughest neighborhoods in this country, in the highest crime neighborhoods in this country, the vast majority of people get up every day and obey the law, pay their taxes, do their best to raise their kids. They deserve people like Kevin Jett. And you're going to be given a chance to give the American people another 100,000 of them, well trained. And I urge you to do it.

You have before you crime legislation which also establishes a police corps to encourage young people to get an education and pay it off by serving as police officers; which encourages retiring military personnel to move into police forces, an inordinate resource for our country; one which has a safe schools provision which will give our young people the chance to walk to school in safety and to be in school in safety instead of dodging bullets. These are important things.

The third thing we have to do is to build on the Brady bill, the Brady law, to take further steps to keep guns out of the hands of criminals. I want to say something about this issue. Hunters must always be free to hunt. Law-abiding adults should always be free to own guns and protect their homes. I respect that part of our culture; I grew up in it. But I want to ask the sportsmen and others who lawfully own guns to join us in this campaign to reduce gun violence. I say to you, I know you didn't create this problem, but we need your help to solve it. There is no sporting purpose on Earth that should stop the United States Congress from banishing assault weapons that out-gun police and cut down children.

Fourth, we must remember that drugs are a factor in an enormous percentage of crimes. Recent studies indicate, sadly, that drug use is on the rise again among our young people. The crime bill contains—all the crime bills contain—more money for drug treatment for criminal addicts and boot camps for youthful offenders that include incentives to get off drugs and to stay off drugs. Our administration's budget, with all its cuts, contains a large increase in funding for drug treatment and drug education. You must pass them both. We need them desperately.

My fellow Americans, the problem of violence is an American problem. It has no partisan or philosophical element. Therefore, I urge you to find ways as quickly as possible to set aside partisan differences and pass a strong, smart, tough crime bill. But further, I urge you to consider this: As you demand tougher penalties for those who choose violence, let us also remember how we came to this sad point. In our toughest neighborhoods, on our meanest streets, in our poorest rural areas, we have seen a stunning and simultaneous breakdown of community, family, and work, the heart and soul of civilized society. This has created a vast vacuum which has been filled by violence and drugs and gangs. So I ask you to remember that even as we say "no" to crime, we must give people, especially our young people, something to say "yes" to.

—Bill Clinton
Address Before a Joint Session of the Congress on the State of the Union,
January 25, 1994.

---

determinant on public opinion of crime as reported in the Gallup poll's "most important problem" time series. This is not to say that television news reports of crime have no impact on public opinion of crime, but rather, presidents influence the collective opinion of what is an important problem facing the country. When the president raises crime as an important issue, the collective American opinion also believes this to be true. Hence, the hypothesis that presidents influence public opinion of crime is once again supported.

DISCUSSION

Although all of the results thus far have supported the key hypothesis, one must consider that the narrowness of the unit of analysis only allows us to apply the findings to current and future presidents. As previously discussed, not only may this provide an understanding of the relationship between the president and the public, it may also provide current and future presidents an understanding of how much impact they have upon the public agenda, specifically in the area of crime. If they can utilize this to push their crime agenda, perhaps in the reverse they could create a sense of safety among the public (although most likely a false sense of safety) by not addressing the crime issue. This can only be stated and applied if in fact the study proves to be both reliable and valid, and it is to these considerations that we now turn.

The first internal validity problem may arise as a result of historical impact.[150] The question arises whether the president actually has the ability to control the agenda or whether it is dictated by events that lie far beyond the president's control. Although it has been found that many foreign and international issues do lie beyond the president's control[151] and such events may push their way to the top of the president's agenda,[152] this is not unique to any of the presidents and all must deal with these varying problems. Johnson was faced with Vietnam, Carter had the energy crisis, and Reagan had a growing unemployment rate. Presidents still must attempt to create an agenda that lies beyond the varying crises, but it is also important to note that these varying crises also find their way into the public's agenda, creating the aforementioned volatility. As there is no intent by these crises to divert attention away from the crime issue, there should be no internal validity threat.

A second internal validity threat may arise as a result of the instruments utilized for operationalizing both presidential activity on crime and the public opinion of crime. There are no indicators that the usage of activity and rhetoric by presidents has changed much in the twentieth century. However, what has changed is the means by which presidents can communicate their agenda. The use of televised speeches such as the State of the Union Address did not occur until the 1960s and may have changed the variable significantly. Also, the Gallup poll's question does not appear to have changed in its format or method of execution over time, except as previously indicated in the years 1945 through 1947. A key threat to internal validity may lie, as in the case of presidential activity, in its ability to tap into the latent variable. Although presidential activity and the Gallup poll's "Most Important Problem" question have both proven to be well utilized in the social sciences, Cook and Campbell's call for multiple measuring devices of the latent variable must be addressed.[153] Although other indicators may prove beneficial to enhancing internal validity, the ability to utilize additional measures is constrained by time and data availability. As these two indicators are perhaps the best available resources because they were well received in the social science literature, and because they appear to be the best indicators available, only one indicator for the key independent variable and one for the dependent variable are utilized to capture the latent variable in this study.

Finally, perhaps the most important threat to internal validity lies in the direction of causality. Although the hypothesis is focused on the fact that the president will influence public opinion of crime, there is the possibility that the counterhypothesis may hold true, that public opinion of crime may influence presidential activity on the issue of crime. In other words, when the public grows concerned that crime is the "most important problem facing the country," the president responds by including the issue on his agenda, generating solutions to the problem, and including policy proposals in his speeches and letters because of public opinion. Some recent research has argued that this is in fact the case. Gonzenbach, in a study of the media, the president, and public opinion on the drug issue from 1984 to 1991, found that public opinion influences the media which in turn influences the president and his agenda.[154] However, as previously stated, several authors have found that presidents have influenced public opinion on the issue of drugs during this same time period, raising a debate as to which is the correct analysis.[155] Although it is true that given a democratic society the public is supposed to give direction to government, the ability of the public to communicate to the president is more constrained than the ability of the president to communicate to the public.[156] Specifically in the use of speeches, presidential activity is most definitely a reflection of what the president finds important to address as well as a reflection of public sentiment. Presidents must remain in touch with the public and must address its needs and concerns. After all, that is why they were elected. Although this may not clarify the causality question completely, it does provide for a stronger causal linkage of president to public. [157]

In order to address the problem of potential reverse causation, the Granger causality test can be utilized to empirically test which variable precedes the other in time. As Gujarati has explained, "since the future cannot predict the past, if variable X (Granger) causes variable Y, then changes in X should precede changes in Y. Therefore, in a regression of Y on other variables, if we include past or lagged values of X and it significantly improves the prediction of Y, then we can say that X (Granger) causes Y."[158] As the research to this point has conducted half of the evaluation, a review of the president variable (X) influencing public opinion (Y) should be reviewed. Employing the simultaneous equation model (see Table 4-9), the one-lag model (see Table 4-10), and the two-lag model (see Table 4-11), it has been demonstrated that all three of these models support the original hypothesis of this study, that presidents influence public opinion of crime. Utilizing the F value for assessing Granger causality,[159] the results indicate that the three models remain robust and it can be stated that presidents "Granger-cause" public opinion of crime (see Table 4-17).

In reversing the key independent and dependent variables to test the hypothesis that public opinion of crime causes presidential activity on crime, a new model was created along with one- and two-lag models to see if these improve the prediction.[160] Because in all three cases, the Durbin-Watson Test for autocorrelation reported that first-order autocorrelation was present, the first-difference method for correcting for autocorrelation was employed.[161] The OLS models were then run for the simultaneous, one-year, and two-year lag models. The results, based upon the F values, indicate that all three of the models assessing the counterhypothesis are not supported (See Table 4-17).[162] In other words, the hypothesis that public opinion of crime influences presidential activity on crime is not supported by the evidence and presidential activity on crime is found to

TABLE 4–17   Causality between Presidential Activity and Public Opinion Related to Crime

Direction of Causality	F value	P value of F	Decision
Pres → PO	10.811	.0000	Do not reject
PO → Pres*	1.109	0.374	Reject
Pres (t−1) → PO	29.786	.0000	Do not reject
PO (t−1) → Pres*	.654	0.708	Reject
Pres (t−2) → PO	9.384	.0000	Do not reject
PO (t−2) → Pres*	.324	.948	Reject

* Transformed data due to inconclusive reporting on Durbin-Watson d-statistic. First-differences was utilized for transforming the data. Berenblutt-Webb g (test) statistic was utilized to validate use of first-difference method. Format for reporting the empirical test is Gujarati, Damodar N. 1995. *Basic Econometrics.* Third Edition. New York: McGraw-Hill, Inc., pp. 620–623.

"Granger-cause" or precede public opinion of crime, providing additional support for the original hypothesis.

Conclusion

Does presidential activity on crime influence the public opinion of crime? As presidents have been found to influence public opinion regarding the public's policy agenda[163] and when presidents give high-profile speeches on a specific policy problem, the problem has been found to rise on the public agenda,[164] it is not, theoretically speaking, a far reach to conclude that presidents can influence the public opinion of crime. As an increase in public concern for crime as the "most important problem facing the country" having been correlated and regressed on presidential activity suggests causation, because increasing the number of time-lags on the presidential variable increases the strength of the model, and because presidential activity is found to "Granger-cause" a rise in public concern for crime, presidents can be said to influence the public on crime. Thus, when the president increases his time and attention to the topic of crime by addressing crime in his speeches, news conferences, and memoranda, he can influence the public perception of crime as an "important problem facing the country" and essentially place it on the public agenda.

In regard to the other hypotheses, the research did find some support for the influence of official crime rates on public opinion of crime. This support may be related to the release of these statistics to the public by the government, through the media,[165] and, in some instances, by the president himself. In the case of the other variables—party affiliation, election year, first year in office, and unemployment—little to no impact was found on public opinion of crime. This is similar to the findings of Marion in two of her studies which found party affiliation, election years, and first-year in office to have little impact upon the presidential agenda on crime.[166] Finally, economic conditions, as operationalized under the official unemployment rates, were not found to have any significant influence on public opinion of crime except when the presidential variable was removed. This, like the impact on the media variable, may demonstrate an interaction between the two variables in question. However, the lack of significance may be more in line with the conclusions of the criminologists Vold and Bernard "that prior research does not conclusively demonstrate that crime rates increase along with absolute measures of economic stress such as the number of poor or unemployed persons."[167]

Finally, it should be noted that the research at hand did indicate a strong relationship between the variables of the president, the media, Congress, and public opinion. The high level of relationship between these variables was not unexpected since there is a highly integrated relationship between these variables in the real world and recent research bears this point out. Cohen has found that "presidents were responsive to public opinion" but only when the speeches were primarily "symbolic."[168] Beckett has found that "both political initiative and media coverage [of crime] continue to be significantly and positively associated with public concern."[169] Gozenbach has found that "when the media speaks, the president listens."[170] Flanagan, based on his research, believes that "the rising tide of media attention captures the attention of political leaders, which promotes even more coverage and which may further increase public concern." He further believes that "action is demanded from political leaders and the criminal justice system, and the salience of crime and justice issues is temporarily increased."[171] Rogers and Dearing have suggested that there is "undoubtedly a two-way, mutually dependent relationship between the public agenda and the media agenda."[172] And finally, a number of authors have highlighted the fact that these are all highly related variables and the true direction of causation is difficult to untangle.[173] Despite the complex web of interconnectedness among these four variables, the research at hand concludes that the president is at least one of the influencing factors on public opinion of crime.

Endnotes

1. Johnson, Lyndon B. 1965. "Statement by the President on the Riots in New York City. July 21, 1964." *Public Papers of the Presidents of the United States.* Washington D.C.: U.S. G.P.O., p. 876. Note: Italics added by author.
2. Sniderman, Paul M. 1993. " The New Look in Public Opinion Research." In *Political Science: The State of the Discipline II.* Ada W. Finifter, ed. Washington D.C.: American Political Science Association, pp. 219–245.
3. Lippmann, Walter. 1925. *The Phantom Public.* New York: Macmillan.
4. Key, V. O., Jr. 1967. *Public Opinion and American Democracy.* New York: Knopf.
5. Campell, Angus, Philip E. Converse, Warren E. Miller, and Donald E. Stokes. 1960. *The American Voter.* New York: Whiley; Converse, Phillip E. 1964. "The Nature of Belief Systems in Mass Publics." In *Ideology and Discontent.* David E. Apter, ed. New York: Free Press, pp. 206–261.

6. Campell, Angus, Philip E. Converse, Warren E. Miller, and Donald E. Stokes. 1960. *The American Voter.* New York: Whiley; Converse, Phillip E. 1964. "The Nature of Belief Systems in Mass Publics." In *Ideology and Discontent.* David E. Apter, ed. New York: Free Press, pp. 206–261.

7. Page, Benjamin I. and Robert Y. Shapiro. 1992. *The Rational Public: Fifty Years of Trends in Americans' Policy Preferences.* Chicago: The University of Chicago Press.

8. Mayer, William G. 1993. *The Changing American Mind: How and Why American Public Opinion Changed Between 1960 and 1988.* Ann Arbor: The University of Michigan Press.

9. Jacobs, Lawrence and Robert Y. Shapiro. 1995. "Public Opinion, Institutions, and Policy Making." *PS: Political Science and Politics.* 27: 9–17.

10. Jacobs, Lawrence and Robert Y. Shapiro. 1995. "Public Opinion, Institutions, and Policy Making." *PS: Political Science and Politics.* 27: 9–17; Page, Benjamin I. and Robert Y. Shapiro. 1983. "Effects of Public Opinion on Policy." *American Political Science Review* 77: 175–190; Page, Benjamin I. and Robert Y. Shapiro. 1992. *The Rational Public: Fifty Years of Trends in Americans' Policy Preferences.* Chicago: The University of Chicago Press; Page, Benjamin I., Robert Y. Shapiro, and Glenn R. Dempsey. 1987. "What Moves Public Opinion?" *American Political Science Review* 81: 23–43; Stimson, James A. 1991. *Public Opinion in America: Moods, Cycles, and Swings.* Boulder: Westview Press.

11. Jacobs, Lawrence and Robert Y. Shapiro. 1995. "Public Opinion, Institutions, and Policy Making." *PS: Political Science and Politics.* 27: 9–17.

12. Cohen, Jeffrey E. 1997. *Presidential Responsiveness and Public Policy-Making.* Ann Arbor: University of Michigan Press; Hill, Kim Quaile. 1998. "The Policy Agendas of the President and the Mass Public: A Research Validation and Extension." *American Journal of Political Science* 42: 1328–1334.

13. Jacobs, Lawrence R. and Robert Y. Shapiro. Forthcoming. *Politicians Don't Pander.* As cited in Morin, Richard. 2000. "Unconventional Wisdom: Pander Gap." *The Washington Post* (March 19): B5.

14. Gaubatz, Kathlyn Taylor. 1995. *Crime in the Public Mind.* Ann Arbor: The University of Michigan Press, p. 10.

15. Hurwitz, Jon and Mark Peffley. 1997. "Public Perceptions of Race and Crime: The Role of Racial Stereotypes." *American Journal of Political Science* 41 (2): 375–401, p. 376.

16. For examples of public opinion and national criminal justice policy, see Flanagan, Timothy J. 1996. "Public Opinion and Public Policy in Criminal Justice." In *Americans View Crime and Justice: A National Public Opinion Survey.* Thousand Oaks: SAGE Publications, pp. 151–158. For examples of public opinion and state criminal justice policy, see Johnson, Bruce and C. Ronald Huff. 1987. "Public Opinion and Criminal Justice Policy Formulation." *Criminal Justice Policy Review* 2: 118–132.

17. Flanagan, Timothy J. and Dennis R. Longmire. 1996. *Americans View Crime and Justice: A National Public Opinion Survey.* Thousand Oaks: SAGE Publications; Roberts, Julian V. and Loretta J. Stalans. 1997. *Public Opinion, Crime, and Criminal Justice.* Boulder: Westview Press.

18. Scheingold, Stuart A. 1995. "Politics, Public Policy, and Street Crime." *The Annals of the American Academy of Political and Social Science* 539: 155–168, p. 163.

19. Haghighi, Bahram and Jon Sorenson. 1996. "America's Fear of Crime," In *Americans View Crime and Justice: A National Public Opinion Survey.* Thousand Oaks: SAGE Publications; Scheingold, Stuart A. 1984. *The Politics of Law and Order.* New York: Longman Press; Scheingold, Stuart A. 1995. "Politics, Public Policy, and Street Crime." *The Annals of the American Academy of Political and Social Science* 539: 155–168; Warr, Mark. 1990. "Dangerous Situations: Social Context and Fear of Victimization," *Social Forces* 68: 891–907; Warr, Mark. 1995. "The Polls—Poll Trends: Public Opinion on Crime and Punishment." *Public Opinion Quarterly* 59: 296–310; Will,

J. A. and J. H. McGrath. 1995. "Crime, Neighborhood Perception, and the Underclass: The Relationship Between Fear of Crime and Class Position." *Journal of Criminal Justice* 23: 163–176.

20. Beckett, Katherine. 1994. "Setting the Public Agenda: 'Street Crime' and Drug Use in American Politics." *Social Problems* 41:425–447; Scheingold, Stuart A. 1991. *The Politics of Street Crime*. Philadelphia: Temple University Press; Wilson, James Q. and Joan Petersilia. 1995. *Crime*, San Francisco, California: ICS Press, see Introduction.

21. Warr, Mark. 1984. "Fear of Victimization: Why are Women and Elderly More Afraid?" *Social Science Quarterly* 65: 681–702.

22. Lavrakas, Paul. 1982. "Fear of Crime and Behavioral Restrictions in Urban and Suburban Neighborhoods." *Population and Environments* 5: 242–264; Lewis, Dan A. and Greta Salem. 1986. *Fear of Crime: Incivility and the Production of a Social Problem*. New Brunswick: Transaction Books; Skogan, Wesley. 1986. "Fear of Crime and Neighborhood Change." In *Communities and Crime*. Albert J. Reiss, Jr. and Michael Tonry, eds. Chicago: University of Chicago Press; Skogan, Wesley. 1993. "The Various Meanings of Fear." In *Fear of Crime and Criminal Victimization*. W. Bilsky, C. Pfeiffer, and P. Wetzels, eds. Stuttgart: Ferdinand Enke Verlag.

23. Ferraro, Kenneth F. 1995. *Fear of Crime: Interpreting Victimization Risk*. Albany: State University of New York Press; LaGrange, Randy L., Kenneth F. Ferraro, and Michael Supanic. 1992. "Perceived Risk and Fear of Crime: Role of Social and Physical Incivilities." *Journal of Research in Crime and Delinquency* 29: 311–335; Meithe, Terance D. and Gary R. Lee. 1984. "Fear of Crime Among Older People: A Reassessment of the Predictive Power of Crime-Related Factors." *Sociological Quarterly* 25: 397–416; Skogan, Wesley G. 1993. "The Various Meanings of Fear." In *Fear of Crime and Criminal Victimization*. W. Bilsky, C. Pfeiffer, and P. Wetzels, eds. Stuttgart: Ferdinand Enke Verlag; Warr, Mark. 1991. "America's Perceptions of Crime and Punishment." In *Criminology: A Contemporary Handbook*. J. F. Sheley, ed. Belmont: Wadsworth.

24. Skogan, Wesley. 1993. "The Various Meanings of Fear." In *Fear of Crime and Criminal Victimization*. W. Bilsky, C. Pfeiffer, and P. Wetzels, eds. Stuttgart: Ferdinand Enke Verlag; Warr, Mark. 1990. "Dangerous Situations: Social Context and Fear of Criminal Victimization." *Social Forces* 68: 891–907.

25. Skogan, Wesley. 1993. "The Various Meanings of Fear." In *Fear of Crime and Criminal Victimization*. W. Bilsky, C. Pfeiffer, and P. Wetzels, eds. Stuttgart: Ferdinand Enke Verlag.

26. Research and Forecasts, Inc. 1983. *America Afraid: How Fear of Crime Changes the Way We Live (The Figgie Report)*. Andy Friedberg, ed. New York: New American Library.

27. Bennack, Frank A., Jr. 1989. *The American Public's Hopes and Fears for the Decade of the 1990s*. New York: The Hearst Company.

28. Warr, Mark. 1995. "The Polls—Poll Trends: Public Opinion on Crime and Punishment." *Public Opinion Quarterly* 59: 296–310.

29. McAney, Leslie. 1993. "The Gallup Poll on Crime." *Gallup Poll Monthly* (December): 18; Miethe, Terance D. 1995. "Fear and Withdrawal from Urban Life." *The Annals of the American Academy of Political and Social Science* 539: 14–140; Scheingold, Stuart A. 1995. "Politics, Public Policy, and Street Crime." *The Annals of the American Academy of Political and Social Science* 539: 155–168.

30. Ferraro, Kenneth and Randy LaGrange. 1987. "The Measurement of Fear of Crime." *Sociological Quarterly* 57: 71–101; Liska, Allen E. and William Baccaglini. 1990. "Feeling Safe by Comparison: Crime in the Newspapers." *Social Problems* 37: 360–374.

31. Warr, Mark. 1995. "The Polls—Poll Trends: Public Opinion on Crime and Punishment." *Public Opinion Quarterly* 59: 296–310.

32. Baumer, Terry L. 1985. "Testing a General Model of Fear of Crime." *Journal of Research in Crime and Delinquency* 22: 239–256; Clemente, F. and M. B. Kleiman. 1977. "Fear of Crime in the United States: A Multivariate Analysis." *Social Forces* 56: 519–531; Ferraro, Kenneth F. 1995. *Fear of Crime: Interpreting Victimization Risk*. New York: State University of New York

Press; Gardner, Carol B. 1990. "Safe Conduct: Women, Crime, and Self in Public Places." *Social Problems* 37: 311–328; Garofalo, James. 1981. "The Fear of Crime: Causes and Consequences." *Journal of Criminal Law and Criminology* 72: 839–857; Haghighi, Bahram and Jon Sorenson. 1996. "America's Fear of Crime." In *Americans View Crime and Justice: A National Public Opinion Survey.* Thousand Oaks: SAGE Publications; Kennedy, Leslie W. and Robert A. Silverman. 1985. "Significant Others and Fear of Crime Among the Elderly." *Journal of Aging and Human Development* 20: 241–256; LaGrange, Randy L., Kenneth F. Ferraro, and M. Supancic. 1992. "Perceived Risk and Fear of Crime: Role of Social and Physical Incivilities." *Journal of Research in Crime and Delinquency* 29: 311–334; Miethe, Terance D. and Gary R. Lee. 1984. "Fear of Crime Among Older People: A Reassessment of the Predictive Power of Crime-Related Factors." *Sociological Quarterly* 25: 397–415; Ortega, Suzanne T. and Jessie L. Myles. 1987. "Race and Gender Effects on Fear of Crime: An Interactive Model with Age." *Criminology* 25: 133–152; Warr, Mark. 1984. "Fear of Victimization: Why are Women and Elderly More Afraid?" *Social Science Quarterly* 65: 681–702; Yin, Peter. 1982. "Fear of Crime as a Problem for the Elderly." *Social Problems* 30: 240–245.

33. Schuman, H. and J. Scott. 1987. "Problems in the Use of Survey Questions to Measure Public Opinion." *Science* 236: 957–959.

34. Gallup, George H. 1996. *The Gallup Poll: Public Opinion.* Wilmington: Scholarly Resources, Inc.

35. Cohen, Jeffrey E. 1995. "Presidential Rhetoric and the Public Agenda." *American Journal of Political Science* 39: 87–107; Lewis-Beck, Michael S. and Tom W. Rice. 1992. *Forecasting Elections.* Washington D.C.: Congressional Quarterly Press; Marion, Nancy E. 1994. *A History of Federal Crime Control Initiatives, 1960–1993.* Westport: Praeger Publishers; Smith, T. 1980. "America's Most Important Problems—A Trend Analysis, 1946–1976." *Public Opinion Quarterly* 44: 164–180.

36. Mayer, William G. 1993. *The Changing American Mind: How and Why American Public Opinion Changed Between 1960 and 1988.* Ann Arbor: The University of Michigan Press; Page, Benjamin I. and Robert Y. Shapiro. 1992. *The Rational Public: Fifty Years of Trends in Americans' Policy Preferences.* Chicago: University of Chicago Press.

37. Gozenbach, William J. 1996. *The Media, The President, and Public Opinion: A Longitudinal Analysis of the Drug Issue, 1984–1991.* Mahwah: Lawrence Erlbaum Associates (publishers), pp. 29–30; Mayer, William G. 1993. *The Changing American Mind: How and Why American Public Opinion Changed Between 1960 and 1988.* Ann Arbor: The University of Michigan Press; Page, Benjamin I. and Robert Y. Shapiro. 1992. *The Rational Public: Fifty Years of Trends in Americans' Policy Preferences.* Chicago: University of Chicago Press.

38. Light, Paul C. 1991. *The President's Agenda: Domestic Policy Choice from Kennedy to Reagan.* Rev. ed. Baltimore: The Johns Hopkins University Press.

39. The specific polls consisted of a CBS News, CBS News/New York Times, The Wirthlin Group, and the Princeton Survey Research Associates surveys. See Warr, Mark. 1995. "The Polls—Poll Trends: Public Opinion on Crime and Punishment." *Public Opinion Quarterly* 59: 296–310.

40. Federal Bureau of Investigation. 1993–1999. *Uniform Crime Reports.* Washington D.C.: U.S. Department of Justice.

41. Hurwitz, Jon and Mark Peffley. 1997. "Public Perceptions of Race and Crime: The Role of Racial Stereotypes." *American Journal of Political Science* 41 (2): 375–401, p. 376; Scheingold, Stuart A. 1995. "Politics, Public Policy, and Street Crime." *The Annals of the American Academy of Political and Social Science* 539: 155–168; Taylor, D. Garth, Kim L. Scheppele, and Arthur L. Stinchcombe. 1979. "Salience of Crime and Support for Harsher Criminal Sanctions." *Social Problems* 26 (4): 413–424; Warr, Mark. 1995. "The Polls—Poll Trends: Public Opinion on Crime and Punishment." *Public Opinion Quarterly* 59: 296–310.

42. Beckett, Katherine. 1997. *Making Crime Pay: Law and Order in Contemporary American Politics.* New York: Oxford University Press; Beckett, Katherine. 1994. "Setting the Public Agenda: 'Street Crime' and Drug Use in American Politics." *Social Problems* 41 (3): 425–447; Beckett, Katherine and Theodore Sasson. 2000. *The Politics of Injustice: Crime and Punishment in America.* Thousand Oaks: Pine Forge Press; Chambliss, William J. 1994. "Policing the Ghetto Underclass: The Politics of Law and Law Enforcement." *Social Problems* 41 (2): 177–194; Gozenbach, William J. 1996. *The Media, The President, and Public Opinion: A Longitudinal Analysis of the Drug Issue, 1984–1991.* Mahwah: Lawrence Erlbaum Associates (publishers); Scheingold, Stuart A. 1984. *The Politics of Law and Order.* New York: Longman; Scheingold, Stuart A. 1991. *The Politics of Street Crime: Criminal Process and Cultural Obsession.* Philadelphia: Temple University Press; Taylor, D. Garth, Kim L. Scheppele, and Arthur L. Stinchcombe. 1979. "Salience of Crime and Support for Harsher Criminal Sanctions." *Social Problems* 26 (4): 413–424.

43. Light, Paul C. 1991. *The President's Agenda: Domestic Policy Choice from Kennedy to Reagan.* Baltimore: The Johns Hopkins University Press, pp. 2–3.

44. Light, Paul C. 1991. *The President's Agenda: Domestic Policy Choice from Kennedy to Reagan.* Baltimore: The Johns Hopkins University Press, p. 3.

45. Light, Paul C. 1991. *The President's Agenda: Domestic Policy Choice from Kennedy to Reagan.* Baltimore: The Johns Hopkins University Press, p. 2.

46. Light, Paul C. 1991. *The President's Agenda: Domestic Policy Choice from Kennedy to Reagan.* Baltimore: The Johns Hopkins University Press, p. 2.

47. Gozenbach, William J. 1996. *The Media, The President, and Public Opinion: A Longitudinal Analysis of the Drug Issue, 1984–1991.* Mahwah: Lawrence Erlbaum Associates (publishers); Graber, Doris. 1982. *The President and the Public.* Philadelphia: Institute for the Study of Human Issues; Hinckley, Barbara. 1994. *Less Than Meets the Eye: Foreign Policy Making and the Myth of the Assertive Congress.* Chicago: A Twentieth Century Fund Book; Hinckley, Barbara. 1990. *The Symbolic Presidency: How Presidents Portray Themselves.* New York: Routledge; Marion, Nancy. 1992. "Presidential Agenda Setting in Crime Control." *Criminal Justice Policy Review* 6 (2): 159–184; Marion, Nancy. 1994. "Symbolism and Federal Crime Control Legislation, 1960–1990." *Journal of Crime and Justice* 17 (2): 69–91; Smith, Craig Allen and Kathy B. Smith. 1994. *The White House Speaks: Presidential Leadership as Persuasion.* Westport: Praeger Publishers.

48. Cohen, Jeffrey E. 1997. *Presidential Responsiveness and Public Policy–Making: The Public and the Policies that Presidents Choose.* Ann Arbor: The University of Michigan Press; Cohen, Jeffrey E. 1995. "Presidential Rhetoric and the Public Agenda." *American Journal of Political Science* 39 (1): 87–107; Kessel, John H. 1974. "Parameters of Presidential Politics." *Social Science Quarterly* 55: 8–24; Light, Paul C. 1991. *The President's Agenda: Domestic Policy Choice from Kennedy to Reagan.* Baltimore: The Johns Hopkins University Press.

49. Cambell, Karlyn Kohrs and Kathleen Hall Jamieson. 1990. *Deeds Done in Words: Presidential Rhetoric and the Genres of Governance.* Chicago: University of Chicago Press; Hart, Roderick P. 1987. *The Sounds of Leadership: Presidential Communication in the Modern Age.* Chicago: University of Chicago Press; Medhurst, Martin J. 1993. *Dwight D. Eisenhower: Strategic Communicator.* Westport: Greenwood Press; Smith, Craig Allen and Kathy B. Smith. 1994. *The White House Speaks: Presidential Leadership as Persuasion.* Westport: Praeger Publishers; Stuckey, Mary E. 1990. *Playing the Game: The Presidential Rhetoric of Ronald Reagan.* New York: Praeger Publishers; Tulis, Jeffrey K. 1987. *The Rhetorical Presidency.* Princeton: Princeton University Press; Windt, Theodore Otto, Jr. 1990. *Presidents and Protestors: Political Rhetoric in the 1960s.* Tuscaloosa: University of Alabama Press.

50. Smith, Craig Allen and Kathy B. Smith. 1994. *The White House Speaks: Presidential Leadership as Persuasion.* Westport: Praeger Publishers.

51. Light, Paul C. 1991. *The President's Agenda: Domestic Policy Choice from Kennedy to Reagan.* Baltimore: The Johns Hopkins University Press, p. 6.

52. Light, Paul C. 1991. *The President's Agenda: Domestic Policy Choice from Kennedy to Reagan.* Baltimore: The Johns Hopkins University Press, p. 160.

53. Gelderman, Charles W. 1995. "All the President's Words." *The Wilson Quarterly* 19: 68–79; Light, Paul C. 1991. *The President's Agenda: Domestic Policy Choice from Kennedy to Reagan.* Baltimore: The Johns Hopkins University Press, p. 160.

54. Kessel, John H. 1975. *The Domestic Presidency: Decision-Making in the White House.* North Scituate: Duxbury Press; Kessel, John H. 1974. "The Parameters of Presidential Politics." *Social Science Quarterly* 55: 8–24; Light, Paul C. 1991. *The President's Agenda: Domestic Policy Choice from Kennedy to Reagan.* Baltimore: The Johns Hopkins University Press; Mumper, M. 1985. "The Presidency and Domestic Policy-Making." *Congress and the Presidency* 12: 75–80; Shull, Steven A. and L. T. LeLoup. 1979. *The Presidency: Studies in Policy-Making.* Brunswick: King's Court Communications; Spitzer, Robert J. 1983. *The Presidency and Public Policy.* University: University of Alabama Press; Spitzer, Robert J. 1993. "Congress and Capital Punishment: An Exercise in Symbolic Politics." *Law and Policy Quarterly* 7: 157–179.

55. Marion, Nancy. 1992. "Presidential Agenda Setting in Crime Control." *Criminal Justice Policy Review* 6 (2): 159–184.

56. Marion, Nancy. 1994. "Symbolism and Federal Crime Control Legislation, 1960–1990." *Journal of Crime and Justice* 17 (2): 69–91.

57. Marion, Nancy E. 1994. *A History of Federal Crime Control Initiatives, 1960–1993.* Westport: Praeger Publishers.

58. Marion, Nancy E. 1997. "Symbolic Policies in Clinton's Crime Control Agenda." *Buffalo Criminal Law Review* 1 (1): 67–108.

59. Edwards, George C. III. 2000. "Building Coalitions." *Presidential Studies Quarterly* 30 (1): 47–78, p. 50.

60. Jacobs, Lawrence R. and Robert Y. Shapiro. 1996. "Public Opinion, Institutions, and Policy Making." *PS: Political Science and Politics* 27: 9–17.

61. Bailey, Frankie and Donna Hale. 1998. *Popular Culture, Crime, and Justice.* Belmont: International Thompson Publishing Company; Baumgartner, Frank D. and Bryan D. Jones. 1993. *Agendas and Instability in American Politics.* Chicago: The University of Chicago Press; Chermak, Steven M. and Alexander Weiss. 1997. "The Effects of the Media on Federal Criminal Justice Policy." *Criminal Justice Policy Review* 8 (4): 323–342; Garofalo, James. 1981. "Crime and the Mass Media: A Selective Review of Research." *Journal of Research in Crime and Delinquency* 18: 319–350; Iyengar, Shanto. 1991. *Is Anyone Responsible? How Television Frames Political Issues.* Chicago: The University of Chicago Press; Iyengar, Shanto and Donald Kinder. 1987. *News that Matters.* Chicago: The University of Chicago Press; Leff, D. R., D. L . Protess, and S. C Brooks. 1986. "Crusading Journalism: Changing Public Attitudes and Policy-Making." *Public Opinion Quarterly* 50: 300–315; Mayer, William G. 1993. *The Changing American Mind: How and Why American Public Opinion Changed Between 1960 and 1988.* Ann Arbor: The University of Michigan Press; Miethe, Terance D. 1995. "Fear and Withdrawal from Urban Life." *Annals of the American Academy of Political and Social Science* 539: 14–28; O'Keefe, G. J. 1985. " 'Taking a Bite Out of Crime': The Impact of a Public Information Campaign." *Communication Research* 12: 147–178; Potter, Gary W. and Victor E. Kappeler. 1998. *Constructing Crime: Perspectives on Making News and Social Problems.* Prospect Heights: Waveland; Surette, Ray. 1998. *Media,*

Crime, and Criminal Justice: Images and Realities. 2d ed. Belmont: International Thompson Publishing Company.

62. Graber, Doris. 1980. *Crime News and the Public.* New York: Praeger Publishers.

63. Savelsburg, Joachim J. 1994. "Knowledge, Domination, and Capital Punishment." *American Journal of Sociology* 99 (4): 911–943.

64. Sacco, Vincent F. 1982. "The Effects of Mass Media on Perceptions of Crime: A Reanalysis of the Issues." *Pacific Sociological Review* 25: 475–493.

65. La Free, Gary. 1998. *Losing Legitimacy: Street Crime and the Decline of Social Institutions in America.* Boulder: Westview Press, p. 25; Potter, Gary W. and Victor E. Kappeler. 1998. *Constructing Crime: Perspectives on Making News and Social Problems.* Prospect Heights: Waveland; Surette, Ray. 1998. *Media, Crime, and Criminal Justice: Images and Realities.* 2d ed. Belmont: International Thompson Publishing Company.

66. La Free, Gary. 1998. *Losing Legitimacy: Street Crime and the Decline of Social Institutions in America.* Boulder: Westview Press; Maier, Mark H. 1995. *The Data Game.* 2d ed. Armonk: M. E. Sharpe.

67. Haynie, Dana L. 1998. "The Gender Gap in Fear of Crime, 1973–1994: A Methodological Approach." *Criminal Justice Review* 23 (1): 29–50; Welch, Michael, Melissa Fenwick, and Meridith Roberts. 1997. "Primary Definitions of Crime and Moral Panic: A Content Analysis of Experts' Quotes in Feature Newspaper Articles on Crime." *Journal of Research on Crime and Delinquency* 34: 474–494.

68. Beattie, R. H. 1955. "Problems of Criminal Statistics in the United States." *Jounral of Criminal Law, Criminology, and Police Science* 46: 178–186; Biderman, A. D. and J. P. Lynch. 1991. *Understanding Crime Incidence Statistics.* New York: Springer-Verlag; Black, Donald J. 1970. "Production of Crime Rates." *American Sociological Review* 35: 733–748; Hindelang, Michael. 1974. "The Uniform Crime Reports Revisited." *Journal of Criminal Justice* 2: 1–17; Kitsuse, John L. and A. V. Cicourel. 1963. "A Note on the Use of Official Statistics." *Social Problems* 11: 131–138; Maier, Mark H. 1995. *The Data Game.* 2d ed. Armonk: M. E. Sharpe; Seidman, David and Michael Couzens. 1974. "Getting the Crime Rate Down: Political Pressure and Crime Reporting." *Law and Society Review* 8: 457–493; Silberman, Charles E. 1978. *Criminal Violence, Criminal Justice.* New York: Random House, see appendix; Skogan, Wesley G. 1974. "The Validity of Official Crime Statistics: An Empirical Investigation." *Social Science Quarterly* 55: 25–38; Wheeler, Stanton. 1967. "Criminal Statistics: A Reformulation of the Problem." *Journal of Criminal Law, Criminology, and Police Science* 58: 317–324.

69. Scheingold, Stuart A. 1995. "Politics, Public Policy, and Street Crime." *The Annals of the American Academy of Political and Social Science* 539: 155–168. To some degree, this belief is still maintained today. See Davey, Joseph Dillon. 1998. *The Politics of Prison Expansion: Winning Elections by Waging War on Crime.* Westport: Praeger Publishers, pp. 48–51, 111.

70. Marion, Nancy E. 1994. *A History of Federal Crime Control Initiatives, 1960–1993.* Westport: Praeger Publishers.

71. Marion, Nancy. 1994. "Symbolism and Federal Crime Control Legislation, 1960–1990." *Journal of Crime and Justice* 17 (2): 69–91.

72. Brace, Paul and Barbara Hinckley. 1992. *Follow the Leader: Opinion Polls and the Modern Presidents.* New York: Basic Books; Kessel, John H. 1975. *The Domestic Presidency: Decision-Making in the White House.* North Scituate: Duxbury Press; Light, Paul C. 1991. *The President's Agenda: Domestic Policy Choice from Kennedy to Reagan.* Rev. ed. Baltimore: The Johns Hopkins University Press; Mezey, Michael L. 1989. *Congress, the President, and Public Policy.* Boulder: Westview Press; Pfiffner, James P. 1996. *The Strategic Presidency: Hitting the Ground Running.* Lawrence: University Press of Kansas.

73. Golden, D. G. and J. M. Porterba. 1980. "The Price of Popularity: The Political Business Cycle Reexamined." *American Journal of Political Science* 24: 696–714; Hibbs, D. A., Jr., R. D. Rivers and N. Vasiltos. 1982. "On the Demand for Economic Outcomes." *Journal of Politics* 43: 426–462; Kernell, Samuel. 1978. "Explaining Presidential Popularity." *American Political Science Review* 72: 506–522; Norpoth, H. 1984. "Unemployment and Crime." *Journal of Criminal Law and Criminology* 71 (2): 181–183; Ragsdale, Lyn. 1998. *Vital Statistics on the Presidency: Washington to Clinton.* Washington D.C.: Congressional Quarterly, Inc.

74. Barlow, David E., Melissa Hickman Barlow, and W. Wesley Johnson. 1996. "The Political Economy of Criminal Justice Policy: A Time-Series Analysis of Economic Conditions, Crime, and Federal Criminal Justice Legislation, 1948–1987." *Justice Quarterly* 13 (2): 223–242; Chiricos, Ted G. 1987. "Rates of Crime and Unemployment: An Analysis of Aggregate Research Evidence." *Social Problems* 34 (2): 187–211; Hagan, John and Ruther Peterson. 1995. *Crime and Inequality.* Stanford: Standford University Press; Nagel, W. G. 1977. "A Statement on Behalf of a Moratorium on Prison Construction." *Crime & Delinquency* 23 (2): 154–172; Orsagh, T. 1980. "Unemployment and Crime." *Journal of Criminal Law and Criminology* 71 (2): 181–183; Vold, George B. and Thomas J. Bernard. 1986. *Theoretical Criminology.* 3d ed. New York: Oxford University Press, p. 141.

75. Cohen, Jeffrey E. 1997. *Presidential Responsiveness and Public Policy-Making: The Public and the Policies that Presidents Choose.* Ann Arbor: The University of Michigan Press; Cohen, Jeffrey E. 1995. "Presidential Rhetoric and the Public Agenda." *American Journal of Political Science* 39: 87–107; Gozenbach, William J. 1996. *The Media, The President, and Public Opinion: A Longitudinal Analysis of the Drug Issue, 1984–1991.* Mahwah: Lawrence Erlbaum Associates (publishers); Lewis-Beck, Michael S. and Tom W. Rice. 1992. *Forecasting Elections.* Washington D.C.: Congressional Quarterly Press; Marion, Nancy E. 1994. *A History of Federal Crime Control Initiatives, 1960–1993.* Westport: Praeger Publishers; Smith, T. 1980. "America's Most Important Problems—A Trend Analysis, 1946–1976." *Public Opinion Quarterly* 44: 164–180.

76. Corbett, Michael. 1991. *American Public Opinion.* New York: Longman, pp. 36–48; Frankel, Martin R. and Lester R. Frankel. 1987. "Fifty Years of Survey Sampling in the United States." *Public Opinion Quarterly* 51: 5127–5138; Freedman, David, Robert Pisani, Roger Purves, and Ani Adhikari. 1991. *Statistics.* 2d ed. New York: W.W. Norton and Company, p. 314.

77. Freedman, David, Robert Pisani, Roger Purves, and Ani Adhikari. 1991. *Statistics.* 2d ed. New York: W.W. Norton and Company, p. 314.

78. Frankel, Martin R. and Lester R. Frankel. 1987. "Fifty Years of Survey Sampling in the United States." *Public Opinion Quarterly* 51: 5127–5138.

79. Gallup, George. 1946–1997. *The Gallup Poll: Public Opinion.* Wilmington: Scholarly Resources, Inc.

80. Marion, Nancy E. 1994. *A History of Federal Crime Control Initiatives, 1960–1993.* Westport: Preager Publishers.

81. Bureau of Justice Statistics. 1980–1997. *Sourcebook of Criminal Justice Statistics.* Washington D.C.: Bureau of Justice Statistics.

82. Gallup, George. 2000. "Gallup Social and Economic Indicators—Most Important Problem." *The Gallup Organization Homepage.* http://www.gallup.com/poll/inidcators/indmip.asp Data was obtained January 2000.

83. Gozenbach, William J. 1996. *The Media, The President, and Public Opinion: A Longitudinal Analysis of the Drug Issue, 1984–1991.* Mahwah: Lawrence Erlbaum Associates (publishers); Graber, Doris. 1982. *The President and the Public.* Philadelphia: Institute for the Study of Human Issues; Heck, E. V. and Steven A. Shull. 1982. "Policy Preferences of Justices and Presidents." *Law and Policy Quarterly* 4: 327–338; Hinckley, Barbara. 1994. *Less Than Meets the*

Eye: Foreign Policy Making and the Myth of the Assertive Congress. Chicago: A Twentieth Century Fund Book; Hinckley, Barbara. 1990. *The Symbolic Presidency: How Presidents Portray Themselves.* New York: Routledge; Marion, Nancy. 1992. "Presidential Agenda Setting in Crime Control." *Criminal Justice Policy Review* 6 (2): 159–184; Marion, Nancy. 1994. "Symbolism and Federal Crime Control Legislation, 1960–1990." *Journal of Crime and Justice* 17 (2): 69–91; Shull, Steven A. and A. C. Ringelstein. 1989. "Presidential Attention, Support, and Symbolism in Civil Rights, 1953–1984." *The Social Science Journal* 26: 45–54; Smith, Craig Allen and Kathy B. Smith. 1994. *The White House Speaks: Presidential Leadership as Persuasion.* Westport: Praeger Publishers.

84. Hinckley, Barbara. 1990. *The Symbolic Presidency: How Presidents Portray Themselves.* New York: Routledge, pp. 17–18.

85. Hinckley, Barbara. 1990. *The Symbolic Presidency: How Presidents Portray Themselves.* New York: Routledge, p. 18.

86. Hinckley, Barbara. 1990. *The Symbolic Presidency: How Presidents Portray Themselves.* New York: Routledge, p. 18.

87. Baumgartner, Frank D. and Bryan D. Jones. 1993. *Agendas and Instability in American Politics.* Chicago: University of Chicago Press; Marion, Nancy E. 1994. "Symbolism and Federal Crime Control Legislation, 1960–1990." *Journal of Crime and Justice* 17: 69–91.

88. The author used a recoding and correlation test similar to the two tests recommended by Gozenbach to determine intercoder reliability. See Gozenbach, William J. 1996. *The Media, The President, and Public Opinion: A Longitudinal Analysis of the Drug Issue, 1984–1991.* Mahwah: Lawrence Erlbaum Associates (publishers), p. 28. The author randomly selected six years (to represent a .10 sample of the total number of cases) and coded the data without referencing the original data collection. A comparison between these six years and their corresponding six years was assessed. A Pearson correlation of .983 was obtained, where p was significant at the .05 level.

89. Baumgartner, Frank R. and Bryan D. Jones. 1993. *Agendas and Instability in American Politics.* Chicago: University of Chicago Press; Chermak, Steven M. and Alexander Weiss. 1997. "The Effect of the Media on Federal Criminal Justice Policy." *Criminal Justice Policy Review* 8 (4): 323–342; Weart, Spencer. 1988. *Nuclear Fear: A History of Images.* Cambridge: Harvard University Press.

90. Best, Joel. 1990. *Threatened Children: Rhetoric and Concern about Crime–Victims.* Chicago: The University of Chicago Press; Brown, Les. 1971. *Television.* New York: Harcourt Brace Jovanovich, Inc.; Danielian, Lucig H. and Stephen D. Reese. 1989. "A Closer Look at Intermedia Influence on Agenda Setting: The Cocaine Issue of 1986." In *Communication Campaigns about Drugs: Government, Media, and the Public.* Pamela J. Shoemaker, ed. Hillsdale: Lawrence Erlbaum Associates, pp. 47–66; Troyer, Ronald J. and Gerald E. Markle. 1983. *Cigarettes, The Battle over Smoking.* New Brunswick: Rutgers University Press; Winter, James P. and Chaim H. Eyal. 1981. "Agenda-Setting for the Civil Rights Issue." In *Agenda Setting: Readings on Media, Public Opinion, and Policymaking.* David L. Protess and Maxwell McCombs, ed. Hillsdale: Lawrence Erlbaum Associates, pp. 101–107.

91. Beniger, J. R. 1978. "Media Content as Social Indicators: The Greenfield Index of Agenda-Setting." *Communication Research* 5: 437–451.

92. See Baumgartner, Frank R. and Bryan D. Jones. 1993. *Agendas and Instability in American Politics.* Chicago: University of Chicago Press, p. 50. See also Mazur, Allan. 1981. *The Dynamics of Technical Controversy.* Washington D.C.: Communications Press; Mazur, Allan. 1981. "Media Coverage and Public Opinion on Scientific Controversies." *Journal of Communication* 31: 106–116; Patterson, Samuel C. and Gregory A. Calderia. 1990. "Standing up for Congress: Variations in Public Esteem Since the 1960s." *Legislative Studies Quarterly* 15: 25–47; Rogers, Everett M., James W. Dearing, and Soonbum Chang. 1991. "AIDS in the 1980s:

The Agenda-Setting Process for a Public Issue." Journalism Monograph No. 126. Lexington: Association for Education and Journalism.

93. Baumgartner, Frank R. and Bryan D. Jones. 1993. *Agendas and Instability in American Politics.* Chicago: University of Chicago Press, p. 50.

94. As the data collection methods employed were the same as Baumgartner and Jones methodology, see Baumgartner, Frank R. and Bryan D. Jones. 1993. *Agendas and Instability in American Politics.* Chicago: University of Chicago Press, "Appendix A—Data Sources."

95. Federal Bureau of Investigation. 1999. *Uniform Crime Reports, 1998.* Washington D.C.: U.S. Department of Justice.

96. LaFree, Gary. 1998. *Losing Legitimacy: Street Crime and the Decline of Social Institutions in America.* Boulder: Westview Press, p. 13.

97. Arson was added to the Part I crimes by act of Congress in 1979.

98. Beckett, Katherine. 1994. "Setting the Public Agenda: 'Street Crime' and Drug Use in American Politics." *Social Problems* 41: 425–447.

99. Haynie, Dana L. 1998. "The Gender Gap in Fear of Crime, 1973–1994: A Methodological Approach." *Criminal Justice Review* 23 (1): 29–50.

100. For a discussion on the use of dummy variables, especially in time-series analysis, see Gujarati, Damodar N. 1995. *Basic Econometrics.* 3d ed. New York: McGraw-Hill, Inc.

101. Ostrom, Charles W., Jr. 1978. *Time Series Analysis: Regression Techniques.* Beverly Hills: SAGE Publications, p. 9.

102. Funkhouser, G. R. 1973. "The Issue of the Sixties: An Exploratory Study of the Dynamics of Public Opinion." *Public Opinion Quarterly* 37: 62–75; Neuman, W. R. 1990. "The Threshold of Public Attention." *Public Opinion Quarterly* 54: 159–176.

103. Flamm, Michael William. 1998. *"Law and Order": Street Crime, Civil Disorder, and the Crisis of Liberalism.* Ph.D. Dissertation, Columbia University.

104. Bertram, Eva, Morris Blachman, Kenneth Sharpe, and Peter Andreas. 1996. *Drug War Politics: The Price of Denial.* Berkeley: The University of California Press.

105. Mahoney, Barry. 1976. *The Politics of the Safe Streets Act, 1965–1973: A Case Study in Evolving Federalism and the National Legislative Process.* Ph.D. Dissertation, Columbia University; Marion, Nancy E. 1994. *A History of Federal Crime Control Initiatives, 1960–1993.* Westport: Praeger Publishers, chapter three, titled "The Johnson Administration: A Continuation and Expansion of Activities from the Kennedy Years."

106. Marion, Nancy E. 1994. *A History of Federal Crime Control Initiatives, 1960–1993.* Westport: Praeger Publishers, chapter eight, titled "The Bush Administration: A Continuation of Reagan's Administration."

107. Jones, Bryan D. 1994. *Reconceiving Decision-Making in Democratic Politics: Attention, Choice, and Public Policy.* Chicago: The University of Chicago Press, pp. 106–108. For similar conclusions, see also Beckett, Katherine and Theodore Sasson. 2000. *The Politics of Injustice: Crime and Punishment in America.* Thousand Oaks: Pine Forge Press, pp. 60–68.

108. Beckett, Katherine. 1997. *Making Crime Pay: Law and Order in Contemporary American Politics.* New York: Oxford University Press; Beckett, Katherine. 1994. "Setting the Public Agenda: 'Street Crime' and Drug Use in American Politics." *Social Problems* 41 (3): 425–447.

109. Chambliss, William J. 1994. "Policing the Ghetto Underclass: The Politics of Law and Law Enforcement." *Social Problems* 41 (2): 177–194.

110. In addition to model specification, the errors were found to be normally distributed as indicated by the tests for Skewness, Kurtosis, and the Omnibus test, the expected values of the error term were set at zero, and there were no signs of heteroskedasticity.

111. Cook, Thomas D. and Donald T. Campbell. 1979. *Quasi-Experimentation: Design & Analysis Issues for Field Settings.* Boston: Houghton Mifflin Company; Gujarati, Damodar N. 1995.

Basic Econometrics. 3d ed. New York: McGraw-Hill, Inc.; Ostrom, Charles W., Jr. 1978. *Time Series Analysis: Regression Techniques.* Beverly Hills: SAGE Publications.

112. Gujarati, Damodar N. 1995. *Basic Econometrics.* 3d edition. New York: McGraw-Hill, Inc., pp. 400–415.

113. Gujarati, Damodar N. 1995. *Basic Econometrics.* 3d edition. New York: McGraw-Hill, Inc., pp. 420–425. In should be noted that the Durbin-Watson test only tests for first-order autocorrelation. Although most time series in the social sciences are first-order autoregressive, this does not mean that the presence of second-order autoregression may not be present. However, because of the frequent changes in presidents, issues, and time and attention by the president, it is not believed that second-order autoregression will be present if first-order autoregression is not detected through the Durbin-Watson test. See also McCleary, R. and R. A. Hay. 1980. *Applied Time Series Analysis for the Social Sciences.* Beverly Hills: SAGE Publications; Ostrom, Charles W., Jr. 1978. *Time Series Analysis: Regression Techniques.* Beverly Hills: SAGE Publications.

114. The Durbin-Watson d-statistic was 1.8397, for which the upper bound value with 52 cases and seven variables ($k = 7$) was 1.692, indicating the absence of first-order autocorrelation.

115. Gujarati, Damodar N. 1995. *Basic Econometrics.* 3d ed. New York: McGraw-Hill, Inc., pp. 319–327.

116. The Pearson correlation between the president and the media was .85 where p is significant at the .05 level.

117. A test to see the level of multicollinearity was conducted by regressing each independent variable on all of the other independent variables in the manner described by Lewis-Beck. The R^2 remained at or below the .8 level. When the president variable was removed from the model, the media variable became positively related, demonstrating that multicollinearity is present between the media and president variables and raising an issue as to which is the cause and which is the effect between these variables. The data do indicate, however, that the president is the stronger influence of public opinion. See Lewis-Beck, Michael. 1980. *Applied Regression: An Introduction.* Newbury Park: SAGE Publications.

118. See similar conclusions by Beckett, Katherine. 1997. *Making Crime Pay: Law and Order in Contemporary American Politics.* New York: Oxford University Press; Beckett, Katherine. 1994. "Setting the Public Agenda: 'Street Crime' and Drug Use in American Politics." *Social Problems* 41 (3): 425–447; Caldeira, Gregory A. 1983. "Elections and the Politics of Crime: Budgetary Choices and Priorities in America." In *The Political Science of Criminal Justice.* Springfield: Charles C. Thomas Publishers, pp. 238–252; Gozenbach, William J. 1996. *The Media, The President, and Public Opinion: A Longitudinal Analysis of the Drug Issue, 1984–1991.* Mahwah: Lawrence Erlbaum Associates (publishers).

119. Achen, Christopher H. 1982. *Interpreting and Using Regression.* Beverly Hills: SAGE Publications, pp. 82–83; Gujarati, Damodar N. 1995. *Basic Econometrics.* 3d edition. New York: McGraw-Hill, Inc., pp. 325–327.

120. Note that these two models cannot be compared, for although the dependent variable remains the same, the sample size n has changed. See Gujarati, Damodar N. 1995. *Basic Econometrics.* 3d ed. New York: McGraw-Hill, Inc., p. 209.

121. The Durbin–Watson d-statistic was 1.7005, for which the upper bound value with 51 cases and seven variables ($k = 7$) was 1.692, indicating the absence of first-order autocorrelation.

122. The Durbin-Watson d-statistic was 2.1080, for which the upper bound value with 50 cases and seven variables ($k = 7$) was 1.692, indicating the absence of first-order autocorrelation.

123. In order to verify the reliability of the new estimates, each of the independent variables remaining in the media-only model were regressed on the other variables with the following R^2 reported: Media = .6000, Party = .2509, Election = .1530, First Year = .1527, Unemployment = .4520, and Crime Rate = .7070. All of these fall under the .8 mark indicating high

multicollinearity. See Lewis-Beck, Michael S. 1980. *Applied Regression: An Introduction.* Thousand Oaks: SAGE Publications, pp. 58–63.

124. Three issues must be noted here. The first is that as long as the same size n and the dependent variable remain the same, R^2 and Adj.R^2 can in fact be compared to determine which model is the better-fitted model. See Gujarati, Damodar N. 1995. *Basic Econometrics.* 3d ed. New York: McGraw-Hill, Inc., p. 209. Second, the author must note that this in turn generates a new problem in that a "willful commission of specification error" has been committed, based on the assumption that the original models, and their lags (see Table 4–9, 4–10, and 4–11) are the correct explanatory models. Third, in order to verify the reliability of the new estimates, each of the independent variables remaining in the president-only model were regressed on the other variables with the following R^2 reported: President = .4855, Party = .2070, Election = .1611, First Year = .1531, Unemployment = .4718, and Crime Rate = .6762. All of these fall under the .8 mark indicating high multicollinearity. See Lewis-Beck, Michael S. 1980. *Applied Regression: An Introduction.* Thousand Oaks: SAGE Publications, pp. 58–63.

125. Marion, Nancy E. 1994. *A History of Federal Crime Control Initiatives, 1960–1993.* Westport: Praeger Publishers.

126. Deering, Christopher and Steven S. Smith. 1997. *Committees in Congress.* 3d ed. Washington D.C.: Congressional Quarterly Press; Fenno, Richard F., Jr. 1973. *Congressmen in Committees.* Boston: Little, Brown and Company; House Judiciary Committee Homepage. Available on line at http://www.house.gov/judiciary. Reviewed January 2000; Marion, Nancy E. 1994. *A History of Federal Crime Control Initiatives, 1960–1993.* Westport: Praeger Publishers; Senate Judiciary Committee Homepage. Available on line at http://www.senate.gov/~judiciary. Reviewed January 2000.

127. Fenno, Richard F., Jr. 1978. *Home Style.* Boston: Little, Brown and Company.

128. LeLoup, Lance T. and Steven A. Shull. 1999. *The President and Congress: Collaboration and Combat in National Policymaking.* Boston: Allyn and Bacon.

129. Baumgartner, Frank R. and Bryan D. Jones. 1993. *Agendas and Instability in American Politics.* Chicago: The University of Chicago Press.

130. Center for American Politics and Public Policy. "Policy Agendas Project." Seattle: The University of Washington. Available on line at http://depts.washington.edu/ampol/index.html Information was downloaded and evaluated September through October 1999.

131. Hunt, Valerie, Bryan Jones, Frank Baumgartner, Michael MacLeod, and T. Jes Feeley. 1999. "Congressional Hearings Data Description." *Policy Agendas Project, Center for American Politics and Public Policy.* Seattle: The University of Washington. Available on line at http://depts.washington.edu/ampol/index.html. Information was downloaded September 1999.

132. Hunt, Valerie, Bryan Jones, Frank Baumgartner, Michael MacLeod, and T. Jes Feeley. 1999. "Congressional Hearings Data Description." *Policy Agendas Project, Center for American Politics and Public Policy.* Seattle: The University of Washington. Available on line at http://depts.washington.edu/ampol/index.html. Information was downloaded September 1999.

133. The data used here were originally collected by Frank R. Baumgartner and Bryan D. Jones with the support of National Science Foundation grant number SBR 9320922, and were distributed through the Center for American Politics and Public Policy at the University of Washington and/or the Department of Political Science at Penn State University. Neither NSF nor the original collectors of the data bear any responsibility for the analysis reported here.

134. In all of the correlations a Pearson's r correlation was used.

135. The Durbin-Watson d-statistic was 1.9321, for which the upper bound value with 49 cases and seven variables ($k = 8$) was 1.748, indicating the absence of first-order autocorrelation.

136. The Durbin-Watson d-statistic was 1.8681, for which the upper bound value with 48 cases and eight variables ($k = 8$) was 1.748, indicating the absence of first-order autocorrelation.

137. In order to verify the reliability of the new estimates, each of the independent variables remaining in the new president-only model were regressed on the other variables with the following R^2 reported: President = .7626, Media = .8154, Party = .2510, Election = .1630, First Year = .1563, Unemployment = .4994, and Crime Rate = .7147. The key variable of concern in the new estimates is the media which exceeds the .8 mark indicating high multicollinearity. However, the other variables all fall below the .8 mark. While multicollinearity remains a problem, the model clarifies the fact that many of the variables are related, but the president-only model remains the better-fitting model. See Lewis-Beck, Michael S. 1980. *Applied Regression: An Introduction.* Thousand Oaks: SAGE Publications, pp. 58–63.

138. In order to verify the reliability of the new estimates, each of the independent variables remaining in the Congress-only model were regressed on the other variables with the following R^2 reported: Congress = .8680, Media = .7881, Party = .2056, Election = .2158, First Year = .2766, Unemployment = .5369, and Crime Rate = .8360. The key variable of concern in the new estimates is both Congress and the crime rates which both exceed the .8 mark indicating high multicollinearity. However, the other variables all fall below the .8 mark. While multicollinearity remains a problem, the model clarifies the fact that many of the variables are related, but the president-only model remains the better-fitting model. See Lewis-Beck, Michael S. 1980. *Applied Regression: An Introduction.* Thousand Oaks: SAGE Publications, pp. 58–63.

139. Baumgartner, Frank R. and Bryan D. Jones. 1993. *Agendas and Instability in American Politics.* Chicago: University of Chicago Press, p. 50; Beniger, J. R. 1978. "Media Content as Social Indicators: The Greenfield Index of Agenda-Setting." *Communication Research* 5: 437–451.

140. Graber, Doris. 1980. *Crime News and the Public.* New York: Praeger Publishers; Potter, Gary W. and Victor E. Kappeler. 1998. *Constructing Crime: Perspective on Making News and Social Problems.* Prospect Heights: Waveland Press, Inc.; Surette, Ray. 1998. *Media, Crime, and Criminal Justice: Images and Realities.* 2d ed. Belmont: International Thompson Publishing Company.

141. Lichter, Robert S. and Linda S. Lichter. 1994. *Media Monitor: 1993—The Year in Review.* vol. 8, no. 1. Washington D.C.: Center for Media and Public Affairs.

142. The Kaiser Family Foundation/Center for Media and Public Affairs. 1998. *Assessing Local Television News Coverage of Health Issues.* Menlo Park: The Kaiser Family Foundation/Center for Media and Public Affairs.

143. The Kaiser Family Foundation/Center for Media and Public Affairs. 1998. *Assessing Local Television News Coverage of Health Issues.* Menlo Park: The Kaiser Family Foundation/Center for Media and Public Affairs.

144. Graber, Doris. 1980. *Crime News and the Public.* New York: Praeger Publishers.

145. Vanderbilt University. *Television News Archive.* Available on line at http://tvnews.vanderbilt.edu/index.html. Information was downloaded January 2000.

146. Vanderbilt University. *Television News Archive.* Available on line at http://tvnews.vanderbilt.edu/index.html. Information was downloaded January 2000.

147. Vanderbilt University. *Television News Archive.* Available on line at http://tvnews.vanderbilt.edu/index.html. Information was downloaded January 2000.

148. The method of correlation was Pearson's *r*.

149. The Durbin-Watson *d*-statistic was 1.9883, for which the upper bound value with 29 cases and seven variables ($k = 7$) was 1.830, indicating the absence of first-order autocorrelation.

150. Cook, Thomas D. and Donald T. Campbell. 1979. *Quasi-Experimentation: Design & Analysis for Field Settings.* Boston: Houghton Mifflin Company, chapter two, titled "Validity."

151. Light, Paul C. 1991. *The President's Agenda: Domestic Policy Choice from Kennedy to Reagan.* Rev. ed. Baltimore: The Johns Hopkins University Press.

152. Rose, Richard. 1991. *The Postmodern President.* 2d ed. Chatham: Chatham House.

153. Cook, Thomas D. and Donald T. Campbell. 1979. *Quasi-Experimentation: Design & Analysis for Field Settings.* Boston: Houghton Mifflin Company, chapter two, titled "Validity."

154. Gonzenbach, William J. 1996. *The Media, The President, and Public Opinion: A Longitudinal Analysis of the Drug Issue, 1984–1991.* Mahwah: Lawrence Erlbaum Associates (publishers), pp. 87–92.

155. Jones, Bryan D. 1994. *Reconceiving Decision-Making in Democratic Politics: Attention, Choice, and Public Policy.* Chicago: The University of Chicago Press, pp. 106–108. For similar conclusions, see also Beckett, Katherine and Theodore Sasson. 2000. *The Politics of Injustice: Crime and Punishment in America.* Thousand Oaks: Pine Forge Press, pp. 60–68.

156. Graber, Doris. 1982. *The President and the Public.* Philadelphia: Institute for the Study of Human Issues.

157. Cohen, Jeffrey E. 1995. "Presidential Rhetoric and the Public Agenda." *American Journal of Political Science* 39: 87–107.

158. Gujarati, Damodar N. 1995. *Basic Econometrics.* 3d ed. New York: McGraw-Hill, Inc., p. 621. See also Cromwell, Jeff B., Michael J. Hannan, Walter C. Labys, and Michael Terraza. 1994. *Multivariate Tests for Time Series Models.* Thousand Oaks: SAGE Publications; Freeman, John R. 1982. "Granger Causality and the Time Series Analysis of Political Relationships." *American Journal of Political Science* 26: 327–358.

159. Gujarati, Damodar N. 1995. *Basic Econometrics.* 3d ed. New York: McGraw-Hill, Inc., pp. 620–623.

160. Gujarati, Damodar N. 1995. *Basic Econometrics.* 3d ed. New York: McGraw-Hill, Inc., p. 621.

161. Gujarati, Damodar N. 1995. *Basic Econometrics.* 3d ed. New York: McGraw-Hill, Inc., p. 428.

162. It should be noted that in each of these three models, in order to determine if the first difference method was applicable, the Berenblutt-Webb tests of the hypothesis that $p = 1$ was utilized. In all three cases the g statistic was reported to be below the Durbin-Watson lower bound limit. In this case, because the null hypothesis assumes that $p = 1$ (rather than $p = 0$), the first difference method is acceptable. See Gujarati, Damodar N. 1995. *Basic Econometrics.* 3d ed. New York: McGraw-Hill, Inc., pp. 429–430.

163. Cohen, Jeffrey E. 1997. *Presidential Responsiveness and Public Policy-Making: The Public and the Policies that Presidents Choose.* Ann Arbor: The University of Michigan Press; Cohen, Jeffrey E. 1995. "Presidential Rhetoric and the Public Agenda." *American Journal of Political Science* 39 (1): 87–107.

164. Behr, Roy L. and Shanto Iyengar. 1985. "Television News, Real-World Cues, and Changes in the Public Agenda." *Public Opinion Quarterly* 49: 38–57.

165. Haynie, Dana L. 1998. "The Gender Gap in Fear of Crime, 1973–1994: A Methodological Approach." *Criminal Justice Review* 23 (1): 29–50.

166. Marion, Nancy. 1992. "Presidential Agenda Setting in Crime Control." *Criminal Justice Policy Review* 6 (2): 159–184; Marion, Nancy. 1994. "Symbolism and Federal Crime Control Legislation, 1960–1990." *Journal of Crime and Justice* 17 (2): 69–91.

167. Vold, George B. and Thomas J. Bernard. 1986. *Theoretical Criminology.* 3d ed. New York: Oxford University Press, p. 141. For quote, see LaFree, Gary. 1998. *Losing Legitimacy: Street Crime and the Decline of Social Institutions in America.* Boulder: Westview Press, p. 120.

168. Cohen, Jeffrey E. 1997. *Presidential Responsiveness and Public Policy-Making: The Public and the Policies that Presidents Choose.* Ann Arbor: The University of Michigan Press, p. 240.

169. Beckett, Katherine. 1997. *Making Crime Pay: Law and Order in Contemporary American Politics.* New York: Oxford University Press, pp. 21–22.

170. Gonzenbach, William J. 1996. *The Media, The President, and Public Opinion: A Longitudinal Analysis of the Drug Issue, 1984–1991.* Mahwah: Lawrence Erlbaum Associates (publishers), p. 90.

171. Flanagan, Timothy J. 1996. "Public Opinion and Public Policy in Criminal Justice." In *Americans View Crime and Justice: A National Public Opinion Survey.* Timothy J. Flanagan and Dennis R. Longmire, eds. Thousand Oaks: SAGE Publications, pp. 156–157.

172. Rogers, Everett M. and James W. Dearing. 1988. "Agenda-Setting Research: Where Has It Been and Where Is It Going?" In *Communication Yearbook.* James A. Anderson, ed. vol. 11. Beverly Hills: SAGE Publications, p. 571.

173. See Calderia, Gregory A. 1983. "Elections and the Politics of Crime: Budgetary Choices and Priorities in America." In *The Political Science of Criminal Justice.* Stuart Nagel, Erika Fairchild, and Anthony Champagne, eds. Springfield: Charles C. Thomas Publishers, pp. 238–252; Scheingold, Stuart A. 1984. *The Politics of Law and Order.* New York: Longman; Scheingold, Stuart A. 1995. "Politics, Public Policy and Street Crime." *The Annals of the American Academy of Political and Social Science* 539: 1155–1168.

President Richard M. Nixon greeting members of the Maryland State Police in the White House Oval Office.

chapter 5

Conclusions

This research began with the theory that presidents influence public opinion and integrated this theory into the hypothesis that presidents influence public opinion of crime. Recognizing that there are inherently several assumptions being made with any hypothesis (or theory), the research attempted to identify the most influential, namely the assumptions that presidents have focused on the issue of crime, that presidents have reasons for engaging in crime-policy, and that presidents have the means to pursue this type of policy. The general conclusion that can be drawn from this study is that all three of these assumptions are valid assumptions.

In the case of the first assumption, it has been demonstrated that presidents do in fact focus on issues of crime. Presidents in the eighteenth and nineteenth centuries were found to be largely relegated to responding to state calls for assistance in domestic disturbances in accordance with the United States Constitution and for dealing with issues of criminality in areas such as the western territories (the traditional era) that had express federal jurisdiction. At the beginning of the twentieth century and until 1928, presidents began to focus on expanding the federal mechanisms for law enforcement, but largely in a reactionary and limited response to social conditions (the responsive period). Commencing with the election of 1928 and the entry of President Hoover into the White House in 1929, presidents began seeking a more active role in issues of crime control not only at the federal level but, finding means to enhance enforcement, at the state and local levels as well (the developmental period). This slow but steady growth of federal intervention in the issues of crime policy (the transitional era) would set the stage for the nationalization of the issue of crime. This would definitively commence with the Johnson and Goldwater debates of the 1964 presidential election and would see presidents, beginning with Johnson, actively engaged in issues of crime, ranging from those clearly under federal jurisdiction down to local street crimes (the nationalization era). Finally, with the presidencies of Reagan, Bush, and Clinton, crime policy has become a mainstay of presidential politics and politically a national issue. As Friedman has so clearly stated, the federal government's "role in the [criminal justice] system has grown to impressive size, starting from a baseline of close to zero."[2] Acknowledging the increased role in crime-control policy by the federal government throughout the history of the United States and recognizing that the presidents themselves are catalysts, support for the assumption that presidents are engaged in crime policy is supported and the assertion of a "law and order" presidency reaffirmed.

In the case of the second assumption—that there are reasons why presidents engage in crime-control policies—it has been found that presidents include crime-control policy on their agenda for a variety of reasons. It has been demonstrated that presidents engage in crime-control policies for three key reasons. The first is because certain crimes reach the level of national attention and the nation looks to the president for guidance and leadership. The president simply responds—fulfilling his role as the nation's leader. This action provides one of the key reasons presidents engage in issues of crime. The second reason is because crime provides presidents with the ability to create and support substantive policy in order to affect the problems of crime. And third, because it is a valence issue, it provides them with an issue that is highly complimentary to the use of symbolic language. And despite the assertions of President Nixon in the opening quote, it has allowed presidents to play on a racial theme thus linking racial prejudice with hatred for criminals. In addition, there are a number of political explanations that clearly show that presidents can gain political benefits from advancing the issue of crime by engaging in crime-control policy. The final reason why presidents engage in crime-control policy comes from the ideological explanation. A president's character—how a president orients himself toward life and his world view, how he sees human nature, the cause and effects of social phenomena, and his morality—all can impact the president's desire to engage in crime-control policy, and more importantly, may explain why he pursues the type of crime-control policy that he does. In sum, presidents have a multitude of reasons for engaging in crime-control policies and while some may be more prevalent than others depending upon the individual president, suffice it to say that a number of these explanations are most likely at work in concert. Recognizing the explanations for why presidents engage in crime-control policy lends credence to the assumption that there are in fact reasons why presidents engage in crime-control policy and further supports the concept of a "law and order" presidency.

The third assumption—that presidents have means by which they can become engaged in crime-control policy—has also been demonstrated to be sound. Although the Constitution provides the president with some enumerated powers to engage in crime-control policy such as his ability to grant pardons, create and administer the federal bureaucracy, and respond to formal requests for assistance in cases of domestic disturbances, it is the implied powers that give the president more methods by which he can engage in crime policy. Presidents of the twentieth-century transitional and nationalization eras have managed to engage in crime policy through presidential elections, adhering to the party platforms, creating White House staff positions dedicated to crime policy, expanding and reorganizing federal bureaucracies oriented toward crime control through the creation of crime commissions and task forces, issuing executive orders on crime, generating legislative proposals including crime expenditures in the budget and, ultimately, through their rhetorical abilities. As a result, the assumption that presidents have the means to engage in crime-control policy is met and the research lends more credence to the concept of a "law and order" presidency.

Having raised and met these three key assumptions of the hypothesis, the study turned to testing the hypothesis that presidents influence public opinion of crime. Utilizing an Ordinary Least Squares time-series regression analysis, the study found ample support for the hypothesis. Controlling for all other influencing factors such as crime, media, congressional activity, and economic conditions, the study found that the president was a significant influence on public opinion of crime. When the model introduced a series of lags, it was found that presidential activity on crime one year influenced public opinion of crime the next year as well as two years later, again controlling for all other influencing factors. The media, Congress, and crime were other significant variables raising the issue that all of these were highly related. In the end, while it cannot be definitively said that the president is the *only* influence on public opinion of crime, it can be said with some assurances of accuracy that he is at least *one* of the influencing factors.

The research also posited the potential for reverse causation, which would argue that given a democratic society, public opinion influences presidential activity on crime. Utilizing the "Granger-causality" test, an analysis of reverse causation was conducted and a number of lags were introduced. There was no support found for public opinion influencing presidential activity on crime, demonstrating continued support for the original hypothesis. This is also in keeping with recent findings that presidents, at least over the past twenty years, are not as responsive to the preferences of the public, hence it is not so much presidents responding to public concern, but rather presidents focusing on a policy issue that becomes one of public concern.[3] In sum, based upon the research oriented on the assumptions of the hypothesis and through the use of a statistical model testing the hypothesis, it is the conclusion of this researcher that presidents do in fact influence public opinion of crime.

There has been some research, however, that has supported the claims that public opinion influenced presidents to become engaged in the issue of crime. James Q. Wilson argued that public opinion spurred President Johnson's activity on the Omnibus Crime Control and Safe Streets Act of 1968 by employing Gallup poll data which articulated crime was the "most important problem facing the country."[4] The problem with Wilson's assertions however is that they were not true. Crime did not become the "most important problem facing the country" until 1994, and as the data alludes to, presidential activity on crime in 1967 and 1968 *preceded* a substantial rise in the issue of crime in the Gallup poll's time-series.[5] More recently, Wisotsky has argued for a similar cause and effect relation to the drug war in that public concern for drugs preceded presidential activity on drugs.[6] In addition, a more analytical approach by Gozenbach, assessing the drug issue from 1984 through 1991, found that the president was "a follower rather than a leader concerning the obtrusive drug issue."[7] Although Gozenbach's findings appear sound, they can only be applied to the drug issue within the specified time frame. Looking at the overall issue of crime including the issue of drugs across a longer time frame, 1945 though 1996, this researcher reached a different conclusion. Therefore, despite Wilson's, Wisotsky's, and Gozenbach's conclusions to the contrary, this study paints a picture of the president as a leader rather than a follower concerning the overall issue of crime.

It must also be noted that supportive research to this researcher's conclusions is also available. Baumgartner and Jones found that "in his first prime-time speech to the nation on September 5, 1989, President Bush unveiled his war on drugs. If his desire was to increase attention to drugs, he surely succeeded. After the speech there was an eightfold increase in the amount of television coverage on drugs."[8] Jones, in a follow-up publication, expanded upon the success of President Bush by raising the salience of the issue of drugs after his "anti-drug speech."[9] Elaine Sharpe also found President Nixon to be highly successful in raising public concern for the issue of drugs in the early 1970s.[10] Finally, Beckett on a number of occasions has demonstrated the point that, whether in regard to "crime" or "drugs," presidential attention to the issue has raised the salience of the issue with the public.[11] This additional research lends further support to the fact that presidents lead public opinion of crime and hence stand in a strong position to shape public opinion of this issue in the future.

This last assertion is significant for a number of reasons which will be addressed, but in terms of presidential success it would appear that crime policy stands as a unique opportunity for the presidency. Brace and Hinckley have explained that presidential success is predicated on the president's ability to influence both the public and Congress[12] Bertram, Blachman, Sharpe, and Andreas have stated that "presidents must win popular and congressional approval to implement their political agenda."[13] It would appear then, in regard to crime policy, the equation is half solved. Presidents have the ability to influence the public in regard to the issue of crime, which most likely feeds into popular approval for their stance on crime. And as George C. Edwards explains, "whether successful or not, the president's efforts to build coalitions among the public are designed to assist

President Lyndon Baines Johnson surrounded by the White House Uniformed Secret Service on November 22, 1968.
PHOTOGRAPH COURTESY OF THE LYNDON BAINES JOHNSON LIBRARY, AUSTIN, TEXAS.

building coalitions in Congress"[14] and because it would appear that presidents are successful with Congress on the issue of crime, the second half of the equation may also be solved although further research is most assuredly needed.

Although this research demonstrates that presidents do influence public opinion of crime and suggests they influence Congress, the ability to mobilize the public and build the coalitions necessary goes deeper then simply stating: presidents talk, people react. Brace and Hinckley in their research have explained that "public mobilization is critical if presidents are to succeed, but our evidence indicates that such mobilization cannot be accomplished through presidential position-taking or success in Congress." They continue to articulate that "approval, critical to influence in Congress, must be derived elsewhere, such as from speeches or dramatic international events,"[15] as well as perhaps dramatic national events. It would also appear that in terms of mobilization, presidents have the ability, as previously detailed in chapter three, to mobilize the public through a variety of means regarding crime policy. Edwards recently stated that "leading the public—changing opinion and mobilizing citizens into action—is perhaps the ultimate resource of the democratic political leader."[16] Crime policy appears to give the president the opportunity to lead the public, change public opinion, and mobilize citizens into supporting the president's policies on crime. Thus, the perplexity expressed by Scheingold that "the movement of crime on and off the political agenda is not readily explicable in terms of salience of the issue to the public,"[17] may be partially explained by the salience of the issue to the president. The fact that presidents lead public opinion of crime further strengthens the argument that has developed out of the presidential penchant for focusing on crime policy—the presence of the "law and order" presidency.

QUALIFICATIONS

While this study argues that presidents are the primary influencing factor on the public opinion of crime, it is not attempting to argue that he is the sole influencing agent. Clearly, it is not as simple as the president speaks and the public simply echoes his words in some Orwellian mind-set. It is therefore acknowledged that there are other influencing factors on the public opinion of crime. However, because this study specified a one-directional influence it did not take fully into account all of the other possibilities of influence on public opinion of crime. While it did control for such influencing factors as the media, Congress, and unemployment, it did not assess the impact of other political entities such as interest groups, the Supreme Court, the bureaucracies, governors, state legislatures, or local politicians such as mayors, sheriffs, and city council members. It is clear then, that these entities may also contribute to the overall understanding of crime by American citizens either directly or, more likely, indirectly. As Meier has explained, "in reality, the relationships between political actors and both citizens and interest groups are reciprocal"[18] and "public opinion can be shaped by politicians, and interest groups can be urged by politicians to respond on key issues."[19] Therefore, it is this complex web of interaction that may be missing from this study and further research may help to unravel the various layers of influence upon public opinion of crime.

The two influencing factors that apparently had some influence on the public opinion of crime in this study, besides the president, must be fully noted. First, the impact that the media has on the public perception of the crime problem cannot be overstated. Although it has become a common theme in academic circles to blame the media for a number of social problems and specifically for sensationalizing issues such as crime, the reality of the matter is that, the media, in all its various forms, does in fact influence and distort public opinion of crime. Whether one is analyzing television news or entertainment, crime is a primary staple of television.[20] As one critic noted approximately fifty years ago, "criminality is still the backbone of broadcasting."[21] This was no less true in the 1950s than it is today. In addition, one cannot overlook the use of crime in the other forms of media, from newspapers and magazines to radio and the internet. As these various mediums have proliferated and become more sophisticated, it is becoming evidently clear that they have had a profound influence on public opinion in general[22] and on public opinion of crime more specifically.

The second influencing factor is that of the official crime rates. While the impact alluded to in this variable was the assessment of crime itself, the subtlety of this factor may be the official crime rates themselves. In other words, official crime rates as published each year by the Federal Bureau of Investigation are utilized to assess the amount of U.S. crime. This may cause the rise and fall of crime and to correlate with the rise and fall of public opinion of crime and it may also be that simply publishing "rising" crime statistics may increase the salience of crime among the public. In either event, crime and crime rates cannot be ignored as an influencing factor on public opinion of crime. This influence, above and beyond the president, should be noted as such.

Although the media and crime rates were assessed within this study, perhaps one of the more significant variables overlooked which should be openly discussed, is the influence that governors have over public opinion of crime, as well as in relation to the issue of crime, crime policy, and their role in the criminal justice system. In fact, recent research has demonstrated that gubernatorial campaigns are rife with the issue of crime and, once elected, governors spend a portion of their time dealing with the crime issue.[23] In addition, other research has demonstrated that "law and order" politics among governors in various states has largely been responsible for the significant increase in prison expansion over the last two decades of the twentieth century.[24] And, despite evidence that this policy has largely failed, governors continue to respond to the perception of public demands to "build more prisons" and "get tough on crime."[25] Although there has been no research to date that has analyzed the impact on public opinion of governors' attention to crime, there is at least enough evidence to suggest that it might be an influencing factor.

In addition to the impact that governors may have on public opinion of crime, another possible influence is the impact that Congress may have. While it was a variable that was taken into consideration during the research, the variable assessed Congress in the aggregate and only through their time and attention to the issue of crime by committee and subcommittee. This does not take into account the activity of the individual congressional members when they return home to campaign and discuss policy issues such as crime with their constituents. As governors may influence those citizens that live within a particular state, members of Congress may influence citizens within their congressional districts. Hence, in those jurisdictions where members of Congress utilize "law and order" rhetoric and allocate some of their time and attention to the issue of crime, the salience of crime may be higher in the minds of the public than in those jurisdictions where members of Congress virtually ignore the topic. So, like the research conducted to date on governors and crime policy, Congress has been found to have an impact upon crime policy,[26] but it is unknown whether or not they have an impact on public opinion of crime. The research at hand suggests they do not, but further research is needed to determine if this suggestion can be substantiated.

It should also be noted that perhaps one of the key influencing factors on public opinion of crime may be found at the local level, through local politicians who may desire to politicize the issue of crime thus trying to raise the salience of the issue among their electorate. While the possibility is real, Scheingold has argued that local politicians cannot address the issue of crime in the same manner as their national counterparts.[27] He explains that "local political leaders and criminal process professionals [e.g., Sheriffs, Police Chiefs, etc.] must to some extent answer for a failure to control crime"[28] which means they do not have as vested an interest to highlight crime policy. In addition, because "the politicization of street crime in urban areas tends to exacerbate social divisions because racial minorities are disproportionately represented in arrest, conviction, and incarceration rates,"[29] and because it is "likely to have an adverse impact on the local business climate,"[30] local politicians are more reserved in their use of crime rhetoric, symbolics, or policy. As Scheingold concludes, "politicization at the local level tends to impose burdens, while at the national level it is likely to confer benefits,"[31] thus local politicians are perhaps less likely to influence public opinion of crime.

Finally, it must be noted that there also lies the possibility that other political variables may influence, either directly or indirectly, public opinion of crime. The courts, and more specifically the United States Supreme Court, has been shown to have some influence upon public opinion, albeit in a very limited fashion.[32] The various bureaucracies within the federal government dealing with the issue of crime, such as the Federal Bureau of Investigation or the United States Custom Service, also stand in a position to potentially influence public opinion of crime.[33] Finally, it must be noted that there is the distinct possibility that interest groups have a significant influence on public opinion of crime.[34]

In sum, it is clear that presidents do not have an absolute command over public opinion of crime and that a number of other political entities may influence citizens' beliefs of the crime issue. It is also clear that the issue of crime is a complex mosaic of interested actors both directly and indirectly influencing each other which assuredly helps to shape and form public opinion in the aggregate. However, despite the complexity of the issue, this does not mean that one actor, namely the president, cannot influence a specific policy within the policy process, thereby influencing the American people. As it has previously been mentioned, the president is one of the most visible political actors and one of the most followed leaders. As Kingdon explains, "no other single actor in the political system has quite the capability of the president to set agendas in given policy areas for all who deal with those policies."[35] Cohen and Collier take this further when they state, "the

President Harry S Truman receiving honorary badges from the Washington D.C. Metropolitan Police, the White House Secret Service, and the U.S. Park Police. From left to right are Robert V. Murry, Mark H. Raspberry, Hobart Francis, and President Harry S Truman.
PHOTOGRAPH TAKEN BY ABBIE ROWE OF THE NATIONAL PARK SERVICES, COURTESY OF THE HARRY S TRUMAN LIBRARY.

president also is at the center of public attention. No other political figure can compete with the president in this regard, and the presidential presence in the public space may be overpowering."[36] Add to this Bosso's assertion that "the presidency . . . is the political system's thermostat, capable of heating up or cooling down the politics of any single issue or of an entire platter of issues,"[37] and one assuredly has the prime situation for a president to take the issue of crime policy, bring it to the American people through his presence, and heat up the crime issue thus raising the salience of crime. Finally, as Friedman explained in his treatment of the history of crime and punishment in America regarding crime policy in the United States, "the big show, the main show, is now Washington, D.C.; and the big gun is the president, not the governor or the mayor."[38] Therefore, the significant findings and conclusions that presidents influence public opinion of crime are not an aberration, but approbatory in nature.

IMPLICATIONS

Recognizing that presidents do influence public opinion of crime raises a number of serious implications related to presidents, crime control policy, and politics. As the more time and attention presidents give to the issue of crime control policy increases the salience of crime among Americans, who then come to consider crime to be the "most important problem facing the country," this demonstrates that presidents have the ability to lead public opinion on at least this single policy issue. Hence, an individual in the position of policy advisor to the president—Louis McHenry Howe to Franklin Roosevelt, Joseph Califano to President Johnson, Al From and Bruce Reed to President-elect Clinton—would be remiss in not advising the president or president-elect to go after the crime issue. After all, they have much to gain and little to lose since presidents are not ultimately responsible nor held accountable for local street crimes.

If presidents are one of the primary influences over the public in regard to crime, this suggests that presidents have the capability of making crime policy a successful part of their agenda. It has been found that "merely mentioning a problem to the public heightens concern with the policy problem."[39] Thus if a president wants to utilize the crime issue, he merely has to mention it often. As Light advises presidents to "move it or lose it,"[40] Pfiffner advises presidents to "hit the ground running"[41] and Cohen advises that they "keep on hitting until the policy process is played out,"[42] it could perhaps be drawn from this study that presidents should "hit the ground running, keep moving, and keep on hitting." If crime is to be their issue, they have the capability of manipulating the public opinion of crime by merely raising the issue and increasing their time and attention toward crime-control policy. They have the ability to lead, to get the word out that crime is a problem, to raise the salience of crime with the American public, to place crime on the government's agenda, and more likely, to garner support for their crime-control policies thus creating legislative victories. Yet, herein lies the problem for good policy.

As one of the ultimate goals of presidents is to implement good, effective policies, presidents and their staff are constantly seeking policy issues in which they can be most effective. Cohen explains that presidents seek out effective policies for two reasons:

> First, desirable policy outcomes boost the confidence of the public, which leads to greater levels of approval and popularity. This may translate into reelection victory, greater influence with Congress, and greater leeway in future policy decisions. Second, desirable policy outcomes will enhance the president's standing in the history books. Desirable policy outcome become one basis of his legacy to the nation.[43]

As a result of the opportunity crime policy affords presidents to influence public opinion by raising the issue and demonstrating that they will "get tough on crime," presidents can benefit from increased public approval and popularity over their stance on crime and gain greater influence with Congress on crime-control policies originating from the White House. In addition, presidential activity in crime-control policy will not go unnoticed in the "history books." Crime-control policies of presidents from Hoover to the current president have become a topic of research as the study at hand will attest. Again, presidents have everything to gain from focusing on crime-control policy and little to lose; therefore many of the problems with the trend toward the nationalization of crime begin to arise.

One of the key problems lies in the recognition that many presidents no longer focus on long-term problems with long-term proposals, but rather they have taken to using a series of short-term proposals.[44] As Simon and Ostrom have explained, presidents face a critical dilemma in trying to improve overall policies which take into consideration solutions for long-term problems, or in engaging in problems of a daily nature which only consider short-term solutions. The problem, they highlight, is that:

> The long-term approach will direct the president's actions and energies toward the solution of principal problems of the day . . . to the extent that such attempts fail to solve problems, the president's resource reservoir will become increasingly shallow as the vicious circle begins to undermine his influence on the policy process. This explains the attractiveness of the short-term approach. The president is relatively unconstrained in relying upon political drama and will welcome the bursts in support which actions on the political stage trigger. However, the impact of such actions are short-lived and, by themselves, can do little but provide bumps and wiggles on the downward course of approval. Therein lies the dilemma.[45]

This has occurred throughout the twentieth century in regard to crime-control policy as it was clear that several presidents, such as Hoover, from a conservative perspective, and Johnson, from a liberal perspective, attempted to incorporate crime-control policy as a part of their overall policy proposals to address long-term social problems. In the case of President Hoover, his was a method of social engineering predicated on "the theory of rational choice, which suggest that decision makers contemplate goals and objectives, alternatives and consequences, ultimately deciding upon that which yields the best results."[46] In respect to President Johnson, his policy proposal was part of his "great society" program for which he explained to Congress in 1966 that "effective law enforcement and social justice must be pursued together, as the foundation of our efforts against crime."[47] Since the presidency of President Johnson, crime-control policy has not been incorporated into a larger policy initiative but rather has become its own policy initiative, isolated from any other social considerations. It has apparently fallen to the short-term solution set rather than the long-term.

The advantage to crime falling into the short-term solution set is that despite our best intentions and efforts, crime will always be with us. As a result, it provides presidents with the "political drama" that they need to respond with their policy proposals. In the tragic death of Matthew Shepherd it was the call for hate crime legislation. In the aftermath of the shooting at the National Zoo in Washington, D.C., it was the call for child safety gun locks. And in the wake of the Oklahoma City bombing, at first it was the call for legislation to address international terrorism, and when it was discovered that it was an act of domestic terrorism, it was the call for legislation that would address both. In all of these tragedies and more, crime presents a short-term problem for which presidents and other politicians can propose their short-term solution set, missing the fact that crime is a long-term problem with many facets of social problems undergirding these events.

In addition to the "high drama" that these crime events provide—highlighted and heavily emphasized by the media—crime also provides Americans, and more importantly the president, with an enemy. Gaubatz has explained that Americans throughout the latter half of the twentieth century slowly lost an enemy in which they could target their negative feelings and needed some place to put them. As she rhetorically asks, "what better place than in strenuous opposition to the acts of criminal offenders?"[48] Hence, with the past targets of American aggression such as minorities and "communists" gone, Americans moved toward targeting their aggression toward criminals. As a result, presidents stood in the envious position of leading the aggressive attack against criminals by utilizing their rhetoric to target these internal security threats in the same manner as past external security threats.

As a result, presidents have come to use their position to engage in the proverbial "war on crime" and to demonstrate to the American people that they can be "tough on crime." More specifically, they have utilized all of the tools of the trade (see chapter three) to demonstrate their hardline stance on crime. Where this has been most evident is in the increased number of speeches mentioning crime and, more importantly in the number of speeches solely dedicated to the topics of crime and drugs. Why this is most significant is found in the conclusions of Lyn Ragsdale who has extensively studied presidential speechmaking, when he explains that "through their speeches, presidents offer the impression that they are in charge of existing political circumstances" and "the public is reassured that someone knows what is to be done."[49] In regard to crime policy, Scheingold has made this same assertion stating that these policies have more to do with reassuring the public that something is being done to address the problem when in fact they largely ignore the underlying problems that contribute to increased levels of crime.[50] As a result, "Congress and the President appear to be doing something when indeed they are not."[51]

Rhetoric, then, is perhaps the key to the presidents' ability to influence public opinion of crime because they can utilize symbolic and valence politics to raise the specter of crime and pledge to get tough on crime without ever having to take any action other than their rhetoric. As Lowi, in his seminal work on *The Personal Presidency*, explained:

> Rhetoric—as any angry ape will testify—is preferable to action; but the relationship between rhetoric and action is a problematic one. Mass pressure on plebiscitary presidents requires results, or the appearance of results, regardless of the dangers. Thus, while there is a difference in principle between diplomatic and military approaches, escalation of the definition of conflicts can reach such a height that it wipes out that difference. Oversell is the rhetorical equivalent of militarism.[52]

Thus, crime rhetoric is preferable to any type of definitive action, but presidents have to ultimately demonstrate that they are doing something, so the appearance of addressing crime, such as adding "100,000 Cops" to the streets of America or supporting "Three Strikes" legislation, provides the appearances presidents need. This acts to the detriment of true substantive policy that would address the true nature and underlying causes of crime, which in turn becomes subservient to symbolic and valence politics because these serve the short-term political needs of presidents. However, make no mistake, symbolic policy solutions generated for real social problems do have an impact, for in the words of Murray Edelman, they "signify who are virtuous and useful and who are dangerous and inadequate, which actions will be rewarded and which penalized."[53] Recent research has rather convincingly demonstrated who, in the words of Edelman, are "dangerous and inadequate" and which actions will be "penalized."

Although the conclusions have proven to be highly controversial,[54] more and more evidence demonstrates that minority groups have become the "dangerous and inadequate" group of people as a result of "symbolic racism."[55] Because overt racism is no longer socially acceptable, a more subtle form of racism has developed that makes it acceptable to target "criminals" when in reality these criminals are often blacks and other minority members.[56] As Michael Tonry has argued, "the War on Drugs and the set of harsh crime-control policies in which it was enmeshed were launched to achieve political, not policy, objectives, and it is the adoption for political purposes of policies with foreseeable disparate impacts, the use of disadvantaged Black Americans as a means to the achievement of politicians' electoral ends, that must in the end be justified, and cannot."[57] This has resulted in the use of a veiled form of racism where it is acceptable to target criminals while attempting to argue that there is no intersection between racial prejudice and the punishment orientation of criminals. In the end, symbolic politics, valence politics, and rhetoric are the victors, and substantive policy to address the true underlying problems of crime becomes the loser. Presidents gain, real crime control loses.

This last statement then feeds into another realization. Crime politics is no longer an ideological issue that presents a dichotomized viewpoint, but rather one that now sustains a one-ideological presentation. A number of researchers have pointed out that the competing liberal and conservative perspectives on causes and solutions to crime have largely vanished. Poveda has stated the "poles (crime prevention versus punishment and due process versus crime control) of the traditional liberal-conservative dialogue have largely disappeared, as measures emphasizing punishment far overshadow any consideration of crime prevention."[58] Walker has argued that the "dichotomy is not as sharp as it was a few years ago," largely because conservatives and liberals are "switching sides" and advocating each other's policies[59] and that "by the 1990s, in fact, the old division between 'conservative' and 'liberal' crime policies had vanished."[60] Scheingold stretches this point further by stating that "a troubling theme in this parade of policy perversity is the increasingly pronounced tendency to federalize crime control-policy" which he explains has wrought "something of a role reversal between conservatives and liberals, with conservatives in the vanguard of federalization and liberals voicing, albeit weakly, reservations."[61] Platt has argued that the cause comes from the fact that "the advocates of 'law and order' have promoted an ideology that focuses on working-class crime and mystifies the causes of crime."[62] However, Dilulio, Smith, and Saiger have argued that we have adopted neither side of the conservative-liberal dichotomy, but have placated both. They state that "if experience is any guide, the national government will continue [to] do something to satisfy each of a diverse set of views on crime policy, without adopting any one, single, overarching vision of how best to combat crime."[63] In sum, it is clear the old dichotomy is assuredly gone. But the question is what has taken its place? Is it one ideology, the switching of sides, a complete role reversal, or a movement toward placating both sides?

This author argues that what has occurred is the creation of a one-ideological phenomenon that is not inherently an all-conservative ideology on the one hand or an all-liberal ideology on the other. Rather, what has been created over the past three decades is an ideological viewpoint based upon a pragmatic mind-set that has generated a national presence in the area of crime in order to demonstrate that the national government is doing something about crime, which has effectively avoided most considerations of the underlying causes of crime or discussions of the best policies to reduce such crime. This has simply been left to the academics. As Theodore Lowi argued in his book *The End of Liberalism*:

> Well before the end of the Democratic era of the 1960s we had established a full-scale, modern national state in the United States. A national presence had been established in all areas of social and economic endeavor. The national presence extended not only to matters pertinent to large corporations and their treatment of employees; it had gone far beyond intervention into the affairs of state governments and their local units. The national presence had for the first time extended even into the streets. Police power had been nationalized in the fullest sense of the word. During the 1960s more federal troops were called up to deal with more local disorders than during the entire nineteenth century.[64]

Lowi then concludes that "the fact seems to be that we had nationalized local disorders, just as we had nationalized commerce. All of the peripheries of this country now felt the glow of national presence."[65] And, in his more recent publication, *The End of the Republican Era,* Lowi reasserts the concept of a national presence and furthers the argument by explaining:

> . . . a more consistent line of argument would be that both political parties had become committed to the positive, discretionary, liberal state and that each administration, regardless of the party, was drawn into doing whatever seemed necessary to cope with the problems of this kind of state. Federal troops and federal regulators were drawn into local matters as the federal government became more and more involved in local transactions. This is inherent in the notion of establishing a national *presence.* Intervention at all levels is built into the logic of this situation, as President Bill Clinton confirmed with his war-on-crime proposals of 1994.[66]

As a result, regardless of political affiliation evident especially in the vast similarities between Reagan and Bush with President Clinton, crime policy has become perhaps the epitome of the "positive, discretionary, liberal state." Hence, crime policy is no longer predicated upon the agreement that crime is a problem and the dichotomy of how best to effectively deal with it, but rather upon the acknowledgment that crime is a problem and what is the best way to pragmatically respond to the political dramas unfolding. Ideology has given way to pragmatism. Or rather, pragmatism *is* the one-ideological view.

The question, more specifically then, is to ask what are the implications of this shift from the ideological to the pragmatic in terms of crime-control policy. The fact that crime has become both politicized and nationalized has most assuredly had an enormous impact on crime policy over the past three decades. Narrowing the focus to just presidential activity on crime over this same time period also reveals the significant impact that presidents have on public opinion and crime policy in the United States. In fact, it is the culmination of the presidents' influence on the public as well as the movement toward the politicization and nationalization of crime control that has created one of the greatest problems of crime control policy, namely the misconception that most people have about crime. As Poveda has articulated, "a common theme in the politics of crime is the exploitation of . . . stereotypes and images to foster a climate of fear and alarm."[67] This had in turn exacerbated the fears of the public who believe that crime rates are on the rise and that crime is the "most important problem facing the nation," and has created various moral panics such as the "war on drugs" and the "crack cocaine epidemic." As evidenced by the Gallup poll, soon after Bush commenced making drugs one of his key issues, drugs became the third most important problem in 1988, the second most important in 1989, and the number one problem facing the country in 1990 (see Table 4–6). In addition, in the wake of President Clinton's efforts to move his crime bill through Congress in 1994, according to the

Gallup poll, crime became the number one problem for two years in a row, 1994 and 1995, falling to second place in 1996 (see Table 4–6). This was at a time when overall official crime rates had been falling for three years in a row and have continued to fall throughout the decade.[68] Why then, at a time when crime rates were falling across the country, was the concern for crime rising? The answer, again, is the politicization of crime highlighted by presidential activity on crime; through the false perception that crime rates were rising largely created by this politicization; through the creation of moral panics such as the "war on drugs;" and by exacerbating stereotypes of criminality which was perhaps epitomized in the Willie Horton ads. What has been created is a politics of fear—a fear that has serious implications for crime policy in the United States.

This fear is detrimental for a number of reasons. First and foremost it presents a highly distorted view of the problems of crime hence creating a situation where facts, reality, and research are ignored and myths are created.[69] People's perceptions of the problem of crime are vastly out of line with the reality of crime in the United States. Several recent studies by criminal justice students who we would hope know better have found that their estimations of the number of homicides per year often exceeds one million and most tend to estimate at least 100,000 per year.[70] Even in our worst year, we have not exceeded 25,000. This demonstrates that the perception of crime has run amok. In the words of Theodore Lowi,[71] there has been a rhetorical "oversell" of crime, promoted by presidents and other politicians, as well as by the entertainment and news media. Americans are saturated with the issue of crime. Extending Lowi's argument further, this rhetorical oversell may be the cause of what has been termed an almost militaristic approach to crime in the United States.[72] In any case, these false perceptions of crime on the part of Americans have serious implications all on their own and can become exacerbated with a little help.

Second, these erroneous impressions of crime create, in the words of Scheingold, "an anxious and malleable public responsive to political leaders who wish to politicize crime."[73] It therefore takes little work on the part of the politicians, or specifically the presidents, to play on these false perceptions of crime by highlighting the problems of crime and how best to respond. If people do not have a firm grasp of the true nature of crime, they cannot possibly hope to have a firm grasp of how best to deal with the problems of crime. Hence, the solutions offered by politicians begin to sound plausible and are thus supported by a vast number of people. In addition, these erroneous impressions may also create unrealistic perceptions of the crime problem and the solutions to crime, thus necessitating that politicians take even bolder stances on the issue of crime and seek out more policies that are attractive to the public such as "100,000 Cops," mandatory sentencing, "Three Strikes" legislation, and boot camps, to name a few. Despite the fact that research has told us time and time again these types of policies would fail or are failing, the false perceptions continue to proliferate and politicians continue to benefit.

Third, it may create a situation in which individuals are more willing to believe that anything other than punishment and retribution will not work. Thus, promulgating the "get tough" measures that have proven to be equally, if not more, dismal in implementation.[74] The problem here lies in the fact that politicians, including the presidents, have largely misrepresented public attitudes toward punishment. They have made the argument that they are simply responding to what the public wants, but as is clear from this research, presidents are often creating the increase in concern for crime. Presidents and other politicians then provide the false perception that American citizens are more punitive in nature than they really are, hence the punitive crime policies become the only ones considered for adoption.[75] In fact, citizens are not as punitive as conventional wisdom would have us believe, but rather hold very complex views of crime and justice that seek a balance between both punishment and rehabilitation.[76]

Fourth, the resulting effect of all of this is the fact that both politicians and citizens will react to any short term policy promise in the wake of a high drama situation, thus promulgating poor criminal justice policy and policy based upon the short term. In other words, our criminal justice policy in the United States, especially at the national level, is created out of political dramas, false perceptions, and a desire to do something, anything, immediately, without the benefits of research, institutional considerations, and thoughtful reflection on the costs, efficiency, effectiveness, and equity of such proposals. A case in point is the call by politicians to build more prisons to lock up more criminals and get them off the street, for which there has been seemingly overwhelming public support.[77] However, research by Marvell and Moody demonstrates that as prison populations continue to grow larger and larger, the offenders that are locked behind bars tend to be, on average, less serious offenders than those previously behind bars.[78] In other words, as we build more prison space, we have the profound ability to continue filling those spaces, but not with those originally intended by the politicians or the public, such as murderers and rapists, but with low-level offenders guilty of crimes such as public intoxication, vagrancy, and simple drug possession.

Fifth, the politicization of crime could provide a way for politicians to divert attention from other more pressing policy problems that are more complex and require greater sacrifices.[79] This creates a situation where the debate over social policy is heavily focused on fighting the various "wars" on crime and drugs at the expense of other social policies such as health care, education, and welfare. Meier gives the example of the earnest efforts of the "war on drugs" in the late 1980s which was met with enthusiasm, while other problems such as a increasing deficits and national debt, health care, and a sluggish economy were not adequately addressed.[80] This is, in some sense, caused by the proliferation of tough talk on crime which has shifted the focus from the causes of crime to the problems of crime. Some call this the movement to a more "managerial" form of crime policy.[81] But in a sense, this is once again a reiteration of the pragmatic theme. No one, other than academics, cares why people commit crime—people just want something done about the criminals. As a result, the sole emphasis is on the criminal justice system for dealing with crime from a managerial perspective while other forms of state intervention into the area of crime are excluded.[82] This, in turn, results in crime policy excluding other types of social issues such as welfare, joblessness, and family breakdown that impact on crime.[83] We then allocate funds to crime-control policy at the expense of other types of social programs that may prevent crime, such as those attempting to treat addiction, increase educational opportunities, improve communities, and strengthen families.[84] In sum, as a society, we are demanding federal intervention through pragmatic crime policy to be implemented solely by the criminal justice system in an attempt to address the systemic problems of crime. We are simply asking too much.

Finally, it also creates a situation where the debate over crime policy is solely focused on street crime at the expense of other, equally serious, crimes such as white collar crime, computer fraud, and organized crime.[85] As Susan Caringella-MacDonald explains, "recent crime control agendas are not, of course, aimed at the crimes of the powerful. It is not the corporations (whose violations kill at least five times as many people as all 'street' murders combined, and whose crimes take

President Gerald R. Ford shakes hands with a California Highway Patrolman in front of Air Force One on a campaign trip to California on May 24, 1976.
PHOTO COURTESY OF THE GERALD R. FORD LIBRARY.

billions more than all 'street' crime taken together) that are the objects of the sweeping . . . reactions to crime." As a result, the nationalization of crime is oriented more toward addressing the problems of street crime—something that has long been under the control of the state and local governments—and does little to address more sophisticated crime problems that are beyond the scope of state and local governments. In addition, because the emphasis within crime policy is on street crime, the responses are again oriented on the pragmatic punishment-oriented solutions, and the solutions found within the areas of crime prevention, treatment, and rehabilitation are virtually ignored. Recognizing the problems of crime policy and the role the president plays in shaping public opinion of crime, these conclusions now turn to the prescriptive measures for dealing with these problems.

PRESCRIPTION

Unfortunately, there is no panacea for what ails us in regard to the problem of crime. The reality is that crime always has been and always will be a problem that plagues any society. As Silberman once remarked, "crime is as American as Jesse James."[86] However, crime, being dealt with at the national level through presidential rhetoric and congressional laws overseeing crimes that were once thought the province of state and local governments, is largely a twentieth-century phenomenon. As we move into the twenty-first century it has become relatively clear that this phenomenon has been vastly expanding over the past four decades and does not appear to be retracting. The national government has established itself in the area of crime policy. The Office of the Presidency has institutionalized the crime issue to such an extent that this author argues what has been wrought is nothing less than a new role for the presidency, namely the "law and order presidency." The question then, for prescriptive purposes, is whether or not this is a good thing?

Writing in the late 1970s, James Calder had the ability to only look back upon the presidential administrations of Hoover through Carter. The three key presidencies that began dealing with the nationalization of crime that he was able to observe at the time of his research were those of the Kennedy, Johnson, and Nixon administrations. Based upon his research however, he was able to conclude that:

> . . . the issue of crime will undoubtedly reappear in future political campaigns. When it does, local, state, and federal politicians will offer canned definitions and pre-packaged solutions, some old and few new. People in small numbers will demand action at various levels of government. Political candidates will awaken to the political appeal of crime's crisis orientation and will alternately put each other on the spot for statements and counterstatements about results. If the problem is widespread or sufficiently advertised by the media, the new crime dilemma will aggregate up to

the presidential level, whereupon it will again be seen not for its grass roots reality, but for its political appeal. Though anti-crime statements will be made, commissions will be formed, legislative proposals will be put forth, and certainly millions of dollars will be spent. Such is the linearity of the ordinary crime problem. Much historical evidence supports this common trend.[87]

Calder's words were very prescient and with only one error in his forecast—that billions and billions of dollars have been spent rather than "millions and millions"—he accurately foretold of the Reagan/Bush/Clinton politicization of the crime issue. This is primarily why Calder rightly concluded that "presidents ought to extricate themselves entirely from the matter of crime control policymaking."[88] To extend this point, he utilized the words of Theodore Roosevelt to highlight the reasons why:

> One of the things one must learn unfortunately, as President or Governor or any like position, is not to jeopardize one's power for doing the good that is possible by efforts to correct evils over which one has no control and with which one is only himself *generally* concerned; save in wholly exceptional instances.[89]

It would seem then to be good advice that presidents should not be involved in the issue of crime-control policy, especially if we are to have sound crime policy in the United States. Others have voiced this similar cry—Ashdown when he argues that "federal involvement in crimes of local concern . . . can create questionable policy decisions,"[90] and Cronin, Cronin, and Milakovich when they bluntly added, "crime in the streets . . . should never have developed at all as an issue in *national* politics."[91] In fact, more recently, a more renowned researcher in the area of crime policy has argued for a moratorium on federal crime policies in order to allow research to determine what politics has wrought.[92] In the end, it would seem that the most philosophically sound argument for dealing with the issue of the nationalization and politicization of crime is to remove it as an area of presidential attention. While philosophically this may sound prudent, it is clearly not politically beneficial.

It is perhaps best articulated by the words of Nancy Marion, a researcher that this author has depended upon heavily, when she explains that "it is expected that crime will be on the systemic agenda of all presidents in the future, and that the federal government will become more involved in crime-control to the extent that it can."[93] In other words, the possibility of completely extricating presidents from crime-control policy, especially after decades of institutionalizing the methods by which they can participate in crime-control policy, is not likely to occur and the reality of the matter is that the "law and order" presidency is here to stay. By all appearances then, it would seem the calls made by the President's Commission on Law Enforcement and Administration of Justice when it stated that "the Commission wants not only to endorse warmly Federal participation in the effort to reduce delinquency and crime, but to urge that it be intensified and accelerated"[94] and the conclusions of Theodore Lowi when he argued that the expansion of the national government into sacrosanct policy areas such as crime is inevitable,[95] have proved all too true. As a result, the political use of crime as a crisis issue by presidents will continue such as is evident in President Clinton's 1992 campaign publication, *Putting People First,* when he and his running mate Al Gore argued:

> Despite all the tough talk we hear from Washington, crime and drug use are expanding dramatically in America. Today more people are victims of violent crime and more addicted to drugs than ever before. We have a national problem on our hands that requires a tough national response. The Clinton-Gore national crime strategy will use the powers of the White House to prevent and punish crime. . . . We need to put more police on the streets and more criminals behind bars.[96]

Crime, as several authors have argued, is a "constant in contemporary politics"[97] and as Gordon has concluded:

> No countervailing symbols to the myth of crime and punishment have been found, no effective language of opposition to the individual perspective on remedies for crime. The values of tolerance, social protection and brotherly love are currently no match for the justifiable fear and outrage over street crime and the law and order politics that exploit them.[98]

In the end, there is little doubt that crime will continue to be nationalized and politicized and that the law and order presidency has become an institutional part of the American presidency. Despite the calls for the extrication of presidents from crime policy or for at least a moratorium, neither of these appear to be a realistic solution to the problem. What is needed is some type of compromise that would continue to secure the nationalization of crime in some areas, but also would continue to secure the traditional rights of state and local governments to oversee local crimes.

Despite all of the discussion thus far about the nationalization and federalization of crime, about the politicization of crime policy, and the institutionalization of the "law and order" presidency, one truism that remains is that the day-to-day responsibility for law enforcement still rests primarily on the local criminal justice system followed by the state system and then, and only then, by the federal system. In other words, the lion's share of responsibility for crime in the United States still remains under the purview of local governments. As Dilulio, Smith, and Saiger have stated, "the national government now has little ability to implement policies that depend almost entirely on state and local governments for their actual day-to-day administration, and which aim at changing the behavior of countless people in government and in the community."[99] Friedman also concludes similarly when he states, "when all is said and done, despite all the hoopla, the federal role in criminal justice is limited, and will stay limited in the foreseeable future."[100] Despite this truism, Marion articulates that "it cannot be suggested that the federal government and future presidents completely delegate crime control to the states [for] as Robert Kennedy argued, there are many issues that the states simply cannot solve alone."[101] Herein lies the key.

While presidents and the national government as a whole will continue to involve themselves in issues of crime control and state and local governments continue to handle the day-to-day management of criminal justice, it is perhaps here that we can find some compromise to the crime policy issue. The state and local government should continue to be primarily responsible for crimes of a local nature, ranging from cases of murder and rape to those that have received much in the way of national attention, such as "car-jackings," driving under the influence, and illegal weapons. Where the national government should be involved is in those areas that are clearly under constitutional authority such as domestic disturbances where the legislature or governor requests assistance.[102] Second, it should limit itself to issues of a strictly federal responsibility, much in the manner presidents did in the nineteenth century with regard to the western territories or issues related to crime in Washington, D.C., or in the United States military.[103] Third, it should relegate itself to dealing with crimes that have a truly "inter-state" applicability and are beyond the means of either state or local governments to effectively deal with these problems such as white-collar crimes,[104] organized crime, internet frauds, and both international and domestic terrorism.[105] One last area of federal responsibility is articulated by Heymann and Moore when they explain that the national government should also be responsible for "matters that local law enforcement may not be willing to undertake [which] includes, prominently, crimes by important local government officials (particularly corruption), crimes by major local industries (particularly environmental crimes), and violations of civil rights or civil liberties carried out or tolerated by the local authorities."[106] While this author agrees with this conclusion, very strict parameters should be placed upon these to avoid any infringement on the rights of state and local governments. These types of national interventions should be shown to have a federal justification, and thus may actually fit into the third category of federal intervention cited above.

The emphasis then, would be for the law and order presidency to use its institutional powers to influence public opinion in the direction of concern for such issues as domestic terrorism, white-collar crime, and internet frauds. By raising awareness of these issues, it may serve to educate the public about these crimes and create a public belief that these crimes are important and thus should be dealt with accordingly by the national government. This would then feed into Zimring and Hawkins "principled basis for federal criminal legislation" which argues that the national government should have a strong interest, a larger interest than state and local governments, a distinct advantage to investigate these types of crimes, and where the state and local governments would be substantially ineffective.[107] This would allow the national government to avoid activity on such crime legislation as federalizing the crime of "car-jackings" and would assist in the passage of more principled legislation such as methods

President George Bush talking with children from the Drug Abuse Resistance Education (D.A.R.E.) Program while signing the National Drug Abuse Resistance Education Day proclamation on September 13, 1989.

PHOTOGRAPH COURTESY OF THE GEORGE BUSH PRESIDENTIAL LIBRARY.

to punish the transfer of child pornography on the world wide web or through the use of the internet to commit wide-spread frauds. Presidential time and activity on these types of crimes may raise their salience and hence both the public and Congress may pay more attention to these pressing issues of our times rather than the local street crimes that local governments are already equipped to handle.

The downside to this use of the law and order presidency however, may lie in the fact that when presidents influence public opinion of crime, they are largely playing on the politics of "street crime" which holds real, or potentially real, fears on the part of Americans. In other words, the public will listen and grow concerned when the presidents speak of "crime in the streets." What they will not respond to are crimes that have no real personal meaning to the vast majority, such as organized crime and white-collar crime. These are crimes that "happen to other people" and "do not affect me." The only way then to address this problem is to call for some means to educate the American people on issues of crime and punishment.

Thomas Jefferson once wrote that "if a nation expects to be both ignorant and free, it expects what never was and never will be." Therefore, it is imperative that the nation becomes properly educated in the area of crime, that they have a realistic understanding of the problem, and that they come to grasp the delicate issues of crime policy in order that they have an understanding of how best to address the problems of crime in the United States. This includes not only educating the public at large, but also educating the politicians and policymakers responsible for the rapid federalization and politicization of crime over the past several decades. Researchers must continue to conduct quality research in the field of criminal justice and the widest possible dissemination of their work must be made available to these politicians and policymakers. Perhaps where researchers may have the greatest impact is through the academy of criminal justice sciences which, still largely in its infancy, is hopefully creating a large body of educated students that can begin filling positions that help formulate, implement, and evaluate criminal justice policy in the United States. Although it would seem that many researchers have made this call for education,[108] and it may sound rather trite at times, it is nonetheless an imperative if we are to have sound criminal justice policy and if we are to remain a free nation.

FUTURE RESEARCH

An extension of the need for public education on the issue of crime and crime policy is the need for continued research into issues of crime, crime control, and crime policy. This research has only begun to explore the notion that presidents have the ability to influence public opinion of crime and has done so with only one operationalization of the variable of presidents. Cook and Cambell have argued for multiple operationalizations of variables[109] and perhaps future research could move to achieve this end. One means by which several researchers have assessed the presidential agenda is through the number of mentions of a particular issue in the State of the Union Address.[110] This type of analysis, while more narrow in focus, may truly assess the president's ability to influence public opinion. In addition, several areas of presidential activity on crime such as the president's use of executive orders on crime, major speeches dedicated to the topic of crime, or news conferences could be isolated to determine what effect it had on public opinion or on crime policy as a whole. Finally, in terms of multiple operationalizations, it may be helpful to isolate the various issues related to crime such as gun control, drugs, and "street crime" rather than utilizing an aggregated variable.

Although additional research in the area of presidential ability to influence public opinion is assuredly needed, the next logical step in research should be to determine if presidents have the ability to influence Congress on crime. As Brace and Hinckley explain that "the president acts, and Congress and the public respond,"[111] within this study the latter half has been demonstrated to be the case. But it is the former that needs further explorations. The research at hand suggests that presidents have the ability to influence Congress, but this is a hypothesis that clearly needs further study. The key then is to compare and contrast the presidential agenda with the agenda of Congress perhaps through the utilization of two measures, often used in the political science literature derived from Congressional Quarterly, which denote vote success and vote concurrence.[112] Other measures, such as a more detailed comparison between presidential activity on crime and congressional activity on crime could also be made by disaggregating the data used to operationalize both of these variables into isolated issue topics such as drugs, gun control, and street crime. Finally, in regard to the variable of Congress, it may prove advantageous to explore their role in crime-control policy more fully.[113]

Continuing this line of thought—that other variables should be more fully explored—it would also be prudent to explore other measures of such variables as economic indicators.[114] In addition, it would assist our understanding of influencing agents on crime policy if additional variables were explored, especially at the national level, such as the impact of interest groups,[115] bureaucracies,[116] and governors on the crime policy process. Moreover, it would prove beneficial to advance the statistical analysis through such techniques as ARIMA modeling to help sort out the direction of causation among such highly interrelated variables as presidential activity, public opinion, and media.[117]

Finally, additional research into two areas that this research inadvertently highlighted may prove beneficial not just in the area of crime policy, but as it relates to the ability of the presidents to influence all policy. The first is the fact that this research found that presidents do influence public opinion of crime. The natural extension to this would be to ask if presidents influence public opinion of other policy areas. Cohen found that presidents do influence public opinion in the policy areas of economic, foreign, and civil-rights policies.[118] But what about energy, environmental, and transportation policies? Do presidents have the same ability to influence public opinion on these issues? If they do, then it may be said that presidents do have the ability to influence public opinion on all issues. But if it is limited to certain issues, then what is it about those issues that give presidents the power to manipulate public opinion? One possibility, and the second area of research needed, may be in the area of symbolic[119] and valence[120] issues. It could be hypothesized that, when policy issues are highly complementary to symbolic politics and when they are clearly valence issues where there is no definitive opposition to the presidents' stance on the issue, circumstances may give the president the ability to more readily manipulate public opinion than in issues that are laden with opposing viewpoints.[121] It is therefore of interest from a larger policy perspective to begin exploring the political potential for both symbolic and valence issues on the part of presidents.

THE LAW & ORDER PRESIDENCY

Despite the fact that the United States Constitution gave the President of the United States little in the way of power over issues of crime, presidents have managed to secure a role for themselves in this particular policy area. This led

Clarence Berdahl over eighty years ago to write about the president's "power of police control."[122] Other influential writers on the American presidency have also reverberated this sentiment. Edward Corwin spoke of "the president as supervisor of law enforcement,"[123] Clinton Rossiter described the president as "protector of peace" (both internal and external),[124] and Joseph Kallenback stated that the president was the "Conservator-in-Chief of Public Order."[125] More recent scholars, such as Calder[126] and Marion,[127] have also explored the role of the chief executive in regard to crime policy and have acknowledged a similar role. Recognizing that the president's attention to crime has increased and his powers enhanced with nearly every presidential succession, this role has changed and evolved over time. Not only do presidents today have a number of reasons *for* and a plethora of means to engage *in* crime-control policy, they have a robust history upon which to draw their role.

Commencing with Thomas Jefferson's use of the phrase "law and order" in his third annual message to Congress and progressing to Ulysses S. Grant's call for the "maintenance of law and order" during reconstruction, and to President Hoover's call for "law and order in the United States," presidents have invoked this phrase for a variety of reasons and have loaded it with layers of meaning.[128] Jefferson spoke in terms of maintaining local law and order as a protection from the British. Grant spoke in terms of protecting Black Southerners from the cruelties and injustices brought upon them by groups such as the Ku Klux Klan during the reconstruction period. Hoover meant it in terms of the lawlessness experienced in the wake of Prohibition. All invoked the same phrase, but all for very different reasons.

Presidents have continued to invoke this phrase throughout the twentieth when century as when Roosevelt called for "law and order" in response to a number of domestic situations involving gangsters and the mafia and when President Kennedy called for "law and order" as a response to open discrimination against blacks during the civil rights movement. Despite the fact that Wallace used the term in the 1964 Presidential election campaign in order "to attract support among northern white ethnic voters in Wisconsin, Indiana, and Maryland"[129] and Goldwater picked up the theme to mobilize a national concern with issues of civil rights demonstrations, riots, and crime in the street, neither of these candidates were able to capitalize enough on the divisiveness of the issue to launch them into office. However, the candidate who attempted to avoid the issue of "law and order" during the campaign, Lyndon B. Johnson, would find himself overseeing one of the biggest national expansions of the concept and would invoke the phrase quite often.

President Nixon followed Johnson in the presidency and would himself heavily invoke the phrase "law and order" as a response to all of the then current social problems from campus unrest to riots in the streets. His use of the phrase however, invoked so often and in a similar vein as Wallace and Goldwater, generated the charge that Nixon was using the phrase "law and order" as code words for repressions of blacks.[130] Although he won the election, Nixon spent much of his time defending his use of the phrase as the opening quote attests. With the resignation of President Nixon, Gerald Ford assumed the Office of the President and attempted to distance himself from the phrase, saying he did not like the phrase, but preferred the phrase "insuring domestic tranquility." Despite his stated preferences, Ford continued to speak in terms of "law and order." Carter's Presidency which followed attempted to avoid similar issues. He would be followed by President Reagan who would revitalize the term in the manner of Goldwater and Nixon. He would invoke the term very often in his speeches attempting to describe his administration's efforts to target organized crime, crime on the street, and drugs. Bush would then use it to his advantage in his renewed "war on drugs." Finally, President Clinton would use the phrase to demonstrate he was "tough on crime" in 1992 and would then invoke the phrase quite often to win public support for his crime bill legislation. In all, the phrase "law and order," like all of the layers of meaning behind it, has become a fixture of the American presidency. The earlier noted roles have developed rapidly over the last four decades into the "law and order" presidency.

The concept of a "law and order" presidency is the recognition of an additional role and responsibility of the American presidency—one that has developed and evolved over the span of forty-two presidents. It stands today as a role that has become institutionalized within the office of the presidency, not particular to any one president, party, or generation, but rather one that has become a permanent fixture of the office itself. Its meaning developed out of a politicized phrase which "had special resonance because it combined an understandable concern over the rising number of traditional crimes—robberies and rapes, mugging and murder—with a host of implicit and explicit attitudes and assumptions toward civil rights, urban rioting, antiwar protest, changing moral values, the Supreme Court, and drug use."[131] It became an amalgam of meanings. As Nicholas Katzenbach wrote after stepping down as Attorney General:

> There are many ingredients to the confusing calls for "law and order," and, while these do not have to be mixed up together, they have become so. In this respect, liberals and conservatives, intellectuals and rednecks, racists and civil libertarians, adults and juveniles are all contributors to confusion.[132]

As a result, the phrase "law and order" became a term with many "layers of meaning virtually impossible to disentangle,"[133] but "what ultimately gave the issue such potency was precisely its amorphous quality, its ability to represent different concerns to different people at different moments."[134] The "law and order presidency" has subsequently been able to capitalize on these amorphous qualities, securing itself a role in anything and everything related to the issue of crime, ranging from local street crimes and low-level drug dealing to issues of international and domestic terrorism and drug trafficking in the United States. In sum, the issue of crime and its nationalization and politicization by past presidents has created a new role for the Office of the Presidency—one focused on addressing nearly any and every criminal act within the United States. It has created the *Law & Order Presidency.*

Standing upon the ashes of the worst terrorist attack on American soil Sept. 14, President Bush pledges that the voices calling for justice from across the country will be heard.

End Notes

1. Nixon, Richard M. 1971. "Remarks at Phoenix, Arizona. October 31, 1970." *Public Papers of the Presidents of the United States.* Washington D.C.: U.S. G.P.O., p. 1037.
2. Friedman, Lawrence M. 1993. *Crime and Punishment in American History.* New York: Basic Books, p. 262.
3. Jacobs, Lawrence R. and Robert Y. Shapiro. Forthcoming. *Politicians Don't Pander.* Chicago: University of Chicago Press.
4. Wilson, James Q. 1975. *Thinking About Crime.* New York: Basic Books, pp. 65–66.
5. See Beckett, Katherine. 1997. *Making Crime Pay: Law and Order in Contemporary American Politics.* New York: Oxford University Press, pp. 15–16; Chambliss, William J. 1994. "Policing the Ghetto Underclass: The Politics of Law and Law Enforcement." *Social Problems* 41 (2): 177–194.
6. Wisotsky, Steven. 1987. "Crackdown: The Emerging 'Drug Exception' to the Bill of Rights." *Hastings Law Journal* 38: 889–926.
7. Gozenbach, William J. 1996. *The Media, The President, and Public Opinion: A Longitudinal Analysis of the Drug Issue, 1984–1991.* Mahwah: Lawrence Erlbaum Associates (publishers), p. 98.
8. Baumgartner, Frank R. and Bryan D. Jones. 1993. *Agendas and Instability in American Politics.* Chicago: The University of Chicago Press, p. 156.
9. Jones, Bryan D. 1994. *Reconceiving Decision-Making in Democratic Politics: Attention, Choice and Public Policy.* Chicago: The University of Chicago Press, pp. 106–108.

10. Sharp, Elaine B. 1994. *The Dilemma of Drug Policy in the United States.* New York: Harper-Collins College Publishers, pp. 23–33.

11. Beckett, Katherine. 1997. *Making Crime Pay: Law and Order in Contemporary American Politics.* New York: Oxford University Press; Beckett, Katherine. 1994. "Setting the Public Agenda: 'Street Crime' and Drug Use in American Politics." *Social Problems* 41 (3): 425–447; Beckett, Katherine and Theodore Sasson. 2000. *The Politics of Injustice: Crime and Punishment in America.* Thousand Oaks: Pine Forge Press.

12. Brace, Paul and Barbara Hinckley. 1992. *Follow the Leader: Opinion Polls and the Modern Presidency.* New York: Basic Books, p. 73.

13. Betram, Eva, Morris Blachman, Kenneth Sharpe and Peter Andreas. 1996. *Drug War Politics: The Price of Denial.* Berkeley: The University of California Press, p. 103.

14. Edwards, George C. III. 2000. "Building Coalitions." *Presidential Studies Quarterly* 30 (1): 47–78, p. 58.

15. Brace, Paul and Barbara Hinckley. 1992. *Follow the Leader: Opinion Polls and the Modern Presidency.* New York: Basic Books, pp. 82–83.

16. Edwards, George C. III. 2000. "Building Coalitions." *Presidential Studies Quarterly* 30 (1): 47–78, p. 48.

17. Scheingold, Stuart A. 1995. "Politics, Public Policy, and Street Crime." *The Annals of the American Academy of Political and Social Science* 539: 155–168, p. 163.

18. Meier, Kenneth J. 1994. *The Politics of Sin: Drugs, Alcohol, and Public Policy.* Armonk: M. E. Sharpe, p. 245.

19. Meier, Kenneth J. 1994. *The Politics of Sin: Drugs, Alcohol, and Public Policy.* Armonk: M. E. Sharpe, p. 245.

20. Bailey, Frankie and Donna Hale. 1998. *Popular Culture, Crime, and Justice.* Belmont: International Thompson Publishing Company; Graber, Doris. 1980. *Crime News and the Public.* New York: Praeger; Stark, Steven D. 1997. *Glued to the Set.* New York: Delta Trade Paperbacks; Surette, Ray. 1998. *Media, Crime, and Criminal Justice: Images and Realities.* 2d ed. Belmont: International Thompson Publishing Company.

21. Morton, Charles. 1951. "Accent on Living." *The Atlantic Monthly.* September: 13–14.

22. Roberts, Julian V. and Loretta J. Stalans. 1997. *Public Opinion, Crime, and Criminal Justice.* Boulder: Westview Press.

23. Gerber, Rudolph J. 1999. *Cruel and Usual: Our Criminal Injustice System.* Westport: Praeger Publishers.

24. Davey, Joseph Dillon. 1998. *The Politics of Prison Expansion: Winning Elections by Waging War on Crime.* Westport: Praeger Publishers; Durham, Alexis M. III. 1994. *Crisis and Reform: Current Issues in American Punishment.* Boston: Little, Brown and Company.

25. Davey, Joseph Dillon. 1998. *The Politics of Prison Expansion: Winning Elections by Waging War on Crime.* Westport: Praeger Publishers; Durham, Alexis M. III. 1994. *Crisis and Reform: Current Issues in American Punishment.* Boston: Little, Brown and Company.

26. Taggart, William A. 1997. "The Nationalization of Corrections Policy in the American States." *Justice Quarterly* 14 (3): 429–444.

27. Scheingold, Stuart A. 1991. *The Politics of Street Crime: Criminal Process and Cultural Obsession.* Philadelphia: Temple University Press.

28. Scheingold, Stuart A. 1991. *The Politics of Street Crime: Criminal Process and Cultural Obsession.* Philadelphia: Temple University Press, p. 178.

29. Scheingold, Stuart A. 1991. *The Politics of Street Crime: Criminal Process and Cultural Obsession.* Philadelphia: Temple University Press, p. 178.

30. Scheingold, Stuart A. 1991. *The Politics of Street Crime: Criminal Process and Cultural Obsession.* Philadelphia: Temple University Press, p. 178.

31. Scheingold, Stuart A. 1991. *The Politics of Street Crime: Criminal Process and Cultural Obsession.* Philadelphia: Temple University Press, p. 178.

32. Baum, Lawrence. 1995. *The Supreme Court.* 5th ed. Washington D.C.: Congressional Quarterly Press; Canon, Bradley C. and Charles A. Johnson. 1999. *Judicial Policies: Implementation and Impact.* 2d ed. Washington D.C.: Congressional Quarterly Press.

33. Meier, Kenneth J. 1993. *Politics and the Bureaucracy: Policymaking in the Fourth Branch of Government.* Belmont: Wadsworth Publishing Company; Peters, B. Guy. 1995. *The Politics of Bureaucracy.* 4th ed. Longman: Longman Publishers.

34. Cigler, Allan J. and Burdett A. Loomis. 1998. *Interest Group Politics.* 5th ed. Washington D.C.: Congressional Quarterly Press.

35. Kingdon, John W. 1995. *Agendas, Alternatives, and Public Policies.* 2d ed. New York: Harper-Collins College Publishers, p. 23.

36. Cohen, Jeffrey and Ken Collier. 1999. "Public Opinion: Reconceptualizing Going Public." In *Presidential Policymaking: An End-of-Century Assessment.* Steven A. Shull, ed. Armonk: M. E. Sharpe, pp. 41–58, pp. 42–43.

37. Bosson, Christopher. 1987. *Pesticides and Politics: The Life Cycle of a Public Issue.* Pittsburgh: University of Pittsburgh Press, p. 261.

38. Friedman, Lawrence M. 1993. *Crime and Punishment in American History.* New York: Basic Books, p. 263.

39. Cohen, Jeffrey E. 1995. "Presidential Rhetoric and the Public Agenda." *American Journal of Political Science* 39 (1): 87–107, p. 102.

40. Light, Paul C. 1991. *The President's Agenda: Domestic Policy Choice from Kennedy to Reagan.* Rev ed. Baltimore: The Johns Hopkins University Press.

41. Pfiffner, James P. 1996. *The Strategic Presidency: Hitting the Ground Running.* 2d ed., rev. Lawrence: University Press of Kansas.

42. Cohen, Jeffrey E. 1995. "Presidential Rhetoric and the Public Agenda." *American Journal of Political Science* 39 (1): 87–107, p. 103.

43. Cohen, Jeffrey E. 1997. *Presidential Responsiveness and Public Policy-Making: The Public and the Policies that Presidents Choose.* Ann Arbor: The University of Michigan Press, p. 234.

44. Light, Paul C. 1991. *The President's Agenda: Domestic Policy Choice from Kennedy to Reagan.* Rev. ed. Baltimore: The Johns Hopkins University Press.

45. Simon, Dennis and Charles Ostrom, Jr. 1985. "The President and Public Support: A Strategic Perspective." In *The Presidency and Public Policy Making.* George Edwards, Steven Shull, and Norman Thomas, eds. Pittsburgh: University of Pittsburgh Press, pp. 65–66.

46. Calder, James D. 1993. *The Origins and Development of Federal Crime Control Policy: Herbert Hoover's Initiatives.* Westport: Praeger Publishers, p. 26.

47. Johnson, Lyndon B. 1967. "Message to Congress. March 9, 1966." *Public Papers of the Presidents of the United States.* Washington D.C.: U.S. G.P.O., p. 299.

48. Gaubatz, Kathlyn Taylor. 1995. *Crime in the Public Mind.* Ann Arbor: The University of Michigan Press, p. 162.

49. Ragsdale, Lyn. 1984. "The Politics of Presidential Speechmaking, 1949–1980." *The American Political Science Review* 78 (4): 971–984, p. 983.

50. Scheingold, Stuart A. 1991. *The Politics of Street Crime: Criminal Process and Cultural Obsession.* Philadelphia: Temple University Press. Ed Meese, former advisor to President Reagan on the issue of crime, has also articulated that "clearly, a major cause of the federalization of criminal law is the desire of some members of Congress to appear tough on crime, though they know well that crime is fought most effectively at the local level." See Meese, Edwin III and Rhett Dehart. 1996. "How Washington Subverts Your Local Sheriff." *Policy Review* 75: 48–56.

51. Marion, Nancy E. 1997. "Symbolic Politics in Clinton's Crime Control Agenda." *Buffalo Criminal Law Review* 1 (1): 67–108, p. 103.

52. Lowi, Theodore J. 1985. *The Personal President: Power Invested, Promise Unfulfilled.* Ithaca: Cornell University Press, p. 173.

53. Edelman, Murray. 1988. *Constructing the Political Spectacle.* Chicago: University of Chicago Press, p. 12.

54. Sniderman, Paul M. 1993. "The New Look in Public Opinion Research." In *Political Science: The State of the Discipline II.* Ada W. Finifter, ed. Washington D.C.: The American Political Science Association, pp. 219–245.

55. Bobo, Lawrence. 1983. "Whites' Opposition to Busing: Symbolic Racism or Realistic Group Conflict?" *Journal of Personality and Social Psychology* 45: 1196–1210; Gilens, Martin. 1995. "Racial Attitudes and Opposition to Welfare." *The Journal of Politics* 57 (4): 994–1014; Kinder, Donald. 1986. "The Continuing American Dilemma: White Resistance to Racial Change Forty Years after Mrydal." *Journal of Social Issues* 42: 151–172; Kuklinski, James H., Paul M. Sniderman, Kathleen Knight, Thomas Piazza, Philip E. Tetlock, Gordon R. Lawrence, and Barbara Mellers. 1997. "Racial Prejudice and Attitudes Toward Affirmative Action." *American Journal of Political Science* 41 (2): 402–419; McConahey, John B. 1986. "Modern Racism, Ambivalence and the Modern Racism Scale." In *Prejudice, Discrimination, and Racism.* John F. Dovido and Samuel L. Gaertner, eds. Orlando: Academic Press; Schuman, Howard, Charlotte Steeh and Lawrence Bobo. 1985. *Racial Attitudes in America: Trends and Interpretations.* Cambridge: Harvard University Press; Sears, David O. 1988. "Symbolic Racism." In *Eliminating Racism.* Phyllis A. Katz and Dalmas A, Taylor, eds. New York: Plenum; Sniderman, Paul M., Thomas Piazza, and Phillip E. Tetlock. 1991. "The New Racism." *American Journal of Political Science* 35: 423–447.

56. Edsall, Thomas Bryne and Mary D. Edsall. 1991. *Chain Reaction: The Impact of Race, Rights, and Taxes on American Politics.* New York: W.W. Norton and Company; Schlosser, Eric. 1998. "The Prison–Industrial Complex." *The Atlantic Monthly* December: 51–77; Tonry, Michael. 1995. *Malign Neglect: Race, Crime, and Punishment in America.* New York: Oxford University Press; Tonry, Michael. 1994. "Racial Politics, Racial Disparities, and the War on Crime." *Crime & Delinquency* 40 (4): 475–495.

57. Tonry, Michael. 1995. *Malign Neglect: Race, Crime, and Punishment in America.* New York: Oxford University Press, p. 123.

58. Poveda, Tony G. 1996. "Clinton, Crime, and the Justice Department." *Social Justice* 21 (3): 73–84, p. 73.

59. Walker, Samuel. 1998. *Sense and Nonsense about Crime and Drugs: A Policy Guide.* 4th ed. Belmont: International Thompson Publishing Company, p. 22.

60. Walker, Samuel. 1998. *Popular Justice: A History of American Criminal Justice.* 2d ed. New York: Oxford University Press, p. 240.

61. Scheingold, Stuart A. 1995. "Politics, Public Policy, and Street Crime." *The Annals of the American Academy of Political and Social Science* 539: 155–168, p. 160.

62. Platt, Tony. 1988. "U.S. Criminal Justice in the Reagan Era: An Assessment." *Crime and Social Justice* 29: 58–69, p. 67.

63. Dilulio, John Jr., Steven K. Smith, and Aaron J. Saiger. 1995. "The Federal Role in Crime Control." In *Crime.* James Q. Wilson and Joan Petersilia, eds. San Francisco: ICS Press, p. 451.

64. Lowi, Theodore. 1979. *The End of Liberalism: The Second Republic of the United States.* 2d ed. New York: W.W. Norton and Company, p. 276.

65. Lowi, Theodore. 1979. *The End of Liberalism: The Second Republic of the United States.* 2d ed. New York: W.W. Norton and Company, p. 277.

66. Lowi, Theodore. 1995. *The End of the Republican Era.* Norman: University of Oklahoma Press, p. 57.

67. Poveda, Tony G. 1996. "Clinton, Crime, and the Justice Department." *Social Justice* 21 (3): 73–84, p. 80.

68. Federal Bureau of Investigation. 1991–1999. *Uniform Crime Reports.* Washington D.C.: U.S. Department of Justice.

69. Kappeler, Victor E., Mark Blumberg, and Gary W. Potter. 1996. *The Mythology of Crime and Criminal Justice.* 2d ed. Prospect Heights: Waveland Press, Inc.

70. Vandiver, Margaret and David Giacopassi. 1997. "One Million and Counting: Students' Estimates of the Annual Number of Homicides in the U.S." *Journal of Criminal Justice Education* 8: 135–143; Oliver, Willard and Tanya Conrad. 1999. "One Million and Still Counting: A Replication Study of Students' Estimation of Homicides in the U.S." *The Dialogue* (September). Available on line at http://www.appstate.edu/~robinsnmb/dialoguesep99woliver.htm

71. Lowi, Theodore J. 1985. *The Personal President: Power Invested, Promise Unfulfilled.* Ithaca: Cornell University Press, p. 173.

72. Kraska, Peter B. 1996. "Enjoying Militarism: Political/Personal Dilemmas in Studying U.S. Police Paramilitary Units." *Justice Quarterly* 13 (3): 405–429; Kraska, Peter B. 1993. "Militarizing the Drug War: A Sign of the Times." In *Altered States of Mind: Critical Observations of the Drug War.* Peter B. Kraska, ed. New York: Garland, pp. 159–206; Kraska, Peter B. and Louis J. Cubellis. 1997. "Militarizing Mayberry and Beyond: Making Sense of American Paramilitary Policing." *Justice Quarterly* 14 (4): 607–629; Kraska, Peter B. and Victor E. Kappeler. 1997. "Militarizing American Police: The Rise and Normalization of Paramilitary Units." *Social Problems* 44: 1–18.

73. Scheingold, Stuart A. 1991. *The Politics of Street Crime: Criminal Process and Cultural Obsession.* Philadelphia: Temple University Press, p. 33.

74. Walker, Samuel. 1998. *Sense and Nonsense about Crime and Drugs.* 4th ed. Belmont: International Thompson Publishing Company.

75. Gaubatz, Kathlyn Taylor. 1995. *Crime in the Public Mind.* Ann Arbor: The University of Michigan Press; Gottfredson, Stephen D., Barbara D. Warner, and Ralph B. Taylor. 1988. "Conflict and Consensus about Criminal Justice in Maryland." In *Public Attitudes to Sentencing.* N. Walker and M. Hough, eds. Brookfield: Gower; Roberts, Julian and Loretta J. Stalans. 1997. *Public Opinion, Crime, and Criminal Justice.* Boulder: Westview Press.

76. Gaubatz, Kathlyn Taylor. 1995. *Crime in the Public Mind.* Ann Arbor: The University of Michigan Press; Roberts, Julian and Loretta J. Stalans. 1997. *Public Opinion, Crime, and Criminal Justice.* Boulder: Westview Press.

77. Schlosser, Eric. 1998. "The Prison-Industrial Complex." *The Atlantic Monthly* December: 51–77.

78. Marvell, Thomas B. and Carlisle E. Moody, Jr. 1994. "Prison Population Growth and Crime Reduction." *Journal of Quantitative Criminology* 10 (2): 109–137.

79. Meier, Kenneth J. 1994. *The Politics of Sin: Drugs, Alcohol, and Public Policy.* Armonk: M. E. Sharpe, p. 255.

80. Meier, Kenneth J. 1994. *The Politics of Sin: Drugs, Alcohol, and Public Policy.* Armonk: M. E. Sharpe, p. 255.

81. Clear, Todd R. 1997. "Societal Responses to the President's Crime Commission: A Thirty-Year Retrospective." *The Challenge of Crime in a Free Society: Looking Back, Looking Forward.* Washington D.C.: U.S. Department of Justice, pp. 131–158.

82. Welch, Michael, Melissa Fenwick, and Meredith Roberts. 1998. "State Managers, Intellectuals, and the Media: A Content Analysis of Ideology in Experts' Quotes in Feature Newspaper Articles on Crime." *Justice Quarterly* 15 (2): 219–241.

83. Currie, Elliott. 1998. *Crime and Punishment in America: Why the Solutions to America's Most Stubborn Social Crisis Have Not Worked—And What Will.* New York: Henry Holt and Company, Inc.; Hannon, Lance and James DeFronzo. 1998. "Welfare and Property Crime." *Justice Quarterly* 15 (2): 273–288; Sherman, Lawrence W., Denise Gottfredson, Doris MacKenzie, John Eck, Peter Reuter, and Shawn Bushway. 1997. *Preventing Crime: What Works, What Doesn't, What's Promising.* Washington D.C.: National Institute of Justice.

84. Chambliss, William J. 1994. "Policing the Ghetto Underclass: The Politics of Law and Law Enforcement." *Social Problems* 41 (2): 177–194; Clear, Todd R. 1997. "Societal Responses to the President's Crime Commission: A Thirty-Year Retrospective." *The Challenge of Crime in a Free Society: Looking Back, Looking Forward.* Washington D.C.: U.S. Department of Justice, pp. 131–158; Cullen, Francis T. 1995. "Assessing the Penal Harm Movement." *Journal of Research in Crime and Delinquency* 32: 338–358; Tonry, Michael. 1995. *Malign Neglect: Race, Crime, and Punishment in America.* New York: Oxford University Press; Zimring, Franklin and Gordon Hawkins. 1997. "Lethal Violence and the Overreach of American Imprisonment." *National Institute of Justice Research Report.* Washington D.C.: U.S. G.P.O.

85. Albanese, Jay. 1995. *White-Collar Crime in America.* Englewood Cliffs: Prentice Hall; Kappeler, Victor E., Mark Blumberg, and Gary W. Potter. 1996. *The Mythology of Crime and Criminal Justice.* 2d ed. Prospect Heights: Waveland Press, Inc.; Rosoff, Stephen M., Henry N. Pontell, and Robert Tillman. 1998. *Profit Without Honor: White-Collar Crime and the Looting of America.* Upper Saddle River: Prentice Hall.

86. Silberman, Charles E. 1978. *Criminal Violence, Criminal Justice.* New York: Vintage Books.

87. Calder, James Doug. 1978. *Presidents and Crime Control: Some Limitations on Executive Policy Making.* Ph.D. Dissertation, Claremont University, pp. 259–260.

88. Calder, James Doug. 1978. *Presidents and Crime Control: Some Limitations on Executive Policy Making.* Ph.D. Dissertation, Claremont University, p. 280.

89. Roosevelt, Theodore. As cited in Calder, James Doug. 1978. *Presidents and Crime Control: Some Limitations on Executive Policy Making.* Ph.D. Dissertation, Claremont University, p. 280, who obtained the citation from Tourtellot, Arthur B. 1970. *The Presidents on the Presidency.* New York: Russell and Russell, p. 404.

90. Ashdown, Gerald G. 1996. "Federalism, Federalization, and the Politics of Crime." *West Virginia Law Review* 98: 787–813.

91. Cronin, Thomas E., Tania Z. Cronin, and Michael E. Milakovich. 1981. *U.S. v. Crime in the Streets.* Bloomington: Indiana University Press, p. 169.

92. Dilulio, John J., Jr. 1999. "Federal Crime Policy: Time for a Moratorium." *Brookings Review* 17 (1): 17–21.

93. Marion, Nancy. 1992. "Presidential Agenda Setting in Crime Control." *Criminal Justice Policy Review* 6 (2): 159–184, p. 181.

94. President's Commission on Law Enforcement and Administration of Justice. 1968. *The Challenge of Crime in a Free Society.* New York: Avon Books, p. 631.

95. Lowi, Theodore. 1979. *The End of Liberalism: The Second Republic of the United States.* 2d ed. New York: W.W. Norton and Company, p. 277.

96. Clinton, Bill and Al Gore. 1992. *Putting People First: How We Can All Change America.* New York: Times Book, p. 71.

97. Chernoff, Harry A., Christopher M. Kelly, and John R. Kroger. 1996. "The Politics of Crime." *Harvard Journal on Legislation* 33 (2): 527–579, p. 577.

98. Gordon, Diana. 1990. *The Justice Juggernaut.* New Brunswick: Rutgers University Press, p. 41.

99. Dilulio, John J., Jr., Steven K. Smith, and Aaron J. Saiger. 1995. "The Federal Role in Crime Control." In *Crime.* James Q. Wilson and Joan Petersilia, eds. San Francisco: ICS Press, p. 461.

100. Friedman, Lawrence M. 1993. *Crime and Punishment in American History.* New York: Basic Books, p. 275.

101. Marion, Nancy E. 1994. *A History of Federal Crime Control Initiatives, 1960–1993.* Westport: Praeger Publishers, p. 251.

102. These would include largely the powers derived from the Constitution, but also those articulated by Clinton Rossiter when he spoke of the president as Protector of the Peace. See Rossiter, Clinton. 1960. *The American Presidency.* Rev. ed. New York: Mentor Books, pp. 113–116.

103. Heymann, Philip B. and Mark H. Moore. 1996. "The Federal Role in Dealing with Violent Street Crime: Principles, Questions, and Cautions." *The Annals of the American Academy of Political and Social Science* 543: 103–115.

104. Pontell, Henry N., Kitty Calavita, and Robert Tillman. 1994. "Corporate Crime and Criminal Justice System Capacity: Government Response To Financial Institution Fraud." *Justice Quarterly* 11 (3): 383–410.

105. Hagan, Frank E. 1997. *Political Crime: Ideology and Criminality.* Boston: Allyn & Bacon; Smith, Brent L. and Kelly R. Damphousse. 1998. "Terroism, Politics, and Punishment: A Test of Structural-Contextual Theory and the 'Liberation Hypothesis' " *Criminology* 36 (1): 67–92.

106. Heymann, Philip B. and Mark H. Moore. 1996. "The Federal Role in Dealing with Violent Street Crime: Principles, Questions, and Cautions." *The Annals of the American Academy of Political and Social Science* 543: 103–115, pp. 110–111.

107. Zimring, Franklin E. and Gordon Hawkins. 1996. "Toward a Principles Basis for Federal Criminal Legislation." *The Annals of the American Academy of Political and Social Science* 543: 15–26.

108. Durham, Alexis M. III. 1994. *Crisis and Reform: Current Issues in American Punishment.* Boston: Little, Brown and Company, p. 348; Roberts, Julian V. and Loretta J. Stalans. 1997. *Public Opinion, Crime, and Criminal Justice.* Boulder: Westview Press, pp. 291–293; Task Force on the Federalization of Criminal Law. 1998. *The Federalization of Criminal Law.* Washington D.C.: American Bar Association, p. 52.

109. Cook, Thomas D. and Donald T. Campbell. 1979. *Quasi-Experimentation: Design and Analysis Issues for Field Settings.* Boston: Houghton Mifflin Company, pp. 61–63.

110. Cohen, Jeffrey E. 1997. *Presidential Responsiveness and Public Policy-Making: The Public and the Policies that Presidents Choose.* Ann Arbor: The University of Michigan Press; Cohen, Jeffrey E. 1995. "Presidential Rhetoric and the Public Agenda." *American Journal of Political Science* 39 (1): 87–107; Light, Paul C. 1991. *The President's Agenda: Domestic Policy Choice from Kennedy to Reagan.* Rev. ed. Baltimore: The Johns Hopkins University Press.

111. Brace, Paul and Barbara Hinckley. 1992. *Follow the Leader: Opinion Polls and the Modern Presidents.* New York: Basic Books, p. 73.

112. Ragsdale, Lyn. 1998. *Vital Statistics on the Presidency: Washington to Clinton.* Rev. ed. Washington D.C.: Congressional Quarterly Press, pp. 369–372.

113. For example, see Stolz, Barbara Ann. 1992. "Congress and the War on Drugs: An Exercise in Symbolic Politics." *Journal of Crime and Justice* 15 (1): 119–136.

114. Carlson, Susan M. and Raymond J. Michalowski. 1997. "Crime, Unemployment, and Social Structure of Accumulation: An Inquiry into Historical Contingency." *Justice Quarterly* 14 (2): 209–241, p. 236.

115. Shaiko, Ronald G. 1998. "Reverse Lobbying: Interest Group Mobilization from the White House and the Hill." In *Interest Group Politics.* 5th ed. Allan J. Ciglar and Burdett A. Loomis, eds. Washington D.C.: Congressional Quarterly Press, pp. 255–282.

116. Windlesham, Lord. 1998. *Politics, Punishment, and Populism.* New York: Oxford University Press.

117. Gonzenbach, William J. 1996. *The Media, The President, and Public Opinion: A Longitudinal Analysis of the Drug Issue, 1984–1991.* Mahwah: Lawrence Erlbaum Associates, (publishers); Gujarati, Damodar N. 1995. *Basic Econometrics.* 3d ed. New York: McGraw-Hill, Inc.

118. Cohen, Jeffrey E. 1995. "Presidential Rhetoric and the Public Agenda." *American Journal of Political Science* 39 (1): 87–107.

119. Edelman, Murray. 1988. *Constructing the Political Spectacle.* Chicago: The University of Chicago Press; Edelman, Murray. 1971. *Politics as Symbolic Action: Mass Arousal and Quiescence.* Chicago: Markham Publishing Company; Edelman, Murray. 1964. *The Symbolic Uses of Politics.* Urbana: University of Illinois Press; Elder, Charles and Roger Cobb. 1983. *The Po-*

litical Uses of Symbols. New York: Longman; Gusfield, Joseph. 1963. *Symbolic Crusade.* Urbana: University of Illinois Press; Hinckley, Barbara. 1990. *The Symbolic Presidency: How Presidents Portray Themselves.* New York: Routledge.

120. Stokes, Donald. 1992. "Valence Politics." *Electoral Politics.* Dennis Kavanagh, ed. Oxford: Clarendon Press.

121. For similar conclusions, see Beckett, Katherine. 1994. "Setting the Public Agenda: 'Street Crime' and Drug Use in American Politics." *Social Problems* 41 (3): 425–447. For research conducted on symbolics and drug policy, see Jensen, Eric L. and Jurg Gerber. 1998. *The New War on Drugs: Symbolic Politics and Criminal Justice Policy,* Cincinnati: Academy of Criminal Justice Sciences/Anderson Publishing.

122. Berdahl, Clarence A. 1920. *War Powers of the Executive in the United States.* Urbana: University of Illinois Press, p. 182. I was first introduced to these early concepts of the president and crime by the works of James D. Calder. See Calder, James D. 1982. "Presidents and Crime Control: Kennedy, Johnson and Nixon and the Influences of Ideology." *Presidential Studies Quarterly* 12: 574–589; Calder, James D. 1978. *Presidents and Crime Control: Some Limitations on Executive Policy Making.* Ph.D. Dissertation, Claremont University.

123. Corwin, Edward S. 1957. *The President and His Powers 1787 to 1957.* 4th ed. New York: New York University Press, p. 79.

124. Rossiter, Clinton. 1960. *The American Presidency.* 2d ed. New York: New American Library, p. 26.

125. Kallenbach, Joseph E. 1966. *The American Chief Executive.* New York: Harper and Row, p. 446.

126. Calder, James D. 1981. "Herbert Hoover's Contributions to the Administrative History of Crime Control Policy." Paper presented at the annual meeting of the Southwest Political Science Association, Dallas, Texas; Calder, James D. 1982. "Presidents and Crime Control: Kennedy, Johnson and Nixon and the Influences of Ideology." *Presidential Studies Quarterly* 12: 574–589; Calder, James D. 1978. *Presidents and Crime Control: Some Limitations on Executive Policy Making.* Ph.D. Dissertation, Claremont University.

127. Marion, Nancy. 1992. "Presidential Agenda Setting in Crime Control." *Criminal Justice Policy Review* 6 (2): 159–184; Marion, Nancy. 1994. "Symbolism and Federal Crime Control Legislation, 1960–1990." *Journal of Crime and Justice* 17 (2): 69–91. Two other works by Nancy Marion do not focus exclusively on the presidents, but include material on presidents and crime: Marion, Nancy E. 1994. *A History of Federal Crime Control Initiatives, 1960–1993.* Westport: Praeger Publishers; Marion, Nancy E. 1995. *A Primer in the Politics of Criminal Justice.* New York: Harrow and Heston Publishers.

128. The concept of "loading the phrase 'law and order' with layers of meaning" comes from Flamm, Michael William. 1998. *"Law and Order": Street Crime, Civil Disorder, and the Crisis of Liberalism.* Ph.D. Dissertation, Columbia University.

129. Flamm, Michael William. 1998. *"Law and Order": Street Crime, Civil Disorder, and the Crisis of Liberalism.* Ph.D. Dissertation, Columbia University, p. 65.

130. Cronin, Thomas E., Tania Z. Cronin, and Michael E. Milakovich. 1981. *U.S. v. Crime in the Streets.* Bloomington: Indiana University Press, pp. 64–65.

131. Flamm, Michael William. 1998. *"Law and Order": Street Crime, Civil Disorder, and the Crisis of Liberalism.* Ph.D. Dissertation, Columbia University. See abstract.

132. Katzenbach as cited in Caplan, Gerald. 1973. "Reflections on the Nationalization of Crime, 1964–1968." *Law and the Social Order* 1973: 583–635, p. 584.

133. Flamm, Michael William. 1998. *"Law and Order": Street Crime, Civil Disorder, and the Crisis of Liberalism.* Ph.D. Dissertation, Columbia University. See abstract.

134. Flamm, Michael William. 1998. *"Law and Order": Street Crime, Civil Disorder, and the Crisis of Liberalism.* Ph.D. Dissertation, Columbia University. See abstract.

Bibliography

103rd Congress, 2nd Session. 1995. "Violence Crime Control and Law Enforcement Act of 1994." *Congressional and Administrative News.* St. Paul: West Publishing.

Abrams, Richard M. 1997. "Theodore Roosevelt." In *The Presidents: A Reference History.* 2d ed. Henry F. Graff, ed. New York: Simon & Schuster Macmillan.

Adams, John. *Messages and Papers of the Presidents of the United States.* Vol. 1. In *American Reference Library.* 1998. CD-ROM. Orem: The Western Standard Publishing Company.

Adler, Freda. 1995. "Who are We? A Self-Analysis of Criminal Justice Specialists." *ACJS Today.* 14(1): 1–21.

Adlow, Elijah. 1955. "Teen-Age Criminals." *The Atlantic Monthly* 196(1): 46–50.

Albanese, Jay. 1995. *White-Collar Crime in America.* Englewood Cliffs: Prentice Hall.

Alpheus, Thomas Mason. 1955. *William Howard Taft: Chief Justice.* New York: Simon & Schuster.

Alvarez, R. Michael, and John Brehm. 1997. "Are Americans Ambivalent Towards Racial Policies?" *American Journal of Political Science* 41(2): 345–374.

Anderson, David C. 1988. *Crimes of Justice: Improving the Police, the Courts, the Prisons.* New York: Times Books.

Anderson, James E. 1990. *Public Policymaking: An Introduction.* Boston: Houghton Mifflin.

Ashdown, Gerald G. 1996. "Federalism, Federalization, and the Politics of Crime." *West Virginia Law Review* 98: 789–813.

Bailey, Frankie, and Donna Hale. 1998. *Popular Culture, Crime, and Justice.* Belmont: International Thompson Publishing Company.

Barber, James D. 1992. *The Presidential Character: Predicting Performance in the White House.* 4th ed. Englewood Cliffs: Prentice Hall.

Barkan, Steven E. and Steven F. Cohn. 1998. "Racial Prejudice and Support by Whites for Police Use of Force: A Research Note." *Justice Quarterly* 15(4): 743–753.

Barlow, David E., Melissa Hickman-Barlow, and W. Wesley Johnson. 1996. "The Political Economy of Criminal Justice Policy: A Time-Series Analysis of Economic Conditions, Crime, and Federal Criminal Justice Legislation, 1948–1987. *Justice Quarterly* 13(2): 223–241.

Barrett, Paul. 1990. "Moving On: Though the Drug War Isn't Over, Spotlight Turns to Other Issues." *Wall Street Journal* 11(November).

Baum, Dan. 1996. *Smoke and Mirrors: The War on Drugs and the Politics of Failure.* Boston: Little, Brown and Company.

Baum, Lawrence. 1998. *The Supreme Court.* 6th ed. Washington D.C.: Congressional Quarterly Press.

Baumer, Terry L. 1985. "Testing a General Model of Fear of Crime." *Journal of Research in Crime and Delinquency* 22: 239–256.

Baumgartner, Frank R., and Bryan D. Jones. 1993. *Agendas and Instability in American Politics.* Chicago: The University of Chicago Press.

Beale, Sara Sun. 1996. "Federalizing Crime: Assessing the Impact on the Federal Courts." *The Annals of the American Academy of Political and Social Science* 543: 39–51.

Beattie, R. H. 1955. "Problems of Criminal Statistics in the United States." *Journal of Criminal Law, Criminology, and Police Science* 46: 178–186.

Beckett, Katherine. 1997. *Making Crime Pay: Law and Order in Contemporary American Politics.* New York: Oxford University Press.

———. 1994. "Setting the Public Agenda: 'Street Crime' and Drug Use in American Politics." *Social Problems* 41(3): 425–447.

Beckett, Katherine, and Theodore Sasson. 2000. *The Politics of Injustice.* Thousand Oaks: Pine Forge Press, p. 70.

Behr, Roy L., and Shanto Iyengar. 1985. "Television News, Real-World Clues, and Changes in the Public Agenda." *Public Opinion Quarterly* 49: 38–57.

Beniger, J. R. 1978. "Media Content as Social Indicators: The Greenfield Index of Agenda-Setting." *Communication Research* 5: 437–451.

Bennack, Frank A., Jr. 1989. *The American Public's Hopes and Fears for the Decade of the 1990s.* New York: The Hearst Company.

Berdahl, Clarence A. 1920. *War Powers of the Executive in the United States.* Urbana: University of Illinois Press.

Bertram, Eva et al. 1996. *Drug War Politics: The Price of Denial.* Berkeley: University of California Press.

Best, Joel. 1990. *Threatened Children: Rhetoric and Concern about Crime-Victims.* Chicago: The University of Chicago Press.

Biderman, A. D., and J. P. Lynch. 1991. *Understanding Crime Incidence Statistics.* New York: Springer-Verlag.

Black, Donald J. 1970. "Production of Crime Rates." *American Sociological Review* 35: 733–748.

Bobo, Lawrence. 1983. "Whites' Opposition to Busing: Symbolic Racism or Realistic Group Conflict?" *Journal of Personality and Social Psychology* 45: 1196–1210.

Bobo, Lawrence, and James R. Kluegal. 1993. "Opposition to Race Targeting: Self-Interest, Stratification Ideology, or Racial Attitudes?" *American Sociological Review* 58: 443–464.

Boehm, Randolph. 1997. *Records of the Wickersham Commission on Law Observance and Enforcement (Research Collections in American Legal History).* New York: University Publications of America.

Booth, Wayne C., Gregory G. Colomb, and Joseph M. Williams. 1995. *The Craft of Research.* Chicago: The University of Chicago Press.

Bordenhamer, David J. 1992. *Fair Trial: Rights of the Accused in American History.* New York: Oxford University Press.

Bosso, Christopher. 1987. *Pesticides and Politics: The Life Cycle of a Public Issue.* Pittsburgh: University of Pittsburgh Press.

Brace, Paul, and Barbara Hinckley. 1992. *Follow the Leader: Opinion Polls and the Modern Presidents.* New York: Basic Books.

———. 1993. "Presidential Activities from Truman through Reagan: Timing and Impact." *Journal of Politics* 55: 382–398.

Bridenbaugh, Carl. 1938. *Cities in the Wilderness: The First Century of Urban Life in America.* New York: The Ronald Press Company.

———. 1955. *Cities in Revolt: Urban Life in America, 1743–1776.* New York: Alfred A. Knopf.

Brown, Les. 1971. *Television.* New York: Harcourt Brace Jovanovich, Inc.

Bryner, Gary. 1998. *Politics and Public Morality.* New York: W.W. Norton and Company, Inc.

Bureau of Justice Assistance. 1992–1998. *Edward Bryne Memorial State and Local Law Enforcement Assistance: Fact Sheet.* Washington D.C.: U.S. Department of Justice.

Burke, John P. 1992. *The Institutional Presidency.* Baltimore: The Johns Hopkins University Press.

Burner, David. 1979. *Herbert Hoover: A Public Life.* New York: Alfred A. Knopf.

———. 1997. "Herbert Hoover." In *The Presidents: A Reference History.* 2d ed. Henry F. Graff, ed. New York: Simon & Schuster Macmillan.

Butler, David, and Donald Stokes. 1974. *Political Change in Britain: The Evolution of Electoral Choice.* 2d ed. New York: Macmillan.

Caldeira, Gregory A. 1983. "Elections and the Politics of Crime: Budgetary Choices and Priorities in America." In *The Political Science of Criminal Justice.* Stuart Nagel, Erika Fairchild, and Anthony Champagne, eds. Springfield: Charles C. Thomas Publishers, pp. 238–252.

Caldeira, Gregory A, and Andrew T. Cowart. 1980. "Budgets, Institutions, and Change: Criminal Justice Policy in America." *American Journal of Political Science* 24: 413–438.

Calder, James D. 1978. *Presidents and Crime Control: Some Limitations on Executive Policy Making.* Ph.D. Dissertation, Claremont University.

———. 1981. "Herbert Hoover's Contributions to the Administrative History of Crime Control Policy." Paper presented at the annual meeting of the Southwest Political Science Association, Dallas, Texas.

———. 1982. "Presidents and Crime Control: Kennedy, Johnson and Nixon and the Influences of Ideology." *Presidential Studies Quarterly* 12: 574–589.

———. 1993. *The Origins and Development of Federal Crime Control Policy: Herbert Hoover's Initiatives.* Westport: Praeger Publishers.

Cambell, Karlyn Kohrs, and Kathleen Hall Jamieson. 1990. *Deeds Done in Words: Presidential Rhetoric and the Genres of Governance.* Chicago: University of Chicago Press.

Campell, Angus, Philip E. Converse, Warren E. Miller, and Donald E. Stokes. 1960. *The American Voter.* New York: Whiley.

Canon, Bradley C., and Charles A. Johnson. 1999. *Judicial Policies: Implementation and Impact.* 2d ed. Washington D.C.: Congressional Quarterly Press.

Caplan, Gerald. 1973. "Reflections on the Nationalization of Crime, 1964–1968." *Law and the Social Order* 1973: 583–635.

Caplan, Lincoln. 1987. *The Tenth Justice: The Solicitor General and the Rule of Law.* New York: Random House.

Caringella-MacDonald, Susan. 1990. "State Crises and the Crackdown on Crime under Reagan." *Contemporary Crises* 14: 91–118.

Carlson, Susan M., and Raymond J. Michalowski. 1997. "Crime, Unemployment, and Social Structure of Accumulation: An Inquiry into Historical Contingency." *Justice Quarterly* 14(2): 209–241.

Carter, Dan T. 1995. *The Politics of Rage: George Wallace, the Origins of the New Conservatism, and the Transformation of American Politics.* New York: Simon & Schuster.

Carter, Jimmy. Various Years. *Public Papers of the Presidents of the United States.* Washington D.C.: U.S. G.P.O.

Ceaser, James W. 1985. "The Rhetorical Presidency Revisited." In *Modern Presidents and the Presidency.* Marc Landy, ed. Lexington: Lexington Books, pp. 15–34.

Ceaser, James W., Glen E. Thurow, Jeffrey Tulis, and Joseph M. Bessette. 1981. "The Rise of the Rhetorical Presidency." *Presidential Studies Quarterly* 11: 158–171.

Chambliss, William J. 1994. "Policing the Ghetto Underclass: The Politics of Law and Law Enforcement." *Social Problems* 41(2): 177–194.

Chermak, Steven M., and Alexander Weiss. 1997. "The Effects of the Media on Federal Criminal Justice Policy." *Criminal Justice Policy Review* 8(4): 323–342.

Chernoff, Harry A., Christopher M. Kelly, and John R. Kroger. 1996. "The Politics of Crime." *Harvard Journal on Legislation* 33(2): 527–579.

Chiricos, Ted. 1998. "The Media, Moral Panics and the Politics of Crime Control." In *The Criminal Justice System: Politics and Policies.* 7th ed. George F. Cole and Marc G. Gertz, eds. Belmont: Wadsworth Publishers, pp. 58–75.

Chiricos, Ted G. 1987. "Rates of Crime and Unemployment: An Analysis of Aggregate Research Evidence." *Social Problems* 34(2): 187–211.

Cigler, Allan J., and Burdett A. Loomis. 1998. *Interest Group Politics.* 5th ed. Washington D.C.: Congressional Quarterly Press.

Clear, Todd. 1997. "Societal Responses to the President's Crime Commission: A Thirty-Year Retrospective." In *The Challenge of Crime in a Free Society: Looking Back, Looking Forward.* Washington D.C.: U.S. Department of Justice, pp. 131–158.

Clemente, F., and M. B. Kleiman. 1977. "Fear of Crime in the United States: A Multivariate Analysis." *Social Forces* 56: 519–531.

Clinton, Bill, and Al Gore. 1992. *Putting People First.* New York: Times Books.

Clinton, William J. Various Years. *Public Papers of the Presidents of the United States.* Washington D.C.: U.S. G.P.O.

Cobb, Roger W., and Charles D. Elder. 1971. "The Politics of Agenda-Building." *Journal of Politics* 33(4): 892–915.

———. 1972. *Participation in American Politics: The Dynamics of Agenda-Building.* Baltimore: The Johns Hopkins University Press.

Cobb, Roger, Jennie-Keith Ross, and Marc Howard Ross. 1976. "Agenda Building as a Comparative Political Process." *American Political Science Review* 70: 126–138.

Cohen, Jeffrey E. 1995. "Presidential Rhetoric and the Public Agenda." *American Journal of Political Science* 39(1): 87–107.

———. 1997. *Presidential Responsiveness and Public Policy-Making.* Ann Arbor: University of Michigan Press.

Cohen, Jeffrey E., and Ken Collier. 1999. *Presidential Policymaking: An End-of-Century Assessment.* Steven A. Shull, ed. Armonk: M. E. Sharpe, p. 43.

Cohen, Stanley. 1980. *Folk Devils and Moral Panics: The Creation of the Mods and Rockers.* New York: St. Martin's Press.

Coletta, Paolo E. 1997. "William Howard Taft." In *The Presidents: A Reference History.* 2d ed. Henry F. Graff, ed. New York: Simon & Schuster Macmillan.

Congressional Digest. 1994. "The Federal Role in Crime Control." *Congressional Digest* 73(6/7): 161–192.

Congressional Information Service. 1995. *CIS Annual 1994.* Bethesda: Congressional Information Service.

Conlan, Timothy. 1988. *New Federalism: Intergovernmental Reform from Nixon to Reagan.* Washington D.C.: The Brookings Institution.

Conley, John A. 1994. *The 1967 President's Crime Commission Report: Its Impact 25 Years Later.* Cincinnati: Anderson Publishing Company/Academy of Criminal Justice Sciences.

Converse, Phillip E. 1964. "The Nature of Belief Systems in Mass Publics." In *Ideology and Discontent.* David E. Apter, ed. New York: Free Press, pp. 206–261.

Cook, Thomas D., and Donald T. Campbell. 1979. *Quasi-Experimentation: Design & Analysis Issues for Field Settings.* Boston: Houghton Mifflin Company.

Corbett, Michael. 1991. *American Public Opinion.* New York: Longman.

Cornwell, Elmer E. 1965. *Presidential Leadership of Public Opinion.* Bloomington: Indiana University Press.

Corwin, Edward S. 1957. *The President and His Powers 1787 to 1957.* 4th ed. New York: New York University Press.

"Crime: Nixon Approach, Its Cost and Results." *Congressional Quarterly Weekly Report.* 29(April 30, 1971): 985–988.

Cronin, Thomas E. 1980. *The State of the Presidency.* Boston: Little, Brown and Company.

Cronin, Thomas E., Tania Z. Cronin, and Michael E. Milakovich. 1981. *U.S. v. Crime in the Streets.* Bloomington: Indiana University Press.

Curriden, Mark, and Leroy Phillips, Jr. 1999. *Contempt of Court: The Turn-of-the-Century Lynching that Launched a Hundred Years of Federalism.* New York: Oxford.

Currie, Elliott. 1998. *Crime and Punishment in America: Why the Solutions to America's Most Stubborn Social Crisis Have Not Worked—And What Will.* New York: Henry Holt and Company, Inc.

Dallek, Robert. 1984. *Ronald Reagan and the Politics of Symbolism.* Cambridge: Harvard University Press.

Daly, Christopher B. 1991. "Massachusetts Seen Near Return to Death Penalty." *Washington Post* (August 18): A4.

Danielian, Lucig H., and Stephen D. Reese. 1989. "A Closer Look at Intermedia Influence on Agenda Setting: The Cocaine Issue of 1986." In *Communication Campaigns about Drugs: Government, Media, and the Public.* Pamela J. Shoemaker, ed. Hillsdale: Lawrence Erlbaum Associates, pp. 47–66.

Davey, Joseph D. 1988. *The Politics of Prison Expansion: Winning Elections by Waging War on Crime.* Westport: Praeger Publishers.

Davidson, Roger H., and Walter J. Oleszek. 1998. *Congress and Its Members.* 6th ed. Washington D.C.: Congressional Quarterly Press.

Davis, David S. 1983. "The Production of Crime Policies." *Crime and Social Justice* (20): 121–137.

Deering, Christopher, and Steven S. Smith. 1997. *Committees in Congress.* 3d ed. Washington D.C.: Congressional Quarterly Press.

DeFrances, Carol J., and Steven K. Smith. 1994. "Federal-State Relations in Gun Control: The 1993 Brady Handgun Violence Prevention Act." *Publius: The Journal of Federalism* 24(Summer): 69–82.

Democratic National Convention. "1992 Democratic Party Platform." Reprinted in World Book Encyclopedia. 1998. *American Reference Library.* CD-ROM. Orem: Western Standard Publishing Company.

Denton, Robert F., Jr., and Dan F. Hahn. 1986. *Presidential Communication.* New York: Praeger Publishers.

Devroy, Ann, and Ruth Marcus. 1992. "Police Group Gives Bush Its Blessing: President Fought for Endorsement." *The Washington Post* (October 10): A1.

DiClerico, Robert E. 1995. *The American President.* 4th ed. Englewood Cliffs: Prentice Hall, Inc.

———. 1996. "Assessing Context and Character." *Society* 33(6): 28–36.

———. 2000. *The American President.* 5th ed. Upper Saddle River: Prentice Hall, Inc.

———. 2000. *Political Parties, Campaigns, and Elections.* Upper Saddle River: Prentice Hall, Inc.

Diegelman, Robert F. 1982. "Federal Financial Assistance for Crime Control: Lessons of the LEAA Experience." *Journal of Criminal Law and Criminology* 73(3): 994–1011.

Dilulio, John J., Jr. 1999. "Federal Crime Policy: Time for a Moratorium." *Brookings Review* 17(1): 17–21.

Dilulio, John J., Jr., Steven K. Smith, and Aaron J. Saiger. 1995. "The Federal Role in Crime Control." In *Crime.* James Q. Wilson and Joan Petersilia, eds. San Francisco: Institute for Contemporary Studies.

Dodd, Lawrence C., and Bruce I. Oppenheimer. 1997. *Congress Reconsidered.* 6th ed. Washington D.C.: Congressional Quarterly, Inc.

Donald, Herbert D. 1995. *Lincoln.* New York: Simon & Schuster.

Donziger, Steven R. 1996. *The Real War on Crime: The Report of the National Criminal Justice Commission.* New York: Harper Perennial.

Downs, Anthony. 1972. "Up and Down with Ecology—The 'Issue Attention Cycle.'" *The Public Interest* 28(Summer): 38–50.

Durham, Alexis M. III. 1994. *Crisis and Reform: Current Issues in American Punishment.* Boston: Little, Brown and Company.

Edelman, Murray. 1964. *The Symbolic Uses of Politics.* Urbana: University of Illinois Press.

———. 1971. *Politics as Symbolic Action: Mass Arousal and Quiescence.* Chicago: Markham Publishing Company.

———. 1988. *Constructing the Political Spectacle.* Chicago: The University of Chicago Press.

Edsall, Thomas Bryne, and Mary D. Edsall. 1991. *Chain Reaction: The Impact of Race, Rights, and Taxes on American Politics.* New York: W.W. Norton.

Edwards, George C. III. 1983. *The Public Presidency: The Pursuit of Popular Support.* New York: St. Martin's Press.

————. 2000. "Building Coalitions." *Presidential Studies Quarterly* 30(1): 47–78.

Edwards, George C. III, and Stephen J. Wayne. 1990. *Presidential Leadership: Politics and Policy Making.* 2d ed. New York: St. Martin's Press.

Edwards, George C. III, Steven A. Shull, and Norman C. Thomas. 1985. *The Presidency and Public Policy Making.* Pittsburgh: University of Pittsburgh Press.

Ehrlichman, John. 1982. *Witness to Power: The Nixon Years.* New York: Simon & Schuster.

Eisenhower, Dwight D. Various Years. *Public Papers of the Presidents of the United States.* Washington D.C.: U.S. G.P.O.

Eisner, Marc Allen. 1993. *Regulatory Politics in Transition.* Baltimore: The Johns Hopkins University Press.

Elder, Charles, and Roger Cobb. 1983. *The Political Uses of Symbols.* New York: Longman.

Ellis, Joseph J. 1997. *American Sphinx: The Character of Thomas Jefferson.* New York: Alfred A. Knopf.

Epstein, Edward. 1977. *Agency of Fear: Opiates and Political Power in America.* New York: Random House.

Fairchild, Erika S., and Vincent J. Webb. 1985. *The Politics of Crime and Criminal Justice.* Beverly Hills: SAGE Publications.

Faucheux, Ron. 1994. "The Politics of Crime." *Campaigns and Elections.* (March): 31–34.

Federal Bureau of Investigation. 1993–1999. *Uniform Crime Reports.* Washington D.C.: U.S. G.P.O.

Feeley, Malcolm M., and Austin D. Sarat. 1980. *The Policy Dilemma: Federal Crime Policy and the Law Enforcement Assistance Administration.* Minneapolis: University of Minnesota Press.

Felkenes, George T. 1992. "Liberty, Restraint, and Criminal Justice: Gerald Ford's Presidential Concerns." *Journal of Criminal Justice* 20: 147–160.

————. 1993. "Domestic Tranquility: President Ford's Policy Positions on Criminal Justice Issues." *Presidential Studies Quarterly* 23(3): 519–532.

Fenno, Richard F., Jr. 1973. *Congressmen in Committees.* Boston: Little, Brown and Company.

Ferraro, Kenneth F. 1995. *Fear of Crime: Interpreting Victimization Risk.* Albany: State University of New York Press.

Ferraro, Kenneth, and Randy LaGrange. 1987. "The Measurement of Fear of Crime." *Sociological Quarterly* 57: 71–101.

Finckenauer, James O. 1978. "Crime as a National Political Issue: 1964–1976." *Crime & Delinquency* 24(1): 13–27.

Fishel, Jeff. 1985. *Presidents and Promises: From Campaign Pledge to Presidential Performance.* Washington D.C.: Congressional Quarterly Press.

Flamm, Michael William. 1998. *"Law and Order": Street Crime, Civil Disorder, and the Crisis of Liberalism.* Ph.D. Dissertation, Columbia University.

Flanagan, Timothy J., and Dennis R. Longmire. 1996. *Americans View Crime and Justice: A National Public Opinion Survey.* Thousand Oaks: SAGE Publications.

Foucault, Michel. 1977. *Discipline and Punish: The Birth of the Prison.* New York: Vintage Press.

Ford, Gerald R. Various Years. *Public Papers of the Presidents of the United States.* Washington D.C.: U.S. G.P.O.

————. 1979. *A Time to Heal: The Autobiography of Gerald R. Ford.* New York: Harper & Row, Publishers and the Reader's Digest Association, Inc.

Frankel, Martin R., and Lester R. Frankel. 1987. "Fifty Years of Survey Sampling in the United States." *Public Opinion Quarterly* 51: 5127–5138.

Freedman, David, Robert Pisani, Roger Purves, and Ani Adhikari. 1991. *Statistics.* 2d ed. New York: W.W. Norton and Company.

Friedman, Lawrence M. 1993. *Crime and Punishment in American History.* New York: Basic Books.

Funkhouser, G. R. 1973. "The Issue of the Sixties: An Exploratory Study of the Dynamics of Public Opinion." *Public Opinion Quarterly* 37: 62–75.

Gallup, George. 1945–1996. *The Gallup Poll: Public Opinion.* Wilmington, Delaware: Scholarly Resources, Inc.

———. 2000. "Gallup Social and Economic Indicators—Most Important Problem." *The Gallup Organization Homepage.* http://www.gallup.com/poll/indicators/indmip.asp.

Gardner, Carol B. 1990. "Safe Conduct: Women, Crime, and Self in Public Places." *Social Problems* 37: 311–328.

Garofalo, James. 1981. "Crime and the Mass Media: A Selective Review of Research." *Journal of Research in Crime and Delinquency* 18: 319–350.

———. 1981. "The Fear of Crime: Causes and Consequences." *Journal of Criminal Law and Criminology* 72: 839–857.

Garraty, John A. 1997. "Grover Cleveland." In *The Presidents: A Reference History.* 2d ed. Henry F. Graff, ed. New York: Simon & Schuster Macmillan.

Gaubatz, Kathlyn Taylor. 1995. *Crime in the Public Mind.* Ann Arbor: The University of Michigan Press.

Gelderman, C. W. 1995. "All the President's Words." *The Wilson Quarterly* 19: 68–79.

Gerber, Rudolph J. 1999. *Cruel and Usual: Our Criminal Injustice System.* Westport: Praeger Publishers.

Gest, Ted, et al. 1996. "Popgun Politics." *U.S. News & World Report* (September 30): 30–42.

Gilens, Martin. 1995. "Radial Attitudes and Opposition to Welfare." *The Journal of Politics* 57(4): 994–1014.

Glaser, Daniel. 1978. *Crime in Our Changing Society.* New York: Holt.

Golden, D. G., and J. M. Porterba. 1980. "The Price of Popularity: The Political Business Cycle Re-examined." *American Journal of Political Science* 24: 696–714.

Goldberg, Raymond. 1997. *Drugs Across the Spectrum.* Englewood: Morton Publishing Company.

Goldwater, Barry. 1964. "Republican Nomination Acceptance Speech." *New York Times* (January 10, 1964): A10.

Gonzenbach, William J. 1996. *The Media, The President, and Public Opinion: A Longitudinal Analysis of the Drug Issue, 1984–1991.* Mahwah: Lawrence Erlbaum Associates, Publishers.

Gordon, Diana. 1990. *The Justice Juggernaut.* New Brunswick: Rutgers University Press.

Gottfredson, Stephen D., Barbara D. Warner, and Ralph B. Taylor. 1988. "Conflict and Consensus about Criminal Justice in Maryland." In *Public Attitudes to Sentencing.* N. Walker and M. Hough, eds. Brookfield: Gower.

Graber, Doris. 1980. *Crime News and the Public.* New York: Praeger Publishers.

———. 1982. *The President and the Public.* Philadelphia: Institute for Study of Human Issues.

———. 1989. *Mass Media and American Politics.* Washington D.C.: Congressional Quarterly Press.

Graham, Hugh D., and Ted R. Gurr, eds. 1969. *A Report to the National Commission on the Causes and Prevention of Violence. Violence in America: Historical and Comparative Perspectives.* Vols. 1 and 2. New York: New American Library Inc.

Gray, Virginia, and Bruce Williams. 1980. *The Organizational Politics of Criminal Justice: Policy In Context.* Lexington: Lexington Books.

Greenburg, Douglas. 1974. *Crime and Law Enforcement in the Colony of New York, 1691–1776.* Ithaca: Cornell University Press.

Greenstein, Fred I. 1974. "The Politics of Persuasion." In *Choosing the President.* James D. Barber, ed. Englewood Cliffs: Prentice Hall, pp. 87–102.

Grossman, Michael B., and Martha Joynt. 1981. *The White House and the News Media.* Baltimore: The Johns Hopkins University Press.

Gujarati, Damodar N. 1995. *Basic Econometrics.* 3d ed. New York: McGraw-Hill, Inc.

Gusfield, Joseph. 1963. *Symbolic Crusade.* Urbana: University of Illinois Press.

Hagan, Frank E. 1997. *Political Crime: Ideology and Criminality.* Boston: Allyn & Bacon.

Hagan, John. 1983. "The Symbolic Politics of Criminal Sanctions." In *The Political Science of Criminal Justice.* Stuart Nagel, Erika Fairchild, and Anthony Champagne, eds. Springfield: Charles C. Thomas Publishers.

Hagan, John, and Ruther Peterson. 1995. *Crime and Inequality.* Stanford: Stanford University Press.

Hagan, Michael G. 1995. "The Crime Issue and the 1994 Elections." Paper presented at the annual meeting of the American Political Science Association, Chicago, August 31–September 3.

Haghighi, Bahram, and Jon Sorenson. 1996. "America's Fear of Crime," In *Americans View Crime and Justice: A National Public Opinion Survey.* Thousand Oaks: SAGE Publications.

Hale, Donna C. 1998. "Presidential Address: Delivered at the 34th Annual Meeting of the Academy of Criminal Justice Sciences, Louisville, Kentucky, March 1997. Criminal Justice Education: Traditions in Transition." *Justice Quarterly* 15(3): 385–394.

Hall, Stuart, Charles Critcher, Tony Jefferson, John Clarke, and Brian Roberts. 1978. *Policing the Crisis: Mugging, the State, and Law and Order.* London: Macmillan.

Hammond, Matthew Carlton. 1997. "The Posse Comitatus Act: A Principle in Need of Renewal." *Washington University Law Quarterly* 72(2). Available at http://www.wulaw.wustl.edu/WULQ/75-2/752-10.html

Handberg, Roger, and Harold F. Hill, Jr. 1980. "Court Curbing, Court Reversals, and Judicial Review: The Supreme Court versus Congress." *Law and Society Review* 14: 309–322.

Hannon, Lance, and James DeFronzo. 1998. "Welfare and Property Crime." *Justice Quarterly* 15(2): 273–288.

Hargrove, Erwin C. 1974. *The Power of the Modern Presidency.* New York: Alfred A. Knopf, Inc.

Hart, Roderick P. 1984. "The Language of the Modern Presidency." *Presidential Studies Quarterly* 14: 249–264.

———. 1987. *The Sounds of Leadership: Presidential Communication in the Modern Age.* Chicago: University of Chicago Press.

Hayes, Rutherford B. *Messages and Papers of the Presidents.* Vol. 6. In *American Reference Library.* 1998. CD-ROM. Orem: The Western Standard Publishing Company.

Haynie, Dana L. 1998. "The Gender Gap in Fear of Crime, 1973–1994: A Methodological Approach." *Criminal Justice Review* 23(1): 29–50.

Heclo, Hugh. 1994. "Ideas, Interests, and Institutions." In *The Dynamics of American Politics: Approaches and Interpretations.* Lawrence C. Dodd and Calvin Jillson, eds. Boulder: Westview Press, pp. 366–392.

Henderson, Phillip. 1988. *Managing the Presidency: The Eisenhower Legacy from Kennedy to Reagan.* Boulder: Westview Publishers.

Hess, Stephen. 2000. "I Am On TV Therefore I Am." In *Media Power in Politics.* Doris A. Graber, ed. Washington D.C.: Congressional Quarterly Press, pp. 246–254.

Heymann, Philip B., and Mark H. Moore. 1996. "The Federal Role in Dealing with Violent Street Crime: Principles, Questions, and Cautions." *The Annals of the American Academy of Political and Social Science* 543: 103–115.

Hibbs, D. A., Jr., R. D. Rivers, and N. Vasiltos. 1982. "On the Demand for Economic Outcomes." *Journal of Politics* 43: 426–462.

Hill, Kim Quaile. 1998. "The Policy Agenda of the President and the Mass Public: A Research Validation and Extension." *American Journal of Political Science* 42: 1328–1334.

Hinckley, Barbara. 1990. *The Symbolic Presidency: How Presidents Portray Themselves.* New York: Routledge.

———. 1994. *Less Than Meets the Eye: Foreign Policy Making and the Myth of the Assertive Congress.* Chicago: A Twentieth Century Fund Book.

Hindelang, Michael. 1974. "The Uniform Crime Reports Revisited." *Journal of Criminal Justice* 2: 1–17.

Hofstadter, Richard, and Michael Wallace, eds. 1971. *American Violence: A Documentary History.* New York: Vintage Books.

Hoover, Herbert. Various Years. *Public Papers of the Presidents of the United States.* Washington D.C.: U.S. G.P.O.

———. 1952. *The Memories of Herbert Hoover: The Cabinet and the Presidency 1920–1933.* New York: The Macmillan Company.

Houston, James, and William W. Parsons. 1998. *Criminal Justice and the Policy Process.* Chicago: Nelson-Hall Publishers.

Hoxie, R. Gordon. 1984. "The Cabinet in the American Presidency, 1789–1984." *Presidential Studies Quarterly* (Spring): 209–230.

Hurwitz, Jon, and Mark Peffley. 1997. "Public Perceptions of Race and Crime: The Role of Racial Stereotypes." *American Journal of Political Science* 41(2): 375–401.

Hyland, Pat. 1995. *Presidential Libraries and Museums: An Illustrated Guide.* Washington D.C.: Congressional Quarterly Books.

Ifill, Gwen. 1992. "Clinton, in Houston Speech, Assails Bush on Crime Issue." *The New York Times* (July 24): A13.

———. 1994. "Clinton Embraces Crime Measure, Ever So Vaguely." *The New York Times* (February 21): A13.

Ifill, Walsh Edward. 1992. "Clinton Charges Bush Uses Crime Issue to Divide." *The Washington Post* (July 24): A16.

Inciardi, James A. 1986. *The War on Drugs: Heroin, Cocaine, Crime and Public Policy.* Palo Alto: Mayfield Publishers.

Iyengar, Shanto. 1991. *Is Anyone Responsible? How Television Frames Political Issues.* Chicago: University of Chicago Press.

Iyengar, Shanto, and Donald R. Kinder. 1987. *News that Matters: Television and American Public Opinion.* Chicago: University of Chicago Press.

Jackson, Andrew. *Messages and Papers of the Presidents of the United States.* Vol. 1. In *American Reference Library.* 1998. CD-ROM. Orem: The Western Standard Publishing Company.

Jacobs, Lawrence, and Robert Y. Shapiro. 1995. "Public Opinion, Institutions, and Policy Making." *PS: Political Science and Politics.* 27: 9–17.

———. 2000. *Politicians Don't Pander.* Chicago: University of Chicago Press.

Jamieson, Kathleen Hall. 1992. *Dirty Politics: Deception, Distraction, and Democracy.* New York: Oxford University Press.

Jefferson, Thomas. *Messages and Papers of the Presidents of the United States.* Vol. 1. In *American Reference Library.* 1998. CD-ROM. Orem: The Western Standard Publishing Company.

Jensen, Eric L., and Jurg Gerber. 1998. "The Social Construction of Drug Problems: An Historical Overview." In *The New War on Drugs: Symbolic Politics and Criminal Justice Policy.* Eric L. Jensen and Jurg Gerber, eds. Cincinnati: Academy of Criminal Justice Sciences and Anderson Publishing.

Johnson, Bruce, and C. Ronald Huff. 1987. "Public Opinion and Criminal Justice Policy Formulation." *Criminal Justice Policy Review* 2: 118–132.

Johnson, Lyndon B. Various Years. *The Public Papers of the Presidents of the United States.* Washington D.C.: U.S. G.P.O.

Johnson, Lyndon Baines. 1971. *The Vantage Point: Perspectives of the Presidency, 1963–1969.* New York: Holt, Rinehart and Winston.

Johnson, Paul. 1997. *A History of the American People.* New York: HarperCollins Publishers.

Jones, Bryan D. 1994. *Reconceiving Decision-Making in Democratic Politics: Attention, Choice and Public Policy.* Chicago: The University of Chicago Press.

Kadish, Sanford H. 1983. "Crime Commissions." *Encyclopedia of Crime and Justice.* Vol. 1. New York: The Free Press.

Kaiser Family Foundation/Center for Media and Public Affairs Report. 1998. *Assessing Local Television News Coverage of Health Issues.* Menlo Park: The Henry J. Kaiser Family Foundation.

Kallenbach, Joseph E. 1966. *The American Chief Executive.* New York: Harper and Row.

Kaminer, Wendy. 1994. "Federal Offense." *The Atlantic Monthly* (June): 102–114.

Kappeler, Victor E., Mark Blumberg, and Gary W. Potter. 1996. *The Mythology of Crime and Criminal Justice.* 2d ed. Prospect Heights: Waveland Press, Inc.

Kemp, Kathleen. 1981. "Symbolic and Strict Regulation in the American States." *Social Science Quarterly* 62: 516–526.

Kennedy, John F. Various Years. *Public Papers of the Presidents of the United States.* Washington D.C.: U.S. G.P.O.

Kennedy, Leslie W. and Robert A. Silverman. 1985. "Significant Others and Fear of Crime Among the Elderly." *Journal of Aging and Human Development* 20: 241–256.

Kennedy, Robert F. 1960. *The Enemy Within.* New York: Harper & Brothers.

Kernell, Samuel. 1978. "Explaining Presidential Popularity." *American Political Science Review* 72: 506–522.

———. 1997. *Going Public: New Strategies of Presidential Leadership.* 3d ed. Washington D.C.: Congressional Quarterly, Inc.

Kessel, John H. 1974. "Parameters of Presidential Politics." *Social Science Quarterly* 55: 8–24.

———. 1977. "Seasons of Presidential Politics." *Social Science Quarterly* 58: 418–435.

Key, V. O., Jr. 1967. *Public Opinion and American Democracy.* New York: Knopf.

Kikendall, Richard S. 1997. "Jimmy Carter." In *The Presidents: A Reference History.* 2d ed. Henry F. Graff, ed. New York: Simon & Schuster Macmillan, pp. 551–567.

Kinder, Donald. 1986. "The Continuing American Dilemma: White Resistance to Racial Change Forty Years after Mrydal." *Journal of Social Issues* 42: 151–172.

Kingdon, John W. 1995. *Agendas, Alternatives, and Public Policies.* 2d ed. New York: HarperCollins College Publishers.

Kitsuse, John L., and A. V. Cicourel. 1963. "A Note on the Use of Official Statistics." *Social Problems* 11: 131–138.

Klein, Joe. 1994. "Crime Bill Garbage Barge." *Newsweek* 123 (February 28): 35.

Kraska, Peter B. 1993. "Militarizing the Drug War: A Sign of the Times." In *Altered States of Mind: Critical Observations of the Drug War.* Peter B. Kraska, ed. New York: Garland, pp. 159–206.

———. 1996. "Enjoying Militarism: Political/Personal Dilemmas in Studying U.S. Police Paramilitary Units." *Justice Quarterly* 13(3): 405–429.

Kraska, Peter B., and Louis J. Cubellis. 1997. "Militarizing Mayberry and Beyond: Making Sense of American Paramilitary Policing." *Justice Quarterly* 14(4): 607–629.

Kraska, Peter B., and Victor E. Kappeler. 1997. "Militarizing American Police: The Rise and Normalization of Paramilitary Units." *Social Problems* 44: 1–18.

Kuklinksi, James H., Paul M. Sniderman, Kathleen Knight, Thomas Piazza, Philip E. Tetlock, Gordon R. Lawrence, and Barbara Mellers. 1997. "Racial Prejudice and Attitudes Toward Affirmative Action." *American Journal of Political Science* 41(2): 402–419.

LaFree, Gary. 1998. *Losing Legitimacy: Street Crime and the Decline of Social Institutions in America.* Boulder: Westview Press.

LaGrange, Randy L., Kenneth F. Ferraro, and Michael Supanic. 1992. "Perceived Risk and Fear of Crime: Role of Social and Physical Incivilities." *Journal of Research in Crime and Delinquency* 29: 311–335.

Lane, Roger. 1976. "Criminal Violence in America: The First Hundred Years." *The Annals of the American Academy of Political and Social Science* 423: 1–13.

Latner, Richard B. 1997. "Andrew Jackson." In *The Presidents: A Reference History.* 2d ed. Henry F. Graff, ed. New York: Simon & Schuster Macmillan.

Lavrakas, Paul. 1982. "Fear of Crime and Behavioral Restrictions in Urban and Suburban Neighborhoods." *Population and Environments* 5: 242–264.

Leff, D. R., D. L. Protess, and S. C. Brooks. 1986. "Crusading Journalism: Changing Public Attitudes and Policy-Making." *Public Opinion Quarterly* 50: 300–315.

LeLoup, Lance T., and Steven A. Shull. 1999. *The President and Congress: Collaboration and Combat in National Policymaking.* Boston: Allyn & Bacon.

Levy, Leonard W., and Louis Fisher, eds. 1994. "Crime, Policy On." *Encyclopedia of the American Presidency.* Vol. 1. New York: Simon & Schuster.

Lewis, Dan A., and Greta Salem. 1986. *Fear of Crime: Incivility and the Production of a Social Problem.* New Brunswick: Transaction Books.

Lewis-Beck, Michael. 1980. *Applied Regression: An Introduction.* Newbury Park: SAGE Publications.

Lewis-Beck, Michael S., and Tom W. Rice. 1992. *Forecasting Elections.* Washington D.C.: Congressional Quarterly Press.

Leyden, Kevin M., Willard M. Oliver, and John C. Kilwein. 1999. "Is Crime Control Policy Another Form of Pork Barrel Politics?" Unpublished paper presented at the annual meeting of the Western Political Science Association, Seattle, Washington.

Leyden, Kevin M., John C. Kilwein, and Willard M. Oliver. 1996. "Public Opinion and Crime: Who Fears Crime and Why?" Unpublished paper presented at the Northeastern Political Science Association's annual meeting, Boston, Massachusetts.

Lichter, Roberts S., and Linda S. Lichter. 1994. *Media Monitor: 1993—The Year in Review.* Vol. 8 No. 1. Washington D.C.: Center for Media and Public Affairs.

Light, Paul C. 1991. *The President's Agenda: Domestic Policy Choice from Kennedy to Reagan.* Rev. ed. Baltimore: The Johns Hopkins University Press.

———. 1993. "Presidential Policy Making." In *Researching the Presidency: Vital Questions, New Approaches.* George C. Edwards III, John H. Kessel, and Bert A. Rockman, eds. Pittsburgh: University of Pittsburgh Press, pp. 161–199.

Lincoln, Abraham. *Messages and Papers of the Presidents.* Vol. 5. In *American Reference Library.* 1998. CD-ROM. Orem: The Western Standard Publishing Company.

Link, Arthur S. 1997. "Woodrow Wilson." In *The Presidents: A Reference History.* 2d ed. Henry F. Graff, ed. New York: Simon & Schuster Macmillan.

Lippmann, Walter. 1925. *The Phantom Public.* New York: Macmillan.

Liska, Allen E., and William Baccaglini. 1990. "Feeling Safe by Comparison: Crime in the Newspapers." *Social Problems* 37: 360–374.

Lowi, Theodore J. 1964. "American Business, Public Policy, Case Studies, and Political Theory." *World Politics* 16(July): 677–715; Lowi, Theodore J. 1972. "Four Systems of Policy, Politics, and Choice." *Public Administration Review* 32(July/August): 298–310.

———. 1979. *The End of Liberalism: The Second Republic of the United States.* 2d ed. New York: W.W. Norton and Company.

———. 1985. *The Personal President: Power Invested, Promises Unfulfilled.* Ithaca: Cornell University Press

———. 1995. *The End of the Republican Era.* Norman: University of Oklahoma Press.

Lumbard, Eliot H. 1971. "State and Local Government Crime Control." In *The Challenge of Crime in a Free Society.* Henry S. Ruth, Jr. et al., eds. New York: De Capo Press, pp. 79–97.

Lyons, William. 1999. *The Politics of Community Policing: Rearranging the Power to Punish.* Ann Arbor: The University of Michigan Press.

MacKuen, Michael B. 1983. "Political Drama, Economic Conditions and the Dynamics of Presidential Popularity." *American Journal of Political Science* 27: 165–192.

Madison, James. *Messages and Papers of the Presidents of the United States.* Vol. 1. In *American Reference Library.* 1998. CD-ROM. Orem: The Western Standard Publishing Company.

Maier, Mark H. 1995. *The Data Game.* 2d ed. Armonk: M. E. Sharpe.

Maguire, Kathleen, and Ann L. Pastore. 1998. *Sourcebook of Criminal Justice Statistics 1997.* Washington D.C.: Bureau of Justice Statistics.

Mahoney, Barry. 1976. *The Politics of the Safe Streets Act, 1965–1973: A Case Study in Evolving Federalism and the National Legislative Process.* Ph.D. Dissertation, Columbia University.

Malone, Dumas. 1970. *Jefferson the President: First Term 1801–1805.* Boston: Little, Brown and Company.

Marion, Nancy E. 1992. "Presidential Agenda Setting in Crime Control." *Criminal Justice Policy Review* 6: 159–184.

———. 1994. "Symbolism and Federal Crime Control Legislation, 1960–1990." *Journal of Crime and Justice* 17(2): 69–91.

————. 1994. *A History of Federal Crime Control Initiatives, 1960–1993*. Westport: Praeger Publishers.

————. 1995. *A Primer in the Politics of Criminal Justice*. New York: Harrow and Heston Publishers.

————. 1997. "Symbolic Policies in Clinton's Crime Control Agenda." *Buffalo Criminal Law Review* 1(1): 67–108.

Marshall, Thomas R. 1993. "Symbolic versus Policy Representation on the U.S. Supreme Court." *Journal of Politics* 55: 140–150.

Martinek, Wendy L., Kenneth J. Meier, and Lael R. Keiser. 1998. "Jackboots or Lace Panties? The Bureau of Alcohol, Tobacco and Firearms." In *The Changing Politics of Gun Control*. John M. Bruce and Clyde Wilcox, eds. Lanham: Rowman & Littlefield Publishers, Inc., pp. 17–44.

Marvell, Thomas B., and Carlisle E. Moody, Jr. 1994. "Prison Population Growth and Crime Reduction." *Journal of Quantitative Criminology* 10(2): 109–137.

Massing, Michael. 1998. *The Fix*. New York: Simon & Schuster.

Mayer, William G. 1993. *The Changing American Mind: How and Why American Public Opinion Changed Between 1960 and 1988*. Ann Arbor: The University of Michigan Press.

Mayhew, David R. 1974. *Congress: The Electoral Connection*. New Haven: Yale University Press.

Mazur, Allan. 1981. *The Dynamics of Technical Controversy*. Washington D.C.: Communications Press.

Mazur, Allan. 1981. "Media Coverage and Public Opinion on Scientific Controversies." *Journal of Communication* 31: 106–116.

McAney, Leslie. 1993. "The Gallup Poll on Crime." *Gallup Poll Monthly* (December): 18.

McCleary, R., and R. A. Hay. 1980. *Applied Time Series Analysis for the Social Sciences*. Beverly Hills: SAGE Publications.

McConahey, John B. 1986. "Modern Racism, Ambivalence and the Modern Racism Scale." In *Prejudice, Discrimination, and Racism*. John F. Dovido and Samuel L. Gaertner, eds. Orlando: Academic Press.

McCoy, Donald R. 1997. "Calvin Coolidge." In *The Presidents: A Reference History*. 2d ed. Henry F. Graff, ed. New York: Simon & Schuster Macmillan.

McKinley, William. *Messages and Papers of the Presidents*. Vol. 8. In *American Reference Library*. 1998. CD-ROM. Orem: The Western Standard Publishing Company.

McWilliams, John C. 1989. "Unsung Partner Against Crime: Harry J. Anslinger and the Federal Bureau of Narcotics, 1930–1962." *The Pennsylvania Magazine of History & Biography* 113(2): 207–236.

————. 1991. "Through the Past Darkly: The Politics and Policies of America's Drug War." *Journal of Policy History* 3(4): 356–392.

Meador, Daniel J. 1980. *The President, the Attorney General, and the Department of Justice*. Charlottesville: White Burkett Miller Center of Public Affairs, University of Virginia.

Medhurst, Martin J. 1993. *Dwight D. Eisenhower: Strategic Communicator*. Westport: Greenwood Press.

Meier, Kenneth J. 1990. "The Politics of Drug Abuse: Laws, Implementation and Consequences." *The Western Political Quarterly* 45: 41–69.

————. 1993. *Politics and the Bureaucracy: Policymaking in the Fourth Branch of Government*. 3d ed. Belmont: Wadsworth Publishing Company.

————. 1994. *The Politics of Sin: Drugs, Alcohol, and Public Policy*. Armonk: M. E. Sharpe.

Meier, Robert F., and Gilbert Geis. 1997. *Victimless Crimes?* Los Angeles: Roxbury Publishing Company.

Meithe, Terance D. 1995. "Fear and Withdrawal from Urban Life." *The Annals of the American Academy of Political and Social Science* 539: 14–140.

Meithe, Terance D., and Gary R. Lee. 1984. "Fear of Crime Among Older People: A Reassessment of the Predictive Power of Crime-Related Factors." *Sociological Quarterly* 25: 397–416.

Mezey, Michael L. 1989. *Congress, the President, and Public Policy.* Boulder: Westview Press.

Michelowski, Raymond. 1993. "Some Thoughts Regarding the Impact of Clinton's Election on Crime and Justice Policy." *The Criminologist* 18(3): 6.

Milakovich, Michael E., and Kurt Weis. 1975. "Politics and Measures of Success in the War on Crime." *Crime and Delinquency* 21(1): 1–10.

Milkis, Sidney M. 1999. "Political Parties and Divided Government." In *Presidential Policymaking: An End-of-Century Assessment.* Steven A. Shull, ed. Armonk: M. E. Sharpe, pp. 79–97.

Miller, Nathan. 1992. *Theodore Roosevelt: A Life.* New York: William Morrow.

Miroff, Bruce. 1982. "Monopolizing the Public Space: The President as a Problem for Democratic Politics." In *Rethinking the Presidency.* Thomas Cronin, ed. Boston: Little Brown and Company, pp. 218–232.

Mondak, Jeffrey. 1993. "Source Cues and Policy Approval: The Cognitive Dynamics of Public Support for the Reagan Agenda." *American Journal of Political Science* 37: 186–212.

Mooney, Christopher Z. 2000. *The Public Clash of Private Values: The Politics of Morality Policy.* New York: Seven Bridges Press.

Moore, John E. 1969. "Controlling Delinquency: Executive, Congressional and Juvenile, 1961–1964." In *Congress and Urban Problems.* Frederick N. Cleaveland, ed. Washington D.C.: Brookings Institution.

Morrison, Samuel E. 1965. *The Oxford History of the American People.* New York: Oxford University Press.

Morton, Charles. 1951. "Accent on Living." *The Atlantic Monthly.* (September): 13–14.

Murray, Robert K. 1997. "Warren G. Harding." In *The Presidents: A Reference History.* 2d ed. Henry F. Graff, ed. New York: Simon & Schuster Macmillan.

Nagel, Stuart, Erika Fairchild, and Anthony Champagne. 1983. *The Political Science of Criminal Justice.* Springfield: Charles C. Thomas.

The National Advisory Commission on Civil Disorders. 1968. *Report of the National Advisory Commission on Civil Disorders.* New York: Bantam Books.

National Archives and Records Administration. 1999. "Executive Orders Disposition Tables." Available on the world wide web at http://www.nara.gov/fedreg/eo.html.

National Commission on the Causes and Prevention of Violence. 1969. *To Insure Domestic Tranquility.* Washington D.C.: U.S. G.P.O.

Navasky, Victor S. 1971. *Kennedy Justice.* New York: Atheneum.

Nelli, Humbert S. 1985. "American Syndicate Crime: A Legacy of Prohibition." In *Law, Alcohol, and Order: Perspectives on National Prohibition.* David E. Kyvig, ed. Westport: Greenwood Press, pp. 123–137.

Nelson, Barbara J. 1984. *Making an Issue of Child Abuse.* Chicago: University of Chicago Press.

Neuman, W. R. 1990. "The Threshold of Public Attention." *Public Opinion Quarterly* 54: 159–176.

Neustadt, Richard E. 1990. *Presidential Power and the Modern Presidents: The Politics of Leadership from Roosevelt to Reagan.* New York: The Free Press.

Nixon, Richard M. Various Years. *Public Papers of the Presidents of the United States.* Washington D.C.: U.S. G.P.O.

Nixon, Richard. 1978. *RN: Memoirs of Richard Nixon.* New York: Grosset and Dunlap.

Norpoth, H. 1984. "Unemployment and Crime." *Journal of Criminal Law and Criminology* 71(2): 181–183.

Novak, Michael. 1974. *Choosing Our King: Powerful Symbols in Presidential Politics.* New York: Macmillan.

Office of National Drug Control Policy. *National Drug Control Strategy, 1996.* Washington D.C.: U.S. G.P.O.

Oliver, Willard M. 1998. "Presidential Rhetoric on Crime and Public Opinion." *Criminal Justice Review* 23(2): 139–160.

Oliver, Willard, and Tanya Conrad. 1999. "One Million and Still Counting: A Replication Study of Students' Estimation of Homicides in the U.S." *The Dialogue* September. Available on line at http://www.appstate.edu/~robinsnmb/dialoguesep99woliver.htm

Oliver, Willard M., Kevin M. Leyden, and John C. Kilwein. 1997. "Drowning: The Subterfuge of Race by the Issue of Crime." Unpublished paper presented at the Southern Criminal Justice Association's annual meeting. Richmond, Virginia.

Omni, Michael, and Howard Winant. 1986. *Racial Formation in the United States.* New York: Routledge.

O'Keefe, G. J. 1985. "'Taking a Bite Out of Crime': The Impact of a Public Information Campaign." *Communication Research* 12: 147–178.

O'Reilly, Kenneth. 1982. "A New Deal for the FBI: The Roosevelt Administration, Crime Control, and National Security." *The Journal of American History* 69(3): 638–658.

Orsagh, T. 1980. "Unemployment and Crime." *Journal of Criminal Law and Criminology* 71(2): 181–183.

Ortega, Suzanne T., and Jessie L. Myles. 1987. "Race and Gender Effects on Fear of Crime: An Interactive Model with Age." *Criminology* 25: 133–152.

Ostrom, Charles W., Jr. 1978. *Time Series Analysis: Regression Techniques.* Beverly Hills: SAGE Publications.

Ostrom, Charles W., Jr., and Dennis M. Simon. 1985. "Promise and Performance: A Dynamic Model of Presidential Popularity." *American Political Science Review* 79: 334–358.

———. 1988. "The President's Public." *American Journal of Political Science* 32: 1096–1119.

———. 1989. "The Man in the Teflon Suit: The Environmental Connection, Political Drama and Popular Support in the Reagan Presidency." *Public Opinion Quarterly* 53: 353–387.

Page, Benjamin I., and Robert Y. Shapiro. 1984. "Presidents as Opinion Leaders: Some New Evidence." *Policy Studies Journal* 12: 649–661.

———. 1985. "Presidential Leadership through Public Opinion." In *The Presidency and Public Policy Making.* George C. Edwards III, Steven A. Shull, and Norman C. Thomas, eds. Pittsburgh: University of Pittsburgh Press, pp. 22–36.

———. 1992. *The Rational Public: Fifty Years of Trends in Americans' Policy Preferences.* Chicago: University of Chicago Press.

Page, Benjamin I., Robert Y. Shapiro, and Glenn R. Dempsey. 1987. "What Moves Public Opinion?" *American Political Science Review* 81: 23–43.

Parmet, Herbert S. 1997. "Gerald R. Ford." *The Presidents: A Reference History.* 2d ed. Henry F. Graff, ed. New York: Simon & Schuster Macmillan.

Patterson, Samuel C., and Gregory A. Caldeira. 1990. "Standing up for Congress: Variations in Public Esteem Since the 1960s." *Legislative Studies Quarterly* 15: 25–47.

Patterson, Samuel C., and Keith R. Eakins. 1998. "Congress and Gun Control." In *The Changing Politics of Gun Control.* John M. Bruce and Clyde Wilcox, eds. Lanham: Rowman and Littlefield Publishers, Inc., pp. 45–73.

Patterson, Thomas E. 1994. *Out of Order.* New York: Vintage Books.

Peffley, Mark, Todd Shields, and Bruce Williams. 1996. "The Intersection of Race and Crime in Television News Stories: An Experimental Study." *Political Communication* 13: 309–327.

Peffley, Mark, Jon Hurwitz, and Paul M. Sniderman. 1997. "Racial Stereotypes and Whites' Political Views of Blacks in the Context of Welfare and Crime." *American Journal of Political Science* 41(1): 30–60.

Pepinsky, Harold E. 1976. "The Growth of Crime in the United States." *The Annals of the American Academy of Political and Social Science* 423: 23–30.

Peterson, Merrill D. 1997. "Thomas Jefferson." In *The Presidents: A Reference History.* 2d ed. Henry F. Graff, ed. New York: Simon & Schuster Macmillan.

Pfiffner, James P. 1996. *The Strategic Presidency: Hitting the Ground Running*. 2d ed, Rev. Lawrence: University Press of Kansas.

Pfiffner, John M. 1929. "The Activities and Results of Crime Surveys." *American Political Science Review* 23: 930–955.

Pfiffner, James P. 1994. *The Modern Presidency*. New York: St. Martin's Press.

Pierce, Franklin. *Messages and Papers of the Presidents*. Vol. 4. In *American Reference Library*. 1998. CD-ROM. Orem: The Western Standard Publishing Company.

Platt, Tony. 1987. "U.S. Criminal Justice in the Reagan Era: An Assessment." *Crime and Social Justice* 29: 58–69.

Polakoff, Keith Ian. 1997. "Rutherford B. Hayes." In *The Presidents: A Reference History*. 2d ed. Henry F. Graff, ed. New York: Simon & Schuster Macmillan.

Pomper, Gerald, and Susan Lederman. 1980. *Elections in America: Control and Influence in Democratic Politics*. 2d ed. New York: Longman.

Pontell, Henry N., Kitty Calavita, and Robert Tillman. 1994. "Corporate Crime and Criminal Justice System Capacity: Government Response To Financial Institution Fraud." *Justice Quarterly* 11(3): 383–410.

Popper, Frank. 1970. *President's Commissions*. New York: Twentieth Century Fund.

Potter, Claire B. 1998. *War on Crime: Bandits, G-Men, and the Politics of Mass Culture*. New Brunswick: Rutgers University Press.

Potter, Gary W., and Victor E. Kappeler. 1998. *Constructing Crime: Perspectives on Making News and Social Problems*. Prospect Heights: Waveland.

Pound, Roscoe, and Felix Frankfurter, eds. 1968 (1922). *Criminal Justice in Cleveland: Reports of Cleveland Foundation Survey of the Administration of Criminal Justice in Cleveland, Ohio*. Montclair: Patterson-Smith.

Poveda, Tony G. 1996. "Clinton, Crime, and the Justice Department." *Social Justice* 21(3): 73–84.

President's Commission on Law Enforcement and Administration of Justice. 1968. *The Challenge of Crime in a Free Society*. New York: An Avon Book.

Ragsdale, Lyn. 1982. *Presidents and Publics: The Dialogue of Presidential Leadership*. Ph.D. Dissertation, University of Wisconsin—Madison.

———. 1984. "The Politics of Presidential Speechmaking, 1949–1980." *American Political Science Review* 78: 971–984.

———. 1987. "Presidential Speechmaking and the Public Audience: Individual Presidents and Group Attitudes." *Journal of Politics* 49: 704–736.

———. 1998. *Vital Statistics on the Presidency: Washington to Clinton*. Rev. ed. Washington D.C.: Congressional Quarterly, Inc.

Ragsdale, Lyn, and Jerrold G. Rusk. 1999. "Elections and Presidential Policymaking." In *Presidential Policymaking: An End-of-Century Assessment*. Steven A. Shull, ed. Armonk: M. E. Sharpe, pp. 98–116.

Reagan, Ronald. 1988. Various Years. *Public Papers of the Presidents of the United States*. Washington D.C.: U.S. G.P.O.

———. 1990. *An American Life*. New York: Simon & Schuster.

Reiman, Jeffrey. 1995. *The Rich Get Richer and the Poor Get Prison: Ideology, Class, and Criminal Justice*. Boston: Allyn & Bacon.

Research and Forecasts, Inc. 1983. *America Afraid: How Fear of Crime Changes the Way We Live (The Figgie Report)*. Andy Friedberg, ed. New York: New American Library.

Ripley, Randall B. 1985. *Policy Analysis in Political Science*. New York: Nelson-Hall, Inc.

Ripley, Randall, and Grace A. Franklin. 1991. *Congress, the Bureaucracy and Public Policy*. California: Brooks/Cole Publishers.

Rivers, Douglas, and Nancy L. Rose. 1985. "Passing the President's Program: Public Opinion and Presidential Influence in Congress." *American Journal of Political Science* 29: 183–196.

Roberts, Julian V., and Loretta J. Stalans. 1997. *Public Opinion, Crime, and Criminal Justice.* Boulder: Westview Press.

Rogers, Everett M., James W. Dearing, and Soonbum Chang. 1991. "AIDS in the 1980s: The Agenda-Setting Process for a Public Issue." *Journalism Monograph* No. 126. Lexington: Association for Education and Journalism.

Rollins, Alfred B., Jr. 1962. *Roosevelt and Howe.* New York: Alfred A. Knopf.

Roosevelt, Franklin D. 1933. *Looking Forward.* Rahway: The John Day Company, Inc.

———. Various Years. *The Public Papers and Addresses of Franklin D. Roosevelt.* New York: Russell and Russell.

Roosevelt, Theodore. *Messages and Papers of the Presidents.* Vol. 10. In *American Reference Library.* 1998. CD-ROM. Orem: The Western Standard Publishing Company.

Rosch, Joel. 1985. "Crime as an Issue in American Politics." In *The Politics of Crime and Criminal Justice.* Erika S. Fairchild and Vincent J. Webb, eds. Beverly Hills: Sage Publications, pp. 19–35.

Rossiter, Clinton. 1960. *The American Presidency.* 2d ed. New York: New American Library.

———. 1961. *The Federalist Papers.* New York: New American Library.

Rosoff, Stephen M., Henry N. Pontell, and Robert Tillman. 1998. *Profit Without Honor: White-Collar Crime and the Looting of America.* Upper Saddle River: Prentice Hall.

Rubin, Richard. 1981. *Press, Party, and Presidency.* New York: W.W. Norton and Company.

Rush, George E. 2000. *The Dictionary of Criminal Justice.* 5th ed. New York: Dushkin/McGraw-Hill.

Sacco, Vincent F. 1982. "The Effects of Mass Media on Perceptions of Crime: A Reanalysis of the Issues." *Pacific Sociological Review* 25: 475–493.

Savelsburg, Joachim J. 1994. "Knowledge, Domination, and Capital Punishment." *American Journal of Sociology* 99(4): 911–943.

Scheingold, Stuart A. 1984. *The Politics of Law and Order: Street Crime and Public Policy.* New York: Longman.

———. 1991. *The Politics of Street Crime: Criminal Process and Cultural Obsession.* Philadelphia: Temple University Press.

———. 1995. "Politics, Public Policy, and Street Crime." *The Annals of the American Academy of Political and Social Science* 539: 141–154.

Schell, Jonathan. 1976. *The Time of Illusion.* New York: Alfred A. Knopf.

Schlosser, Eric. 1998. "The Prison-Industrial Complex." *The Atlantic Monthly* (December): 51–77.

Schoenberg, Robert J. 1992. *Mr. Capone.* New York: William Morrow and Company, Inc.

Schuman, H., and J. Scott. 1987. "Problems in the Use of Survey Questions to Measure Public Opinion." *Science* 236: 957–959.

Schuman, Howard, Charlotte Steeh, and Lawrence Bobo. 1985. *Racial Attitudes in America: Trends and Interpretations.* Cambridge: Harvard University Press.

Schurr, Edwin M. 1965. *Crimes Without Victims.* Englewood Cliffs: Prentice Hall.

Scigliana, Robert. 1971. *The Supreme Court and the Presidency.* New York: The Free Press.

Scruggs, Donald Lee. 1980. *Lyndon Baines Johnson and the National Advisory Commission on Civil Disorders (The Kerner Commission): A Study of the Johnson Domestic Policy Making System.* Ph.D. Dissertation, The University of Oklahoma.

Sears, David O. 1988. "Symbolic Racism." In *Eliminating Racism.* Edited by Phyllis A. Katz and Dalmas A. Taylor, eds. New York: Plenum.

Segal, Jeffrey A. 1984. "Predicting Supreme Court Decisions Probabilistically: The Search and Seizure Cases (1962–1981)." *American Political Science Review* 78: 891–900.

———. 1988. "Amicus Curiae Briefs by the Solicitor General During the Warren and Burger Courts." *Western Political Quarterly* 41: 135–144.

———. 1990. "Supreme Court Support for the Solicitor General: The Effect of Presidential Appointments." *Western Political Quarterly* 43: 137–152.

Segal, Jeffrey A., and Cheryl D. Reedy. 1988. "The Supreme Court and Sex Discrimination: The Role of the Solicitor General." *Western Political Quarterly* 41: 553–568.

Segal, Jeffrey A., and Robert M. Howard. 1999. "Justices and Presidents." In *Presidential Policymaking: An End-of-Century Assessment.* Steven A. Shull, ed. Armonk: M. E. Sharpe, pp. 168–182.

Seidman, David, and Michael Couzens. 1974. "Getting the Crime Rate Down: Political Pressure and Crime Reporting." *Law and Society Review* 8: 457–493.

Shaiko, Ronald G. 1998. "Reverse Lobbying: Interest Group Mobilization from the White House and the Hill." In *Interest Group Politics.* 5th ed. Allan J. Ciglar and Burdett A. Loomis, eds. Washington D.C.: Congressional Quarterly Press, pp. 255–282.

Sharp, Elaine B. 1994. *The Dilemma of Drug Policy in the United States.* New York: HarperCollins College Publishers.

Sherman, Lawrence W., Denise Gottfredson, Doris MacKenzie, John Eck, Peter Reuter, and Shawn Bushway. 1997. *Preventing Crime: What Works, What Doesn't, What's Promising.* Washington D.C.: National Institute of Justice.

Shull, Steven A. 1983. *Domestic Policy Formation: Presidential-Congressional Partnership?* Westport: Greenwood Press.

Shull, Steven A., and A. C. Ringelstein. 1989. "Presidential Attention, Support, and Symbolism in Civil Rights, 1953–1984." *The Social Science Journal* 26: 45–54.

Sigelman, Lee. 1980. "Gauging the Public Response to Presidential Leadership." *Presidential Studies Quarterly* 10: 427–433.

Silberman, Charles E. 1978. *Criminal Violence, Criminal Justice.* New York: Vintage Books.

Simon, David R., and Stanley D. Eitzen. 1993. *Elite Deviance.* 4th ed. Boston: Allyn & Bacon.

Simon, Dennis M., and Charles W. Ostrom, Jr. 1985. "The President and Public Support: A Strategic Perspective." In *The Presidency and Public Policy Making.* George C. Edwards III, Steven A. Shull, and Norman C. Thomas, eds. Pittsburgh: University of Pittsburgh Press.

———. 1988. "The Politics of Prestige: Popular Support and the Modern Presidency." *Presidential Studies Quarterly* 18: 741–759.

Simon, John Y. 1997. "Ulysses S. Grant." In *The Presidents: A Reference History.* 2d ed. Henry F. Graff, ed. New York: Simon & Schuster Macmillan.

Skogan, Wesley G. 1974. "The Validity of Official Crime Statistics: An Empirical Investigation." *Social Science Quarterly* 55: 25–38.

———. 1986. "Fear of Crime and Neighborhood Change." In *Communities and Crime.* Edited by Albert J. Reiss, Jr. and Michael Tonry, eds. Chicago: University of Chicago Press.

———. 1993. "The Various Meanings of Fear." In *Fear of Crime and Criminal Victimization.* W. Bilsky, C. Pfeiffer, and P. Wetzels, eds. Stuttgart: Ferdinand Enke Verlag.

Smith, Brent L., and Kelly R. Damphousse. 1998. "Terrorism, Politics, and Punishment: A Test of Structural-Contextual Theory and the 'Liberation Hypothesis'" *Criminology* 36(1): 67–92.

Smith, Craig Allen, and Kathy B. Smith. 1994. *The White House Speaks: Presidential Leadership as Persuasion.* Westport: Praeger Publishers.

Smith, Daniel A., Kevin M. Leyden, and Stephen A. Borrelli. 1998. "Predicting the Outcomes of Presidential Commissions: Evidence from the Johnson and Nixon Years." *Presidential Studies Quarterly* 28(2): 269–285.

Smith, T. 1980. "America's Most Important Problems—A Trend Analysis, 1946–1976." *Public Opinion Quarterly* 44: 164–180.

Smith, William French. 1991. *Law and Justice in the Reagan Administration: Memoirs of an Attorney General.* Stanford: Hoover Institution Press.

Sniderman, Paul M. 1993. " The New Look in Public Opinion Research." In *Political Science: The State of the Discipline II.* Ada W. Finifter, ed. Washington D.C.: American Political Science Association, pp. 219–245.

Sniderman, Paul M., and Thomas Piazza. 1993. *The Scar of Race.* Cambridge: Harvard University Press.

Sniderman, Paul M., Thomas Piazza, Philip E. Tetlock, and Ann Kendrick. 1991. "The New Racism." *American Journal of Political Science* 35: 423–447.

Spitzer, Robert J. 1987. "Promoting Policy Theory: Revising the Arenas of Power." *Policy Studies Journal* 15: 675–689.

———. 1995. *The Politics of Gun Control.* Chatham: Chatham House Publishers, Inc.

Stark, Rodney. 1972. *Police Riots.* Belmont: Wadsworth Publishing Company.

Stark, Steven D. 1997. *Glued to the Set.* New York: Delta Trade Paperbacks.

Stein, Robert M., and Kenneth M. Bickers. 1995. *Perpetuating the Pork Barrel.* Cambridge: Cambridge University Press.

Stiles, Lela. 1954. *The Man Behind Roosevelt: The Story of Louis McHenry Howe.* Cleveland: The World Publishing Company.

Stimson, James A. 1991. *Public Opinion in America: Moods, Cycles, and Swings.* Boulder: Westview Press.

Stokes, Donald. 1992. "Valence Politics." In *Electoral Politics.* Dennis Kavanagh, ed. Oxford: Clarendon Press.

Stolz, Barbara Ann. 1992. "Congress and the War on Drugs: An Exercise in Symbolic Politics." *Journal of Crime and Justice* 15(1): 119–136.

Stuckey, Mary E. 1990. *Playing the Game: The Presidential Rhetoric of Ronald Reagan.* New York: Praeger Publishers.

Sundquist, James N. 1969. *Politics and Policy: The Eisenhower, Kennedy, and Johnson Years.* Washington D.C.: Brookings Institution.

Surette, Ray. *Media, Crime, and Criminal Justice: Images and Realities.* 2d ed. Belmont: West/Wadsworth Publishers.

Taft, William H. *Messages and Papers of the Presidents.* Vol. 10. In *American Reference Library.* 1998. CD-ROM. Orem: The Western Standard Publishing Company.

Taggart, William A. 1997. "The Nationalization of Corrections Policy in the American States." *Justice Quarterly* 14(3): 429–444.

Task Force on the Federalization of Criminal Law. 1998. *The Federalization of Criminal Law: Defending Liberty, Pursuing Justice.* Washington D.C.: American Bar Association.

Tatalovich, Raymond, and Bryon Daynes. 1988. *Social Regulatory Policy.* Boulder: Westview Press.

———. 1998. *Moral Controversies in American Politics.* Armonk: M. E. Sharpe.

Taylor, D. Garth, Kim L. Scheppele, and Arthur L. Stinchcombe. 1979. "Salience of Crime and Support for Harsher Criminal Sanctions." *Social Problems* 26(4): 413–424.

Thomas, Norman C., and Joseph A. Pika. 1996. *The Politics of the Presidency.* 4th ed. Washington D.C.: Congressional Quarterly Press.

Tonry, Michael. 1994. "Racial Politics, Racial Disparities, and the War on Crime." *Crime & Delinquency* 40(4) 475–494.

———. 1995. *Malign Neglect: Race, Crime, and Punishment in America.* New York: Oxford University Press.

Tourtellot, Arthur B. 1970. *The Presidents on the Presidency.* New York: Russell and Russell.

Troyer, Ronald J., and Gerald E. Markle. 1983. *Cigarettes, The Battle over Smoking.* New Brunswick: Rutgers University Press.

Truman, Harry S. *Public Papers of the Presidents of the United States.* In *American Reference Library.* 1998. CD-ROM. Orem: The Western Standard Publishing Company.

Tulis, Jeffrey K. 1987. *The Rhetorical Presidency.* Princeton: Princeton University Press.

Tyler, John. *Messages and Papers of the Presidents.* Vol. 3. In *American Reference Library.* 1998. CD-ROM. Orem: The Western Standard Publishing Company.

U.S. Department of Justice, Office of Justice Programs. 1997. *The Challenge of Crime in a Free Society: Looking Back, Looking Forward.* Washington D.C.: U.S. Department of Justice.

U.S. Senate. 1955. *Juvenile Delinquency: Hearings Before the Special Subcommittee on Juvenile Delinquency of the Senate Committee on Labor and Public Welfare.* 84th Congress, 1st Session.

Van Buren, Martin. *Messages and Papers of the Presidents.* Vol. 2. In *American Reference Library.* 1998. CD-ROM. Orem: The Western Standard Publishing Company.

Vandiver, Margaret, and David Giacopassi. 1997. "One Million and Counting: Students' Estimates of the Annual Number of Homicides in the U.S." *Journal of Criminal Justice Education* 8: 135–143.

Vold, George B., and Thomas J. Bernard. 1986. *Theoretical Criminology.* 3d ed. New York: Oxford University Press.

Walker, Samuel. 1978. "Reexamining the President's Crime Commission: The Challenge of Crime in a Free Society after Ten Years." *Crime & Delinquency* (January): 1–12.

———. 1994. *Sense and Nonsense about Crime and Drugs: A Policy Guide.* 3d ed. Belmont: Wadsworth Publishing Company.

———. 1998. *Popular Justice: A History of American Criminal Justice.* 2d ed. New York: Oxford University Press.

Walker, Samuel, Cassia Spohn, and Miriam DeLone. 1996. *The Color of Justice: Race, Ethnicity, and Crime in America.* Belmont: Wadsworth Publishing Company.

Wallace, Henry Scott. 1992. "Clinton's Real Plan on Crime." *National Law Journal* 12:15.

Walsh, Edward. 1992. "Clinton Charges Bush Uses Crime Issue to Divide." *The Washington Post* (July 24): A16.

Warr, Mark. 1984. "Fear of Victimization: Why are Women and Elderly More Afraid?" *Social Science Quarterly* 65: 681–702.

———. 1990. "Dangerous Situations: Social Context and Fear of Victimization." *Social Forces* 68: 891–907.

———. 1991. "America's Perceptions of Crime and Punishment." In *Criminology: A Contemporary Handbook.* J. F. Sheley, ed. Belmont: Wadsworth.

———. 1995. "The Polls—Poll Trends. Public Opinion on Crime and Punishment." *Public Opinion Quarterly* 59: 296–310.

Warshaw, Shirley Anne. 1997. *The Domestic Presidency: Policy Making in the White House.* Boston: Allyn & Bacon.

———. 1999. "Staffing Patterns in the Modern White House." In *Presidential Policymaking: An End-of-Century Assessment.* Steven A. Shull, ed. Armonk: M. E. Sharpe, pp. 131–149.

Warshaw, Shirley Anne, and John Robert Greene. 1994. "'Brushfires': The Departments, the Domestic Council, and Policy Agendas in the Ford White House." *Congress & The Presidency* 21(2): 83–97.

Washington, George. *Messages and Papers of the Presidents of the United States.* Vol. 1. In *American Reference Library.* 1998. CD-ROM. Orem: The Western Standard Publishing Company.

Wattenberg, Ben J. 1996. *Values Matter Most: How Democrats or Republicans or a Third Party Can Win and Renew the American Way of Life.* New York: Regnery Publishing, Inc.

Wattenberg, Martin P. 1991. *The Rise of Candidate-Centered Politics.* Cambridge: Harvard University Press.

Waxman, Seth P. 1998. "'Presenting the Case of the United States As It Should Be': The Solicitor General in Historical Context." Address to the Supreme Court Historical Society. Available online at http://www.usdoj.gov/osg/aboutosg/sgarticle.html

Weart, Spencer. 1988. *Nuclear Fear: A History of Images.* Cambridge: Harvard University Press.

Welch, Michael, Melissa Fenwick, and Meridith Roberts. 1997. "Primary Definitions of Crime and Moral Panic: A Content Analysis of Experts' Quotes in Feature Newspaper Articles on Crime." *Journal of Research on Crime and Delinquency* 34: 474–494.

West, Darrell M. 1997. *Air Wars: Television Advertising in Election Campaigns 1952–1996.* 2d ed. Washington D.C.: Congressional Quarterly, Inc.

West, William F. 1995. *Controlling the Bureaucracy: Institutional Constraints in Theory and Practice.* Armonk: M. E. Sharpe.

Wheeler, Stanton. 1967. "Criminal Statistics: A Reformulation of the Problem." *Journal of Criminal Law, Criminology, and Police Science* 58: 317–324.

White, Theodore H. 1965. *The Making of the President 1964.* New York: Atheneum Publishers.

Wiecek, William M. 1972. *The Guarantee Clause of the U.S. Constitution*. Ithaca: Cornell University Press.

Wildavsky, Aaron. 1992. *The New Politics of the Budgetary Process*. 2d ed. New York: HarperCollins Publishers.

Will, J. A., and J. H. McGrath. 1995. "Crime, Neighborhood Perception, and the Underclass: The Relationship Between Fear of Crime and Class Position." *Journal of Criminal Justice* 23:163–176.

Wilson, James Q. 1968. *Varieties of Police Behavior*. Cambridge: Harvard University Press.

————. 1975. *Thinking About Crime*. New York: Basic Books, Inc.

————. 1976. "Crime and Punishment, 1776 to 1976. Bicentennial Essay." *Time* (April 26): 82–85.

Wilson, Woodrow. 1973. *Congressional Government*. Cleveland: World Publishing.

Windlesham, Lord. 1998. *Politics, Punishment, and Populism*. New York: Oxford University Press.

Windt, Theodore Otto, Jr. 1990. *Presidents and Protestors: Political Rhetoric in the 1960s*. Tuscaloosa: University of Alabama Press.

Winter, James P., and Chaim H. Eyal. 1981. "Agenda-Setting for the Civil Rights Issue." In *Agenda Setting: Readings on Media, Public Opinion, and Policymaking*. David L. Protess and Maxwell McCombs, eds. Hillsdale: Lawrence Erlbaum Associates, pp. 101–107.

Wisotsky, Steven. 1987. "Crackdown: The Emerging 'Drug Exception' to the Bill of Rights." *Hastings Law Journal* 38: 889–926.

Yin, Peter. 1982. "Fear of Crime as a Problem for the Elderly." *Social Problems* 30: 240–245.

Zimring, Franklin E., and Gordon Hawkins. 1996. "Toward a Principles Basis for Federal Criminal Legislation." *The Annals of the American Academy of Political and Social Science* 543: 15–26.

————. 1997. "Lethal Violence and the Overreach of American Imprisonment." *National Institute of Justice Research Report*. Washington D.C.: U.S. G.P.O.

Zuckman, Jill. 1993. "The President's Call to Serve is Clear but Undefined." *Congressional Quarterly Weekly Report* 218: 51.

Index

Page numbers in *italics* indicate photographs.